Lecture Notes in Computer Science 15897

Founding Editors

Gerhard Goos
Juris Hartmanis

The series Lecture Notes in Computer Science (LNCS), including its subseries Lecture Notes in Artificial Intelligence (LNAI) and Lecture Notes in Bioinformatics (LNBI), has established itself as a medium for the publication of new developments in computer science and information technology research, teaching, and education.

LNCS enjoys close cooperation with the computer science R & D community, the series counts many renowned academics among its volume editors and paper authors, and collaborates with prestigious societies. Its mission is to serve this international community by providing an invaluable service, mainly focused on the publication of conference and workshop proceedings and postproceedings. LNCS commenced publication in 1973.

Osvaldo Gervasi · Beniamino Murgante ·
Chiara Garau · Yeliz Karaca ·
Maria Noelia Faginas Lago · Francesco Scorza ·
Ana Cristina Braga
Editors

Computational Science and Its Applications – ICCSA 2025 Workshops

Istanbul, Turkey, June 30 – July 3, 2025
Proceedings, Part XII

 Springer

Editors
Osvaldo Gervasi ⓘ
University of Perugia
Perugia, Italy

Beniamino Murgante ⓘ
University of Basilicata
Potenza, Italy

Chiara Garau ⓘ
University of Cagliari
Cagliari, Italy

Yeliz Karaca ⓘ
University of Massachusetts
Worcester, MA, USA

Maria Noelia Faginas Lago ⓘ
University of Perugia
Perugia, Italy

Francesco Scorza ⓘ
University of Basilicata
Potenza, Italy

Ana Cristina Braga ⓘ
University of Minho
Braga, Portugal

ISSN 0302-9743   ISSN 1611-3349 (electronic)
Lecture Notes in Computer Science
ISBN 978-3-031-97659-9   ISBN 978-3-031-97660-5 (eBook)
https://doi.org/10.1007/978-3-031-97660-5

This Springer imprint is published by the registered company Springer Nature Switzerland AG
The registered company address is: Gewerbestrasse 11, 6330 Cham, Switzerland

If disposing of this product, please recycle the paper.

Preface

The compiled 14 volumes (LNCS volumes 15886–15899) consist of the peer-reviewed papers from the 68 Workshops of the 2025 International Conference on Computational Science and Its Applications (ICCSA 2025), which was held between June 30 – July 3, 2025 in Istanbul (Türkiye). The peer-reviewed papers of the main conference tracks are published in a separate set made up of three volumes (LNCS 15648–15650).

The conference was held in a hybrid form, with the large majority of participants in presence, hosted by Galatasaray University, Istanbul, Türkiye. We enabled virtual participation for those who did not attend the event in person due to logistical, political and economic problems, by adopting a technological infrastructure via open-source software (jitsi + riot) and a commercial Cloud infrastructure.

With the 2025 edition, ICCSA celebrated its 25th anniversary, a quarter of a century as a memorable moment that is harmoniously aligned with Istanbul, an extraordinary city located at the crossroads and acting as a bridge connecting Asia and Europe, representing different cultures, beliefs as well as lifestyles, which highlights its intercultural fabric.

ICCSA 2025 marked another fruitful and thought-provoking academic event in the International Conferences on Computational Science and Its Applications (ICCSA) conference series, previously held in Hanoi, Vietnam (2024), Athens, Greece (2023), Málaga, Spain (2022), Cagliari, Italy (hybrid with a few participants in presence in 2021 and completely online in 2020), whilst earlier editions took place in Saint Petersburg, Russia (2019), Melbourne, Australia (2018), Trieste, Italy (2017), Beijing, China (2016), Banff, Canada (2015), Guimaraes, Portugal (2014), Ho Chi Minh City, Vietnam (2013), Salvador, Brazil (2012), Santander, Spain (2011), Fukuoka, Japan (2010), Suwon, South Korea (2009), Perugia, Italy (2008), Kuala Lumpur, Malaysia (2007), Glasgow, UK (2006), Singapore (2005), Assisi, Italy (2004), Montreal, Canada (2003), and (as ICCS) Amsterdam, the Netherlands (2002) and San Francisco, USA (2001).

Computational Science constitutes the main pillar of most present research, industrial and commercial applications, and plays a unique role in exploiting ICT innovative technologies, and the ICCSA conference series has, accordingly, provided ample opportunities to researchers and industry practitioners to discuss new ideas, to share complex problems and their solutions, and to shape new trends in Computational Science. As the conference mirrors society from a scientific point of view, this year's undoubtedly dominant theme was large language models, machine learning and Artificial Intelligence (AI) and their applications in the most diverse technological, economic and industrial fields, amongst the others.

The ICCSA 2025 conference was structured in six general tracks covering the fields of computational science and its applications: Computational Methods, Algorithms and Scientific Applications – High Performance Computing and Networks – Geometric Modeling, Graphics and Visualization – Advanced and Emerging Applications – Information Systems and Technologies – Urban and Regional Planning. In addition, the conference consisted of 68 workshops, focusing on topical issues of utmost importance to science, technology and society: from new computational approaches for earth science, to mathematical methods for image processing, new statistical and optimization methods, several Artificial Intelligence approaches, sustainability issues, smart cities and related technologies, to name some.

In the Workshops' proceedings, we accepted 362 full papers, 37 short papers and 2 Ph.D. Showcase papers from total of 1043 submissions (Acceptance rate 38.4%). In the Main Conference Proceedings, we accepted 71 full papers, 6 short papers and 1 Ph.D. Showcase paper from 269 submissions to the General Tracks of the Conference (with an acceptance rate of 29.9%). We would like to convey our sincere appreciation to the workshops' chairs and co-chairs and program committee members for their diligent work, commitment and dedication.

The success and consistent maintenance of the ICCSA conference series in general, and of ICCSA 2025 in particular, rely upon the support of many people: authors, presenters, participants, keynote speakers, workshop chairs, session chairs, organizing committee members, student volunteers, Program Committee members, Advisory Committee members, International Liaison chairs, reviewers and other individuals in various roles. Thus, we take this opportunity to wholehartedly thank each and everyone.

We additionally wish to thank publisher Springer for their agreement to publish the proceedings, besides sponsoring part of the best papers awards and for their kind assistance and cooperation during the editing process.

We would cordially like to invite you to refer to the ICCSA website https://iccsa.org, where you can find the relevant details regarding this academic endeavor and event of ours.

June 2025

Osvaldo Gervasi
Yeliz Karaca
Beniamino Murgante
Chiara Garau

A Welcome Message from the Organizers

The International Conference on Computational Science and Its Applications (ICCSA) reflects a culmination of meticulous and dedicated efforts and academic endeavors toward the progress of science and technology.

One of the most noteworthy aspects of ICCSA is its fostering of a collective spirit, bringing together a plethora of participants from all over the world. Correspondingly, this merging power manifests itself in the 25th anniversary of ICCSA, which is a quarter of a century, in Istanbul, Türkiye, which connects and acts as a bridge between two continents, namely Asia and Europe. This unique location in the world hosts the 25th year of ICCSA at Galatasaray University, located on Çırağan Avenue by Istanbul's Bosphorus, which is an established international university bestowed with a distinctive past of teaching tradition, research and education exceeding five centuries.

Istanbul, having served as the capital city of four empires, namely the Roman Empire (330–395), the Byzantine Empire (395–1204 and 1261–1453), the Latin Empire (1204–1261) and the Ottoman Empire (1453–1922), is an exceptional city of the Republic of Türkiye founded by Mustafa Kemal Atatürk.

Situated at a strategic location along the historic Silk Road, Istanbul is at the core of extending rail networks which span across Europe and West Asia along with the only sea route between the Black Sea and the Mediterranean.

The cultural, historical and economic pulses of the country are evident in Istanbul whose rooted origins have embraced varying beliefs, lifestyles and populace, which highlights the city's mosaic quality with blended fabric in a constant harmonious flow. This has enabled cultures to grow and be nurtured, which is profoundly rooted in its urban culture.

Computational Science constitutes the main pillar of most present research, industrial and commercial activities besides manifesting a unique role in exploiting and addressing innovative Information and Communication Technologies. Thus, the 25-year-old ICCSA conference series provides remarkable opportunities to get acquainted with leading researchers, scientists, scholars, practitioners and many more while exchanging innovative ideas and initiating new partnerships, associations and bonds.

With the hosting of Galatasaray University, I would personally and on behalf of the Local Organizing Committee, with the members Emre Alptekin, Gülfem Işıklar Alptekin, Cengiz Kahraman, Abdullah Çağrı Tolga and Ayberk Zeytin, like to convey our sincere gratitude and thanks to everyone who exerted their efforts in and contributed to the realization of ICCSA 2025. With these notes and remarks, welcome to Istanbul!

Cordially yours,

On behalf of the Local Organizing Committee.

June 2025   Yeliz Karaca

Organization

Honorary General Chairs

Bernady O. Apduhan	Kyushu Sangyo University, Japan
Kenneth C. J. Tan	Sardina Systems, UK

General Chairs

Yeliz Karaca	University of Massachusetts, USA
Osvaldo Gervasi	University of Perugia, Italy
David Taniar	Monash University, Australia

Program Committee Chairs

Beniamino Murgante	University of Basilicata, Italy
Chiara Garau	University of Cagliari, Italy
Ana Maria A. C. Rocha	University of Minho, Portugal
A. Çağrı Tolga	Galatasaray University, Turkey

International Advisory Committee

Jemal Abawajy	Deakin University, Australia
Dharma P. Agarwal	University of Cincinnati, USA
Rajkumar Buyya	Melbourne University, Australia
Claudia Bauzer Medeiros	University of Campinas, Brazil
Manfred M. Fisher	Vienna University of Economics and Business, Austria
Pierre Frankhauser	University of Franche-Comté/CNRS, France
Marina L. Gavrilova	University of Calgary, Canada
Sumi Helal	University of Florida, USA & Lancaster University, UK
Bin Jiang	University of Gävle, Sweden
Yee Leung	Chinese University of Hong Kong, China

International Liaison Chairs

Ivan Blečić	University of Cagliari, Italy
Giuseppe Borruso	University of Trieste, Italy
Elise De Donker	Western Michigan University, USA
Maria Noelia Faginas Lago	University of Perugia, Italy
Maria Irene Falcão	University of Minho, Portugal
Robert C. H. Hsu	Chung Hua University, Taiwan
Yeliz Karaca	University of Massachusetts Chan Medical School, USA
Tae-Hoon Kim	Zhejiang University of Science and Technology, China
Vladimir Korkhov	Saint Petersburg University, Russia
Takashi Naka	Kyushu Sangyo University, Japan
Rafael D. C. Santos	National Institute for Space Research, Brazil
Maribel Yasmina Santos	University of Minho, Portugal
Anastasia Stratigea	National Technical University of Athens, Greece

Workshop and Session Organizing Chairs

Beniamino Murgante	University of Basilicata, Italy
Chiara Garau	University of Cagliari, Italy

Award Chair

Wenny Rahayu	La Trobe University, Australia

Publicity Committee Chairs

Elmer Dadios	De La Salle University, Philippines
Nataliia Kulabukhova	Saint Petersburg University, Russia
Daisuke Takahashi	Tsukuba University, Japan
Shangwang Wang	Beijing University of Posts and Telecommunications, China

Local Organizing Committee Chairs

Emre Alptekin	Galatasaray University, Turkey
Gülfem Işıklar Alptekin	Galatasaray University, Turkey
Cengiz Kahraman	İstanbul Technical University, Turkey
A. Çağrı Tolga	Galatasaray University, Turkey
Ayberk Zeytin	Galatasaray University, Turkey

Technology Chair

Damiano Perri	University of Perugia, Italy

Program Committee

Vera Afreixo	University of Aveiro, Portugal
Vladimir Alarcon	Northern Gulf Institute, USA
Filipe Alvelos	University of Minho, Portugal
Debora Anelli	Polytechnic University of Bari, Italy
Hartmut Asche	Hasso-Plattner-Institut für Digital Engineering Ggmbh, Germany
Nizamettin Aydın	İstanbul Technical University, Turkey
Ginevra Balletto	University of Cagliari, Italy
Nadia Balucani	University of Perugia, Italy
Socrates Basbas	Aristotle University of Thessaloniki, Greece
David Berti	ART SpA, Italy
Michela Bertolotto	University College Dublin, Ireland
Sandro Bimonte	CEMAGREF, TSCF, France
Ana Cristina Braga	University of Minho, Portugal
Tiziana Campisi	Kore University of Enna, Italy
Yves Caniou	Université Claude Bernard Lyon 1, France
Alessandra Capolupo	Polytechnic University of Bari, Italy
José A. Cardoso e Cunha	Universidade Nova de Lisboa, Portugal
Rui Cardoso	University of Beira Interior, Portugal
Leocadio G. Casado	University of Almería, Spain
Mete Celik	Erciyes University, Turkey
Maria Cerreta	University of Naples Federico II, Italy
Ta Quang Chieu	Thuyloi University, Vietnam
Rachel Chien-Sing Lee	Sunway University, Malaysia
Birol Ciloglugil	Ege University, Turkey
Mauro Coni	University of Cagliari, Italy

Florbela Maria da Cruz Domingues Correia — Polytechnic Institute of Viana do Castelo, Portugal

Alessandro Costantini — INFN, Italy

Roberto De Lotto — University of Pavia, Italy

Luiza De Macedo Mourelle — State University of Rio De Janeiro, Brazil

Marcelo De Paiva Guimaraes — Federal University of Sao Paulo, Brazil

Frank Devai — London South Bank University, UK

Joana Matos Dias — University of Coimbra, Portugal

Aziz Dursun — Virginia Tech University, USA

Laila El Ghandour — Heriot-Watt University, UK

Rafida M. Elobaid — Canadian University Dubai, United Arab Emirates

Maria Irene Falcao — University of Minho, Portugal

Florbela P. Fernandes — Polytechnic Institute of Bragança, Portugal

Paula Odete Fernandes — Polytechnic Institute of Bragança, Portugal

Adelaide de Fátima Baptista Valente Freitas — University of Aveiro, Portugal

Valentina Franzoni — University of Perugia, Italy

Andreas Fricke — University of Potsdam, Germany

Raffaele Garrisi — Centro Operativo per la Sicurezza Cibernetica, Italy

Ivan Gerace — University of Perugia, Italy

Maria Giaoutzi — National Technical University of Athens, Greece

Salvatore Giuffrida — University of Catania, Italy

Teresa Guarda — Universidad Estatal Peninsula de Santa Elena, Ecuador

Sevin Gümgüm — Izmir University of Economics, Turkey

Malgorzata Hanzl — Technical University of Lodz, Poland

Maulana Adhinugraha Kiki — Telkom University, Indonesia

Clement Ho Cheung Leung — Chinese University of Hong Kong, China

Andrea Lombardi — University of Perugia, Italy

Marcos Mandado Alonso — University of Vigo, Spain

Ernesto Marcheggiani — Katholieke Universiteit Leuven, Belgium

Antonino Marvuglia — Luxembourg Institute of Science and Technology, Luxembourg

Michele Mastroianni — University of Salerno, Italy

Hideo Matsufuru — High Energy Accelerator Research Organization, Japan

Fernando Miranda — Universidade do Minho, Portugal

Giuseppe Modica — University of Reggio Calabria, Italy

Majaz Moonis — University of Massachusetts, USA

Nadia Nedjah — State University of Rio de Janeiro, Brazil

Paolo Nesi — University of Florence, Italy

Workshops

Workshop on Advancements in Applied Machine-Learning and Data Analytics (AAMDA 2025)

Workshop Organizers

Alessandro Costantini	INFN, Italy
Daniele Cesini	INFN, Italy
Elisabetta Ronchieri	INFN, Italy
Barbara Martelli	INFN, Italy

Workshop Program Committee Members

Alessandro Costantini	Istituto Nazionale di Fisica Nucleare (INFN), Italy
Daniele Cesini	Istituto Nazionale di Fisica Nucleare (INFN), Italy
Elisabetta Ronchieri	Istituto Nazionale di Fisica Nucleare (INFN), Italy
Barbara Martelli	Istituto Nazionale di Fisica Nucleare (INFN), Italy
Luca Dell'Agnello	Istituto Nazionale di Fisica Nucleare (INFN), Italy

Advanced and Innovative Web Apps 2025 (AIWA 2025)

Workshop Organizers

Damiano Perri	University of Perugia, Italy
Osvaldo Gervasi	University of Perugia, Italy
Stelios Kouzeleas	International Hellenic University, Greece
Sergio Tasso	University of Perugia, Italy

Workshop Program Committee Members

David Berti	ART SpA, Italy
JungYoon Kim	Gachon University, South Korea
TaiHoon Kim	Zhejiang University of Science and Technology, China

Advanced Processes of Mathematics and Computing Models in Complex Data-Intensive Computational Systems (AMCM 2025)

Workshop Organizers

Yeliz Karaca	University of Massachusetts Chan Medical School and Massachusetts Institute of Technology, USA
Dumitru Baleanu	Lebanese American University, Lebanon
Osvaldo Gervasi	University of Perugia, Italy
Yudong Zhang	University of Leicester, UK
Majaz Moonis	University of Massachusetts Chan Medical School and Massachusetts Institute of Technology, USA

Workshop Program Committee Members

TaeHoon Kim	Zhejiang University of Science and Technology, China
Martin Bohner	Missouri University of Science and Technology, USA
Shuihua Wang	University of Leicester, UK
Khan Muhammad	Sungkyunkwan University, South Korea
Mahmoud Abdel-Aty	Sohag University, Egypt
Aziz Dursun	Virginia Polytechnic Institute and State University, USA
Kemal Güven Gülen	Namık Kemal University, Turkey
Akif Akgül	Hitit Üniversitesi, Turkey

Advanced Numerical Approaches for Assessment and Design of No-Tension Masonry Structures (ANAMS 2025)

Workshop Organizers

Antonino Iannuzzo	Universitá degli studi del Sannio, Italy
Carlo Olivieri	Universitá Telematica Pegaso, Italy
Andrea Montanino	CIMNE, Spain
Elham Mousavian	University of Edinburgh, UK

Workshop Program Committee Members

Pietro Meriggi	Roma Tre University, Italy
Francesca Perelli	University of Naples Federico II, Italy
Marialuigia Sangirardi	University of Oxford, UK
Sam Cocking	University of Cambridge, UK

Matteo Salvalaggio	University of Minho, Portugal
Vittorio Paris	University of Bergamo, Italy
Luigi Sibille	Norwegian University of Science and Technology, Norway
Natalia Pingaro	Politecnico di Milano, Italy
Martina Buzzetti	Politecnico di Milano, Italy
Generoso Vaiano	Pegaso Telematic University, Italy
Alessandra Capolupo	Politecnico di Bari, Italy
Amal Gerges	Università degli Studi di Cagliari, Italy
Fabian Orozco	National Autonomous University of Mexico, Mexico
Nathanael Savalle	Polytech Clermont and Université Clermont Auvergne, France
Luca Umberto Argiento	University of Naples Federico II, Italy
Bartolomeo Pantó	Durham University, UK

Unveiling the Synergies Between Air Quality and Climate PlAnning (AQCliPA 2025)

Workshop Organizers

Angela Pilogallo	University of L'Aquila, Italy
Luigi Santopietro	University of Basilicata, Italy
Filomena Pietrapertosa	IMAA CNR, Italy
Monica Salvia	IMAA CNR, Italy
Carlo Trozzi	IMAA CNR, Italy
Valeria Scapini	Central University of Chile, Chile

Workshop Program Committee Members

Lucia Saganeiti	IMAA-CNR, Italy
Lorena Fiorini	University of L'Aquila, Italy
Antonio Mazza	IMAA-CNR, Italy
Gabriele Nolè	IMAA-CNR, Italy
Carmen Guida	University of Naples "Federico II", Italy
Floriana Zucaro	University of Naples "Federico II", Italy
Sabrina Lai	University of Cagliari, Italy
Chiara Garau	University of Cagliari, Italy

Advancements in Spatial assessment of Socio-Ecological SystemS (ASSESS 2025)

Workshop Organizers

Daniele Cannatella	TU Delft, The Netherlands
Giuliano Poli	University of Naples Federico II, Italy
Eugenio Muccio	TU Delft, The Netherlands
Claudiu Forgaci	TU Delft, The Netherlands

Workshop Program Committee Members

Daniele Cannatella	TU Delft, The Netherlands
Giuliano Poli	University of Naples Federico II, Italy
Eugenio Muccio	University of Naples Federico II, Italy
Claudiu Forgaci	TU Delft, The Netherlands
Maria Cerreta	University of Naples Federico II, Italy
Maria Somma	University of Naples Federico II, Italy
Laura Di Tommaso	University of Naples Federico II, Italy
Sabrina Sacco	Politecnico di Milano, Italy
Piero Zizzania	University of Naples Federico II, Italy
Gaia Daldanise	CNR IRISS, Italy
Benedetta Grieco	University of Naples Federico II, Italy
Giuseppe Ciciriello	University of Naples Federico II, Italy
Marta Dell'Ovo	Politecnico di Milano, Italy
Francesco Piras	University of Cagliari, Italy
Diana Rolando	Politecnico di Torino, Italy
Stefano Cuntò	University of Naples Federico II, Italy
Ludovica La Rocca	University of Naples Federico II, Italy

Blockchain and Distributed Ledgers: Technologies and Applications (BDLTA 2025)

Workshop Organizers

Vladimir Korkhov	Saint Petersburg State University, Russia
Elena Stankova	Saint Petersburg State University, Russia
Nataliia Kulabukhova	Saint Petersburg State University, Russia

Workshop Program Committee Members

Adam Belloum	University of Amsterdam, the Netherlands
Dmitrii Vasiunin	Deutsche Telekom Cloud Services E.P.E., Greece
Serob Balyan	Osensus Arm LLC, Armenia
Suren Abrahamyan	Osensus Arm LLC, Armenia
Ashot Sergey Gevorkyan	NAS of Armenia, Armenia

Michal Hnatic	Univerzita Pavla Jozefa Šafárika v Košiciach, Slovakia
Michail Panteleyev	Saint Petersburg Electrotecnical University, Russia
Martin Vala	Univerzita Pavla Jozefa Šafárika v Košiciach, Slovakia
Nodir Zaynalov	Tashkent University of Information Technologies named after Muhammad al Khwarizmi, Uzbekistan
Michail Panteleyev	Saint Petersburg Electrotecnical University, Russia
Alexander Degtyarev	Saint Petersburg University, Russia
Alexander Bogdanov	St. Petersburg State University, Russia

Bio and Neuro Inspired Computing and Applications (BIONCA 2025)

Workshop Organizers

Nadia Nedjah	State University of Rio de Janeiro, Brazil
Luiza de Macedo Mourelle	State University of Rio de Janeiro, Brazil

Workshop Program Committee Members

Nadia Nedjha	State University of Rio de Janeiro, Brazil
Luiza de Macedo Mourelle	State University of Rio de Janeiro, Brazil
Luigi Maciel Ribeiro	State University of Rio de Janeiro, Brazil
Joelmir Ramos	Federal University of Rio de Janeiro, Brazil
Rogério Moraes	Brazilian Navy, Brazil
Marcos Santana Farias	Institute of Nuclear Energy, Brazil
Luneque Silva Jr.	Federal University of ABC, Brazil
Alan Oliveira	University of Lisboa, Portugal
Brij Bhooshan Gupta	Asia University, Taiwan

Computational and Applied Mathematics (CAM 2025)

Workshop Organizers

Maria Irene Falcão	University of Minho, Portugal
Fernando Miranda	University of Minho, Portugal

Workshop Program Committee Members

Fernando Miranda	University of Minho, Portugal
Graça Tomaz	Polytechnic of Guarda, Portugal
Helmuth Malonek	University of Aveiro, Portugal

Isabel Cacao	University of Aveiro, Portugal
João Morais	Autonomous Technological Institute of Mexico, Mexico
Lidia Aceto	University of Eastern Piedmont, Italy
Luís Ferrás	University of Porto, Portugal
M. Irene Falcão	University of Minho, Portugal
Patrícia Beites	University of Beira Interior, Portugal
Paulo Amorim	FGV EMAp, Brazil
Regina de Almeida	University of Trás-os-Montes e Alto Douro, Portugal
Ricardo Severino	University of Minho, Portugal

Computational and Applied Statistics (CAS 2025)

Workshop Organizer

Ana Cristina Braga	ALGORITMI Research Centre, LASI, University of Minho, Portugal

Workshop Program Committee Members

Adelaide Freitas	University of Aveiro, Portugal
Andreas Futschik	Johannes Kepler University Linz, Austria
Ana Cristina Braga	University of Minho, Portugal
Ângela Silva	University of Minho, Portugal
Arminda Manuela Gonçalves	University of Minho, Portugal
Carina Silva	Polytechnic Intitute of Lisbon, Portugal
Elisete Correia	University of Trás-os-Montes e Alto Douro, Portugal
Frank Westad	Norwegian University of Science and Technology, Norway
Isabel Natario	New University of Lisbon, Portugal
Irene Oliveira	University of Trás-os-Montes e Alto Douro, Portugal
Ivan Rodriguez Conde	University of Vigo, Spain
Joaquim Gonçalves	Instituto Politécnico do Cávado e do Ave, Portugal
Lino Costa	University of Minho, Portugal
Marco Reis	University of Coimbra, Portugal
Maria Filipa Mourão	Polytechnic Institute of Viana do Castelo, Portugal
Maria João Polidoro	Polytechnic Institute of Porto, Portugal
Martin Perez Perez	University of Vigo, Spain
Michal Abrahamowicz	McGill University, Canada
Vera Afreixo	University of Aveiro, Portugal

Werner G. Müller	Johannes Kepler University Linz, Austria
Bruna Silva Ramos	University Lusiada de Famalicão, Portugal
Inês Sousa	University of Minho, Portugal
Luís Miguel Rocha Matos	University of Minho, Portugal
Manuel Carlos Figueiredo	University of Minho, Portugal

Cyber Intelligence and Applications (CIA 2025)

Workshop Organizer

Gianni D'Angelo	University of Salerno, Italy

Workshop Program Committee Members

Gianni D'Angelo	University of Salerno, Italy
Francesco Palmieri	University of Salerno, Italy
Massimo Ficco	University of Salerno, Italy
Arcangelo Castiglione	University of Salerno, Italy

Computational Methods for Business Analytics (CMBA 2025)

Workshop Organizers

Cláudio Alves	Universidade do Minho, Portugal
Telmo Pinto	Universidade do Minho, Portugal

Workshop Program Committee Members

Abdulrahim Shamayleh	American University of Sharjah, United Arab Emirates
Ana Rocha	University of Minho, Portugal
Angelo Sifaleras	University of Macedonia, Greece
Cristóvão Silva	University of Coimbra, Portugal
José Valério de Carvalho	University of Minho, Portugal
Miguel Vieira	Universidade Lusófona, Portugal
Rita Macedo ˙	Université de Lille, France
Ana Moura	Universidade de Aveiro, Portugal
Cristina Lopes	ISCAP, Portugal
Eliana Costa e Silva	Instituto Politécnico do Porto, Portugal

Computational Methods, Statistics and Industrial Mathematics (CMSIM 2025)

Workshop Organizers

Maria Filomena Teodoro	IST ID, Instituto Superior Técnico, Portugal
Marina Alexandra Pedro Andrade	ISCTE – Lisbon University Institute, Portugal
Paula Simões	University of Lisbon, Portugal
Teresa A. Oliveira	IST ID, Instituto Superior Técnico, Portugal

Workshop Program Committee Members

Amilcar Oliveira	Universidade Aberta and Universidade de Lisboa, Portugal
Victor Lobo	Escola Naval and NOVA IMS Almada, Portugal
António Pacheco	IST Universidade de Lisboa, Portugal
Eliana Costa	Escola Superior de Tecnologia e Gestão IPPorto, Portugal
Aldina Correia	Escola Superior de Tecnologia e Gestão IPPorto, Portugal
Fernando Carapau	University of Évora, Portugal
Ricardo Moura	Portuguese Naval Academy, Portugal
Ana Borges	Escola Superior de Tecnologia e Gestão IPPorto, Portugal
Cristina Lopes	ISCAP IPPorto, Portugal
Fernanda Costa	University of Minho, Portugal
Cabrita Carlos	IPBeja, Portugal
Maria Luísa Morgado	University of Trás os Montes e Alto Douro and University of Lisboa, Portugal
Rosário Ramos	Universidade Aberta, Portugal
Sofia Rézio	Iscal, Instituto Politécnico de Lisboa, Portugal
Matteo Sacchet	University of Turin, Italy
Marina Marchisio Conte	University of Turin, Italy
António Seijas-Macias	University of Coruña, Spain
Luís F. A. Teodoro	University of Glasgow, UK and University of Oslo, Norway
Christos Kitsos	University of West Attica, Greece
M. Filomena Teodoro	Universidade de Lisboa, Portugal
Marina A. P. Andrade	Instituto Universitário de Lisboa, Portugal
Paula Simões	Military Academy and Universidade Nova de Lisboa, Portugal
Teresa Oliveira	Universidade Aberta and Universidade de Lisboa, Portugal

Computational Optimization and Applications (COA 2025)

Workshop Organizers

Ana Rocha	ALGORITMI Research Centre, LASI, University of Minho, Portugal, Portugal
Humberto Rocha	ALGORITMI Research Centre, LASI, University of Minho, Portugal, Portugal

Workshop Program Committee Members

Florbela Fernandes	Polytechnic Institute of Bragança, Portugal
Clara Vaz	Polytechnic Institute of Bragança, Portugal
Ana Pereira	Polytechnic Institute of Bragança, Portugal
Filipe Alvelos	University of Minho, Portugal
Joana Dias	University of Coimbra, Portugal
Eligius M. T. Hendrix	University of Málaga, Spain
Emerson José de Paiva	Federal University of Itajubá, Brazil
Ana Paula Teixeira	University of Trás-os-Montes and Alto Douro, Portugal
Lino Costa	Universidade do Minho, Portugal

Coastal Cities Versus Inland Areas. Hypotheses for Sustainable Regeneration Through Ecosystem Services of 'Hooking' and Rehabilitation of Brownfield Sites (CoastalCities_VS_InlandAreas 2025)

Workshop Organizers

Celestina Fazia	Università di Enna Kore, Italy
Angrilli Massimo	University of Chieti-Pescara, Italy
Valentina Ciuffreda	University of Chieti-Pescara, Italy
Maurizio Oddo	Università di Enna Kore, Italy
Marcello Sestito	Università di Enna Kore, Italy
Clara Stella Vicari Aversa	University of Reggio Calabria, Italy

Workshop Program Committee Members

Alessandro Camiz	Università d'Annunzio, Italy
Thowayeb Hassan	King Faisal University, Saudi Arabia
Alessandro Barracco	Università Kore di Enna, Italy
Mario Morrica	University of Urbino, Italy
Mariana Ratiu	University of Oradea, Romania
Alanda Akamana	Mohammed VI Polytechnic University, Morocco
Kaoutare Amini Alaoui	Mohammed VI Polytechnic University, Morocco

Computational Astrochemistry 2025 (CompAstro 2025)

Workshop Organizers

Marzio Rosi	University of Perugia, Italy
Daniela Ascenzi	University of Trento, Italy
Nadia Balucani	University of Perugia, Italy
Stefano Falcinelli	University of Perugia, Italy

Workshop Program Committee Members

Dario Campisi	Università degli Studi di Perugia, Italy
Giacomo Giorgi	Università degli Studi di Perugia, Italy
Andrea Giustini	Università degli Studi di Perugia, Italy
Luca Mancini	Università degli Studi di Perugia, Italy
Albert Rimola	Universitat Autònoma de Barcelona, Spain
Gianmarco Vanuzzo	Università degli Studi di Perugia, Italy
Dimitrios Skouteris	Master-Tec, Italy
Piero Ugliengo	Università degli Studi di Torino, Italy
Franco Vecchiocattivi	Università degli Sudi di Perugia, Italy
Giacomo Pannacci	Università degli Studi di Perugia, Italy
Costanza Borghesi	Università degli Studi di Perugia, Italy
Marco Parriani	Università degli Studi di Perugia, Italy
Marta Loletti	Università degli Studi di Perugia, Italy
Fernando Pirani	Università degli Studi di Perugia, Italy
Andrea Lombardi	Università degli Studi di Perugia, Italy
Noelia Faginas Lago	Università degli Studi di Perugia, Italy
Paolo Tosi	Università di Trento, Italy
Cecilia Coletti	Università degli Studi Chieti-Pescara, Italy
Nazzareno Re	Università degli Studi Chieti-Pescara, Italy
Linda Podio	Osservatorio Astrofisico di Arcetri INAF, Italy
Claudio Codella	Osservatorio Astrofisico di Arcetri INAF, Italy
Gabriella Di Genova	Università degli Studi di Perugia, Italy

Computational Methods for Porous Geomaterials (CompPor 2025)

Workshop Organizers

Vadim Lisitsa	IPGG SB RAS, Russia
Evgeniy Romenski	IPGG SB RAS, Russia

Workshop Program Committee Members

Vadim Lisitsa	Institute of Petroleum Geology and Geophysics SB RAS, Russia
Evgeniy Romenski	Sobolev Institute of Mathematics SB RAS, Russia
Vladimir Cheverda	Sobolev Institute of Mathematics SB RAS, Russia
Tatyana Khachkova	IPGG SB RAS, Russia
Dmitry Prokhorov	IPGG SB RAS, Russia
Mikhail Novikov	Sobolev Institute of Mathematics SB RAS, Russia
Sergey Solovyev	Sobolev Institute of Mathematics SB RAS, Russia
Kirill Gadylshin	LLC RNBashNIPIneft, Russia
Olga Stoyanovskaya	Lavrentev Institute of Hydrodynamics SB RAS, Russia
Yerlan Amanbek	Nazarbaev University, Kazakstan

Workshop on Computational Science and HPC (CSHPC 2025)

Workshop Organizers

Elise de Doncker	Western Michigan University, USA
Hideo Matsufuru	High Energy Accelerator Research Organization, Japan

Workshop Program Committee Members

Elise de Doncker	Western Michigan University, USA
Hideo Matsufuru	High Energy Accelerator Research Organization (KEK), Japan
Fukuko Yuasa	KEK, Japan
Issaku Kanamori	RIKEN, Japan
Hiroshi Daisaka	Hitotsubashi University, Japan
Norikazu Yamada	KEK, Japan
Naohito Nakasato	University of Aizu, Japan
Robert Makin	Western Michigan University, USA

Cities, Technologies and Planning 2025 (CTP 2025)

Workshop Organizers

Giuseppe Borruso	University of Trieste, Italy
Beniamino Murgante	University of Basilicata, Italy
Malgorzata Hanzl	Lodz University of Technology, Poland
Anastasia Stratigea	National Technical University of Athens, Greece
Ljiljana Zivkovic	Republic Geodetic Authority, Serbia
Ginevra Balletto	University of Trieste, Italy

Workshop Program Committee Members

Giuseppe Borruso	University of Trieste, Italy
Beniamino Murgante	University of Basilicata, Italy
Malgorzata Hanzl	Lodz University of Technology, Poland
Anastasia Stratigea	National Technical University of Athens, Greece
Ljiljiana Zivkovic	Republic Geodetic Authority of Serbia, Serbia
Ginevra Balletto	University of Cagliari, Italy
Silvia Battino	University of Sassari, Italy
Mara Ladu	University of Cagliari, Italy
Maria del Mar Munoz Leonisio	University of Cádiz, Spain
Ahinoa Amaro Garcia	University of Las Palmas of Gran Canaria, Spain
Maria Attard	University of Malta, Malta
Enrico D'agostini	World Maritime University, Sweden
Francesca Krasna	University of Trieste, Italy
Brisol Garcia Garcia	Polytechnic University of Quintana Roo, Mexico
Tu Anh Trinh	UEH University, Vietnam
Giovanni Mauro	Università degli Studi della Campania, Italy
Maria Ronza	University of Naples Federico II, Italy
Massimiliano Bencardino	University of Salerno, Italy
Tomasz Bradecki	Silesian University of Technology, Poland
Dorota Kamrowska-Załuska	Gdańsk University of Technology, Poland
Iwona Jażdżewska	University of Lodz, Poland
Yiota Theodora	National Technical University of Athens, Greece
Apostolos Lagarias	University of Thessaly, Greece
George Tsilimigkas	University of the Aegean, Greece
Akrivi Leka	National Technical University of Athens, Greece
Maria Panagiotopoulou	National Technical University of Athens, Greece
Andrea Gallo	Ca' Foscari University of Venice, Italy
Francesca Sinatra	University of Trieste, Italy

Digital Transition: Effects on Housing Mobility, Market, Land Governance (DIGITRANS 2025)

Workshop Organizers

Fabrizio Battisti	University of Florence, Italy
Fabiana Forte	University of Campania, Italy
Orazio Campo	Sapienza University of Rome, Italy
Alessio Pino	Kore University of Enna, Italy
Carlo Pisano	University of Florence, Italy
Mariolina Grasso	Kore University of Enna, Italy

Workshop Program Committee Members

Fabrizio Battisti	University of Florence, Italy
Fabiana Forte	Università della Campania Luigi Vanvitelli, Italy
Orazio Campo	University of Rome "La Sapienza", Italy
Alessio Pino	Kore University of Enna, Italy
Carlo Pisano	University of Florence, Italy
Mariolina Grasso	Università Kore di Enna, Italy

Evaluating Inner Areas Potentials (EIAP 2025)

Workshop Organizers

Diana Rolando	Politecnico di Torino, Italy
Alice Barreca	Politecnico di Torino, Italy
Manuela Rebaudengo	Politecnico di Torino, Italy
Giorgia Malavasi	Politecnico di Torino, Italy

Workshop Program Committee Members

John Accordino	Virginia Commonwealth University, USA
Francesco Bruzzone	Università Iuav di Venezia, Italy
Maria Cerreta	Università degli Studi di Napoli Federico II, Italy
Maddalena Chimisso	Università degli Studi del Molise, Italy
Chiara Chioni	Università degli Studi di Trento, Italy
Annalisa Contato	Università degli Studi di Palermo, Italy
Cristina Coscia	Politecnico di Torino, Italy
Marta Dell'Ovo	Politecnico di Milano, Italy
Benedetta Di Leo	Università Politecnica delle Marche, Italy
Sara Favargiotti	Università degli Studi di Trento, Italy
Maddalena Ferretti	Università Politecnica delle Marche, Italy
Salvo Giuffrida	Università degli Studi di Palermo, Italy
Barbara Lino	Università degli Studi di Palermo, Italy
Umberto Mecca	Politecnico di Torino, Italy
Beatrice Mecca	Politecnico di Torino, Italy
Giuliano Poli	Università degli Studi di Napoli Federico II, Italy
Marco Rossitti	Politecnico di Milano, Italy
Alexandra Stankulova	Politecnico di Torino, Italy
Elena Todella	Politecnico di Torino, Italy
Asja Aulisio	Politecnico di Torino, Italy
Giulia Datola	Politecnico di Milano, Italy

Francesco Calabrò · Università degli Studi Mediterranea di Reggio
Calabria, Italy
Valeria Saiu · Università degli Studi di Cagliari, Italy
Maria Rosa Trovato · Università di Catania, Italy

Econometric and Multidimensional Evaluation in Urban Environment (EMEUE 2025)

Workshop Organizers
Maria Cerreta · University of Naples Federico II, Italy
Carmelo Maria Torre · Polytechnic University of Bari, Italy
Pierluigi Morano · Polytechnic University of Bari, Italy
Simona Panaro · University of Naples Federico II, Italy
Felicia Di Liddo · University of Naples Federico II, Italy
Debora Anelli · University of Naples Federico II, Italy

Workshop Program Committee Members
Carmelo Maria Torre · Polytechnic University of Bari, Italy
Maria Cerreta · University of Naples Federico II, Italy
Pierluigi Morano · Polytechnic University of Bari, Italy
Francesco Tajani · Sapienza University of Rome, Italy
Simona Panaro · University of Naples Federico II, Italy
Felicia di Liddo · Polytechnic University of Bari, Italy
Debora Anelli · Sapienza University of Rome, Italy
Giuliano Poli · University of Naples Federico II, Italy
Maria Somma · University of Naples Federico II, Italy
Simona Panaro · University of Campania Luigi Vanvitelli, Italy
Laura Di Tommaso · University of Naples Federico II, Italy
Caterina Loffredo · University of Naples Federico II, Italy
Ludovica La Rocca · University of Naples Federico II, Italy
Sabrina Sacco · Politecnico di Milano, Italy
Piero Zizzania · University of Naples Federico II, Italy
Gaia Daldanise · CNR IRISS, Italy
Benedetta Grieco · University of Naples Federico II, Italy
Giuseppe Ciciriello · University of Naples Federico II, Italy
Marta Dell'Ovo · Politecnico di Milano, Italy
Daniele Cannatella · TU Delft University, The Netherlands
Eugenio Muccio · University of Naples Federico II, Italy
Sveva Ventre · University of Naples Federico II, Italy

Governance of Energy Transition: Environmental, Landscape, Social and Spatial Planning (ENERGY_PLANNING 2025)

Workshop Organizers

Mara Ladu	University of Cagliari, Italy
Ginevra Balletto	University of Cagliari, Italy
Emilio Ghiani	University of Cagliari, Italy
Alessandra Marra	University of Salerno, Italy
Roberto De Lotto	University of Pavia, Italy
Balázs Kulcsár	Chalmers University of Technology, Sweden

Workshop Program Committee Members

Riccardo Trevisan	University of Cagliari, Italy
Marco Naseddu	University of Cagliari, Italy
Giuseppe Borruso	University of Trieste, Italy
Andrea Gallo	University of Trieste, Italy
Francesca Sinatra	University of Trieste, Italy
Maria Attard	University of Malta, Malta
Tu Anh Trinh	UEH University Ho Chi Minh City, Vietnam
Marcello Tadini	University of Eastern Piedmont, Italy
Luigi Mundula	University for Foreigners of Perugia, Italy
Silvia Battino	University of Sassari, Italy
Maria del Mar Munoz Leonisio	University of Cádiz, Spain
Anna Richiedei	University of Brescia, Italy
Michele Pezzagno	University of Brescia, Italy
Federico Mertellozzo	University of Firenze, Italy
Marco Mazzarino	IUAV University Venice, Italy

Ecosystem Services in Spatial Planning for Climate Neutral Urban and Rural Areas (ESSP 2025)

Workshop Organizers

Sabrina Lai	University of Cagliari, Italy
Francesco Scorza	University of Basilicata, Italy
Corrado Zoppi	University of Cagliari, Italy
Beniamino Murgante	University of Basilicata, Italy
Carmela Gargiulo	University of Naples Federico II, Italy
Floriana Zucaro	University of Naples Federico II, Italy

Workshop Program Committee Members

Alfonso Annunziata	University of Basilicata, Italy
Ginevra Balletto	University of Cagliari, Italy
Ivan Blečić	University of Cagliari, Italy
Giuseppe Borruso	University of Trieste, Italy
Barbara Caselli	University of Parma, Italy
Maria Cerreta	University of Naples Federico II, Italy
Chiara Garau	University of Cagliari, Italy
Carmen Guida	University of Naples Federico II, Italy
Federica Isola	University of Cagliari, Italy
Francesca Leccis	University of Cagliari, Italy
Federica Leone	University of Cagliari, Italy
Silvia Rossetti	University of Parma, Italy
Luigi Santopietro	University of Basilicata, Italy
Carmelo Torre	Polytechnic of Bari, Italy

The 15th International Workshop on Future Information System Technologies and Applications (FiSTA 2025)

Workshop Organizers

Bernady O. Apduhan	Kyushu Sangyo University, Japan
Rafael Santos	Brazilian National Institute for Space Research, Brazil

Workshop Program Committee Members

Agustinus Borgy Waluyo	Monash University, Australia
Andre Ricardo Abed Grégio	Federal University of Paraná, Brazil
Eric Pardede	La Trobe University, Australia
Kai Cheng	Kyushu Sangyo University, Japan
Ching-Hsien Hsu	Asia University, Taiwan
Fenghui Yao	Tennessee State University, USA
Yusuke Gotoh	Okayama University, Japan
Alvaro Fazenda	Federal University of São Paulo, Brazil
Kazuaki Tanaka	Kyushu Institute of Technology, Japan
Tengku Adil	MARA Technological University, Malaysia
Toshihiro Yamauchi	Okayama University, Japan
Yasuaki Sumida	Kyushu Sangyo University, Japan
Earl Ryan Aleluya	MSU-Iligan Institute of Technology, Philippines
Cherry Mae G. Villame	MSU-Iligan Institute of Technology, Philippines
Anton Louise De Ocampo	Batangas State University, Philippines
Krishnamoorthy Ranganthan	Chennai Institute of Technology, India

Flow Management in Urban Contexts (FMUC 2025)

Workshop Organizers

Alessio Pino	Kore University of Enna, Italy
Giovanna Acampa	Kore University of Enna, Italy

Workshop Program Committee Members

Giovanna Acampa	University of Florence, Italy
Alessio Pino	Kore University of Enna, Italy
Mariolina Grasso	Università Kore di Enna, Italy
Fabrizio Battisti	University of Florence, Italy
Fabrizio Finucci	Roma Tre University, Italy
Antonella G. Masanotti	Roma Tre University, Italy
Daniele Mazzoni	Roma Tre University, Italy

Geographical Analysis, Urban Modeling, Spatial Statistics 2025 (Geog-And-Mod 2025)

Workshop Organizers

Beniamino Murgante	University of Basilicata, Italy
Giuseppe Borruso	University of Trieste, Italy
Hartmut Asche	University of Potsdam, Germany
Rodrigo Tapia McClung	CentroGeo, Mexico
Andreas Fricke	University of Potsdam, Germany

Workshop Program Committee Members

Giuseppe Borruso	University of Trieste, Italy
Beniamino Murgante	University of Basilicata, Italy
Hartmut Asche	University of Potsdam, Germany
Rodrigo Tapia-McClung	Centro de Investigación en Ciencias de Información Geoespacial (CentroGeo), Mexico
Andreas Fricke	University of Potsdam, Germany
Malgorzata Hanzl	Lodz University of Technology, Poland
Anastasia Stratigea	National Technical University of Athens, Greece
Ljiljiana Zivkovic	Republic Geodetic Authority of Serbia, Serbia
Ginevra Balletto	University of Cagliari, Italy
Silvia Battino	University of Sassari, Italy
Mara Ladu	University of Cagliari, Italy
Maria del Mar Munoz Leonisio	University of Cádiz, Spain
Ahinoa Amaro Garcia	University of Las Palmas of Gran Canaria, Spain
Maria Attard	University of Malta, Malta

Enrico D'agostini	World Maritime University, Sweden
Francesca Krasna	University of Trieste, Italy
Brisol García García	Polytechnic University of Quintana Roo, Mexico
Tu Anh Trinh	UEH University, Vietnam
Giovanni Mauro	Università degli Studi della Campania, Italy
Maria Ronza	University of Naples Federico II, Italy
Massimiliano Bencardino	University of Salerno, Italy
Andrea Gallo	Ca' Foscari University of Venice, Italy
Francesca Sinatra	University of Trieste, Italy
Salvatore Dore	University of Trieste, Italy

Geogames for Sustainable Development (Geogames 2025)

Workshop Organizer

Alenka Poplin	Iowa State University, USA

Workshop Program Committee Members

Alenka Poplin	Iowa State University, USA
Bruno Amaral de Andrade	Portucalense University, Portugal
Brian Tomaszewski	Rochester Institute of Technology, USA
Deepak Marhatta	Tribhuvan University, Nepal
Alessandro Plaisant	University of Sassari, Italy
David Schwartz	Rochester Institute of Technology, USA
Silvia Rossetti	University of Parma, Italy
Floriana Zucaro	University of Naples Federico II, Italy
Alfonso Annunziata	University of Basilicata, Italy
Reza Askarizad	University of Cagliari, Italy
Chiara Garau	University of Cagliari, Italy
Tanja Congiu	University of Sassari, Italy

Geomatics for Resource Monitoring and Management (GRMM 2025)

Workshop Organizers

Alberico Sonnessa	Politecnico di Bari, Italy
Eufemia Tarantino	Politecnico di Bari, Italy
Alessandra Capolupo	Politecnico di Bari, Italy

Workshop Program Committee Members

Umberto Fratino	Politecnico di Bari, Italy
Valeria Monno	Politecnico di Bari, Italy

Antonino Maltese	Università degli studi di Palermo, Italy
Athos Agapiou	Cyprus University of Technology, Cyprus
Michele Mangiameli	Università di Catania, Italy
Angela Gorgoglione	Universidad de la República de Uruguay, Uruguay
Roberta Ravanelli	University of Liège, Belgium
Ester Scotto di Perta	Università degli studi di Napoli Federico II, Italy
Giacomo Caporusso	CNR, Italy
Andrea Montanino	International Centre for Numerical Methods in Engineering of Barcelona, Spain
Antonino Iannuzzo	Università degli studi del Sannio, Italy
Alessandro Pagano	Politecnico di Bari, Italy
Francesco Di Capua	Università degli Studi della Basilicata, Italy
Albertini Cinzia	CNR-IREA, Italy
Alessandra Saponieri	Università degli studi del Salento, Italy
PierFrancesco Recchi	Università degli studi di Napoli Federico II, Italy
Vincenzo Totaro	Politecnico di Bari, Italy
Stefania Santoro	CNR Water Research Institute, Italy
Francesco Bimbo	University of Foggia, Italy
Cristina Proietti	Istituto Nazionale di Geofisica e Vulcanologia, Italy
Carla Cavallo	University of Salerno, Italy
Gaetano Falcone	Università degli Studi di Napoli Federico II, Italy
Valeria Belloni	Sapienza University of Rome, Italy
Alessandra Mascitelli	University of Chieti-Pescara, Italy

HERitage and CLIMAte neutrality. Resilient approach for nature centered/based sustainable cities (HERCLIMA 2025)

Workshop Organizers

Celestina Fazia	Università di Enna Kore, Italy
Angrilli Massimo	University of Chieti-Pescara, Italy
Clara Stella Vicari Aversa	University of Reggio Calabria, Italy
Dorina Camelia Ilies	University of Oradea, Romania
Mariana Ratiu	University of Oradea, Romania

Workshop Program Committee Members

Alessandro Camiz	Università d'Annunzio, Italy
Mario Morrica	University of Urbino, Italy
Thowayeb Hassan	King Faisal University, Saudi Arabia
Alessandro Barracco	Università Kore di Enna, Italy
Kaoutare Amini Alaoui	Mohammed VI Polytechnic University (UM6P), Morocco

| Mariana Ratiu | University of Oradea, Romania |
| Valentina Ciuffreda | Università Chieti-Pescara, Italy |

International Workshop on Information and Knowledge in the Internet of Things (IKIT 2025)

Workshop Organizers

Teresa Guarda	Universidad Estatal Península de Santa Elena, Ecuador
Luis Enrique Chuquimarca Jimenez	Universidad Estatal Península de Santa Elena, Ecuador
Gustavo Gatica	Universidad Andrés Bello, Chile
Filipe Mota Pinto	Polytechnic Institute of Leiria, Portugal
Arnulfo Alanis	Instituto Tecnológico de Tijuana, Mexico
Luis Mazon	Universidad Estatal Península de Santa Elena, Spain

Workshop Program Committee Members

Arnulfo Alanis	Instituto Tecnológico de Tijuana, Mexico
Bruno Sousa	University of Coimbra, Portugal
Carlos Balsa	Instituto Politécnico de Bragança, Portugal
Filipe Mota Pinto	Instituto Politécnico de Leiria, Portugal
Gustavo Gatica	Universidad Andrés Bello, Chile
Isabel Lopes	Instituto Politécnico de Bragança, Portugal
José-María Díaz-Nafría	Universidad a Distancia, Spain
Maria Fernanda Augusto	BiTrum Research Group, Spain
Maria Isabel Ribeiro	Instituto Politécnico Bragança, Portugal
Modestos Stavrakis	University of the Aegean, Greece
Simone Belli	Universidad Complutense de Madrid, Spain
Walter Lopes Neto	Instituto Federal de Educação, Brazil

International Workshop on territorial Planning to integrate Risk prevention and urban Ontologies (IWPRO 2025)

Workshop Organizers

Beniamino Murgante	University of Basilicata, Italy
Roberto De Lotto	University of Pavia, Italy
Elisabetta Maria Venco	University of Pavia, Italy
Caterina Pietra	University of Pavia, Italy

Workshop Program Committee Members

Stefano Borgo	Consiglio Nazionale delle Ricerche ISTC, Italy
Valentina Costa	Università di Genova, Italy
Hamid Danesh Pajouh	Middle East Technical University, Turkey
Ilaria Delponte	Università di Genova, Italy
Lorena Fiorini	Università de L'Aquila, Italy
Veronica Gazzola	Politecnico di Milano, Italy
Ghazaleh Goodarzi	Islamic Azad University, Iran
Michele Grimaldi	Università degli Studi di Salerno, Italy
Alessandra Marra	Università degli Studi di Salerno, Italy
Naghmeh Mohammadpourlima	Åbo Akademi University, Finland
Francesca Pirlone	Università di Genova, Italy
Silvia Rossetti	Università di Parma, Italy
Bahareh Shahsavari	University of Minnesota, USA
Ilenia Spadaro	Università di Genova, Italy
Maria Rosaria Stufano Melone	Politecnico di Bari, Italy

Regional Connectivity, Spatial Accessibility and MaaS for Social Inclusion (MaaS 2025)

Workshop Organizers

Mara Ladu	University of Cagliari, Italy
Ginevra Balletto	University of Cagliari, Italy
Gianfranco Fancello	University of Cagliari, Italy
Tanja Congiu	University of Sassari, Italy
Patrizia Serra	University of Cagliari, Italy
Francesco Piras	University of Cagliari, Italy

Workshop Program Committee Members

Marco Naseddu	University of Cagliari, Italy
Italo Meloni	University of Cagliari, Italy
Giuseppe Borruso	University of Trieste, Italy
Andrea Gallo	University of Trieste, Italy
Francesca Sinatra	University of Trieste, Italy
Maria Attard	University of Malta, Malta
Tu Anh Trinh	UEH University, Vietnam
Marcello Tadini	University of Eastern Piedmont, Italy
Luigi Mundula	University for Foreigners of Perugia, Italy
Silvia Battino	University of Sassari, Italy
Brunella Brundu	University of Sassari, Italy
Veronica Camerada	University of Sassari, Italy

Maria del Mar Munoz Leonisio	University of Cádiz, Spain
Anna Richiedei	University of Brescia, Italy
Michele Pezzagno	University of Brescia, Italy
Marco Mazzarino	IUAV University Venice, Italy

The Development of Urban Mobility Management, Road Safety and Risk Assessment (MANTAIN 2025)

Workshop Organizers

Antonio Russo	Università degli Studi di Enna, Italy
Corrado Rindone	University of Reggio Calabria, Italy
Antonio Polimeni	University of Messina, Italy
Florin Rusca	Politehnica University of Bucharest, Romania
Grigorios Fountas	Aristotle University of Thessaloniki, Greece
Antonio Comi	University of Rome Tor Vergata, Italy

Workshop Program Committee Members

Massimo Di Gangi	University of Messina, Italy
Orlando Marco Belcore	University of Messina, Italy
Antonio Polimeni	University of Messina, Italy
Socrates Basbas	Aristotle University of Thessaloniki, Greece
Claudia Caballini	Polytechnic of Torino, Italy
Efstathios Bouhouras	Aristotle University of Thessaloniki, Greece
Stefano Ricci	Sapienza University of Rome, Italy
Marina Zanne	University of Lubljana, Slovenia
Kh Md Nahiduzzaman	Mohammed VI Polytechnic University, Morocco
Alexsandra Deluka Tibljaš	University of Rijeka, Croatia
Guilhermina Torrao	Aston University, UK

Multidimensional Evolutionary Evaluations for Transformative Approaches (MEETA 2025)

Workshop Organizers

Maria Cerreta	University of Naples Federico II, Italy
Giuliano Poli	University of Naples Federico II, Italy
Maria Somma	University of Naples Federico II, Italy
Gaia Daldanise	CNR IRISS, Italy
Ludovica La Rocca	University of Naples Federico II, Italy

Workshop Program Committee Members

Maria Cerreta	University of Naples Federico II, Italy
Giuliano Poli	University of Naples Federico II, Italy
Maria Somma	University of Naples Federico II, Italy
Laura Di Tommaso	University of Naples Federico II, Italy
Sabrina Sacco	Politecnico di Milano, Italy
Piero Zizzania	University of Naples Federico II, Italy
Gaia Daldanise	CNR IRISS, Italy
Benedetta Grieco	University of Naples Federico II, Italy
Giuseppe Ciciriello	University of Naples Federico II, Italy
Marta Dell'Ovo	Politecnico di Milano, Italy
Daniele Cannatella	TU Delft, The Netherlands
Eugenio Muccio	University of Naples Federico II, Italy
Francesco Piras	University of Cagliari, Italy
Diana Rolando	Politecnico di Torino, Italy
Sveva Ventre	University of Naples Federico II, Italy
Caterina Loffredo	University of Naples Federico II, Italy
Ludovica La Rocca	University of Naples Federico II, Italy
Simona Panaro	University of Campania Luigi Vanvitelli, Italy

Building Multi-dimensional Models for Assessing Complex Environmental Systems (MES 2025)

Workshop Organizers

Vanessa Assumma	University of Bologna, Italy
Caterina Caprioli	Politecnico di Torino, Italy
Giulia Datola	Politecnico di Milano, Italy
Federico Dell'Anna	University of Bologna, Italy
Marta Dell'Ovo	Politecnico di Milano, Italy
Marco Rossitti	Politecnico di Milano, Italy

Workshop Program Committee Members

Vanessa Assumma	Università di Bologna, Bologna
Caterina Caprioli	Politecnico di Torino, Italy
Giulia Datola	DAStU Politecnico di Milano, Italy
Federico Dell'Anna	Politecnico di Torino, Italy
Marta Dell'Ovo	Politecnico di Milano, Italy
Marco Rossitti	Politecnico di Milano, Italy
Francesca Torrieri	Politecnico di Milano, Italy
Mariarosaria Angrisano	Università Telematica Pegaso, Italy
Maksims Feofilovs	Riga Technical University, Latvia

Danny Caprini	Politecnico di Milano, Italy
Giulio Cavana	Politecnico di Torino, Italy
Sebastiano Barbieri	Politecnico di Torino, Italy
Marta Bottero	Politecnico di Torino, Italy
Francesco Cosentino	Politecnico di Milano, Italy
Silvia Ronchi	Politecnico di Milano, Italy
Chiara Mazzarella	TU Delft, Netherlands
Marco Volpatti	Politecnico di Torino, Italy
Chiara D'Alpaos	Università degli Studi di Padova, Italy
Alessandra Oppio	Politecnico di Milano, Italy
Alessia Crisopulli	Politecnico di Milano, Italy
Domenico D'Uva	Politecnico di Milano, Italy
Giorgia Malavasi	Politecnico di Torino, Italy
Rubina Canesi	Università degli Studi di Padova, Italy
Elena Todella	Politecnico di Torino, Italy
Beatrice Mecca	Politecnico di Torino, Italy
Giulia Marzani	University of Bologna, Italy
Isabella Giovanetti	University of Bologna, Italy
Lucia Petronio	University of Bologna, Italy
Franco Corti	University of Padova, Italy
Salvatore De Pascalis	Politecnico di Milano, Italy
Valeria Vitulano	Politecnico di Torino, Italy
Lorenzo Diana	Università degli studi di Napoli Federico II, Italy
Maksims Feofilovs	Riga Technical University, Latvia
Marco De Luca	Politecnico di Torino, Italy
Ilaria Cazzola	Politecnico di Torino, Italy
Andrea De Toni	Politecnico di Milano, Italy
Eugenio Muccio	University of Naples Federico II, Italy
Giuliano Poli	University of Naples Federico II, Italy
Francesco Sica	University "La Sapienza" of Rome, Italy
Elena Di Pirro	Università degli Studi del Molise, Italy
Riccardo Alba	Università di Torino, Italy
Irene Regaiolo	Università di Torino, Italy
Francesca Cochis	Università di Torino, Italy

Modelling Liveable Cities: Techniques, Methods, Challenges, and Perspectives Behind the 'X-Minute' City (MLC 2025)

Workshop Organizers

Federico Mara	University of Pisa, Italy
Valerio Cutini	University of Pisa, Italy
Alessandro Araldi	Université Côte d'Azur, France

| Flávia Lopes | Chalmers University of Technology, Sweden |
| Giovanni Fusco | Université Côte d'Azur, France |

Workshop Program Committee Members

Simone Rusci	University of Pisa, Italy
Lorena Fiorini	University of L'Aquila, Italy
Chiara Di Dato	University of L'Aquila, Italy
Francesco Zullo	University of L'Aquila, Italy
Alfonso Annunziata	University of Basilicata, Italy
Beniamino Murgante	University of Basilicata, Italy
Alessandro Araldi	Universitè Côte d'Azur, France
Chiara Garau	University of Cagliari, Italy
Giampiero Lombardini	Università di Genova, Italy
Flavia Lopes	Chalmers University of Technology, Sweden
Giovanni Fusco	Universitè Côte d'Azur, France

Mathematical Methods for Image Processing and Understanding 2025 (MMIPU 2025)

Workshop Organizers

Ivan Gerace	Università degli Studi di Perugia, Italy
Gianluca Vinti	Università degli Studi di Perugia, Italy
Arianna Travaglini	Università degli Studi della Basilicata, Italy

Workshop Program Committee Members

Ivan Gerace	University of Perugia, Italy
Gianluca Vinti	University of Perugia, Italy
Arianna Travaglini	University of Basilicata, Italy
Marco Baioletti	University of Perugia, Italy
Marco Donatelli	University of Insubria, Italy
Anna Tonazzini	C.N.R. Pisa, Italy
Muhammad Hanif	Ghulam Ishaq Khan Institute of Engineering Sciences and Technology, Pakistan
Francesco Marchetti	University of Padua, Italy
Wolfgang Erb	University of Padua, Italy
Danilo Costarelli	University of Perugia, Italy
Francesco Santini	University of Perugia, Italy
Valentina Giorgetti	University of Perugia, Italy

Mobility Opportunities Bridging Inequalities: Social Inclusion and Gender Equity Initiatives Strategies Against Fragmentation and Complexity of Mobility (MOBIL-EGI 2025)

Workshop Organizers

Tiziana Campisi	University of Enna Kore, Italy
Guilhermina Torrao	Aston University, UK
Socrates Basbas	Aristotle University of Thessaloniki, Greece
Tanja Congiu	University of Sassari, Italy
Stefanos Tsigdinos	National Technical University of Athens, Greece
Florin Nemtanu	Politehnica University of Bucharest, Romania

Workshop Program Committee Members

Massimo Di Gangi	University of Messina, Italy
Orlando Marco Belcore	University of Messina, Italy
Francesco Russo	Mediterranean University of Reggio Calabria, Italy
Alexandros Nikitas	University of Huddersfield, UK
Marilisa Nigro	Rome Tre University, Italy
Kh Md Nahiduzzaman	Mohammed VI Polytechnic University, Morocco
Efstathios Bouhouras	Aristotle University of Thessaloniki, Greece
Antonio Comi	University of Rome Tor Vergata, Italy
Edouard Ivanjko	University of Zagreb, Slovenia
Osvaldo Gervasi	University of Perugia, Italy
Beniamino Murgante	University of Basilicata, Italy
Chiara Garau	University of Cagliari, Italy

MOdels and indicators for assessing and measuring the urban settlement deVElopment in the view of NET ZERO by 2050 (MOVEto0 2025)

Workshop Organizers

Lorena Fiorini	University of L'Aquila, Italy
Lucia Saganeiti	CNR-IMAA, Italy
Angela Pilogallo	CNR-IMAA, Italy
Alessandro Marucci	University of L'Aquila, Italy
Francesco Zullo	University of L'Aquila, Italy

Workshop Program Committee Members

Ginevra Balletto	University of Cagliari, Italy
Giuseppe Borruso	University of Trieste, Italy
Chiara Garau	University of Cagliari, Italy

Beniamino Murgante	University of Basilicata, Italy
Giulia Desogus	University of Cagliari, Italy
Ljiljana Zivkovic	Republic Geodetic Authority, Serbia
Luigi Santopietro	University of Basilicata, Italy
Ilaria Delponte	University of Genoa, Italy
Carmen Guida	University of Naples Federico II, Italy
Chiara Di Dato	University of L'Aquila, Italy

5th Workshop on Privacy in the Cloud/Edge/IoT World (PCEIoT 2025)

Workshop Organizers

Lelio Campanile	Università degli Studi della Campania Luigi Vanvitelli, Italy
Mauro Iacono	Università degli Studi della Campania Luigi Vanvitelli, Italy
Michele Mastroianni	Università degli Studi di Foggia, Italy

Workshop Program Committee Members

Arcangelo Castiglione	Università degli Studi di Salerno, Italy
Maria Ganzha	Warsaw University of Technology, Poland
Daniel Grzonka	Cracow University of Technology, Poland
Antonio Iannuzzi	Università degli Studi Roma Tre, Italy
Armando Tacchella	Università degli Studi di Genova, Italy
Biagio Boi	University of Salerno, Italy
Marco De Santis	University of Salerno, Italy
Fiammetta Marulli	Università degli Studi della Campania "L. Vanvitelli", Italy
Christian Riccio	Università degli Studi della Campania "L. Vanvitelli", Italy
Luigi Piero Di Bonito	Università degli Studi di Napoli Federico II, Italy

Preserving Our Past: Spatial and Remote Sensing Technologies for Cultural Heritage in a Changing Climate (POP 2025)

Workshop Organizers

Maria Danese	CNR-ISPC, Italy
Nicola Masini	CNR-ISPC, Italy
Rosa Lasaponara	CNR-IMAA, Italy

Workshop Program Committee Members

Maria Danese	CNR-ISPC, Italy
Nicola Masini	CNR-ISPC, Italy
Rosa Lasaponara	CNR-IMAA, Italy
Dario Gioia	CNR-ISPC, Italy
Giuseppe Corrado	Università degli Studi della Basilicata, Italy
Canio Sabia	CNR-ISPC, Italy

Processes, methods and tools towards RESilient cities and cultural and historic sites prone to SOD and ROD disasters (RES 2025)

Workshop Organizers

Elena Cantatore	Polytechnic University of Bari, Italy
Dario Esposito	Polytechnic University of Bari, Italy
Alberico Sonnessa	Polytechnic University of Bari, Italy

Workshop Program Committee Members

Elena Cantatore	Politecnico di Bari, Italy
Dario Esposito	Politecnico di Bari, Italy
Alberico Sonnessa	Politecnico di Bari, Italy
Valeria Belloni	Sapienza University of Rome, Italy
Michela Ravanelli	Sapienza University of Rome, Italy
Silvano Dal Sasso	University of Basilicata, Italy
Francesco Chiaravalloti	CNR - IRPI, Italy
Roberta Ravanelli	University of Liège, Belgium
Alessandra Mascitelli	University of Chieti-Pescara, Italy
Francesco Di Capua	University of Basilicata, Italy
Gabriele Bernardini	Università Politecnica delle Marche, Italy
Vito Domenico Porcari	University of Basilicata, Italy
Carmen Rosa Fattore	University of Basilicata, Italy
Stefania Santoro	Water Research Institute, Italy

Scientific Computing Infrastructure (SCI 2025)

Workshop Organizers

Vladimir Korkhov	Saint Petersburg State University, Russia
Elena Stankova	Saint Petersburg State University, Russia
Nataliia Kulabukhova	Saint Petersburg State University, Russia

Workshop Program Committee Members

Adam Belloum	University of Amsterdam, the Netherlands
Dmitrii Vasiunin	Deutsche Telekom Cloud Services E.P.E., Greece
Serob Balyan	Osensus Arm LLC, Armenia
Suren Abrahamyan	Osensus Arm LLC, Armenia
Ashot Sergey Gevorkyan	NAS of Armenia, Armenia
Michal Hnatic	Univerzita Pavla Jozefa Šafárika v Košiciach, Slovakia
Michail Panteleyev	Saint Petersburg Electrotecnical University, Russia
Martin Vala	Univerzita Pavla Jozefa Šafárika v Košiciach, Slovakia
Nodir Zaynalov	Tashkent University of Information Technologies named after Muhammad al Khwarizmi, Uzbekistan
Michail Panteleyev	Saint Petersburg Electrotecnical University, Russia
Alexander Degtyarev	Saint Petersburg University, Russia
Alexander Bogdanov	St. Petersburg State University, Russia

Ports and Logistics of the Future - Smartness and Sustainability (SmartPorts 2025)

Workshop Organizers

Andrea Gallo	Università degli Studi di Trieste, Italy
Gianfranco Fancello	University of Cagliari, Italy
Giuseppe Borruso	Università degli Studi di Trieste, Italy
Enrico D'agostini	World Maritime University, Sweden
Silvia Battino	Università degli Studi di Sassari, Italy
Veronica Camerada	Università degli Studi di Sassari, Italy

Workshop Program Committee Members

Giuseppe Borruso	University of Trieste, Italy
Beniamino Murgante	University of Basilicata, Italy
Ginevra Balletto	University of Cagliari, Italy
Silvia Battino	University of Sassari, Italy
Mara Ladu	University of Cagliari, Italy
Maria del Mar Munoz Leonisio	University of Cádiz, Spain
Ahinoa Amaro Garcia	University of Las Palmas of Gran Canaria, Spain
Maria Attard	University of Malta, Malta
Enrico D'agostini	World Maritime University, Sweden
Francesca Krasna	University of Trieste, Italy

Tu Anh Trinh	UEH University - Ho Chi Minh City, Vietnam
Giovanni Mauro	Università degli Studi della Campania, Italy
Maria Ronza	University of Naples Federico II, Italy
Massimiliano Bencardino	University of Salerno, Italy
Andrea Gallo	Ca' Foscari University of Venice, Italy
Francesca Sinatra	University of Trieste, Italy
Salvatore Dore	University of Trieste, Italy
Veronica Camerada	University of Sassari, Italy
Brunella Brundu	University of Sassari, Italy
Gianfranco Fancello	University of Cagliari, Italy
Marcello Tadini	University of Eastern Piedmont, Italy
Marco Mazzarino	IUAV University Venice
José Ángel Hernández Luis	University of Las Palmas de Gran Canaria, Spain
Marco Naseddu	University of Cagliari, Italy
Maurizio Cociancich	Adriafer, Italy
Giovanni Longo	University of Trieste, Italy
Luca Toneatti	University of Trieste, Italy
Martina Sinatra	University of Cagliari, Italy
Enrico Vanino	University of Sheffield, UK
Patrizia Serra	University of Cagliari, Italy
Agostino Bruzzone	University of Genoa, Italy
Marco Petrelli	University of Roma 3, Italy

Smart Transport and Logistics - Smart Supply Chains (SmarTransLog 2025)

Workshop Organizers

Francesca Sinatra	University of Trieste, Italy
Maria del Mar Munoz	Universidad de Cádiz, Spain
Brunella Brundu	University of Sassari, Italy
Patrizia Serra	University of Cagliari, Italy
Salvatore Dore	University of Trieste, Italy
Marco Naseddu	University of Cagliari, Italy

Workshop Program Committee Members

Giuseppe Borruso	University of Trieste, Italy
Beniamino Murgante	University of Basilicata, Italy
Ginevra Balletto	University of Cagliari, Italy
Silvia Battino	University of Sassari, Italy
Mara Ladu	University of Cagliari, Italy
Maria del Mar Munoz Leonisio	University of Cádiz, Spain
Ahinoa Amaro Garcia	University of Las Palmas of Gran Canaria, Spain

Maria Attard	University of Malta, Malta
Enrico D'agostini	World Maritime University, Sweden
Francesca Krasna	University of Trieste, Italy
Tu Anh Trinh	UEH University, Vietnam
Giovanni Mauro	Università degli Studi della Campania, Italy
Maria Ronza	University of Naples Federico II, Italy
Massimiliano Bencardino	University of Salerno, Italy
Andrea Gallo	Ca' Foscari University of Venice, Italy
Francesca Sinatra	University of Trieste, Italy
Salvatore Dore	University of Trieste, Italy
Veronica Camerada	University of Sassari, Italy
Brunella Brundu	University of Sassari, Italy
Gianfranco Fancello	University of Cagliari, Italy
Marcello Tadini	University of Eastern Piedmont, Italy
Marco Mazzarino	IUAV University Venice
José Ángel Hernández Luis	University of Las Palmas de Gran Canaria, Spain
Marco Naseddu	University of Cagliari, Italy
Maurizio Cociancich	Adriafer, Italy
Giovanni Longo	University of Trieste, Italy
Luca Toneatti	University of Trieste, Italy
Martina Sinatra	University of Cagliari, Italy
Enrico Vanino	University of Sheffield, UK
Patrizia Serra	University of Cagliari, Italy
Agostino Bruzzone	University of Genoa, Italy
Marco Petrelli	University of Roma 3, Italy

Smart Tourism (SmartTourism 2025)

Workshop Organizers

Silvia Battino	University of Sassari, Italy
Francesca Krasna	University of Trieste, Italy
Ainhoa Amaro	University of Las Palmas de Gran Canaria, Spain
Maria del Mar Munoz	University of Cádiz, Spain
Brisol García García	Polytechnic University of Quintana Roo, Mexico
Marta Meleddu	University of Sassari, Italy

Workshop Program Committee Members

Giuseppe Borruso	University of Trieste, Italy
Beniamino Murgante	University of Basilicata, Italy
Gianfranco Fancello	University of Cagliari, Italy
Mara Ladu	University of Cagliari, Italy

Martina Sinatra	University of Cagliari, Italy
Salvatore Dore	University of Trieste, Italy
Marco Mazzarino	IUAV University Venice, Italy
Veronica Camerada	University of Sassari, Italy
Brunella Brundu	University of Sassari, Italy
Maria Attard	University of Malta, Malta
Ginevra Balletto	University of Cagliari, Italy
Giovanni Mauro	University degli Studi della Campania, Italy
Salvatore Lampreu	University of Sassari, Italy
Maria Ronza	University of Naples, Italy
Massimiliano Bencardino	University of Salerno, Italy

Sustainable evolution of long-Distance frEight and paSsenger Transport (SOLIDEST 2025)

Workshop Organizers

Francesco Russo	University of Reggio Calabria, Italy
Andreas Nikiforiadis	Democritus University of Thrace, Greece
Orlando Marco Belcore	University of Messina, Italy
Antonio Comi	University of Rome Tor Vergata, Italy
Tiziana Campisi	Kore University of Enna, Italy
Aura Rusca	Politehnica University of Bucharest, Romania

Workshop Program Committee Members

Massimo Di Gangi	University of Messina, Italy
Orlando Marco Belcore	University of Messina, Italy
Antonio Polimeni	University of Messina, Italy
Socrates Basbas	Aristotle University of Thessaloniki, Greece
Efstathios Bouhouras	Aristotle University of Thessaloniki, Greece
Marina Zanne	University of Lubljana, Slovenia
Marilisa Nigro	Rome Tre University, Italy
Edoardo Marcucci	Molde University College, Norway
Eugen Rosca	Polytechnic University of Bucharest, Romania
Kh Md Nahiduzzaman	Mohammed VI Polytechnic University, Morocco
Beniamino Murgante	University of Basilicata, Italy
Chiara Garau	University of Cagliari, Italy

Sustainability Performance Assessment: Models, Approaches, and Applications Toward Interdisciplinary and Integrated Solutions (SPA 2025)

Workshop Organizers

Francesco Scorza	University of Basilicata, Italy
Sabrina Lai	University of Cagliari, Italy
Francesco Rotondo	Università Politecnica delle Marche, Italy
Jolanta Dvarioniene	Kaunas University of Technology, Lithuania
Michele Campagna	University of Cagliari, Italy
Corrado Zoppi	University of Cagliari, Italy

Workshop Program Committee Members

Federico Amato	University of Lausanne, Switzerland
Ferdinando Di Carlo	University of Basilicata, Italy
Maddalena Floris	University of Cagliari, Italy
Federica Isola	University of Cagliari, Italy
Giuseppe Las Casas	University of Basilicata, Italy
Federica Leone	University of Cagliari, Italy
Giampiero Lombardini	University of Genoa, Italy
Federico Martellozzo	University of Florence, Italy
Alessandro Marucci	University of L'Aquila, Italy
Ana Clara Moura	Universidade Federal de Minas Gerais, Brazil
Beniamino Murgante	University of Basilicata, Italy
Silviu Nate	Lucian Blaga University of Sibiu, Romania
Anastasia Stratigea	National Technical University of Athens, Greece
Francesco Zullo	University of L'Aquila, Italy
Luigi Santopietro	University of Basilicata, Italy
Benedetto Manganelli	University of Basilicata, Italy

Specifics of Smart Cities Development in Europe (SPEED 2025)

Workshop Organizers

Chiara Garau	University of Cagliari, Italy
Katarína Vitálišová	Matej Bel University, Slovak Republic
Marco Fanfani	University of Florence, Italy
Anna Vaňová	Matej Bel University, Slovak Republic
Kamila Borsekova	Matej Bel University, Slovak Republic
Paola Zamperlin	University of Florence, Italy

Workshop Program Committee Members

Claudia Loggia	University of KwaZulu-Natal, South Africa
Francesca Maltinti	University of Cagliari, Italy
Alessandro Plaisant	University of Sassari, Italy
Alenka Poplin	Iowa State University, USA
Silvia Rossetti	University of Parma, Italy
Gerardo Carpentieri	University of Naples Federico II, Italy
Carmen Guida	University of Naples Federico II, Italy
Floriana Zucaro	University of Naples Federico II, Italy
Anastasia Stratigea	National Technical University of Athens, Greece
Yiota Theodora	National Technical University of Athens, Greece
Giovanna Concu	University of Cagliari, Italy
Paolo Nesi	University of Florence, Italy
Emanuele Bellini	University of Roma Tre, Italy
Mana Dastoum	Polytechnic University of Madrid, Spain
Barbara Caselli	University of Parma, Italy
Martina Carra	University of Brescia, Italy
Alfonso Annunziata	University of Basilicata, Italy
Elisabetta Venco	University of Pavia, Italy
Caterina Pietra	University of Pavia, Italy
Enrico Collini	University of Florence, Italy
Luciano Alessandro Ipsaro Palesi	University of Florence, Italy

Smart, Safe, and Healthy Cities (SSHC 2025)

Workshop Organizers

Chiara Garau	University of Cagliari, Italy
Gerardo Carpentieri	University of Naples Federico II, Italy
Carmen Guida	University of Naples Federico II, Italy
Tanja Congiu	University of Sassari, Italy
Martina Carra	University of Brescia, Italy
Alenka Poplin	Iowa State University, USA

Workshop Program Committee Members

Rosaria Battarra	Istituto di Studi sul Mediterraneo, Italy
Barbara Caselli	University of Parma, Italy
Francesca Maltinti	University of Cagliari, Italy
Romano Fistola	Università degli Studi di Napoli Federico II, Italy
Alessandro Plaisant	University of Sassari, Italy
Silvia Rossetti	University of Parma, Italy
Marco Fanfani	University of Florence, Italy
Reza Askarizad	University of Cagliari, Italy

Floriana Zucaro	University of Naples Federico II, Italy
Anastasia Stratigea	National Technical University of Athens, Greece
Yiota Theodora	National Technical University of Athens, Greece
Giovanna Concu	University of Cagliari, Italy
Francesco Zullo	University of L'Aquila, Italy
Paola Zamperlin	University of Florence, Italy
Vincenza Torrisi	University of Catania, Italy
Tiziana Campisi	University of Enna Kore, Italy
Katarína Vitálišová	Matej Bel University, Slovakia
Tazyeen Alam	University of Cagliari, Italy
Mana Dastoum	Polytechnic University of Madrid, Spain
Martina Carra	University of Brescia, Italy
Alfonso Annunziata	University of Basilicata, Italy
Elisabetta Venco	University of Pavia, Italy
Caterina Pietra	University of Pavia, Italy

Smart and Sustainable Island Communities (SSIC 2025)

Workshop Organizers

Chiara Garau	University of Cagliari, Italy
Anastasia Stratigea	National Technical University of Athens, Greece
Yiota Theodora	National Technical University of Athens, Greece
Giovanna Concu	University of Cagliari, Italy

Workshop Program Committee Members

Milena Metalkova-Markova	University of Portsmouth, UK
Tarek Teba	University of Portsmouth, UK
Alenka Poplin	Iowa State University, USA
Gerardo Carpentieri	University of Naples Federico II, Italy
Carmen Guida	University of Naples Federico II, Italy
Floriana Zucaro	University of Naples Federico II, Italy
Silvia Rossetti	University of Parma, Italy
Barbara Caselli	University of Parma, Italy
Martina Carra	University of Brescia, Italy
Alfonso Annunziata	University of Basilicata, Italy
Maria Panagiotopoulou	National Technical University of Athens, Greece
Apostolos Lagarias	University of Thessaly, Greece
Paola Zamperlin	University of Florence, Italy
Vincenza Torrisi	University of Catania, Italy
Giuseppina Vacca	University of Cagliari, Italy
Roberto Minunno	Curtin University, Australia
Marco Zucca	University of Cagliari, Italy

Elisabetta Venco	University of Pavia, Italy
Caterina Pietra	University of Pavia, Italy
Pietro Crespi	Politecnico di Milano, Italy

From STreet Experiments to Planned Solutions (STEPS 2025)

Workshop Organizers

Silvia Rossetti	Università degli Studi di Parma, Italy
Angela Ricciardello	Kore University of Enna, Italy
Francesco Pinna	Università degli Studi di Cagliari, Italy
Chiara Garau	Università degli Studi di Cagliari, Italy
Tiziana Campisi	Kore University of Enna, Italy
Vincenza Torrisi	University of Catania, Italy

Workshop Program Committee Members

Martina Carra	University of Brescia, Italy
Barbara Caselli	University of Parma, Italy
Tanja Congiu	University of Sassari, Italy
Gabriele D'Orso	University of Palermo, Italy
Matteo Ignaccolo	University of Catania, Italy
Md Kh Nahiduzzaman	Mohammed VI Polytechnic University, Morocco
Muhammad Ahmad Al-Rashid	University of Malaya, Malaysia
Alessandro Plaisant	University of Sassari, Italy
Marianna Ruggieri	University of Enna Kore, Italy
Michele Zazzi	University of Parma, Italy

Sustainable Tourism Evaluations: approaches, methods and indicators (STEva 2025)

Workshop Organizers

Mariolina Grasso	Università Kore di Enna, Italy
Fabrizio Finucci	Roma Tre University, Italy
Daniele Mazzoni	Roma Tre University, Italy
Antonella G. Masanotti	Roma Tre University, Italy
Giovanna Acampa	University of Florence, Italy

Workshop Program Committee Members

Giovanna Acampa	University of Florence, Italy
Fabrizio Finucci	Roma Tre University, Italy
Mariolina Grasso	"Kore" University of Enna, Italy

Alberto Marzo	Ministero della Cultura, Italy
Antonella G. Masanotti	Roma Tre University, Italy
Daniele Mazzoni	Roma Tre University, Italy
Rocco Murro	Sapienza University of Rome, Italy
Claudio Piferi	University of Florence, Italy
Alessio Pino	"Kore" University of Enna, Italy
Nicoletta Setola	University of Florence, Italy
Laura Calcagnini	Roma Tre University, Italy
Antonio Magarò	Roma Tre University, Italy
Janos Ghyerghyak	University of Pécs, Hungary
Ágnes Borsos	University of Pécs, Hungary
Fabrizio Battisti	University of Florence, Italy

Sustainable Development of Ports (SUSTAINABLEPORTS 2025)

Workshop Organizers

Tiziana Campisi	University of Enna KORE, Italy
Giuseppe Musolino	University of Reggio Calabria, Italy
Efstathios Bouhouras	Aristotle University of Thessaloniki, Greece
Elen Twrdy	University of Ljubljana, Slovenia
Elena Cocuzza	University of Catania, Italy
Aura Rusca	Politehnica University of Bucharest, Romania

Workshop Program Committee Members

Massimo Di Gangi	University of Messina, Italy
Orlando Marco Belcore	University of Messina, Italy
Antonio Polimeni	University of Messina, Italy
Claudia Caballini	Polytechnic of Torino, Italy
Gianfranco Fancello	University of Cagliari, Italy
Marina Zanne	University of Lubljana, Slovenia
Stefano Ricci	Sapienza University of Rome, Italy
Beniamino Murgante	University of Basilicata, Italy
Chiara Garau	University of Cagliari, Italy

Theoretical and Computational Chemistry and Its Applications (TCCMA 2025)

Workshop Organizers

Noelia Faginas Lago	Università di Perugia, Italy
Andrea Lombardi	Università di Perugia, Italy
Marcos Mandado Alonso	University of Vigo, Spain

Workshop Program Committee Members

Noelia Faginas-Lago	University of Perugia, Italy
Andrea Lombardi	University of Perugia, Italy
Marcos Mandado	University of Vigo, Spain
Angeles Peña	University of Vigo, Spain
Luca Mancini	Universiy of Perugia, Italy
Massimiliano Bartolomei	CSIC, Spain
Cecilia Coletti	University of Chieti-Pescara, Italy
Iñaki Tuñón	Universidad de Valencia, Spain
Albert Rimola Gilbert	Universitat Autònoma de Barcelona, Spain
Stefano Falcinelli	University of Perugia, Italy
Dario Campisi	University of Perugia, Italy
Ernesto García Para	University of the Basque Country, Spain
Giacomo Giorgi	University of Perugia, Italy
Tomás González Lezana	IFF CSIC, Spain
Enrique M. Cabaleiro Lago	Universidade de Santiago de Compostela, Spain
Aurora Costales	Universidad de Oviedo, Spain
Angel Martin	Universidad de Oviedo, Spain
Jose Manuel	University of Vigo, Spain
Annarita Laricchiuta	CNR ISTP Bari, Italy
Fernando Pirani	University of Perugia, Italy

Transport Infrastructures for Smart Cities (TISC 2025)

Workshop Organizers

Francesca Maltinti	University of Cagliari, Italy
Mauro Coni	University of Cagliari, Italy
Benedetto Barabino	University of Brescia, Italy
Nicoletta Rassu	University of Cagliari, Italy
James Rombi	University of Cagliari, Italy

Workshop Program Committee Members

Francesco Pinna	University of Cagliari, Italy
Chiara Garau	University of Cagliari, Italy
Mauro D'Apuzzo	University of Cassino, Italy
Roberto Minunno	Curtin University, Australia
Tiziana Campisi	University of Enna Kore, Italy
Roberto Ventura	University of Brescia, Italy
Alessandro Plaisant	University of Sassari, Italy
Massimo Di Francesco	University of Cagliari, Italy

Vincenza Torrisi   University of Catania, Italy
Paola Zamperlin   University of Florence, Italy

Transforming Urban Analytics: The Impact of Crowdsourced Mapping and Advanced AI Techniques on Future Cities (Tr-UrbAna 2025)

Workshop Organizers

Ayse Giz Gulnerman Gengec   Ankara Hacı Bayram Veli University, Turkey
Müslüm Hacar   Tildiz Technical University, Turkey
Himmet Karaman   Istanbul Technical University, Turkey

Workshop Program Committee Members

Beniamino Murgante   University of Basilicata, Italy
Abdulkadir Memduhoğlu   Harran University, Turkey
Zeynel Abidin Polat   İzmir Katip Çelebi University, Turkey
Güzide Miray Perihanoğlu   Van Yüzüncü Yıl University, Turkey
Tugba Memisoglu Baykal   Ankara Hacı Bayram Veli University, Turkey

From structural to TRAnsformative-change of City Environment: challenges and solutions and perspectives (TRACE 2025)

Workshop Organizers

Pierluigi Morano   Polytechnic University of Bari, Italy
Maria Rosaria Guarini   Sapienza University of Rome, Italy
Francesco Sica   Sapienza University of Rome, Italy
Francesco Tajani   Sapienza University of Rome, Italy
Marco Locurcio   Polytechnic University of Bari, Italy
Debora Anelli   Polytechnic University of Bari, Italy

Workshop Program Committee Members

Felicia di Liddo   Politecnico di Bari, Italia
Valeria Saiu   Università di Cagliari, Italia
Emma Sabatelli   Sapienza Università di Roma, Italia
Antonella Roma   Sapienza Università di Roma, Italia
Giuseppe Cerullo   Sapienza Università di Roma, Italia
Lucia della Spina   Università di Reggio Calabria, Italia
Alejandro Segura de la Cal   Politecnico di Madrid, Spain
Yilsy Nuñez   Politecnico di Madrid, Spain
Gabriella Maselli   Università di Salerno, Italy
Maria Rosa Trovato   Università di Catania, Italy

Manuela Rebaudengo	Politecnico di Torino, Italy
Pierfrancesco De Paola	Università di Napoli Federico II, Italy
Daniela Tavano	Università della Calabria, Italy
Maria Saez	University of Granada, Spain
Paola Amoruso	LUM "Giuseppe Degennaro" University, Italy

Temporary Real Estate management: Approaches and methods for Time-integrated impact assessments and evaluations (TREAT 2025)

Workshop Organizers

Chiara Mazzarella	TUDelft, The Netherlands
Hilde Remoy	TUDelft, The Netherlands
Maria Cerreta	University of Naples Federico II, Italy

Workshop Program Committee Members

Chiara Mazzarella	TU Delft, The Netherlands
Hilde Remoy	TU Delft, The Netherlands
Maria Cerreta	University of Naples Federico II, Italy
Maria Somma	University of Naples Federico II, Italy
Simona Panaro	University of Campania Luigi Vanvitelli, Italy
Laura Di Tommaso	University of Naples Federico II, Italy
Caterina Loffredo	University of Naples Federico II, Italy
Ludovica La Rocca	University of Naples Federico II, Italy
Sabrina Sacco	Politecnico di Milano, Italy
Piero Zizzania	University of Naples Federico II, Italy
Gaia Daldanise	CNR IRISS, Italy
Benedetta Grieco	University of Naples Federico II, Italy
Giuseppe Ciciriello	University of Naples Federico II, Italy
Marta Dell'Ovo	Politecnico di Milano, Italy
Daniele Cannatella	TU Delft, The Netherlands
Eugenio Muccio	University of Naples Federico II, Italy
Sveva Ventre	University of Naples Federico II, Italy

Supporting the Transition to Ecological Economy in Cities Regeneration: Circular Model Tools for Reusing Architecture and Infrastructures (TReE 2025)

Workshop Organizers

Mariarosaria Angrisano	Pegaso University, Italy
Giulio Cavana	Politecnico di Torino, Italy
Francesca Buglione	CNR-ISPC, Italy

Antonia Gravagnuolo	CNR-ISPC, Italy
Piera Della Morte	Pegaso University, Italy

Workshop Program Committee Members

Giulia Datola	Politecnico di Milano, Italy
Vanessa Assumma	University of Bologna, Italy
Marco Volpatti	Politecnico di Torino, Italy
Sebastiano Barbieri	Politecnico di Torino, Italy
Caterina Caprioli	Politecnico di Torino, Italy
Marta Dell'Ovo	Politecnico di Milano, Italy
Federico Dell'Anna	Politecnico di Torino, Italy
Elena Todella	Politecnico di Torino, Italy
Danny Casprini	Politecnico di Milano, Italy
Grazia Neglia	Università Telematica Pegaso, Italy
Francesca Nocca	Università degli Studi di Napoli Federico II, Italy
Giulio Cavana	Politecnico di Torino, Italy
Francesca Buglione	CNR-IPSC, Italy
Marco Rossitti	Politecnico di Milano, Italy
Jhon Escorcia	Politecnico di Torino, Italy
Beatrice Mecca	Politecnico di Torino, Italy
Sara Biancifiori	Politecnico di Torino, Italy

Urban Digital Twins and Data Spaces: Shaping the Future of Sustainable Cities (TwinAbleCities 2025)

Workshop Organizers

Dessislava Petrova Antonova	Sofia University, GATE Institute, Bulgaria
Beniamino Murgante	University of Basilicata, Italy
Senthil Rajendran	RMSI, Bahrain
Tiziana Campisi	Kore University of Enna, Italy
Mila Koeva	University of Twente, The Netherlands

Workshop Program Committee Members

Dessislava Petrova-Antonova	Sofia University, Bulgaria
Mila Koeva	The University of Twente, The Netherlands
Beniamino Murgante	University of Basilicata, Italy
Senthil Rajendran	RMSI, Bahrain
Tiziana Campisi	Kore University of Enna, Italy

Urban Regeneration: Innovative Tools and Evaluation Model (URITEM 2025)

Workshop Organizers

Fabrizio Battisti	University of Florence, Italy
Giovanna Acampa	University of Florence, Italy
Orazio Campo	Sapienza University of Rome, Italy
Melania Perdonò	University of Florence, Italy

Workshop Program Committee Members

Fabrizio Battisti	University of Florence, Italy
Giovanna Acampa	University of Florence, Italy
Orazio Campo	University of Rome "La Sapienza", Italy
Melania Perdonò	Università degli Studi di Firenze, Italy

Urban Space Accessibility and Mobilities (USAM 2025)

Workshop Organizers

Chiara Garau	DICAAR, University of Cagliari, Italy
Alessandro Plaisant	University of Sassari, Italy
Barbara Caselli	University of Parma, Italy
Mauro D'Apuzzo	University of Cassino and Southern Lazio, Italy
Gabriele D'Orso	University of Palermo, Italy
Matteo Ignaccolo	University of Catania, Italy

Workshop Program Committee Members

Mauro Coni	University of Cagliari, Italy
Martina Carra	University of Brescia, Italy
Tiziana Campisi	University of Enna Kore, Italy
Tanja Congiu	University of Sassari, Italy
Francesca Maltìnti	University of Cagliari, Italy
Silvia Rossetti	University of Parma, Italy
Barbara Caselli	University of Parma, Italy
Angela Pilogallo	University of L'Aquila, Italy
Lorena Fiorini	University of L'Aquila, Italy
Reza Askarizad	University of Cagliari, Italy
Francesco Pinna	University of Cagliari, Italy
Aime Tsinda	University of Rwanda, Rwanda
Youssef El Ganadi	International University of Rabat, Morocco
Marco Migliore	University of Palermo, Italy
Alessio Salvatore	Italian National Research Council, Italy
Giuseppe Stecca	Italian National Research Council, Italy

Paola Zamperlin	University of Florence, Italy
Vincenza Torrisi	University of Catania, Italy
Gerardo Carpentieri	University of Naples Federico II, Italy
Carmen Guida	University of Naples Federico II, Italy
Floriana Zucaro	University of Naples Federico II, Italy
Alfonso Annunziata	University of Basilicata, Italy
Elisabetta Venco	University of Pavia, Italy
Caterina Pietra	University of Pavia, Italy
Tazyeen Alam	University of Cagliari, Italy
Valerio Cutini	University of Pisa, Italy

UX Mobility 2025: Placing User Experience at the Center of Urban Mobility: Methods and Frameworks (UXM 2025)

Workshop Organizers

Carmen Guida	Università degli Studi di Napoli Federico II, Italy
Gerardo Carpentieri	Università degli Studi di Napoli Federico II, Italy
Federico Messa	Systematica srl, Italy
Lamia Abdelfattah	Systematica srl, Italy

Workshop Program Committee Members

Rosaria Battarra	Istituto di Studi sul Mediterraneo CNR, Italy
Romano Fistola	Università degli Studi di Napoli Federico II, Italy
Lucia Saganeiti	IMAA-CNR, Italy

Virtual Reality and Augmented reality and applications (VRA 2025)

Workshop Organizers

Damiano Perri	University of Perugia, Italy
Osvaldo Gervasi	University of Perugia, Italy
Chau Ma Thi	University of Engineering and Technology, Vietnam National University, Hanoi, Vietnam
Paolo Nesi	University of Florence, Italy
Pierfrancesco Bellini	University of Florence, Italy

Workshop Program Committee Members

| David Berti | ART SpA, Italy |
| JungYoon Kim | Gachon University, South Korea |

TaiHoon Kim	Zhejiang University of Science and Technology, China
Marcelo de Paiva Guimares	Federal University of São Paulo, Brazil
Sergio Tasso	University of Perugia, Italy

Workshop on Advanced and Computational Methods for Earth Science Applications (WACM4ES 2025)

Workshop Organizers

Luca Piroddi	University of Cagliari, Italy
Patrizia Capizzi	University of Palermo, Italy
Marilena Cozzolino	University of Molise, Italy
Sebastiano D'Amico	University of Malta, Malta
Chiara Garau	University of Cagliari, Italy
Giuseppina Vacca	University of Cagliari, Italy

Workshop Program Committee Members

Andrea Angelini	CNR ISPC, Italy
Ilaria Barone	Università degli Studi di Padova, Italy
Patrizia Capizzi	University of Palermo, Italy
Luigi Capozzoli	CNR, Italy
Alberto Carletti	University of Cagliari, Italy
Emanuele Colica	University of Malta, Malta
Marilena Cozzolino	Università del Molise, Italy
Sebastiano D'Amico	University of Malta, Malta
Chiara Garau	University of Cagliari, Italy
Luciano Galone	University of Malta, Malta
Peter Iregbeyen	University of Malta, Malta
Mariano Lisi	Basilicata Aerospace Cluster CLAS, Italy
Raffaele Martorana	Università di Palermo, Italy
Paolo Mauriello	Università del Molise, Italy
Veronica Pazzi	University of Florence, Italy
Raffaele Persico	Università della Calabria, Italy
Luca Piroddi	University of Cagliari, Italy
Sina Saneiyan	Binghamton University, USA
Mercedes Solla	Universidade de Vigo, Spain
Deodato Tapete	ASI, Italy
Giuseppina Vacca	University of Cagliari, Italy
Enrica Vecchi	University of Cagliari, Italy

Sponsoring Organizations

ICCSA 2025 would not have been possible without the tremendous support of many organizations and institutions, for which all organizers and participants of ICCSA 2025 express their sincere gratitude:

Galatasaray University, Istanbul, Türkiye
(https://gsu.edu.tr/en)

African Mathematical Union
(https://www.africanmathunion.org/)

Springer Nature Switzerland AG, Switzerland
(https://www.springer.com)

The University of Massachusetts, USA
(https://www.umass.edu/)

University of Perugia, Italy
(https://www.unipg.it)

University of Basilicata, Italy
(http://www.unibas.it)

Monash University, Australia
(https://www.monash.edu/)

Kyushu Sangyo University, Japan
(https://www.kyusan-u.ac.jp/)

Universidade do Minho
Escola de Engenharia

University of Minho, Portugal
(https://www.uminho.pt/)
Venue
ICCSA 2025 took place in: **Galatasaray University, Istanbul, Türkiye**

Additional Reviewers

Reviewers
The review tasks for each workshop have been carried out by the workshop Organizers
and the members of the workshop Program Committee.

Plenary Lectures

Sky Safe with GAI and Post-quantum Computing

Elizabeth Chang

Professor of Cyber Security and Head of Discipline, University of the Sunshine Coast, Australia

Abstract. Professor Chang's talk in this presentation has two distinct parts. To start, she will introduce the landscape of cybersecurity development, attacks, threats, and vulnerabilities, as well as state-of-the-art cyber protection, cyber defence, and cyber incident prevention. This is followed by a discussion of the impact of Generative AI (GAI) and quantum-safe cryptographic computing, highlighting the major issues and challenges in research, education, and training. In conclusion, she will present a vision for Sky Safe solutions, aiming to achieve cyber resilience that supports business and economic stability, enhances human capabilities, and promotes environmental sustainability.

Disaster Preparedness and Risk Profiling in the Digital Era from Earth Observation Lens

Jagannath Aryal

Department of Infrastructure Engineering, University of Melbourne, Australia

Abstract. Natural hazards which turn into disasters result in severe losses of lives, infrastructure, and property. Disasters such as earthquakes and landslides and their impacts on transportation safety, infrastructure resilience, and displacement of people to new places are challenges. To address such challenges, earth observation data and intelligent methods can provide potential solutions in developing decision support systems. This talk will present the state of the art in Earth observation for disaster resilience using intelligent methods. In the Earth observation space, digitalisation has revolutionised the way we map, monitor, and develop decision support systems. Global case study examples covering earthquake-induced landslides from the Himalayan region will cover the digital capabilities. The digital capabilities will embrace object recognition, interpretation, and their accurate and precise capture to integrate into digital models. The developed digital models from representative case studies can be leveraged in other jurisdictions in profiling risks to protect lives and infrastructure and creating disaster preparedness in the era of digital age and digital economy.

Intelligent Image Enhancement for Real-World Applications in Adverse Atmospheric Conditions

Khan Muhammad

Department of Global Convergence, Sungkyunkwan University, South Korea

Abstract. The adverse impacts of atmospheric conditions such as haze, fog, and low-light environments pose significant challenges for real-world applications reliant on computer vision, including autonomous driving, surveillance, and remote sensing. This keynote explores cutting-edge advancements in intelligent image enhancement, drawing insights from two pivotal studies. The first introduces HazeSpace2M, a comprehensive dataset and novel classification-guided dehazing framework that improves image clarity across diverse atmospheric conditions, addressing the gap between synthetic and real-world dehazing performance. The second focuses on LoLI-Street, a benchmark for low-light image enhancement tailored to urban environments, extending beyond enhancement to enable robust object detection and scene understanding. Taken together, these contributions demonstrate how integrating domain-specific datasets, advanced algorithms, and performance benchmarks can significantly elevate the reliability of computer vision systems under challenging weather and lighting conditions. Attendees will gain valuable insights into the methodologies, datasets, and practical applications driving innovation in this field, with implications for research and industry alike.

In Memory of Carmelo Torre

Unfortunately, Professor Carmelo Torre, one of the cornerstones of the ICCSA Conference, passed away last December, leaving everyone stunned and deeply saddened. His loss has created a profound void within our academic community. Carmelo was not only a respected scholar and dedicated contributor to the success and growth of ICCSA, but also a generous colleague, mentor, and friend to many. His intellectual rigor, warm personality, and unwavering commitment to advancing research will be remembered with great admiration. As we continue the work he helped shape, we honor his legacy and the indelible mark he left on all of us. Carmelo Torre graduated in engineering at the Polytechnic of Bari with a thesis on urban planning under Dino Borri's guidance. He began his research career by collaborating with Franco Selicato. During his PhD at the University of Naples Federico II under Luigi Fusco Girard, he specialized in real estate market analysis and multi-criteria evaluation methods. He explored the social impacts of urban transformations with his lifelong friend Maria Cerreta. His first ICCSA participation was in Perugia in 2008, in the session Geographical Analysis, Urban Modeling, Spatial Statistics. Instantly captivated by the conference, his charisma enabled him to involve various Italian scientific communities, including those in real estate and statistics. ICCSA became a yearly commitment for him, where he valued the high editorial quality of the proceedings and the dynamic post-presentation discussions and debates he passionately and expertly enriched. In 2012, alongside Maria Cerreta and Paola Perchinunno, he organized the workshop Econometrics and Multidimensional Evaluation in the Urban Environment (EMEUE), fostering dialogue on critical topics. His influence steadily grew, drawing numerous research groups to ICCSA and establishing real estate and assessment as one of the conference's leading fields. A pillar of ICCSA, he was involved across all facets of the event. Torre's contributions to academic discourse were marked by intellectual rigor and innovative thinking. His conference interventions consistently challenged conventional wisdom, offering insights transcending disciplinary boundaries. Beyond the conference, he passionately advocated for equity and social justice. His left-leaning ideology, though firm, earned respect from those with differing views, thanks to his sincerity and loyalty. He was creative, generous, and always willing to help, even at a personal cost. Despite battling illness, he maintained his characteristic optimism, warmth, cheerfulness, and commitment, supported by his partner, Caterina Rinaldo. His legacy lives on in his ideas, dedication, and unmatched generosity.

Contents – Part XII

Theoretical and Computational Chemistry and its Applications (TC-CMA 2025)

Computational Insights into Perovskite Materials: Classical Molecular Dynamics and Ab Initio Approaches

Noelia Faginas-Lago[1,3], Luca Mancini[1], Andrea Lombardi[1,3],
Fernando Pirani[2], Amanda Covarelli[3(✉)], Bernardino Tirri[4],
and Filippo De Angelis[1,3]

[1] Dipartimento di Chimica, Biologia e Biotecnologie,
Università degli Studi di Perugia, 06123 Perugia, Italy
noelia.faginaslago@unipg.it
[2] Dipartimento di Ingegneria Civile ed Ambientale, Università degli Studi di Perugia,
06125 Perugia, Italy
[3] Istituto CNR di Scienze e Tecnologie Chimiche "Giulio Natta" (CNR-SCITEC),
06123 Perugia, Italy
amanda.covarelli@dottorandi.unipg.it
[4] Eni S.p.A, Via Emilia 1, 20097 San Donato Milanese Milan, Italy

Abstract. In the last years, Perovskite materials emerged as promising candidates for applications in photovoltaics and photocatalysis due to their exceptional optoelectronic properties, cost-effective synthesis, and structural tunability. However, their long-term stability and interaction with external molecules, such as CO_2, remain critical challenges for commercialization. In this study, we integrate classical molecular dynamics (MD) simulations and ab initio calculations to investigate the structural, electronic, and dynamical properties of perovskites. Density functional theory (DFT) is employed to optimize the geometry and compute atomic charge distributions, while MD simulations provide insights into system behavior under varying thermodynamic conditions. We preliminary analyze the role of non-covalent interactions between perovskites and CO_2 molecules, utilizing the canonical Lennard-Jones potential model. The obtained results suggest how to achieve a more accurate representation of long-range attraction and short-range repulsion, that leads to the development of refined force fields, enhancing the predictive accuracy of computational models for perovskite-based energy and environmental applications. This study lays the groundwork for future theoretical and experimental advancements aimed at optimizing perovskite materials for sustainable energy conversion and CO_2 reduction technologies.

Keywords: Perovskite · Molecular Dynamics · Ab Initio
Calculations · Density Functional Theory · Non-Covalent Interactions ·
Photovoltaics · CO_2 Reduction · Force Field Development

© The Author(s), under exclusive license to Springer Nature Switzerland AG 2026
O. Gervasi et al. (Eds.): ICCSA 2025 Workshops, LNCS 15897, pp. 3–16, 2026.
https://doi.org/10.1007/978-3-031-97660-5_1

1   Introduction

Perovskite, originally considered the mineral name of calcium titanate (CaTiO3) [1], was discovered for the first time by Russian mineralogist Lev Perovskiy. Perovskites are used in photovoltaics because of their increasing power conversion efficiency (PCE), low-cost materials constituents, simple solution fabrication process [2], high absorption coefficient in a wide wavelength range and relatively high carrier mobility of free electrons and holes [1]. Initiated In 2009 with an efficiency of 3.8 % [2], Perovskite solar cells (PSCs) have now achieved a lab-scale power conversion efficiency of 26.7 % [3], competing with the performance of commercial silicon solar cells. Perovskites have a general chemical formula of ABX_3, where A is usually an organic cation such as methylammonium (MA) or formamidinium (FA), B is a metallic cation like tin or lead and X is an halide, such as I, Br or Cl [4]. The A-site cation is coordinated to 12 X anions, forming a cuboctahedron, while the 6-fold-coordinated B-site cation has an octahedral geometry [1], as shown in Fig. 1.

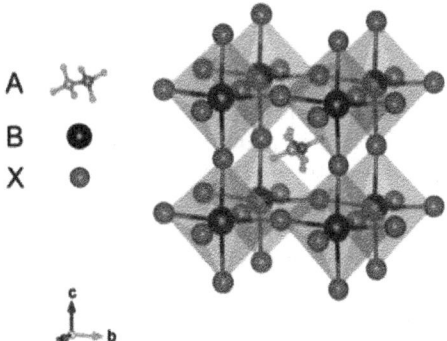

Fig. 1. Crystal structure of an organicâĂŞinorganic metal halide perovskite [5].

Tipically, PSCs have a layered device structure that includes a transparent conductive oxide (TCO)-coated glass substrate, an n-type semiconductor as the electron transport layer (ETL), a perovskite absorber layer, a p-type semiconductor as the hole transport layer (HTL), and a back-contact (metal, TCO or carbon) [2]. However, in spite of all the advantages, perovskites have a problem of stability that impedes rapid commercialization. The main issues causing instability are moisture, UV light and temperature [5]. The irreversible degradation of the perovskite layer is a problem for the lifetime of photovoltaic cells. As with multiple other solar cell technologies, also illumination with UV light can cause degradation in perovskite solar cells. Transient adsorption spectroscopy (TAS) showed that the charge collection efficiency for encapsulated perovskite cells deteriorated when exposed to UV light [5]. Exposure to elevated temperatures also causes degradation of the perovskite layer. Phillippe et al. [6] investigated the influence of elevated temperatures on both $MAPbI_3$ and $MAPbI_{3-x}Cl_x$ films. The authors used hard X-ray photoelectron spectroscopy (XPS), rather than X-ray diffraction (XRD), to explain the film decomposition, as this allows for a determination of the chemical content regardless of the crystallinity of the sample. In this experiment, the films were heated in an analysis chamber under an ultra-high vacuum. Removing the presence of water and air allowed for the isolation of the effect of temperature on the film degradation. The films were characterised using the I/Pb and N/Pb ratios, extracted from XPS. A reduction of these ratios indicates the conversion of the perovskite into PbI_2. Heating at $100\,°C$ for 20 min let to a significant reduction of both ratios. Further heating at $200\,°C$ caused both ratios to drop to a minimum, 2 and 0, respectively. This is indicative of a film composed 100% of PbI_2. To overcome the stability issues, different strategies for stabilizing the active layer have been explored, including compositional engineering, controlled morphology, grain size control, perovskite deposition techniques, interfacial engineering, and many others [7]. An easy-to-implement approach is the use of additives, which in small quantities fine-tune the materials properties and increase the stability of the devices [7].

In the last years, perovskites have been considered as promising materials for different applications, including water splitting and CO_2 reduction [8]. Considering the rapid and alarming increasing of the level of atmospheric carbon dioxide, mainly due to the increase of antropic activities [9–12], photoelectrochemical CO_2 reduction represents an intriguing alternative for the reduction of the amount of CO_2, thus contributing to the field of carbon neutrality techniques. Different works have been performed to analyse and improve the efficiency of perovskites as possible catalysts for CO_2 reduction [13–18] and the actual mechanism of the process is still matter of study and debate. One of the first step of the process, which is common of all chemical processes, is represented by the long-range interaction of the CO_2 molecule with the surface of the perovskite. Such interaction will then lead to different configurations of the weakly bound precursor state of the system, which drives the species involved along specific chanels of the reactivity. Therefore, a detailed analysis of the long-range interaction and of the intermolecular forces driving the initial process can be pivotal for a better understanding of all the reactive process. In order to properly characterize the initial interaction between the two interacting species, a valid approach consists in the use of Molecular Dynamics (MD) simulations considering the appropriate range of thermodynamic conditions. As a first step, it is pivotal to implement the most accurate description of the interactions of the involved molecules through the development of a Force Field (FF), which represents a challenging task [19–21] since the choice of a correct intermolecular force field, modelling the intermolecular forces, crucially influences the realism and feasibility of the simulation studies [21]. Different functions can be used to describe the non electrostatic component of the intermolecular interaction, including the classical Lennard-Jones potential [22], but also the more accurate *Improved Lennard-Jones* (ILJ) formulation [23], which allow for a better representation of long range attraction and short range repulsion. In the present contribution we performed preliminary MD calculation for the system composed of a perovskite layer, composed of 408 atoms in total, with 40 Pb atoms, 112 I atoms and 32 methylammonium ions ($CH_3NH_3^+$), both isolated and interacting with a CO_2 molecule using a LJ force field. The work constitutes a starting point toward the development of more accurate force field based on the physical properties of the interacting molecules.

2   Theoretical Methods

2.1   Ab Initio Calculations

Ab initio calculations have been performed at the DFT level of theory for the perovskite system. In depth, the structure of the perovskite has been optimized using the PBE functional and ultrasoft pseudopoptentials. The same computational strategy has been adopted for the optimization of the CO_2 molecule and the system composed of a carbon dioxide molecule interacting with the perovskite slab. All calculations have been performed with the Quantum Espresso package [24–26].

In order to establish the main properties of the CO_2 molecule, necessary to properly set the MD simulations, a well established computational strategy based on DFT theory has been used [27–32]. In details, the geometry has been optimized using the B3LYP functional and the aug-cc-pVTZ basis set and the atomic (Mulliken) charges have been evaluated at the same level of theory.

2.2   Molecular Dynamics

Classical molecular dynamics simulations have been performed considering both the isolated Perovskite system and the system composed of the Perovskite with a carbon dioxide molecule. In detail, the DL_POLY [33] simulation package has been used considering the NVT ensamble, where the number of particles (N), volume (V) and temperature (T) are kept constant. For this purpose, a Hoover-Nose thermostat [34] has been used, with a relaxation constant of 1 ps. Parallelepiped boundary conditions have been used, considering the shape and dimensions commisurated with the unit cell of the structure (see Sect. 3 for details). NVT simulations have been performed considering a temperature of 300 K and a pressure of 1 atm. An initial equilibration period of 1 ns has been performed, considering a total simulation time of 3 ns.

2.3   Non-covalent Interactions: Potential Energy Surface

In order to obtain a reliable Force Field to be used in the simulation, the global intermolecular interaction energy (V_{Tot}) has been considered as a combination of an electrostatic contribution (V_{Elec}) and a non-electrostatic contribution (V_{Nelec}):

$$V_{Tot} = V_{Elec} + V_{Nelec} \tag{1}$$

where the electrostatic contribution has been calculated taking into account the atomic charge distribution of the system, evaluated at the DFT level of theory and reported in Table 1. In the case of the CO_2 molecule, the atomic charges reported in Fig. 7 are consistent with the electric molecular quadrupole (Fig. 2).

Table 1. Average atomic (Mulliken) charges calculated for the structure reported in Fig. 3.

Atom	Charge
Pb	+0.317
I	−0.339
N	+0.282
C	−0.222
H	+0.112

-0.326

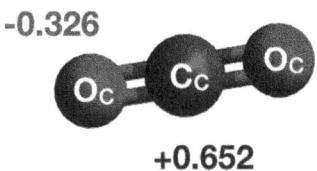

+0.652

Fig. 2. Atomic charges evaluated for the CO_2 molecule.

The non-electrostatic component of the intermolecular interaction has been evaluated considering the *Lennard-Jones* formulation [22]. The LJ potential model for a pair of neutral particles can be formulated as follows:

$$V_{LJ} = 4\varepsilon \left[\left(\frac{\sigma}{r} \right)^{12} - \left(\frac{\sigma}{r} \right)^{6} \right] \tag{2}$$

where σ represents the intermediate distance where the potential V goes to zero. Moreover, the long-range attraction coefficient is defined as:

$$C_6 = 4\varepsilon\sigma^6 \tag{3}$$

In this model, the potential well, describing the intermolecular binding energy and its characteristics arise from a balance between attraction and repulsion forces. Despite the simplicity of the formulation, the LJ model is still widely used in molecular dynamics simulations today due to its simplicity, exportability and differentiability of the adopted function. The pair parameters, obtained starting from literature values [35–37], were evaluated considering the combination rules proposed initially by Lorentz and Berthelot [38, 39] are reported in Table 2 for the Perovskite system, while in Table 3 are reported the parameters for the Perovskite - CO_2 interaction.

Table 2. List of the Lennard-Jones parameters evaluated for the Perovskite system.

Interacting Pair	σ (Å)	ε (kcal)
Pb - Pb	3.188	0.1015
Pb - I	2.884	0.1387
Pb - C	3.604	0.0118
Pb - N	3.524	0.0174
Pb - H	2.124	0.0084
I - I	2.580	0.0108
I - C	3.300	0.0039
I - N	3.220	0.0057
I - H	1.820	0.0027
C - N	3.940	0.0020
C - H	2.540	0.00096
N - N	3.860	0.0029
N - H	2.460	0.0014
H - H	1.060	0.00069

Table 3. List of the Lennard-Jones parameters evaluated for the Perovskite - CO_2 system.

Interacting Pair	σ (Å)	ε (kcal)
Pb - C_C	2.969	0.0106
Pb - O_C	3.109	0.0193
I - C_C	2.660	0.0037
I - O_C	2.805	0.0063
N - C_C	3.305	0.0019
N - O_C	3.445	0.0033
C - C_C	3.385	0.0013
C - O_C	3.525	0.0022
H - C_C	1.905	0.00094
H - O_C	2.045	0.0015

3 Results and Discussion

The global Perovskite system used in the present work is composed of four layers with a total of 408 atoms, including 40 Pb atoms, 112 I atoms and 32 methylammonium ions ($CH_3NH_3^+$), which can be considered as a good prototype for the lead halide perovskite [40] The global structure is reported in Fig. 3. As can be seen from the representation reported in the figure, the structure of the perovskite is composed by five layers in which lead and iodine atoms form an octahedral structure, generating spaces which are occupied by methylammonium cations.

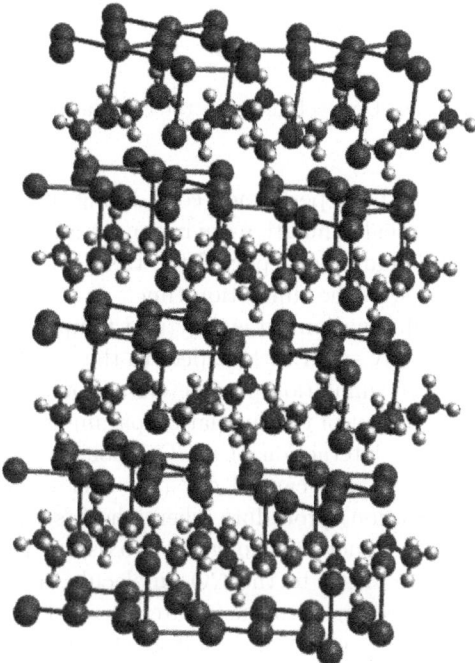

Fig. 3. 3D representation of the structure of the Perovskite used for the present analysis.

In order to run a proper MD simulation, it is pivotal to set appropriate values for the periodic boundary conditions, and, therefore, to analyze the accurate unit cell to be repeated during the simulation. In the present case, as reported also in Sect. 2, parallelepiped boundary conditions have been used, considering a unit cell whose dimensions are $9 \times 9 \times 13$ Å. A schematic representation of the unit cell used for the preliminary MD calculations is reported in Fig. 4.

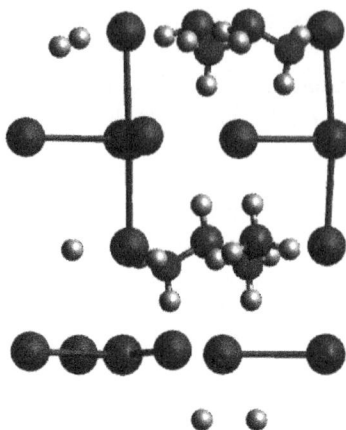

Fig. 4. Unit cell used for the calculations.

An initial analysis has been performed considering only the perovskite system, in order to set the ideal simulation environment and check the stability of the simulation. In Figs. 5 and 6 are reported the trends of the Total Energy and Temperature as a function of the simulation time.

As can be seen, the fluctuations of energy and temperature during the MD calculations are considerably small with respect to the absolute value, thus indicating the goodness of the simulation parameters adopted.

After the initial assessment of the simulation parameters, a new analysis was performed considering the interaction of a CO_2 molecule with the perovskite. An initial *ab initio* analysis was carried out (see Sect. 2 for details) considering a relaxation (optimization) procedure where the first three layers from the bottom of the perovskite structure (along the z-axis)are kept rigid, while the last two layers, which are closer to the CO_2 molecule, are able to relax. The same strategy has been used for both the isolated perovskite and the perovskite interacting with the CO_2 molecule. The resulting strucure, obtained through *ab initio* calculations, is reported in Fig. 7

The energy of the system can be easily calculated, allowing to quantify the strength of the interaction between the CO_2 molecule in the gas phase and the surface of the perovskite. In details, the adsorption energy can be evaluated as follows:

$$E_{ads} = E_{tot} - E_{per} - E_{CO_2} \tag{4}$$

where E_{tot} is the energy deriving from the optimized structure of the perovskite with the CO_2 molecule, while E_{per} and E_{CO_2} represent the energies of the perovskite and CO_2 optimized separately, obtained at the DFT level of theory. Following the formulation reported in Eq. 4, a value of $E_{ads} = -5.07\,kcal/mol$ was obtained. The value can be compared with the results derived from a preliminary MD analysis, performed considering a *Lennard-Jones* formulation of

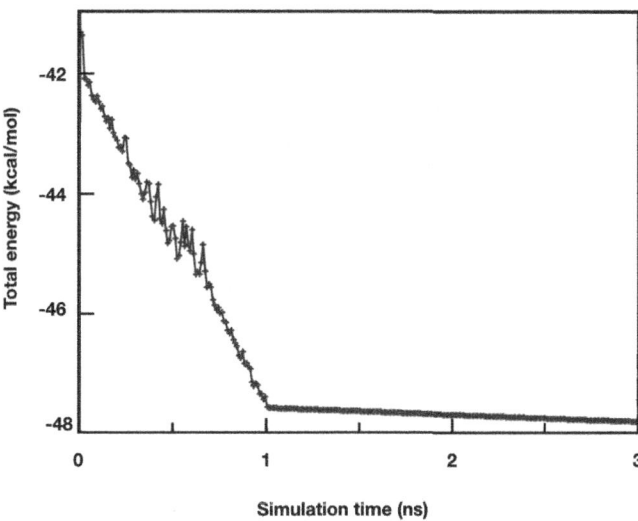

Fig. 5. Trend of the total energy (in kcal/mol) as a function of the simulation time (ns) for the Perovskite system, obtained through MD calculations.

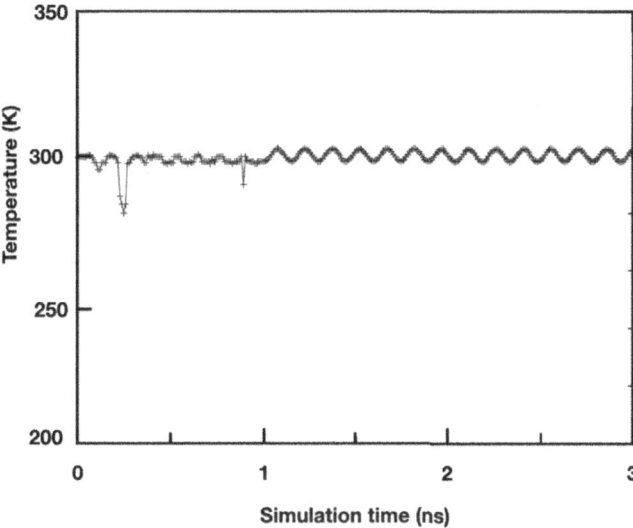

Fig. 6. Trend of the temperature (in K) as a function of the simulation time (ns) for the Perovskite system.

the non-electrostatic interaction (see Table 3 for details). Also in this case, the interaction energy was evaluated considering the difference between the configurational energy of the perovskite+CO_2 system and the configurational energy of the two interacting species, calculated separately. The value obtained from clas-

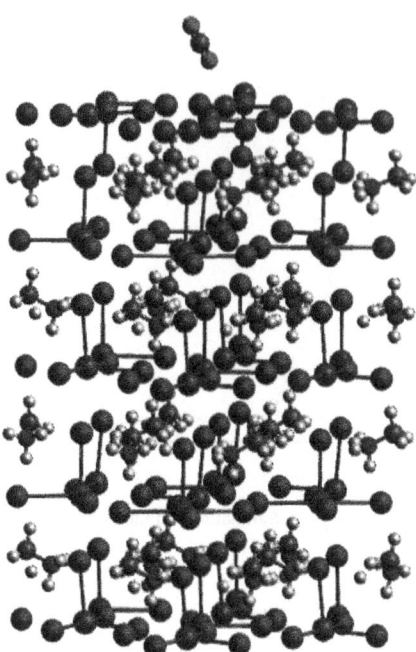

Fig. 7. 3D representation of the structure of the perovskite system interacting with a CO_2 molecule.

sical MD calculation is equal to $-3.54\,\text{kcal/mol}$, differing of around $1.5\,\text{kcal/mol}$ with respect to the value coming from *ab initio* calculations. An additional analysis can be performed considering the geometry resulting from *ab initio* calculations, and in particular taking into account the distance between the CO_2 molecule and the Perovskite layer. In Table 4 are reported the main distances obtained through accurate *ab initio* calculations.

The results reported in Table 4 can be directly compared with the σ parameters of the LJ formulation (see Table 3). As can be seen, the main interaction distances estimated using the Lennard-Jones formulation are considerably lower than the ones obtained from the *ab initio* calculations. The most important deviation can be appreciated considering the I-C$-C$ interaction, where the difference is around 2 . One of the reasons of the disagreement between accurate *ab initio* calculations and classical molecular dynamics simulations can be attributed to the force field adopted for the simulations. In particular, a different formulation of both the electrostatic and the non-electrostatic potential can be used to properly take into account the effect of the chemical environment in the description of the atom-atom interactions. For this purpose, the *Improved Lennard-Jones* [23] formulation of the potential can be of great help, since the main parameters governing the interactions are related to fundamental physical quantities, such as charge distribution and atomic/moleculear polarizabilities. In order to have a proper representation of all the interaction centers with a limited computational

Table 4. Atom-atom distances (in Å) between the CO_2 molecule and the first layer of the perovskite structure, obtained through DFT calculations (see Sect. 2.1 for details).

Interacting Pair	dist. (Å)
C_C - Pb	4.021
O_C - I	2.996
C_C - Pb	4.628
O_C - I	4.188

cost, in the case of complex systems, it can be necessary to consider different moieties globally as effective atoms, each one having polarizability equal to the average molecular component, in order to provide a simplified formulation of the multidimensional Potential Energy Surface (PES).

4   Conclusions

In the present contribution, we performed a preliminary molecular dynamics (MD) analysis of the interaction between CO_2 and perovskites, using the canonical Lennard-Jones potential function to model the non-covalent interactions. The obtained results were compared with high level *ab initio* calculations, to evaluate the quality of the results. The obtained results show a slight disagreement between classical MD simulations and *ab initio* resulting, suggest that the initial force field needs to be adjusted to better represent the non-covalent interactions. A first refinement can be done modeling the electrostatic contribution considering a different charge distribution on the perovskite, where the atomic charges are +2 for the Pb atoms, −1 for the I and +1 for the CH_3NH_3 cation. Additionally, in order to achieve a more accurate representation of long-range attraction and short-range repulsion, a different computational models can be used, namely the *Improved Lennard-Jones* formulation, where the parameters are linked to physical properties, such as dipole moment and electric dipole. The present study lays the basis of a future characterization, allowing to properly represent the interaction between perovskyte systems and small molecules, with particular relevance in the field of energy storage.

Acknowledgments. This work has been funded by the European Union - NextGenerationEU under the Italian Ministry of University and Research (MUR) National Innovation Ecosystem grant ECS00000041 - VITALITY - CUP J97G22000170005. N.F.L, A.L. and F. DA acknowledge funding by the Italian Ministry of Environment and Energy Security in the framework of the Project GoPV (CSEAA_00011) for Research on the Electric System. A.C., from UniPG, acknowledges the financial support of Eni S.p.A. for research activities conducted within the PhD cycle XXXIX.

Disclosure of Interests. The authors have no competing interests to declare that are relevant to the content of this article.

References

1. Kim, J.Y., Lee, J.W., Jung, H.S., Shin, H., Park, N.G.: High-efficiency perovskite solar cells. Chem. Rev. **120**(15), 7867–7918 (2020)
2. Rong, Y., et al.: Challenges for commercializing perovskite solar cells. Science **361**(6408), eaat8235 (2018)
3. Mao, L., Xiang, C.: A comprehensive review of machine learning applications in perovskite solar cells: materials discovery, device performance, process optimization and systems integration. Mater. Today Energy, 101742 (2024)
4. Correa-Baena, J.P., et al.: Promises and challenges of perovskite solar cells. Science **358**(6364), 739–744 (2017)
5. Wang, D., Wright, M., Elumalai, N.K., Uddin, A.: Stability of perovskite solar cells. Sol. Energy Mater. Sol. Cells **147**, 255–275 (2016)
6. Philippe, B., Park, B.W., Lindblad, R., Oscarsson, J., Ahmadi, S., Johansson, E.M., Rensmo, H.: Chemical and electronic structure characterization of lead halide perovskites and stability behavior under different exposures a photoelectron spectroscopy investigation. Chem. Mater. **27**(5), 1720–1731 (2015)
7. Valero, S., Soria, T., Marinova, N., Delgado, J.L.: Efficient and stable perovskite solar cells based on perfluorinated polymers. Polym. Chem. **10**(42), 5726–5736 (2019)
8. Bienkowski, K., et al.: Halide perovskites for photoelectrochemical water splitting and co2 reduction: challenges and opportunities. ACS Catal. **14**(9), 6603–6622 (2024)
9. Harfoot, M.B., et al.: Present and future biodiversity risks from fossil fuel exploitation. Conserv. Lett. **11**(4), e12448 (2018)
10. Deutz, S., et al.: Cleaner production of cleaner fuels: wind-to-wheel-environmental assessment of co_2-based oxymethylene ether as a drop-in fuel. Energy Environ. Sci. **11**(2), 331–343 (2018)
11. Marques, A.C., Fuinhas, J.A., Pereira, D.A.: Have fossil fuels been substituted by renewables? An empirical assessment for 10 European countries. Energy Policy **116**, 257–265 (2018)
12. Rogelj, J., et al.: Scenarios towards limiting global mean temperature increase below 1.5 c. Nat. Climate Change **8**(4), 325–332 (2018)
13. Tang, C., Chen, C., Xu, W., Xu, L.: Design of doped cesium lead halide perovskite as a photo-catalytic co 2 reduction catalyst. J. Mater. Chem. A **7**(12), 6911–6919 (2019)
14. Shyamal, S., Pradhan, N.: Halide perovskite nanocrystal photocatalysts for co2 reduction: successes and challenges. J. Phys. Chem. Lett. **11**(16), 6921–6934 (2020)
15. Chen, J., Dong, C., Idriss, H., Mohammed, O.F., Bakr, O.M.: Metal halide perovskites for solar-to-chemical fuel conversion. Adv. Energy Mater. **10**(13), 1902433 (2020)
16. Zhang, X., Tang, R., Li, F., Zheng, R., Huang, J.: Tailoring inorganic halide perovskite photocatalysts toward carbon dioxide reduction. Solar RRL **6**(6), 2101058 (2022)
17. Yuan, J., Liu, H., Wang, S., Li, X.: How to apply metal halide perovskites to photocatalysis: challenges and development. Nanoscale **13**(23), 10281–10304 (2021)
18. Chen, S., Yin, H., Liu, P., Wang, Y., Zhao, H.: Stabilization and performance enhancement strategies for halide perovskite photocatalysts. Adv. Mater. **35**(6), 2203836 (2023)

19. Marques, J., et al.: A global optimization perspective on molecular clusters. Phil. Trans. R. Soc. A: Math. Phys. Eng. Sci. **375**(2092), 20160198 (2017)
20. Cappelletti, D., Falcinelli, S., Pirani, F.: The dawn of hydrogen and halogen bonds and their crucial role in collisional processes probing long-range intermolecular interactions. Phys. Chem. Chem. Phys. **26**, 7971–7987 (2024)
21. Marques, J.M., Prudente, F.V., Pirani, F.: Intermolecular forces: from atoms and molecules to nanostructures (2022)
22. Lennard-Jones, J., Hall, G.: Je lennard-jones proc. Roy. Soc. Lond. A. **106**, 441 (1924)
23. Pirani, F., Brizi, S., Roncaratti, L.F., Casavecchia, P., Cappelletti, D., Vecchiocattivi, F.: Beyond the lennard-jones model: a simple and accurate potential function probed by high resolution scattering data useful for molecular dynamics simulations. Phys. Chem. Chem. Phys. **10**(36), 5489–5503 (2008)
24. Giannozzi, P., et al.: Quantum espresso: a modular and open-source software project for quantum simulations of materials. J. Phys. Conden. Matt. **21**(39), 395502 (2009). http://www.quantum-espresso.org
25. Giannozzi, P., et al.: Advanced capabilities for materials modelling with quantum espresso. J. Phys. Conden. Matter **29**(46), 465901 (2017). http://stacks.iop.org/0953-8984/29/i=46/a=465901
26. Giannozzi, P., et al.: Quantum espresso toward the exascale. J. Chem. Phys. **152**(15), 154105 (2020)
27. Pannacci, G., et al.: A combined crossed molecular beam and theorerical study of the $O(^3P, {}^1D)$ + acrylonitrile (CH_2CHCN) reactions and implications for combustion and extraterrestrial environments. Phys. Chem. Chem. Phys. **25**(30), 20194–20211 (2023)
28. Liang, P., et al.: Oh (2π)+ c2h4 reaction: a combined crossed molecular beam and theoretical study. J. Phys. Chem. A **127**(21), 4609–4623 (2023)
29. Rosi, M., et al.: Electronic structure and kinetics calculations for the Si+SH reaction, a possible route of SiS formation in star-forming regions. In: Misra, S., et al. (eds.) ICCSA 2019. LNCS, vol. 11621, pp. 306–315. Springer, Cham (2019). https://doi.org/10.1007/978-3-030-24302-9_22
30. Liang, P., et al.: Combined crossed molecular beams and computational study on the n (2d)+ hcccn (x1σ+) reaction and implications for extra-terrestrial environments. Mol. Phys. **120**(1–2), e1948126 (2022)
31. Vanuzzo, G., et al.: The n (2d)+ ch2chcn (vinyl cyanide) reaction: a combined crossed molecular beam and theoretical study and implications for the atmosphere of titan. J. Phys. Chem. A **126**(36), 6110–6123 (2022)
32. Vanuzzo, G., Mancini, L., Pannacci, G., Liang, P., Marchione, D., Recio, P., Tan, Y., Rosi, M., Skouteris, D., Casavecchia, P., et al.: Reaction n (2d)+ ch2cch2 (allene): an experimental and theoretical investigation and implications for the photochemical models of titan. ACS Earth Space Chem. **6**(10), 2305–2321 (2022)
33. Smith, W., Yong, C., Rodger, P.: Dl_poly: application to molecular simulation. Mol. Simul. **28**(5), 385–471 (2002)
34. Hoover, W.G.: Canonical dynamics: equilibrium phase-space distributions. Phys. Rev. A **31**(3), 1695 (1985)
35. Poling, B.E., Prausnitz, J.M., O'connell, J.P., et al.: The Properties of Gases and Liquids, vol. 5. Mcgraw-hill, New York (2001)
36. Maghfiroh, C.Y., Arkundato, A., Maulina, W., et al.: Parameters (σ, ε) of lennard-jones for fe, ni, pb for potential and cr based on melting point values using the molecular dynamics method of the lammps program. In: Journal of Physics: Conference Series. vol. 1491, p. 012022. IOP Publishing (2020)

37. Freindorf, M., Shao, Y., Furlani, T.R., Kong, J.: Lennard-jones parameters for the combined qm/mm method using the b3lyp/6-31g*/amber potential. J. Comput. Chem. **26**(12), 1270–1278 (2005)
38. Lorentz, H.: About the application of the virial theorem in the kinetic theory of gases. Ann. Phys. **248**(1), 127–136 (1881)
39. Berthelot, D., Amoreux, G.: Comptes rendus acad (1898)
40. Canil, L., et al.: Halogen-bonded hole-transport material suppresses charge recombination and enhances stability of perovskite solar cells. Adv. Energy Mater. **11**(35), 2101553 (2021)

Comparative Evaluation of Molecular Representation Models for Simulation of Methane Adsorption on Graphtriyne Sheet

Noelia Faginas-Lago[1,2(✉)] ⓘ, Yusuf Bramastya Apriliyanto[3(✉)] ⓘ,
Luca Mancini[1] ⓘ, and Andrea Lombardi[1,2] ⓘ

[1] Dipartimento di Chimica, Biologia e Biotecnologie,
Università degli Studi di Perugia, 06123 Perugia, Italy
noelia.faginaslago@unipg.it
[2] Istituto CNR di Scienze e Tecnologie Chimiche "Giulio Natta" (CNR-SCITEC),
06123 Perugia, Italy
[3] Department of Chemistry, Indonesia Defense University,
Kampus Unhan Komplek IPSC Sentul, 16810 Bogor, Indonesia
yusuf.bramastya@gmail.com

Abstract. Reducing greenhouse gas emissions by employing advanced porous adsorbents is critical for mitigating anthropogenic contributions to the climate change. In this study, molecular dynamics (MD) simulations were performed to investigate the adsorption performance of graphtriyne sheet as a potential methane adsorbent. A comparative analysis of two molecular representation models—united-atom and atomistic—was conducted using the Improved Lennard-Jones (ILJ) potential function. The results indicated that the united-atom model yielded a higher permeation rate and diffusion coefficient but exhibited lower gas uptake than the atomistic model. The lack of orientation effects in the united-atom model led to reduced steric hindrance, facilitating methane permeation; whereas the atomistic model's stronger orientation effects lowered permeance. These findings highlight the significant influence of molecular representation on the accuracy of MD simulation results and emphasize the importance of selecting well-validated force field parameters for methane adsorption studies.

Keywords: MD simulations · graphynes · graphtriyne · methane capture

1 Introduction

Reducing greenhouse gases emissions is crucial in mitigating possible anthropic contributions to climate change and global warming. Methane (CH_4), a potent greenhouse gas, has been reported having a global warming potential (GWP) 84–87 times higher than carbon dioxide (CO_2) over a 20-year period and 28–36 times higher over a 100-year period [1,2]. Methane emissions contribute to about 30%

O. Gervasi et al. (Eds.): ICCSA 2025 Workshops, LNCS 15897, pp. 17–27, 2026.
https://doi.org/10.1007/978-3-031-97660-5_2

of global warming, with annual emissions reaching approximately 570 million metric tons [3]. One effective strategy for reducing greenhouse gases emissions is the capture and storage of methane from anthropogenic sources such as landfills, coal mines, and natural gas processing facilities. Among various methane capture technologies, adsorption using advanced porous materials have actively been explored and garnered significant interest in the past few years due to its high efficiency, low energy consumption, and environmental sustainability [4–6].

Carbon-based materials bearing intrinsic pores currently have emerged as promising adsorbents for greenhouse gases due to their exceptional surface area, tunable porosity, and high chemical stability [7–9]. One notable form of carbon allotrope is graphene, a two-dimensional carbon-based nanomaterial. Unlike conventional porous adsorbents such as activated carbon, zeolites, and metal-organic frameworks (MOFs), graphene and its derivatives exhibit superior properties by having low density and robust structures originated from lightweight elements linked by strong covalent bonds [10]. Furthermore, functionalized graphene materials, including graphene oxide (GO) and reduced graphene oxide (rGO), have been studied for their enhanced adsorption properties, offering potential for large-scale methane capture and storage applications [11,12]. However, one significant limitation of graphene is its tendency to form aggregates, which restricts its gas uptake capacity. γ-graphynes are class of two-dimensional carbon allotropes that share several properties with graphene but offer the advantage of uniformly distributed and tunable pores [13]. Unlike graphene, γ-graphynes exhibit weaker dispersion forces, reducing aggregation. This characteristic makes them particularly effective for greenhouse gas capture [10,14]. Unfortunately, the effective way to experimentally synthesize graphines is not yet actively explored [15,16]. Within this gap, computational chemistry and molecular simulations have played a vital role in the development of carbon-based adsorbents for methane capture [17].

Density Functional Theory (DFT) calculations and Grand Canonical Monte Carlo (GCMC) simulations have been widely employed to predict methane adsorption behaviour, optimize pore structures, and enhance material performance [12,18]. These computational techniques provide valuable insights into the mechanisms of adsorption at the atomic level, facilitating the rational design of high-performance carbon-based adsorbents. Furthermore, molecular dynamics (MD) simulations have been increasingly utilized to investigate the dynamic interactions between methane molecules and graphene surfaces under different environmental conditions [19,20]. These simulations enable the analysis of key properties such as diffusion coefficients, adsorption energies, and interaction potentials, providing deeper insight into the stability and efficiency of graphene-based adsorbents for methane capture. MD simulations allow study of the adsorption kinetics, diffusion behavior, and structural stability of adsorbents over time, complementing the insights provided by the DFT and GCMC approaches [21]. Recent computational studies reported that graphtriyne (a form of graphynes, in which each benzene ring is connected to each of six others through a chain composed of three acetylenic bonds) [22] showed potential as a carbon-based adsorbent for gas capture and separation under post-combustion conditions [23–26].

A critical aspect of computational simulations is the accurate representation of interatomic interactions as well as structural modeling of materials, which requires well-validated force field parameters [17,19]. The choice of force field influences the accuracy of adsorption predictions. Therefore, in this work, a comparative study of the two widely used molecular representations to model van der Waals interactions between methane and carbon-based materials is evaluated using extended MD simulations. The results could provide insights into the adsorption performance of graphtriyne for methane capture, by evaluating factors such as adsorption capacity and thermodynamic behaviour that contribute to the development of efficient methane adsorption technologies.

2 Theoretical Methods

For modelling the intermolecular interactions, the total potential energy of the system is split into electrostatic and non-electrostatic contributions. The electrostatic contribution is treated using a standard Coulombic summation, by assigning point charges of the interacting molecules as the following:

$$V_{tot}(r) = \sum_{i,j}^{n} \frac{q_i q_j}{r_{ij}} + \sum_{i}^{n} V_{ILJ}(r_i) \tag{1}$$

On the other hand, the non-electrostatic term is expressed using the following Improved Lennard-Jones (ILJ) potential [27] which requires four parameters (r_0, ε, m and β) to be specified as given by

$$V_{ILJ}(r_i) = 4\varepsilon \left[\left(\frac{m}{m(r) - m} \right) \left(\frac{r_0}{r} \right)^{n(r)} - \frac{n(r)}{n(r) - m} \left(\frac{r_0}{r} \right)^{m} \right] \tag{2}$$

with

$$n(r) = \beta + 4.0 \left(\frac{r}{r_0} \right)^2 \tag{3}$$

The r_0 and ε are pair specific parameter representing the equilibrium distance and the depth of potential well, respectively. The m parameter takes the value of 6 for describing interactions between neutral molecules. The β is an adjustable dimensionless parameter describing the hardness of the interaction. The ILJ formulation incorporates anisotropic effects and high-order interaction terms that refine the accuracy of intermolecular interactions, thus make ILJ as a versatile function that improve not only at equilibrium distance but also at short- and long-range parts of the potential compared to the Lennard-Jones (LJ) function [28].

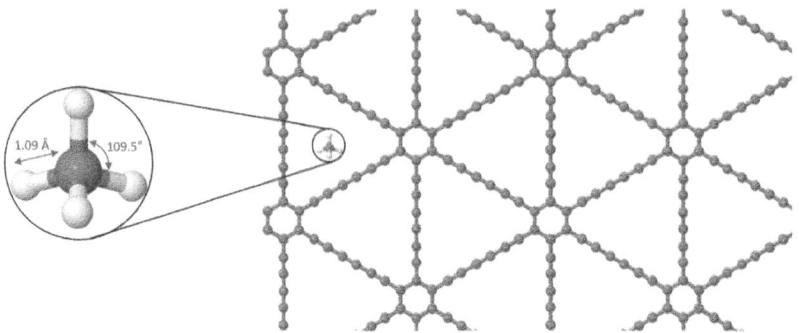

Fig. 1. Molecular geometry of methane and graphtriyne used in this study.

The methane molecular geometry has been optimized employing DFT at B3LYP/def2-TZVP level. The same computational strategy, based on DFT investigations, has been adopted in the past for several works [29–32], resulting as a valid compromise between chemical accuracy and computational cost. The graphtriyne structure is taken from Ref. [25] where it had been fully relaxed by using periodic DFT optimization. Figure 1 ilustrates the geometrical structure of methane and grapfhtriyne used in the MD simulations. Following computational approach reported in Ref. [20], a united-atom and an atomistic model were selected to represent methane molecule. The united-atom model treats the CH_4 molecule as a sphere by putting one interaction center on the center of mass of CH_4. On the other hand, the atomistic model puts an interaction center on all atoms of the CH_4 molecule. For the united-atom model, charges were calculated by the Hirshfeld population analysis [33] (−0.148 e on the carbon atom and 0.037 e on the hydrogen atoms). Meanwhile, for the atomistic model, the atomic charges of CH_4 molecule were not included meaning that all intermolecular interactions were operated by using only the ILJ potential. All parameters used for the simulations in this study (listed in Table 1) was taken from the parameters reported in Ref. [20].

Figure 2 shows the simulation box with dimension of $72.210 \times 62.523 \times 280.0$ $\mathring{A}^3$. A total of 100 CH_4 molecules were randomly distributed inside the simulation box, where graphtriyne sheet with a dimension of 72.210×62.523 $\mathring{A}^2$ was set in the center of the box. The cut-off distances for the ILJ and electrostatic interactions were set to 15 $\mathring{A}$, where the Ewald method [34] was applied for the calculation of electrostatic interactions. The graphtriyne were considered as a frozen framework and the gas molecules were treated as rigid bodies. Periodic boundary conditions were implemented in all directions of axes. Each simulation was performed for 5 ns after 0.5 ns equilibration period with a fixed time step of 1 fs. The statistical data and trajectory were collected at every 1 ps. All the MD simulations is performed by using DL_POLY package [35] in the canonical (NVT) ensemble employing the Nose-Hoover algorithm to maintain the applied

Table 1. Interaction parameters used for representing the intermolecular potentials in methane-graphtryne system. C_m indicates the C of the methane molecule.

Model	Type	ε (kcal mol^{-1})	$r_0(\mathring{A})$	β	Charges (e)
United atom	Cm–Cm	0.421	4.168	8.215	–
	Cm–C	0.210	3.938	8.185	–
	Cm	–	–	–	–0.148
	H	–	–	–	0.037
Atomistic	Cm–Cm	0.109	3.800	8.027	–
	Cm–C	0.195	3.671	7.745	–
	Cm–H	0.075	3.628	4.932	–
	C–H	0.099	3.727	5.476	–
	H–H	0.005	3.419	4.363	–

temperatures at 300K. The graphical representations and the molecular trajectories were processed by using VMD program [36].

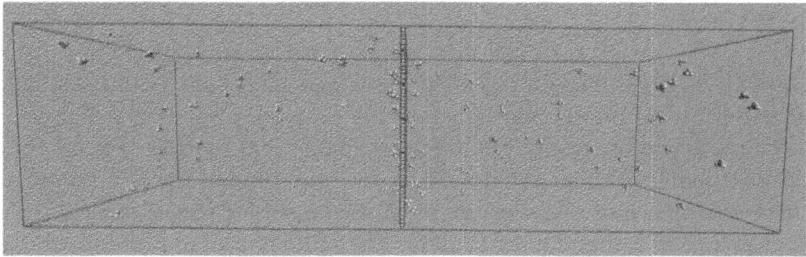

Fig. 2. Snapshoot of the simulation box filled with CH_4 molecules where the graphytriyne is located at the centre of simulation box.

3   Results and Discussion

Production runs of MD simulations were started after 0.5 ns equilibration time in which the energy and temperature convergence were checked as an indication of equilibrated system. Statistical data along with the z-density and the radial distribution function (RDF) profiles were then monitored. Figure 3 depicts the fluctuation of configurational energy during the simulation period. We obtained the average configuration energy or potential energy for the united atom model of –45.59 kcal mol^{-1} with a percent deviation of about 12% or equal to 5.63 kcal mol^{-1}. On the other hand, the average value for the atomistic model is about –360.60 kcal mol^{-1} with 7% deviation or equal to 25.28 kcal mol^{-1}. This confirmed that classical MD simulations of diverse models exhibited different energy fluctuations; in this case, the united atom model had more potential energy fluctuation at the equilibrium. Interestingly, the atomistic model produced more converge and more negative potential energy surface at the equilibrium that could be an early indication of high adsorption phenomenon.

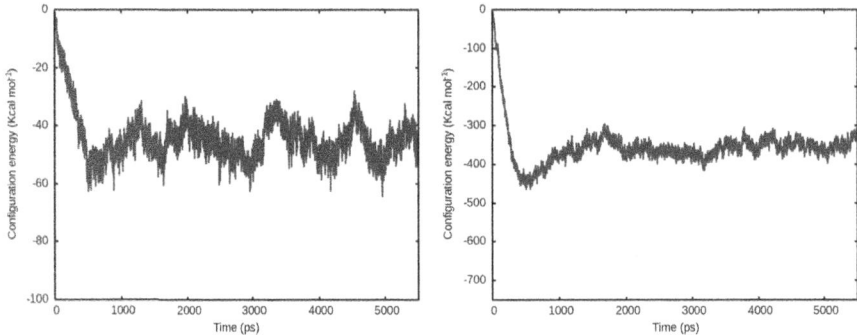

Fig. 3. Configurational energy fluctuation of united atom (left panel) and atomistic model (right panel) during MD simulations.

The CH_4 molecules could cross the layer multiple times from both sides of the layer during the production runs (see the snapshoot reported in Fig. 2). The number of permeation events was then calculated and plotted as a function of simulation time. The slope of this plot is an estimation of the CH_4 permeation rate measured in a unit of molecules ps^{-1}. Figure 4 (left panel) depicts the permeation events as a function of time for the united-atom and atomistic model of CH_4. It is clear that the number of permeation events of CH_4 represented by using united-atom model is higher than the atomistic model. Quantitatively, permeation rate of CO_2 for the united-atom model is 1.419×10^{-1} molecules ps^{-1}, almost 60% higher than its counterpart by only 0.905×10^{-1} molecules ps^{-1}.

Figure 4 (right panel) shows a plot of the mean number density of CH_4 along the z-axis (i.e. the z-density profile), where the z-axis is perpendicular with the graphtriyne surface. As it can be seen from the z-density profile, there are sharp peaks at a region below 5 Å from the surface. This region is the location where CH_4 molecules are highly adsorbed by the graphtriyne, thus it is normally called as the adsorption region. Surprisingly, a high permeation rate of CH_4 for the united-atom model is inversely related to the CH_4 adsorption on the graphtriyne surface (Fig. 4, right panel). As reported in our previous works [23–25], the permeation events are closely related to the adsorption of gas over the surfaces of membrane. The more gas is adsorbed over the surfaces, the higher is its probability to permeate the graphtriyne sheet. However, the number of adsorbed molecules also can diminish the gas permeance by saturating the pores and blocking other molecules to cross the membrane. Apparently, this

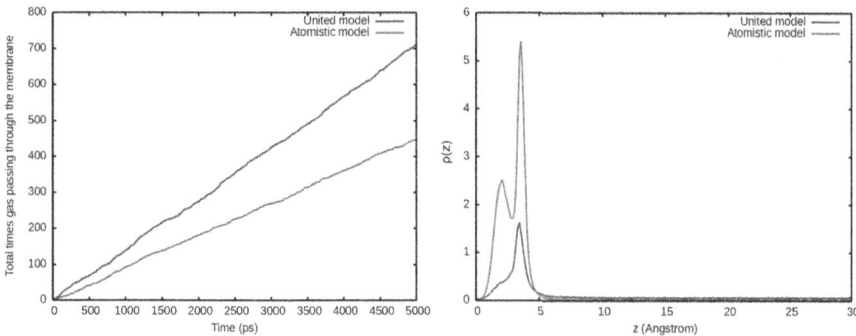

Fig. 4. Permeation events as a function of time (left panel) and the z-density profiles (right panel) for CH_4 represented as united-atom and atomistic model.

phenomenon happened for the case of CH_4 treated using atomistic model, where the atomistic model produced stronger attraction forces combined with orientation requirement for crossing the graphtriyne leading to lower gas permeance than the united-atom model.

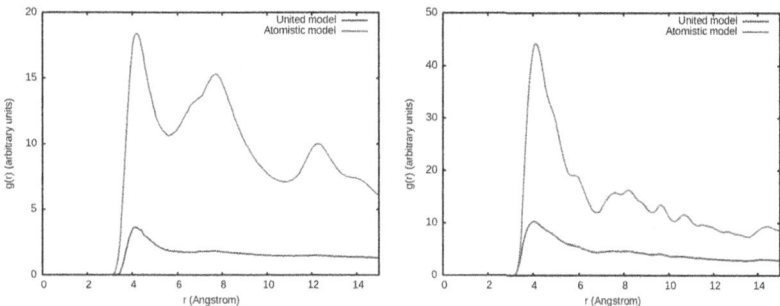

Fig. 5. Radial distribution functions (RDF) between CH_4 molecules (right) and CH_4 molecules with respect to graphtryne (left) for united-atom and atomistic model.

Stronger attraction forces for the case of atomistic model can also be verified by looking at the radial distribution functions (RDF) reported in Fig. 5. According to RDF, atomistic model has the largest and highest peaks meaning that CH_4 molecules are more likely to be located near the C atoms of graphtriyne and near other CH_4 molecules. In other words, high and broad peaks of RDF presented in Fig. 5 correspond to the deep and wide of CH_4 potential well, meaning a strong long-ranged attractions, when CH_4 is represented by using atomistic model. In addition to the RDF reported in Fig. 5, the stronger attraction for atomistic model is also reflected in configuration and vdW energies listed in Table 2. The atomistic model produced more negative energies, even two orders of magnitude lower than the united-atom model. Table 2 also shows that for the case of united model, the contribution of Coulombic energy is quite small; this indicates the electrostatic interactions between non-polar molecules are weak and negligible in comparison with the van der Waals forces. Therefore, the adsorption dynamics of CH_4 molecules on grapthriyne sheet is mainly governed by van der Waals intermolecular interactions.

Table 2. Several key properties of methane adsorption on graphtriyne obtained from the MD simulations

Parameters	United Model	Atomistic model
Configuration Energy (kcal mol^{-1})	-4.559×10^1	-3.606×10^2
vdW Energy (kcal mol^{-1})	-4.559×10^1	-3.606×10^2
Couloumb Energy (kcal mol^{-1})	-1.493×10^{-4}	-
Diffusion Coefficient (10^{-9} m^{2}s^{-1})	3.211×10^3	1.415×10^3
Adsorbed Molecules (molecules)	24.669	80.621
Gas Permeation Rate (molecules ps^{-1})	1.419×10^{-1}	0.905×10^{-1}

We also calculated the average of CH_4 uptakes by integrating the z-density profiles at the adsorption region. The adsorption region is an area located in the range of 5 Å from the surface of graphtriyne. We found that the atomistic model yielded a much stronger methane adsorption by capturing about 81 molecules. The united-atom model, on the other hand, showed a lower methane uptake of 25 molecules (Table 2). This trend is in good agreement with the results reported in Ref. [20], where the atomistic model of methane predicted more CH_4 adsorption on graphene surface. Furthermore, by calculating the diffusion coefficient of methane (defined as the rate of CH_4 movement inside the simulation box), we confirm that the atomistic model exhibits stronger adsorption by the fact that attraction forces could impede the movement of CH_4 molecules, decreasing the diffusion coefficient value (Table 2). As a final remark, both molecular representation models reveal the potential application of graphtriyne for methane adsorption. However, it is clear that the choice of force field influences the accuracy of adsorption predictions; therefore, it is crucial to use the appropriate set of force fields to guarantees a quantitative description of the interactions and trustable results for the adsorption dynamics.

4   Conclusions

Graphtriyne sheet has been investigated for the purpose of methane capture employing extensive MD simulations based on two distinct formulation of force fields. The results showed that graphtriyne sheet could be considered as a potential porous adsorbent for methane gas uptake. Comparative analysis of two molecular representation models of CH_4 (i.e. united-atom and atomistic) revealed that the united-atom model produced higher permeation rate and diffusion coefficient than the later. Conversely, the united-atom model exhibited lower gas uptake than the atomistic model. The united-atom model did not take into account orientation effects for the representation of CH_4 molecules. Therefore, within this model, adsorbed molecules around the pores did not spent time too long for crossing the graphtriyne sheet; in other words, there was no steric hindrance that preventing permeation events. However, the orientation effects were found stronger for the atomistic gas model, lowering the CH_4 permeance. In addition, we found that the adsorption dynamics of CH_4 molecules on grapthriyne sheet was mainly governed by van der Waals forces. The type of molecular representation highly influences the accuracy of MD simulations results, yet more details representation requires more computational time. Considering all those results, the choice of well-validated force field parameters is a critical aspect of molecular simulations. Improving future force fields should focus on incorporating molecular orientation effects and steric barriers into simplified models to enhance the accuracy of adsorption and diffusion studies, while still optimizing computational efficiency.

Acknowledgments. This work has been funded by the European Union - NextGenerationEU under the Italian Ministry of University and Research (MUR) National Innovation Ecosystem grant ECS00000041 - VITALITY - CUP J97G22000170005. N.F.L thanks financial support under the National Recovery and Resilience Plan (NRRP), Mission 4, Component 2, Investment 1.1, Call for tender No. 104 published on 2.2.2022 by the Italian Ministry of University and Research (MUR), funded by the European Union – NextGenerationEU – Project Title 2022JC2Y93 ChemicalOrigins: linking the fossil composition of the Solar System with the chemistry of protoplanetary disks – CUP J53D23001600006 - Grant Assignment Decree No. 962 adopted on 30/06/2023 by the Italian Ministry of University and Research (MUR). A.L. acknowledges funding by the Italian Ministry of Environment and Energy Security in the framework of the Project GoPV (CSEAA_00011) for Research on the Electric System. YBA acknowledges support from the Department of Chemistry Unhan RI

Disclosure of Interests. The authors have no competing interests to declare that are relevant to the content of this article.

References

1. WRI: How methane emissions contribute to climate change. https://www.wri.org/. Accessed 01 Mar 2025
2. UNEP: Global methane assessment: Benefits and costs of mitigating methane emissions. unep & climate and clean air coalition. https://www.unep.org/resources. Accessed 01 Mar 2025
3. IEA: Methane tracker 2021: Methane and climate change. https://www.iea.org/reports/methane-tracker-2021. Accessed 01 Mar 2025
4. Alonso, A., et al.: Critical review of existing nanomaterial adsorbents to capture carbon dioxide and methane. Sci. Total Environ. **595**, 51–62 (2017).

https://doi.org/10.1016/j.scitotenv.2017.03.229. https://www.sciencedirect.com/science/article/pii/S004896971730760X

5. Roohollahi, H., Zeinalzadeh, H., Kazemian, H.: Recent advances in adsorption and separation of methane and carbon dioxide greenhouse gases using metalâorganic framework-based composites. Ind. Eng. Chem. Res. **61**(30), 10555–10586 (2022). https://doi.org/10.1021/acs.iecr.2c00664

6. Ko, V.Y., Wang, J., He, I., Ryan, D., Zhang, X., Lan, C.: Adsorption of methane on biochar for emission reduction in oil and gas fields. Biochar **5**(1), 15 (2023)

7. Memetova, A., et al.: Porous carbon-based material as a sustainable alternative for the storage of natural gas (methane) and biogas (biomethane): a review. Chem. Eng. J. **446**, 137373 (2022). https://doi.org/10.1016/j.cej.2022.137373. https://www.sciencedirect.com/science/article/pii/S1385894722028613

8. Singh, R., Wang, L., Ostrikov, K.K., Huang, J.: Designing carbon-based porous materials for carbon dioxide capture. Adv. Mater. Interfaces **11**(4), 2202290 (2024). https://doi.org/10.1002/admi.202202290. https://advanced.onlinelibrary.wiley.com/doi/abs/10.1002/admi.202202290

9. Deng, H., Li, T., Li, H., Dang, A., Han, Y.: Carbon-based adsorbents for co2 capture: a systematic review. J. Ind. Eng. Chem. (2024). https://doi.org/10.1016/j.jiec.2024.12.026. https://www.sciencedirect.com/science/article/pii/S1226086X24008396

10. de Oliveira, R.B., Borges, D.D., Machado, L.D.: Mechanical and gas adsorption properties of graphene and graphynes under biaxial strain. Sci. Rep. **12**(1), 22393 (2022). https://doi.org/10.1038/s41598-022-27069-y

11. Szczniak, B., Choma, J., Jaroniec, M.: Gas adsorption properties of graphene-based materials. Adv. Colloid Interface Sci. **243**, 46–59 (2017). https://doi.org/10.1016/j.cis.2017.03.007. https://www.sciencedirect.com/science/article/pii/S0001868617300039

12. Arango Hoyos, B.E., et al.: Exploring the capture and desorption of co2 on graphene oxide foams supported by computational calculations. Sci. Rep. **13**(1), 14476 (2023). https://doi.org/10.1038/s41598-023-41683-4

13. James, A., et al.: Graphynes: indispensable nanoporous architectures in carbon flatland. RSC Adv. **8**, 22998–23018 (2018). https://doi.org/10.1039/C8RA03715A

14. Azizi, K., Vaez Allaei, S.M., Fathizadeh, A., Sadeghi, A., Sahimi, M.: Graphyne-3: a highly efficient candidate for separation of small gas molecules from gaseous mixtures. Sci. Rep. **11**(1), 16325 (2021). https://doi.org/10.1038/s41598-021-95304-z

15. Desyatkin VG, Martin WB, A.A.: Scalable synthesis and characterization of multilayer -graphyne, new carbon crystals with a small direct band gap. J. Am. Chem. Soc. **144**(39), 17999–18008 (2022). https://doi.org/10.1021/jacs.2c06583

16. Li, J., Han, Y.: Artificial carbon allotrope γ-graphyne: synthesis, properties, and applications. Giant **13**, 100140 (2023)

17. Vekeman, J., Cuesta, I. G., Faginas-Lago, N., Wilson, J., Snchez-Marn, J., Snchez de Mers, A.: Potential models for the simulation of methane adsorption on graphene: development and ccsd(t) benchmarks. Phys. Chem. Chem. Phys. **20**, 25518–25530 (2018). https://doi.org/10.1039/C8CP03652G

18. Rugarabamu, J.R., Zhao, D., Li, S., Diao, R., Song, K.: Structure modeling of activated carbons used for simulating methane adsorption- a review. Petrol. Res. **8**(1), 103–117 (2023)

19. Vekeman, J., Sanchez-Marin, J., Sanchez de Meras, A., Garcia Cuesta, I., Faginas-Lago, N.: Flexibility in the graphene sheet: the influence on gas adsorption from molecular dynamics studies. J. Phys. Chem. C **123**(46), 28035–28047 (2019)

20. Vekeman, J., Faginas-Lago, N., Lombardi, A., Sánchez de Merás, A., García Cuesta, I., Rosi, M.: Molecular dynamics of ch_4/n_2 mixtures on a flexible graphene layer: adsorption and selectivity case study. Front. Chem. **7**, 386 (2019)
21. Faginas-Lago, N., Apriliyanto, Y.B., Lombardi, A.: Confinement of co_2 inside carbon nanotubes. Eur. Phys. J. D **75**(5), 161 (2021)
22. Bartolomei, M., Carmona-Novillo, E., Giorgi, G.: First principles investigation of hydrogen physical adsorption on graphynes' layers. Carbon **95**, 1076–1081 (2015)
23. Faginas-Lago, N., Apriliyanto, Y.B., Lombardi, A.: Molecular simulations of $co_2/n_2/h_2o$ gaseous mixture separation in graphtriyne membrane. In: Misra, S., et al. (eds) ICCSA 2019. Lecture Notes in Computer Science, pp. 374–387. Springer, Heidelberg (2019)
24. Faginas-Lago, N., Apriliyanto, Y.B., Lombardi, A.: Carbon capture and separation from co2/n2/h2o gaseous mixtures in bilayer graphtriyne: a molecular dynamics study. In: Gervasi, O., et al. (eds.) ICCSA 2020. LNCS, vol. 12255, pp. 489–501. Springer, Cham (2020). https://doi.org/10.1007/978-3-030-58820-5_36
25. Apriliyanto, Y.B., et al.: Multilayer graphtriyne membranes for separation and storage of co2: Molecular dynamics simulations of post-combustion model mixtures. Molecules **27**(18), 5958 (2022)
26. Bartolomei, M., Giorgi, G.: A novel nanoporous graphite based on graphynes: first-principles structure and carbon dioxide preferential physisorption. ACS Appl. Mater. Interfaces **8**, 27996–28003 (2016). https://doi.org/10.1021/acsami.6b08743
27. Pirani, F., Brizi, S., Roncaratti, L.F., Casavecchia, P., Cappelletti, D., Vecchiocattivi, F.: Beyond the lennard-jones model: a simple and accurate potential function probed by high resolution scattering data useful for molecular dynamics simulations. Phys. Chem. Chem. Phys. **10**(36), 5489–5503 (2008)
28. Bramastya Apriliyanto, Y., Lombardi, A., Mancini, L., Pirani, F., Faginas-Lago, N.: Revisiting numerical solutions of weakly bound noble gases' vibrational energy levels modeled by the improved lennard-jones potential. ChemPhysChem **25**(20), e202400223 (2024)
29. Pannacci, G., et al.: A combined crossed molecular beam and theorerical study of the o (3 p, 1 d)+ acrylonitrile (ch 2 chcn) reactions and implications for combustion and extraterrestrial environments. Phys. Chem. Chem. Phys. **25**(30), 20194–20211 (2023)
30. Liang, P., et al.: Oh (2π)+ c2h4 reaction: a combined crossed molecular beam and theoretical study. J. Phys. Chem. A **127**(21), 4609–4623 (2023)
31. Giani, L., et al.: Revised gas-phase formation network of methyl cyanide: the origin of methyl cyanide and methanol abundance correlation in hot corinos. Mon. Not. R. Astron. Soc. **526**(3), 4535–4556 (2023)
32. Richardson, V., et al.: Fragmentation of interstellar methanol by collisions with he+: an experimental and computational study. Phys. Chem. Chem. Phys. **24**(37), 22437–22452 (2022)
33. Hirshfeld, F.: Bonded-atom fragments for describing molecular charge densities. Theor. Chim. Acta **44**, 129–138 (1977). https://doi.org/10.1007/BF00549096
34. Ewald, P.P.: Die berechnung optischer und elektrostatischer gitterpotentiale. Annalen der Physik **369**(3), 253–287 (1921). https://doi.org/10.1002/andp.19213690304. https://onlinelibrary.wiley.com/doi/abs/10.1002/andp.19213690304
35. Smith, W., Yong, C.W., Rodger, P.M.: Dl_poly: application to molecular simulation. Molec. Simul. **28**, 385 – 471 (2002). https://api.semanticscholar.org/CorpusID:95419206
36. Humphrey, W., Dalke, A., S.K.: VMD: visual molecular dynamics. J. Mol. Graph. **14**, 33–28 (1996). https://doi.org/10.1016/0263-7855(96)00018-5

Permeation of Polychlorinated Biphenyls Through Lipid Membranes: Classical MD and QM/MM-EDA Analysis

Nicolás Ramos-Berdullas$^{(\boxtimes)}$ (ID), Álvaro Pérez-Barcia (ID), and Lorena Ruano (ID)

Department of Physical Chemistry, University of Vigo, Lagoas-Marcosende s/n, 36310 Vigo, Spain
nicolas.ramos@uvigo.es

Abstract. Persistent organic compounds, particularly those of industrial origin, are highly toxic, bioaccumulative, persistent, and capable of traveling long distances. The World Health Organization even considers some of them potential carcinogens. In the marine environment, polychlorinated biphenyls (PCBs) accumulate in sediments, leading to continuous exposure and potentially causing adverse effects on ecosystems and food chains. In particular, concentrations of seven key PCBs (IUPAC numbers 28, 52, 101, 118, 138, 153 and 180) are usually closely monitored. Despite advances in understanding the metabolic processes of PCBs, their absorption and diffusion mechanisms across cell membranes remain insufficiently understood. These membranes act as reservoirs for PCBs, prolonging chronic exposure. In this study, we investigate the permeation process of these compounds across lipid membranes by means of classical molecular dynamics (CMD) in combination with the umbrella sampling approach, using a model composed of 128 1,2-dioleoyl-sn-glycero-3-phosphocholine lipids (DOPC). The free energy profile shows the penetration process is largely favoured thermodynamically, with a progressively decrease of the energy until reaching the energy minima close to the centre of the membrane. The analysis of key regions along the diffusion pathway is particularly relevant for studying intermolecular interactions between PCBs and lipid bilayers. Therefore, the characterization of contaminant-membrane interactions was initially conducted using a combination of quantum mechanics/molecular mechanics (QM/MM) calculations and energy decomposition analysis (EDA). This approach provides deeper insight into the underlying mechanisms, including the contributions of electrostatic, exchange, repulsion, and polarization interactions, which together elucidate the permeation process.

Keywords: Persistent Organic Pollutants · Polychlorinated Biphenyls · Lipid Membranes · Molecular Dynamics · QM/MM · EDA

1 Introduction

In the present world, pollution represents one of the greatest challenges for the global population. The international community has developed regulations to control and reduce pollutant emissions and existing contamination, with an emphasis on studying the action mechanisms to detect and eliminate chemical agents, such as persistent organic pollutants (POPs) [1]. These compounds, mainly of industrial origin, are characterized by their high toxicity, resistance to natural degradation, high bioaccumulation, and significant ability to travel long distances [2], posing an environmental and health risk, according to the Stockholm Convention and the WHO [3].

In the marine environment, persistent pollutants can enter through the atmosphere or from urban and industrial inputs [4, 5], associating with organic particles and accumulating on the seabed for years. This process exposes living organisms to these compounds through ingestion, leading to their introduction into the food chain, or through the resuspension of sediments, causing negative effects on ecosystems and, by extension, on health. Among persistent organic pollutants, polychlorinated biphenyls (PCBs) stand out due to their significant presence in this environment. These substances, lipophilic in nature, preferentially accumulate in the fatty tissues of living organisms [6, 7]. They form a group of 209 congeners with various ecotoxicological properties, which vary depending on the degree of chlorination and the position of chlorine atoms in the molecule. Additionally, several studies conducted along the western coast of Europe reveal that marine sediments in this area exceed the maximum acceptable ecotoxicological values [8, 9], identifying it as a significant source of PCB contamination. It is important to note that, in marine pollution monitoring and control programs, only seven of the most representative congeners are included: six non–dioxin-like (NDL-PCB) (IUPAC no. 28, 52, 101, 138, 153, and 180), and one dioxin-like (DL-PCB) (IUPAC no. 118) (see Fig. 1). The sum of the concentrations of these compounds is referred to as SCB7 and is used as the main indicator of PCB contamination.

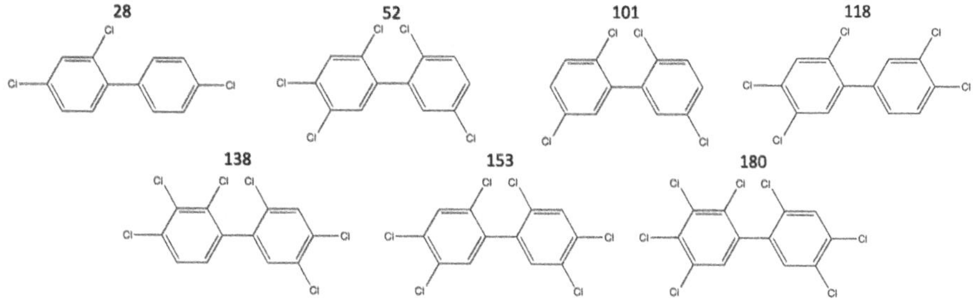

Fig. 1. Schematic representation of the PCBs that make up the SCB7 set.

Despite advances in the study of PCB metabolism, the absorption and diffusion process of these compounds across cell membranes remains insufficiently understood. Understanding this mechanism is critical for elucidating the toxicokinetics of PCBs and assessing the risks associated with their exposure. Cell membranes, in addition to acting as a barrier, function as reservoirs for PCB storage, becoming an internal source of chronic exposure to these contaminants [6]. In this context, computational simulations using classical methods provide valuable information on the thermodynamics and kinetics of dehydration and diffusion processes of PCBs across membranes. Quantum mechanical models, on the other hand, represent a promising tool for analyzing molecular interactions between pollutants and cell membranes, facilitating a more precise description of the structural and functional changes these compounds induce in the biological environment.

Herein, a comparative study of the permeation of the aforementioned PCBs molecules through a lipid membrane model has been conducted using umbrella sampling combined with classical molecular dynamics (CMD) in order to evaluate the role that membrane permeability plays in the relative toxicity of these compounds. The aim of our work has been extended to shed more light on the origin and nature of the intermolecular interactions governing the process, particularly at the free energy minima, where the molecular environment changes due to the hydrophilic and hydrophobic regions of the lipid bilayer. To this end, a hybrid QM/MM energy decomposition analysis (QM/MM-EDA) has been initially applied at the free energy minima along the permeation path of PCBs through biological membranes (both DL-PCB and NDL-PCB). This approach has been successfully applied to other persistent organic pollutants such as chlorinated dibenzo-p-dioxins and dibenzofurans, but this is the first time that the permeation of PCBs through biological membranes has been studied at the quantum mechanical level. Finally, the results presented here also serve to assess the capability of classical force fields to represent the intermolecular interactions of these molecules with the lipid bilayer and evaluate strategies to accurately simulate the interactions involved in biological systems.

2 Methodology

2.1 CMD Simulations

The dynamic simulations of the absorption and distribution process of the compounds that make up SCB7 was carried out using a lipid membrane composed of 1,2-dioleoyl-sn-glycero-3-phosphatidylcholine (DOPC) units. The bilayer contained 128 DOPC lipids, evenly distributed between the upper and lower layers. The membrane was placed in a rectangular box with periodic boundary conditions applied in all three spatial dimensions. Additionally, to mimic physiological conditions, the membrane was solvated by including a water layer of 22.5 Å on each side (approximately 37 water molecules per lipid) and a 0.15 M concentration of KCl ions. The Lipid17 force field [10] was used to describe the lipid bilayer, while the TIP3P model was used to describe the water molecules. The K^+ and Cl^- ions were represented using appropriate Amber parameters.

The resulting structure underwent a relaxation process to ensure system stability before further analysis. Initially, a 10,000-step minimization was performed, transitioning from a steepest descent to a conjugate gradient minimization midway through the simulation. This was followed by a sequential heating phase: a 5 ps run increased the temperature to 100 K in the constant temperature and volume ensemble (NVT), followed by a 100 ps run that heated the system to 303 K in the constant temperature and pressure ensemble (NPT). Positional restraints were applied to the lipid molecules throughout the heating process.

Next, ten sequential runs of 500 ps were performed to ensure the equilibration of the periodic boundary conditions of the system, followed by a production step that lasted 125 ns. These simulations were conducted in the NPT ensemble under the same conditions as the second heating step. Finally, a randomly selected snapshot was extracted from the production step to represent the final configuration of the system.

Each PCB was inserted at 32 Å from the center of mass of the relaxed DOPC membrane, with the intramolecular and Lennard-Jones parameters of the compounds provided by the General Amber Force Field (GAFF) [11]. To calculate the atomic charges, the geometries of the previously obtained conformational minima were optimized using the M06-2X functional and the 6-311G(d,p) basis set, followed by the application of the Merz-Singh-Kollman scheme at the same level of theory.

Next, a minimization of 20,000 steps was performed, again using the conjugate gradient method in the second half. The system was then heated to 303 K, imposing certain positional restraints of 10 kcal/mol·Å^2 and 5 kcal/mol·Å^2 on the lipid bilayer and the PCB, respectively. The heating was carried out in the NVT ensemble for 1 ns. Subsequently, four 5 ns runs were performed in the NPT ensemble to equilibrate the system before the accelerated simulation. Each run maintained the pressure and temperature at the desired values of 1 bar and 303 K, respectively, while gradually reducing the initial positional restraints mentioned earlier on the lipid bilayer and the PCB. Molecular dynamics simulations were executed using the pmemd CUDA implementation of the Amber program [12].

Once the system was equilibrated, the permeation processes of two conformers with different degrees of chlorination were simulated using umbrella sampling, except for PCB no. 28, which, due to its symmetry, has only one conformer. The reaction coordinate was defined as the distance along the z-axis (perpendicular to the lipid bilayer) between the contaminant's center of mass and the membrane, with 0 Å representing the contaminant at the center of the membrane. The initial reaction coordinate was set at 32.0 Å from the membrane center and was divided into 32 windows, each spanning 1.0 Å. As a result, the full simulation of contaminant penetration from the aqueous phase to the membrane center lasted 640 ns, with each window simulated for 20 ns. Finally, the Weighted Histogram Analysis Method (WHAM) was applied to obtain the free energy profiles [13].

2.2 QM/MM EDA Calculations

The interaction energy, E_{int}, between two molecular systems A and B is defined as:

$$E_{int} = E_{AB} - \left(E_A^{AB} - E_B^{AB} \right) \tag{1}$$

where E_{AB}, represents the energy of the complex, and E_A^{AB} and E_B^{AB} correspond to the energies of the isolated systems, calculated in the same geometry and using the same basis set as in the complex.

The EDA scheme used in this study to analyze non-covalent interactions partitions the complex energy, expressed in terms of the one-electron density, density matrix, and exchange-correlation density (see Eq. 2), into perturbed and unperturbed components [14]. Additionally, a second-order perturbation approach is applied to further decompose the polarization energy [15]. Consequently, the total interaction energy from Eq. (1) is divided into electrostatic (E_{elec}), Pauli repulsion (E_{Pau}), induction (E_{ind}), and dispersion

(E_{disp}) contributions.

$$E_{int} = E_{elec} + E_{Pau} + E_{ind} + E_{disp} \tag{2}$$

When a QM/MM electrostatic embedding is introduced in the calculations, the electrostatic potential, $\hat{V}_{MM}(r)$, associated to the MM charges, q_i,

$$\hat{V}_{MM}(r) = \sum_{i=1}^{NA_{MM}} \frac{q_i}{|r - R_i|} \tag{3}$$

must be added to both or one of the nuclei potential operators, $\hat{v}_{N_A}(r)$ and $\hat{v}_{N_B}(r)$, as well as to the nuclear repulsion energy in order to get the energy decomposition of Eq. (2) at QM/MM level of theory.

This scheme, used in the study of membrane-pollutant interactions, requires the system to be divided into two subsystems as the pollutant molecule (A) and the DOPC membrane together with water molecules and ions (B). Additionally, this analysis also requires a description of the interaction region using a QM theory level, combined with a classical approach as the electrostatic embedding to represent the environmental effects. The optimal QM region should include the pollutant and the minimum number of DOPC molecules necessary to ensure the convergence of the total pollutant-lipid interaction energy and its components. Thus, subsystem A is fully described at the QM level, whereas the complex and subsystem B are described at QM/MM level. In our particular case, $\hat{V}_{MM}(r)$, has been added to $\hat{v}_{N_B}(r)$ and to the nuclear term of the electrostatic energy as follows [16, 17],

$$\hat{v}_{N_B}^{MM}(r) = \hat{v}_{N_B}(r) + \hat{V}_{MM}(r) \tag{4}$$

QM/MM calculations were performed using the Gaussian16 software package [18], employing density functional theory (DFT) with the M06-2X functional and 6-31G(d,p) basis set—well-suited for non-covalent interactions without empirical dispersion corrections [19]. The QM/MM-EDA scheme required three electronic structure calculations: one for the full complex (pollutant plus solvated membrane), one for the solvated membrane, and one for the pollutant alone. Gaussian input files were automatically generated using MoBioTools [20, 21], ensuring the complete basis set was applied to prevent basis set superposition errors. Electrostatic embedding was applied, incorporating atomic charges from the MM region, which were extracted from Amber CMD simulations and included in Gaussian input files via MoBioTools. The interaction energy and its components were computed using the EDA-NCI program [22].

3   Results and Discussion

3.1   Optimization Geometrical and Energy Stabilization

The geometric optimization and vibrational analysis of the PCB set were performed using the Gaussian16 software [18]. The optimized geometries and ground-state energies were obtained at the density functional theory (DFT) level, employing the M06-2X functional [19] in combination with the 6-311G(d,p) basis set.

The rotation between the phenyl groups of different PCBs was analyzed due to its importance in estimating and examining free energy profiles during the entry and diffusion of these compounds. The inclusion of an additional reaction coordinate, beyond that associated with membrane penetration, increases the complexity of the study, as it necessitates analyzing a free energy surface rather than a one-dimensional profile. To address this issue, DFT calculations were performed by varying the angle between the phenyl rings, thereby obtaining the potential energy profiles associated with the torsional coordinate (see Fig. 2).

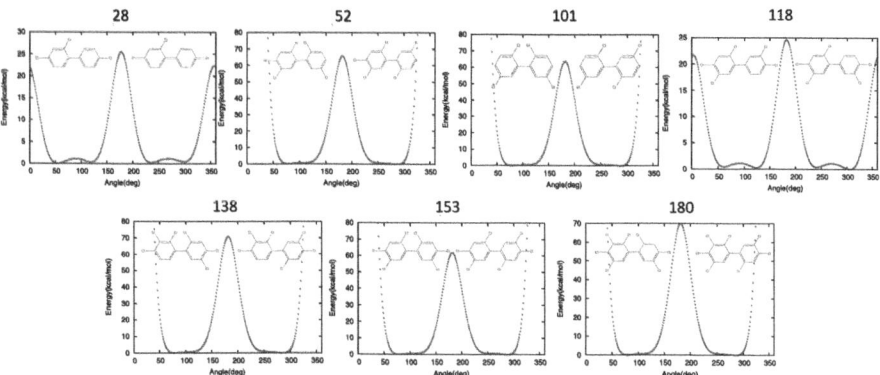

Fig. 2. Potential energy profiles of different PCBs, including schematic representations of the resulting structures with dihedral angles less than 180° and greater than 180°.

The calculation results revealed that PCBs with substituents in the ortho position exhibit a significantly higher energy barrier compared to those lacking chlorination in these positions. Nevertheless, in all cases, symmetric profiles with substantial energy barriers around 180° were observed, as reported in Table 1.

Table 1. Energy barriers (kcal/mol) for the relative maxima around 180°.

IUPAC no.	Angle	Energy	IUPAC no.	Angle	Energy
28	177	25.52	138	182	70.95
52	181	65.82	153	181	61.79
101	182	63.81	180	182	70.21
118	183	24.62			

Furthermore, the energy values and configurations obtained through quantum calculations proved to be sufficiently stable. This suggests that the force field used in the molecular dynamic simulations should be appropriate and capable of accurately analyzing the entry and diffusion process of these compounds.

3.2 Molecular Dynamics Simulations

As mentioned in the previous section, the permeation of pollutants through the membrane was simulated using CMD in combination with the umbrella sampling technique. The free energy profiles obtained via WHAM from simulations conducted separately for each of the studied PCBs are presented in Fig. 3.

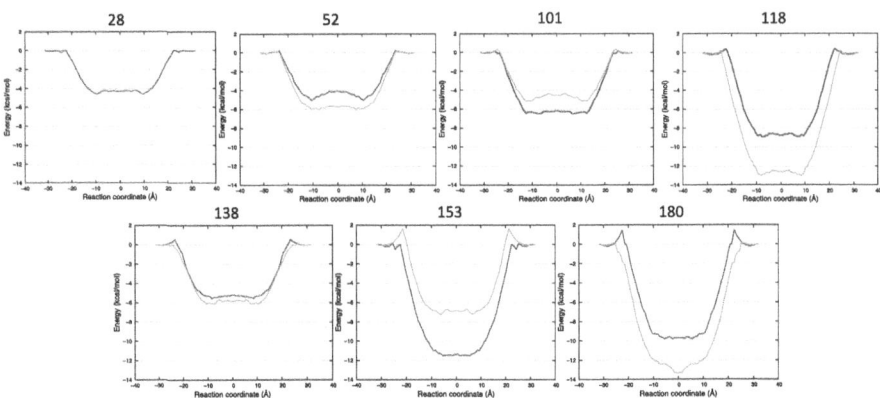

Fig. 3. Free energy diffusion profiles. Conformer with an angle smaller than 180° (blue line) and conformer with an angle greater than 180° (orange line).

The hydrophobic nature of the contaminants facilitates their penetration through the lipid bilayer, with a progressive decrease in free energy observed from the water-lipid interface to the hydrophobic region. Most of the conformers have their free energy minimum located about 7 Å from the center of the membrane, except for one conformer of PCB 180, which is situated near the center of the bilayer. In the other cases, a small increase in free energy is observed at the center of the membrane, resulting in slight local maxima. When comparing the conformers of different biphenyls, small shifts in the free energy minima are observed, indicating their preferred positions in the membrane. The most significant discrepancy is observed in the absolute values of the free energy minima, which in some cases reach up to 4 kcal/mol. This suggests that the entry may be slightly more favorable depending on the contaminant's conformation.

Destabilizations within the bilayer and shifts toward the more hydrophilic regions can be attributed to differences in the polar character of the conformers. Those exhibiting higher dipole moments tend to be less stable in the hydrophobic environment of the membrane. Furthermore, a direct correlation is observed between the free energy of the most stable conformation and the number of chlorine substitutions across the different biphenyls. However, PCB 118 deviates from this trend, displaying a lower free energy than more highly chlorinated compounds.

To demonstrate that the conformational barrier is energetically sufficient to ensure the existence of two conformers during entry into the lipid bilayer, Fig. 4 overlays the torsional potential energy profiles of biphenyls with 5, 6, and 7 substitutions, based on the torsional variation along the umbrella sampling simulation of each conformer. In all cases, the stability of the conformer was confirmed throughout the trajectory, with no interchange between them at any point.

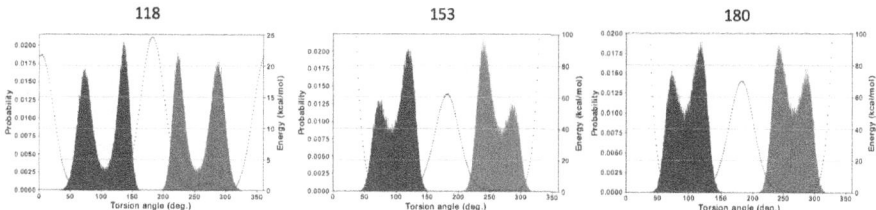

Fig. 4. Potential energy profiles (red dots) and dihedral angle count along the umbrella sampling. Conformer with an angle smaller than 180° (blue color) and conformer with an angle greater than 180° (green color).

3.3   Interaction Energy Decomposition Analysis

As explained above, a hybrid QM/MM method, which includes DFT for the QM region and electrostatic embedding for the QM/MM interaction, has been used to calculate the interaction energies. Specifically, the energetic analysis of intermolecular interactions between PCBs and the membrane was conducted in the regions of minimum free energy. The electrostatic, Pauli, induction, and dispersion contributions of the interaction energy were then obtained using the QM/MM-EDA scheme outlined in Methodology Section.

The first step in the QM/MM calculations is to determine the optimal size of the QM region. In this case, the QM region must include the pollutant and the minimum number of DOPC molecules required to ensure convergence of the total pollutant-lipid interaction energy and its individual components with respect to region size. Similar studies on other pollutants have determined this number using an arbitrary snapshot taken around the free energy minimum, ensuring that all energetic components converge within ±1 kcal/mol when 10 residues are included in the QM region [23]. Once the number of lipids has been established, QM/MM-EDA calculations are performed at the free energy minima by sampling 34 geometries from the minima of the previous CMD simulations. In recent studies on the permeation of other systems through the same lipid membrane, the average values of the different interaction energy components were found to converge well after considering 100 geometries [17, 23]. However, more recent refinements have reduced this number to just over 30 geometries, balancing computational efficiency and accuracy in QM/MM calculations for systems with nearly a thousand atoms [24].

The preliminary mean values of total interaction energy and its components for PCB 118 and PCB 180 at the energy minima are summarized in Table 2. As observed, these values indicate that the previously reported anomaly in the energy profiles of PCB 118 disappears. A clear correlation is observed between the total interaction energy and the number of chlorine substituents. Dispersion energy emerges as the primary driving force behind intermolecular interactions within the lipid bilayer, consistent with the nonpolar nature and hydrophobic character of PCBs. An increase in chlorine substituents leads to higher dispersion energy, which, in turn, enhances the total interaction energy.

Table 2. Mean interaction energy and contribution values (kcal/mol) at the free energy minima for conformers with angles smaller and greater than 180°.

	E_{elec}	E_{Pau}	E_{disp}	E_{ind}	E_{int}
118 (<180°)	−16.49	46.10	−50.13	−6.77	−27.28
118 (>180°)	−17.34	49.45	−51.58	−6.99	−26.14
180 (<180°)	−19.57	55.06	−55.63	−7.35	−27.46
180 (>180°)	−18.32	51.28	−53.79	−6.87	−27.68

However, the energies obtained at the QM/MM level exhibit discrepancies compared to the classical free energy profile. In this case, conformer 2 of PCB 118 appears slightly more stable than conformer 1. Additionally, a significant increase in interaction energy is detected at the minima of both contaminants, suggesting that this difference may be attributed to entropic factors reflected in the free energy profiles.

In general, the small differences observed in the PCB entry processes, both in molecular dynamics simulations and QM/MM-EDA calculations, suggest that absorption and diffusion through the cell membrane are not the primary factors responsible for the differences in toxicity. Instead, the divergence appears to be linked to PCB metabolism.

In this context, affinity for the AhR receptor could explain the relative toxicity of these compounds. This receptor regulates the expression of genes associated with various disorders and diseases. When polychlorinated compounds enter the cell and bind to AhR, they induce changes in gene transcription, leading to toxic effects. Therefore, the affinity of PCBs for AhR may play a critical role in determining their toxicity and warrants further investigation in future studies. In the case of PCB 118, a PCB with dioxin-like toxicological properties, it exhibits a high affinity for AhR, while other SCB7 congeners show low or no affinity for the receptor.

4   Conclusions

In this work, a comparative study was conducted on the permeation of the contaminants that make up the SCB7 set through a lipid membrane formed by DOPC molecules, using a combination of classical molecular dynamics simulations, accelerated dynamics methods such as umbrella sampling, and a QM/MM-EDA approach. The molecular dynamics simulations demonstrated that the hydrophobic nature of PCBs favors their incorporation into the lipid bilayer, and that, in certain cases, differences between the conformers of PCBs are significant in terms of free energy. On the other hand, QM/MM-EDA calculations initially indicate that the number of chlorine substituents in the different biphenyls affects the interaction energy. In conclusion, the results suggest that absorption and diffusion steps through the cell membrane do not explain the toxicity differences measured for the SCB7 set, despite the small variations observed in the entry processes.

Acknowledgments. The authors thank the funding and support from the Diputación de Pontevedra and the University of Vigo. They also acknowledge the BioEDA project (PID2021-128180NB-I00) and GRC Xunta (ED431C 2024/21). N.R.B. thanks the University of Vigo for a postdoctoral fellowship under the "Retención de Talento Investigador da Universidade de Vigo 2023" program. A.P.B. thanks the Xunta de Galicia for funding through the ED481A-2022/228 predoctoral fellowship.

Disclosure of Interests. The authors have no competing interests to declare that are relevant to the content of this article.

References

1. Ritter, L., Solomon, K.R., Forget, J., Stemeroff, M., O'Leary, C.: A review of selected persistent organic pollutants. In: International Programme on Chemical Safety (IPCS) PCS/95.39, p. 66. World Health Organization, Geneva (1995)
2. Wania, F., MacKay, D.: Tracking the distribution of persistent organic pollutants. Environ. Sci. Technol. **30**(9), 390A–396A (1996)
3. Van Den Berg, M., Birnbaum, L., Bosveld, A.T.C., Brunström, B., Cook, P., Feeley, M., Giesy, J.P., Hanberg, A., Hasegawa, R., Kennedy, S.W., Kubiak, T., Larsen, J.C., Van Leeuwen, F.X.R., Liem, A.K.D., Nolt, C., Peterson, R.E., Poellinger, L., Safe, S., Schrenk, D., Tillitt, D., Tysklind, M., Younes, M., Wærn, F., Zacharewski, T.: Toxic equivalency factors (TEFs) for PCBs, PCDDs, PCDFs for humans and wildlife. Environ. Health Perspect. **106**(12), 775–792 (1998)
4. Rappe, C.: Dioxin, patterns and source identification. Fresenius J. Anal. Chem. **348**(1–2), 63–75 (1994)
5. Beck, H., Droß, A., Eckart, K., Mathar, W., Wittkowski, R.: PCDDs, PCDFs and related compounds in paper products. Chemosphere. **19**(1–6), 655–660 (1989)
6. Merrill, M.L., Emond, C., Kimi, M.J., Antignaci, J.-P., Bizeci, B.L., Birnbaum, K.C.L.S., Barouki, R.: Toxicological function of adipose tissue: Focus on persistent organic pollutants. Environ. Health Perspect. **121**(2), 162–169 (2013)
7. Regnier, S.M., Sargis, R.M.: Adipocytes under assault: environmental disruption of adipose physiology. Biochim. Biophys. Acta Mol. basis Dis. **1842**(3), 520–533 (2014)
8. Nunes, T., González-Quijano-Mosteiro, A., Viñas, L.: Determinación de compuestos organoclorados en sedimentos de la Ría de Vigo. Procesos biogeoquímicos en sistemas costeros hispano-lusos. In: Prego, R., Fernández-Álvarez, J.M. (eds.) Diputación Provincial de Pontevedra, Vigo (1997)
9. González-Quijano, A., García, A., Fumega, J., González, J.: Temporal variation of PCB concentrations in mussel tissue in two areas of Santander Bay (Spain). Cienc. Mar. **32**(2B), 465–469 (2006)
10. Dickson, C.J., Madej, B.D., Skjevik, Å.A., Betz, R.M., Teigen, K., Gould, I.R., Walker, R.C.: Lipid14: the Amber lipid force field. J. Chem. Theory Comput. **10**(2), 865–879 (2014)
11. Wang, J., Wolf, R.M., Caldwell, J.W., Kollman, P.A., Case, D.A.: Development and testing of a general amber force field. J. Comput. Chem. **25**(9), 1157–1174 (2004)
12. Case, D.A., Belfon, K., Ben-Shalom, I.Y., Brozell, S.R., Cerutti, D.S., Cheatham III, T.E., Cruzeiro, V.W.D., Darden, T.A., Duke, R.E., Giambasu, G., et al.: AMBER 2020. University of California, San Francisco, CA (2020)
13. Kumar, S., Rosenberg, J.M., Bouzida, D., Swendsen, R.H., Kollman, P.A.: The weighted histogram analysis method for free-energy calculations on biomolecules. I. The method. J. Comput. Chem. **13**(8), 1011–1021 (1992)
14. Mandado, M., Hermida-Ramón, J.M.: Electron density based partitioning scheme of interaction energies. J. Chem. Theory Comput. **7**(3), 633–641 (2011)

15. Ramos-Berdullas, N., Pérez-Juste, I., Van Alsenoy, C., Mandado, M.: Theoretical study of the adsorption of aromatic units on carbon allotropes including explicit (empirical) DFT dispersion corrections and implicitly dispersion-corrected functionals: The pyridine case. Phys. Chem. Chem. Phys. **17**, 575–587 (2014)

16. Pérez-Barcia, A., Cárdenas, G., Nogueira, J.J., Mandado, M.: Effect of the QM size, basis set and polarisation on QM/MM energy decomposition analysis. J. Chem. Inf. Model. **63**(3), 882–897 (2023)

17. Alvarado, R., Cárdenas, G., Nogueira, J.J., Ramos-Berdullas, N., Mandado, M.: On the permeation of polychlorinated dibenzodioxins and dibenzofurans through lipid membranes: classical MD and hybrid QM/MM-EDA analysis. Membranes. **13**(28), 1–14 (2023)

18. Frisch, M.J., Trucks, G.W., Schlegel, H.B., Scuseria, G.E., Robb, M.A., Cheeseman, J.R., Scalmani, G., Barone, V., Petersson, G.A., Nakatsuji, H., et al.: Gaussian 16 Revision C.01. Gaussian, Inc., Wallingford, CT (2016)

19. Zhao, Y., Truhlar, D.G.: The M06 suite of density functionals for main group thermochemistry, thermochemical kinetics, non-covalent interactions, excited states, and transition elements: two new functionals and systematic testing of four M06-class functionals and 12 other functionals. Theor. Chem. Accounts. **120**, 215–241 (2008)

20. Cárdenas, G., Lucia-Tamudo, J., Mateo-delaFuente, H., Palmisano, V.F., Anguita-Ortiz, N., Ruano, L., Pérez-Barcia, A., Díaz- Tendero, S., Mandado, M., Nogueira, J.J.: MoBioTools: a toolkit to setup QM/MM calculations. J. Comput. Chem. **44**(4), 516–533 (2022)

21. Cárdenas, G. MoBioTools: https://github.com/mobiochem/MoBioTools, last accessed 20 March 2025

22. Mandado, M., Van Alsenoy, C. EDA-NCI: Energy Decomposition Analysis of Non-Covalent Interactions: https://github.com/marcos-mandado/EDA-NCI, last accessed 20 March 2025

23. Cárdenas, G., Pérez-Barcia, A., Mandado, M., Nogueira, J.J.: Characterization of cisplatin/membrane interactions by QM/MM energy decomposition analysis. Phys. Chem. Chem. Phys. **23**, 20533–20540 (2021)

24. Ruano, L., Pérez-Barcia, Á., Palmisano, V.F., Nogueira, J.J., Mandado, M., Ramos-Berdullas, N.: Unravelling the Role Played by Non-Covalent Interactions in the Action Mechanism of PCDDs within Cells, in preparation (2025)

On the Mechanism Responsible of the Varying Adsorption Affinities of CO_2, N_2 and H_2O on Graphtriyne Membranes

Yusuf Bramastya Apriliyanto[1] ![ORCID], Luca Mancini[2] ![ORCID], Noelia Faginas-Lago[2] ![ORCID], and Marcos Mandado[3(✉)] ![ORCID]

[1] Department of Chemistry, The Republic of Indonesia Defense University, Kampus Unhan Komplek IPSC Sentul, 16810 Bogor, Indonesia
[2] Department of Chemistry, Biology and Biotechnology, University of Perugia, & UdR INSTM di Perugia, Via Elce di Sotto 8, 06123 Perugia, Italy
[3] Department of Physical Chemistry, University of Vigo, Lagoas-Marcosende s/n, 36310 Vigo, Spain
mandado@uvigo.es

Abstract. Deformation Density based Energy Decomposition Analysis (DD-EDA) of the interaction energy between CO_2, N_2, and H_2O and graphtriyne membranes was performed at the DFT-D3 level to elucidate the energy components responsible for the differences in adsorption affinity. Previous explanations at a qualitative level were based on electric dipole and polarizability scales. Surprisingly, neither electrostatic nor polarization interactions primarily account for CO_2's strongest adsorption affinity to a monolayer membrane. Instead, Pauli repulsion governs the adsorption affinity, with CO_2 experiencing the lowest Pauli repulsion energy, not showing the more negative polarization or electrostatic energies. The stability of these three molecules within a trilayer membrane follows the same order as in a monolayer. However, in this case, CO_2 exhibits the highest Pauli repulsion energy, which is largely offset by its more negative polarization and electrostatic energies. This variation can be attributed to the distinct trends observed in the energy-versus-distance profiles of these gases with a monolayer membrane. These preliminary results, derived from static simulations, should be further validated against those obtained from dynamic simulations.

Keywords: Graphtriyne Membrane · Gas Adsorption · Energy Decomposition Analysis · Density Functional Theory · Computational Chemistry

1 Introduction

Membrane technology has gained significant attention as a highly energy-efficient and scalable solution for gas separation and storage, particularly in industries such as hydrogen production, natural gas purification, and carbon capture [1, 3]. Among various membrane materials, carbon-based membranes have emerged as a promising class due to their unique structural properties, high thermal and chemical stability, and tunable selectivity.

© The Author(s), under exclusive license to Springer Nature Switzerland AG 2026
O. Gervasi et al. (Eds.): ICCSA 2025 Workshops, LNCS 15897, pp. 39–52, 2026.
https://doi.org/10.1007/978-3-031-97660-5_4

Over the past few decades, extensive research efforts have been dedicated to optimizing their microstructure, improving separation performance, and enabling large-scale applications [4, 5].

The development of carbon molecular sieve (CMS) membranes marked a pivotal advancement, as these materials demonstrated exceptional size-selective gas transport due to their precisely controlled microporous structures. Further innovations in porous carbon materials, including activated and templated carbons, enhanced gas adsorption capacity and selectivity by tailoring pore architecture. The advent of two-dimensional materials, such as graphene and graphene oxide (GO), introduced ultrathin membranes with exceptionally high gas permeability while maintaining precise molecular sieving capabilities [6–8]. Additionally, carbon nanotube (CNT) membranes have exhibited near-frictionless gas transport, enabling ultrafast diffusion rates while maintaining strong selectivity [9].

Beyond these fundamental advancements, hybrid and composite membranes integrating carbon materials with polymers and metal-organic frameworks (MOFs) have enhanced mechanical stability and separation efficiency [10]. Meanwhile, microporous carbon membranes tailored for CO_2 capture have demonstrated superior selectivity and permeability, offering a viable approach for mitigating industrial emissions [11]. More recently, research has focused on improving the scalability, durability, and cost-effectiveness of carbon-based membranes, addressing challenges related to fabrication and industrial integration. Among these, graphynes, a family of two-dimensional (2D) carbon materials featuring sp- and sp^2-hybridized carbon atoms, have attracted increasing attention due to their unique structural and electronic characteristics [12, 13]. Unlike graphene, which consists entirely of sp^2-hybridized carbon atoms, graphynes incorporate acetylenic linkages between benzene rings, resulting in a tunable band gap, intrinsic porosity, and anisotropic transport properties. These features make graphynes highly promising for applications in gas separation, catalysis, and nanoelectronics [14, 15].

Theoretical studies have predicted various graphyne allotropes, including α-, β-, γ-, and 6,6,12-graphyne, each with distinct lattice structures and electronic behaviors [16]. Computational simulations suggest that these materials exhibit superior gas selectivity, particularly for hydrogen and carbon dioxide, due to their well-defined nanopores [17]. Additionally, their intrinsic semiconducting nature and high carrier mobility position them as candidates for next-generation electronic and optoelectronic devices [18]. Despite their promising properties, the experimental realization of graphynes remains a significant challenge due to the difficulty in achieving large-scale synthesis with precise structural control.

To date, graphdiyne [13], a closely related structure containing diacetylenic linkages, has been successfully synthesized and demonstrated exceptional chemical stability, high porosity, and strong adsorption capabilities [19]. This breakthrough has paved the way for experimental investigations into the gas separation, energy storage, and catalytic properties of sp–sp^2 hybridized carbon materials. However, the synthesis of pure graphyne structures beyond graphdiyne remains an ongoing challenge, with research efforts focused on templated growth, catalytic coupling reactions, and bottom-up organic synthesis strategies.

Recent theoretical studies have shown that mono and multilayer graphtriyne membranes exhibit high hydrogen permeability [20], making them promising candidates for hydrogen purification and energy storage applications. Computational simulations have confirmed that their sub-nanometer pores allow selective H_2 diffusion, while effectively blocking larger gas molecules like CO_2, N_2 and H_2O [21]. Furthermore, graphtriyne has shown a strong affinity for CO_2 adsorption, followed by H_2O and N_2 [22, 23]. These studies have also hypothesized that the binding energy order can be broadly explained by the relative electric dipole moments and polarizabilities of the different gases [21]. Beyond the qualitative nature of these conclusions, key aspects of intermolecular forces—such as the role of Pauli repulsion, which includes spin repulsion and intermolecular electron exchange, as well as multipolar electrostatic interactions—may significantly influence the interaction between these gases and the membrane. This study investigates the role of these factors, along with dispersion and inductive phenomena, in the adsorption of CO_2, N_2, and H_2O by graphtriyne membranes through interaction energy decomposition analysis. The results presented here are preliminary, based on static calculations. As a next step they must be validated against those obtained from dynamic simulations, which enable a more comprehensive exploration of the configurational space and incorporate thermal effects into the analysis.

2 Methodology

In this study, we investigated the adsorption of three gases, CO_2, N_2, and H_2O, using monolayer and trilayer graphtriyne membranes. The adsorption pores of these membranes were simulated based on molecular models depicted in Fig. 1, which are consistent with those used in previous studies. The geometrical parameters of both the membrane models and gas molecules were kept fixed throughout the calculations, with the most relevant parameters also presented in the figure. Regarding the monolayer and trilayer models: each layer is represented by a octadecadehydrotribenzo annulene molecule with D_3h symmetry and the C-C and C-H distances shown in Fig. 1, which corresponds to those previously obtained from DFT periodic calculations [20, 21]. In the trilayer model, the interlayer distance is 3.45 Å, and the layers are intercalated with a displacement of 1.6 Å between the geometric centers of the inner and outer layers (parameters also illustrated in Fig. 1).

The calculations were performed at the Density Functional Theory (DFT) level using the M06-2X functional combined with the 6-311++G(2df,pd) basis set. This functional was shown to be suitable to investigate non-covalent interactions [24] and has been shown to accurately capture most of the dispersion energy in complexes involving carbon allotropes, including graphene, when compared to other functionals [25]. The basis set employed is sufficiently large to ensure an accurate representation of the electron polarization. Explicit D3 dispersion corrections, as developed by Grimme et al. [26], were also included in the calculations. Interaction energies were computed using the supermolecule approach and further decomposed into electrostatic, Pauli repulsion, and polarization contributions via Deformation Density-based Energy Decomposition Analysis (DD-EDA) [25, 27]. To account for Basis Set Superposition Error (BSSE), all energies were corrected using the counterpoise method of Boys and Bernardi [28].

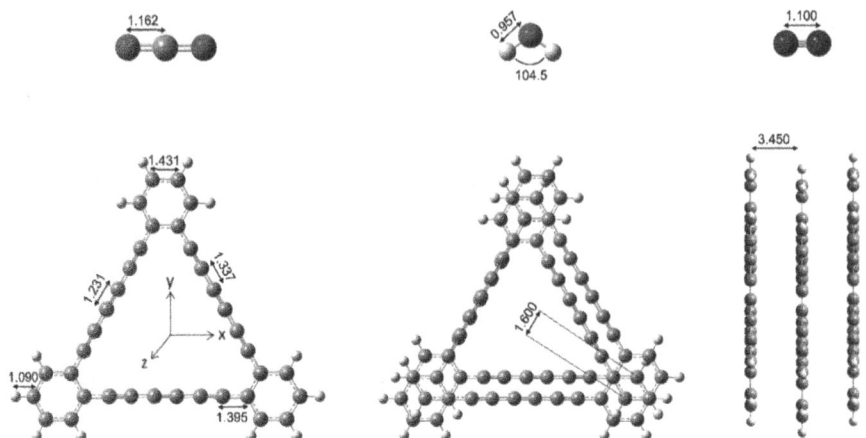

Fig. 1. Main geometrical parameters of the molecules, monolayer and trilayer models of the graphtriyne membranes. Distances in Angstroms and angles in degrees.

Electron densities were calculated with the Gaussian 16 software package [29], and the DD-EDA was performed with the EDA-NCI program [30].

The Pauli repulsion energy was further decomposed into its attractive component (intermolecular exchange) and its repulsive component (spin repulsion) using the DD-EDA method. Additionally, the polarization energy was divided into induction and dispersion contributions. However, this decomposition relies on defining molecular fragments within the Hilbert space of the basis functions, requiring the use of basis sets without diffuse functions to ensure reliable results. To address this, calculations were repeated using the 6-311G(d,p) basis set, allowing for a detailed analysis of the dispersion and induction contributions to polarization energy. This smaller basis set also provided a means to assess the influence of polarization and diffuse functions on the computed energy terms.

3   Results

3.1   Monolayer Membrane

The initial step was to determine the most stable orientation of the molecules within the monolayer membrane pore by calculating the relative strength of the interaction at the pore center. This was followed by a scan along the perpendicular direction to the membrane surface for the most stable orientation, starting from the pore center up to a distance of 3.2 Å. This approach builds upon the previous analysis conducted by Bartolomei et al. [21] but extends it to include the different interaction energy components, providing deeper insight into the adsorption mechanisms and relative stabilities of the molecules within the pore.

The interaction energy values and their components for CO_2, N_2, and H_2O molecules positioned at the center of the monolayer membrane—with their main symmetry axis aligned along the x, y, or z directions—are presented in Table 1. Figure 1 illustrates the orientation of the Cartesian axes in the monolayer. As observed, the most stable orientation for CO_2 and N_2 is with the molecular axis aligned along the z direction, while for H_2O, it is with the C_2 symmetry axis aligned along the y direction, consistent with the findings of Bartolomei et al. [21]. The EDA analysis reveals that the destabilization in the other two orientations in CO_2 and N_2 is primarily due to a significant increase in spin repulsion energy, which is not offset by corresponding increases (in negative terms) in electrostatic, polarization, and intermolecular exchange energies. Given the well-known relationship between Pauli energy and steric hindrance, this suggests that these molecules orient themselves within the membrane pore to minimize steric interactions as much as possible. In contrast, for H_2O, the most favorable orientation is the one with greater (more negative) electrostatic, polarization, and intermolecular exchange energies, which compensate for the increased spin repulsion.

Table 1. Total interaction energy and its different components for the interaction of the monolayer membrane with CO_2, N_2, and H_2O positioned at the center of the monolayer membrane and oriented with their main symmetry axis aligned along the x, y, or z directions (see Fig. 1). Elec, Exch, Rep, Pol and Tot, refer to electrostatic, intermolecular exchange, spin repulsion, polarization and total energies, respectively. Atrac is the summation of all attractive energy terms, namely, Elec, Exch and Pol.

	Elec	Exch	Rep	Pol	Atrac	Tot
CO_2						
X^a	−11.07	−40.53	76.16	−12.03	−63.63	12.53
Y^a	−12.29	−41.38	80.19	−12.28	−65.95	14.24
Z	−2.09	−7.14	10.74	−5.13	−14.36	−3.61
N_2						
X^a	−1.67	−9.46	15.88	−2.86	−14.00	1.87
Y^a	−1.67	−9.50	16.02	−2.82	−13.99	2.03
Z	−1.68	−8.47	13.04	−4.92	−15.07	−2.03
H_2O						
X^a	0.50	1.49	−2.54	0.64	2.63	0.09
Y	−2.15	−10.98	16.61	−6.07	−19.20	−2.60
Z^a	1.02	2.47	−4.41	1.83	5.33	0.92

[a] These are less stable orientations and their energies are given relative to the most stable one.

Figure 2 compares the interaction energy and its components as the molecules are moved along the perpendicular direction to the membrane plane. CO_2 exhibits the most favorable adsorption, as its interaction energy remains more negative than that of the other two molecules throughout the scan. However, in the 1.2–1.8 Å range, its values are very close to those of H_2O. At the limiting distance of 3.2 Å considered in this study, the interaction energies of all three molecules converge, with H_2O and N_2 showing nearly identical values.

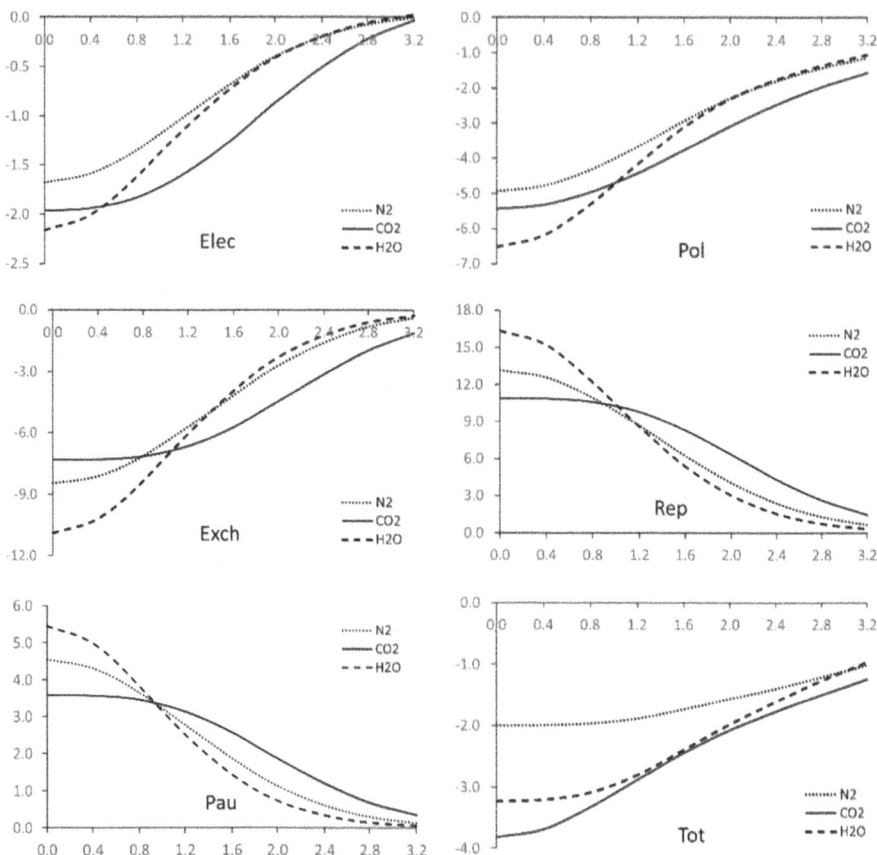

Fig. 2. Electrostatic (Elec), polarization (Pol), intermolecular exchange (Exch), spin repulsion (Rep), Pauli (Pau) and total (Tot) interaction energies vs the distance between the geometrical center of the molecule and that of the monolayer membrane in the perpendicular detachment of the adsorption complex. Energies were obtained with the 6-311++G(2df,pd) basis set and are expressed in kcal/mol, distances are expressed in Angstroms.

The behavior of the interaction energy components is somewhat unexpected, as their contributions to the relative stability of the complexes change along the scan. At short distances from the membrane center, CO_2's greater stability arises from its lower spin repulsion energy, even though the attractive terms are consistently stronger for H_2O, and even for N_2 in the case of intermolecular exchange. However, beyond 1.0 Å, spin repulsion increasingly destabilizes CO_2 relative to H_2O and N_2. This destabilization is counterbalanced by attractive forces, which become more negative for CO_2 beyond 0.6 Å, 1.0 Å, and 1.1 Å for electrostatic, polarization, and intermolecular exchange energies, respectively. These findings suggest that CO_2 adsorption is initially driven by the attractive intermolecular forces but, at closer distances, is stabilized by a reduction in repulsion forces.

An unexpected result is that H_2O exhibits a larger (more negative) polarization energy than CO_2 and N_2 at distances below 1.0 Å, despite having only one heavy atom, compared to three in CO_2 and two in N_2. Given H_2O's lower overall polarizability, a lower polarization energy would typically be expected. This anomaly is explained by the orientation of H_2O within the pore, with its most polarizable atom, oxygen, positioned at the center. In contrast, CO_2 has its carbon atom at the center, with oxygen atoms positioned at a distance of 0.957 Å, while N_2 has no central atom, with each nitrogen positioned 0.55 Å away. As the molecules move perpendicularly to the membrane, the oxygen atom in H_2O shifts away from the center while one of CO_2's oxygen atoms moves closer, reversing the polarization energy trend between these two molecules.

Figure 3 further decomposes the polarization energy into induction and dispersion terms using a basis set that excludes diffuse functions, as described in the methodology. The polarization energy scan closely resembles the one obtained with the basis set including diffuse functions, suggesting that the partitioning into induction and dispersion can be reasonably extrapolated to the larger basis set.

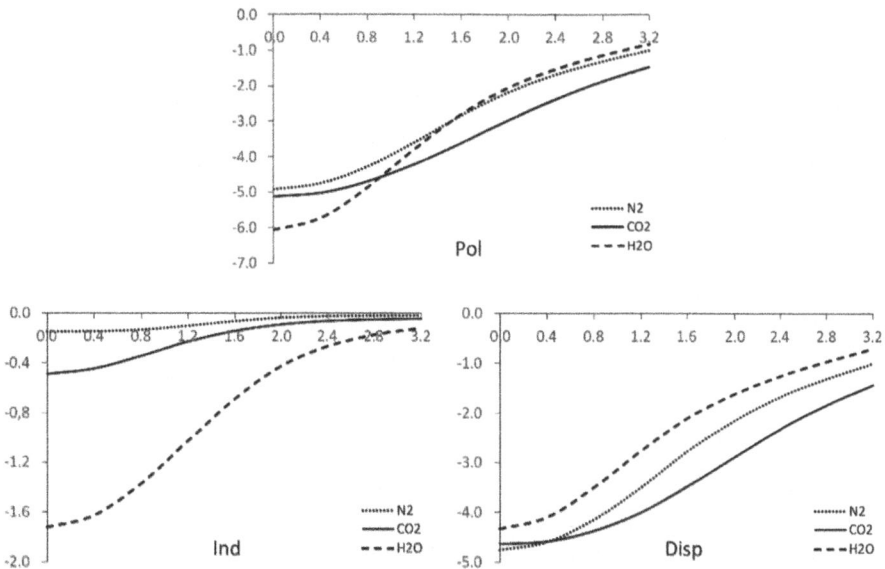

Fig. 3. Polarization (Pol), induction (Ind) and dispersion (Disp) energies vs the distance between the geometrical center of the molecule and that of the monolayer membrane in the perpendicular detachment of the adsorption complex. Energies were obtained with the 6-311G(d,p) basis set and are expressed in kcal/mol, distances are expressed in Angstroms.

From the induction energy scan, we observe that H_2O consistently exhibits the most negative induction energy, as expected due to its large dipole moment and its orientation relative to the membrane plane. CO_2 follows, as it has bond dipole moments but is oriented perpendicularly to the membrane plane. Lastly, N_2 shows a negligible induction energy due to the nonpolar nature of its single bond.

Regarding the dispersion term, CO_2 and N_2 exhibit more negative values than H_2O throughout the scan. When positioned near the center of the membrane, CO_2 and N_2 have nearly identical dispersion energies. However, at larger distances, CO_2 shows a more negative dispersion energy than N_2.

The relative stability order of $CO_2 > H_2O > N_2$ can be also qualitatively understood by examining the spin repulsion and polarization densities, which correspond to the Pauli and polarization energies, respectively. Figure 4 compares the spin repulsion and polarization densities at the center of the membrane pore for the three molecules. As shown in the figure, spin repulsion exhibits negative values, representing electron depletion, in the intermolecular region due to the overlap between the electron clouds of the molecule and the membrane. Conversely, positive values, representing electron accumulation, are observed near the atoms of both the molecule and the membrane. The negative regions are slightly more pronounced in H_2O, followed by N_2 and then CO_2, aligning with the Pauli and spin repulsion energy trends shown in Fig. 2 at short distances from the membrane center.

The polarization densities shown in Fig. 4 reveal distinct characteristics for CO_2, N_2, and H_2O. In CO_2 and N_2, the polarization densities reflect the typical behavior of highly dispersive interactions, with electron density migrating from the molecules to the intermolecular region. In H_2O, induced dipoles are also observed along the molecular skeleton of the membrane and within the O-H bonds, highlighting the significant contribution of induction interactions. The magnitude of polarization density follows the trend: $N_2 < CO_2 < H_2O$, aligning with the order of polarization energies obtained at the center of the membrane.

Regarding the total densities, which result from the superposition of spin repulsion and polarization, it is observed that for the most stable complexes—CO_2 and H_2O—the total deformation density more closely resembles the polarization component than the spin repulsion. In contrast, for N_2, the total deformation density aligns more closely with the spin repulsion, which qualitatively accounts for the lower stability of this complex.

3.2 Trilayer Membrane

The next step in our analysis was to construct a trilayer membrane (see Fig. 1), following the same procedure as Bartolomei et al. [20, 21], and perform a DD-EDA of the interaction energy for CO_2, N_2, and H_2O at the three most relevant positions within the membrane: the center of the inner layer, the center of the interlayer region, and the center of one of the outer layers. These positions are illustrated in Fig. 5 for the N_2 molecule. For consistency, the most stable orientation of each molecule in the monolayer membrane was used in the trilayer study.

Table 2 presents the results obtained for the interaction energy and its main components, calculated using the 6-311++G(2df,pd) and 6-311G(d,p) basis sets. The total interaction energy differences between these basis sets are negligible in the case of N_2, more significant in CO_2, and relevant in H_2O, with maximum deviations of 2.3%, 9.7% and 20.4%, respectively. However, differences in polarization energies are smaller, with maximum deviations of 2.4%, 4.9% and 9.0%. It should be noted that the larger basis set produces more negative interaction energies in all cases.

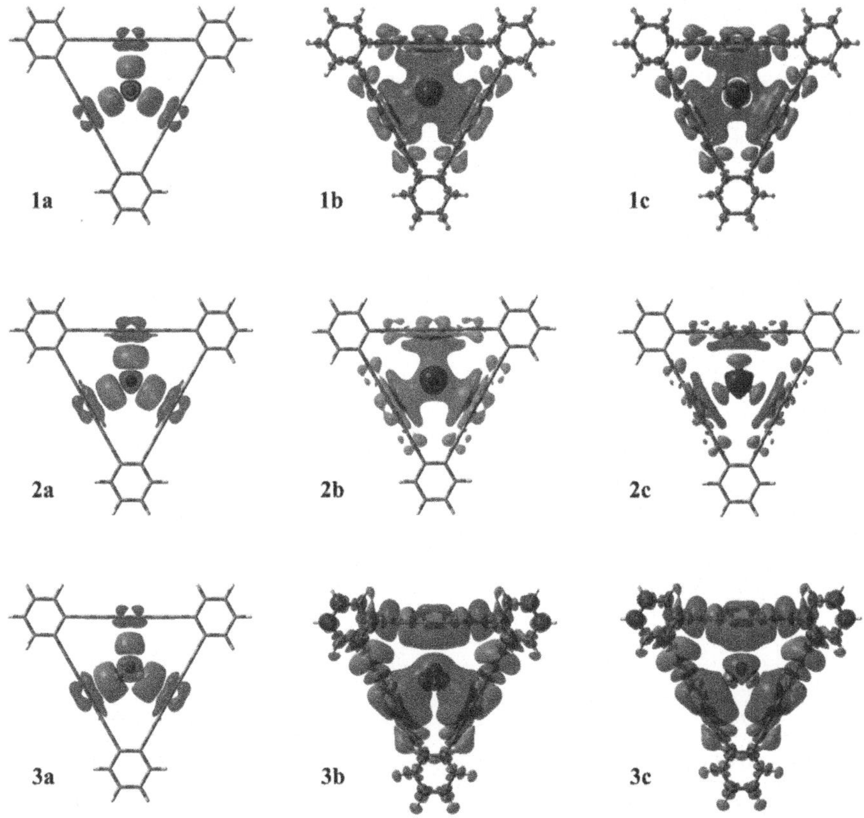

Fig. 4. Spin repulsion (**a**), polarization (**b**) and total deformation (**c**) densities arising from the interaction of CO$_2$ (**1**), N$_2$ (**2**) and H$_2$O (**3**) molecules with a monolayer membrane of graphtriyne. In all cases, the complex corresponds to the lowest energy conformation. Brown and magenta colors represent electron density depletion and accumulation, respectively. Plots were represented with an isosurface value of $5 \cdot 10^{-4}$ Densities were obtained with the 6-311++G(2df,pd) basis set.

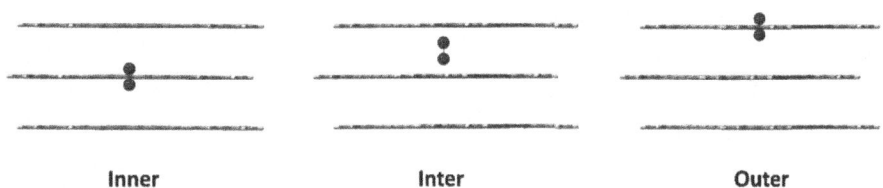

Inner   **Inter**   **Outer**

Fig. 5. Positions selected within the trilayer membrane model for the N2 molecule. These are same positions selected for CO$_2$ and H$_2$O.

Given that a basis set without diffuse functions is required to decompose polarization into induction and dispersion, and that the differences in polarization energy remain below 9.0%, we will use the larger basis set to analyze all energy components except induction and dispersion, for which the smaller basis set will be employed.

Table 2. Total interaction energy and its different components for the interaction of the trilayer membrane of graphtriyne with a CO_2, N_2 and H_2O molecule located at the geometric center of the inner layer, the outer layer and between the inner and an outer layers. All energies in kcal/mol.

	Inner[a]	Inter[a]	Outer[a]	Inner[b]	Inter[b]	Outer[b]
CO_2						
Elec	−2.51	−4.76	−2.14	−2.57	−4.85	−2.21
Pau	6.83	13.01	5.21	6.81	13.04	5.21
Exch	−14.33	−21.24	−10.85	−14.05	−21.19	−10.62
Rep	21.17	34.25	16.06	20.87	34.23	15.84
Pol	−10.20	−11.35	−7.92	−9.70	−10.99	−7.54
Ind	−4.19	−3.67	−2.69	−0.75	−0.70	−0.61
Disp	−6.02	−7.68	−5.23	−8.96	−10.29	−6.93
Tot	−5.88	−3.10	−4.85	−5.46	−2.80	−4.53
N_2						
Elec	−1.73	−2.54	−1.63	−1.77	−2.61	−1.68
Pau	5.42	8.12	4.98	5.42	8.05	4.99
Exch	−10.97	−14.30	−9.77	−10.81	−14.08	−9.64
Rep	16.38	22.42	14.75	16.23	22.13	14.63
Pol	−7.55	−8.45	−6.31	−7.43	−8.25	−6.25
Ind	−0.61	0.14	−0.03	−0.23	−0.48	−0.20
Disp	−6.94	−8.59	−6.28	−7.20	−7.78	−6.05
Tot	−3.86	−2.87	−2.96	−3.77	−2.81	−2.94
H_2O						
Elec	−1.87	−2.15	−1.95	−1.86	−2.13	−1.94
Pau	5.67	6.01	5.54	5.82	6.12	5.71
Exch	−11.92	−12.46	−11.40	−11.72	−12.25	−11.33
Rep	17.59	18.47	16.94	17.53	18.37	17.04
Pol	−8.31	−8.08	−7.45	−7.56	−7.39	−6.86
Ind	−2.39	−2.19	−1.95	−1.76	−1.44	−1.72
Disp	−5.92	−5.89	−5.50	−5.80	−5.95	−5.13
Tot	−4.52	−4.22	−3.86	−3.60	−3.40	−3.09

[a] Values calculated with the 6-311++(2df,pd) basis set.
[b] Values calculated with the 6-311(d,p) basis set.

Based on the data in Table 2, it can be concluded that CO_2 is the most stabilized molecule at the center of both the inner and outer layers, while H_2O is more stabilized at the interlayer position. As observed in the monolayer case, N_2 is the least stabilized molecule within the trilayer membrane. Unlike the monolayer case, the greater stability of CO_2 at the center of a layer (either inner or outer) in the trilayer membrane results from more negative values of all attractive terms, with the most significant contributions coming from intermolecular exchange and dispersion energies. In contrast, the spin repulsion for CO_2 is larger than that for N_2 and H_2O. These differences, compared to the monolayer case—where the largest stabilization of CO_2 is attributed to a decrease in spin repulsion—highlight the significant impact of interactions with neighboring layers in a multilayer membrane.

The greater stability of H_2O at the center of the interlayer region results from a significant increase in spin repulsion energy for CO_2, and to a lesser extent for N_2, which is not compensated by the attractive terms. As a result, CO_2 experiences a notable decrease in stability from the center of the inner and outer layers to the interlayer region, suggesting that the orientation of these molecules may not be optimal in the interlayer region. This points to the need for a more thorough exploration of the potential energy surface, along with a dynamic study, as mentioned at the end of the Introduction section. In contrast, the stability of H_2O remains relatively stable along the trilayer, with a slight increase as the molecule penetrates deeper into the membrane.

The results obtained for CO_2 differ from those reported in Reference 21 for the total interaction energies, where the value at the center of the interlayer region is nearly identical to that at the center of the inner layer. This discrepancy may stem from the different computational approaches used, DFT-D3 in this study and MP2C in Reference 21. However, the exact cause remains unclear and could be attributed to an underestimation of spin repulsion in the interlayer region at the MP2C level, an underestimation of dispersion energy at the DFT-D3 level, or even the use of the counterpoise correction in Reference 21. In principle, the counterpoise correction is not recommended for post-SCF methods involving multi determinant wave functions, unless it is used in conjunction with a complete basis set extrapolation scheme [31]. This will be particularly relevant for large systems like the trilayer membrane model. Further investigation is needed to clarify the differences observed between these computational approaches.

Finally, it is important to highlight the effect of diffuse functions on the decomposition of polarization into induction and dispersion terms. In CO_2, the largest molecule, there is a clear overestimation of the induction energy, a smaller overestimation in H_2O, and no discernible trend in N_2. This overestimation occurs due to the extensive penetration of diffuse functions, located on atoms of one molecule, into the spatial regions of nearby atoms in the other molecule. A potential solution would be to perform a real-space partition of the molecular domains instead of a Hilbert space partition, though this approach is computationally more expensive and could be impractical for very large molecular systems.

4 Conclusions

In this preliminary study, we explored the differences previously observed in the adsorption affinities of graphtriyne membranes for CO_2, N_2, and H_2O gas molecules. Analyzing the main components of the interaction energy by means of DD-EDA, we characterized the intermolecular forces governing the relative stability of these molecules when interacting with both monolayer and trilayer membranes.

Our findings indicate that spin repulsion plays a crucial role in the greater stability of CO_2 near the pore center of a monolayer membrane. In contrast, during the initial stages of the adsorption process, the attractive terms—electrostatics, intermolecular exchange, and polarization—primarily dictate the relative stability of the different gases.

For interactions with a trilayer membrane, CO_2 remains the most stabilized molecule, primarily due to stronger attraction by the different layers, despite experiencing greater spin repulsion compared to the other two gases. The stability order follows the same trend as in the monolayer membrane: $CO_2 > H_2O > N_2$.

Acknowledgments. M This work has been funded by the European Union—Next Generation EU under the Italian Ministry of University and Research (MUR) National Innovation Ecosystem grant ECS00000041 - VITALITY - CUP J97G22000170005. N.F.L acknowledges funding by the Italian Ministry of Environment and Energy Security in the framework of the Project GoPV (CSEAA_00011) for Research on the Electric System. M.M.A. thanks Ministerio de Ciencia e Innovación for financial support through the project PID2022-138023NB-I00 and Xunta de Galicia for financial support through the project GRC2024/27.

Disclosure of Interests. The authors have no competing interests to declare that are relevant to the content of this article.

References

1. Baker, R.W., Lokhandwala, K.: Natural gas processing with membranes: an overview. Ind. Eng. Chem. Res. **47**, 2109–2121 (2008)
2. Bernardo, P., Drioli, E., Golemme, G.: Membrane gas separation: a review/state of the art. Ind. Eng. Chem. Res. **48**, 4638–4663 (2009)
3. Hou, R., Fong, C., Freeman, B.D., Hill, M.R., Xie, Z.: Current status and advances in membrane technology for carbon capture. Sep. Purif. Technol. **300**, 121863 (2022)
4. Genduso, G., Ogieglo, W., Wang, Y., Pinnau, I.: Carbon molecular sieve gas separation materials and membranes: a comprehensive review. J. Membr. Sci. **699**, 122533 (2024)
5. Liu, Z., Qiu, W., Quan, W., Koros, W.J.: Advanced carbon molecular sieve membranes derived from molecularly engineered cross-linkable copolyimide for gas separations. Nat. Mat. **22**, 109–116 (2023)
6. Bunch, J.S., Verbridge, S.S., Alden, J.S., van der Zande, A.M., Parpia, J.M., Craighead, H.G., McEuen, P.L.: Impermeable atomic membranes from graphene sheets. Nano Lett. **8**, 2458–2462 (2008)
7. Koenig, S.P., Wang, L., Pellegrino, J., Bunch, J.S.: Selective molecular sieving through porous graphene. Nat. Nanotechnol. **7**, 728–732 (2012)
8. Chumakova, N., Kokorin, A.: Graphene oxide membranes—synthesis, properties, and applications. Mambranes. **13**, 771 (2023)
9. Yazid, A.F., Mukhtar, H., Nasir, R., Mohshim, D.F.: Incorporating carbon nanotubes in nanocomposite mixed-matrix membranes for gas separation: a review. Membranes. **12**, 589 (2022)

10. Dassouki, K., Dasgupta, S., Eddy Dumas, E., Steunou, N.: Interfacing metal organic frameworks with polymers or carbon-based materials: from simple to hierarchical porous and nanostructured composites. Chem. Sci. **14**, 12898–12925 (2023)

11. Lei, L., Bai, L., Lindbråthen, A., Pan, F., Zhang, X., He, X.: Carbon membranes for CO_2 removal: status and perspectives from materials to processes. Chem. Eng. J. **401**, 126084 (2020)

12. Malko, D., Neiss, C., Viñes, F., Görling, A.: Competition for graphene: Graphynes with direction-dependent Dirac cones. Phys. Rev. Lett. **108**, 086804 (2012)

13. Li, Y., Xu, L., Liu, H., Li, Y.: Graphdiyne and graphyne: from theoretical predictions to practical construction. Chem. Soc. Rev. **43**, 2572–2586 (2014)

14. Cranford, S.W., Buehler, M.J.: Selective hydrogen purification through graphyne membranes: theory meets experiment. Nanoscale. **4**, 4587–4593 (2012)

15. Qian, X., Li, Y., Li, Y.: Graphyne-based membranes for gas separation. ACS Nano. **12**, 11836–11844 (2018)

16. Perkgoz, N.K., Sevik, C.: Vibrational and thermodynamic properties of α-, β-, γ-, and 6, 6, 12-graphyne structures. Nanotechnology. **25**, 185701 (2014)

17. Azizi, K., Allaei, S.M.V., Fathizadeh, A., Sadeghi, A., Sahimi, M.: Graphyne-3: a highly efficient candidate for separation of small gas molecules from gaseous mixtures. Sci. Rep. **11**, 16325 (2021)

18. Majidi, R.: Irida-graphyne: a promising material for optoelectronic applications. Mater. Today Commun. **38**, 107641 (2024)

19. Li, S., Zhao, Y., Wang, D.: Progress in graphdiyne-based membrane for gas separation and water purification. ChemPhysMater. (2025). https://doi.org/10.1016/j.chphma.2025.02.007

20. Bartolomei, M., Carmona-Novillo, E., Giorgi, G.: First principles investigation of hydrogen physical adsorption on graphynes' layers. Carbon. **95**, 1076–1081 (2015)

21. Bartolomei, M., Giorgi, G.: A novel Nanoporous graphite based on graphynes: first-principles structure and carbon dioxide preferential physisorption. ACS Appl. Mater. Interfaces. **8**, 27996–28003 (2016)

22. Apriliyanto, Y.B., Faginas-Lago, N., Lombardi, A., Evangelisti, S., Bartolomei, M., Leininger, T., Pirani, F.: Nanostructure selectivity for molecular adsorption and separation: the case of graphyne layers. J. Phys. Chem. C. **122**, 16195–16208 (2018)

23. Apriliyanto, Y.B., Faginas-Lago, N., Evangelisti, S., Bartolomei, M., Leininger, T., Pirani, F., Pacifici, L., Lombardi, A.: Multilayer graphtriyne membranes for separation and storage of CO2: molecular dynamics simulations of post-combustion model mixtures. Molecules. **27**, 5958 (2022)

24. Zhao, Y., Truhlar, D.G.: The M06 suite of density functionals for main group thermochemistry, thermochemical kinetics, noncovalent interactions, excited states, and transition elements: two new functionals and systematic testing of four M06-class functionals and 12 other functionals. Theor. Chem. Account. **120**, 215–241 (2008)

25. Ramos-Berdullas, N., Pérez-Juste, I., Van Alsenoy, C., Mandado, M.: Theoretical study of the adsorption of aromatic units on carbon allotropes including explicit (empirical) DFT dispersion corrections and implicitly dispersion-corrected functionals: the pyridine case. Phys. Chem. Chem. Phys. **17**, 575–587 (2015)

26. Grimme, S., Antony, J., Ehrlich, S., Krieg, H.: A consistent and accurate ab initio parametrization of density functional dispersion correction (DFT-D) for the 94 elements H-Pu. J. Chem. Phys. **132**, 154104 (2010)

27. Mandado, M., Hermida-Ramón, J.M.: Electron density based partitioning scheme of interaction energies. J. Chem. Theory Comput. **7**, 633–641 (2011)

28. Boys, S.F., Bernardi, F.: The calculation of small molecular interactions by the differences of separate total energies. Some procedures with reduced errors. Mol. Phys. **19**, 553–566 (1970)

29. Frisch, M.J., et al: Gaussian 16 Revision C.01. (2016)
30. Mandado, M., Van Alsenoy, C.: EDA-NCI: Energy Decomposition Analysis of Non-Cova-lent Interactions. https://github.com/marcos-mandado/EDA-NCI, last accessed 27 March 2025
31. Halkier, A., Klopper, W., Helgaker, T., Jörgensen, P., Taylor, P.R.: Basis set convergence of the interaction energy of hydrogen-bonded complexes. J. Chem. Phys. **111**, 9157–9167 (1999)

Accurate Force Field for Dimer Interactions: From Acetone to Dimethylsulfoxide

Luca Mancini[1]([✉])(iD), Andrea Lombardi[1,3](iD), Fernando Pirani[2](iD),
Leonardo Pacifici[3](iD), Marzio Rosi[2,3](iD), and Noelia Faginas-Lago[1,3](iD)

[1] Dipartimento di Chimica, Biologia e Biotecnologie,
Università degli Studi di Perugia, 06123 Perugia, Italy
luca.mancini@unipg.it
[2] Dipartimento di Ingegneria Civile ed Ambientale, Università degli Studi di Perugia,
06125 Perugia, Italy
[3] Istituto CNR di Scienze e Tecnologie Chimiche "Giulio Natta", (CNR-SCITEC),
06123 Perugia, Italy

Abstract. Acetone (CH_3COCH_3) and dimethylsulfoxide (CH_3SOCH_3,
DMS) are known for their peculiar properties and applications in different fields. The ability of acetone to dissolve an extensive number of chemical species with different physico-chemical properties makes this molecule
an excellent solvent in various processes. On the other hand, due to its
significant pharmacological potential, dimethylsulfoxide is regarded as an
important species in medical chemistry and biology. Along with playing
a crucial part in cryoprotection, it is also regarded as a significant species
in the fields of radioprotection and anti-inflammatory medicine. For these
reasons, the accurate analysis of the interaction between molecules, leading to the formation of dimers, trimers and clusters represents an important starting point for the detailed characterization of chemical properties of acetone and DMSO solutions. Within this framework, classical
Molecular Dynamics simulations can be of great help to elucidate the
main properties of the system and its behavior under the influence of
different conditions. In this contribution we analyze the robustness of
a new force field, developed for the acetone-acetone and DMSO-DMSO
interaction, identified as a combination of electrostatic and non electrostatic contribution, the last one formulated using the *Improved Lennard-
Jones* potential. A comparison with the data obtained through *Ab Initio*
calculations allowed us to demonstrate the reliability of the developed
force field.

Keywords: Acetone · Dimethylsulfoxide · Improved Lennard-Jones ·
Molecular Dynamics · Force Field

1 Introduction

Acetone is extremely soluble in water and may dissolve a variety of chemical compounds, including polar, nonpolar, and polymeric substances. These properties

© The Author(s), under exclusive license to Springer Nature Switzerland AG 2026
O. Gervasi et al. (Eds.): ICCSA 2025 Workshops, LNCS 15897, pp. 53–66, 2026.
https://doi.org/10.1007/978-3-031-97660-5_5

made acetone an useful and important solvent for different applications, ranging from laboratory studies to industrial processes [1,2]. Within the industrial framework, planning and increasing the effectiveness of technologically significant operations need a detailed understanding of the macroscopic and microscopic characteristics of acetone [3–5]. In the last years, different works have been performed in order to implement accurate force fields for the study of various systems involving acetone molecules. One example is represented by the analysis of complex mixtures, mainly composed of aldehides and chetones, to obtain important information of phase equilibrium properties [6–8]. Moreover, thermodinamic properties of liquid acetone were investigated through the use of classical molecular dynamics, obtaining a good agreement between theoretical predictions and experimental analysis [9]. Furthermore, given the high level of miscibility, the properties of acetone-water mixtures were extensively studied, including the effect of the variation of the dipole moment in acqueous solutions [10].

A similar molecule, dimethylsulfoxide (DMSO, CH_3SOCH_3), was analysed considering the analogies with acetone. The different chemical properties of sulfur, with respect to the carbon, are responsible for a different physical and chemical behavior of DMSO mixtures. Dimethylsulfoxide is particularly used in the field of cryopreservation, since it is not toxic and shows, together with a low molecular weight, a high solubility in acqueous solutions [11]. Being able to penetrate cell membranes, DMSO was proposed as cryopreservant for the preparation and storage of cells samples to be subjected to RNA sequencing [12]. Together with cryoprotective actions [13–15], DMSO also shows strong prophylactic and radioprotective properties [16]. Additional pharmacological applications of DMSO include anti-inflammatry and bacteriostatic activity, as well as analgesia [17]. One of the key aspects of the reactivity of both acetone and DMSO is related to their ability to form small aggregates and clusters [18]. Therefore, in order to unveil the reaction mechanism, a detailed understanding of the first step of the aggregation process, mainly driven by long-range non-covalent interactions, is pivotal.

A valid approach, considered as a satisfactory compromise between chemical accuracy and computational cost, is represented by classic molecular dynamics (MD) calculations. This last is regarded as a valuable technique for modeling the structure and predicting features of large systems, that are challenging or impossible to examine through precise *ab initio* research and/or experimental investigations. By using straightforward formulas based on Newton's laws of motion, molecular dynamics simulations enable the prediction of the positions of the various atoms in a system as a function of time. The most important step to be taken into account when setting the MD simulation is the implementation of the force field (FF), which describes the non covalent part of the interaction. The choice of the accurate parameters to describe the energy function is driven from both laboratory experiment and theoretical calculations. The electrostatic (Coulombic) contribution between atoms and the non-electrostatic one are the two primary components of MD force field, which is required to address non-covalent interactions. The proper modeling of intermolecular interactions (non-electrostatic contribution), in particular the van der Waals component, which is always present and crucial for the overall dynamics, is one of the most difficult tasks in implementing accurate force fields.

In the last years, a new formulation of the intermolecular potential was presented to better take into account the effect of both long-range attraction and short-range repulsion. The formulation, named *Improved Lennard-Jones (ILJ)* [19], was obtained considering a sinergy between high level *ab initio* calculations and experimental investigations, performed through molecular beams scattering techniques [20–22]. A detailed description of the potential is reported in the next section (see Sect. 2.1 for details). One of the main advantages of the ILJ formulation is the relation with physical properties of the interacting systems, which gives a high level of transferability to the system. Recently, the same formulation was employed in different fields, ranging from astrochemistry [23, 24] to material chemistry for energy applications [25, 26]. It is also important to note that the *Improved Lennard-Jones* formulation, giving the first (force) and second (force constant) derivates in an analytical form, provides a physically grounded force field formulation, with a still limited computational cost.

In the present contribution, we report a comparison between the force field, developed through the ILJ formulation of the intermolecular potential, for the acetone-acetone interaction and the DMSO-DMSO one. A comparison with the data obtained via *ab initio* calculations is reported, in order to check the validity of the proposed potential. Previous analysis were already performed to study the interaction of acetone molecules in the formation of clusters [27] and to model the DMSO-water interaction [28]. The present work can indeed be considered as a continuation of the analysis already presented, with the aim of building a robust and appropriate potential functions.

2   Theoretical Methods

2.1   Potential Energy Surface for the Intermolecular Interactions

As already discussed, one of the key aspects for the correct execution of MD simulations is the accurate definition of the intermolecular interactions, which are essential components of the Force Field. In this work, we developed the Force Field taking into account that the total potential (V_{tot}) can be composed of two dominant contributions: the electrostatic potential (V_{elec}), evaluated in accordance with Coulomb's law, considering the atomic charges calculated for each molecule (reported in Fig. 1) and a second term (V_{nelec}), accounting for the non-electrostatic contribution of the interaction.

$$V_{tot}(r) = V_{elec} + V_{nelec} \qquad (1)$$

This last term, V_{nelec}, was evaluated making use of the *Improved Lennard-Jones (ILJ)* model [19, 27, 29–31], associated to different molecular centers, each one identified as an effective atom - effective atom contribution, evaluated at a separation distance r. Accordingly, the total interaction is decomposed considering a series of pair-addictive contributions, which can be formulated taking into account the strength of induced dipoles attraction and the average molecular sizes repulsion, and formulated as follows:

$$V_{nelec} = V_{ILJ} = \varepsilon \left[\frac{m}{n(r) - m} \left(\frac{r_m}{r} \right)^{n(r)} - \frac{n(r)}{n(r) - m} \left(\frac{r_m}{r} \right)^{m} \right] \tag{2}$$

where ε and r_m describes the well depth and its position, respectively, associated to each interaction pair, while m assumes the value of 6 in the case of neutral-neutral systems. The ε and r_m values are estimated on the basis of the molecular polarizabilty partition in components assigned to each interaction center. The newly implemented $n(r)$ shows a dependence on the distance r, defined as:

$$n(r) = \beta + 4 \left(\frac{r}{r_m} \right)^2 \tag{3}$$

where the β parameter represents the hardness of the two interacting fragments, whose value can be properly modulated to indirectly include the role of further interaction components that can add to dispersion attraction and size repulsion effects. As a consequence, the ILJ potential may now enhance the Lennard-Jones function in asymptotic regions and it can indirectly include, through the modulation of the β parameter, for the perturbation effects due to additional interaction components as induction and charge transfer attractions.

2.2   Molecular Dynamics

In order to validate the efficiency of the Force Field, we run classical molecular dynamics simulations for both the dimethylsulfide and the acetone dimers. The DL_POLY [32] simulation package was used, considering the NVT ensamble, where the number of particles (N), volume (V) and temperature (T) are kept constant and using a Hoover-Nose thermostat [33] with a relaxation constant of 1 ps. After an initial equilibration period of 1 ns, all the simulations were performed for a total time of 3 ns, considering a pressure of 1 atm and for different values of temperature, ranging from 10 K to 300 K. Finally, the value of configurational energy (which refers to the potential energy associated to a specific configuration of the system), directly obtained from the OUTPUT of the MD calculations, was extrapolated to 0 K in order to compare the data with the results of *Ab Initio* calculations (see next section for details).

2.3   *Ab Initio* calculations

The final validation was performed considering the comparison between the results obtained from the MD calculations and the data coming from accurate electronic structure calculations. As already shown in several cases before [34–40], *ab initio* calculations based on DFT theory appear to be a good compromise between chemical accuracy and computational cost. Following this suggestion, using the *Gaussian09* [41] software, geometry optimization was performed at the

B3LYP [42,43] level of theory, with the inclusion of the Grimme's D3BJ disper-sion [44] (B3LYP-D3). The 6-311++G(d,p) [45,46] basis set was used for this purpose, while single point energy calculations were performed with the same B3LYP-D3 functional with the more accurate aug-cc-pVTZ [47] basis set.

3 Results

3.1 Implementation of the Force Field

As a first step for the correct implementation of the ILJ interaction parameters, the dipole and/or quadrupole moments of the molecules in the gas phase must be accurately represented through the computation of atomic charges for the two interacting species. In Fig. 1, the atomic charges used to represent the dypole moment of the acetone and DMSO molecules are reported.

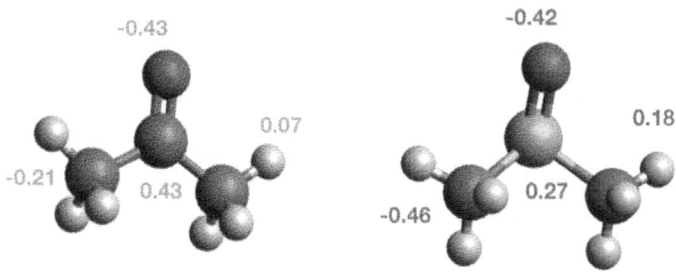

Fig. 1. Atomic charges used for the analysis of the electrostatic potential for both the acetone (left hand side) and the DMSO (right hand side) molecules.

The values shown in Fig. 1 are compatible with the experimental value of dipole moment for acetone and DMSO, which appears to be equal to 2.88 D and 3.96 D, respectively [48]. Additionally, the molecular polarizability, which repre-sents a key properties for the determination of the ILJ parameters, is equal to 6.1 Å^3 for acetone [49] and 8.1 Å^3 for dimethylsulfoxide [28]. The values of the elec-tric dipole moment and of the molecular polarizabilty of DMSO are greater than those of acetone, therefore we can expect considerable differences in the main interaction parameters for the DMSO dimer, with respect to those in acetone-acetone one. As already discussed (see Sect. 2 for details) the ILJ parameters are linked to the fundamental quantities related to the intermolecular potential [50], including the dipole moment (μ) and atomic/molecular polarizability (α). In details, the ε and r_m parameters for neutral-neutral systems are obtained as follows [51]:

$$r_m(\text{Å}) = 1.767 \frac{\alpha_1^{1/3} + \alpha_2^{1/3}}{(\alpha_1 \alpha_2)^{0.095}} \tag{4}$$

$$\varepsilon(meV) = 0.720\frac{C_{6,eff}}{r_m^6} \tag{5}$$

where $C_{6,eff}$ is the long-range attraction coefficient, evaluated considering the number of electrons, effectively undergoing polarization, of the two interacting particles (expressed as N_1 and N_2)

$$C_{6,eff}(meV\mathring{A}^6) = 15700\frac{\alpha_1\alpha_2}{\left(\frac{\alpha_1}{N_1}\right)^{1/2} + \left(\frac{\alpha_2}{N_2}\right)^{1/2}} \tag{6}$$

The direct relation between the ILJ parameters and physical properties of the interacting system leads to a high degree of transferability, allowing to move easily from a system to a similar one, without particular changes in the parameters. Additionally, the derived parameters lead to a high level of portability of the formulation, allowing also to study complex systems, by simply decomposing the main molecular structure in different moieties. Considering the relations previously presented, the ILJ parameters for the interaction between two acetone molecules, as well as the ones for the DMSO-DMSO, were calculated. The final parameters are reported in Tables 1 and 2, respectively.

Table 1. List of the Improved Lennard-Jones parameters (well depth, ε, and equilibrium distance, r_m) evaluated for the acetone-acetone system. (Adapted from the work presented by N. Faginas-Lago et al. [27])

Interacting Pair	r_m (Å)	ε (kcal/mol)
C_{CH_3} - C_{CH_3}	4.053	0.262
C_{CO} - C_{CO}	3.628	0.150
O - O	3.398	0.119
C_{CO} - O	3.521	0.130

Table 2. List of the Improved Lennard-Jones parameters (well depth, ε, and equilibrium distance, r_m) evaluated for the DMSO-DMSO system. (Adapted from the work presented by L. Mancini et al. [28])

Interacting Pair	r_m (Å)	ε (kcal/mol)
C_{CH_3} - C_{CH_3}	4.053	0.262
S - S	4.075	0.325
O - O	3.534	0.150
S - O	3.847	0.201

As can be seen, the ε parameter for the DMSO-DMSO interaction assumes, in general, values different from those derived for the acetone dimer, especially the ones associated to the interaction pairs involving the sulfur atom are significantly higher. This reflects the higher value of the molecular polarizability of DMSO, with respect to the case of acetone itself. The β parameter can be appropriately modulated in the V_{elec} changes and is typically thought to be in the range of 8.5 $\pm$ 2.5. Furthermore, other distinct contributions that are less significant and not directly included in the formulation–such as additional additive components of the interaction at long distances that are indirectly included–can be compensated for and included using the same parameter.

3.2   Validation of the Force Field

In order to assess the viability of the developed force field for both the dimer interactions, we run MD calculations, as outlined in Sect. 2.2. As a first step, we evaluated the interaction energy of the dimer by performing MD calculations at different temperatures and extrapolating the value of the configurational (or potential) energy (E_{cfg}) at 0 K. It is possible to consider this last value as an estimate of the binding energy. In Fig. 2 the values of E_{cfg} obtained for the acetone dimer at different temperatures (represented by the marked points) are shown, together with the linear extrapolation (dashed line) used to obtain the value at 0 K. Our results predict a configurational energy of - 4.92 kcal/mol.

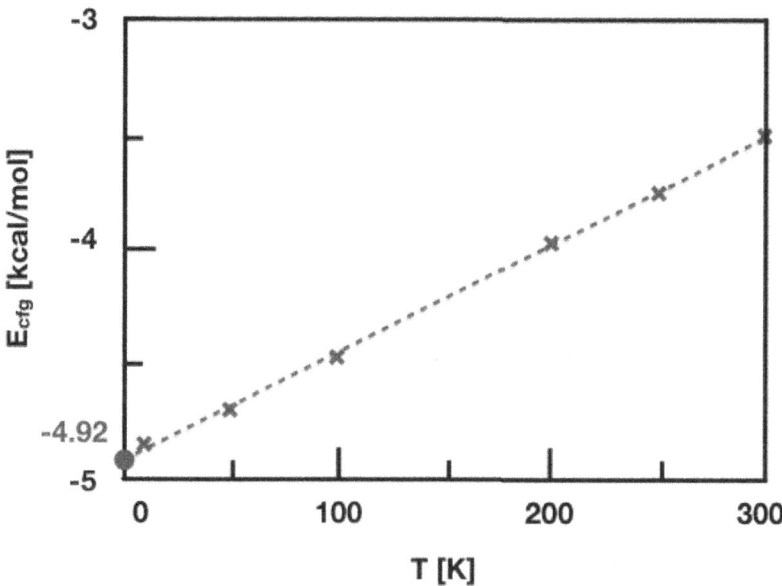

Fig. 2. Configurational energy (E_{cfg}) as a function of the temperature for the acetone dimer.

This value can be directly compared with the data obtained by *ab initio* calculations. The analysis performed at the B3LYP-D3/aug-cc-pVTZ level of theory lead to a value of energy of -5.89 kcal/mol, in agreement with the data obtained extrapolating MD results. A similar procedure was carried out for the case of the DMSO dimer. The results obtained from the analysis performed through classical MD simulations are reported in Fig. 3, obtaining a value of configurational energy at a temperature of 0 K equal to - 10.35 kcal/mol.

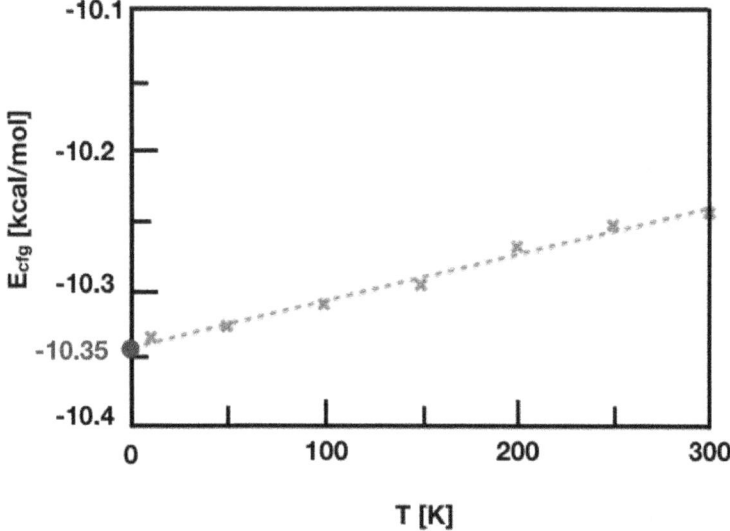

Fig. 3. Configurational energy (E_{cfg}) as a function of the temperature for the DMSO dimer.

Also in this case, the value can be compared with the data obtained at the B3LYP-D3/aug-cc-pVTZ level of theory, which reported a value of energy of -11.4 kcal/mol, showing once again the agreement between classical MD predictions and *ab initio* calculations, within the range of accuracy due to the different types of calculations. In Table 3 are reported the energies obtained through classical MD calculation and *ab initio* analysis for a direct comparison.

Table 3. Electrostatic (E_{coul}), non-electrostatic (E_{ILJ}) and configurational (potential) energy (E_{cfg}), in kcal/mol, obtained from the extrapolation at 0 K from classical MD calculations E_{cfg} compared with the *ab initio* energy, evaluated at the B3LYP-D3/aug-cc-pVTZ level of theory E_{B3LYP} for both the acetone and DMSO dimer.

Dimer	MD			*Ab initio*
	E_{coul}	E_{ILJ}	E_{cfg}	$E_{B3LYP-D3}$
Acetone-Acetone	−2.82	−2.08	−4.92	−5.89
DMSO-DMSO	−7.99	−2.32	−10.35	−11.4

As can be noticed from the data reported in Table 3, the interaction energy is higher for the DMSO dimer, with respect to the case of acetone. The reason of such a difference is related to both the electrostatic contribution of the interaction, due to the higher value of dipole moment of DMSO, and the non-electrostatic contribution, since the value of polarizability of DMSO is considerably higher than the one of acetone.

Finally, a comparison between the geometry of the adducts can be performed in order to assess the force field used to describe the intermolecular forces. In details, the geometry obtained from the last frame of the trajectory carried out at 10 K was used as a starting point for a geometry optimization, carried out at the B3LYP-D3/6-311++G(d, p) level of theory. In Table 4 the main atom-atom distances for both the acetone dimer and the DMSO dimer are reported, while Fig. 4 shows a 3D representation of the structure of the dimer for both acetone and DMSO.

Table 4. Main atom-atom distances for both the acetone dimer and the DMSO dimer, resulting from MD calculations and DFT (B3LYP-D3/6-311++G(d,p) level of theory.

Atom-Atom	r_{MD} (Å)	r_{DFT} (Å)
Acetone-Acetone		
C_{CO}-C_{CO}	3.746	3.222
O-O	3.953	3.495
C_{CH_3}-C_{CH_3}	3.840	3.907
DMSO-DMSO		
S-S	4.450	4.390
O-O	3.963	3.498
C_{CH_3}-C_{CH_3}	3.677	3.943

As can be seen from the data reported in Table 4, the values of distances between the two molecules of each dimer derived from MD calculations are comparable with the DFT data. The main deviations are lower than 0.52 Å for the acetone dimer and lower than 0.47 Å for the DMSO-DMSO interaction, pointing

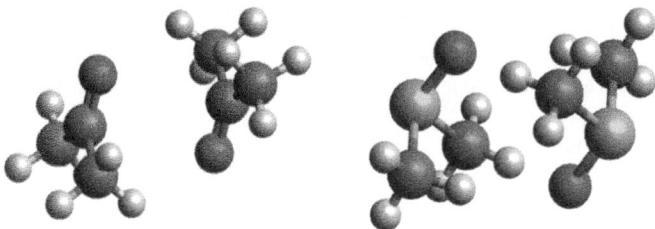

Fig. 4. 3D representation of the structure of the dimer for acetone (left) and DMSO (right) optimized at the B3LYP-D3/6-311++G(d, p) level of theory.

out a good agreement between the two methods and, therefore, confirming the validity and robustness of the presented force field.

4   Conclusions

The development of accurate force fields, which determines the interaction energy and the geometry associated to the dimers aggregation, represents a crucial first step of relevance for the formation of liquids and solutions. In particular, we presented the parameters for the ILJ formulation of the long-range potential for both the acetone-acetone and the DMSO-DMSO interactions. Moreover, the binding energies obtained for the DMSO dimer appear to be significantly stronger than the ones between acetone molecules. This finding is a direct consequence of the higher value of the molecular polarizability and electric dipole of DMSO with respect to those of acetone. The data obtained performing classical MD simulations were compared with the results of DFT calculations, showing a general good agreement of both the configurational energy and the final geometry of the system, considering the main differences in the two approaches. Further refinement of the ILJ parameters can be considered in order to get a better agreement with the *ab initio* data. In particular, a fine-tuning of the β parameter can be useful for the purpose. It is possible to conclude, therefore, that the present work sets the stage for a more complex analysis and the parameters used for the formulation of both the electrostatic and non-electrostatic components of the interactions are reasonable and can be used for the development of the force field. An additional analysis will be performed in the case of bulk systems, which will be the purpose of a future work, where the outcome of the MD calculations will be compared with physico-chemical properties of teh system. Additionally, more accurate *ab initio* calculations will be performed at a higher level of theory in order to set reference data for the complete validation of the force field. The same strategy can be applied to the study of different systems, with a wide range of applications, including the study of nanomaterials for energy storage and carbon neutrality techniques, allowing to properly describe the interaction of small molecules with adsorbing substrates.

Acknowledgments. This work has been funded by the European Union - NextGenerationEU under the Italian Ministry of University and Research (MUR) National Innovation Ecosystem grant ECS00000041 - VITALITY - CUP J97G22000170005. LP acknowledges financial support from the European Union - Next Generation EU, National Centre for HPC, Big Data and Quantum Computing – HPC project - Centro Nazionale – CN0000013: CUP:B93C22000620006

Disclosure of Interests. The authors have no competing interests to declare that are relevant to the content of this article.

References

1. Nagai, K.: Appl. Catal., A: Gen. **221**, 367 (2001)
2. Uglea, C.V., Negulescu, I.I.: Synthesis and Characterization of Oligomers. CRC Press (1991)
3. Asada, M., Fujimori, T., Fujii, K., Kanzaki, R., Umebayashi, Y., Ishiguro, S.I.: Solvation structure of magnesium, zinc, and alkaline earth metal ions in n, n-dimethylformamide, n, n-dimethylacetamide, and their mixtures studied by means of Raman spectroscopy and DFT calculations–ionic size and electronic effects on steric congestion. J. Raman Spectrosc.: Int. J. Original Work Aspects Raman Spectrosc. Includ. High. Order Process. Brillouin Rayleigh Scatter. **38**(4), 417–426 (2007)
4. Palombo, F., Paolantoni, M., Sassi, P., Morresi, A., Giorgini, M.G.: Molecular dynamics of liquid acetone determined by depolarized Rayleigh and low-frequency Raman scattering spectroscopy. Phys. Chem. Chem. Phys. **13**(36), 16197–16207 (2011)
5. Mollner, A.K., Brooksby, P.A., Loring, J.S., Bako, I., Palinkas, G., Fawcett, W.R.: Ion- solvent interactions in acetonitrile solutions of lithium iodide and tetrabutylammonium iodide. J. Phys. Chem. A **108**(16), 3344–3349 (2004)
6. Ferrando, N., Lachet, V., Boutin, A.: Monte Carlo simulations of mixtures involving ketones and aldehydes by a direct bubble pressure calculation. J. Phys. Chem. B **114**(26), 8680–8688 (2010)
7. Stubbs, J.M., Potoff, J.J., Siepmann, J.I.: Transferable potentials for phase equilibria. 6. United-atom description for ethers, glycols, ketones, and aldehydes. J. Phys. Chem. B **108**(45), 17596–17605 (2004)
8. Hantal, G., Jedlovszky, P., Hoang, P.N., Picaud, S.: Investigation of the adsorption behaviour of acetone at the surface of ice. A grand canonical Monte Carlo simulation study. Phys. Chem. Chem. Phys. **10**(42), 6369–6380 (2008)
9. Ghatee, M.H., Taslimian, S.: Investigation of temperature and pressure dependent equilibrium and transport properties of liquid acetone by molecular dynamics simulation. Fluid Phase Equilib. **358**, 226–232 (2013)
10. Pereyra, R.G., Asar, M.L., Carignano, M.A.: The role of acetone dipole moment in acetone-water mixture. Chem. Phys. Lett. **507**(4–6), 240–243 (2011)
11. Lovelock, J.E., Bishop, M.W.: Prevention of freezing damage to living cells by dimethyl sulphoxide. Nature **183**(4672), 1394–1395 (1959)
12. Wohnhaas, C.T., et al.: DMSO cryopreservation is the method of choice to preserve cells for droplet-based single-cell RNA sequencing. Sci. Rep. **9**(1), 10699 (2019)
13. Chaytor, J.L., et al.: Inhibiting ice recrystallization and optimization of cell viability after cryopreservation. Glycobiology **22**(1), 123–133 (2012)

14. Wolfe, J., Bryant, G.: Freezing, drying, and/or vitrification of membrane-solute-water systems. Cryobiology **39**(2), 103–129 (1999)
15. Wolfe, J., Bryant, G.: Cellular cryobiology: thermodynamic and mechanical effects. Int. J. Refrig **24**(5), 438–450 (2001)
16. Jacob, S.W., Herschler, R.: Pharmacology of DMSO. Cryobiology **23**(1), 14–27 (1986)
17. Pope, D., Oliver, W.: Dimethyl sulfoxide (DMSO). Can. J. Comp. Med. Vet. Sci. **30**(1), 3 (1966)
18. Malloum, A., Conradie, J.: Non-covalent interactions in dimethylsulfoxide (DMSO) clusters and DFT benchmarking. J. Mol. Liq. **350**, 118522 (2022)
19. Pirani, F., Brizi, S., Roncaratti, L.F., Casavecchia, P., Cappelletti, D., Vecchiocattivi, F.: Beyond the lennard-jones model: a simple and accurate potential function probed by high resolution scattering data useful for molecular dynamics simulations. Phys. Chem. Chem. Phys. **10**(36), 5489–5503 (2008)
20. Pirani, F., Maciel, G.S., Cappelletti, D., Aquilanti, V.: Experimental benchmarks and phenomenology of interatomic forces: open-shell and electronic anisotropy effects. Int. Rev. Phys. Chem. **25**(1–2), 165–199 (2006)
21. Pirani, F., Albertı, M., Castro, A., Teixidor, M.M., Cappelletti, D.: Atom-bond pairwise additive representation for intermolecular potential energy surfaces. Chem. Phys. Lett. **394**(1–3), 37–44 (2004)
22. Cappelletti, D., Ronca, E., Belpassi, L., Tarantelli, F., Pirani, F.: Revealing charge-transfer effects in gas-phase water chemistry. Acc. Chem. Res. **45**(9), 1571–1580 (2012)
23. Richardson, V., et al.: Fragmentation of interstellar methanol by collisions with He^+: an experimental and computational study. Phys. Chem. Chem. Phys. **24**(37), 22437–22452 (2022)
24. Mancini, L., et al.: Destruction of interstellar methyl cyanide CH_3CN via collisions with He^+ ions. Astron. Astrophys. **691**, A83 (2024)
25. Apriliyanto, Y.B., Faginas Lago, N., Lombardi, A., Evangelisti, S., Bartolomei, M., Leininger, T., Pirani, F.: Nanostructure selectivity for molecular adsorption and separation: the case of graphyne layers. J. Phys. Chem. C **122**(28), 16195–16208 (2018)
26. Faginas-Lago, N., Apriliyanto, Y.B., Lombardi, A.: Confinement of CO_2 inside carbon nanotubes. Eur. Phys. J. D **75**(5), 161 (2021)
27. Faginas Lago, N., Albertí, M., Lombardi, A., Pirani, F.: A force field for acetone: the transition from small clusters to liquid phase investigated by molecular dynamics simulations. Theoret. Chem. Acc. **135**, 1–9 (2016)
28. Mancini, L., Lombardi, A., Pirani, F., Pacifici, L., Rosi, M., Faginas-Lago, N.: A computational analysis of the DMSO-water interaction: toward the implementation of an accurate force field. In: International Conference on Computational Science and Its Applications, pp. 361–374. Springer (2024)
29. Lombardi, A., Laganà, A., Pirani, F., Palazzetti, F., Faginas-Lago, N.: Carbon oxides in gas flows and earth and planetary atmospheres: state-to-state simulations of energy transfer and dissociation reactions. In: LNCS, PART 2, vol. 7972, pp. 17–31 (2013). https://doi.org/10.1007/978-3-642-39643-4_2
30. Lombardi, A., Faginas-Lago, N., Gaia, G., Federico, P., Aquilanti, V.: Collisional energy exchange in CO_2–N_2 gaseous mixtures. In: Gervasi, O., et al. (eds.) ICCSA 2016. LNCS, vol. 9786, pp. 246–257. Springer, Cham (2016). https://doi.org/10.1007/978-3-319-42085-1_19

31. Albertí, M., Faginas-Lago, N.: Ion size influence on the AR solvation shells of $M^+C_6F_6$ clusters (M = Na, K, Rb, Cs). J. Phys. Chem. A **116**(12), 3094–3102 (2012). https://doi.org/10.1021/jp300156k

32. Smith, W., Yong, C., Rodger, P.: Dl_poly: application to molecular simulation. Mol. Simul. **28**(5), 385–471 (2002)

33. Hoover, W.G.: Canonical dynamics: equilibrium phase-space distributions. Phys. Rev. A **31**(3), 1695 (1985)

34. Pannacci, G., et al.: A combined crossed molecular beam and theorerical study of the $O(^3P, {}^1D)$ + acrylonitrile (CH_2CHCN) reactions and implications for combustion and extraterrestrial environments. Phys. Chem. Chem. Phys. **25**(30), 20194–20211 (2023)

35. Liang, P., et al.: OH (2π)+ C_2H_4 reaction: a combined crossed molecular beam and theoretical study. J. Phys. Chem. A **127**(21), 4609–4623 (2023)

36. Rosi, M., et al.: Electronic structure and kinetics calculations for the $Si+SH$ reaction, a possible route of SiS formation in star-forming regions. In: Computational Science and Its Applications–ICCSA 2019: 19th International Conference, Saint Petersburg, Russia, 1–4 July 2019, Proceedings, Part III 19, pp. 306–315. Springer (2019)

37. Liang, P., et al.: Combined crossed molecular beams and computational study on the $N(^2D)$ + $HCCCN(X^1\Sigma^+)$ reaction and implications for extra-terrestrial environments. Mol. Phys. **120**(1–2), e1948126 (2022)

38. Vanuzzo, G., et al.: The N (^2D) + CH_2CHCN (vinyl cyanide) reaction: a combined crossed molecular beam and theoretical study and implications for the atmosphere of titan. J. Phys. Chem. A **126**(36), 6110–6123 (2022)

39. Vanuzzo, G., et al.: Reaction N (^2D) + CH_2CCH_2 (allene): an experimental and theoretical investigation and implications for the photochemical models of titan. ACS Earth Space Chem. **6**(10), 2305–2321 (2022)

40. Recio, P., et al.: A crossed molecular beam investigation of the N (^2D) + pyridine reaction and implications for prebiotic chemistry. Chem. Phys. Lett. **779**, 138852 (2021)

41. Frisch, M., et al.: Fox: Gaussian 09, Revision A. 02, 2009. Gaussian. Inc., Wallingford (2009)

42. Becke, A.D.: Density functional thermochemistry. III. The role of exact exchange. J. Chem. Phys. **98**(7), 5648–5652 (1993). https://doi.org/10.1063/1.464913

43. Stephens, P.J., Devlin, F.J., Chabalowski, C.F., Frisch, M.J.: *Ab Initio* calculation of vibrational absorption and circular dichroism spectra using density functional force fields. J. Phys. Chem. **98**(45), 11623–11627 (1994). https://doi.org/10.1021/j100096a001

44. Grimme, S., Ehrlich, S., Goerigk, L.: Effect of the damping function in dispersion corrected density functional theory. J. Comput. Chem. **32**(7), 1456–1465 (2011)

45. Krishnan, R., Binkley, J.S., Seeger, R., Pople, J.A.: Self-consistent molecular orbital methods. XX. A basis set for correlated wave functions. J. Chem. Phys. **72**(1), 650–654 (1980)

46. McLean, A., Chandler, G.: Contracted gaussian basis sets for molecular calculations. I. Second row atoms, z= 11–18. J. Chem. Phys. **72**(10), 5639–5648 (1980)

47. Dunning Jr., T.H.: Gaussian basis sets for use in correlated molecular calculations. I. the atoms boron through neon and hydrogen. J. Chem. Phys. **90**(2), 1007–1023 (1989). https://doi.org/10.1063/1.456153

48. Nelson, R., Lide, D., Margott, A.: Selected values of electric dipole moments for molecules in the gas phase NSRDS-NBS10. Washington, DC (1967)

49. Olney, T.N., Cann, N., Cooper, G., Brion, C.: Absolute scale determination for photoabsorption spectra and the calculation of molecular properties using dipole sum-rules. Chem. Phys. **223**(1), 59–98 (1997)
50. Maitland, G., Rigby, M., Smith, E., Wakeham, W., Henderson, D.: Intermolecular forces: their origin and determination (1987)
51. Cambi, R., Cappelletti, D., Liuti, G., Pirani, F.: Generalized correlations in terms of polarizability for van der Waals interaction potential parameter calculations. J. Chem. Phys. **95**(3), 1852–1861 (1991)

Sustainable Tourism Evaluations: Approaches, Methods and Indicators (STEva 2025)

Tourism Ecosystems New Challenges

Teresa Guarda[1,2(✉)] ⓘ, Maria Fernanda Augusto[3] ⓘ, Datzania Villao[1] ⓘ,
and Isabel Lopes[4,5] ⓘ

[1] Universidad Estatal Península de Santa Elena, La Libertad, Ecuador
tguarda@gmail.com
[2] Facultad de Sistemas y Telecomunicaciones, La Libertad, Ecuador
[3] BiTrum Research Group, Leon, Spain
[4] Instituto Politécnico de Bragança, Campus de Santa Apolónia, Bragança, Portugal
[5] Applied Management Research Unit (UNIAG), Instituto Politécnico de Bragança (IPB),
Bragança, Portugal

Abstract. The global challenges in terms of climate change, sustainability and traveler behavior are having a profound impact on tourism ecosystems, which are evolving. This paper identifies these challenges and recommends novel governance solutions to enable sustainable tourism ecosystem ports. Through an integration of ecological balance and economic efficiency, they underscore the importance of interdisciplinary approaches that account for environmental, cultural and socioeconomic aspects. Examples such as the sustainable management of the Galápagos Islands highlight the feasibility of integrating conservation and tourism development within fragile ecosystems. This research highlights the importance of aligning global tourism trends with local characteristics through an investigation of emerging trends and key sustainability principles. The results indicate that multi-stakeholder collaboration, adaptive strategies, and technology-driven innovations are necessary for successful tourism ecosystem management, balancing conservation with economic growth.

Keywords: Tourism Ecosystems · Sustainability · Governance · Challenges

1 Introduction

Tourism has long been seen as a system focused on destinations and destination networks, which are currently identified as tourism ecosystems, due to certain distinct characteristics, as they have some unique features, specifically the ecological components they encompass [1, 2]. The relationship between the traditional economy, the participatory industry, the natural environment, and intangible culture is currently being emphasized [3].

The physiology and pathophysiology of tourism systems suggest that should be understood as unique ecosystems, where physical and intangible components coexist and interact interdependently, producing a summative system of considerable significance [4]. Understanding their important role today; the forms they have assumed; and the

O. Gervasi et al. (Eds.): ICCSA 2025 Workshops, LNCS 15897, pp. 69–77, 2026.
https://doi.org/10.1007/978-3-031-97660-5_6

meanings they have acquired over the centuries have evolved from the practices of these diverse but overlapping systems [1].

The era of globalization has seen evolutionary developments that involve a greater emphasis on and more advanced elements in tourist services [5]. Growing interest in conservation and sustainability suggests that the ecosystem perspective remains crucial for understanding natural, manufactured, and productive goods in tourism [3]. Environmental policy in Europe increasingly shares the notion that systems and environmental issues are global and interconnected [6]. Protected natural ecosystems, such as the Galápagos Islands, illustrate how tourism ecosystems can be successfully managed to balance environmental preservation with socio-economic development.

Tourism assessment sciences have often neglected the dynamic and interactive aspects of tourist systems, preferring to view them from a compartmentalized perspective, particularly concerning their most important subsystems [7]. The macro-subsystems relevant to this dimension of tourism ecosystems theory are essentially twofold: one has a biological-natural matrix, which loses much of its ecological aspect to become a naturalistic ecosystem type, while the other is of a socio-cultural matrix, characterized by relatively rapid evolutionary processes compared to the first-mentioned system [8]. In a spatial perspective, the characteristics of the territory interact systemically as individual components, including the landscape and human creations that belong to that territory. In some instances, the landscape represents a culturally produced entity, emphasizing the intangible aspects [9].

2 Tourism Ecosystems

Modern definitions of tourism propose that the concept "tourism ecosystem" incorporates various entities and processes. It is accept that the so-called tourism system or tourism industry is too narrow for understanding the tourism phenomenon and its significant influences on the structure and functioning of different social, environmental, and economic systems [1].

The tourism ecosystem (TE) is a system composed of several critical components, which are dynamic, influenced, and influenced by each other (Table 1). Is it possible to see the tourism ecosystem as a complex network composed by various interrelated components from natural and cultural environments. These components include physical landscapes, biodiversity, local communities, and socio-economic activities that interact within the tourism sector [5]. Addressing the new issues that tourism ecosystems face in the context of sustainability requires an understanding of these relationships. With this knowledge, stakeholders may create plans that benefit local people, encourage natural balance, and improve the overall experience of tourists. Resource depletion and climate change provide new difficulties that the tourism industry may solve by implementing sustainable practices and technologies [9]. It is essential to understand the interconnections between the various stakeholders, such as local communities, government entities, and also tourists. The adoption of a more conscious travel style should be encouraged as a way of preserving and protecting natural resources and thus strengthening the resilience of tourist ecosystems [10]. Only in this way can we ensure that tourism prospers and benefits the environment and society, encouraging cooperation and implementing sustainable practices. This strategy will ensure the protection of natural and cultural resources for future generations while also enhancing the visitor experience [5]. Ecological protection and economic growth can coexist in harmony when sustainable practices are integrated into tourism ecosystems [9]. This integration not only enhances the tourist experience but also ensures the natural environment for future generations.

Table 1. Key Components of Tourism Ecosystems.

Key component	Description
Natural resources	Physical landscapes, biodiversity, and natural environments that attract visitors.
Cultural resources	Cultural environments, local communities' knowledge, attitudes, and traditions that attract tourists.
Local communities	Functional elements managing resources and affected by the ecosystem's functioning.
Infrastructure	Systems interconnecting communities and resources, also part of tourist services.
Services	Experiences provided to visitors, influenced by preferences, expectations, and decisions.
Stakeholders	Entities ensuring the ecosystem is functioning, interacting with other members and the market.
Market	External entity demanding and consuming the ecosystem's resources.
Environment	External entity impacted by the functioning of the tourism ecosystem.

Local communities are the recognizable functional elements of the tourism ecosystem. They are responsible for resource management, and their well-being are affect by the functioning of the other components of the ecosystem. Natural and cultural resources attract visitors, and their state reflects local communities' tacit knowledge, cultures, and attitudes [1, 3]. Infrastructure interconnects communities and resources are part of the services offered to tourists. Services refer to the experiences visitors' encounter, which depend on the preferences, expectations, and decisions of both visitors and local citizens [4, 9]. Stakeholders are responsible for the functioning of the entire tourism ecosystem. They interact with other members of the ecosystem and the market [6, 11]. The market is saw as the outer entity that demands and consumes the resources of the tourism ecosystem, while the environment is the outer entity affected by the functioning of the tourism ecosystem. Understanding the functioning of tourism ecosystems by recognizing their different components can contribute to developing sustainable tourism policies and practices [7].

3 Tourism Ecosystems Challenges

Academics and experts who face new challenges today are particularly interested in tourism ecosystems. One of the most debated topics are over tourism, which causes a destination's tourist attractions to become overcrowded.

The implications of over tourism are multiple and manifest both at social and economic levels. Indeed, it infringes upon the sustainability of the tourism ecosystem of a destination. Another major and more long-term consequence of over tourism is the gradual degradation of the natural and built environment, the loss of authenticity of that destination, and, consequently, a diminishing tourist experience (Table 2) [1]. This also fuels alienation and discontent within the host community, and a reduction in their quality of life. The last decade has seen an increase in attention towards the environmental implications of the travel phenomenon. Indeed, the travel industry is known as an industry with extremely detrimental environmental footprints [3]. There are two ways, at least, that the environmental problem can be framed. It can vary from the pollution created by traffic to the destruction of cultural heritage and the biosphere at a larger level [4]. The shifting winds in the market towards environmentalism have also led to the development of several green and responsible tourism movements; other derivative movements include ecotourism, community-based tourism, and so forth. Society is transforming towards greater inequalities of incomes and living standards as well as opportunities. Multi-layered, these are also mirrored in the tourism ecosystem [5]. Climate change is the major long-term problem that will affect the sustainability of many tourism ecosystems. Climate variations and extreme weather events have generated shifts in the approach towards tourism. Thus, no longer treating climate as merely a high or low season issue, it has focused on the need to address day-to-day crowding and the various economically damaging crises such as forest fires, cyclones, and tsunamis [9]. The sudden outbreak of the pandemic in 2020 demonstrated the risks inherent to human life, communities, economic systems, and the tourism ecosystem [7].

Table 2. Challenges Faced by Tourism Ecosystems.

Challenges Faced by Tourism Ecosystems	Description
Over tourism	Leads to congestion at destinations, degradation of natural and built environments, and loss of authenticity, diminished tourist experience, and reduced quality of life for host communities.
Environmental impact	Tourism industry generates pollution (e.g., traffic-related), destruction of cultural heritage, and harm to the biosphere.
Climate change	Climate variations and extreme weather events (e.g., forest fires, cyclones, and tsunamis) disrupt tourism ecosystems and impact long-term sustainability.
Income inequality	Societal inequalities in income, living standards, and opportunities are reflected in tourism ecosystems, exacerbating disparities.
Pandemic global crises	COVID-19 pandemic had caused disruptions (border closures, lockdowns, and travel restrictions) that affecting the global mobility and tourism economies.
Technological and managerial barriers	Lack of innovations, tools, and strategies hinders adaptive capacity and sustainable stewardship within tourism ecosystems.
Sustainability challenges	Requires new strategies to balance economic goals with ethical and aesthetic frameworks of sustainable tourism.

In the first decade of the twenty-first century, especially with the outbreak of the pandemic, the contentious issue that brought about various changes, and has been discussed in management literature is innovations, managerial and enterprise strategies, tools, technology, and applications for the breaking of adaptive barriers and stewardship sustainability issues [4]. The move from economic openness and globalization to a triaging of health security marked a break with patterns of travel, affecting those who derive from global mobility. As the tourism sector operates as one of the mainstays of numerous economies, its disruption within the ecosystem and the widespread disruptions it produced generated alterations to support sustainable tourism that required managerial and production strategies, within the aesthetic and ethical framework of stewardship [1, 3] behavior. Ecosystem migration occurred in terms of targets probed, strategies, high-tech, logistic systems, tools, technologies, and experiences [7].

4   Strategies for Sustainable Tourism Development

The share of research focusing on innovative solutions for the development of cultural and natural tourist ecosystems is currently confronting a variety of increasing challenges and threats. These are multifaceted and include issues related to cultural heritage preservation, the adverse effects of climate change, and the rising number of tourists that exacerbate the pressure on these delicate [12, 13]. In light of these circumstances, the development of robust and long-term strategies for managing these areas is not just beneficial but indeed an urgent necessity [14]. Strategies should be designed around the principles of environmental preservation and socio-economic sustainability, as these elements are crucial for the effective management of tourist ecosystems [15] (Table 3).

Table 3.   Strategies for Sustainable Tourism Development.

Category	Strategy	Objective
Environmental preservation	• Promotion of ecotourism in areas of natural and cultural significance • Implementation of green infrastructure • Reforestation projects • Sponge city designs and flood embankments • Green payments for environmental services • Capacity enhancements through effective catchment management	• Emphasize conservation by focusing on relatively untouched ecosystems • Support restoration and preservation of ecosystems • Restore natural ecosystems • Enhance resilience against flooding and support environmental conservation • Incentivize conservation efforts through financial mechanisms • Improve water resource management
Socio-economic Sustainability	• Community-based tourism initiatives • Promoting local culture and heritage through tourism	• Empower local residents, promote economic development, foster cultural preservation, and ensure environmental stewardship • Enhance community involvement, economic benefits, and preservation of traditions
Stakeholder Collaboration	• Fostering partnerships between governments, businesses, and community groups • Engaging stakeholders at all levels • Integrating local knowledge and practices into tourism planning	• Develop a more sustainable tourism model that benefits visitors and residents alike • Identify shared goals to create innovative solutions and enhance stakeholder collaboration • Foster cultural authenticity and support economic resilience

(continued)

Table 3. (*continued*)

Category	Strategy	Objective
Education and awareness	• Community engagement and education on sustainable practices • Promoting responsible travel practices	• Build awareness and encourage sustainable tourism behaviors • Mitigate negative impacts on natural resources and local communities
Economic development	• Ensuring local communities benefit directly from tourism revenues	• Support social and environmental Well-being through sustainable economic models

It is estimated that the tourism industry will support approximately 10% of the global GDP, along with the provision of one in every eight jobs worldwide; therefore, ensuring the sustainability and resilience of this sector is vital for the overall health of economies across the globe [16].

Ideally, tourism should not only generate substantial economic benefits for the destination community but also strive to maintain the integrity of cultural and historical sites while ensuring environmental conservation [17, 18]. Achieving an optimal balance between harnessing the economic potential of tourism as an engine for growth and safeguarding endangered tourist destinations is inherently a challenging and complex endeavor [19]. One increasingly popular strategy being leveraged to mitigate the detrimental impacts associated with traditional mass tourism is the promotion of eco-tourism in areas noted for their natural and cultural significance [20]. Protected areas, particularly insular ecosystems such as the Galápagos Islands, offer important examples where eco-tourism practices have been successfully integrated with strict conservation frameworks, supporting both biodiversity preservation and local socio-economic development. The primary focus of ecotourism revolves around travel to relatively untouched or pristine segments of the natural ecosystems, thereby emphasizing [14]. Consequently, existing literature supports and verifies the need for creating environments that prioritize restoration and preservation initiatives [12]. Strategies that aim to restore and protect natural ecosystems while maintaining profitability include an amalgamation of nature-based approaches. These strategies encompass green infrastructure, ecotourism practices, reforestation projects, as well as a blend of low-tech hybrid and high-tech applications [21]. These may include mechanisms such as green payments for environmental services, the organization of community-based tourism in strategically selected areas across various regions, and the implementation of more engineering-oriented solutions [22]. Several case studies confirm the functionality and success of these diverse strategies in promoting sustainable tourism and ecosystem preservation [23].

Several real-world projects show how the strategies discussed above have been put into practice. In the Galápagos Islands (Ecuador), ecotourism is managed through visitor limits, conservation fees, and the involvement of local communities. These measures protect biodiversity while supporting the local economy. In China, the Sponge City program uses green infrastructure to improve flood control in urban areas, including places that attract tourists [25]. In Andro Village, Manipur (India), community-based tourism has given local residents the responsibility to manage visitor activities, helping to protect the environment and preserve cultural traditions [21]. These examples show that it is possible to connect environmental protection, local development, and cooperation between stakeholders in tourism ecosystems.

5 Conclusion and Future Directions

The study emphasizes that tourist ecosystems are complex, dynamic systems that require integrated strategies for management to ensure sustainability.

Insights indicate that implementing community-based tourism, utilizing technological innovations, and encouraging cross-sector collaboration can greatly improve the sustainability of tourism systems. In addition, we must develop adaptive governance models that involve stakeholders and allow for data-informed decision-making to tackle them. Thus, we call for future studies with quantitative models for assessing the long-term effects of sustainability strategies in tourism ecosystems.

Recent examples, such as sustainable tourism initiatives in the Galápagos Islands, Sponge City infrastructure projects in China, and community-led tourism in Andro Village, demonstrate that these strategies are already being successfully applied in diverse contexts.

In the end, it will be responsible tourism practices that will enable tourism ecosystems to flourish and effectively protect their environmental and cultural assets for future generations.

Future studies must be directed to quantitative approaches to model the long-term effectiveness of sustainability strategies in tourism ecosystems. In conclusion, the scientific community cannot disentangle itself from the influences of tourism; it must work on responsible tourism practices that enable tourism elements and systems to flourish but with protection of their environmental and cultural-assets now for future generations.

References

1. Ivars-Baidal, J.A., Celdrán-Bernabeu, M.A., Femenia-Serra, F., Perles-Ribes, J.F., Giner-Sánchez, D.: Measuring the progress of smart destinations: the use of indicators as a management tool. J. Destin. Mark. Manag. **19**, 1–20 (2021). https://doi.org/10.1016/j.jdmm.2020.100531
2. Katuk, N., Ku-Mahamud, K.R., Kayat, K., Abdul Hamid, M.N., Zakaria, N.H., Purbasari, A.: Halal certification for tourism marketing: the attributes and attitudes of food operators in Indonesia. J. Islam. Market. **12**(5), 1043–1062 (2021). https://doi.org/10.1108/jima-03-2020-0068
3. Bianchi, R.V., de Man, F.: Tourism, inclusive growth and decent work: A political economy critique. In: Jamal, E.T., Higham, J. (eds.) Justice and Tourism, pp. 220–238. Routledge (2021). https://doi.org/10.4324/9781003143055
4. Garanti, Z.: Value co-creation in smart tourism destinations. Worldwide Hosp. Tour. Themes. **15**(5), 468–475 (2023). https://doi.org/10.1108/WHATT-06-2023-0070
5. Safarov, B., Al-Smadi, H.M., Buzrukova, M., Janzakov, B., Ilieş, A., Grama, V., Dávid, L.D.: Forecasting the volume of tourism services in Uzbekistan. Sustain. For. **14**(13), 1–187 (2022). https://doi.org/10.3390/su14137762
6. Buhagiar, K.: Interorganizational learning in the tourism industry: conceptualizing a multi-level typology. Learn. Organ. **28**(2), 208–221 (2021). https://doi.org/10.1108/TLO-01-2020-0016

7. Meza-Osorio, Y.T., Mendoza-González, G., Martínez, M.L.: Sun and sand ecotourism Management for Sustainable Development in sisal, Yucatán, Mexico. Sustainability. **16**(20), 1–18 (2024). https://doi.org/10.3390/su16208807
8. Rachmiatie, A., Setiawan, E., Zakiah, K., Saud, M., Martian, F.: Halal tourism ecosystem: networks, institutions and implementations in Indonesia. J. Islam. Market. **15**(11), 3247–3265 (2024). https://doi.org/10.1108/jima-09-2023-0286
9. Wang, B., Hu, C., Li, J.: Coupling and coordination relationship between the tourism economy and ecosystem service value in southern Jiangsu, China. Int. J. Environ. Res. Public Health. **19**(23), 1–17 (2022). https://doi.org/10.3390/ijerph192316136
10. Suparjo, S., Dana, Y.A., Kumala, C.M., Sunarsih, E.S.: Stakeholder collaboration in sustainable tourism development in tana toraja, South Sulawesi province, Indonesia: efforts to improve tourist visits. J. Econ. Fin. Manag. Stud. **7**(06), 3669–3677 (2024). https://doi.org/10.47191/jefms/v7-i6-58
11. Suksmawati, H., Rahmatin, L.S., Firdaus, P.: Implementation of conservation tourism in supporting the protection of the essential turtle ecosystem area at Taman Kili-Kili Beach Wonocoyo, Panggul. E-J. Tour. **9**(2), 196–209 (2022). https://doi.org/10.24922/eot.v9i2.91384
12. Trišić, I., Štetić, S., Privitera, D.: The importance of nature-based tourism for sustainable development-A report from the selected biosphere reserve. J. Geograp. Inst. Jovan Cvijic. **71**(2), 203–209 (2021). https://doi.org/10.2298/IJGI2102203T
13. Akorio, F.A., Turyamureeba, S., Tugume, A., Eze, V.H.: Rural tourism and socio-economic development in Kalapatta Sub County Kabong District of Uganda. J. Hum. Soc. Sci. **6**(1), 31–38 (2024). https://doi.org/10.36079/lamintang.jhass-0601.606
14. Nazirullah, Som, A.P., Shariffuddin, N.S., Zain, W.M., Al Qassem, A.: The influence of socio-cultural and economic impact on tourism support: A mediating role of community value. Plann. Malaysia J. **21**, 1–17 (2023). https://doi.org/10.21837/pm.v21i25.1230
15. Berondo, R.G.: The impact of socio–economic and traditional practices of the local folks in the tourism industry. Cult. Landsc. Insights. **1**(2), 57–63 (2023). https://doi.org/10.59762/cli901324531220231205131244
16. Tiwari, S., Tomczewska-Popowycz, N., Gupta, S.K., Swart, M.P.: Local community satisfaction toward tourism development in pushkar region of Rajasthan, India. Sustainability. **13**(23), 1–20 (2021). https://doi.org/10.3390/su132313468
17. Kudumoviç, L.: Cultural landscape preservation in Bosnia and Herzegovina in the frame of tourism development. TEM J. **9**(2), 740–749 (2020). https://doi.org/10.18421/tem92-42
18. Khusainova, I., Gasimova, A.A., Mammadova, I.I., Yekimov, S., Tahirzade, J.F., Khalilova, R.F., Sobirov, B.: Studying the principles of sustainable tourism development in Karabakh. BIO Web Conf. **9, 93**, 1–8 (2024). https://doi.org/10.1051/bioconf/20249305003
19. Popova, P., Petrova, M., Попов, В., Маринова, К., Сущенко, О.: Potential of the digital ecosystem for the sustainable development of the tourist destination. IOP Conf. Ser. Earth Environ. Sci. **1126**(1), 1–11 (2023). https://doi.org/10.1088/1755-1315/1126/1/012021
20. Escamis, J.E.: Community-based tourism implementation as mediator on the relationship between community participation and socio-economic sustainability of tourism. Am. J. Tour. Hosp. **2**(1), 93–104 (2024). https://doi.org/10.54536/ajth.v2i1.3629
21. Ursa, T., Arunkumar, M.C.: Residents' perceptions and outcomes of community-based tourism in andro village of Manipur. Dera Natung Govern. Coll. Res. J. **8**(1), 169–179 (2023). https://doi.org/10.56405/dngcrj.2023.08.01.12
22. Ilieva, L., Todorova, L.: Role of technological innovation for sustainable management of tourism organizations. IOP Conf. Ser. Earth Environ. Sci. **1269**(1), 1–13 (2023). https://doi.org/10.1088/1755-1315/1269/1/012038

23. Christiani, L.C., Ikasari, P.N., Nisa, F.K.: Creative tourism development through storynomics tourism model in borobudur. J. Stud. Komunikasi (Indonesian J. Commun. Stud.). **6**(3), 871–884 (2022). https://doi.org/10.25139/jsk.v6i3.4682

24. UNESCO: Conservation and Sustainable Tourism in the Galápagos Islands. UNESCO World Heritage Centre (2023) https://whc.unesco.org/en/news/2562

25. Chan, F.K.S., Griffiths, J.A., Higgitt, D., Xu, S., Zhu, F., Tang, Y.T., Xu, Y., Thorne, C.R.: "Sponge City" in China—A breakthrough of planning and flood risk management in the urban context. Land Use Policy. **76**, 772–778 (2018). https://doi.org/10.1016/j.landusepol.2018.03.005

Towards a User-Centered *Ex-Post* Evaluation: Monitoring Jubilee 2025

Antonio Magarò⬤, Antonella G. Masanotti(✉) ⬤, and Marina Tonolo⬤

Roma Tre University, Rome 00154,, Italy
antonella.masanotti@uniroma3.it

Abstract. The impact evaluation of major events on cities represents an opportunity to understand the urban and social transformations resulting from strategic interventions. The tangible and intangible legacy of such events, as demonstrated by the XXXIII Olympic Games in Paris, highlights the importance of monitoring for measuring outcomes. This monitoring originates from a broader evaluation process, spanning from *ex-ante* to *ex-post* phases. A central aspect is the definition of the user profile as a guiding framework for the assessment, ensuring that benefits and impacts are analysed from the perspective of different user categories. The Jubilee of Rome 2025 emerges as a strategic event due to the substantial investments in urban and infrastructural transformations aimed at enhancing the pilgrimage experience while also leaving a material legacy for the citizens of Rome. Accordingly, this study introduces, as a first step in the monitoring process, a classification of the main intervention categories, which is essential for an organised representation of the funding framework. Subsequently, it focuses on the User-Centered approach as a key element in constructing the user profile for ex-post evaluation, thereby ensuring an inclusive perspective. Finally, the study proposes an evaluation dashboard designed to monitor the Jubilee-related projects in Rome. In doing so, it seeks to support decision-making processes and foster a deeper understanding of urban transformations within the context of strategic interventions.

Keywords: *Ex-post* evaluation · User-centered evaluation · Rome Jubilee 2025

1 Introduction

Major events represent strategic opportunities for host countries and cities, as they enhance international visibility, attract investment, and stimulate infrastructural development. Also referred to as mega-events, they provide a significant occasion to initiate profound processes of urban transformation [1], while at the same time posing the risk of excessive touristification of the territory. The organisational aspects associated with such events require substantial public investment and involve complex decision-making dynamics that engage institutional, economic, and social actors. Indeed, public investments of this kind are often regarded as crucial catalysts for economic recovery and urban renewal, as well as effective instruments for the implementation of long-term strategic

© The Author(s), under exclusive license to Springer Nature Switzerland AG 2026
O. Gervasi et al. (Eds.): ICCSA 2025 Workshops, LNCS 15897, pp. 78–96, 2026.
https://doi.org/10.1007/978-3-031-97660-5_7

policies [2]. Cost-benefit analysis has frequently been employed for the economic evaluation of public projects. However, this method adopts a relatively narrow conception of strategic success and is not always considered a reliable tool by policymakers [3]. It is therefore essential to adopt evaluation approaches capable of integrating multiple criteria, taking into account the diverse dimensions relevant to public project management. Such approaches, including the Five Case Model[1] used in the United Kingdom [4] and sustainability impact assessments across its three dimensions [5], belong to the broader category of multi-criteria evaluations. Nevertheless, these approaches are predominantly applied in the *ex-ante* phase, relying on forecasts and assumptions, while their *ex-post* application, based on concrete data and empirical evidence, remains limited [2]. Within this framework, strategic projects linked to major events play a central role, as they generate long-term economic and territorial effects.

Furthermore, while major events can foster economic development, in highly attractive urban contexts experiencing growing tourist flows, they contribute to the ongoing debate on overtourism [6]. This phenomenon, characterised by unsustainable mass tourism practices, increasingly leads to a perception of discomfort arising from tourist saturation [7]. The progressive transformation of historic city centres is one of the most evident examples of touristification processes [8]. Certain forms of tourism fail to integrate with residents' daily lives, consequently altering the urban landscape and making the cost of living affordable only for wealthier social classes [9]. As a result, integrating Human-Centred and User-Centred approaches in *ex-post* evaluations represents a first step towards implementing an assessment system that more effectively considers the needs and well-being of users. In this regard, the survey conducted immediately after the event within the European Capital of Culture (ECoC) project, specifically analysing the case of Matera 2019 [10], proved to be a valuable tool for examining possible causal links between the levels of satisfaction expressed by the local community and the actions and programmes implemented. The findings revealed that, while the event significantly enhanced the city's tourism appeal and economic fabric, it also generated partial dissatisfaction regarding citizen participation in the programme and the redevelopment of public spaces, leading to a phenomenon of gentrification, particularly of a commercial nature. Among the most recent examples there is Paris, host city of the XXXIII Olympic Games, where an *ex-post* evaluation would be highly desirable to precisely investigate the impact of the mega-event on the city and its inhabitants [1].

For the city of Rome, major events have historically constituted a crucial opportunity for urban development and the regeneration of specific areas, giving rise to a unique process of urban evolution. This dynamic has made contemporary planning processes particularly complex, as it is necessary to reconcile the preservation of historical memory with innovation [11]. Ultimately, Rome represents an urban environment of remarkable complexity, enriched by stylistic elements and overlapping works accumulated over the centuries, the result of the stratification of different civilisations and cultures that have shaped its history [12]. The Jubilee of 2025 is undoubtedly part of these intricate dynamics and, as such, serves as the case study for this contribution.

---

[1] The Five Case Model is a decision-support method based on five evaluation dimensions: strategic, economic, commercial, financial, and managerial.

2 The Role of Ex-Post Evaluation in Major Event Projects

Systematic *ex-post* evaluations following major events are rarely conducted. Notable exceptions include the post-opening evaluation system for major projects used in Norway and the United Kingdom's Post-Opening Project Evaluation (POPE), both of which employ dedicated *ex-post* assessment frameworks to measure outcomes [13]. When carried out, such evaluations typically cover less than 5 years, while long-term assessments remain infrequent. However, they serve as valuable tools to verify whether projects have effectively delivered the expected benefits and to identify which interventions have yielded results above or below initial projections, as well as the causes of these outcomes [14].

The effectiveness of *ex-post* evaluation is particularly evident when conducted in conjunction with *ex-ante* assessments, as this allows for a direct comparison between anticipated and actual effects, thereby enabling the identification of any deviations [15]. This comparison is essential not only for assessing the accuracy of initial forecasts and the effectiveness of interventions but also for distinguishing the specific effects of public policies from those driven by external factors, which may influence project outcomes even when planning has been carried out correctly [16]. Specifically, *ex-post* evaluation can be framed at two distinct moments during the operational phase: it is possible to define an *ex-post* results analysis, which provides an account of the activities undertaken, and an *ex-post* impact assessment, conducted after an adequate time interval to evaluate direct or indirect effects.

In this context, various evaluation methods can support decision-making in the *ex-post* phase, including direct survey tools such as questionnaires and interviews, econometric modelling, cost-benefit analysis, and multi-criteria evaluation methods [17]. This paper focuses on the latter, as they can accommodate conflicting attributes within a given decision-making context [18, 19]. These attributes, also referred to as evaluation criteria, represent specific aspects that, if necessary, can be aggregated into macro-criteria or evaluation dimensions. Such criteria are defined using specific indicators, a measurement scale (quantitative and/or qualitative), and an objective function (positive or negative). In *ex-post* evaluation, the alternatives—corresponding to individual interventions—are compared based on their performance relative to the selected criteria. The aforementioned evaluation components are structured using operational tools derived from linear algebra, specifically matrices, where columns represent the criteria and rows represent the alternatives. Furthermore, both evaluation and decision-making processes must be oriented towards a specific objective, which reflects the perspective of a decision-maker (e.g., an economic operator, an interest group, a technical expert, etc.) and, if necessary, can be explored under different scenarios [20].

Adopting an evaluation approach that focuses on user perceptions and engagement is essential for a deeper understanding of the impact of major events on those who live and experience cities [21]. The assessment of effects and impacts cannot be limited to the construction of a quantitative evaluation framework; instead, it should incorporate qualitative dimensions capable of capturing the experiential and social value created for the local community [10]. To achieve this, it is necessary to integrate a User-Centred approach into the evaluation process, ensuring that the intangible costs and benefits of major events on cities and their residents are also considered [22].

2.1 Ex-Post User-Centered Evaluation

The concept of designing based on the needs of users emerged in the 1970s, developing through different methods and applications depending on the field of intervention. In the domain of computer science, Rob Kling's 1997 publication *The Organizational Context of User-Centered Software Designs* is widely regarded as the moment when the term User-Centered Design (UCD) was formally codified [23]. In the field of architecture, the UCD approach serves as both a design and evaluation methodology, involving users in all phases of project development to address their specific needs and requirements [24].

The 2019 ISO standard [25], *Ergonomics of Human-System Interaction – Human-Centred Design for Interactive Systems*, establishes principles and activities for a design process that places users at the centre, enhancing their experience through direct involvement. However, a distinction must be made between Human-Centered Design and User-Centered Design (UCD), despite their shared focus on shifting attention from the product or process being designed to the end user and their needs. The former adopts a holistic perspective, considering users' physical, mental, and emotional needs, whereas the latter takes a more functionalist approach, concentrating on the user as an operator with specific functional requirements [26].

Integrating UCD principles into *ex-post* evaluation enables a more comprehensive understanding of the impact of major events through an iterative approach that considers users' perceptions of a programme or project. This type of evaluation involves gathering subjective feedback on usability, satisfaction, the quality of the work delivered, and the impact on users' health and well-being. An evaluation system structured on multiple levels, that considers the objectives established in the *ex-ante* phase, the degree of participation, the sense of belonging developed during the event, and user perceptions in the *ex-post* phase, is crucial for a comprehensive understanding of programme outcomes. Such an approach serves as a tool for examining the relationship between the local community's satisfaction levels and the actions or programmes implemented [10].

3   The Jubilee Works in Rome

This paper aims to structure a monitoring proposal for the ex-post evaluation of major events, using the Jubilee as a case study and assessing user satisfaction.

The history of significant events in modern Rome begins with the Ordinary Jubilee of 1900 [27]. One hundred and twenty-five years later, the inauguration of the Holy Year takes place within a broader development perspective, as the city of Rome is called upon to plan the management of increasingly diverse tourist flows. The objective is to attract new market segments linked to major cultural and sporting events while simultaneously preparing for the 2025 Jubilee [28]. In this regard, the Capital city is experiencing a phase of significant expansion in the tourism sector: since the end of the Covid-19 pandemic, growth indicators have shown a positive trend, reaffirming tourism as a strategic driver of the city's economic development. In 2023, foreign tourist expenditure in Italy reached €51,688,000, marking a 16.8% increase compared to 2022 [29].

The specific interventions planned for the Jubilee primarily aim to rethink the relationship between consolidated areas, particularly the historic centre, and emerging peripheral hubs [28]. This event has already prompted the launch and partial completion of numerous construction projects, supported financially by the National Recovery and Resilience Plan (PNRR) through the *"Caput Mundi"* investment. This plan allocates substantial resources for the enhancement of Rome's archaeological, historical, artistic, and environmental heritage. Funding is directed towards coordinated interventions, including extensive conservation and enhancement works across the city. The focus is not only on Vatican City and the major basilicas but also on lesser-known religious and tourist sites, intending to restore urban decorum from both a touristic and religious perspective. At the same time, efforts are being made to improve transport services and mobility infrastructure [27].

The complexity of urban dynamics, which encompasses economic, cultural, and social dimensions [30], prevents a straightforward interpretation of their effects. Distinguishing the reciprocal influences of major events, extraordinary funding, and routine urban policies is particularly challenging. In this context, the local administration must simultaneously manage the demands of daily life, preparations for the 2025 Jubilee, and the implementation of numerous projects financed through the PNRR [27].

3.1 Funding for the Jubilee Projects

The Intervention Plan for the Jubilee 2025 aims to ensure adequate reception for the tens of millions of pilgrims who will arrive in Rome, making the city more accessible, sustainable, and inclusive [31]. For Rome, this plan represents an extraordinary opportunity, not only to guarantee the efficient management of the global influx of visitors but also to implement structural interventions capable of enhancing the city and leaving a tangible legacy for its residents. The interventions are divided into two categories: those deemed non-deferrable, to be completed in time for the Jubilee celebrations, and those essential for the long-term improvement of the city's infrastructure, which will have a lasting impact on the quality of life for both citizens and pilgrims [31] (Fig. 1).

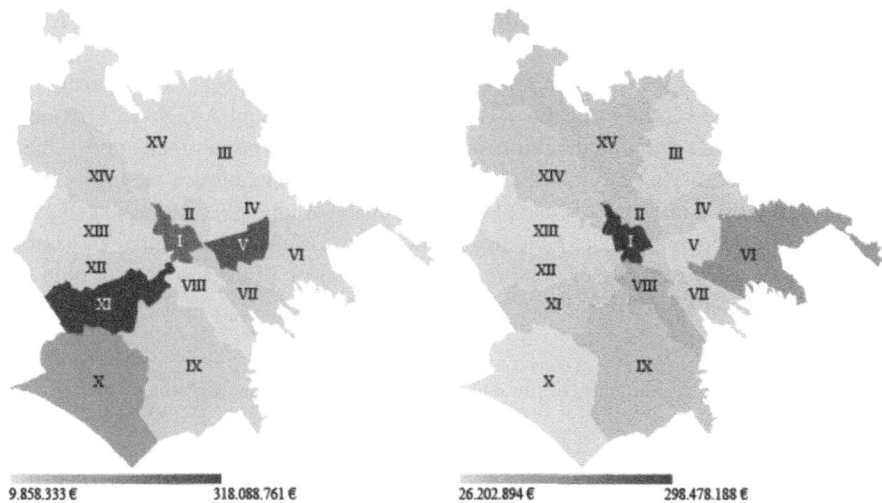

9.858.333 €   318.088.761 €   26.202.894 €   298.478.188 €

Fig. 1. Distribution of total funding by administrative Municipalities for essential interventions (left) and non-deferrable interventions (right), authors' analysis.

Table 1. Summary of intervention types by Municipality, authors' analysis.

Municipality	Essential interventions	Non-deferrable interventions
I (Centro)	227.770.089 €	298.478.189 €
II (Parioli)	14.485.594 €	44.602.758 €
III (Monte Sacro)	9.858.333 €	33.202.895 €
IV (Tiburtino)	11.433.333 €	39.352.895 €
V (Prenestino-Casilino)	264.448.665 €	30.849.561 €
VI (delle Torri)	20.558.333 €	141.454.228 €
VII (Appio-Tuscolano)	26.254.062 €	38.952.895 €
VIII (Ostiense-Ardeatino)	10.283.333 €	63.269.450 €
IX (EUR-Laurentino)	22.933.333 €	50.246.894 €
X (ostia-Acilia)	111.675.865 €	26.202.895 €
XI (Arvalia Portuense)	318.088.761 €	40.647.629 €
XII (Gianicolense)	16.505.903 €	34.393.875 €
XIII (Aurelio)	10.358.333 €	27.048.416 €
XIV (Monte Mario)	17.910.863 €	39.990.187 €
XV (Milvio)	10.933.333 €	47.310.228 €
Beyond the City of Rome	504.872.527 €	52.431.787 €
Purchase and equipments	120.349.000 €	1.030.295.309 €
Total	1.718.719.664 €	2.038.730.090 €

If the 2022 planning included a total of 88 interventions with an allocated budget of 2.337.000.000 €, the latest revision has established a total public expenditure of

4.306.249.75 €, of which 1.766.800.000 € is allocated to Jubilee grant, covering a total of 326[2] interventions.

In the history of Rome's urban transformations for past Jubilees, two recurring elements emerge: the centrality of the axis connecting Castel Sant'Angelo to St. Peter's Basilica, aimed at facilitating the influx and mobility of pilgrims, and the improvement of their routes between the city's basilicas [27]. The current Jubilee strategy can be evaluated through a mapping of funded interventions by municipal distribution (Fig. 2). Notably, within the total Jubilee funding, Municipality I dominates resource allocation, accounting for 22% of the total funding (Table 1) and 36% of the resources within the administrative boundaries of Rome's Metropolitan City.[3]

Table 2. Summary of funding by Municipality, authors' analysis.

Municipality	Total funding	Of which Jubilee funding
I (Centro)	559.581.611 €	393.198.189 €
II (Parioli)	92.421.686 €	41.172.758 €
III (Monte Sacro)	76.394.561 €	34.477.895 €
IV (Tiburtino)	84.119.561 €	39.682.895 €
V (Prenestino-Casilino)	328.631.560 €	62.619.561 €
VI (delle Torri)	195.345.895 €	93.822.228 €
VII (Appio-Tuscolano)	98.540.290 €	30.847.895 €
VIII (Ostiense-Ardeatino)	106.886.117 €	47.700.894 €
IX (EUR-Laurentino)	106.513.561 €	56.096.894 €
X (ostia-Acilia)	171.212.093 €	58.302.895 €
XI (Arvalia Portuense)	392.069.723 €	50.517.895 €
XII (Gianicolense)	84.233.111 €	35.441.495 €
XIII (Aurelio)	70.740.082 €	36.539.895 €
XIV (Monte Mario)	91.234.383 €	49.871.869 €
XV (Milvio)	91.576.895 €	57.910.228 €
Beyond the City of Rome	557.304.314 €	101.655.314 €
Purchase and equipments	1.199.444.309 €	576.941.201 €
Total	4.306.249.754 €	1.766.800.000 €

[2] The planned interventions, excluding those funded by the PNRR "*Caput Mundi*" programme, amount to 325. Therefore, it is assumed that the total number of interventions, including those financed by the PNRR, is higher.

[3] The data analysis preliminary to the mapping was conducted by the authors based on the interventions outlined in the document published by the *Osservatorio PNRR e Giubileo Roma,* available at: https://www.osservatoriopnrrgiubileoroma.it/giubileo-2025/ (Last accessed: 27 February 2025). The areas involved beyond the boundaries of Rome's Metropolitan City include the provinces of Frascati, Viterbo, and Frosinone.

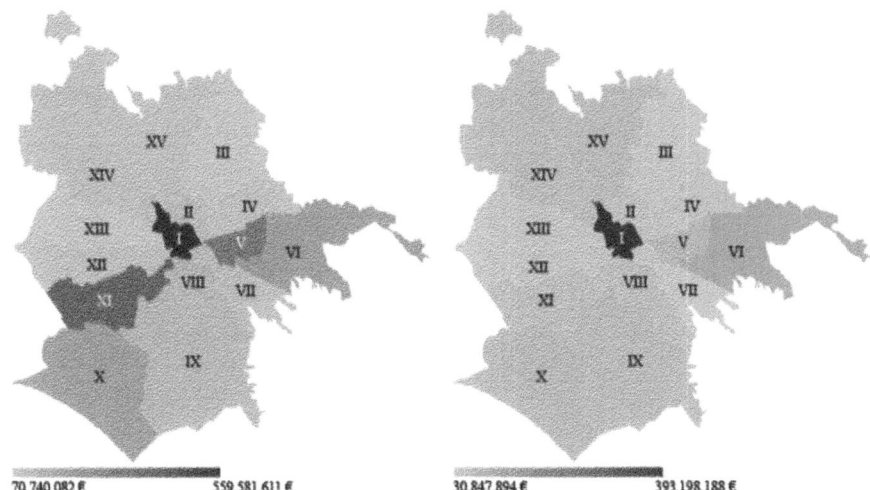

70.740.082 €   559.581.611 €   30.847.894 €   393.198.188 €

Fig. 2. Distribution of total funding (left) and Jubilee funding (right) by Municipality, authors' analysis.

For *ex-post* evaluation purposes, it is essential to identify the intervention categories (Table 2) described in the Intervention Plan for the Jubilee 2025 [31], briefly outlined below.

The thematic macro-area of Requalification and Enhancement includes 121 interventions divided into three specific domains: the requalification of public spaces, the enhancement of Jubilee sites, and the revitalisation of suburban areas. The macro-area of Accessibility and Mobility comprises 44 interventions aimed at improving accessibility and mobility both within the city and in the surrounding areas. These interventions include actions and strategies designed to strengthen public transport infrastructure, promote soft and sustainable mobility, and optimise private transport. The macro-area of Hospitality and Participation consists of 70 interventions, further categorised into: interventions dedicated to welcoming pilgrims and visitors, those focused on supporting vulnerable individuals, initiatives aimed at fostering participatory processes, and measures to enhance reception in healthcare facilities. The macro-area of Environment and Territory reflects the Jubilee's commitment to preserving and enhancing the city's natural heritage, with 24 interventions focused on water routes and parks, to integrate them harmoniously and sustainably with the urban environment and its inhabitants. The macro-area of Hospitality Programme encompasses 66 interventions divided across various sectors: public order and safety, healthcare, mobility, telecommunications, volunteering and logistics, tourism, culture, and urban maintenance. Additionally, by precisely identifying each intervention, it has been possible to map the distribution of funding across municipalities based on each thematic macro-area (Fig. 3; Table 3).

Table 3. Summary of Jubilee Funding by Thematic Macro-Area

Thematic Macro-Area	Interventions	Total Funding	Of which Jubilee Funding
Requalification and enhancement	121	976.621.050 €	717.671.321 €
Accessibility and mobility	44	1.809.631.703 €	545.776.473 €
Hospitality and participation	70	676.221.556 €	222.878.000 €
Environment and territory	24	60.965.000 €	60.400.000 €
Hospitality programme	66	278.310.446 €	215.574.206 €
Other (Rome *Caput Mundi*)	1	4.500.000 €	0 €
Total	326	4.306.249.754 €	1.766.800.000 €

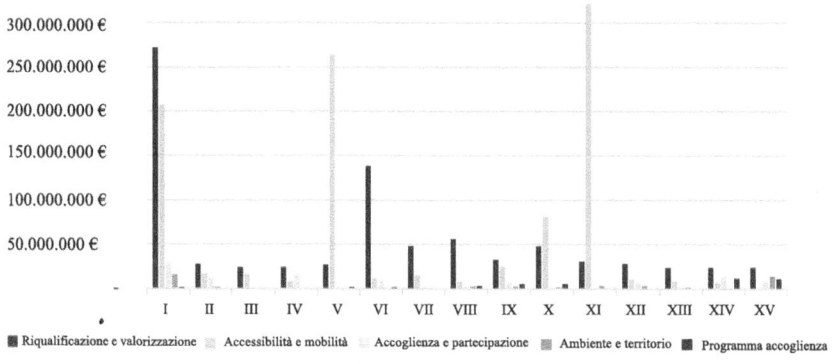

Fig. 3. Distribution of total funding by Municipality, for each thematic macro-area, authors' analysis.

It is evident that the Intervention Plan for the Jubilee 2025 represents an extraordinary opportunity for public investment in the city of Rome. With the exception of the resources allocated to Municipality I, the funding is distributed almost evenly across the territory of Rome's Metropolitan City. This is further confirmed by the high concentration of construction sites throughout the city, albeit with some differences between central and peripheral areas, reflecting the ambitious commitment to requalify and modernise the urban fabric. Not only the historic centre but also the suburbs and surrounding areas are targeted by these interventions, fostering widespread and inclusive urban transformation.[4] The Plan's cross-sectoral approach—ranging from the requalification of public

---

[4] Through the portal https://romasitrasforma.it/il-progetto, it is possible to estimate that by September 2024, approximately 400 construction sites were simultaneously active in the capital.

spaces to the enhancement of historical and cultural heritage, as well as improvements in infrastructure and services—highlights the interconnected nature of the various areas of intervention.

4   Monitoring Proposal

The analysis focuses on the impact of the interventions by adopting a User-Centered approach, assessing the material legacy anticipated by the Intervention Plan for the Jubilee 2025. The initial research results provide a preliminary evaluation of the implementation status of Jubilee projects, based on the distribution of funding by type and Municipality (Table 4).

Table 4. Progress status of Jubilee projects by type of intervention and municipal distribution, authors' analysis (The data processing was carried out based on the total amount listed in Table 1).

Municipality	Essential interventions		Non-deferrable interventions	
	Completed	Ongoing	Completed	Ongoing
I (Centro)	0%	66%	64.0%	31.5%
II (Parioli)	0%	59%	4.4%	92.3%
III (Monte Sacro)	0%	4%	3.4%	93.7%
IV (Tiburtino)	0%	13%	2.9%	92.1%
V (Prenestino-Casilino)	0%	62%	6.4%	84.1%
VI (delle Torri)	0%	2%	24.1%	64.5%
VII (Appio-Tuscolano)	0%	38%	2.9%	79.2%
VIII (Ostiense-Ardeatino)	0%	54%	25.9%	67.4%
IX (EUR-Laurentino)	0%	39%	2.3%	95.8%
X (Ostia-Acilia)	0%	9%	4.4%	92.0%
XI (Arvalia Portuense)	0%	3%	2.8%	92.5%
XII (Gianicolense)	0%	30%	3.3%	90.5%
XIII (Aurelio)	0%	9%	4.2%	83.6%
XIV (Monte Mario)	0%	2%	19.1%	72.5%
XV (Milvio)	0%	13%	2.4%	80.9%
Total	0%	34%	27.6%	65.3%

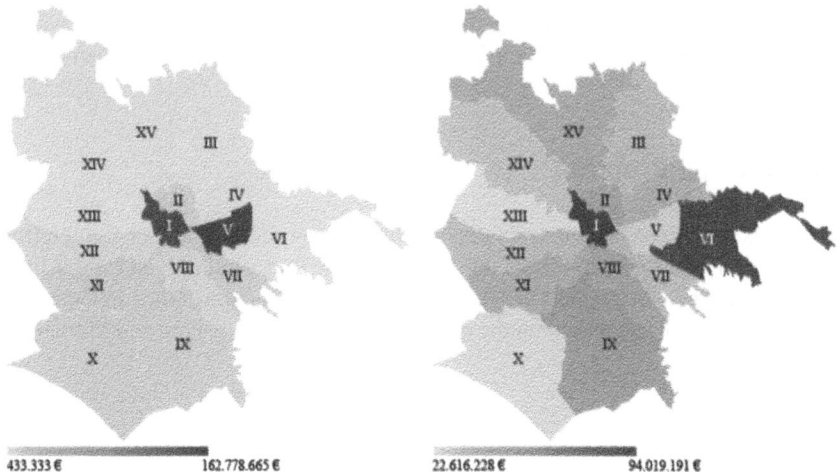

Fig. 4. Distribution of Jubilee projects under construction as of March 2025, by Municipality, with essential interventions (left) and indispensable interventions (right), authors' analysis.

Fig. 5. Archaeological Monumental Centre, Piazza di Porta Capena: ongoing, completion expected in the first quarter of 2025. Photo by the authors.

The entirety of the Jubilee projects has completed the design phase. Among the non-deferrable interventions, only 27.6% have been completed, 65.3% are in the construction phase, and the majority of works are expected to be completed between the third and fourth quarters of 2025. These projects mainly involve extraordinary maintenance of primary roads, restoration works, and infrastructural developments. The remaining 7.1% still need to complete the tendering process to award the construction contracts.[5]

In contrast, none of the essential interventions have been completed, and only 13% are currently under construction; the remaining 87% still need to finalize the tendering process. These interventions are primarily infrastructural in nature, with completion expected between 2026 and 2029 (Figs. 4 and 5).

Moreover, the research outlined the operational aspects for a future monitoring proposal, envisioning the following steps:

1. Selection of thematic areas involving funding directly allocated to the territory of Rome's Metropolitan City.
2. Definition of key aspects contributing to ex-post evaluation.
3. Assessment of impact (high, medium, low) on users for each thematic area, based on evaluation criteria.
4. Development of a set of criteria for the ex-post evaluation of each thematic area to structure the evaluation matrix.

The first phase involves defining the thematic areas to be considered for the evaluation, based on public spending carried out in the territory for Jubilee projects.[6]

For each macro-area, the completed interventions are highly diverse, both in terms of scale and type of the projects carried out. Within the thematic macro-area of Requalification and Enhancement, one of the most significant completed projects is the construction of the new underpass at Castel Sant'Angelo, along with the redevelopment of the overlying Piazza Pia, by pedestrianizing the area between Castel Sant'Angelo and St. Peter's Basilica. In the thematic macro-area of Accessibility and Mobility, one of the most important undertakings is the expansion of cycling infrastructure, with particular emphasis on a new pedestrian-cycle path linking the Monte Mario and Monte Ciocci cycle route to St. Peter's. As for the thematic macro-area of Hospitality and Participation, the establishment of a new youth hostel within the premises of the former Psychiatric Hospital of Santa Maria della Pietà in Rome, that has resulted in the creation of approximately 70 beds for pilgrims. Within the thematic macro-area of Environment and Territory, among the most impactful completed works is the creation of new riverside parks along the Tiber River, such as the park at Lungotevere delle Navi, which features a wooden walkway with rest areas and open spaces designed for educational and nature-based activities. Finally, as part of the Hospitality Programme, substantial investments have been made in the transport sector, including the renewal of regional railway lines and the acquisition of new public transport vehicles (Table 5).

The aspects contributing to the *ex-post* evaluation in the second phase are framed with the objective of assessing the overall well-being of the population. The adopted reference is the "Benessere Equo e Sostenibile" (BES) report [32], which evaluates quality of life in a multidimensional way. The areas analyzed in the report include

---

[5] The data reported are the result of a direct survey on all the interventions analysed and through consultation of the platform www.romasitrasforma.it.

[6] The following are excluded: communication areas, public order and security, essential and emergency technical services, and telecommunications related to the macro-area of the Hospitality Program.

Table 5. Definition of thematic areas and identification of interventions within the investment framework.

Thematic Macro-Area	Thematic Area	Interventions Under Evaluation	Excluded Investments	Total
Requalification and enhancement	Public space	56	4	60
	Jubilee sites	15	0	15
	Peripheries	46	0	46
Accessibility and mobility	Soft	8	0	8
	Public	16	1	17
	Private	13	6	19
Hospitality and participation	Pilgrims and visitors	18	1	19
	Vulnerable individuals	2	0	2
	Participation	15	0	15
Environment and territory	Urban decor	1	1	2
	Historical parks	3	0	3
	Tiber river	18	1	19
Hospitality programme	City maintenance	1	2	3
	Mobility	6	7	13
	Healthcare	4	2	6
	Setups	3	0	3
	Tourism and culture	3	4	7
	Volunteering	1	8	9

12 dimensions of wellbeing: "Health," "Education and training," "Work and work-life balance," "Economic Well-being," "Social relationships," "Politics and institutions," "Safety," "Subjective wellbeing," "Landscape and cultural heritage," "Environment," "Innovation, research, and creativity," and "Quality of services."

In the third phase, the evaluation grid is structured into an assessment matrix composed of thematic areas (rows) and evaluation aspects (columns). The entries in the matrix correspond to the impact on users for each thematic area based on each evaluation aspect (Table 6). The impact assessment is expressed on a three-level qualitative measurement scale (low, medium, high), thus making it possible to define a priority vector of evaluation aspects for each thematic area.

Finally, for each evaluation aspect derived from the BES report [32], criteria were defined based on the strategies adopted in the research by Bosone and Ciampa [33] and identified in the first European Commission document, *"Human-Centred City"* [34].

Table 6. Human-Centered impact matrix.

Thematic Area	1. Health	2. Education and training	3. Work and life-time balance	4. Economic well-being	5. Social relations	6. Politic and institutions	7. Safety	8. Subjective well-being	9. Landscape and cultural heritage	10. Environment	11. Innovation, research and creativity	12. Quality of services
Public space	•	○	○	•	•	•	•	•	•	•	○	•
Jubilee sites	○	.	.	•	○	•	•	○	•	•	•	•
Peripheries	•	•	•	•	•	•	•	•	○	•	•	•
Soft Mobility	•	○	•	•	.	•	.	•	.	•	.	•
Public Mobility	•	○	•	•	.	•	.	•	.	•	.	•
Private Mobility	•	○	○	•	.	○	.	○	.	○	.	.
Pilgrims and visitors	○	.	.	•	○	•	•	•	•	.	.	•
Vulnerable individuals	•	○	○	○	•	○	•	•	•	.	.	•
Participation	○	•	○	•	•	○	•	•	○	.	○	•
Urban decor	○	.	○	○	○	○	•	•	.	○	.	•
Historical parks	○	.	○	•	○	.	○	.	○	○	.	.
Tiber river	•	○	○	○	○	.	.	.	.	•	.	.
City Maintenance	•	○	•	•	○	•	•	•	.	•	○	•
Mobility	○	○	•	•	•	•	•	•	.	○	○	•
Healthcare	•	.	•	•	•	○	○	•	.	○	.	•
Setups	○	.	•	○	○	.	○	.	.	○	.	.
Tourism and culture	○	○	•	•	•	•	○	•	•	○	•	•

| • = high user impact | ○ = medium user impact | . = low user impact |

This document emphasizes the importance of citizen engagement in the planning, design, implementation, and dissemination phases of any research and innovation initiative, highlighting the critical transition toward Human-Centered cities aimed at providing equal opportunities for all (Table 7).

Table 7. Human-Centered Aspects and Criteria of the Evaluation.

Aspect	Criterion	Description
1. Health	1.1. Health-resilience plans	The impact of the intervention in improving access to healthcare services, strengthening public health.
	1.2. Circularity	The effect of circular economy practices triggered by the intervention on public health.
	1.3. Equal opportunities	The initiation of policies capable of reducing healthcare inequalities as a result of the interventions.
2. Education and training	2.1. Population training	Effects on improving the population's skills and increasing accessibility to educational opportunities.
	2.2. Bridge educational and income gaps	Reduction of disparities in access to education and economic opportunities between different territories and citizens.
3. Work and life-time balance	3.1. Governance and participatory process	Citizen engagement activated by the intervention.
	3.2. Urban inclusion	Impacts and effects on the inclusion of all individuals in urban contexts.
4. Social relations	4.1. Inclusive cities	Impact of urban works on social inclusion and the reduction of marginalization of vulnerable groups.
	4.2. Cultural diversity	Influence of interventions on social cohesion and the quality of urban lifestyle.
	4.3. Social bonding	Strengthening of social networks and solidarity within communities.
5. Politic and institutions	5.1. Citizen engagement	The level of active citizen participation in public policy development and implementation.

(*continued*)

Table 7. (*continued*)

Aspect	Criterion	Description
	5.2. Urban innovation systems	Urban innovation systems that improve quality of life and enhance service efficiency.
6. Safety and subjective Well-being	6.1. Built environment	Impact of the built environment on urban safety, psychological wellbeing, and overall quality of life.
7. Landscape and cultural heritage	7.1. Cultural and natural heritage resilience plans	Community resilience and the safeguarding of ecosystems.
8. Environment	8.1. Adaptation and mitigation	Effectiveness of interventions in reducing emissions and adapting infrastructures to climate change impacts.
	8.2. Develop resources	Efficiency in the use and management of natural, technological, and human resources, and its impact on sustainable development.
	8.3. Decarbonisation	Success in reducing CO_2 emissions and the transition to low-emission technologies.
9. Innovation, research and creativity	9.1 Infrastructure-resilience plans	Infrastructure capacity to withstand extreme events and maintain functionality during crises.
10. Quality of services	10.1 Accessible services	Accessibility of services for all individuals, ensuring equal opportunities in accessing vital resources.

Finally, the evaluation of the performance of each previously considered intervention, categorized within its respective Macro-Area (Table 8), is planned. To this end, the next implementation phase will focus on defining specific indicators for each criterion, along with identifying the essential metrics required to monitor the progress of the interventions over time and assess their effects and impacts.

Table 8. Human-centered evaluation matrix for the Macro-Area Requalification and Enhancement.

	Evaluation Aspects																		
	1.			2.		3.		4.			5.		6.	7.	8.			9.	10.
Area of intervention	1.1.	1.2.	1.3.	2.1.	2.2.	3.1.	3.2.	4.1.	4.2.	4.3.	5.1.	5.2.	6.1.	7.1.	8.1.	8.2.	8.3.	9.1.	10.1.
Public space																			
(Intervention n.)																			
Jubilee sites																			
(Intervention n.)																			
Peripheries																			
(Intervention n.)																			

5 Conclusions

In recent decades, *ex-post* evaluations of major events have raised critical concerns regarding the actual accuracy of *ex-ante* studies, especially those commissioned by event promoters, which often tend to overestimate net benefits while underestimating costs. This tendency has given rise to what economist Martin Müller [22] terms the "mega-event syndrome." The economic literature on major events questions their long-term impact on the built environment and the host city's population. Consequently, such transformations require an evaluation based on a User-Centered Design (UCD) approach, prioritizing the needs of residents and visitors alike to balance tourist appeal with daily urban livability [22].

In the case of the Jubilee Year 2000 in Rome, one major critical issue was the lack of a structured ex-post evaluation. According to Montanari [35], this absence hindered a comprehensive understanding of the long-term effects of the event's material legacy on the host city and its inhabitants. A thorough *ex-post* evaluation could have yielded valuable insights to enhance the planning and management of future events, thus ensuring long-lasting benefits for the local community.

In the context of the 2025 Jubilee, *ex-post* evaluation emerges as an essential tool, urging decision-makers to adopt sound governance practices and remain accountable for the measured impacts and outcomes of their choices. Additionally, it increases transparency concerning the event's actual results.

In the absence of structured *ex-ante* and ongoing evaluations for the current case study, the research thus far has focused on defining an evaluative framework and identifying relevant thematic areas toward a proposed *ex-post* monitoring process. The UCD approach has enabled attention to be directed toward the legacy that the Jubilee 2025 could leave behind, particularly in terms of sustainable, equitable, and inclusive urban development. One notable challenge is the limited direct comparability between expected outcomes and actual post-event results. However, by combining qualitative and quantitative techniques, it becomes possible to measure the value of urban transformations, documenting investments and project timelines in terms of urban well-being.

In this light, the contribution aims to advance a user-centered proposal, which implies active engagement of users. Therefore, when evaluating the impacts of future events, it is essential to develop consistent tools. Future developments could involve creating an instrument to assess the effects of Jubilee 2025 based on specific criteria and indicators co-designed and measured with users.

Such an approach would not only deepen the understanding of the tangible benefits and challenges linked to urban transformations but also refine the decision-making process for future events, promoting greater transparency and ensuring a long-term positive impact on the city and its residents.

References

1. Messina, G., Nicosia, E., Porto, C.M.: Mega eventi e spazi urbani: Parigi, Olympic City 2024. Documenti Geografici. **2**, 75–94 (2024)
2. Volden, G.H., Welde, M.: Public project success? Measuring the nuances of success through ex post evaluation. Int. J. Proj. Manag. **40**(6), 703–714 (2022)
3. Volden, G.H.: Assessing public projects' value for money: an empirical study of the usefulness of cost–benefit analyses in decision-making. Int. J. Proj. Manag. **37**, 549–564 (2019)
4. HM Treasury: Public Sector Business Cases Using the Five Case Model: Green Book Supplementary Guidance on Developing Public Value from Spending Proposals. HM Treasury (2013)
5. OECD: Guidance on Sustainability Impact Assessment. OECD Publishing, Paris (2010)
6. Mohanty, P.P., Mishra, N.R.: Overtourism in religious places: is it a myth or a journey towards faith, a reflection from Golden triangle (Bhubaneswar-Puri-Konark) of Odisha, India. In: Sharma, A., Hassan, A. (eds.) Overtourism as Destination Risk: Impacts and Solutions, pp. 235–260. Emerald, Leeds (2021)
7. Colomb, C., Novy, J.: Protest and Resistance in the Tourist City. Routledge, London (2016)
8. Celata, F.: La "Airbnbificazione" delle città: gli effetti a Roma tra centro e periferia. Memotef, Roma (2017)
9. Celata, F., Romano, A.: Overtourism and online short-term rental platforms in Italian cities. In: Platform-Mediated Tourism, pp. 70–89. Routledge, London (2022)
10. Salone, C., Arfò, F.: Città e grandi eventi: il programma Matera Capitale Europea della Cultura 2019 nella percezione dei resident. Rivista Geografica Italiana. **2020**(3), 5–29 (2020)
11. Insolera, I., Berdini, P.: Roma moderna. Due secoli di storia urbanistica. Nuova edizione ampliata, Einaudi, Turin (2024)
12. Maggioli, M.: Paesaggi urbani. In: Morri, R., et al. (eds.) Piazza Tiburtino III. Società Geografica Italiana, Rome (2012)
13. Nicolaisen, M.S., Driscoll, P.A.: An international review of ex-post project evaluation schemes in the transport sector. JEAPM. **18**, 1650008 (2016)
14. de Jong, G., Vignetti, S., Pancotti, C.: Ex-post evaluation of major infrastructure projects. Transp. Res. Procedia. **42**, 75–84 (2020)
15. Pennisi, G.: Tecniche di valutazione degli investimenti pubblici, 2nd edn. Istituto Poligrafico e Zecca dello Stato, Libreria dello Stato, Rome (1991)
16. Bezzi, C.: Glossario della ricerca sociale e valutativa. Rassegna Italiana di Valutazione. **11** (2011)
17. Bottero, M., Mondini, G., Oppio, A.: Decision support systems for evaluating urban regeneration. Procedia. Soc. Behav. Sci. **23**, 923–928 (2016)
18. Miccoli, S., Finucci, F., Murro, R.: Assessing project quality: A multidimensional approach. Adv. Mater. Res. **1030-1032**, 2519 (2014)
19. Diana, L., D'Auria, S., Acampa, G., Marino, G.: Assessment of disused public buildings: strategies and tools for reuse of healthcare structures. Sustain. For. **14**, 2361 (2022)

20. Borsos, A., Finucci, F., Gyergyák, J., Masanotti, A.: Evaluation in green building design for conversion projects: case studies and comparative approaches. E3S Web Conf. **436** (2023)
21. Bianchini, F., Albano, R., Bollo, A.: The regenerative impacts of the European City/Capital of Culture events. In: Leary, M.E., McCarthy, J. (eds.) The Routledge Companion to Urban Regeneration, pp. 515–526. Routledge (2013)
22. Gruppioni, G.: I grandi eventi e i loro benefici: analisi del caso Expo Milano 2015. Master's Degree Thesis. Università Ca' Foscari Venezia (2017)
23. Kling, R.: The organizational context of user-centered software designs. MIS Q. **1**(4), 41 (1977)
24. Cellucci, C., Di Sivo, M.: F.A.AD. CITY "Città Fiendly, Active, Adaptive". University Press, Pisa (2018)
25. ISO 9241: Ergonomics of human-system interaction - Part 210: Human-centred design for interactive systems. (s.d.)
26. Tartaglia, A.: Human/user-centered design. In: Baratta, A., Conti, C. (eds.) Manifesto lessicale per l'Accessibilità Ambientale. 50 parole per progettare l'inclusione, Anteferma, Conegliano, pp. 190–193 (2023)
27. Morri, R., Pallottino, C.: The Rome of "great events": mapping and diachronic analysis at the city-territory scale. The impact of a century and a half of extraordinary interventions. Documenti Geografici. **2**, 95–123 (2024)
28. Bozzato, S.: Re-think Rome, re-generate the peripheries. The Jubilee 2025. Documenti Geografici. **2**, 125–141 (2024)
29. Federalberghi: Il barometro del turismo (2024). Disponibile da: https://www.ebnt.it/studi-e-ricerche/osservatori/osservatorio-barometro-del-turismo-di-federalberghi/, last accessed 27 Feb 2025
30. Finucci, F., Masanotti, A.G., Mazzoni, D.: Preliminary evaluation approaches in the urban regeneration of Corviale in Rome. Lect. Notes Netw. Syst. **1186**, 128–141 (2024)
31. Decreto del Presidente del Consiglio dei Ministri (DPCM) dell'11 giugno 2024. Relazione illustrativa. Disponibile da: https://www.osservatoriopnrrgiubileoroma.it/giubileo-2025/, last accessed 27 Feb 2025
32. ISTAT: BES 2023. Il benessere equo e sostenibile in italia. Istituto Nazionale di Statistica, Roma (2023)
33. Bosone, M., Ciampa, F.: Human-centred indicators (HCI) to regenerate vulnerable cultural heritage and landscape towards a circular city: from the Bronx (NY) to Ercolano (IT). Sustain. For. **13**(10), 5505 (2021)
34. European Commission: The Human-Centred City: Opportunities for Citizens through Research and Innovation. European Commission, Luxembourg (2019)
35. Montanari, A.: Grandi eventi, marketing urbano e realizzazione di nuovi spazi turistici. Bollettino della Società Geografica Italiana. **XII**(7), 757–782 (2002)

Overtourism and Hostile Architecture: Preliminary Assessments of the Effects in Major Italian Cities

Adolfo F. L. Baratta[1]([✉]) [iD], Daniele Mazzoni[1] [iD], and Valeria Tatano[2] [iD]

[1] Roma Tre University, 00154 Rome, Italy
adolfo.baratta@uniroma3.it
[2] Iuav University of Venice, 30135 Venice, Italy

Abstract. The term *overtourism* is used when the number of visitors in each location becomes disproportionate to the capacity of the site to sustainably manage tourist flows. According to the United Nations World Tourism Organization (UNWTO), overtourism denotes the negative impact of tourism on a destination, affecting both the visitor experience and, more significantly, the quality of life of residents.

To better assess the impact that overtourism has had on major Italian cities over the past decade, it is essential to understand the political strategies implemented by local administrations and the resulting urban and social transformations.

City administrators in the most attractive tourist destinations have adopted solutions that encourage tourist consumption while contributing to the displacement of residents. Among these strategies, hostile architecture stands out as a measure designed to control and influence the behaviour, attitudes, and well-being of specific groups of people within public spaces.

In this context, several aspects can be evaluated: the weakening of local public transportation (explicit hostile architecture), the removal or alteration of benches (implicit hostile architecture), the disappearance of public restrooms (denied architecture), and other similar interventions.

After establishing the general framework of reference, this study presents an assessment based on direct survey techniques, aiming to preliminarily identify the impact of overtourism-induced discomfort on tourist decision-making. This type of consultation, targeting key industry stakeholders as well as directly affected individuals both tourists and residents focuses on hostile solutions to foster a deeper understanding of the ongoing transformations.

Keywords: Overtourism · Hostile architecture · Public spaces · Preliminary assessments

1 Overtourism as a Phenomenon of Urban Decay

The term *overtourism* is used when the number of visitors in each location becomes disproportionate to the site's capacity to sustainably manage tourist flows. According to the United Nations World Tourism Organization (UNWTO), overtourism denotes the negative impact of tourism on a destination, affecting both the visitor experience and, more significantly, the quality of life of residents.

O. Gervasi et al. (Eds.): ICCSA 2025 Workshops, LNCS 15897, pp. 97–113, 2026.
https://doi.org/10.1007/978-3-031-97660-5_8

Tourist overcrowding is a phenomenon that has affected many European cities in the last decade, leading to problems in the management of people (residents and visitors), spaces and services. Tourist activities generate important material and immaterial transformations determined by the need to organise and design activities that require the provision of places capable of welcoming, transforming, visitors.

Cities such as Venice, Barcelona, Amsterdam, and Dubrovnik exemplify destinations that have faced substantial challenges related to overtourism. In Dubrovnik, for instance, the influx of tourists has led to a rise in the cost of living, infrastructure congestion, and a gradual loss of local identity. Barcelona has witnessed protests by residents lamenting their displacement from neighborhood due to rising rents and the conversion of residential properties into tourist accommodations. Amsterdam has implemented measures such as restrictions on short-term rentals and the promotion of lesser-known areas to better distribute tourist flows.

Overtourism, primarily driven by the growth of global tourism and the widespread promotion of low-cost travel offers, significantly impacts the quality of life in the historic centers of Italian cities, regardless of their geographic location or size. In Venice's historic center, fewer than 50,000 residents remain, yet on certain days, visitor numbers exceed 80,000, with 80% consisting of day-trippers. The consequences include environmental degradation, damage to cultural heritage, and a decline in residents' quality of life.

The effects of overtourism manifest in various ways, including environmental deterioration particularly pronounced in fragile contexts such as Venice the loss of cultural authenticity due to the disappearance of local traditions, infrastructure overload, and an increase in both the cost of living and urban decline. These factors contribute to the depopulation of historic centers and the migration of residents toward peripheral areas.

To better assess the impact that overtourism has had on major Italian cities over the past decade, it is crucial to examine the political strategies adopted by local administrations and the resulting urban and social transformations. In many cases, the massive influx of tourists has compelled local governments to implement measures aimed at managing tourist flows and mitigating their negative effects on the urban and social fabric.

To counter the effects of overtourism, administrations in the most affected cities have increasingly resorted to measures such as raising tourist taxes, introducing daily entrance fees, and imposing restrictions on tourist access. At the regional level, an additional strategy involves promoting alternative, lesser-known destinations to redistribute tourism. Short term rental regulations have also been introduced, as exemplified by the city of Florence, which has been actively enforcing a ban on the opening of new short-term rental properties in its historic center.

Overtourism represents a complex challenge for Italy, necessitating a balance between the economic benefits of tourism and the imperative to preserve cultural heritage, the environment, and residents' quality of life. Through careful planning and the implementation of sustainable strategies, it is possible to mitigate negative effects and ensure that future generations can continue to appreciate the country's rich cultural and natural beauty.

2   Hostile Spaces and Architectures

As highlighted by a study conducted by United Cities and Local Governments (UCLG), "public space is the place where all citizens, regardless of their income or personal circumstances, can feel equal and cared for" [1].[1]

However, in his book "Defensible Space, People and Design in the Violent City" [2], Oscar Newman develops the idea that crime can be controlled and prevented through the proper design of collective spaces and the management of public property. The book examines the social dynamics within public spaces associated with large residential complexes, focusing on the Pruitt-Igoe neighbourhood in St. Louis, built in 1954, which became notorious for its high crime rates, severe poverty, and racial segregation. Newman highlights how public spaces were vandalized in contrast to the care and attention given to private spaces. Based on these observations, he argues that it is possible to create environmental conditions that act as a deterrent to crime.

The instrument of control can therefore be identified in environmental governance, understood as the extent to which individuals' needs and expectations are acknowledged and addressed.

Barriers, walls, and fences have long been used to divide and protect spaces by keeping out unwanted individuals or enclosing others [3]. The built environment can thus be modified to restrict or complicate the actions of certain individuals. These are not arbitrary decisions or design flaws but rather strategies and solutions aimed at discouraging behaviours deemed undesirable and at limiting or excluding certain groups of people, with the stated goal of protecting public space, maintaining order, and preventing deviant behaviours and crime [4, 5].

Hostile architecture, therefore, seeks to keep out individuals who, more than others, rely on public space because they lack a private one such as homeless individuals and young people. Hostile architecture, understood as both the built environment and urban spaces with their associated furnishings, constitutes a system of strategies designed to limit undesirable behaviours in cities. Different categories and varying intensities of hostile architecture exist. A distinction can be made between explicit or overt hostility, which prevents the use of a space or its furnishings unless at the risk of personal discomfort or harm, and implicit or latent hostility, which renders their use inconvenient.

The first category includes gates, spikes, and sharp protrusions placed on walking surfaces, windowsills, or parapets to prevent individuals from lingering or sitting. These interventions are particularly recognizable, as their presence appears incongruous with the surrounding context and is often visually unappealing. A clear example is a recent intervention in Rome ahead of the 2025 Jubilee Year, in Viale Petroselli, where a fence has been installed near the Aurelian Walls to prevent homeless from gathering (Fig. 1).

---

[1] "That public space is where all citizens, regardless of their income and personal circumstances, can feel equal and cared for".

The second category includes benches specifically designed to make lying down or sleeping impossible, or at the very least highly uncomfortable. Their seating surfaces are often interrupted by armrests, contoured, inclined, or made slippery, while some feature extremely low backrests. These strategies are intended to discourage such practices but ultimately render the benches uncomfortable for all users (Fig. 2). These solutions, which may go unnoticed by those who do not regularly frequent a certain space, are referred to as *silent agents* precisely because of this characteristic.

To the two previously mentioned categories, one must add the strategy of *negation*. For instance, removing seating from railway stations is certainly more effective and cost-efficient than modifying benches, as it directly eliminates a functionality for all individuals. However, such a drastic measure creates inconvenience for the entire community, particularly for elderly people or individuals with disabilities who may require resting spots when moving through public spaces.

Fig. 1. Installation of a gate near the Aurelian Walls in Rome to prevent homeless from settling (Author: Daniele Mazzoni).

At times, these strategies can significantly alter the configuration of public space, reshaping the very structure of places. A particularly concerning example is the strategy implemented in 2022 by the Municipality of Rome to prevent homeless individuals from resting. The intervention, as show in Fig. 3 below, involved sealing the openings between the pillars of the Pettinelli underpass at Termini Central Station in Rome, designed by the architect and engineer Angiolo Mazzoni del Grande.

Although practices aimed at protecting public spaces from perceived threats posed by their users are neither new nor unique, the solutions and justifications employed to achieve these objectives have proliferated in recent years [6].

Wave-shaped, bent, or broken benches, speed bumps and deterrents to curb illegal parking or skateboarding, barriers against terrorist actions, and metal spikes to prevent sitting these elements are scattered across our cities, shaping our behaviours, sometimes to correct misconduct, other times merely in response to basic human needs, with very different approaches.

Fig. 2. Public bench with "anti-loitering" armrests in Gallarate (Author: Daniele Mazzoni).

Since 2007, the Municipality of Verona has installed armrests on public benches to make them "anti-loitering," effectively preventing their use as overnight accommodation for homeless [7, 8]. In contrast, in 2018, the city of Ulm introduced *Ulmer Nests* [9], small capsules placed in parks to provide shelter for homeless suffering from the harsh German winters.

Hostile architecture has a negative impact on the well-being of many people, but it is particularly harmful to the most vulnerable groups. It is undeniable that its negative effects outweigh its benefits. Making an urban environment inhospitable fosters isolation and marginalization, ultimately making life "a little worse for everyone" [10] and diminishing the potential for generating social value [11].

Removing benches from areas with high tourist density has an additional consequence: denying tourists the possibility to sit and rest means forcing them to sit in bars and restaurants, turning them into paying consumers of outdoor seating that occupy the same public spaces from which they are excluded.

A similar effect occurs with the limited availability of public restrooms, which, when available, are not properly advertised by cities as services for both tourists and residents, who once again resort to public establishments.[2]

Fig. 3. Sealing of openings between the pillars of the Pettinelli underpass, near Termini Central Station in Rome (Author: Daniele Mazzoni).

---

[2] In the case of Venice, information about the location and availability of public sanitary facilities is spread across several web pages, making it difficult to quickly locate them. https://www.comune.venezia.it/it/content/igiene-urbana, last accessed 2 March 2025.

3   Hostile Architecture as a Tool for Conditioning Tourists and Limiting Residents

If it is true that "by introducing changes to the environment that enhance accessibility, it is possible to positively influence a person's well-being, their ability to develop their life plan, and their direct and personal participation in collective life and the growth of society" [12], it is equally true the opposite.

Among the measures adopted by the public administration, hostile architecture has emerged as a controversial tool, used not only to influence the behaviour of tourists but also to limit access to and use of public spaces by residents and vulnerable groups, such as homeless people. These strategies are therefore implemented to control and influence the behaviour, attitudes, and health of specific groups within public spaces. Such measures are primarily adopted in the central areas of cities, where there are many tourist attractions and consequently the flow of people is higher. The effect produced is often a de-naturalisation of the historic centre, accentuated by the adoption of solutions that encourage tourist consumption, thereby contributing to the expulsion of residents.

The economic influence of tourism-related activities has led local administrators, particularly in cities lacking a substantial alternative productive sector, to adopt tools for conditioning tourists, even at the expense of residents. Strategies are therefore employed that lead to the elimination of neighbourhood retail stores in favour of souvenir shops, pizza slices, ice cream parlours, and minimarkets. The result is that visitors are conditioned to "consume" the city as economic operators, rather than "living" it by immersing themselves beneath its surface.

Residents, weary of the spaces, services, and consequently the life that is offered to them in such a context, choose to leave the historic centres in favour of areas where they can, at least partially, find the conditions that are missing in their places of origin. This represents a new form of mobility that links tourism to short-distance migration, simultaneously changing the actors and the relationship between temporary inhabitants and urban spaces. In doing so, the desire for interaction both emotional and social between temporary inhabitants and the places and their residents is wiped out and leads the residents themselves to use 'hostile' solutions to protect themselves from the excess of tourists (Fig. 4, 5).

Mass mobility, whether it involves daily visitors such as commuters or tourists, brings a growing and diverse number of city users: this widening of the user base leads people with more fragmented lifestyles to compete for already limited public space, making the design and management of such spaces more complex. The complexity of redefining the qualities of these spaces involves a multidimensional consideration, an integrated vision [13], the implications of which are varied and require the optimisation of resources [14].

Tourism thus induces the transformation of places, generating new urban spaces and new architectures, becoming one of the main agents in the process of globalisation, which can be identified in the dominant trend towards standardisation, facilitated by the information and transportation technologies widely used in the sector [15].

Carolina Gestri points out that while "the tourists of the Grand Tour collected and recorded on-site the peculiarities of the landscape" [16], thereby identifying the distinctive characteristics of Italy, those whom Boris Groys refers to as "the artists of the post-romantic era," using modern communication tools, are not forced to adapt "to the tastes and cultural orientations of the local population" [17].

Tourists, increasingly seeking a genuine experience of daily life rather than specific cultural attractions, look for residents and their usual gathering places, while the residents themselves are pushed out of such places and forced to seek new spaces that are not overrun by tourists [18].

Public space thus becomes the arena in which these lifestyles are consumed, and administrators are forced to adopt strategies to manage and enhance spaces for the public good.

Fig. 4. Deterrent installed on the entrance steps of a private studio in Venice to prevent tourists from sitting (Author: Valeria Tatano).

Fig. 5. Installation of a gate in a 'public' alley in Venice to prevent tourists and daily visitors from misusing the space (Author: Valeria Tatano).

4   The Impact Assessment of Overtourism and the Conditioning of Hostile Architecture

The assessment and monitoring of the impact of overtourism has become crucial to highlight how this phenomenon contributes to altering value systems, behaviours, attitudes, perceptions, and organisational structures within cities [19]. According to statistical analysis conducted on the previous year, the Centre for Tourist Studies in Florence has reported a continued growth in tourism within Italy, estimating a 2.5% increase in arrivals compared to 2023 [20]. This equates to over 458.5 million overnight stays, with tourists predominantly coming from abroad. This figure confirms the trend of recent years, with the previous year surpassing levels reached before the Covid-19 pandemic.

In Italy, the Observatory on the Demographics of Enterprises in Italian Cities has been monitoring the development of commercial establishments and accommodation and catering activities since 2015, observing how these clusters move within urban centres and peripheral areas. The Observatory analyses changes in the municipal network of consumer services and the resulting issues, such as the risk of commercial desertification and crises within urban economies. The scope of the analysis is sufficiently broad, as it includes 120 medium- and large-sized municipalities, which together are home to 13.4 million inhabitants, approximately 23% of the Italian population.

Between 2012 and 2023, the analysis by the Observatory in Italian cities and historic centres has focused on:

– Retail trade related to eleven product categories, including food products, household goods, toys, clothing and footwear, cultural items, pharmacies, tobacco, etc.
– Accommodation services, such as hotels and bed & breakfasts, and catering services, such as bars and restaurants.

It emerges that, from the 120 municipalities under analysis, over 110,000 retail stores and 24,000 street trading activities (-17%) have been deactivated. This phenomenon is only partially due to the decline in population, which has decreased by 2%, and more so to the increase in accommodation services driven by tourist flows [21].

The constant trend over the last decade is therefore a contraction in the number of active businesses in retail trade and a strong growth in accommodation and catering activities. Notably, there has been an exponential growth in bed & breakfasts in the historic centres of the South (+168%) and Central-Northern regions (+87%). The result is commercial desertification, which diminishes the liveability and attractiveness of our cities (Table 1).

To counter this phenomenon, actions are needed that recognise proximity economies as a public interest service[3] and sustainable urban regeneration projects that enhance public spaces. For the enhancement and regeneration of urban areas, such as neighbourhood markets, and a more effective management of urban mobility and logistics, it is necessary to restore the balance between the various uses of the city.

Table 1. Percentage variation in the number of retail, accommodation, and food service units in some of the main historic centers in Italy (Data for Milan, Naples, and Rome are not available because these are multicentric cities, where it is not possible to distinguish between the historic center and non-historic areas.)

Historic Centre	Retail trade (%)	Accommodation and restaurants (%)
Bologna	−21.31	+21.74
Florence	−18.94	+14.08
Palermo	−41.34	+72.88
Turin	−22.14	+2.28
Venice	−19.46	+15.23

---

[3] It is interesting to note that half of the new foreign employment in Italy's entire economy comes from these sectors: approximately 240,000 new jobs, which makes commerce the main avenue for integration for foreigners.

Only recently have initiatives been launched to combat commercial desertification in Italian cities, promoting the development of the social value of proximity economies.

4.1 Tools and Methods: Direct Observation Techniques

To better understand the impact of urban transformations carried out in cities, often through the adoption of hostile architectures, on the quality of life of residents and the quality of the visit for tourists, an analysis is proposed using direct observation techniques. This methodological approach allows for the collection of empirical data useful for assessing perceptions, critical issues, and the socioeconomic implications of the strategies adopted. Such a tool becomes essential, especially when evaluation processes are linked to the decision support system [22].

The choice of the type of observation should be made in relation to the context, the objective to be achieved, and the type of research to be conducted, which can be either qualitative or quantitative. Specifically, qualitative research proves capable of answering questions that traditional quantitative methods cannot or can only do so in a limited and non-exhaustive manner [23]. These observations are carried out using direct consultation techniques, which involve critically listening to the opinions of different individuals to expand the knowledge base related to the problem being evaluated. Among the most used techniques in the literature are formal consensus techniques, focus groups, interviews, and questionnaires. The following are the definitions of these techniques outlined by Foglia and Vanzago [23]:

- Formal Consensus Techniques: (Consensus Conference, Nominal Group Technique, Delphi Method, etc.): Consensus-building techniques play a specific role and are applied to support the decision-making process when the research context is characterised by a lack of scientific evidence, or when such evidence is not demonstrated or fully shared, or when there are contradictions regarding the evidence itself or the sources that generated them. In such cases, the frameworks are not fully defined, and there is a need to find a reference point or shared guidelines.
- Focus Group: this involves a discussion conducted among a limited number of experts in the presence of an evaluator, usually supported by a facilitator, with the aim of describing the nature and main dimensions of a problem.
- Interviews: qualitative interviews are, therefore, "extended" conversations between the researcher and the interviewee, during which the researcher aims to obtain as detailed and in-depth information as possible on the research topic.
- Questionnaire: an observational tool used to quantify and compare information collected from a population sample chosen according to the characteristics of the evaluation.

In this paper among the aforementioned methods, the use of a questionnaire was selected. Two different questionnaires were developed, one for residents and one for tourists, to assess the impact of overtourism and hostile architecture in cities from the perspectives of both residents and visitors. Specifically, as shown in the following Table 2, the questionnaire for residents was divided into 4 sections, while the one for tourists was divided into 3 sections.

Table 2. Organization and structure of the questionnaire administered to residents and tourists.

Questionnaire for resident

Section 1: Respondent profile

Q. 1	Which category best represents your age?	Multiple answer
Q. 2	What is your level of education?	Multiple answer
Q. 3	Which is your employment?	Multiple answer
Q. 4	What city do you live in?	Open answer
Q. 5	What part of the city do you live in?	Multiple answer
Q. 6	How many years have you lived in this city?	Multiple answer

Section 2: Overtourism and quality of life

Q. 7	Have you perceived a significant increase in tourism in your city in recent years?	Multiple answer
Q. 8	What are the most obvious impacts of overtourism on daily life in your city?	Multiple and open answer
Q. 9	Do you think your city's current policies are effective in managing tourism?	Multiple answer
Q. 10	Have you ever thought of moving to another area or city because of excessive tourism?	Multiple and open answer

Section 3: Hostile architecture and urban transformation

Q. 11	Have you ever noticed changes in public space that make the city less accessible or welcoming?	Multiple and open answer
Q. 12	Have these changes negatively affected your quality of life?	Multiple answer
Q. 13	Have any Airbnb's recently opened in the building where he lives?	Multiple answer
Q. 14	Do you think these transformations are designed more to regulate tourism than to improve the lives of residents?	Multiple answer

Section 4: Improvements and suggestions

Q. 15	Do you think that the increase in tourism has pushed some residents to leave the city?	Multiple answer
Q. 16	What strategies should administrations adopt to better balance tourism and urban quality of life?	Multiple and open answer
Q. 17	What aspects of your city would you like to see improved for residents?	Open answer

Questionnaire for resident

(*continued*)

Table 2. (*continued*)

Section 1: Respondent profile		
Q. 1	Which category best represents your age?	Multiple answer
Q. 2	What is your level of education?	Multiple answer
Q. 3	Which is your employment?	Multiple answer
Q. 4	What is your country of origin?	Open answer
Section 2: Overtourism, Quality of Experience, and Hostile Architecture		
Q. 5	Are you just starting your visit or about to leave?	Multiple and open answer
Q. 6	How many times have you visited this city?	Multiple answer
Q. 7	How would you rate the level of crowding in the city you visited?	Multiple answer
Q. 8	How would you rate the level of crowding at the tourist sites you visited?	Multiple answer
Q. 9	How much has overcrowding affected your travel experience?	Multiple answer
Q. 10	Have you noticed elements in public spaces that make the city less accessible or welcoming?	Multiple and open answer
Q. 11	Have you noticed structures designed to prevent people from stopping or resting in the city you visited?	Multiple answer
Q. 12	In which contexts have you noticed the use of hostile architecture the most?	Multiple and open answer
Section 3: Improvements and suggestions		
Q. 13	Has the presence of hostile architecture affected your travel experience?	Multiple answer
Q. 14	Do you plan to visit this city again in the future?	Multiple answer
Q. 15	If you answered 'no' or 'I don't know,' what are the main reasons?	Multiple and open answer

4.2 Assessment Results

The total number of responses collected from both administered questionnaires amounts to 245, specifically 170 from residents and 75 from tourists. It is important to emphasize that, to refine the evaluation, particularly concerning the analysis of the data referring to the first category of respondent's, responses have been categorized based on the respondents' city of residence. This classification was conducted according to the size and tourism attractiveness of the city. Specifically, data were gathered from the cities of Rome, Florence, and Venice.

The first assessment presented concerns the perception of increased tourism. As illustrated in Fig. 6, in all cases examined, over 80% of the surveyed residents perceived, either moderately or significantly, a notable increase in tourism.

This increase also affects the impacts of overtourism on residents' daily lives. Among the most prominent consequences are rising rental costs, changes in the types of commercial services available, overcrowding in public spaces, and, most notably, the loss of authenticity and transformation of neighbourhoods.

It is particularly interesting to analyze the relationship between the area of residence within the city and the perception of increasing tourism. Taking as an example the responses from residents of Rome, only 11% of those who perceived an increase in tourism reside in the historic city center, while 52% live in the semi-central area (defined as the area adjacent to the historic center), 32% in the peripheral area, 3% in the suburban area, and 2% in the extra-urban zone.

These findings highlight that the perception of increasing tourism is not solely an issue affecting historic city centers.

As outlined in previous sections, the administrations of major art cities are implementing different policies related to tourism management, which, in most cases, also have significant repercussions for residents.

Over 75% of respondents to the questionnaires concerning residents of Rome, Florence, and Venice believe that their cities' policies are ineffective in managing tourism, with more than 30% advocating for stricter measures. When such policies affect the configuration of public space, they often make the city less accessible and welcoming. Among the most frequently observed changes reported by residents are the removal or reduction of seating and benches, the installation of devices to restrict certain uses, the placement of barriers to limit access to specific areas, and the closure or removal of public sanitary facilities. As illustrated in Fig. 7, in all cases examined, over 70% of respondents stated that these spatial changes have negatively impacted their quality of life.

The most striking case is that of Florence, where 18% of respondents reported a significant impact, 73% noted a mild impact, and only 9% stated that these changes had no effect on their quality of life.

To refine the evaluation of the questionnaires administered to tourists, responses from individuals who had visited or were in the process of visiting Rome, Florence, and Venice were taken into consideration, accounting for 88% of the total responses received.

The first data finding aligns with the initial assessment of residents' responses regarding the perception of increasing tourism. Specifically, 27% of tourist respondents stated that the city they visited was extremely crowded, 51% considered it very crowded, 14% moderately crowded, and only 8% slightly crowded.

The issue of overtourism, therefore, also affects tourists themselves, worsening the quality of their visit. Indeed, 12% of respondents reported that overcrowding had an extreme impact on their experience, while 42% indicated a significant effect. However, city overcrowding was not the only factor influencing the quality of the visit.

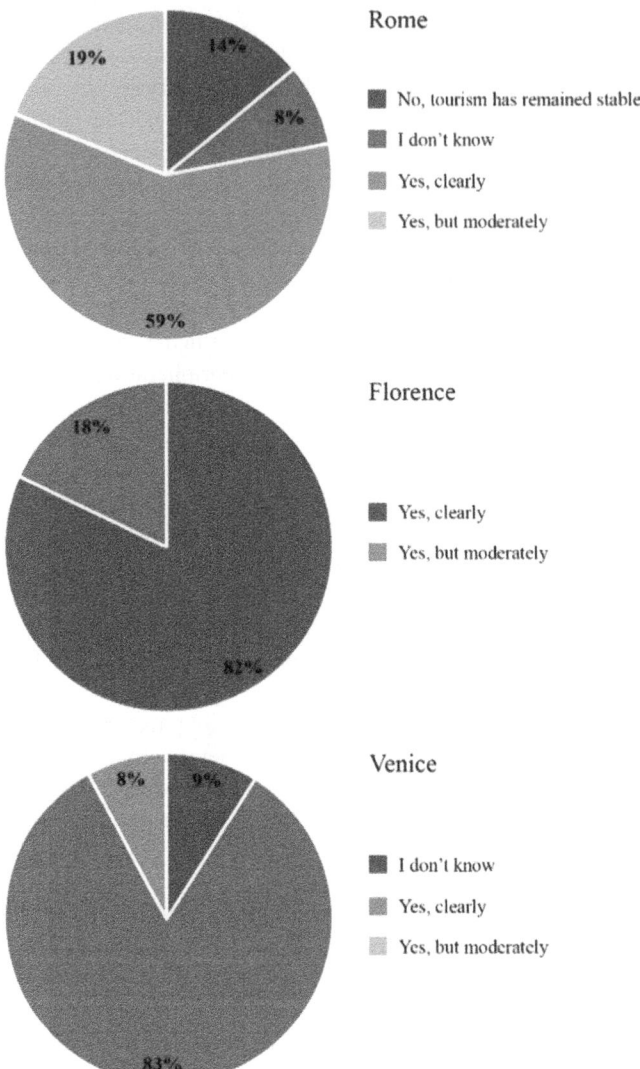

Fig. 6. Perception of the increase in tourism in the cities of Rome, Florence, and Venice (Data processing: Daniele Mazzoni).

As show in Fig. 8, 59% of tourists reported that the presence of hostile architecture negatively affected their experience, with 9% describing the impact as highly negative.

This finding highlights the increasing visibility of hostile architecture within cities. This is further confirmed by the fact that 67% of visitors stated that they had noticed such structures, particularly near public transport stops, in squares and public spaces, or in the vicinity of monuments and tourist attractions.

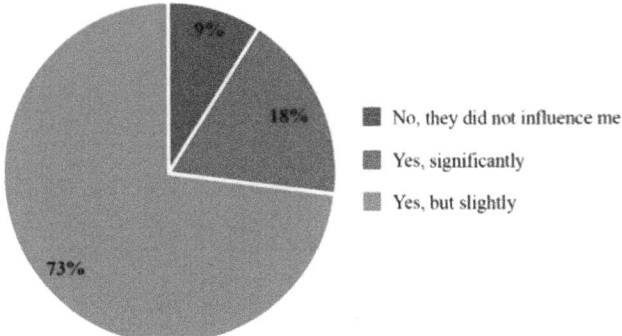

Fig. 7. Impact of spatial changes in the cities of Rome, Florence, and Venice on residents' quality of life (Data processing: Daniele Mazzoni).

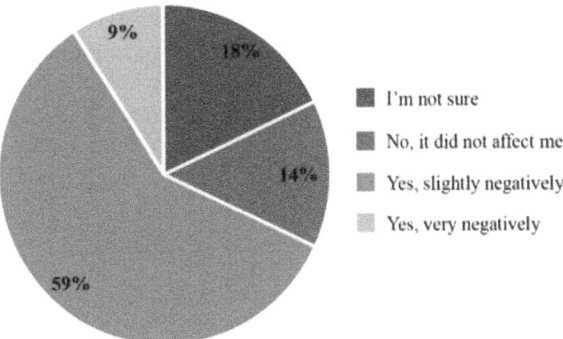

Fig. 8. Impact of hostile architecture in the cities of Rome, Florence, and Venice on the quality of the visitor experience (Data processing: Daniele Mazzoni).

5   Conclusion

Although this research allows only for preliminary reflections, the results emerging from the questionnaires, whose administration is ongoing to enhance representativeness, already provide valuable insights for further consideration. As a concluding remark, it is important to highlight a particularly alarming finding from the evaluation: the need for more effective policies that consider the needs of both tourists and residents. Notably, 24% of resident respondents stated that they are considering relocating to another area or city. The complexity of cities and public spaces cannot be addressed solely through restrictions; rather, it requires a broader vision and interventions that safeguard everyone's right to access and enjoy these spaces. This approach aligns with the principles of inclusive architecture, which seeks to meet the needs of the widest possible audience [24].

While 66% of tourist respondents intend to visit the city again, 34% are either uncertain or have already decided not to return (Fig. 9).

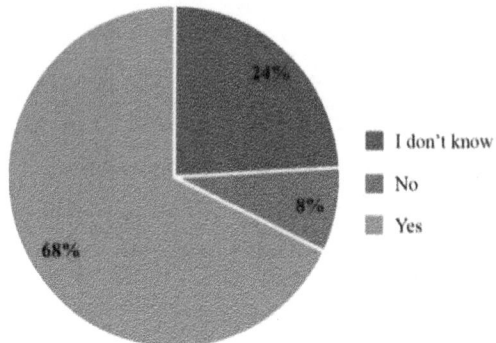

Fig. 9. Percentage of tourists intending to revisit the city in the future (Data processing: Daniele Mazzoni).

Among the main reasons cited by tourists who responded negatively to the question, *"Do you plan to visit this city again in the future?"*, the most prominent, aside from the high cost of the visit, include the perception that the city is overly crowded (46%), and that the presence of hostile architecture makes the environment unwelcoming (39%).

This analysis clearly underscores the need to rethink urban public space as a place where both residents and tourists recognise not only their rights but also their responsibilities, fostering an approach in which tourists are regarded as temporary citizens rather than mere consumers. The solution must involve reimagining tourism, its related activities, residents, and the services essential to them as integral parts of the city's ecosystem rather than as competing interests.

A fundamental objective, as noted by Pietro Garau, is to "adopt an urban strategy centred on public space [...], a place where all citizens, regardless of their income or personal circumstances, can feel equal and cared for" [1]. Many administrations are implementing strategies aimed at decentralising tourism by enhancing the attractiveness of peripheral areas of the city. This approach aligns with the urban model of well-established smart cities, promoting urban regeneration processes, improving neglected areas, and revitalising the outskirts [25].

References

1. Garau, P.: Public space. In: Think Piece. UCLG, Barcelona (2014)
2. Newman, O.: Defensible Space: People and Design in the Violent City. Architectural Press (1973)
3. Baratta, A., Tatano, V.: Hostile architecture. In: Baratta, A., Conti, C., Tatano, V. (eds.) Lexical Manifesto for Environmental Accessibility: 50 Words for Designing Inclusion, pp. 73–78. Anteferma Edizioni (2023)
4. Savic, S., Savicic, G.: Unpleasant design: designing out unwanted behaviour. In: Proceedings of the 5th STS Italia Conference: A Matter of Design, pp. 975–988. Making Society Through Science and Technology (2014)
5. Binnington, C., Russo, A.: Defensive landscape architecture in modern public spaces. Riv. Res. Landsc. Archit. **19**(2), 238–255 (2022)

6. Petty, J.: The London spikes controversy: homelessness, urban securitisation, and the question of hostile architecture. Int. J. Crime Justice Soc. Democr. **5**(1), 67–81 (2016)

7. Comune di Verona: Homepage. https://ufficiostampa.comune.verona.it/nqctent.cfm?a_id=9561&id_com=29908, last accessed 20 Feb 2025

8. Tatano, V.: Panchine per tutti tra inclusione e design ostile. In: Atti del convegno Specie di Spazi, Conegliano, pp. 46–53. Anteferma (2023)

9. Ulmer Nest: Homepage. http://www.ulmer-nest.de, last accessed 20 Feb 2025

10. Andreou, A.: Anti-homeless spikes: sleeping rough opened my eyes to the city's barbed cruelty. The Guardian. (2015). https://www.theguardian.com/society/2015/feb/18/defensive-architecture-keeps-poverty-unseen-and-makes-us-more-hostile, last accessed 20 Feb 2025

11. Acampa, G., Pino, A.: Village repopulation: analysis of extra-economic indicators to evaluate and valorise social generativity in ecovillages. In: Lecture Notes in Networks and Systems, vol. 1186, pp. 257–266. LNNS (2024). https://doi.org/10.1007/978-3-031-74679-6_25

12. Lauria, A.: Environmental design & accessibility: notes on the person-environment relationship and design strategies. Dent. Tech. **13**, 55–62 (2017)

13. Finucci, F., Masanotti, A.G., Mazzoni, D.: Preliminary evaluation approaches in the urban regeneration of Corviale in Rome. Lect. Notes Netw. Syst. **1186**, 128–141 (2023). https://doi.org/10.1007/978-3-031-74679-6_13

14. Acampa, G., Pino, A.: Optimal computing budget allocation for urban regeneration: an unprecedented match between economic/extra-economic evaluations and urban planning. In: Lecture Notes in Computer Science (including subseries Lecture Notes in Artificial Intelligence and Lecture Notes in Bioinformatics), vol. 14112, pp. 69–79. LNCS (2023). https://doi.org/10.1007/978-3-031-37129-5_6

15. Di Campli, A., Gabbianelli, A.: The design tourist space: strategies of ephemerality and rootedness. GOtoECO (2016)

16. Gestri, C.: Touring through the frontiers of forms. Kabul Magazine, pp. 1–7. (2016). https://www.kabulmagazine.com/il-turismo-attraverso-i-confini-delle-forme/

17. Groys, B.: Art power. Postmediabooks, Milan (2012)

18. Richards, G.: Rethinking Cultural Tourism. Edward Elgar Publishing, Cheltenham (2021)

19. Fluperi, S.: The tourist-resident relationship in the Po Delta context: first definition of a measurement tool. Tour. Psychol. **1**, 61–76 (2008)

20. Centro Studi Turistici Firenze: Homepage. https://centrostudituristicifirenze.it/ricerca/studi-rapporti/, last accessed 20 Feb 2025

21. Bella, M.: Cities and business demographics. In: Paper Presented at the 9th Edition of the Conference on Business Demography in Italian Cities, Rome (2024)

22. Finucci, F., Masanotti, A.G.: Crowdmapping: inclusive cities and evaluation. In: Lecture Notes in Computer Science (including subseries Lecture Notes in Artificial Intelligence and Lecture Notes in Bioinformatics), vol. 14112, pp. 80–90 (2023). https://doi.org/10.1007/978-3-031-37129-5_7

23. Foglia, E., Vanzago, A.: Methodology and Methods of Qualitative Research. Center for Research in Economics and Management in Health and Social Services (2011)

24. Clarkson, P.J., Coleman, R.: History of inclusive design in the UK. Appl. Ergon. **46**, 235–247 (2015)

25. Baratta, A.F.L., Mariani, M., Mazzoni, D.: The National Innovative Program for housing quality (PINQuA): strategies and indicators for design quality. In: Lecture Notes in Computer Science (including subseries Lecture Notes in Artificial Intelligence and Lecture Notes in Bioinformatics), vol. 14104, pp. 635–646 (2023). https://doi.org/10.1007/978-3-031-37105-9_42

Sustainable Development of Ports (SUSTAINABLEPORTS 2025)

Assessing Ship Emissions: An Estimation Approach Applied to the Port of Catania (Italy)

Antonio Barbagallo[1]([✉]), Vincenza Torrisi[2]([✉]), Stefano Ricci[3], Elen Twrdy[4], and Matteo Ignaccolo[1]

[1] Department of Civil Engineering and Architecture, University of Catania, Viale Andrea Doria, 6, 95125 Catania, Italy
antonio.barbagallo@phd.unict.it
[2] Department of Electrical, Electronic and Computer Engineering, University of Catania, Viale Andrea Doria, 6, 95125 Catania, Italy
vincenza.torrisi@unict.it
[3] Department of Civil, Construction and Environmental Engineering, Sapienza University of Roma, 09129 Rome, Italy
[4] Faculty of Maritime Studies and Transport, University of Ljubljana, Pot pomorščakov 4, 6320 Portoroz, Slovenia

Abstract. In recent years, reducing emissions from maritime transport has become a priority for many port cities. Indeed, ships are a significant source of pollutants such as carbon dioxide (CO_2), nitrogen oxides (NOx), sulphur dioxide (SO_2), particulate matter (PM) and other pollutants that contribute to air pollution and climate change. The problem is particularly relevant in ports, where ships spend long periods at berth with their engines running to keep on-board systems running, an operational phase known as hoteling. To address this problem, there are different methods of monitoring ship emissions. One approach is direct monitoring, which involves the use of sensors that are installed on ships or in the vicinity of port areas to measure the amount of pollutants being emitted. Although it provides very accurate data, this approach involves high costs and requires specialized equipment. Another methodology is the fuel consumption-based emission inventory, which uses data declared by ship operators. However, this approach may be affected by inconsistencies in reporting and does not always provide precise emission estimates for specific ship activities and operating conditions. In this work, emissions are estimated using available data, including technical characteristics (such as gross tonnage, engine power, etc.) and ship operational information (such as arrival and departure times, dwell time, etc.). Special attention is paid to the time at hoteling, i.e. the period during which the auxiliary engines remain active while the ship is at hoteling, as it contributes significantly to the total emissions. The estimation is based on regression curves and considers variables such as load factor and pollutant-specific emission factors. The necessary information was obtained from databases such as the Automatic Identification System (AIS) and international studies. In this context, the port of Catania was chosen as a case study to analyze the contribution of Ro-Ro ships to local emissions. This type of ship, used to transport vehicles and rolling stock, is among the main sources of pollution. Estimates show that fuel consumption and emissions vary significantly depending on the size and frequency of ship trips, highlighting the importance of

© The Author(s), under exclusive license to Springer Nature Switzerland AG 2026
O. Gervasi et al. (Eds.): ICCSA 2025 Workshops, LNCS 15897, pp. 117–130, 2026.
https://doi.org/10.1007/978-3-031-97660-5_9

targeted strategies to reduce environmental impact. This analysis thus provides a useful framework for understanding the dynamics of maritime pollution and represents a first step towards a more detailed and in-depth quantification of emissions, taking the selected case study as a reference.

Keywords: Vessel emissions · Maritime transport · Air quality · Estimation models

1 Introduction

Maritime transport plays a key role in global trade and economic development, enabling the movement of goods and passengers over long distances. However, it is also a significant source of air pollution, contributing to emissions of carbon dioxide (CO_2), nitrogen oxides (NOx), sulphur oxides (SOx), particulate matter (PM) and other harmful pollutants [1]. These emissions, mainly generated by marine engines and fossil fuel combustion, have serious environmental implications, especially in coastal and port areas where shipping activities are concentrated [2].

Among the various operational phases of ships, hoteling, i.e. the period during which ships remain docked with their auxiliary engines running to ensure power on board, is one of the main causes of local pollution [3, 4]. This problem is particularly relevant in ports located near urban centers [5, 6], where ship emissions directly affect air quality and public health [7, 8]. Indeed, emissions in ports are a growing challenge for environmental sustainability, which has integrated the environmental impact of ports into European and international policies [9, 10]. In this context, reducing emissions is closely linked to the Sustainable Development Goals of the 2030 Agenda [11], including Goal 11 (Sustainable cities and communities), Goal 13 (Combating climate change) and Goal 9 (Industry, innovation and infrastructure) [12]. Measures such as dock electrification (cold ironing) [13], the use of clean fuels, logistical optimisation and emissions monitoring are now key tools for the greening of ports [14, 15].

In this context, effective methods for assessing and estimating ship-generated emissions are essential for the definition of effective operational strategies and environmental policies [16]. Several approaches have been explored [17], including direct monitoring through sensors installed on board ships or in port areas, and indirect methods based on fuel consumption data [14, 18]. Although direct monitoring offers high accuracy, it requires specialized equipment [15, 19] and many ports cannot afford to install sensors due to the high costs associated with their purchase, maintenance, and operation [20, 21]. On the other hand, emission inventories based on fuel consumption may be subject to inconsistencies in reported data, limiting the accuracy of emission estimates for specific activities and operating conditions [22].

In this regard, we proposed a data-efficient approach based on the work of Albo-López et al., 2023 [23] to estimate the emissions generated by Ro-Ro vessels during the hoteling phase in the port of Catania. The choice of this specific case study is based on several reasons: the port of Catania is a medium sized port with mainly Ro-Ro traffic, a characteristic common to many ports in the Mediterranean basin, making it representative for the validation of the proposed model. These conditions allowed a solid application experiment, useful to verify the effectiveness of the method in a realistic operational context. The approach adopted is based on a bottom-up methodology with low information requirements, based on the use of ship technical and operational data (AIS), and is designed to be replicable in other port contexts, both nationally and internationally. It allows not only to estimate emissions as a function of docking time, but also to assess the relative influence of variables such as ship size and docking time.

It is characterized by low data requirements, relying on the technical characteristics of ships and on operational data. The approach uses information provided from the Automatic Identification System (AIS) and emission estimation models to quantify the environmental impact of ship operations. Additionally, it assesses the relative influence of various factors, such as ship size and the time spent in port, on emission levels.

The reminder of the paper is organized as follows: after the introduction in Sect. 1, Sect. 2 analyses the case study of the port of Catania, describing its geographical and operational characteristics and the importance of Ro-Ro traffic in this area. After that, in Sect. 3, the methodological approach is detailed through the data collection process, the emission estimation models and the use of regression analysis to refine the calculations. The results obtained, summarised in Sect. 4, highlight the main trends in emissions and the reliability of the estimation methods applied. Finally, the study concludes with a discussion of possible implications and indications for future research aimed at improving the accuracy of the estimates and supporting more sustainable maritime policies.

2   Case Study

2.1   Territorial Framework

Within this section we introduce the analyzed case study of the port of Catania, a strategic infrastructure for maritime traffic in the Mediterranean basin, located on the east coast of Sicily (Fig. 1).

The strategic geographical position of the port of Catania extends its influence over the entire regional territory. As an important hub, it supports a land area represented by six of the nine Sicilian provinces, with a total population of three million inhabitants [24]. Its management falls under the jurisdiction of the Port System Authority of the Sea of Eastern Sicily, which also oversees the port of Augusta.

The port of Catania is located close to the historical city center, a characteristics that has influenced both urban development and local socio-economic dynamics (Fig. 2). This proximity creates opportunities for port-city integration, while also posing challenges in spatial planning and historical heritage preservation. Moreover, it raises concerns about pollutant emissions and their impact on urban air quality. The main sources of emissions in the port include docked ships, cargo handling activities and associated vehicular traffic. This study focuses on the docking phase, which has the greatest influence on the emission impact.

In this context, the port of Catania represents a particularly important case study: its strategic location, proximity to the city centre and the nature of its predominantly ro-ro traffic make it an emblematic example for assessing the local impact of ship emissions. These characteristics, together with the possibility of accessing operational data,

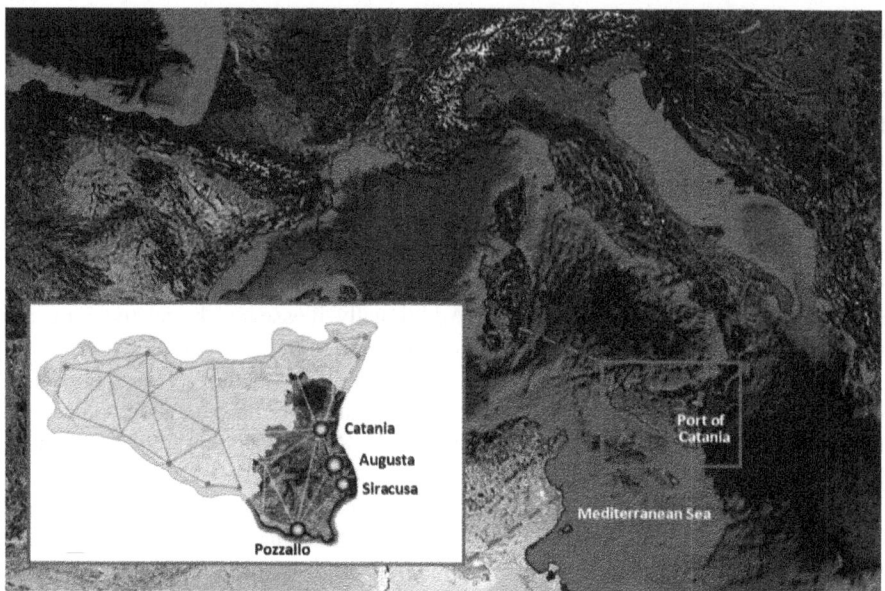

Fig. 1. Territorial framework. Source: Author elaboration from Google Earth

Fig. 2. Port layout and proximity to the city center. Source: Author elaboration from Google Earth

make it an ideal test-bed for testing replicable estimation methods in ports with similar configurations.

2.1.1 Traffic

The port of Catania has a total area of approximately one million squares meters (i.e. land and water areas). The land areas cover 470,000 sqm, the cargo storage yards 280,000 sqm and the total length of the berths of the 26 operational quays is 4200 ml.

It is characterized by predominantly handling Ro-Ro (Roll-on/Roll-off) ships, as well as ferries and cargo units. A total volume of around 7.5 million tons was recorded in 2023, handling over 6.6 million tons for Ro-Ro, followed by containers (around 528,000 tons) and dry goods (over 419,000 tons). The number of containers handled, expressed in Twenty-foot Equivalent Units (TEUs), was 53,212, (Table 1).

Table 1. Traffic within the Port of Catania. Source: Port Authority System [24]

	2020	2021	2022	2023
TOTAL TONS	8.324.867	8.064.127	7.862.342	7.585.488
LIQUID GOODS tons	0	0	0	0
DRY GOODS tons	342.724	373.203	355.995	419.842
GENERAL CARGO tons	7.982.143	7.690.924	7.506.347	7.165.646
Of which				
Container	568.429	557.413	499.225	527.954
Ro-Ro	**7.413.714**	**7.133.511**	**7.004.137**	**6.637.329**
Other	0	0	2.985	363
NUMBER OF SHIPS	1.551	1.380	1.392	1.410
PASSENGER SHIPS RO-RO RO-PAX	56.945	8.118	5.553	4.682
CRUISE PASSENGERS	4.673	12.273	154.152	221.558
Disembarked/embarked in port	711	730	34.454	57.696
In transit	3.962	11.543	119.698	163.862
NUMBER OF CONTAINERS (in TEU)	62.177	58.471	51.666	53.212

The Port Authority's strategy for the future is to further diversify traffic. The plan is to increase the share of dry bulk and containers and gradually reduce the dependence on liquid bulk, which is traditionally less sustainable. An important step in this direction is the transfer of container traffic to the Port of Augusta, which has more space and infrastructure better suited to this type of activity.

From an infrastructure point of view, significant measures are being implemented to improve the port's competitiveness. These include the rehabilitation of the commercial dock and a dock electrification project. With an investment exceeding €56 million, the electrification initiative will reduce ship emissions while at dock, contributing to the port's environmental sustainability.

As stated above, the Port of Catania is an important hub for Ro-Ro transport, allowing the rapid movement of trucks and trailers between Sicily and the rest of the Mediterranean, reinforcing the port's role in the Motorways of the Sea (from Italian "Autostrade del Mare"). The timing of operations for these Ro-Ro ships can vary depending on several factors, including the specific type of operation carried out and the frequency of sea connections [25, 26]. This variability adds complexity to the estimation of emissions, as it can influence the ship's hoteling time within the port. In this regard, we propose a data-efficient approach based on real data provided by the Automatic Identification System (AIS).

3   Methodological Approach

We propose an estimation approach, which uses ship-specific data to estimate port emissions from one of the operational phases, i.e. the hoteling one. The method considers the structural characteristics of the ships and the operational parameter linked to the hoteling phase, retrieved from AIS data. Among those, we consider (i) the *time of hoteling (T_h)*, and (ii) the *Gross Tonnage (GT)*.

The methodological approach is characterized by three phases:

1. Data collection;
2. Model emission estimation;
3. Estimation using regression curves.

3.1   Data Collection

Structural characteristics and operational parameter of ship is retrieved from AIS data, collected through the Vessel Finder platform [27]. AIS provides a wide range of information, which can be divided into three main categories: static data, dynamic data, and operational data. For this work, the *Gross Tonnage (GT)* which represents a measure of a ship's internal volume and can influence energy consumption and emissions during the hoteling phase. It has been directly exported by AIS data. Additionally, we retrieved other information such as the dimensions of the ship in terms of length and width, drawing which indicates how deep the ship is in the water and depends on the cargo carried, Deadweight (DWT) which is the total carrying capacity of the ship and IMO number, as the unique identification code of each ship. These data provide an overview of the main characteristics of each ship, useful for identifying cargo capacity, size and international registration.

We also collected the *time of hoteling (T_h)*, which refers exclusively to the duration of the berthing phase, during which the ship remains at the berth with the auxiliary engines running to ensure on-board services (hoteling). It does not include the waiting, manoeuvring or handling phases. This choice is motivated by the fact that emissions from auxiliary engines during the hoteling phase are a significant contributor to local pollution in ports..

3.2 Model Emission Estimation

Typically, commercial ship estimations are estimated based on each trip, considering the different phases of the journey: cruising, maneuvering and hoteling. In this work, the hoteling phase is considered in relation to the cruising and maneuvering phases because, while the latter involve movement and operations at sea that generate emissions, the hoteling phase occurs when the ship is stationary in port, using auxiliary engines (AEs) to generate electricity powering onboard services. During this phase, the ship continues to consume fuel and emit pollutants without moving, making it a significant source of local pollution, which is especially relevant for ports located near city centers, as in the case study analyzed.

The estimation of the emissions for AEs during hoteling phase $E_{Hoteling,\,i}$ is calculated with Eq. (1), according to [23]:

$$E_{Hoteling,i} = \frac{T_h P_{AE} LF_{AE} EF_i}{10^3} \tag{1}$$

where:

i: pollutant (NOx, SO2, CO2, VOC, PM, CO, N2O);

T_h: time for hoteling (h);

P_{AE}: auxiliary engine nominal power (kW);

LF_{AE}: auxiliary engine load factor;

EF_i: emission factor of "i" pollutant (kg/kW).

From the World Fleet 2010, which relates to Ro-Ro Cargo ships we calculate power of the installed main engine P_{ME} as a function of GT [22] (Eq. 2):

$$P_{ME}(kW) = 164{,}578 \cdot GT^{0,4350} \tag{2}$$

Then, to obtain the auxiliary engine power for hoteling P_{AE}, P_{ME} must be multiplied by the estimated average auxiliary/main engine ratio (AE/ME) of 0.24, again according to Trozzi per ship type [28].

The accuracy of port emission estimates is highly dependent on the reliability of the emission factors available in the literature, which have significant uncertainties related to vessel type, engine and operating conditions. For the purposes of this paper, emission factors have been taken from [29], which presents a recent and comprehensive study related to emission factors considering the above mentioned features. For ships docking in European ports, ships with engines that can only use marine fuel with a sulphur content limit of 0.1% by mass, such as marine gas oil (MGO) of 0.1%, are considered, (Table 2). Furthermore, for the sole purpose of comparing results due to uncertainty in emission factors, other emission factors from different literature sources are used, in particular the emission factors for hoteling for auxiliary engines from 'USA EPA 2009', (Table 3) [30] and 'ENTEC 2010', (Table 4) [31].

3.3 Estimation Using Regression Curves

Finally, emission estimation based on regression curves is used to establish empirical relationships between the technical parameters of ships and generated emissions.

Table 2. AE emission factors (g/kWh) for hoteling. Source [29].

Engine/Fuel Type	NOx	PM10	PM2.5	SOx	CO_2	VOC	CO	N2O	CH4
Medium-speed/0.1% MGO	12.2	0.19	0.17	0.42	696	0.4	1.1	0.029	0.008

Table 3. AE emission factors (g/kWh) for hoteling USA EPA 2009. Source [30]

Fuel Type	NOx	PM10	PM2.5	SOx	CO_2	VOC	CO
0.1% MGO	13.9	0.18	0.17	0.42	690.71	0.4	1.1

Table 4. AE emission factors (g/kWh) for hoteling ENTEC 2010. Source: [31]

Engine/Fuel Type	NOx Pre-2000 Engine	NOx Fleet Average	SO_2	CO_2	VOC	PM10-PM2.5
Medium-speed/0.1% MGO	13.9	13	0.9	690	0.4	0.3

The main objective of using regression is to create a model that allows emissions to be estimated from readily available variables. This approach is useful when direct data on ship-specific emissions are not available.

The reliability of the model is assessed through statistical indicators, Correlation coefficient R^2 and standard error of the regression.

4   Implementation and Results

The emission estimation was conducted on Ro-Ro vessels operating in the port of Catania, focusing on the hoteling phase, during which the auxiliary engines remain switched on to produce electricity.

First, AIS data were collected from the ships that called at the port of Catania and among those, only Ro-Ro Cargo ships were selected. These data refer to a 10-day period between October and November 2023 (Table 5):

As shown in the table, ships are generally similar in size, except for EcoItalia, which belongs to a new generation. According to Eq. (2) we calculated P_{ME}, and by multiplying it for the estimated average auxiliary/main engine ratio (AE/ME) we obtained P_{AE} (see Table 6). From Fig. 3 it can be observed that also for EcoItalia, the P_{AE} is higher than other ships.

Once P_{AE} for each ship was obtained, the estimation of $E_{Hoteling, i}$ of Ro-Ro ships was carried out using Eq. (1) (Table 7), considering a (LF$_{AE}$) of 0.4 corresponding to the stay in port (i.e. hoteling) [23], in applying emission factors from the Port of Los

Table 5. Structural characteristics and operational parameter of selected Ro-Ro ships. Source: Authors' Data Retrieval from VesselFinder.com

Ship list	length/width	Drawing	GT [t]	DWT [t]	N. IMO	T_h [h]
ECO ITALIA	238 / 34 m	6.9 m	67,311	18,080	IMO 9859612	46
EUROCARGO ALEXANDRIA	201 / 26 m	7.6 m	32,843	10,773	IMO 9465540	20
EUROCARGO CATANIA	193 / 26 m	6.3 m	29,429	11,320	IMO 9503627	55
EUROCARGO MALTA	200 / 26 m	7.3 m	32,841	10,787	IMO 9465514	66
EUROCARGO ROMA	200 / 26 m	7.5 m	32,839	10,786	IMO 9465526	24
EUROCARGO SAVONA	193 / 25 m	6.4 m	29,429	11,415	IMO 9457191	57
EUROCARGO VENEZIA	200 / 26 m	7.8 m	32,841	10,765	IMO 9465552	37

Table 6. Estimated power consumption of main and auxiliary engines (kW).

Ship list	P_{ME} [kW]	P_{AE} [kW]
ECO ITALIA	20729.52	4975.08
EUROCARGO ALEXANDRIA	15171.36	3641.13
EUROCARGO CATANIA	14464.02	3471.37
EUROCARGO MALTA	15170.95	3641.03
EUROCARGO ROMA	15170.55	3640.93
EUROCARGO SAVONA	14464.02	3471.37
EUROCARGO VENEZIA	15170.95	3641.03

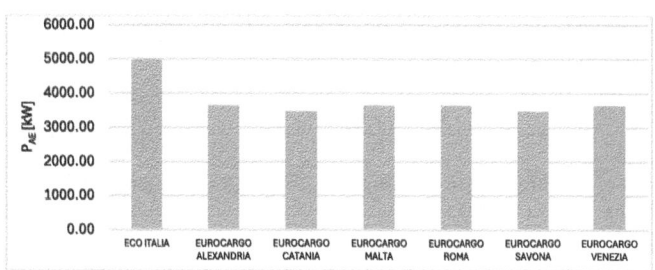

Fig. 3. Auxiliary engines' consumed power (kW)

Angeles 2020 [29]. Results are summarized in Table 7, which provides an overview of the contribution of this category of ships to port air pollution.

Table 7. Emissions (t) estimated from engine power by the emission factors of 'Port of Los Angeles 2020'.

Ship list	Nox [t]	PM10 [t]	PM2.5 [t]	SOx [t]	CO_2 [t]	VOC [t]	CO [t]	N_2O [t]	CH_4 [t]	Total per Ship [t]
ECO ITALIA	1.12	0.02	0.02	0.04	63.71	0.04	0.10	0.00	0.00	65.04
EUROCARGO ALEXANDRIA	0.36	0.01	0.00	0.01	20.27	0.01	0.03	0.00	0.00	20.70
EUROCARGO CATANIA	0.93	0.01	0.01	0.03	53.15	0.03	0.08	0.00	0.00	54.26
EUROCARGO MALTA	1.17	0.02	0.02	0.04	66.90	0.04	0.11	0.00	0.00	68.30
EUROCARGO ROMA	0.43	0.01	0.01	0.01	24.33	0.01	0.04	0.00	0.00	24.83
EUROCARGO SAVONA	0.97	0.02	0.01	0.03	55.09	0.03	0.09	0.00	0.00	56.24
EUROCARGO VENEZIA	0.66	0.01	0.01	0.02	37.51	0.02	0.06	0.00	0.00	38.29

Figure 4 shows how these emissions vary with *Th* and *GT*, for each pollutant:

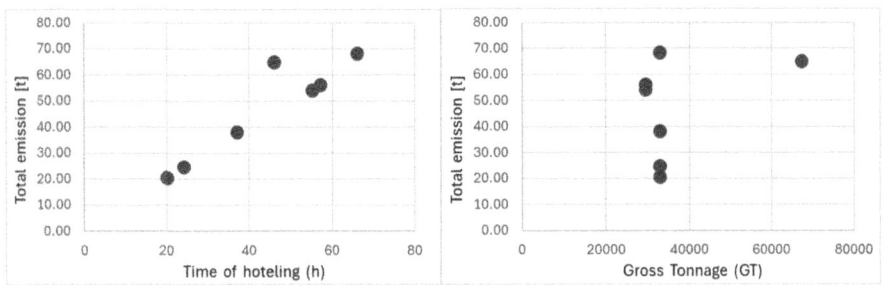

Fig. 4. Analysis of the influence of hoteling time (Th) and GT in emission estimation. Source: Author elaboration.

From these graphs, it can be seen that emissions increase as the hours spent in berth increase, but this is not the case for GT. In fact, in the estimation of total emissions, the weight of hours spent at berth is greater than that of GT. Therefore, the option of performing a simple regression based only on T_h is also considered. These regression curves are implemented by using the Data Analysis tool and coefficients are reported in Table 8.

Table 8. Regression curves. Source: Author elaboration.

Regression Type	Equation	R^2
Simple linear	$E_{total} = 1.021th + 2.3213$	0.8632
2nd-degree polynomial	$E_{total} = -0.0141th^2 + 2.2026th - 18.837$	0.8885

Results are influenced by the limited number of measurements included in the methodological application. Nevertheless, we can observe that the second-degree polynomial curve has a slightly higher reliability.

If one compares the total emissions obtained with those resulting from the regression curves using Eq. (1), one can see that, for the "Eurocargo" ships, the values obtained with the regression curves are very similar to those calculated, for the "EcoItalia" ship, on the other hand, lower values are found (Table 9).

Table 9. Results comparison of the total emissions (t) estimation with model and applying regression.

Ship list	GT [t]	T_h [h]	Total emissions [t]	Linear Regression [t]	2nd-degree Regression [t]
ECO ITALIA	67,311	46	65.04	49.29	52.65
EUROCARGO ALEXANDRIA	32,843	20	20.70	22.74	19.58
EUROCARGO CATANIA	29,429	55	54.26	58.48	59.65
EUROCARGO MALTA	32,841	66	68.30	69.71	65.12
EUROCARGO ROMA	32,839	24	24.83	26.83	25.90
EUROCARGO SAVONA	29,429	57	56.24	60.52	60.90
EUROCARGO VENEZIA	32,841	37	38.29	40.10	43.36

This demonstrates that a different type of ship influences the correlation with emission estimates, thus, we need to analyze similar ships to enhance a better understanding of this phenomenon. This simplified method would be much quicker and more useful when making an initial estimate of the total emissions from Ro-Ro ships in the port of Catania.

The analysis also showed that hoteling time (Th) has a greater impact on emissions than other parameters, such as gross tonnage (GT). This result can be attributed to the relatively homogeneous composition of the Ro-Ro fleet operating in the port of Catania, where ships present similar dimensions and little variation in GT values. This homogeneity limits the predictive effectiveness of GT in the regression models applied, while Th shows greater variability and is confirmed as the most significant explanatory variable for estimation purposes.

5   Conclusions and Future Research

This study proposed the implementation of a data-efficient methodology prosed in literature for estimating emissions from Ro-Ro vessels in the port of Catania, focusing on the phase in which ships remain docked in port with their auxiliary engines running to ensure the operation of on-board systems, i.e. hoteling. Based on the analysis of AIS data and emission estimation models, it was possible to quantify the environmental impact of these ships. This methodology is applied when no emission data from sensors are available or when no other type of data is available, as it uses readily available data such as AIS data.

A key finding of the study is that time of hoteling (T_h) has a more significant impact on total emissions than Gross Tonnage (GT), suggesting that emission reduction strategies should focus on limiting docking time or the possible adoption of more sustainable technologies, such as cold ironing (shore power). A regression model was then used to establish correlations between ship operating parameters and emissions. The results showed that second-degree polynomial regression provided better reliability than linear regression, although the difference between the two models was not significant.

This method makes it possible to obtain an initial assessment of the environmental impact of maritime traffic without having to carry out complex calculations. However, emission factors must be taken into account, as these present significant uncertainties.

This type of analysis can provide concrete support to port authorities and local authorities in defining strategies to reduce environmental impacts in line with European sustainability and decarbonisation objectives. The flexibility and scalability of the model also allows it to be applied to other ports with similar characteristics, making the method replicable in different geographical contexts and easily integrated into environmental planning tools.

Future research could be expanded to include several type of ships and longer observation periods, as well as the integration of more detailed data on engine operating characteristics. In addition, the implementation of more advanced predictive models could further improve the accuracy of estimates, contributing to a more sustainable management of maritime transport and emissions in ports.

Acknowledgements. This work was developed and supported by the research project 'Design of Maritime Sustainable Terminals (DEMASTER)' developed by the University of Rome 'La Sapienza' in close cooperation with teams from the University of Catania and the University of Ljubljana (Slovenia). The work of Vincenza Torrisi is funded by the European Union (NextGenerationEU), through the MUR-PNRR project SAMOTHRACE (ECS00000022).

References

1. Sihaloho, S.M., Saftarina, F.: Analysis of factors causing air pollution on ships. J. Soc. Res. **2**(7), 2304–2311 (2023)
2. Barberi, S., Campisi, T., Neduzha, L.: The role of cold ironing in maritime transport emissions. In: AIP Conference Proceedings (Vol. 2611, No. 1). AIP Publishing (2022, November)
3. Micheli, D., Clemente, S., Taccani, R.: Energy systems on board ships. In: Sustainable Energy Systems on Ships, pp. 27–78. Elsevier (2022)
4. Virgili, S., Rizza, U., Tommasi, M., DI Nisio, S.I.L.V.I.A., Passerini, G.: Air pollution from cruise ships during hotelling in ports: a case study in Ancona harbour, Italy. WIT Trans. Ecol. Environ. **263**, 221–227 (2024)
5. Giuffrida, N., Ignaccolo, M., Inturri, G., Torrisi, V.: Port-city shared areas to improve freight transport sustainability. In: International Conference on Computational Science and Its Applications, pp. 67–82. Springer International Publishing, Cham (2020, July)
6. Ignaccolo, M., Inturri, G., Giuffrida, N., Torrisi, V., Cocuzza, E.: Sustainability of freight transport through an integrated approach: the case of the eastern Sicily port system. Transp. Res. Procedia. **45**, 177–184 (2020)
7. Sorte, S., Arunachalam, S., Naess, B., Seppanen, C., Rodrigues, V., Valencia, A., et al.: Assessment of source contribution to air quality in an urban area close to a harbor: case-study in Porto, Portugal. Sci. Total Environ. **662**, 347–360 (2019)
8. Peddi, K.P., Ricci, S., Rizzetto, L.: Reduction potential of gaseous emissions in European ports using cold ironing. Appl. Sci. **14**(15), 6837 (2024)
9. Alamoush, A.S., Ölçer, A.I., Ballini, F.: Port greenhouse gas emission reduction: port and public authorities' implementation schemes. Res. Transp. Bus. Manag. **43**, 100708 (2022)
10. Puig, M., Azarkamand, S., Wooldridge, C., Selén, V., Darbra, R.M.: Insights on the environmental management system of the European port sector. Sci. Total Environ. **806**, 150550 (2022)
11. Alamoush, A.S., Ballini, F., Ölçer, A.I.: Revisiting port sustainability as a foundation for the implementation of the United Nations sustainable development goals (UN SDGs). J. Shipp. Trade. **6**, 1–40 (2021)
12. https://www.agenziacoesione.gov.it/comunicazione/agenda-2030-per-lo-sviluppo-sosten ibile/
13. Kelmalis, A., Dimou, A., Lekkas, D.F., Vakalis, S.: Cold ironing and the study of RES utilization for maritime electrification on lesvos Island port. Environments. **11**(4), 84 (2024)
14. Barberi, S., Sambito, M., Neduzha, L., Severino, A.: Pollutant emissions in ports: a comprehensive review. Inf. Dent. **6**(8), 114 (2021)
15. Freire, W.P., Melo Jr., W.S., do Nascimento, V.D., Nascimento, P.R., de Sá, A.O.: Towards a secure and scalable maritime monitoring system using blockchain and low-cost IoT technology. Sensors. **22**(13), 4895 (2022)
16. Fan, L., Yang, H., Zhang, X.: Targeting the effectiveness assessment of the emission control policies on the shipping industry. Sustain. For. **16**(6), 2465 (2024)
17. Lambas, M.L., Ricci, S.T.E.F.A.N.O., Rizzetto, L.U.C.A.: Reduction of gaseous emissions from ships: comparative overview of methods and technologies. WIT Trans. Built Environ. **204**, 93–104 (2021)
18. Cammin, P., Yu, J., Heilig, L., Voß, S.: Monitoring of air emissions in maritime ports. Transp. Res. Part D: Transp. Environ. **87**, 102479 (2020)
19. Zhou, F., Fan, Y., Zou, J., An, B.: Ship emission monitoring sensor web for research and application. Ocean Eng. **249**, 110980 (2022)
20. Chen, R., Meng, Q., Jia, P.: Container port drayage operations and management: past and future. Transp. Res. Part E Logist. Transp. Rev. **159**, 102633 (2022)

21. Yang, Y.C., Hsieh, Y.H.: The critical success factors of smart port digitalization development in the post-COVID-19 era. Case Stud. Transp. Policy. **17**, 101231 (2024)
22. Kramel, D., Muri, H., Kim, Y., Lonka, R., Nielsen, J.B., Ringvold, A.L., et al.: Global shipping emissions from a well-to-wake perspective: the MariTEAM model. Environ. Sci. Technol. **55**(22), 15040–15050 (2021)
23. Albo-López, A.B., Carrillo, C., Díaz-Dorado, E.: An approach for shipping emissions estimation in ports: the case of ro–ro vessels in port of Vigo. J. Mar. Sci. Eng. **11**(4), 884 (2023)
24. https://www.adspmaresiciliaorientale.it/porto-di-catania/
25. Piano regolatore portuale di Catania, le previsioni dei traffici - Live Sicilia
26. https://www.adspmaresiciliaorientale.it/wp-content/uploads/2024/12/POTREV.2024.pdf
27. VesselFinder: Disponibile online: https://www.vesselfinder.com/
28. Trozzi, C.: Emission Estimate Methodology for Maritime Navigation, p. 780. Techne Consulting, Rome (2010)
29. Starcrest Consulting Group LLC: Port of Los Angeles. Air Emissions Inventory—2020, p. 114. Starcrest Consulting Group LLC, Albuquerque, NM (2021)
30. https://www.epa.gov/sites/default/files/2016-06/documents/2009-port-inventory-guidance.pdf
31. https://uk-air.defra.gov.uk/reports/cat15/1012131459_21897_Final_Report_291110.pdf

ICT Factors Affecting Ship Times in Container Ports: Experimental Analysis at Country Level

Giuseppe Musolino[✉], Girolamo Pedà, and Francesco Russo

DIIES, Università Mediterranea di Reggio Calabria, 89100 Reggio Calabria, Italy
giuseppe.musolino@unirc.it

Abstract. One of the characteristics of container ports' performances, on the sea side, is the time of ships in port from the arrival and entrance to the departure from the port. The time of the ship in a container port, by considering the largest ports of a country, is therefore a synthetic indicator of the ability of each country-system to compete in international trade challenges. It is useful to investigate what are the significant characteristics, aggregated at the country level, that determine the average ship time in port. The paper presents an experimental analysis aimed to evaluate the incidence of the Information and Communication Technology (ICT) and structural port factors on the average ship time in container ports at country level. Some quantitative indicators are used in the evaluation, such as the calibrated parameters, the substitution rates, the elasticities; the observed vs estimated values.

The results of the experimentation show that the parameters associated with the attributes considered are negative, i.e. the higher is their value, the shorter is the port time. They are interesting for national port systems, because they could support general policies and financial investments on physical and/or digital port infrastructures in order to improve the performances of a national port system in the global competition.

Keywords: commercial ports · ship times in container ports · vessel turnaround time · Information and Communication Technology (ICT) · structural factors · models estimation

1 Introduction

Since ancient times maritime transport has been a vital and strategic factor in the social and economic development of the Mediterranean peoples. It can be said that the history of civilization coincides with the evolution of maritime transport. The innovations in maritime transport played a fundamental role in trade among peoples, reducing the distances among them.

The evolution of ports was classified according to a series of criteria identified by UN Trade and Development (UNCTAD), named as generations [1, 2]. The initial classification of UNCTAD was followed in the later years by an intense scientific debate, a brief summary of which is reported below.

First-generation ports [3–5] were born in ancient times, in proximity to the cities to which they were directly connected. The cities develop where the port is located, that is, the port is born first and then the city close it, which grows in symbiosis with the port. Second-generation ports [6] developed after the settlement of large industrial plants after the end of the Second World War. Those ports were built near large industrial areas of steel, petrochemicals, power plants. The territorial paradigm was reversed compared to first-generation ports: initially, the industrial plant was established, and subsequently, the port was built to serve its needs. Third-generation ports [7–9] emerged with the rise of container transport in the final decade of the XX century, maritime container shipping definitively became the most competitive transport option.

The transport cost was drastically reduced and port became generators of added value by manipulating the goods in transit. Fourth-generation ports [7–9] are port systems, generally composed of two main ports, in which port stakeholders cooperate creating alliances on market segments, or sharing infrastructures and services. The creation of port systems concurs to the solution of the problem of centrality ports in the maritime service at international scale [10–12]. The drivers of the cooperation are: the alliances between shipping companies, the naval gigantism and the sharing land infrastructures in the port hinterlands. The main characteristic of fifth generation ports [13, 14] is the use of emerging Information and Communication Technology (ICT) in the interaction among the port stakeholders. Their introduction has shown that ICT is a further pillar of port competitiveness, such as the position near a city or an industrial plant, the capacity to generate added value, the shared infrastructures and services. A tool that enhances inter-action among port stakeholders is the Port Community System (PCS), which has been largely studied in recent years in order to assess its benefits, particularly in increasing the utilities of port operations.

In the above context, the paper presents the results of an experimental analysis of container ship port times, also called vessel turnaround time, in the potential fifth-generation ports. The focus is on the overall performance of a country's port system. Although some papers have been published on the topic of ship turnaround times (see [15, 16]), the paper examines the interplay between the maximum capacity of the container ships, the dotation of ICT infrastructures, and the number of port calls.

The results of the experimentation show that the parameters associated with the attributes considered are negative, i.e. the higher is their value, the shorter is the port time. Furthermore, the results of the substitution rates between the two types of factors, ICT and infrastructural, and the elasticities of the individual attributes on port time are particularly interesting. They could support general policies and financial investments on physical and/or digital port infrastructures in order to improve the performances of a national port system.

The remaining part of the paper is structured as follows. Section 2 presents the characteristics of the fifth generation ports, focusing on the role of Port Community Systems (PCS). Section 3 reports the specification of indicators to evaluate the incidence of different factors, both ICT and infrastructural, on the values of ship times in container ports. Section 4 reports some experimental results of the specified indicators calculated on a set of countries. Finally, the discussion and the research perspectives.

2 Fifth-Generation Ports: The Role of the Port Community Systems (PCSs)

Fifth generation ports are characterized by horizontal and vertical integration among the port stakeholders, that it is possible by means of emerging ICT technologies such as Internet-of-Things (IoT), Artificial Intelligence (AI), blockchain, big-data, digital twin. The emerging ICT technologies in ports are one of the pillars of ports competitiveness, together with their position close to the city or to industrial plants; the capacity to generate added value in the port hinterland; the cooperation among stakeholders [13, 17, 18].

Today financial and information transactions in ports are generally supported by the adoption of stand-alone ICT systems, sometimes vertically integrated. They increase the efficiency operations of the single private stakeholder, or of the single public service, but do not resolve the interactions between different stakeholders. Interactions between stakeholders are relevant to facilitate the three main flows present in the port: goods, information and financial. The cargo flow relies on data exchange to optimize port operations (e.g. dock and yard operations) for thousands of containers.

The traditional approaches generate low capacity utilization of ships and port infrastructures, that have reflections of ship times. The information flow id mainly related to authorization operations: the paper-based solutions represent a strong constraint for international banks, as defined by the Logistics Performance Index, especially in ports (The World Bank, 2014). The potentialities offered by emerging ICT may be emphasized by means of the Port Community Systems (PCSs) [17, 19–21]. PCSs increase the cooperation among the port stakeholders, and consequently increase their competitiveness as a community compared to other ports. The cooperation is possible due to the integration of procedures and the sharing of information and documents.

3 Ship Times in Container Ports: Specification of Indicators

It is recalled firstly that the general function average ship time in port, t, belongs to the class of functions formalized in (Eq. 1). The function presents a structure commonly used to calculate the transport costs on the elements (e.g. links) of a road network and it is studied in the different load conditions of the links: un-congested and congested (see [22, 23]).

The general function for ship time in port is the following:

$$t = t_0 + t(f/\text{Cap}) \qquad (1)$$

where

t_0, average ship time in free-flow conditions, or when there is no congestion in port on the seaside;

$t()$, function;

f, ship flow arriving at the port (e.g. ship/day);

Cap, port capacity, or maximum value of ship flow serving at the port (e.g. ship/day).

The following statistical indicators have been considered in the analysis presented in this work:

(a) calibrated parameters
(b) substitution rate
(c) elasticity;
(d) observed vs estimated values of ship time in ports.

a. Calibrated parameters

The experimental model presented in [24, 25] concerns the calibration of the aliquot of average ship time in free-flow conditions arriving at the single port, t_0:

$$t_0 = t_0 (\mathbf{x}; \boldsymbol{\beta}) + \varepsilon \tag{2}$$

where
   $\mathbf{x}$ is a vector of attributes,
   $\boldsymbol{\beta}$ is a vector of unknown parameters;
   $t_0()$ is a function;
   ε is the error term.
   A linear specification of Eq. (2) is the following:

$$t_0 = \Sigma_j \beta_j x_j + \varepsilon \tag{3}$$

where:
   x_j is the generic attribute of vector $\mathbf{x}$;
   β_j are components of vector $\boldsymbol{\beta}$.
   The vector of unknown parameters, $\boldsymbol{\beta}$, has been calibrated by means of the Least Squares (LS) method, which allows to identify the optimal vector, among the different configurations of $\boldsymbol{\beta}$, that minimizes the sum of the squares of the deviations between the observed values of ship times and the values of ship time calculated with Eq. (3).

b. Substitution rate

The literature on discrete choice models [22, 23, 26] considers the substitution rates between the level-of-service attributes a significant indicators to evaluate the choice behaviour of individuals. Among these, the substitution rate with the monetary cost are particularly relevant. Thus, for example, given the parameters of travel time, β_t, and of the monetary cost β_c respectively, the Value of Time (e.g. in modal choice behaviour) is equal to: VoT $= \beta t / \beta c$, expressed in monetary units per unit of time.

According to the above definitions and extending them to an aggregate context, in general terms the substitution rate may be expressed as:

$$s = \beta_{x1}/\beta_{y2} \tag{4}$$

with
   s, substitution rate
   β_{x1}, parameter associated to attribute x_1;
   β_{y2}, parameter associated to attribute x_2.

c. Elasticity

Elasticity provides information on the percentage change in the dependent variable (port ship time) to the percentage change of one independent variable attribute. The calculation of direct point elasticity related to an attribute x_k is executed for infinitesimal variations and calculated according to the following equation:

$$\varepsilon_k = (\partial t/t)/(\partial x_k/x_k) \tag{5}$$

where

x_k is the value of the attribute k;

t is the value of port ship time.

The calculation of direct link elasticity related to an attribute x_k is executed for finite variations and calculated according the following equation:

$$E_k = (\Delta t/t)/(\Delta x_k/x_k) \tag{6}$$

where

x_k is the value of the attribute k;

t is the value of port ship time.

d. Observed vs. estimated values

The comparison between observed and estimated values of ship time in ports has been used to verify the capacity of the model to reproduce the observed values. There are several indicators to compare the two classes data. In this work this comparison has been executed in a qualitative way by building radar diagrams showing the difference between the estimated and observed value of ship time for a group of selected countries.

4   Ship Times in Container Ports: Experimental Results

The following attributes, among the others, are considered in the experimentation (see [24] for details):

- Maximum Capacity of container Ship (MCS) [TEU/10^3], maximum number of TEUs transported by a container ship touching the ports of the country in the period considered (e.g. year);
- Number of Ship Calls (NSC), [ship/year*10^3], number of port calls in all ports of the country;
- ICT Technology Index (ITI) [0–1], level of ICT equipments of a country.

The values of attributes are obtained from the UNCTADSTAT data-base referred to the year 2019 (unctadstat.unctad.org). Figures 1, 2 and 3 present the scatterplots, respectively, between:

- the average ship time in port and the maximum capacity (MCS) (Fig. 1), where a declining trend appears and a reducing dispersion of ship times for increasing values of maximum capacity;
- the average ship time in port and the ICT Technology Index (Fig. 2), where, also in this case, a declining trend appears and a reducing dispersion of ship times for increasing values of ICT technology Index;
- the average ship time in port and the number of ship calls (Fig. 3), where a quick decline of ship times appears for increasing number of ship calls until a value of 5000 ship/year followed by slightly declining values.

Table 1 reports the maximum, minimum and average values of the examined attributes among the set of examined countries.

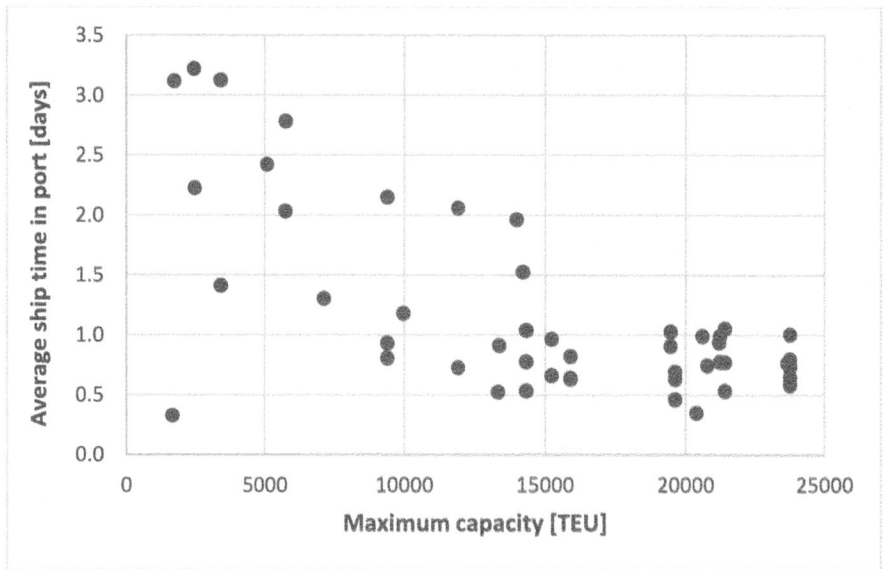

Fig. 1. Scatterplot between average ship time in port and maximum capacity.

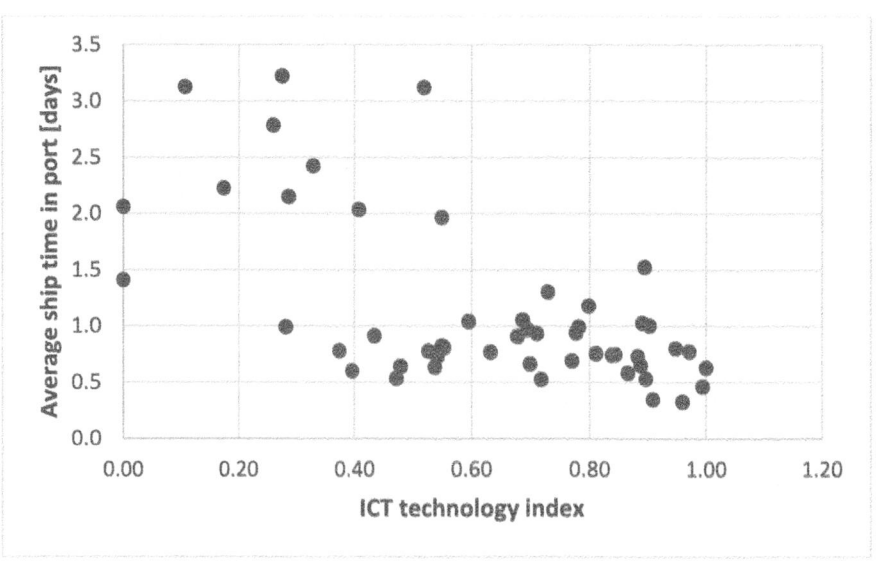

Fig. 2. Scatterplot between average ship time in port and ICT technology index.

4.1 Calibrated Parameters

The model parameters (Eq. 3) were estimated using the LS method [24, 25]. Table 2 shows the values of the estimated parameters, β_j, and the values of r^2 and $\underline{r}^2$.

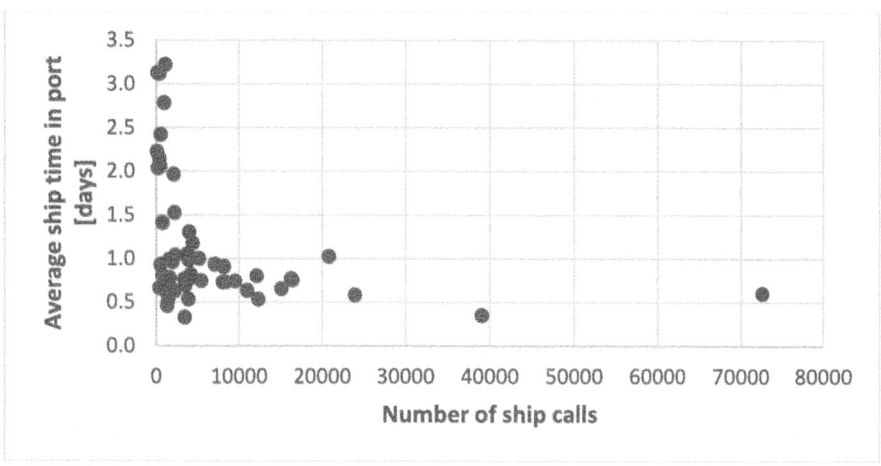

Fig. 3. Scatterplot between average ship time in port and number of ship calls.

Table 1. Maximum, minimum and medium values of examined attributes

		Max	Min	Average
MCS	[TEU*10^3]	23.76	19.46	22.07
NSC	[ship/year*10^3]	72.58	3.78	17.74
ITI	[0,1]	0.95	0.40	0.74

Table 2. Calibrated parameters

	UdM	1	2
β_0	[days]	2.56	2.55
β_{MCS}	[TEU/10^3]	−0.069	−0.067
β_{NSC}	[ship/year*10^3]	–	−0.0015
β_{ITI}	[0,1]	−0.52	−0.46
r^2	–	0.60	0.60
$\underline{r}^2$	–	0.58	0.57

The initial considerations concern the model 1 which can be assumed as the reference model. The value of $\beta_0 = 2.56$ [days] defines the reference threshold of the average ship time in port for all countries. The value of the parameter of the attribute MCS ($\beta_{MSC} = -0.07$) indicates that the average ship time in port reduces when the country id equipped with ports capable of hosting container ships of high capacity. It is important to highlight the sign and the value of the parameter associated to ITI attribute, $\beta_{ITI} = -0.52$. The parameter indicates that the average ship time in port reduces as the country's digital technology equipment increases.

The model 2 introduces the NSC attribute, whose associated parameter is negative. In this case, an increase of the number of ship calls could be associated with a better organization of the country's port system, that leads to reduced average ship times in port. It is worth noting that the parameter associated to the ITI attribute is similar among the two models and, therefore, confirms the role and importance of the country's digital technology equipment.

4.2 Substitution Rate

The substitution rate between the parameters associated with the ITI and MSC attributes, $s = \beta_{ITI}/\beta_{MSC}$, is equal to 7.4 in model 1 and 7.6 in model 2. Therefore, an increase in the value of 0.1 of the ITI attribute corresponds to an increase of between 740 TEUs and 960 TEUs of the maximum capacity of container ships that can potentially be hosted in the ports of a country. The substitution rate between the parameters associated with the ITI and NSC attributes, $s = \beta_{ITI}/\beta_{NSC}$, is equal to 446 [ships/year]. Therefore, an increase in the value of 0.1 of the ITI attribute corresponds to an increase of 446 [ships/year] ship calls in the ports of a country.

4.3 Elasticity

Model 1 and 2 are considered for the calculation of direct link elasticity by means of Eq. (6) for eight countries considering an increase of 5% (=100 $\Delta x_k / x_k$) for each attribute. Among the eight countries, two of them belong to the Northern European range: Belgium and The Netherland; four countries belong to the Mediterranean Basin: Italy, Spain, Greece and Morocco. Moreover, China and United States are considered individually. Table 3 presents the values of the estimated direct link elasticities. Considering the average values of elasticity per single attribute, the following elements emerge. Both models are rigid with respect to the attribute ITI: $\varepsilon_{ITI} = 0.61$ for model 1 and $\varepsilon_{ITI} = 0.67$ for model 2, Both models are elastic with respect to the attribute MCS: $\varepsilon_{MCS} = 2.45$ for model 1 and $\varepsilon_{ITI} = 2.64$ for model 2.

Let' consider the individual values of elasticity for each attribute and country. As far as concerns ITI attribute, the models are basically rigid for the Mediterranean countries: the range is from $E_{ITI} = 0.34;0.36$ for Morocco to $E_{ITI} = 0.51;0.53$ for Greece, except for Spain where $E_{ITI} = 1.06–1.19$. The models are elastic for the Northern European countries: the range is from $E_{ITI} = 1.10;1.19$ of Belgium to $E_{ITI} = 1.22;1.37$ for The Netherland. The models are rigid for China ($E_{ITI} = 0.30; 0.37$) and United States ($E_{ITI} = 0.63; 0.69$). As far as concerns MCS attribute, the models are elastic for all the examined countries: the range is from $E_{MCS} = 1.61;1.67$ of Italy to $E_{MCS} = 4.11;4.54$ for The Netherland. As far as concerns NCS attribute, model 2 is highly rigid for all the examined countries: the range is from $E_{NCS} = 0.02$ of Italy and Belgium to $E_{NCS} = 0.19$ of China.

4.4 Observed Vs. Estimated Values of Ship Times

The results of the comparison between observed values of attributes (see Figs. 1, 2 and 3) vs. estimated values of attributes by means of models 1 and 2 is graphically presented

Table 3. Link elasticity of models 1 and 2 vs. increases of attribute of +5%

	Country	Model 1		Model 2		
		ITI	MCS	ITI	MCS	NCS
Increment 5%	Italy	−0.42	−1.61	−0.44	−1.67	−0.02
	Belgium	−1.10	−3.89	−1.19	−4.15	−0.02
	The Netherland	−1.22	−4.11	−1.37	−4.54	−0.05
	Spain	−1.06	−3.81	−1.19	−4.22	−0.06
	Greece	−0.51	−2.13	−0.53	−2.20	−0.01
	Morocco	−0.34	−1.86	−0.36	−1.91	−0.01
	China	−0.30	−2.41	−0.37	−2.93	−0.19
	USA	−0.63	−1.85	−0.69	−1.99	−0.05
	Average value	*−0.61*	*−2.45*	*−0.67*	*−2.64*	*−0.05*

in the radar diagrams of Figs. 4 and 5. The following elements may be highlighted. In both models the estimated values are lower than the observed ones.

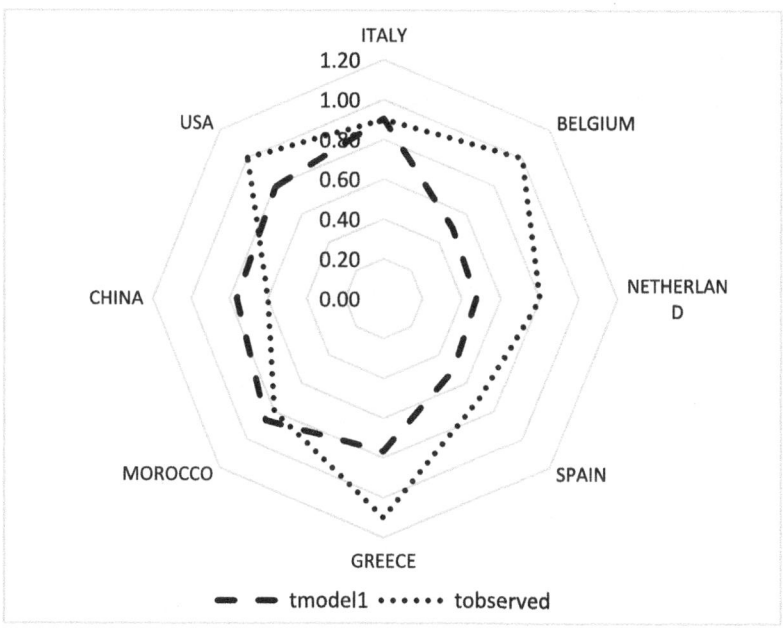

Fig. 4. Comparison between observed and estimated values of ship time in port (days): radar diagrams for model 1.

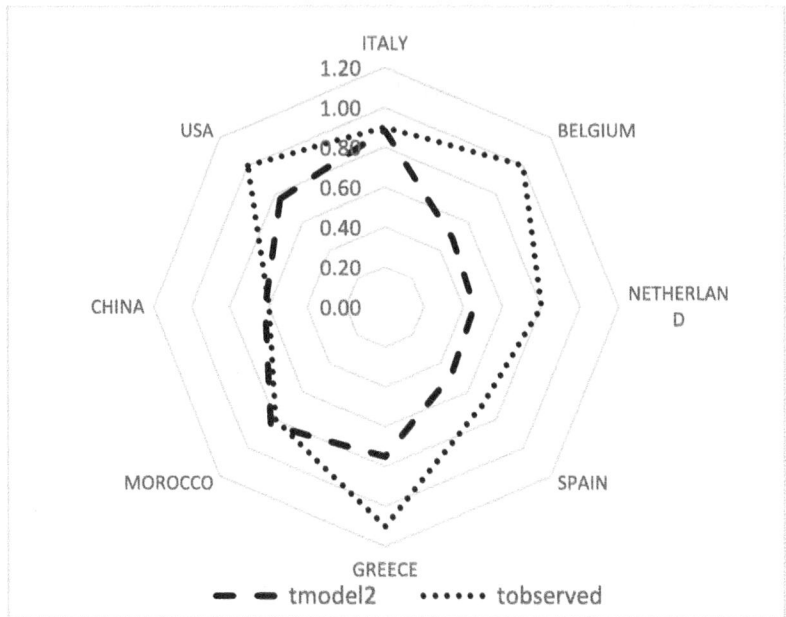

Fig. 5. Comparison between observed and estimated values of ship time in port (days): radar diagrams for model 2.

5 Discussion and Further Research

The performances of container ports are characterized, on the sea side, by the time of ships in port, which may be considered as a synthetic indicator of the capacity of a national port system to compete in the international trade.

The paper investigates the factors belonging to two main categories that generate impacts on ship times in container ports. The first factor belongs to the category of physical (material) components and the second one to the category of intangible (or immaterial) components. In particular, an experimental analysis has been executed to evaluate the incidence of the structural and ICT port factors through some quantitative statistic indicators: calibrated parameters, substitution rates, direct elasticities; observed vs estimated values.

The calibration of the parameters shows that a reference lower threshold of 2.56 days may be assumed as average ship time for the ports of the examined countries. If a country has ports equipped to handle container ships of higher capacity, the ship time reduces. This attribute could be considered as a proxy of the infrastructural dotation of a country in terms of container ports, that allow better performances in handling container ships on the seaside. Moreover, the average ship time decreases for countries that present a higher ICT dotation. This aggregate result is in line with some disaggregate studies about the role of emerging ICT in facilitating the interactions among port stakeholders and, therefore, increasing their shared utility [13].

The calculation of the substitution rates could provide an interesting insight on costs of investments in container ports regarding physical and digital infrastructures. According to the estimated values, national investments in digital technology that increase the ITI attribute of 10% (ΔITI $= +0.1$) determine a fallout in container ports of the following order of magnitude. On the side of maximum capacity of ships, an increase of 1000 TEU in the average size of container ships that can be hosted (for example in Italian ports). On the side of number ship calls, an increase of 446 ships/year handled in ports. It is worth noting that the dredging costs to deepen the port seabed in order to host ships of higher dimensions (ΔMCS $= +1000$ TEUs) could be estimated in at least 50 million euros per port. Such an intervention, for example, on the twenty container ports operating in Italy would entail an expense of one billion euros.

The estimated values of direct elasticities per single attribute lead to the following considerations. The models are, on average, rigid with respect to the ICT attribute and elastic with respect to the infrastructural attributes. The values of elasticities for single countries do not provide clear indications, and they need to be further investigated.

The comparison between observed and estimated values of ship times show that the estimated values are generally lower than the observed ones.

Further developments are necessary on two main research directions. The first direction concerns the investigation about the influence of further ICT attributes in order to evaluate the impacts of different generations of PCS. The second direction regards the comparison with the results of other theoretical approaches, like network models and time series models.

Acknowledgements. This study is carried out within the research project "National and local factors affecting times of ships in container ports", Piano Nazionale di Ripresa e Resilienza (PNRR), Next Generation EU, Progetti di Rilevante Interesse Nazionale PRIN_2022_PNRR_P202292YFW, CUP: C53D2300878001. This presentation reflects only the authors' views and opinions, neither the European Union nor the European Commission can be considered responsible for them.

References

1. UNCTAD: Port Marketing and the Challenge of the Third Generation Port, (1994)
2. UNCTAD: Fourth-Generation Port: Technical Note, (1999)
3. Balletto, G., Borruso, G., Campisi, T.: Not Only Waterfront. The Port-City relations between peripheries and inner harbors. In: Gervasi, O., Murgante, B., Misra, S., Rocha, A.M.A.C., Garau, C. (eds.) Computational Science and Its Applications – ICCSA 2022 Workshops, pp. 196–208. Springer International Publishing, Cham (2022). https://doi.org/10.1007/978-3-031-10548-7_15
4. Giuffrida, N., Ignaccolo, M., Inturri, G., Torrisi, V.: Port-City shared areas to improve freight transport sustainability. In: Gervasi, O., Murgante, B., Misra, S., Garau, C., Blečić, I., Taniar, D., Apduhan, B.O., Rocha, A.M.A.C., Tarantino, E., Torre, C.M., Karaca, Y. (eds.) Computational Science and Its Applications – ICCSA 2020, pp. 67–82. Springer International Publishing, Cham (2020). https://doi.org/10.1007/978-3-030-58820-5_6
5. Russo, F., Musolino, G.: Port-city interactions: models and case studies. In: Transportation Research Procedia (Forthcoming). Elsevier, Rome (2022)

6. Russo, F., Musolino, G.: Industrial and oil ports: case studies and theoretical approaches. In: Transportation Research Procedia (Forthcoming), Rome (2022)
7. Russo, F., Musolino, G.: Case studies and theoretical approaches in port competition and coop-eration. In: Gervasi, O., Murgante, B., Misra, S., Garau, C., Blečić, I., Taniar, D., Apduhan, B.O., Rocha, A.M.A.C., Tarantino, E., Torre, C.M. (eds.) Computational Science and Its Applications – ICCSA 2021, pp. 198–212. Springer International Publishing, Cham (2021). https://doi.org/10.1007/978-3-030-87016-4_15
8. Russo, F., Musolino, G.: Transportation system models to analyse ports competition and cooperation. WMU J. Marit. Affairs. **23**, 393–413 (2024). https://doi.org/10.1007/s13437-024-00345-6
9. Roumboutsos, A., Sys, C., Vanelslander, T.: Imitation, co-opetition and open innovation in network industries: cases from ports. Case Stud. Transp. Policy. **10**, 1627–1639 (2022). https://doi.org/10.1016/j.cstp.2022.06.002
10. Campisi, T., Russo, A., Trwdy, E., Zanne, M., Tesoriere, G.: The importance of the centrality of ports for passenger transport in the Adriatic-Ionian Basin. In: Gervasi, O., Murgante, B., Garau, C., Taniar, D., Rocha, A.M.A.C, and Faginas Lago, M.N. (eds.) Computational Science and Its Applications – ICCSA 2024 Workshops. pp. 269–282. Springer Nature Switzerland, Cham (2024). doi: https://doi.org/10.1007/978-3-031-65329-2_18
11. Giuffrida, N., Fazio, M., Inturri, G., Ignaccolo, M.: Fostering ports synergies by centrality measures: an approach based on automated identification systems. In: Gervasi, O., Murgante, B., Misra, S., Garau, C., Blečić, I., Taniar, D., Apduhan, B.O., Rocha, A.M.A.C., Tarantino, E., Torre, C.M. (eds.) Computational Science and Its Applications – ICCSA 2021, pp. 177–187. Springer International Publishing, Cham (2021). https://doi.org/10.1007/978-3-030-87016-4_13
12. Tocchi, D., Sys, C., Papola, A., Tinessa, F., Simonelli, F., Marzano, V.: Hypergraph-based centrality metrics for maritime container service networks: a worldwide application. J. Transp. Geogr. **98**, 103225 (2022). https://doi.org/10.1016/j.jtrangeo.2021.103225
13. Russo, F., Musolino, G.: The role of emerging ICT in the ports: increasing utilities according to shared decisions. Front. Fut. Transp. **2**, 722812 (2021). https://doi.org/10.3389/ffutr.2021.722812
14. Carlan, V., Sys, C., Vanelslander, T.: How port community systems can contribute to port competitiveness: developing a cost–benefit framework. Res. Transp. Bus. Manag. **19**, 51–64 (2016). https://doi.org/10.1016/j.rtbm.2016.03.009
15. Ducruet, C., Itoh, H.: Spatial network analysis of container port operations: the case of ship turnaround times. Netw. Spat. Econ. **22**, 883–902 (2022). https://doi.org/10.1007/s11067-022-09570-z
16. Mazibuko, D.F., Mutombo, K., Kuroshi, L.: An evaluation of the relationship between ship turnaround time and key port performance indicators: a case study of a Southern African port. WMU J. Marit. Affairs. **23**, 499–524 (2024). https://doi.org/10.1007/s13437-024-00330-z
17. Musolino, G., Peda, G., Russo, F.: Emerging ICT and port community systems: A survey of scientific literature. Presented at the, Valencia, Spain November (2022). https://doi.org/10.2495/UMT220111
18. Carlan, V., Coppens, F., Sys, C., Vanelslander, T., Van Gastel, G.: Blockchain technology as key contributor to the integration of maritime supply chain? In: Maritime Supply Chains, pp. 229–259. Elsevier (2020). https://doi.org/10.1016/B978-0-12-818421-9.00012-4
19. Caldeirinha, V., Felício, J.A., Salvador, A.S., Nabais, J., Pinho, T.: The impact of port com-munity systems (PCS) characteristics on performance. Res. Transp. Econ. **80**, 100818 (2020). https://doi.org/10.1016/j.retrec.2020.100818
20. Moros-Daza, A., Amaya-Mier, R., Paternina-Arboleda, C.: Port community systems: a struc-tured literature review. Transp. Res. A Policy Pract. **133**, 27–46 (2020). https://doi.org/10.1016/j.tra.2019.12.021

21. Barasti, D., Troscia, M., Lattuca, D., Tardo, A., Barsanti, I., Pagano, P.: An ICT prototyping framework for the "port of the future". Sensors. **22**, 246 (2021). https://doi.org/10.3390/s22010246
22. Ortúzar, S.J.D., Willumsen, L.G.: Modelling Transport. John Wiley, Chichester/New York, NY (2001)
23. Cascetta, E.: Transportation Systems Engineering Theory and Methods. Springer US, S.l. (2013)
24. Russo, F., Peda, G., Musolino, G.: Container ports in country systems: calibration of the aggregate function for the time of the ship in port. Int. J. TDI. **6**, 415–427 (2022). https://doi.org/10.2495/TDI-V6-N4-415-427
25. Russo, F., Pedà, G., Musolino, G.: Attributes influencing port times of container ships. WMU J. Marit. Affairs. **23**, 375–392 (2024). https://doi.org/10.1007/s13437-024-00336-7
26. Ben-Akiva, M.E., Lerman, S.R.: Discrete Choice Analysis: Theory and Application to Travel Demand. MIT Press, Cambridge, MA (1985)

National and Local Factors Affecting Ship Time in Container Ports: System of Models at Country and Port Levels

Giuseppe Musolino[1]([⊠]), Paola Panuccio[2], Corrado Rindone[1], Francesco Russo[1], and Antonino Vitetta[1]

[1] DIIES, Università Mediterranea di Reggio Calabria, 89100 Reggio Calabria, Italy
giuseppe.musolino@unirc.it
[2] dAeD, Università Mediterranea di Reggio Calabria, 89100 Reggio Calabria, Italy

Abstract. Ship time in port may be considered as an indicator of the performance of a port, and of a country, in order to compete in the international trade challenge. The general objective of the research concerns the development of a system of models that correlates the average ship times in port with various factors, or attributes, related to the port or to the country that hosts the port.

The attributes are related, in general, to the position and role of the ports; the organization of the maritime services; the administration and legislation of the country to which the port belong; the material and immaterial infrastructures of the port; the port accessibility of the land side. The system of models proposed include models to evaluate maritime services, based on a network approach; to evaluate path choices of commercial vehicles travelling to/from the ports, based on discrete choice models; and to evaluate land use of the port hinterland, according to the smart paradigm. The developed models rely upon the Transport Systems Models theory, that in general simulate the interaction between transport users and (congested) networks generating flows and costs. The paper presents the methodological background and the expected results of the proposed system of models implemented inside the research project.

Keywords: commercial ports · times of ships in container ports · Transport System Models (TSMs) · Spatial Economic Models (SEMs) · quantitative models

1 Introduction

Commercial ports are classified according to different criteria in the scientific and technical literature. The challenge in establishing a universally accepted classification is due to their heterogeneous nature. UNCTAD introduced the concept of port-generation and sketched three generations of port in 1994 [1]. Port belonging to the first generation are historic multipurpose/multifunction ports that are located close to the urban centres. The second generation includes industrial ports strategically located in proximity to great power and steel production facilities. The third generation includes ports which handle relevant volumes of containerized traffic and increase the added value of freight

© The Author(s), under exclusive license to Springer Nature Switzerland AG 2026
O. Gervasi et al. (Eds.): ICCSA 2025 Workshops, LNCS 15897, pp. 144–155, 2026.
https://doi.org/10.1007/978-3-031-97660-5_11

in transit. UNCTAD later sketched the characteristics of the fourth-generation ports [2], which change their attitude with closer ports from a competitive into a cooperative one. The study in [3] introduces a theoretical model that allow to evaluate the competitive and/or cooperative attitudes among two ports Lastly, the fifth-generation port was introduced which incorporate emerging information and communication technology that acts as integrator for different port actors and functions. Some details about the above scientific debate may be found in several publications of the authors ([4–8], and references included).

The research on ports belonging to the third-generation focused on the port areas, where handling and transport operations take place, and the port hinterland, where manufacturing activities may be located increasing the added value of handled freight inside the port. Two recent studies [9, 10] compare some aggregate characteristics of different countries showing relevant differences in import/export times, as reported in the study [11]. The case of Europe is emblematic, where the export times of goods show a great variability between countries compared to the average value of 10 days. Afterwards, the Italian Prime Minister presented an analysis of the time components related to export procedures: documentation, customs, handling and transportation [12]. The analysis showed that differences in average export times of freight depend on documentation and handling times in each country, while times for custom operation seem to be similar in the examined countries.

Given the above context, two main research questions arise: which are the determinants that affects time of ships in container ports? Is it possible to estimate models that relate time of ships in container ports to national and local factors?

The main objective of the ongoing research project aims to respond to the above research questions by providing a spatial analysis of ship times across container ports of the world. The methodologies that are used in the research project have their theoretical background in Transport Systems Models (TSMs) and Spatial Economic Models (SEMs) ([13–17]; among the others).

The following part of the paper will be articulated as follows. Section 2 reports the state of the art about models composing the modelling framework adopted in the research project. Section 3 briefly sketches each model's characteristics in terms of theoretical background and reference equations. The last section presents the expected results of the project.

2   State of the Art

The existing literature reveals the absence of systematic studies where the relationship between the ship times in container ports and national and local factors is analysed. Existing analyses concentrate on individual ports or terminals with few comparative studies [18–21]. In particular, the study in [19] reveals that ship times are influenced by attributes belonging to three homogeneous classes: the size of the ships; the level of the economy, the logistic services and maritime connections.

The literature about freight transport modelling concerns two levels [16, 17, 22, 23]. Commodity-based models estimate the amount of freight produced and consumed, focusing on aggregate costs of production, consumption and trade. Vehicle-based models estimate the mode/service/route used to transport the freight in relation to transportation and logistics costs.

The analysis on the literature about the two above level of model reveals the presence of quantitative methods and models grouped into two frameworks: TSM and SEMs.

TSMs simulate how passengers, or freight transport operators, use the transport infrastructures and services. TSMs are composed by three modelling elements: the supply, the travel demand, and the assignment models.

The supply model calculates the costs of transport connected to the use of infrastructures and services. Transport supply models may be classified in [20, 24]:

- analytic, adopting a representation of maritime and terrestrial infrastructures and services in an aggregate form;
- topologic, adopting a network model by constricting a graph (nodes and links) and relative cost functions.

The supply models allow to study the level of centrality that each port has in the maritime services system at international scale. The study of the different types of centrality is carried out using the formulation produced in the context of network analysis (see [25–27], and references included).

The travel demand models estimate the choices of users based on the transport costs. Freight demand models can be divided into three categories.

- Statistical-descriptive models calculate maritime flows of freight according to attributes connected to the level of service of the existing network and to the level of economy of production-consumption regions.
- Time series models calculate maritime flows of freight by means of historical data about flows and other attributes.
- Partial-share models calculate the structure of choices in terms of trip generation/attraction, distribution, maritime service and port, maritime line (seaside), and path (landside).

In particular, the path choice model evaluates the percentage of choice that the user assigns to each available alternative. Based on the model proposed in [28], the main models proposed belong to the category of random [14], fuzzy [29, 30] and quantum [31] utility models.

The supply-demand interaction models allow the calculation of the interaction between the user's choices and the costs of transport infrastructures and services. The model in urban area and for ordinary conditions generally relies on the concept of equilibrium [14, 32].

SEMs simulate one or more components of the spatial economic system. They generally refer to the so-called production–consumption paradigm, composed of two modelling components.

- The generation models calculate the a-spatial production and consumption levels. They belong to two classes: the microeconomic one calculates the behaviour of individuals though individual demand and production theories; the macroeconomic one calculates the average behaviour of groups of individuals through variables and relationships that exist between them.

- The location models calculate the amount of freight produced and consumed in a region. The location models belong to two main categories: aggregated models are generally based on entropy maximisation theory; disaggregated models may rely to random utility theory.

SEMs and TSMs are jointly used to calculate the relationships between economic and transport systems, which are called Spatial Economic Transport Interactions (SETI) models. The SE component calculates the level and spatial distribution of production-consumption of freight among regions that concur to the configuration of freight flows; while the T component calculates the transport and logistic costs that influences the fright production-consumption location ([14, 15, 17], and references included).

SETI models are grouped into two classes According to the spatial scale examined. National Economic Transport Interaction (NETI) models are used for the country or regional scales, while Land Use Transport Interaction (LUTI) models are used for the urban scale. In particular, land use models developed for port areas support the evaluation of the integration of the port functions with the infrastructural system of the surrounding area. The port has an added value if it speeds up the transit of goods by taking advantage of efficient correlations with territorial system and service facilities, such as dotation of material and immaterial infrastructures and a research centre.

3   Methods

The methodologies that are used in the research project have their theoretical background in TSMs and SEMs frameworks, briefly recalled in the previous section.

The methodologies used in the research project operate at country and port levels (Fig. 1).

The methodologies concern the following elements:

- maritime services, constructing network topology of the main connections provided by the existing container line services;
- port ship times, identifying and calculating the determinants of ship times in container ports based on various attributes on different nature: infrastructural, technological and operational;
- path choice, building path choice models for users that can model and simulate choice behaviour in the road transport system;
- land use, evaluating the land use of the port hinterland, according to the smart paradigm.

3.1   Maritime Services Models

Maritime services are represented adopting the topologic approach, supported by the information deriving from AIS data [33]. Maritime transport supply model consists of a network constituted by:

- a set of nodes that represent ports and way points for identify sea routes connecting couple of ports;

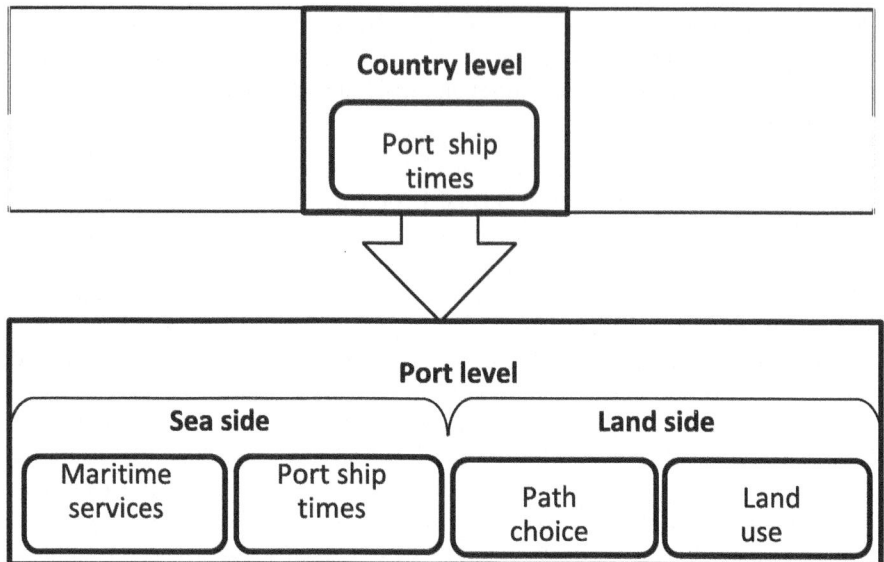

Fig. 1. Modelling framework for the evaluation of port ship times.

- a set of links connecting the nodes representing the sea routes or the sequence of nodes that, with a generic service, connects two ports;
- a set of cost functions for representing performances of ports and sea routes (times, costs, …).

By selecting a specific port, AIS data can be used for reconstructing the main maritime services (e.g. containerships lines) that connect the port with other terminals. By using clustering methods, it is possible to individuate nodes and links. Cost functions can be specified and calibrated in relation to the final aim of the applications.

By following the TSM approach, the topology is represented with the following elements [34]:

δ_{ak}, element of the link-path incidence matrix;
c_a, cost on link a (e.g. travel time);
$g_k = \Sigma_a \, \delta_{ak} \, c_a$, additive cost on path k;
g_k^{NA}, non additive cost on path k;
f_a, flow on link a;
h_k, flow on path k.

According to the above elements, the maritime transport network model is represented with the following formulations.

- Link and path generalized costs:

$$g_k = \Sigma_a \, \delta_{ak} \, c_a \; + g_k^{NA} \tag{1}$$

- Link and path flows:

$$f_a = \Sigma_k \, \delta_{ak} \, h_k \qquad (2)$$

- Link cost functions:

$$c_a = \gamma(f_a)$$

where
$\gamma(\cdot)$ is the link–cost flow function.

3.2   Port Ship Times Models

The models used in the research belong to the class of statistical-descriptive. The relationship defined is supposed to be one-way cause-and-effect.

Ship times in container ports are generally influenced by the following factors:

- role of the port in the supply-chain (e.g. hub port, feeder port) and structure maritime services;
- organization of administration and legislation (e.g. documentation, custom operations);
- port infrastructures (e.g. quays, dock, draught, last-mile connections);
- Information and Communication Technologies (e.g. port community systems, internet-of-things, digital twins).

The general functional form of the model is:

$$t = t\,(\mathbf{x}; \boldsymbol{\beta}) + \varepsilon \qquad (3)$$

where
$\mathbf{x}$ is a vector of port and ship attributes, where the port attributes may belong to the different categories described above;
t is the ship time;
$\boldsymbol{\beta}$ is a vector of unknown parameters;
$t()$ is a function;
ε is the error term.
By assuming that $t()$ is linear, Eq. (3) is specified as follows:

$$t = \beta_0 + \Sigma_j \, \beta_j \, x_j + \varepsilon \qquad (4)$$

where:
x_j is the generic attribute;
β_0 and β_j are components of vector $\boldsymbol{\beta}$.
The vector of parameters, $\boldsymbol{\beta}$, is calibrated by means of the Least Squares (LS) method. A vector $\boldsymbol{\beta}_{LS}$ is estimated which minimizes the distances between the observed values t_i and the values calculated with (4).

The method may be applied both at country and port levels (see Fig. 1). In case of application at country level, the ship times observed, $t_{obs,i}$, and calculated with Eq. (4), and the attributes, $x_{j,i}$, are average values calculated for each country.

3.3 Path Choice Models

Ports can also enable the transfer of goods to and from the mainland. The transfer can mainly take place with the use of two modes of transport: road and rail. Road is used for medium-short distances considering that the mode transfer is more flexible than by rail and, in general, there are no constraints on the use of road infrastructure; rail is used for long distances to allow where possible to amortise the costs of intermodal transfers, the composition and completion of train loads, and the slots available on rail.

The route choice on rail is constrained and decided by the company that organizes the services according to the train paths made available and planned over the long term. Path choice in the road system, on the other hand, is left to the operator who transports the goods, with or without the support of systems that advise or impose the pre-trip and/or en-route. Therefore, it is necessary to build path choice models for users that can model and simulate choice behaviour in the road transport system. These models can support the decision maker in estimating the effects on the road system resulting from freight vehicles with destination or origin in ports [35].

The path choice model considers two levels of choice referred to in this paper as Perception (P) and Choice (C). At each of the two levels, a utility function and a choice model are defined.

For an alternative, the utility function, $v(\mathbf{x}, \boldsymbol{\beta})$, depends on measurable attributes (vector $\mathbf{x}$) and parameters to be calibrated (vector $\boldsymbol{\beta}$). The utility function is non-deterministic (e.g. random, fuzzy, quantum) considering that the analyst does not know exactly how the users' behaviour and the user and analyst do not know exactly the characteristics of the transport system. It is therefore possible to calculate the percentage of choice, $p()$, of each alternative (probability in the random and quantum case and possibility in the fuzzy case) by comparing the utilities of the different alternatives.

Considering the two levels of choice denoted by subscript P and C respectively, the probability of choice of a k route alternative is obtained using the following model [28]:

$$p(k|v_P(\cdot), v_C(\cdot)) = \sum_{I_i} p_P(I_i|v_P(\cdot)) \cdot p_C(k|I_i, \cdot v_C(\cdot)) \qquad (5)$$

having indicated with I_i the generic perceived set of choice and with $v(\cdot)$ the vector containing the utility functions, separated for levels P and C.

If only one perceived set is considered, the previous model degenerates into a single level, with only the choice model applied to the only perceived set I:

$$p(k|v_C(\cdot)) = p_C(k|I, \cdot v_C(\cdot)) \qquad (6)$$

Starting from path choice models, the land-side accessibility can be evaluated.

3.4 Land Use Models

The literature on examples of ports confirms that an important transport infrastructure, such as the case of the port system, must interact with urban and regional areas to maximize profits [36–38].

The big transport nodes such as high-speed railway stations, international airports, inter-continental ports, are often new constructions that invade an already defined territory. The node overlaps with a pre-existing territorial system with considerable difficulties of integration.

The huge project remains closed inside its own limit, inside a system organized exclusively for the function it performs. Therefore, although it is a production system of considerable value, it is not proactive for the territory. This is a limitation, both for the territory that must suffer a massive structure, and for the node that does not use external service infrastructures.

Not having connections, other to causing a conflict with the territory and a strong negative impact, does not permit to benefit from the fruit of relationships, which would instead transform the productive value into added value, increasing its efficiency.

The closed port in itself does not trigger added value. The activities take place within the boundary of the structure and do not increase the benefits.

It is crucial to create proactive connections between the mega infrastructure and the surrounding territorial system.

The lack of integration, with existing or potential systems, does not allow us to take advantage of the opportunities that the territory owns.

The mega structure, without the smart planning process, is unable to integrate into the territory, use services, trigger new development opportunities.

The input that the territory can give is to provide centralized services, production factors of increase for the development of the port.

The key objectives to consider are:

- agile and frequent connections between the node and the territorial network;
- an intermodal exchange infrastructure;
- ability to trigger new functions;
- offer of services and activities, integrated between the node and the neighboring territorial systems.

4   Expected Results and Future Work

Some expected results will be obtained by means of Automatic Identification System (AIS) data, which were initially used to avoid ship collision accidents and, later, their usage expanded to monitor the ships along their maritime routes and inside ports.

The application of AIS data ranges from navigation analysis to ships flow estimation, from pollutant emissions estimation to the evaluation of the ship performances. AIS provides a huge amount of data about ships (e.g., real-time position, route followed) that can be combined with supplementary data (e.g., ports and ships characteristics). AIS data represents the spatial characterization of the trips made by ships. In particular, the AIS provides (among the other ones) the arrival/departure times of the ships from/to the port, allowing to analyse the ship time in port, also called vessel turnaround time, and providing the inputs to define a model able to relate such a time to a set of attributes [39, 40].

The following part of the paragraph reports the expected results in each modelling component of the framework.

The adopted network approach for modelling maritime transport networks, supported by AIS data, will allow to estimate the current performances of port infrastructure and maritime line services. Different configurations of maritime infrastructure and services can be defined by evaluating the main issues of the current network. In the future, it will be possible to experiment different specifications of cost functions of maritime transport networks to better represent current configurations as the volume and variety of AIS big data increases.

The route choice models will make it possible to estimate the percentages of choice in the different alternatives and, thus, also the possibility of estimating the additional load on the road transport network, assuming known travel demand to and from the port broken down by vehicle type and time slot. The route choice model allows also the estimation of the land-side accessibility. The results of the research project concern the type of models to be adopted in the two levels of perception-choice. One could also investigate the possibility of applying different types in the two levels of choice (e.g. quantum and random).

If the port produces value only from transport activities, the convenience will be limited to the supply of the system organized within the limit of its structure. The smart planning process will be tested to plan the integration between the node and the territorial system and to implement the port's supply. The plan proposes useful connections to use existing or potential services and to facilitate port operations. The plan designs new scenarios to meet complex objectives, decisive for integrated opportunities for sustainable development and new smart territories.

Finally, the ship time in port may be a synthetic indicator of the performance of each country and of each container port to compete in the international trade challenges. Specifically, ship times in port are a useful benchmark for evaluating countries and ports' ability to efficiently handle container flows within their terminals. At European level, these times influence competition between Northern and Southern range gateways. The gateways are relevant elements of Trans-European Networks – Transport (TEN-T) and relative infrastructural and commercial corridors (Railway Freight Corridors-RFCs). The research's products contribute to increase knowledge about TEN-T perspectives in terms of effects produced by planned interventions on links (e.g. railway links) and nodes (e.g. ports).

The approach proposed in the research project will be also fruitful in terms of knowledge improvements because it will allow to test the level of dependency of ship times in ports upon national and local attributes both at country level and port levels, provided by international institutes.

Acknowledgements. This study is carried out within the research project "National and local factors affecting times of ships in container ports", Piano Nazionale di Ripresa e Resilienza (PNRR), Next Generation EU, Progetti di Rilevante Interesse Nazionale PRIN_2022_PNRR_P202292YFW, CUP: C53D2300878001. This presentation reflects only the authors' views and opinions, neither the European Union nor the European Commission can be considered responsible for them.

References

1. UNCTAD: Port Marketing and the Challenge of the Third Generation Port, (1994)
2. UNCTAD: Fourth-Generation Port: Technical Note, (1999)
3. Russo, F., Musolino, G.: Transportation system models to analyse ports competition and cooperation. WMU J. Marit. Affairs. **23**, 393–413 (2024). https://doi.org/10.1007/s13437-024-00345-6
4. Russo, F., Musolino, G.: Quantitative characteristics for port generations: the italian case study. Int. J. TDI. **4**, 103–112 (2020). https://doi.org/10.2495/TDI-V4-N2-103-112
5. Russo, F., Musolino, G.: The role of emerging ICT in the ports: increasing utilities according to shared decisions. Front. Fut. Transp. **2**, 722812 (2021). https://doi.org/10.3389/ffutr.2021.722812
6. Russo, F., Musolino, G.: Port-city interactions: models and case studies. In: Transportation Research Procedia (Forthcoming). Elsevier, Rome (2022)
7. Russo, F., Musolino, G.: Industrial and oil ports: case studies and theoretical approaches. Transp. Res. Procedia. **69**, 703–710 (2023). https://doi.org/10.1016/j.trpro.2023.02.226
8. Russo, F., Musolino, G., Assumma, V.: Ro-ro and lo-lo alternatives between Mediterranean countries: factors affecting the service choice. Case Stud. Transp. Policy. **11**, 100960 (2023). https://doi.org/10.1016/j.cstp.2023.100960
9. Pellicanò, D.S., Trecozzi, M.R.: Special economic zones planning for sustainable ports: general approach for administrative simplifications and a test case. In: Gervasi, O., Murgante, B., Misra, S., Rocha, A.M.A.C., Garau, C. (eds.) Computational Science and Its Applications ICCSA 2022 Workshops, pp. 47–59. Springer International Publishing, Cham (2022). https://doi.org/10.1007/978-3-031-10548-7_4
10. Musolino, G., Cartisano, A., Chilà, G., Fortugno, G., Trecozzi, M.R.: Evaluation of structural factors in a third-generation port: methods and applications. Int. J. Transp. Dev. Integrat., 347–362 (2022)
11. International Finance Corporation: Doing business 2014: Understanding Regulations for Small and Medium-Size Enterprises, (2013)
12. Presidenza del Consiglio dei Ministri: Iniziativa Di Studio Sulla Portualità italiana, (2014)
13. Ortúzar S.JD, , Willumsen, L.G.: Modelling Transport. John Wiley, Chichester/New York, NY (2001)
14. Cascetta, E.: Transportation Systems Engineering Theory and Methods. Springer, US, S.l. (2013)
15. Russo, F., Musolino, G.: A unifying modelling framework to simulate the spatial economic transport interaction process at urban and national scales. J. Transp. Geogr. **24**, 189–197 (2012). https://doi.org/10.1016/j.jtrangeo.2012.02.003
16. De Jong, G., Vierth, I., Tavasszy, L., Ben-Akiva, M.: Recent developments in national and international freight transport models within Europe. Transportation. **40**, 347–371 (2013). https://doi.org/10.1007/s11116-012-9422-9
17. Tavasszy, L., de Jong, G.: Modelling Freight Transport. Elsevier (2014). https://doi.org/10.1016/C2012-0-06032-2
18. Ducruet, C., Itoh, H.: Spatial network analysis of container port operations: the case of ship turnaround times. Netw. Spat. Econ. **22**, 883–902 (2022). https://doi.org/10.1007/s11067-022-09570-z
19. Russo, F., Peda, G., Musolino, G.: Container ports in country systems: calibration of the aggregate function for the time of the ship in port. Int. J. Transp. Dev. Integrat. **6**, 415–427 (2022). https://doi.org/10.2495/TDI-V6-N4-415-427
20. Russo, F., Pedà, G., Musolino, G.: Attributes influencing port times of container ships. WMU J. Marit. Affairs. **23**, 375–392 (2024). https://doi.org/10.1007/s13437-024-00336-7

21. Mazibuko, D.F., Mutombo, K., Kuroshi, L.: An evaluation of the relationship between ship turnaround time and key port performance indicators: a case study of a Southern African port. WMU J. Marit. Affairs. **23**, 499–524 (2024). https://doi.org/10.1007/s13437-024-00330-z
22. Ogden, K.W.: Urban Goods Movement: A Guide to Policy and Planning. Ashgate, Aldershot (1992)
23. Russo, F., Musolino, G., Assumma, V.: An integrated procedure to estimate demand flows of maritime container transport at international scale. IJSTL. **6**, 112 (2014). https://doi.org/10.1504/IJSTL.2014.059566
24. Ducruet, C.: The geography of maritime networks: a critical review. J. Transp. Geogr. **88**, 102824 (2020). https://doi.org/10.1016/j.jtrangeo.2020.102824
25. Russo, A., Campisi, T., Bouhouras, E., Basbas, S., Tesoriere, G.: Sustainable maritime passenger transport: a network analysis approach on a national basis. In: Gervasi, O., Murgante, B., Rocha, A.M.A.C., Garau, C., Scorza, F., Karaca, Y., Torre, C.M. (eds.) Computational Science and Its Applications – ICCSA 2023 Workshops, pp. 195–207. Springer Nature, Cham (2023). https://doi.org/10.1007/978-3-031-37120-2_13
26. Campisi, T., Russo, A., Trwdy, E., Zanne, M., Tesoriere, G.: The importance of the centrality of ports for passenger transport in the Adriatic-Ionian Basin. In: Gervasi, O., Murgante, B., Garau, C., Taniar, D., Rocha, A.M.A.C., Faginas Lago, M.N. (eds.) Computational Science and Its Applications – ICCSA 2024 Workshops, pp. 269–282. Springer Nature, Cham (2024). https://doi.org/10.1007/978-3-031-65329-2_18
27. Rindone, C., Russo, A.: A network analysis for HSR services in the south of Italy. (submitted to) International Conference on Computational Science and Its Applications-ICCSA 2024. (2024)
28. Manski, C.F.: The structure of random utility models. Theor. Decis. **8**, 229–254 (1977). https://doi.org/10.1007/BF00133443
29. Quattrone, A., Vitetta, A.: Random and fuzzy utility models for road route choice. Transp. Res. Part E Logist. Transp. Rev. **47**, 1126–1139 (2011). https://doi.org/10.1016/j.tre.2011.04.007
30. Henn, V.: Route choice making under uncertainty: a fuzzy logic based approach. In: Verdegay, J.-L. (ed.) Fuzzy Sets Based Heuristics for Optimization, pp. 277–292. Springer, Berlin, Heidelberg (2003). https://doi.org/10.1007/978-3-540-36461-0_18
31. Vitetta, A.: A quantum utility model for route choice in transport systems. Travel Behav. Soc. **3**, 29–37 (2016). https://doi.org/10.1016/j.tbs.2015.07.003
32. Cantarella, G.E.: Dynamics and Stochasticity in Transportation Systems: Tools for Transportation Network Modelling. Elsevier, Amsterdam, Netherlands (2019)
33. Rindone, C.: AIS data for building a transport maritime network: a pilot study in the Strait of Messina. Presented at the (submitted to) Conference ICCSA 2024: Computational Science and Its Applications
34. Cascetta, E.: Transportation Systems Analysis: Models and Applications. Springer US, Boston, MA (2009). https://doi.org/10.1007/978-0-387-75857-2
35. Vitetta, A.: Path choice in transport systems: comparing random, quantum, and fuzzy utility models in a small network. Front. Fut. Transp. **6**, 1544947 (2025). https://doi.org/10.3389/ffutr.2025.1544947
36. Panuccio, P.: Smart planning: from city to territorial system. Sustain. For. **11**, 7184 (2019). https://doi.org/10.3390/su11247184
37. Russo, F., Panuccio, P., Rindone, C.: Structural factors for A third-generation port: between hinterland regeneration and smart town In Gioia Tauro, Italy. In: Urban and Maritime Transport 2021, WIT Transactions on the Built Environment, vol. 204, pp. 79–90 (2021). https://doi.org/10.2495/UT210071
38. Russo, F., Rindone, C., Panuccio, P.: External interactions for A third generation port: urban and research developments. Int. J. Transp. Dev. Integrat., 253–270 (2022)

39. Polimeni, A., Belcore, O.M.: Times of ship in container ports: AIS data for maritime transport and ports applications. Presented at the (submitted to) Conference ICCSA 2024: Computational Science and Its Applications (2024)
40. Marco Belcore, O., Polimeni, A., Di Gangi, M.: Performance analysis for a maritime port with high-frequency services: an Italian case study. Case Stud. Transp. Policy. **17**, 101263 (2024). https://doi.org/10.1016/j.cstp.2024.101263

Enhancing Port Accessibility: Challenges, Measures, and Sustainability in Terminal Design

Elena Cocuzza[1]([✉])(iD), Matteo Ignaccolo[1](iD), Cristiano Marinacci[2](iD), Stefano Ricci[2](iD), Elen Twrdy[3](iD), and Maja Stojaković[3]

[1] Department of Civil Engineering and Architecture, University of Catania, Catania, Italy
elena.cocuzza@unict.it
[2] Department of Civil, Building and Environmental Engineering, Sapienza University of Rome, Rome, Italy
[3] Faculty of Maritime Studies and Transport, University of Ljubljana, Portoroz, Slovenia

Abstract. Port accessibility is a crucial factor in promoting sustainable development, as it directly impacts the three pillars of sustainability: economic growth, environmental quality, and social equity. Within the port context, accessibility plays a significant role in shaping operational performance, competitiveness, and the integration of the port with its surrounding environment. This study critically examines the main challenges and measures related to accessibility, delving into its distinct dimensions concerning both people and freight. For individuals, accessibility focuses on enabling citizens and tourists to easily and comfortably access the port and its associated urban or leisure activities. For freight, it emphasizes the necessity of an efficient multimodal transport network that facilitates the swift entry, handling, and departure of goods, with seamless connections to inland terminals.

The methodology includes an overview of the main challenges in understanding the role of accessibility in port terminals, the challenges and the definition of the criteria for accessibility in port terminals by the different stakeholders involved in the process. This approach provides a foundation for addressing accessibility-related issues and proposing measures that foster the development of competitive, integrated, and sustainable ports.

Keywords: Port Accessibility · Sustainable Development · Network analysis · Port Competition · Terminal Design

1 Introduction

The increasing attention in sustainable development has underlined the importance of accessibility as a valuable criterion for each of the three pillars of sustainability: economic growth, environmental quality and social equity. It is well known that the application of the concept of accessibility to a port has significant potential in determining and explaining the operational performance, competitiveness and economic performance of port (Wang and Cullinane, 2008), therefore accessibility is a core component of port development. Moreover, accessibility directly affects port-city relationships.

Port accessibility concerns:

O. Gervasi et al. (Eds.): ICCSA 2025 Workshops, LNCS 15897, pp. 156–166, 2026.
https://doi.org/10.1007/978-3-031-97660-5_12

- people, as citizens and tourists should have the possibility to simply and comfortably access the port and the leisure or urban life related activities located into;
- freight, indeed a competitive port is a node of an efficient transport network that allow easy and rapid entrance-handle-departure of merchandise, so an adequate accessibility with road and rail have to be assured, as well as the connection with inland terminals.

Therefore, the accessibility is not limited to the physical connection between port and hinterland but includes the facilitation of the movement of goods and people, the elimination of architectural barriers, modal integration, and the availability of digital and information services. Thus, an analysis of accessibility should require information about the maritime/road/railway transport network, geographical constraints, costs and the distribution of potential origin/destination sites.

Especially for freight transport, the location problem is essential because freight cannot act like a person selecting one destination from a group of potential locations for one purpose (Michalk et al., 2011). Moreover, elements affecting accessibility for freight transport are quite different from those of public or private transport of people, as shown in Fig. 1.

mode / elements	car	public transport	bicycle/walk	freight
time	walking to parking place	hidden waiting time	travel time	loading
	in veichle travel time	travel time of access / egress mode	bicycle parking	transport documents
	congestion time	waiting time at station		transport time (diff. modes)
	finding a parking place	in veichle travel time		transhipment
	walking to destination	transfer time		waiting at ramp, unloading
costs	fixed costs	cost of tickets/ fares	fixed costs	driver costs
	fuel costs		maintenance costs	depreciation
	maintenance costs			fuel and maintenance
	parking costs			rail/road use pricing
	raod pricing costs			insurance
effort	level of dis(comfort)	level of dis(comfort)	level of dis(comfort)	quality of transport
	physical effort	physical effort	physical effort	supply chain / network
	reliability	reliability	social safety	administration
	stress	stress		energy consumption
	accident risk	accident risk		reliability
	information	social safety		accident and theft risks
	status	information		tracking and tracing
		status		value added services

Fig. 1. Differences between elements affecting accessibility for personal and freight transport (Source: Michalk et al., 2011).

Besides that, port accessibility also depends on port types; among classifications within literature (Lam and Iskounen, 2010; Notteboom, 2009; Park and Medda, 2010; Siviero, 2004) based on various criteria (e.g. hierarchy, generation) are relevant the functional definitions of hub port, gateway port and feeder ports.

However, the focus is often on the one hand on the quality of the maritime connections (linking the ports together; another approach has been defined by the PAI - Port Accessibility Index), which takes into account the characteristics of the port, and on the other hand on the internal accessibility of the port (Fancello et al., 2023).

An ideal situation for a port is to have a good accessibility both for people and for freight; generally, it should have a direct relationship with the city center thanks to high quality pedestrian and cycling paths and areas, with a reduced interference with vehicular traffic, as well as good transit accessibility (Giuffrida et al., 2020). At the same time, the port should assure a high quality to commercial and operational activities that require adequate transport infrastructures for vehicular traffic.

In the European context, the Green Deal and the Sustainable and Smart Mobility Strategy place the maritime sector at the heart of the ecological and digital transition (European Commission, 2020). Strengthening port accessibility is thus part of a systemic vision that includes the decarbonization of transport, sustainable intermodality, the digitization of logistics services and the reduction of inequalities in access to infrastructure.

Therefore, it is crucial to ensure that maritime terminals are accessible, efficient and sustainable, in response to a growing global demand for inclusive mobility and environmentally friendly freight transport. Port accessibility needs to be considered in the infrastructural domain (e.g. intermodal connections, architectural barriers), in the logistical and operational domain (e.g. flow management, smart technologies) and in the environmental and social domain (e.g. impact on local communities, equality in the use of port space).

In the context of intensifying trade flows, for both people and goods, and increasing focus on sustainable development objectives, ports face complex challenges involving the design, operational management and environmental impact of terminal infrastructures.

Therefore, this research analyses the main critical issues of accessibility in order to promote a systemic and sustainable vision of port terminal design, aiming to combine economic efficiency, reduced environmental impact and social inclusion, in line with the Sustainable Development Goals (SDGs), specifically SDG 9 (Industry, Innovation and Infrastructure), SDG 11 (Sustainable Cities and Communities) and SDG 13 (Climate Action) supported by EU (European Commission, 2020).

A novel element of the research is an integrated and multidimensional approach, which simultaneously addresses passenger and freight accessibility within port terminals. Through the inclusion of stakeholder-defined and sustainability-related criteria, the study serves as a useful reference to support the planning and design of inclusive, resilient and future-oriented port infrastructure.

2 Methodology

Port accessibility is a crucial element not only to ensure the operational efficiency and competitiveness of a port, but also to foster a harmonious relationship with the city and local communities. While a well accessible port can stimulate international trade and the flow of goods, a port design that takes into account urban integration and environmental sustainability can transform an industrial center into a dynamic and positive hub for the entire surrounding area. The challenges related to improving the accessibility of ports are multiple and interconnected.

Part of the methodology was implemented as part of the Design of Maritime Sustainable Terminals (DEMASTER) project, during which groups of potential stakeholders were identified to better define and tune the strategic objectives for the design of port terminals. Furthermore, different ports, organized into a large cluster focused on the Adriatic-Ionian area (Fig. 2), were selected as case studies in order to validate the design methodology.

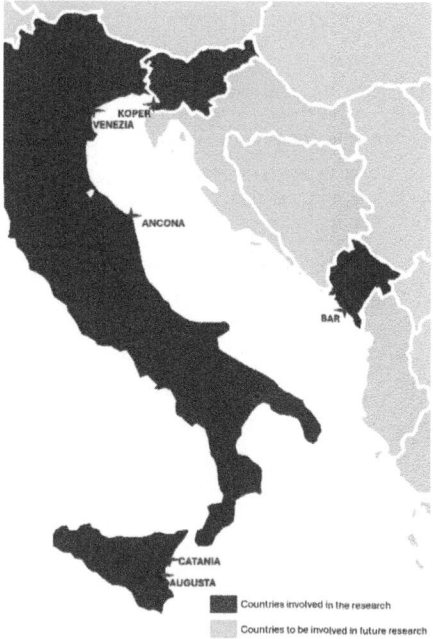

Fig. 2. Case studies of DEMASTER project (Source: Authors' elaboration).

In order to identify the main challenges, measures and considerations for sustainability in the design of the terminals, a qualitative research approach was chosen, centered on the use of thematic focus groups in some ports of the cluster. This method made it possible to gather in-depth insights and different perspectives from a variety of port-related stakeholders. Figure 3 shows the different stages of the implemented methodology.

A series of focus group discussions were organized, each addressing specific topics such as accessibility, environmental impact, operational efficiency and user involvement. The thematic approach allowed participants to engage in focused dialog and the research team to gather detailed qualitative data on the practical and strategic dimensions of terminal design.

Participants were selected based on their roles and importance within the port ecosystem to ensure a heterogeneous mix of perspectives. The selection included:

- Port authorities and terminal operators
- Shipping and logistics companies (including ship owners and cargo operators)
- Trade and professional associations
- Urban planners and environmental consultants
- Representatives of civil society, including citizens' groups.

This diversification of profiles helped to ensure that both institutional priorities and social concerns were equally represented, allowing for a holistic understanding of terminal design challenges and potential solutions.

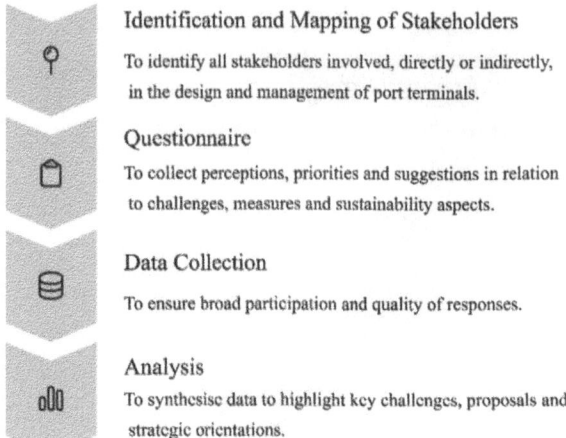

Identification and Mapping of Stakeholders

To identify all stakeholders involved, directly or indirectly, in the design and management of port terminals.

Questionnaire

To collect perceptions, priorities and suggestions in relation to challenges, measures and sustainability aspects.

Data Collection

To ensure broad participation and quality of responses.

Analysis

To synthesise data to highlight key challenges, proposals and strategic orientations.

Fig. 3. Stakeholder Engagement Process (Source: Authors' elaboration).

3   Results and Discussions

The focus group sessions were semi-structured and led by facilitators familiar with port planning and logistics. Where appropriate, findings from the focus groups were cross-referenced with findings from secondary data sources such as policy reports, academic literature and regulatory guidelines to validate and enrich the qualitative analysis.

The results are divided into three tables dealing with the role of accessibility in port terminals (Table 1), the challenges for accessibility in port terminals (Table 2) and the criteria for accessibility in port terminals (Table 3).

Each group of stakeholders brings a unique perspective. For maritime and logistics stakeholders, the focus is on streamlining operations, i.e. shortening waiting times for ships, improving multimodal connections and reducing congestion. But achieving these goals often requires extensive infrastructure upgrades and the integration of new digital tools. This is difficult when many different players and systems have to work in sync.

For institutional and public entities, the challenges are often related to administration—aligning strategies, securing long-term funding and managing complex regulations. Port projects are closely linked to urban development, environmental goals and sometimes even geopolitics. This can lead to slow, fragmented decision-making and delays in important investments.

On the social and end-user side, the conversation is more personal. Accessibility is not just about infrastructure, but also about equity, safety and dignity. When ports serve both cargo and people, it's a constant balancing act to keep things efficient and make them welcoming and safe, especially for those who have difficulty with access, such as older travelers, people with disabilities or visitors who are unfamiliar with the area.

Improving port accessibility requires more than just building new infrastructure—it requires a coordinated effort that considers efficiency, connectivity and inclusivity (Fig. 4).

Table 1. Results of Role of Accessibility in port terminals (Source: Authors' elaboration).

Stakeholder category	Results
Maritime Stakeholders	Terminal accessibility improves loading and unloading times for goods and embarking and disembarking times for people by reducing waiting times and costs.
Operational/Logistics Stakeholders	Multimodal accessibility is crucial for the sorting of goods; bottlenecks cause delays and high costs; port accessibility on both sea and land sides optimizes loading and unloading times and improves competitiveness; smooth connections with hinterland and freight hub are crucial.
Institutional/Public Stakeholders	Accessibility is key to attractiveness and efficient logistics; port accessibility affects local economic and employment development.
Social/End-User Stakeholders	Accessibility with public transport and pedestrian infrastructures is essential for passenger terminals, especially for the most vulnerable groups; well-accessible ferry and cruise terminals are crucial for enhancing the travel experience.

Table 2. Results of Accessibility Challenges in Port Terminals (Source: Authors' elaboration).

Stakeholder category	Results
Maritime Stakeholders	Terminal congestion; limited access slots; insufficient infrastructure for larger vessels.
Operational/Logistics Stakeholders	Inadequate space; inefficient flows of incoming and outgoing goods; delays in access; long waiting times at gates; inadequate road connections; lack of traffic management systems; unpredictable flow times of goods; difficulties in tracking shipments between nodes; bottlenecks in rail and road interconnections; insufficient integration with logistics hubs.
Institutional/Public Stakeholders	Obsolete infrastructure; complex approval processes for new access projects. Urban traffic congestion; environmental impact; balancing port growth with city needs.
Social/End-User Stakeholders	Lack of public transport links; architectural barriers in passenger terminals; inadequate signage; poor accessibility without private transportation.

For the maritime stakeholders ports should focus on improving and modernizing their infrastructure. This includes the expansion of berths, the deepening of waterways

Table 3. Results of Accessibility Criteria in Port Terminals (Source: Authors' elaboration).

Stakeholder category	Results
Maritime Stakeholders	Adequate quay and terminal access for large vessels; Congestion-free berthing and turnaround zones; Availability of shore-side electricity (cold ironing); Digital coordination with land transport schedules.
Operational/Logistics Stakeholders	Smart gate systems and buffer zones for trucks; Scalable terminal layouts for cargo peaks; Charging infrastructure for electric trucks and handling equipment; Seamless cargo flow (sea-rail-road); IoT tracking and warehouse connectivity; Digitalization of cargo and equipment process, and gate status.
Institutional/Public Stakeholders	Electrification of quays (cold ironing) to reduce vessel emissions at berth; Integrated multimodal access (road, rail, sea, public transport); Environmental sustainability standards; Efficient customs zones and traffic flows; Port Community Systems (PCS) for integrated data sharing among actors - Digital customs clearance systems and pre-arrival notifications; compatibility with urban planning goals.
Social/End-User Stakeholders	Barrier-free passenger pathways (elevators, ramps, signage); - Easy public transport access; Centralized services (ticketing, waiting areas, info points); Integration with electric mobility (e-bus, EV charging stations); Passenger information systems (real-time schedules, notifications).

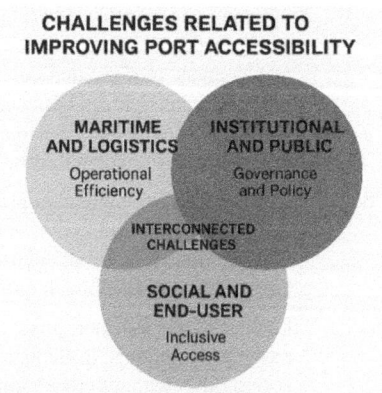

Fig. 4. Interconnected challenges between stakeholders (Source: Authors' elaboration).

for larger vessels and the introduction of intelligent planning systems that help to reduce congestion. Collaboration with private partners can also help accelerate infrastructure modernization and share financial responsibility.

Improving the flow of goods and connectivity is crucial for logistics and operational stakeholders. Expanding road and rail links to the port, especially seamless connectivity to inland freight hubs, will help reduce delays. The introduction of intelligent traffic management systems at the port gates can streamline truck movements and reduce waiting times. Digitizing shipment tracking across the supply chain will improve visibility and coordination. In addition, the development of nearby logistics parks or dry ports can help reduce congestion in the port's core area.

There is a clear need for institutional and public stakeholders to simplify the regulatory and approval processes for new access projects. Faster and more transparent planning can help overcome delays and ensure timely implementation. Urban and port development should be closely coordinated, especially in the border areas between city and port, to avoid conflicts and promote mutual benefits. Environmental concerns need to be addressed proactively, with clear strategies to reduce noise, air pollution and traffic. It is also important to involve and inform the public throughout the development process to build trust and support.

From a social and end-user stakeholder perspective, ports need to become more inclusive and user-friendly. Improving access to passenger terminals by public transport is crucial, especially for people who do not have access to private vehicles. Removing physical and architectural barriers will make it easier for all users, including people with disabilities, to navigate the terminals. Improved signage, available in multiple languages, and intuitive wayfinding systems will also help to improve the user experience. Ports should offer special services and spaces that meet the needs of vulnerable travelers, such as the elderly or people with reduced mobility.

To focus these efforts, it is recommended that ports develop a comprehensive port accessibility plan that includes infrastructure, logistics, technology and inclusive design. Regular stakeholder engagement should be encouraged through roundtables and consultation processes to ensure that decisions take into account the needs of all users. Pilot projects and innovation initiatives can serve as testing grounds for new ideas before they are implemented on a broader scale. Finally, ports should actively seek funding opportunities from regional, national or EU programs to support strategic improvements, especially those with long-term social and environmental benefits.

To improve port accessibility, we need to meet the real needs of the people who use, manage and depend on ports every day. In Table 3 are the answers for each affected group.

For maritime stakeholders ports need to be ready for modern ships—both in terms of size and technology. This means expanding berths and upgrading terminals so that larger ships can dock without delay. It is equally important to reduce congestion at the berths so that ships can enter and leave more smoothly. The installation of shore power (cold ironing) allows ships to turn off their engines while in port, reducing emissions and noise. For all this to run efficiently, ports should use digital tools to stay in sync with truck and train schedules so that everything comes together in real time.

For operational and logistics stakeholders the focus is on speed, efficiency and reliability. Introducing smart gate systems and creating buffer zones for trucks can reduce long queues and improve flow at peak times. Terminals should be flexibly designed to handle peak loads without causing chaos. As part of the shift to greener logistics, it is also important to install charging stations for electric trucks and equipment. On the technical side, the integration of real-time tracking systems and digital warehouse connections will keep goods moving and make the whole process more transparent and predictable.

Public authorities play an important role in shaping the accessibility and sustainability of ports. Investments in shore power systems support cleaner port operations and are in line with environmental goals. Smooth customs procedures are crucial and can be improved by digital pre-arrival systems that reduce waiting times. Data exchange between all parties via a Port Community System (PCS) also improves coordination. And importantly, all of this needs to be aligned with urban planning so that ports grow in harmony with the surrounding cities.

For social and end-user stakeholders the port areas—especially passenger terminals—should be welcoming and accessible to everyone. This means creating barrier-free pathways with ramps, elevators and clear signage for people with reduced mobility. It also means making it easy to get to and from the port by public transport, not just by car. Within the terminal, centralized services such as ticket counters, information points and comfortable waiting areas should be available and easy to find. And with real-time information systems, travelers can find out about timetables, changes and available services.

By bringing together these improvements—better infrastructure, cleaner technologies, smarter systems and more thoughtful design—we can create ports that are not only efficient and competitive, but also welcoming, sustainable and future-proof. This requires collaboration, investment and a shared commitment to building ports that truly work for everyone.

4 Conclusion

The design and development of port terminals are no longer just a question of infrastructure and logistics—they are complex, multi-dimensional challenges that must meet economic, environmental, social and technological requirements. This paper highlights the link between port accessibility, sustainability and stakeholder involvement and emphasizes that sustainable terminals require a holistic, collaborative approach.

In thematic focus groups, various stakeholders—including port authorities, logistics companies, trade associations, urban planners and citizen groups—identified key barriers, such as infrastructure constraints, congestion, policy fragmentation and gaps in inclusive design. These findings underscore the need for a coordinated approach that balances efficiency and inclusiveness, operational speed and long-term sustainability.

To address these challenges, the paper makes a number of practical and forward-looking recommendations, from modernizing port infrastructure and digitizing logistics flows to improving public transport links and integrating clean energy solutions. Transportation planning is no longer conceivable without the use of modern technologies, smart solutions and intelligent services (Stojaković and Twrdy, 2024). The introduction of smart port technologies—such as AI, IoT and real-time dashboards for accessibility—is proving to be a crucial factor that can transform terminals into dynamic, adaptable systems.

The integration of Artificial Intelligence (AI) and Internet of Things (IoT) technologies into port operations offers significant potential to improve efficiency and responsiveness. These technologies can be used to predict congestion patterns, optimize traffic and cargo routes in real time and support proactive decision-making. By dynamically coordinating resources, smart port systems contribute to smoother operations, shorter waiting times and improved throughput, supporting both operational efficiency and environmental goals (Acciaro et al., 2014).

Ultimately, the success of terminal design lies in its ability to serve all users efficiently, equitably and sustainably. Achieving this goal requires more than just investment in hardware. It requires ongoing stakeholder collaboration, a clear policy framework and a commitment to innovation that puts people and the environment at the heart of port development.

To address the environmental impact of port transportation, ports should explore solutions for low-emission last-mile connectivity, such as the integration of bike-sharing systems, electric shuttle services and other forms of green mobility. These measures not only help to reduce congestion and emissions in urban areas adjacent to the port, but also improve accessibility for port workers and passengers, which fits into broader strategies for sustainable urban transport (OECD, 2014).

The development of publicly accessible digital dashboards that display real-time accessibility data is a forward-looking approach to stakeholder engagement and operational transparency. These platforms can provide live updates on access conditions, traffic flows and modal connectivity, helping logistics providers, authorities and end users to make informed decisions. Such tools also support joint planning and improve accountability by giving stakeholders better insight into the performance and accessibility of port systems (European Commission, 2020).

The research was conducted on a selection of case studies analysed within the DEMASTER project. Consequently, the results obtained reflect the limitations related to the number and specificity of the contexts examined. However, this analysis offers a solid basis for future in-depth analysis and expansion, which could include a larger number of cases, involving other countries in the identified geographical cluster (as shown in Fig. 4). The results obtained represent a useful contribution to improving planning and design processes in the sector, orienting them towards principles of environmental sustainability, social equity and climate crisis mitigation.

Acknowledgments. This research has been partially funded by Sapienza University of Rome under the project Design of Maritime Sustainable Terminals (DEMASTER) n. protocollo RG1231888CA06675, 2023.

References

Acciaro, M., Vanelslander, T., Sys, C., Ferrari, C., Roumboutsos, A., Giuliano, G., Kapros, S.: Environmental sustainability in seaports: a framework for successful innovation. Res. Transp. Bus. Manag. **8**, 1–10 (2014). https://doi.org/10.1016/j.rtbm.2014.01.001

European Commission: EU Ports Policy: Port Services and Financial Transparency. European Commission. (2020). https://transport.ec.europa.eu

Fancello, G., Serra, P., Vitiello, D.A.N.I.E.L.: A port accessibility index for Mediterranean container terminals. Europ. Transp. **90**, 1–11 (2023)

Ferrari, C., Parola, F., Gattorna, E.: Measuring the quality of port hinterland accessibility: the Ligurian case. Transp. Policy. **18**(2), 382–391 (2011). https://doi.org/10.1016/j.tranpol.2010. 10.003

Giuffrida, N., Cocuzza, E., Ignaccolo, M., Inturri, G.: A comprehensive index to evaluate non-motorized accessibility to port-cities. Int. J. Sustain. Dev. Plann. **15**(5), 743–749 (2020)

Lam, L., Iskounen, A.: Feeder ports, Inland ports and Corridors – Time for a closer look. Portek Articles in Industry Journals, Article in HTG Yearbook (2010)

LNCS Homepage: (n.d.). http://www.springer.com/lncs, last accessed 25 Oct 2023

Michalk, P., Meimbresse, B., Schmidt, C.: Benchmarking accessibility of ports and inland terminals in European corridor projects. In: 3rd IEEE International Symposium on Logistics and Industrial Informatics (LINDI), vol. 149, no. 158, pp. 25–27 (2011)

Notteboom, T., Rodrigue, J.P.: Port regionalization: towards a new phase in port development. Marit. Policy Manag. **32**(3), 297–313 (2005). https://doi.org/10.1080/03088830500139885

Notteboom, T.: Path dependency and contingency in the development of multi-port gateway regions and multi-port hub regions. In: Notteboom, T., Ducruet, C., de Langen, P.W. (eds.) Ports in Proximity: Competition and Coordination among Adjacent Seaports. Aldershot, Ashagate (2009)

OECD: The Competitiveness of Global Port-Cities. OECD Publishing (2014). https://doi.org/10. 1787/9789264205271-en

Papanikolaou, A., Lekakou, M., Remoundos, I.: Port accessibility for persons with disabilities: the case of passenger ports in Greece. Marit. Policy Manag. **44**(6), 760–775 (2017). https:// doi.org/10.1080/03088839.2017.1341062

Park, Y.; Medda, F. Classification of Container Ports on the Basis of Networks, 12th WCTR, July 11–15, 2010 – Lisbon, Portugal (2010)

Siviero L: Itinerari trasversali mediterranei ed intermodalità mare-ferro, in: I trasporti e l'Europa. Politiche, infrastrutture, concorrenza, a cura di G. Polidori, E. Musso e E. Marcucci. Atti della VII Riunione scientifica annuale della Società Italiana degli Economisti dei Trasporti, Genova 18–20 novembre 2004, Franco Angeli, Milano (2004)

Stojaković, M., Twrdy, E.: Urban transport—synergies between city and the port: the example of the city of Koper. Put i saobraćaj. **70**(1), 9–14 (2024). https://doi.org/10.31075/PIS.70.01.02

Wang, Y., Cullinane, K.: Measuring container port accessibility: an application of the principal eigenvector method (PEM). Marit. Econ. Logist. **10**, 75–89 (2008)

World Bank: Port Development and Competitiveness: Emerging Trends and Best Practices. World Bank.. (2021). https://www.worldbank.org/en/topic/transport/publication

Spatial-Temporal Simulation of Routes Connecting Containers Ports

Massimo Di Gangi⬡, Orlando M. Belcore(✉)⬡, and Antonio Polimeni⬡

Department of Engineering, University of Messina, Messina, Italy
{mdigangi,obelcore,antonio.polimeni1}@unime.it

Abstract. Ports are crucial in global trade, and shipping trade is relevant for all industries. Even more so now that we are experiencing political and social stresses, a situation which means that maritime routes are increasingly less safe and economically more expensive. Inefficiency emerged as a fundamental factor in the competitiveness of a maritime terminal, and research on container ships plays a relevant role in understanding and assessing the competitiveness of the infrastructure. Consequently, the time elapsed between entering and leaving the port can express the capacity of the infrastructure to handle loading and unloading operations, thus representing a measure of receptiveness. Obtaining detailed data for different ports requires a deep understanding of ship turnaround time, workloads at the yard, and company priorities, thus relying on direct interviews with port workers. Due to the exploratory nature of the study and to overcome the costly and time-consuming on-field surveys, this paper analyzed the performance through a simulation process. As input, typical waiting and handling time probability curves for major container ports are derived from a large dataset of Automatics Information Systems, and some of the most crowded and longest commercial routes are analyzed to evaluate route performances in terms of exchanged numbers of containers, waiting time at the anchoring, and berth operations. The proposed framework involves multiple steps concerning (i) possible route stops, (ii) berth occupation, and (iii) route speed variation with the final goal of reducing the loss of time and increasing the exchanged number of containers for the terminal.

Keywords: maritime logistics · AIS · container ports · mesoscopic simulation

1 Introduction

The quantity of freight moved by maritime transport in 2023 was more than 12,000 million tons (with an increase of approximately 2.4% compared to the previous year) and the trade by containers was close to 160 million exchanged TEUs (but with a decrease of 0.14% with respect to 2022) [1]. With reference to the main maritime routes, the East–West routes (Trans-Pacific, Asia-Europe, Transatlantic) in 2023 handled more than 36% of global containerized trade volumes. In the coming years, growth is expected both in the total quantity transported and in the number of containers moved [2, 3]. Therefore, the development of ports [4–6] and the efficient movement of containers across ports are

© The Author(s), under exclusive license to Springer Nature Switzerland AG 2026
O. Gervasi et al. (Eds.): ICCSA 2025 Workshops, LNCS 15897, pp. 167–180, 2026.
https://doi.org/10.1007/978-3-031-97660-5_13

a cornerstone of global logistics. This aspect is treated in the literature from many points of view: technological [7, 8], economic [9, 10], and environmental [11, 12]. One of the approaches used to analyze the container market is the representation of the shipping network as a multi-layer graph, where (in general) each layer corresponds to a set of specific routes. Such a type of representation allows us to analyze the shipping network in order to individuate weak points and evaluate indicators on the performance of the network. Defining the structure of the network, many authors refer to centrality measures (derived from graph theory) to analyze them [13, 14], as an example of measuring the importance of a port in the related geographic area [15] while others focused on the uncertainty of the travel time [16, 17].

In this work, attention is focused on the trip of the single container from the origin to the destination, taking into account key operational events such as ship arrivals, loading and unloading operations, and port transitions. To achieve this goal, after representing the network with graph theory, a mesoscopic simulation approach is implemented. Key aspects include ship-port interactions, container tracking, and statistical analysis. Efficient routing and scheduling are essential to minimize costs and environmental impact. Public transport simulation techniques, commonly used in urban transit systems, provide a promising framework for modeling maritime shipping networks. The model considers container shipping lines (e.g., RTW, pendulum, feeder) as collective transport routes. A frequency is associated with each line, and distances between ports on the same line are calculated. Using graph theory, optimal routes are determined between origin-destination port pairs, treating the problem as a hyper-path computation. The proposed approach facilitates network optimization, efficiency analysis, and dynamic simulations. The approach allows the following:

- defining a transport network composed of ports and shipping lines;
- calculating distances between ports and travel times;
- constructing a graph representation of the shipping network;
- computing optimal routes between all port pairs.

Referring to supply chain resilience, this approach can be useful to assess failure scenarios, that is, when a service fails (partially or completely) and it is required to define a new route to reach the destination.

The paper is structured as follows. In Sect. 2 the literature review, Sect. 3 contains the description of the proposed methodology, while Sect. 4 reports the results of a test application. Finally, the conclusions in Sect. 5.

2 Literature Review

The transport revolution based on the use of containers [18] drastically reduced the cost of maritime freight transport and has caused the birth of a global liner shipping network that allows even small importers/exporters to exchange goods internationally [19]. In this context, the connectivity between different ports plays a crucial role in international container trade, affecting the value of export and the volume of transshipment [19].

International maritime trade requires that the global shipping network allows effective port access in any country [20], therefore, it is necessary to analyze the network and define some indicators to assess its performance. Bartholdi et al. [21] proposed an index to measure the connectivity of a port considering both the topology of the shipping network and the movements of containers between ports in the network. Wang et al. [22] implemented an approach to extract the global shipping network from historical data collected with the automatic identification system (AIS) of the ships; the aim is to analyze the freight flows at different geographical levels. Tsiotas and Ducruet [23] provided a methodological framework able to analyze the global container shipping network in relation to distance and identified three different geographical levels in its structure: local connectivity, international connectivity and intercontinental connectivity. Pan et al. [24] used a graph-based approach to quantify container shipping network connectivity and improve it by adding new links between ports (a gravity model is applied for this scope) if necessary. Jiang et al. [25] proposed a learning method to analyze the container shipping network and provided the results of a cluster analysis. Representing the global container shipping network as a multilayer network (where each layer represents the route of a shipping company), Xu et al. [26] used an AIS data set to identify the global container shipping network and introduced some indices to compare ports within the network. Focusing on European ports, Liu et al. [27] calculated three service-based centrality indices (degree, closeness and betweenness centrality) to compare the centrality of each port with respect to liner services with China. Wang and Cullinane [28] proposed a framework to calculate the centrality measures of a container port, taking into account the characteristics of the port and its role in the entire network (for example, market coverage). The aim is to identify the importance of a port in the network (at regional and/or global level) in relation to the centrality measures.

A study on the container network robustenss is report in Want et al. [29], which developed an analysis based on network evolution over the time. Chen et al. [30] proposed a definition of resilience (calculated from the perspective of shippers) for a local container shipping network and provided a measurement model to assess it. Viljoen and Joubert [31] discussed the vulnerability of the shipping container network when some links are removed to simulate a disruption; the results demonstrated that the container shipping network remains functional, although it is disrupted, even a change in the service configuration is required. Starting from the consideration that there are shipping routes that cross the main channels of the world (e.g., Panama, Suez), Wu et al. [32] analyzed the vulnerability of the entire shipping network by removing the routes that require the use of one of the channels. Some network metrics are used to quantify vulnerability. Huang et al. [33] proposed a shipping hub-and-spoke network design problem to optimize the position of the hub and spoke ports considering the risk of failure (complete or partial) of the port and the port congestion. Calatayud et al. [34] noted that the vulnerability of the shipping flows depends on the position occupied by the countries in the network. In particular, they explored the case of containerships and liner shipping services to highlight the dependence and vulnerability of international trade emerging from the network structure.

3   Methodology

The goal of the proposed is to model the movements of the containers across different ports: given a container, the procedure finds the best route to get it from the port of origin to the port of destination using the available shipping lines. To do this, in addition to having information on ports and lines, it is necessary to simulate the supply system and the operations that take place in the port. Figure 1 shows schematically the proposed approach. The procedure consists of three blocks: the identification of the *shipping network*, voted to calculate the *shortest paths*; a *mesoscopic approach* that takes as input the shortest paths, and the result of a *discrete event simulation* aimed at simulating the events that occur from the ship's arrival in port until its departure. The first operation is data collection, aimed at obtaining information on *ports* (e.g., position) and *shipping lines* (e.g., frequency). The next step is the characterization of the supply: the *graph construction* takes as input the port positions (that represent the nodes of the graph) putted in the set V, and the shipping lines (that represent the arcs of the graph), putted in the set E. After the graph $G(E, V)^1$ is obtained, the shipping network $T(V, E, c)$ is identified by associating a cost at each arc, considering the characteristics of the shipping lines. To evaluate the arc costs (vector c), the arcs are divided into three sets (disjoint), with the same approach used for public transport lines ([35]):

1. *on-board* arcs (set E_1), that link two ports, the associated cost is the travel time
   $c_1 = d/v$, where d is the distance between two ports and v is the average ship speed;
2. *loading arcs* (set E_2), which simulate the load of the container on the ship, the associated cost (under the assumption that the shipping line is perfectly regular) is the waiting time $c_2 = 1/2 \cdot \phi$, where ϕ is the shipping line frequency;
3. *unloading arcs*, whit cost c_3 linked with the handling/transshipment operations.

Then, starting from $T(V, E, c)$, the *shortest paths* are calculated using a procedure for the search for the shortest path (in our case, the Dijkstra's algorithm). In shortest path calculation, the cost considered is the sum of the previously defined costs, as follows:

$$c = c_1 + c_2 + c_3 \tag{1}$$

The procedure described up to this point therefore allows us to obtain the shortest paths that the ships will follow during the simulation; note that these paths remain fixed for the entire simulation.

The shortest paths, the container *demand*, and the results of a discrete *event simulation* are the input for the *mesoscopic simulation* of the system. Focusing on the discrete event simulation approach, it is applied to simulate the events related to the status of the ship; then four different of them can be considered:

- ship arrival, the ship arrives at the port and prepares for the anchoring phase,
- ship at anchor, the ship waits at anchor until it is time to enter port,

---

[1] A graph is defined by a set of elements called nodes and by a set of pairs of nodes belonging to the nodes. The links in a graph modeling a transportation system represent phases and/or activities of possible trips [35].

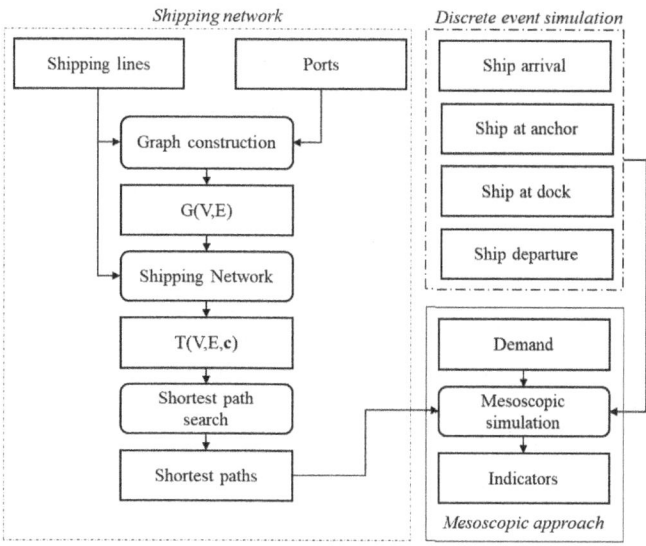

Fig. 1. The proposed approach

- ship at dock, the ship is stationary at the dock during loading/unloading operations,
- ship departure, the ship has finished loading/unloading operations and, respecting the scheduled departure time, is leaving for the next port.

In general, the mesoscopic approach works by grouping elements in packets elements with homogeneous characteristics and simulating the movements of such packets. The approach proposed in this paper considers as a packet a single container that travels from the origin to the destination following the shortest path. Since the simulation is dynamic, the demand values also have a time coordinate, this means that for each container, it is considered the instant t_0 of arrival at port and the instant t_1 of departure from port. Between these two time instants, the instant t_3 in which the container is loaded on the ship must be considered. The *indicators* obtained as output of the simulation are the following:

- the waiting time of the container, intended as the difference between the instant of arrival at port ant the instant when the container is embarked;
- the travel time;
- the transshipment time, to be considered only in the case when to move from one port to another one it is necessary to use at least two different shipping lines.

The proposed approach is scalable to take into account other specific situations: in fact, the graph approach described below allows each situation to be represented both in terms of topology (shipping arcs) and costs (in general, at each arc the cost of a maritime operation can be associated).

4 Test Application

The test application reported in the next paragraph aims to illustrate the applicability of the proposed method, without claiming to build the global container shipping network. In fact, only a subset of shipping lines is considered (Sect. 4.1), at the international and local levels.

4.1 Supply Network

The supply network consists of some lines selected on the web from the data made available by shipping companies. In this particular case, 2 shipping lines have been considered, and they were identified among those offered by the CMA CGM company. The lines considered are as follows:

- Amerigo (*AMERIGO,* Fig. 2), a line operating from Mediterranean Sea and North America (East Coast) and vice versa;
- SSLMED Cross Med Service (*CROSSMED,* Fig. 3), Intra Mediterranean (Spain, Morocco, Italy, Turkey, Egypt, Lebanon, Syria).

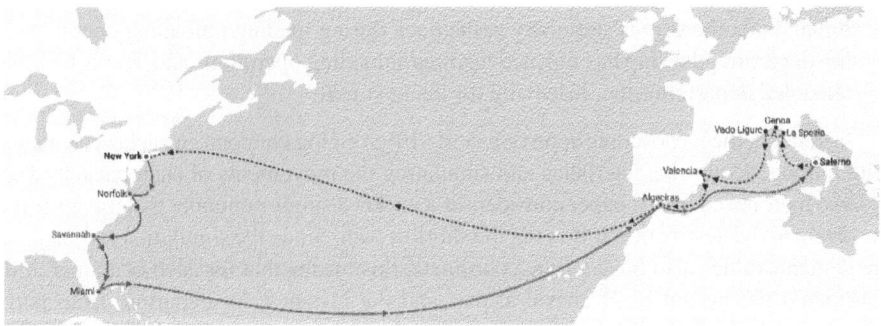

Fig. 2. The Amerigo route

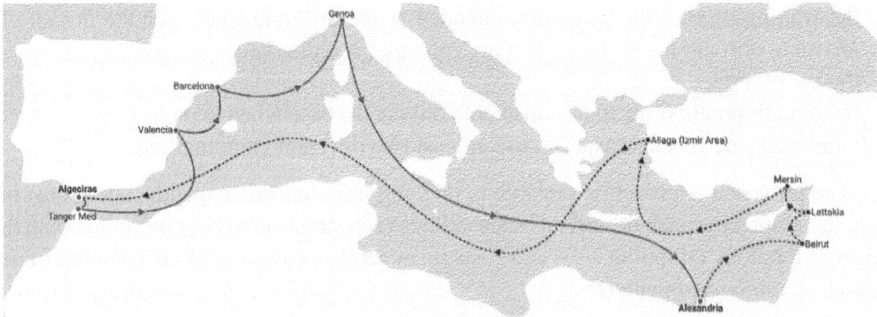

Fig. 3. The Crossmed route

Table 1 reports some characteristics of the shipping routes reported above. In particular, data as frequency, number of ships operating in the route, number of port calls and duration of the navigation are listed.

Table 1. Main characteristics of the considered shipping lines

Name	Frequency [days]	Ship fleet	Ports of call	Duration [days]
AMERIGO	7	7	11	49
CROSSMED	7	4	10	28

4.2 Graph Model

Maritime routes are schematized using a graph-based supply model similar to the one used to represent transit lines, as shown in Fig. 4. With reference to Fig. 4, each port ($P1,...P5$) corresponds to a stop that is connected to the corresponding node of the line representing the stationing of the line itself in the port ($L1, L2$) by means of a pair of arcs, one representing the loading/embarkation (the purple ones) and the other representing the unloading/disembarkation (the black ones). The different stationing nodes of the lines in the ports are connected to each other by arcs (the blue ones) that represent navigation.

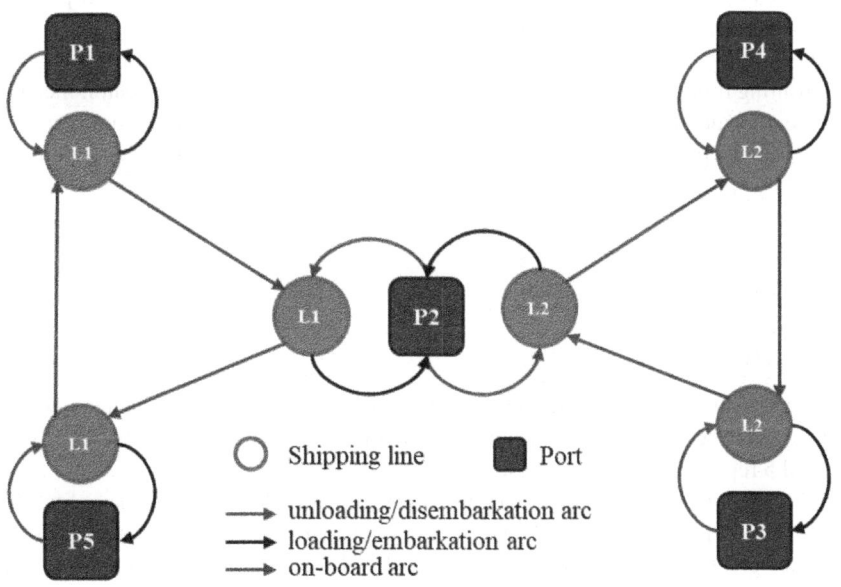

Fig. 4. Representation of the graph

A travel cost is associated with each kind of arc. The navigation time necessary to make the trip from port to port is associated with arcs representing the lines (the blue ones in Fig. 4). Such a time is evaluated considering the day of departure from the port of origin and the day of arrival at the port of destination, as scheduled and without considering the weather conditions.

The average waiting time (generally ½ of the intertime between two successive passages of the same line at the port) is associated with the loading arcs (the purple ones); a fictitious time, representing the handling time, is associated with the unloading arcs (the black ones).

The routes on which the containers are routed to reach the port of destination from the port of origin are computed as the minimum cost paths connecting origin to destination in the graph considering the costs above defined for each arc.

With reference to Fig. 4, the route that containers follow to reach port *P3* starting from port *P5* corresponds to boarding on line *L1*, up to port *P2* where they are unloaded and the transshipment takes place boarding successively on line *L2* to reach the port *P3* of destination.

4.3 Results

The simulation covers 60 days and considers as origin-destination the ports belonging to the shipping lines reported in Table 1. The ports considered in this small test are 17 (Fig. 5), and the origin-destination pairs considered are 272, of which 109 involve at least one transfer.

The distance *d* between them varies from values less than 100 nautical miles to values greater than 4000 miles. In particular (Fig. 6) for 39.71% of the o/d pairs, the travel distance is greater than 4000 nautical miles.

The indicators considered in this test are linked with the time, in particular the travel time, waiting time, and transshipment time are considered. For each indicator, mean and variance are calculated and the coefficient of variation c_v was chosen to summarize the results. Taking into account the distance classes defined above, for each of them c_v is grouped by value as follows:

- $c_v \in [0\%, 5\%)$,
- $c_v \in [5\%, 10\%)$,
- $c_v \in [10\%, 15\%)$,
- $c_v \in [15\%, 20\%)$,
- $c_v \geq 20\%$.

By crossing distance and coefficient of variation classes, it is individuated how much o/d pairs fall in such intervals of distance and coefficient of variation. Tables from Table 2, 3, 4, and 5 report the results of these analyzes.

Table 2 is on the total time, it can be observed that there are 96 *o/d* pairs for which the value of c_v is in the range of [5%, 10%), in particular revealing a low variation for the routes greater than 4000 nautical miles (41 o/d pairs, i.e. the 15% of them, fall in this situation). In addition, there are 88 *o/d* pairs for which the value of c_v is less than 5%, and 53 of them (about 20% of the total pairs) are in the distance range greater than 4000 miles.

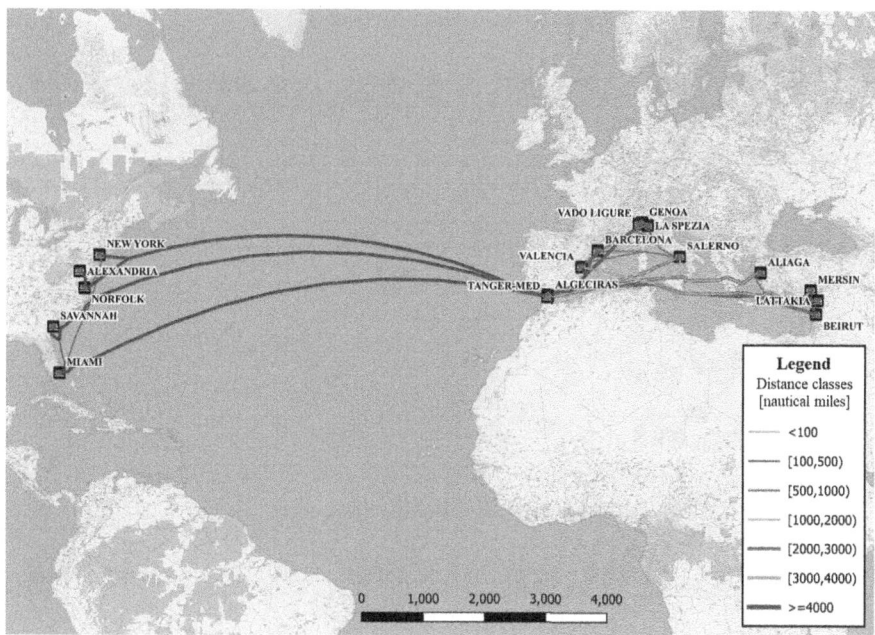

Fig. 5. The ports and the routes considered in the test application

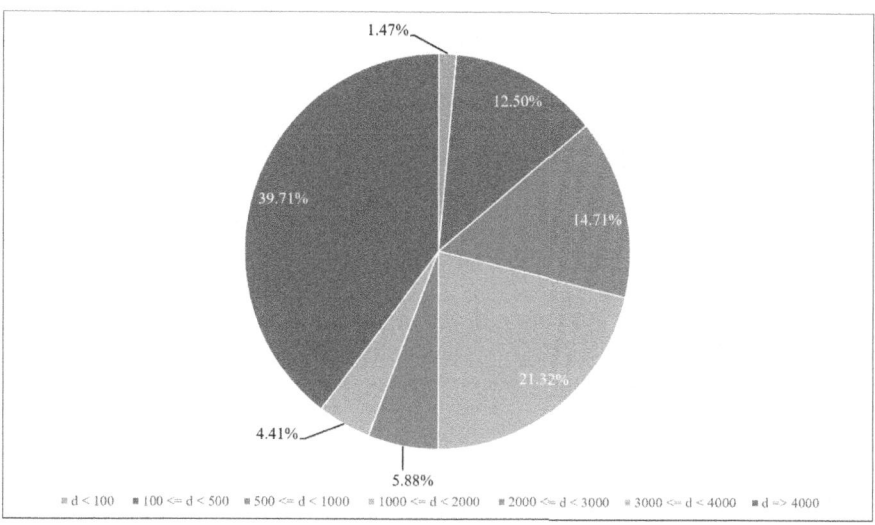

Fig. 6. Travel distance classes (distance d in nautical miles)

Table 3 reports the travel time; in this case for 259 out of 272 pairs, the coefficient cv is less than 5%, the pairs are distributed over different distance classes, with a peak (about 37% of all pairs) for distances greater than 4000 miles.

Table 2. Analysis of the total time

d^*/c_v	[0%, 5%)	[5%, 10%)	[10%, 15%)	[15%, 20%)	≥20%	*Total*
<100	1			1	2	*4*
[100,500)	10	7	1	2	14	*34*
[500,1000)	11	11	5	4	9	*40*
[1000,2000)	11	29	13	5		*58*
[2000,3000)		4	12			*16*
[3000,4000)	2	4	5	1		*12*
≥4000	53	41	5	6	3	*108*
Total	*88*	*96*	*41*	*19*	*28*	*272*

*Distance in nautical miles

Table 3. Analysis of the travel time

d/c_v	[0%, 5%)	[5%, 10%)	[10%, 15%)	[15%, 20%)	≥20%	*Total*
<100	4					*4*
[100,500)	31	2		1		*34*
[500,1000)	39	1				*40*
[1000,2000)	57	1				*58*
[2000,3000)	16					*16*
[3000,4000)	12					*12*
≥4000	100	3	5			*108*
Total	*259*	*7*	*5*	*1*	*0*	*272*

Table 4. Analysis of the waiting time

d/c_v	[0%, 5%)	[5%, 10%)	[10%, 15%)	[15%, 20%)	≥20%	*Total*
<100					4	*4*
[100,500)	1	3	3	4	23	*34*
[500,1000)	1	8	5	1	25	*40*
[1000,2000)	1	2	13	8	34	*58*
[2000,3000)			2	4	10	*16*
[3000,4000)		2	2		8	*12*
≥4000	11	24	17	10	46	*108*
Total	*14*	*39*	*42*	*27*	*150*	*272*

Table 5. Analysis of the transshipment time

d/c_v	[0%, 5%)	[5%, 10%)	[10%, 15%)	[15%, 20%)	≥20%	*Total*
<100	1					*1*
[100,500)	6	1			4	*11*
[500,1000)	7	3	1		2	*13*
[1000,2000)	20	1	1		4	*26*
[2000,3000)						*0*
[3000,4000)	3				1	*4*
≥4000	31	2			21	*54*
Total	*68*	*7*	*2*		*32*	*109*

Table 4 relies with the waiting time, for this component of time most *o/d* pairs fall in the range with a coefficient c_v greater than 20%, the range distance between 1000 and 2000 miles, and the range greater than 4000 miles are worth highlighting.

Finally, Table 5 reports the values of the transshipment time (note that the values in this table are limited to the 109 o/d pairs for which the transshipment is possible). In this case, 68 od/pairs (about 62% of the total) have a c_v less than 5% (about 28% are in the distance range greater than 4000 miles, about 18% in the range between 1000 and 2000 miles). There are also 32 cases (29%) for which the coefficient of variation assumes values greater than 20%.

5   Conclusions

This study presents a simulation framework for modeling container movements across ports based on a novel application of public transport simulation techniques transferred to container shipping. In fact, shipping routes are represented as public transport, considering specific arcs for loading/unloading and handling operations. A procedure based on three blocks has been developed: (1) the shipping network identification (considering both routes and frequencies); (2) a discrete event simulator, to simulate the procedures that are activated when the ship arrives at the port; (3) a mesoscopic simulation procedure to simulate dynamically the travel of a container (it is assumed that the packet to move in the simulation is the container) assessing the performances of the shipping services.

The proposed approach is applied to a test case, considering some existing shipping routes with related frequencies, and, for each simulated container belonging to an o/d pair, its travel is followed during simulation. Such travel can be direct or not, in this last case, the container is transferred from one ship to another (also belonging to different companies) to reach the destination. In particular, the simulation has been performed for a time horizon of 60 days (i.e., the demand is spread over 60 days and the simulation continues until the last container has arrived at its destination), for 17 ports and 272 o/d pairs (109 of them involve the transshipment). The coefficient of variation of the time has been chosen as an indicator to assess the procedure.

The model offers valuable insight into logistics operations and forms the basis for further research in this domain.

The limitations of this work are the size of the database and the fact that the data comes from only one shipping company. Both aspects can be easily overcome in future research developments.

Future work will focus on integrating real-time data, visualizations, and economic factors to further optimize global supply chain efficiency also considering the analysis of a case study. In addition, the procedure could be improved by introducing a procedure that allows the paths to be modified during the travel (re-routing).

Acknowledgments. This study is carried out within the research project "National and local factors affecting times of ships in container ports", Piano Nazionale di Ripresa e Resilienza (PNRR), Next Generation EU. Progetti di Rilevante Interesse Nazionale PRIN_2022_PNRR_P202292YFW. CUP: C53D2300878001. This piece of work reflects only the authors' views and opinions, neither the European Union nor the European Commission can be considered responsible for them.

Disclosure of Interests. The authors have no competing interests to declare that are relevant to the content of this article.

References

1. United Nations Conference on Trade and Development: Review of Maritime Transport 2024. (2024)
2. Russo, F., Musolino, G., Assumma, V.: Ro-ro and lo-lo alternatives between Mediterranean countries: factors affecting the service choice. Case Stud. Transp. Policy. **11**, 100960 (2023). https://doi.org/10.1016/j.cstp.2023.100960
3. Russo, F., Musolino, G., Assumma, V.: An integrated procedure to estimate demand flows of maritime container transport at international scale. Int. J. Shipp. Transp.Logist. **6**, 112–132 (2014). https://doi.org/10.1504/IJSTL.2014.059566
4. Musolino, G., Trecozzi, M.R.: Structural factors for a third-generation port: planning interventions for agri-food logistics in Gioia Tauro, Italy. WIT Trans. Built Environ. **204**, 43–52 (2021)
5. Tsolakis, N., Zissis, D., Papaefthimiou, S., Korfiatis, N.: Towards AI driven environmental sustainability: an application of automated logistics in container port terminals. Int. J. Prod. Res. **60**, 4508–4528 (2022)
6. Song, Z.-Y., Lin, C.-W., Feng, X., Lee, P.T.-W.: An empirical study of the performance of the sixth generation ports model with smart ports with reference to major container ports in mainland China. Transp. Res. Part E Logist. Transp. Rev. **184**, 103460 (2024). https://doi.org/10.1016/j.tre.2024.103460
7. Xiang, X., Liu, C.: Modeling and analysis for an automated container terminal considering battery management. Comput. Ind. Eng. **156**, 107258 (2021). https://doi.org/10.1016/j.cie.2021.107258
8. Yue, L., Fan, H.: Dynamic scheduling and path planning of automated guided vehicles in automatic container terminal. IEEE/CAA J. Autom. Sin. **9**, 2005–2019 (2022). https://doi.org/10.1109/JAS.2022.105950

9. An, Y., Park, N.: Economic analysis for investment of public sector's automated container terminal: Korean case study. J. Mar. Sci. Eng. **9**, 459 (2021). https://doi.org/10.3390/jmse90 50459
10. Jiang, Z., Yang, B., Lv, B.: Evaluation of environmental and economic performance of terminal equipment considering alternative fuels. Transp. Res. Part D: Transp. Environ. **135**, 104385 (2024). https://doi.org/10.1016/j.trd.2024.104385
11. Li, X., Peng, Y., Huang, J., Wang, W., Song, X.: Simulation study on terminal layout in automated container terminals from efficiency, economic and environment perspectives. Ocean Coastal Manag. **213**, 105882 (2021). https://doi.org/10.1016/j.ocecoaman.2021.105882
12. Wan, Z., Zhang, T., Sha, M., Guo, W., Jin, Y., Guo, J., Liu, Y.: Evaluation of emission reduction strategies for berthing containerships: a case study of the Shekou container terminal. J. Clean. Prod. **299**, 126820 (2021). https://doi.org/10.1016/j.jclepro.2021.126820
13. Ducruet, C., Lee, S.-W., Ng, A.K.Y.: Centrality and vulnerability in liner shipping networks: revisiting the Northeast Asian port hierarchy. Marit. Policy Manag. **37**, 17–36 (2010). https://doi.org/10.1080/03088830903461175
14. Ducruet, C., Notteboom, T.: The worldwide maritime network of container shipping: spatial structure and regional dynamics. Global Netw. **12**, 395–423 (2012). https://doi.org/10.1111/j.1471-0374.2011.00355.x
15. González Laxe, F., Jesus Freire Seoane, M., Pais Montes, C.: Maritime degree, centrality and vulnerability: port hierarchies and emerging areas in containerized transport (2008–2010). J. Transp. Geogr. **24**, 33–44 (2012). https://doi.org/10.1016/j.jtrangeo.2012.06.005
16. Kuhlemann, S., Ksciuk, J., Tierney, K., Koberstein, A.: The stochastic liner shipping fleet repositioning problem with uncertain container demands and travel times. EURO J. Transp. Logist. **10**, 100052 (2021). https://doi.org/10.1016/j.ejtl.2021.100052
17. Jia, H., Lee Lam, J.S., Tran, N.K.: Spatial variation of travel time uncertainty in container shipping. Transp. Res. Procedia. **48**, 1740–1749 (2020). https://doi.org/10.1016/j.trpro.2020.08.210
18. Cascetta, E., Henke, I.: The seventh transport revolution and the new challenges for sustainable mobility. J. Urban Mobil. **4**, 100059 (2023). https://doi.org/10.1016/j.urbmob.2023.100059
19. Fugazza, M., Hoffmann, J.: Liner shipping connectivity as determinant of trade. J. Shipp. Trade. **2**, 1 (2017). https://doi.org/10.1186/s41072-017-0019-5
20. Pan, J.-J., Bell, M.G.H., Cheung, K.F., Perera, S., Yu, H.: Connectivity analysis of the global shipping network by eigenvalue decomposition. Marit. Policy Manag. **46**, 957–966 (2019). https://doi.org/10.1080/03088839.2019.1647587
21. Bartholdi, J.J., Jarumaneeroj, P., Ramudhin, A.: A new connectivity index for container ports. Marit. Econ. Logist. **18**, 231–249 (2016). https://doi.org/10.1057/mel.2016.5
22. Wang, Z., Claramunt, C., Wang, Y.: Extracting global shipping networks from massive historical automatic identification system sensor data: a bottom-up approach. Sensors. **19**, 3363 (2019). https://doi.org/10.3390/s19153363
23. Tsiotas, D., Ducruet, C.: Measuring the effect of distance on the network topology of the global container shipping network. Sci. Rep. **11**, 21250 (2021). https://doi.org/10.1038/s41598-021-00387-3
24. Pan, J.-J., Zhang, Y.-F., Fan, B.: Strengthening container shipping network connectivity during COVID-19: a graph theory approach. Ocean Coastal Manag. **229**, 106338 (2022). https://doi.org/10.1016/j.ocecoaman.2022.106338
25. Jiang, L., Chen, L., Wang, W., Wei, W., Lv, Z., Wang, H.: Advanced network representation learning for container shipping network analysis. IEEE Netw. **35**, 182–187 (2021). https://doi.org/10.1109/MNET.011.2000444
26. Xu, Y., Peng, P., Lu, F., Claramunt, C.: Uncovering the multiplex network of global container shipping: insights from shipping companies. J. Transp. Geogr. **120**, 103991 (2024). https://doi.org/10.1016/j.jtrangeo.2024.103991

27. Liu, Q., Yang, Y., Ke, L., Ng, A.K.Y.: Structures of port connectivity, competition, and shipping networks in Europe. J. Transp. Geogr. **102**, 103360 (2022). https://doi.org/10.1016/j.jtrangeo.2022.103360

28. Wang, Y., Cullinane, K.: Determinants of port centrality in maritime container transportation. Transp. Res. Part E: Logist. Transp Rev. **95**, 326–340 (2016). https://doi.org/10.1016/j.tre.2016.04.002

29. Wang, N., Wu, N., Dong, L., Yan, H., Wu, D.: A study of the temporal robustness of the growing global container-shipping network. Sci. Rep. **6**, 34217 (2016). https://doi.org/10.1038/srep34217

30. Chen, H., Cullinane, K., Liu, N.: Developing a model for measuring the resilience of a port-hinterland container transportation network. Transp. Res. Part E Logist. Transp. Rev. **97**, 282–301 (2017). https://doi.org/10.1016/j.tre.2016.10.008

31. Viljoen, N.M., Joubert, J.W.: The vulnerability of the global container shipping network to targeted link disruption. Phys. A Stat. Mech. Appl. **462**, 396–409 (2016). https://doi.org/10.1016/j.physa.2016.06.111

32. Wu, D., Wang, N., Yu, A., Wu, N.: Vulnerability analysis of global container shipping liner network based on main channel disruption. Marit. Policy Manag. **46**, 394–409 (2019). https://doi.org/10.1080/03088839.2019.1571643

33. Huang, L., Tan, Y., Guan, X.: Hub-and-spoke network design for container shipping considering disruption and congestion in the post COVID-19 era. Ocean Coastal Manag. **225**, 106230 (2022). https://doi.org/10.1016/j.ocecoaman.2022.106230

34. Calatayud, A., Mangan, J., Palacin, R.: Vulnerability of international freight flows to shipping network disruptions: a multiplex network perspective. Transp. Res. Part E Logist. Transp. Rev. **108**, 195–208 (2017). https://doi.org/10.1016/j.tre.2017.10.015

35. Cascetta, E.: Transportation Systems Analysis: Models and Applications. Springer US (2009). https://doi.org/10.1007/978-0-387-75857-2

Smart and Sustainable Island Communities (SSIC 2025)

On the Application of the New Italian Bridge Guidelines: The Case of Sardinia Region

Marco Zucca$^{(\boxtimes)}$ ⓘ, Flavio Stochino ⓘ, Mario Lucio Puppio ⓘ,
and Giovanna Concu ⓘ

Department of Civil, Environmental Engineering and Architecture, University of Cagliari,
09123 Cagliari, Italy
`marco.zucca2@unica.it`

Abstract. Considering the collapses which have involved several existing bridges in Italy during the last years, specific new guidelines on risk classification and management, safety assessment and monitoring of existing bridges have been issued in 2020. These guidelines are organized in six levels (from level 0 to 5), that are characterized by different activities: (i) level 0 is defined by the census of the fundamental properties of the bridge, (ii) level 1 involves the visual inspection of the structure to obtain defects and the main geometric parameters of the viaduct, and the hydraulic and geo-morphological properties of the site, (iii) level 2 defines the Class of Attention of the bridge calculated considering the hazard, the vulnerability and the exposure parameters obtained from the previous levels, (iv) level 3 is a preliminary assessment of the bridge to evaluate the need to proceed with the level 4 analyses, (v) level 4 is characterized by an accurate evaluation of the structural elements of the viaduct according to the Italian Design Code and (vi) level 5 concerns the evaluation of the robustness of the road network.

In this paper, the application of the first three levels of analysis of the new guidelines to a stock of bridges located in Sardinia is presented. The census analysis, visual inspection and the definition of the Class of Attention of bridges were performed. The results obtained are analyzed from a critical point of view in order to highlight the limitations of the proposed procedure.

Keywords: Existing Bridges · Italian Bridge Guidelines · Class of Attention

1 Introduction

During the last 10 years, the total or partial bridges collapses occurred in Italy have caused the death of 52 people and the injury of 38 other people [1]. In particular, after the well-known collapse of Polcevera viaduct, that led to the death of 43 people, the management and maintenance of existing bridges has become a topic of considerable interest [2, 3].

It is important to highlight that the identification process of infrastructures maintenance interventions has always been more widespread in North America than in Europe. In fact, in North America the AASHTO Commonly Recognized Standard Element System general rules are well defined and implemented in PONTIS software [4] while

© The Author(s), under exclusive license to Springer Nature Switzerland AG 2026
O. Gervasi et al. (Eds.): ICCSA 2025 Workshops, LNCS 15897, pp. 183–196, 2026.
https://doi.org/10.1007/978-3-031-97660-5_14

in Europe most of the highway management companies have developed their bridge management procedures, but they do not offer the acquired knowledge and developed products for commercial use [5]. Only a part of them have developed a national Bridge Management System (BMS) such as DANBRO in Denmark. Moreover, these BMSs are useful only for the collection of data of the considered bridges but they are not useful to define the risk level of bridges. Large-scale approaches which take into account the main intrinsic characteristics of bridges and the degradation level are generally used to define the maintenance interventions scheduling [6–8].

In Italy there are about 60 k motorway bridges and most of these were built between 1960s and 1970s in reinforced concrete (RC) and consequently require several interventions to maintain an adequate safety levels both under static and dynamic loads. It is important to highlight that the viaducts are generally handled by different companies who may not have detailed information about all their assets.

For these reasons, in 2020 the Italian Ministry of Sustainable Infrastructures and Mobility (MIT) has released the new Italian Bridge Guidelines (IBGs) for the classification and the risk management, safety evaluation and monitoring of existing bridges [9]. The guidelines were updated in 2022.

The guidelines are characterized by a multi-level approach which develops at 6 different levels characterized by the following activities:

- Level 0. Definition of the most important properties of the bridge and verification of existing design documentation.
- Level 1. Running of a series of visual inspections of the structure useful for identifying the presence of: (i) defects, (ii) the structural and geometric properties of the bridge and (iii) the geo-morphological and hydraulic characteristics of the area.
- Level 2. Evaluation of the Class of Attention (CoA) of the bridge considering the definition of hazard, vulnerability and exposure parameters obtained from previous levels. The definition of the different CoAs (Structure and Foundation (CoA-SF), Seismic (CoA-S), Landslide (CoA-L) and Flood (CoA-F)) can be high, medium-high, medium, medium-low and low. Starting from the evaluation of the Classes of Attention, different actions are applicable as a function of the CoAs level. Specific inspections plans will have to be scheduled for structures having medium or medium-high CoAs while a deep structural assessment is needed for bridge having high CoAs.
- Level 3. Structure preliminary assessment useful to identify the aspects useful to perform a Level 4 analysis. The numerical analysis required at Level 3 aim to evaluate the minimum resistance ensured by the codes at the time of construction of the bridge compared with the resistance required by the present code Italian Design Code (NTC2018) [10].
- Level 4. Detailed assessment of the structure considering as reported in NTC18.
- Level 5 is related to the evaluation of the robustness of the road network but currently it is not described in the guidelines.

In this paper, the application of the first three levels of the IBGs to a stock of existing bridges located in Sardinia have been presented. Taking into account the results obtained from the visual inspections, the CoAs of the analyzed bridges have been obtained to define the management of the interventions.

The main goal of this research work is to analyze the different steps of the qualitative evaluation process proposed by the IBGs, in order to highlight the possible critical aspects that may influence the correct safety evaluation of the analyzed existing bridges.

2 Italian Bridge Guidelines

Based on the risk analysis theory, the fundamental parts useful for the evaluation of the CoAs of the viaduct are: (i) hazard, (ii) vulnerability and (iii) exposure. It is possible to classify each risk parameter as high, medium-high, medium, medium-low or low. Table 1 summarizes the primary and secondary parameters that regulate the definition of these components.

Table 1. Parameters that regulate structure-foundation and seismic risks.

CoA	Component	Primary Parameters	Secondary Parameters
Structure-foundation	Hazard	Expected traffic loads, frequency of commercial vehicles	
	Vulnerability	Level of defectiveness, static behavior, number and length of the spans, type of material	Degradation speed, design code
	Exposure	Average daily traffic, mean span length	Road alternative, bypassed entity
Seismic	Hazard	PGA (Peak Ground Acceleration)	Soil class
	Vulnerability	Level of defectiveness, static scheme, number and length of the spans, material	Seismic design criteria
	Exposure	Exposure obtained for structure-foundation CoA	Importance of the bridge

2.1 Structure-Foundation CoA

The parameters which influence the hazard that defines the structure-foundation risk are: (i) the maximum permissible mass of vehicles and (ii) the frequency of transits of commercial vehicles. The influence of the vehicle mass is related to the possible presence of vehicles with a tow characterized by an important weight which causes greater risk than a same bridge but used only for ordinary traffic. Considering the maximum permissible mass of vehicles, the IBGs divide viaducts into five classes: A, B, C, D, and E. The maximum mass for bridges in class A is obtained according to the NTC 2018 requirements for new bridges which is represented by double axe concentrated loads equal to 600 kN.

The classes B, C, D and E are defined by a mass equal to 73%, 43%, 13% and 6% of that obtained for class A, respectively. According to the IBGs, it is possible to classify the frequency of transits of commercial vehicles per lane as low, medium or high. The frequency is considered low if lower than 300 vehicles/day and high if higher than 700 vehicles/day. The hazard class is calculated through a table that depends on the class of the road determined considering the maximum permissible mass and on the frequency of transits of commercial vehicles.

The vulnerability depends on: (i) the defectiveness level, (ii) the rate of degradation, (iii) the design code used (also considering the seismic design criteria), (iv) the static behavior, the materials and the maximum span length.

Considering the defects observed during the execution of the visual inspections, the level of defectiveness of the bridge is defined as a function of the importance, the rate of intensity of the identified defects.

The rate of degradation is calculated as a function of the level of defectiveness related to the construction period of the structure. The definition of the bridge construction period is significant if the structure has never undergone important maintenance interventions. However, if the bridge was subjected to important maintenance interventions that have influenced the degradation process, the year of the last significant maintenance intervention should be considered. Three different categories are defined considering the bridge construction period or the time of the execution of the last important maintenance intervention: (i) prior to 1945, (ii) from 1945 to 1980 and (iii) later than 1980.

The vulnerability level is strictly related to the hypotheses used during the design phase, in particular by the considered traffic load models. In fact, it is important to highlight that the evolution of the Italian design code has led to a variation in traffic load schemes over the years. For this reason, it is possible to divide the first category bridges, designed in the past considering the transit of civil and military vehicles, from the second category bridges, designed considering only the presence of civil vehicles. It is important to highlight that the effects of the civil vehicles considered up to 1980 have been much less severe than now reported within the NTC2018, while the effects of the military vehicles considered from 1952 onwards are about equal to the loads currently used. The influence of the traffic loads on the structural behavior of the analyzed bridge is regulated by different parameters such as the characteristics of the span and the width of the deck. Without more accurate evaluation, the IBGs identify three different classes (A, B or C) defined by the design period, the category of the bridge and the span length.

Moreover, vulnerability is influenced by the most important structural properties of the bridge. The fundamental parameters considered in the IBGs are the redundancy of the static layout, the susceptibility of the formation of brittle collapse mechanisms and the possible development of the materials degradation phenomena. Also in this case, after the definition of the static scheme, the material that characterizes the deck and the maximum span length, it is possible to obtain the vulnerability level of the structure with a table that considers the related main structural characteristics. The class of vulnerability is defined through a flow-chart which summarizes the results of the previously discussed aspects.

Exposure is obtained considering the effects of the following primary and secondary parameters: (i) the average daily traffic and the average span length and (ii) the presence of alternative routes and the type of the bypassed subject. In particular, the expected traffic volume, defined considering the Average Daily Traffic (ADT), is obtained by means of specific evaluation or using the data obtained from the management company. The IBGs classify the ADT level as high, medium and low. The low level presents an ADT not higher than 10,000 vehicles/day while the high level is characterized by an ADT not lower than 25,000 vehicles/day. Another parameter which influences the exposure is the average length of the span (ASL). Considering this aspect, IBGs define three classes of bridges having long spans (ASL higher than 50 m), medium spans (ASL higher than 20 m and lower than 50 m) and low spans (ASL lower than 20 m). The effects of ADT and ASL are considered using a table presents within the IBGs.

Closure or traffic restriction generates disruptions and economic losses. In the evaluation of the exposure, according to the IBGs, have to consider the possible presence and the adequacy of road alternatives in the case of bridge closure. The class of exposure obtained considering the combination of the ADT and ASL effects increases if no alternative routes are possible. Another aspect to consider is the type of the bypassed entity defined by means of three different classes: high, medium and low. The class of exposure which characterizes the viaduct is calculated through a flow chart considering the above-defined parameters.

The final structure-foundation CoA of the bridge is obtained by means tables considering the classes of vulnerability and exposure.

2.2 Seismic CoA

The hazard related to the seismic risk is regulated by (i) the value of the PGA and the topographic category of the site and (ii) by the subsoil category. In particular, the PGA is evaluated considering rigid soils and a probability of exceedance equal to 10% in 50 years. Five hazard classes (high, medium-high, medium, medium-low, low) are considered for PGA and topographic category. The determination of the subsoil category is based on the execution of special surveys if there is no detailed evaluation in the design documents. On the contrary, if it is impossible to obtain the above-mentioned information, the subsoil category is assumed to be the worst possible for the area under consideration. The hazard class is calculated through a table as a function of the classes considering these primary and secondary parameters. In this case, the vulnerability for the seismic risk is defined considering (i) the level of defectiveness, (ii) the use of seismic design criteria and (iii) the static behavior, the materials and the maximum span length.

The defectiveness level is determined considering the results of visual inspections of Level 1 but focusing attention on the structural elements that influence the seismic behavior of the analyzed structure. Also in this case, the IBGs identify five distinct levels of defectiveness, according to what was done for the evaluation of structure-foundation vulnerability class but taking into account the seismic behavior of the structure.

The seismic behavior of a bridge is related to the redundancy of the static layout, on the type and number of elements vulnerable to the seismic action and on the mass of the bridge. Also in this case, the IBGs consider five different classes of vulnerability that depend on static behavior, span length and material.

Moreover, the dynamic performance of existing viaducts is strictly related to the design code used during the design phase. In fact, it is important to distinguish between bridges designed considering seismic action and bridge designed only to resist vertical loads. The class of vulnerability is evaluated through a flow chart that considers the results of the previously mentioned parameters.

The exposure to seismic risk is obtained considering as obtained for the structure-foundation risk and the strategic importance of the structure when a seismic event occurs. The IBGs consider the importance of bridges that must guarantee their operability during seismic events for civil protection purposes. In fact, the level of seismic exposure is increased by one level with respect to those obtained for the structure-foundation risk if the bridge is defined as being of strategic interest for emergencies following an earthquake.

The seismic CoA of the bridge is obtained using tables related to the classes of vulnerability and exposure.

3   Case Studies in Sardinia

The stock of bridges analyzed in this research work is composed of ten existing bridges located in north Sardinia.

Figure 1 shows the location of the bridges under study.

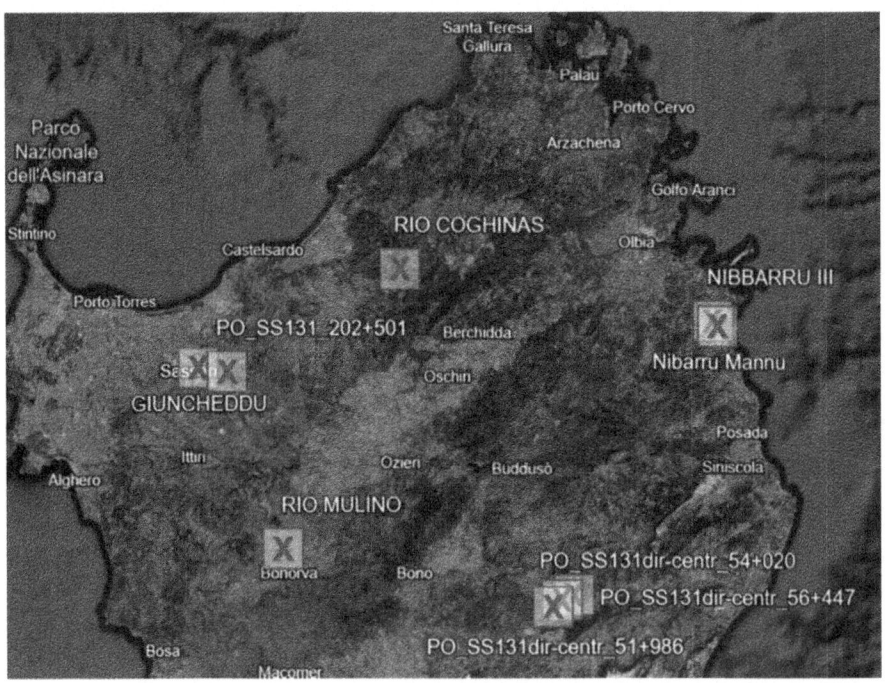

Fig. 1. Localization of the 10 bridges.

Fig. 2. (1) Giuncheddu bridge, (2) PO_SS131_202 + 501, (3) Rio Mulino bridge, (4) Nibbaru III, (5) PO_SS131dir-centr_51 + 986, (6) PO_SS131dir-centr_54 + 020, (7) PO_SS131dir-centr_56 + 447_DX, (8) PO_SS131dir-centr_56 + 447_SX, (9) Nibbaru Mannu, (10) Rio Coghinas bridge.

In particular, three of these bridges (Giuncheddu bridge, PO_SS131_202 + 501 and Rio Mulino bridge) are part of the main highway of Sardinia that connects Cagliari to Sassari (SS 131) while other seven (Nibbaru III, PO_SS131dir-centr_51 + 986, PO_SS131dir-centr_54 + 020, PO_SS131dir-centr_56 + 447_DX, PO_SS131dir-centr_56 + 447_SX, Nibbaru Mannu) are located in a recent branch of the same highway called SS 131 DCN. Only, Rio Coghinas bridge is in correspondence to SS 672 highway. Figure 2 shows the considered case studies, selected by the High Council of Public Works (CSLLPP).

As shown in Fig. 3, five of these bridges are characterized by simply supported spans while the other five are long span bridges. As reported in previous Sect. 2, another important aspect that influences the CoA of the bridge is the materials that characterize the main structural elements. In this case, only two bridges (Nibarru III and Nibarru Mannu) present a deck realized in mixed steel-concrete structure while the other eight analyzed bridges are characterized by a deck composed of prestressed longitudinal concrete I-beams and prestressed transverse rectangular beams with a 0.20 m concrete slab (Fig. 4).

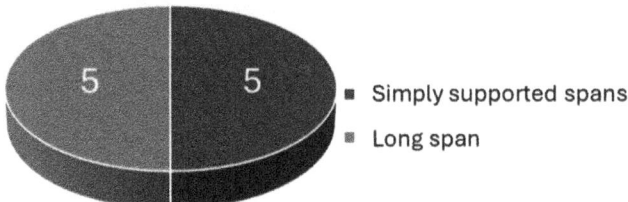

Fig. 3. Static scheme subdivision.

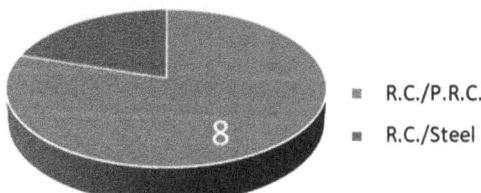

Fig. 4. Bridges materials subdivision.

Figures 5 and 6 report the relative frequency of the maximum girder length and of the maximum piers' height, respectively. It is possible to notice that the maximum value of girder length ranging between 68 m and 31 m. In particular, the maximum values of girder length (68 m and 60 m) characterize the two bridges having the deck realized by a mixed steel-concrete structure. The distribution of the relative frequency of the maximum values of the height of the piers shows appreciable differences, showing values ranging from 9.8 m and 58.08 m.

3.1 Structure and Foundation Risk

Hazard. The hazard related to the structure-foundation risk is evaluated considering the maximum permissible vehicles mass and the frequency of transits of commercial vehicles.

The value of the maximum permissible vehicles mass is determined considering the state of conservation of the structure and it is defined by the highway management company. Considering the analyzed case studies, the maximum permissible mass of vehicles is taken equal to as reported in the Italian Design Code [10] for the new bridges and consequently are in class A.

To evaluate the frequency of transits of commercial vehicles, in terms of number of commercial vehicles per day on single lane, the data obtained from specific traffic studies have been considered. In particular, Nibarru Mannu, Nibarru III, Rio

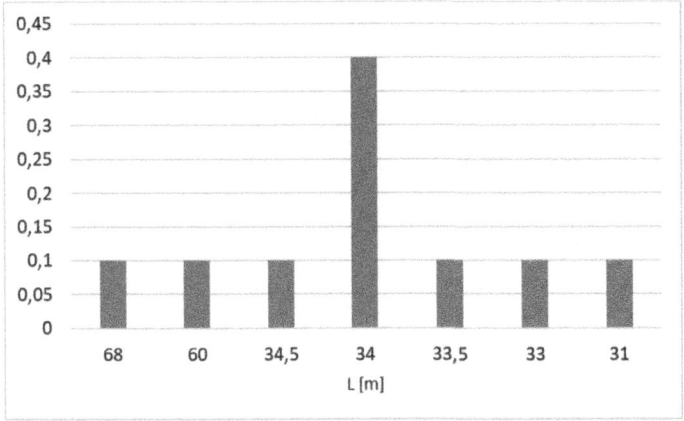

Fig. 5. Maximum girder length relative frequency.

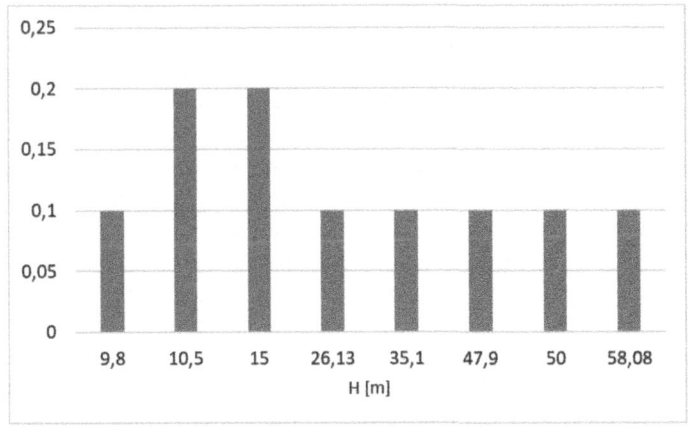

Fig. 6. Maximum piers height relative frequency.

Coghinas, PO_SS131dir-centr_56 + 447_DX and PO_SS131dir-centr_56 + 447_SX are characterized by low traffic frequency (≤300 vehicles/day), PO_SS131dir-centr_51 + 986, PO_SS131dir-centr_54 + 020 and Rio Mulino have a medium traffic frequency (300 ≤ vehicles/day <700) while Giuncheddu and PO_SS131_202 + 501 present a high traffic frequency (≥700 vehicles/day).

Vulnerability. The vulnerability useful for the definition of the structure-foundation risk depends on defectiveness level, rate of degradation, design code used, static behavior, maximum span length and material. In particular, the defectiveness level represents a fundamental parameter for the definition of the vulnerability level. According to as reported in the IBGs, if the defectiveness level is high, the vulnerability is also defined as high. As mentioned before, the defectiveness level is defined considering the results of the visual inspections, considering the criteria listed in Fig. 7.

Defectiveness level	Classification criteria
High	*"Defects with high or medium–high grade (G = 5 or G = 4) and any intensity grade on critical elements or presence of critical conditions"*
Medium-High	*"Defects with high or medium–high grade (G = 5 or G = 4) and high intensity grade on elements whose failure can undermine the statics of the bridge"*
Medium	*"Defects with high or medium–high grade (G = 5 or G = 4) and high intensity grade on elements whose failure cannot undermine the statics of the bridge or defects with high importance grade (G = 5) and medium–low intensity grade"*
Medium-Low	*"Defects with medium–high grade (G = 4) and medium–low intensity grade or many defects with either medium or low grade (G = 3, 2 or 1) and any intensity grade"*
Low	*"A few defects with either medium or low grade (G = 3, 2 or 1) and any intensity grade"*

Fig. 7. Definition of defectiveness level.

The IBGs introduce different types of forms depending on the type of analyzed element (e.g. beams, piers, bearings, slabs, joints, etc..). Each row of the form reports the code, the detailed description and the assigned grade ($1 \leq G \leq 5$) of the observed defect. Furthermore, the different forms are characterized by the presence of several checkboxes which can flag or not by the inspector. These checkboxes define if the considered defect is present in the analyzed element and if this defect compromises or not the load-bearing capacity of the structure. For each identified defect, the inspector must define the related extension (k_1) and intensity (k_2) grade, assigning a value equal to 0.2, 0.5 or 1. For some defects, k_1 and/or k_2 are defined directly by the IBGs.

Moreover, the IBGs identifies a series of critical elements that are considered as important and extended damage states or elements particularly prone to degradation phenomena. These elements (e.g. half-joints, prestressing tendons, etc.) if subject to important degradation can significantly affect the structural capacity of the bridges both under static and dynamic loads. The presence of damage in one critical element leads to a high level of defectiveness, according to as reported in previous Table 2.

Focusing attention on the analyzed case studies, three of them are characterized by a Medium-High defectiveness level, one presents a Medium defectiveness level while the other seven are defined by a Medium-Low defectiveness level. The structural elements that show the most critical defects are the R.C. piers, the P.R.C beams and the bearings.

The degradation rate is defined as a function of the defectiveness level and the construction period of the bridge. According to the IBGs application, eight of the analyzed bridges have been built from 1945 to 1980 while for the other two (Nibarru Mannu and Nibarru III) the construction period is subsequent to 1980.

Another important aspect for the definition of the vulnerability is the design code in force during the bridge design phase or to design the most recent significant structural interventions. Considering the classification of the IBGs, all the bridges fall into class B, that is characterized by first category bridges designed using design code in force from 1952 to 1990 and having spans of <10 m or designed with design code in force from 1952 to 2005 and having spans longer than 10 m.

All the bridges present maximum span length greater than 25 m. As reported in Fig. 3, eight of these are characterized by P.R.C. structures while the other two are realized with mixed steel-concrete structure.

Exposure. The exposure of the structure-foundation risk is defined as a function of the average daily traffic and the average span length, the possible presence of alternative routes and the entity of the bypassed element.

Considering to as reported in the IBGs, the average daily traffic (ADT) can be classified as high, medium or low in relation to the number of commercial vehicles transiting each day on the entire width of the carriageway. Considering as obtained from the highway management company, the ADT is low for all the viaducts.

Regarding the average span length (ASL) of the bridge, as can be seen in previous Fig. 4, eight of the bridges present a medium ASL value (20 m < ASL < 50 m) while the other two are characterized by a high ASL value (ASL > 50 m).

The presence of alternative routes and the type of bypassed entity are two fundamental aspects that regulate the possible social and economic consequences due to the interruption of the traffic. Alternative routes are present for five of the analysed bridges. The class that defines the importance of the bypassed entity can be high, medium or low, according to as reported in the IBGs. Seven of the bridges are interested by bypassed entity classified as low. The bypassed entity of the other three bridges as classified as medium for two bridges and high for the other.

3.2 Seismic Risk

Similarly, to was what reported for structure-foundation risk, the seismic risk has been evaluated starting from the definition of hazard, vulnerability and exposure.

Hazard. The hazard related to the seismic risk is defined starting from the PGA value that characterize the site where the bridge was built. As mentioned before, all the bridges are located in Sardinia which is a low seismic risk area. For this reason, a PGA ≤ 0.05 g has been considered for the ten bridges. Other important parameters that regulate the hazard are the topographic category and the soil class.

The topographic category is defined according to as reported in [10] and in this case four bridges are in areas characterized by a topographic category equal to T1, other four in sites with T2 topographic category while the last two are realized in zones having T3 topographic category.

The soil class that characterizes the sites is defined according to Eurocode 8 [11]. Seven of the case studies are built in areas with A soil class while the other three are realized in sites having soil class equal to B.

Vulnerability. The vulnerability of the seismic action is strictly related to the defectiveness level, the possible use of design codes taking into account seismic action, the static layout, the maximum length of the span and the material.

Also in this case, the defectiveness level is calculated considering the results of the visual inspection with the only difference that the critical elements that influence the seismic performance of the structure are slightly different compared to those considered for the evaluation of the structure-foundation risk.

The IBGs divide bridges designed only considering vertical loads from those designed to resist seismic loads. Considering the age of the analysed bridges, all the case studies fall into the first group.

The other parameters which influence the vulnerability to seismic action are like those already defined for the evaluation of the vulnerability of the structure-foundation risk. The only difference is the definition of the static layout that is related to the number of spans of the bridge. Also in this case, the IBGs evaluate the vulnerability related to the structural characteristics by means of a table.

Exposure. The exposure useful to define the seismic risk is obtained considering the results of the structure-foundation risk that are corrected taking into account the strategic function of the considered viaduct when a seismic event occurs. All the analysed bridges are considered as strategic structures.

3.3 Definition of the CoA

Figure 8 summarizes the Class of Attention obtained considering the structure-foundation risk and the seismic risk of the ten case studies.

Bridge	Structure-foundation CoA	Seismic CoA
1	Medium-High	High
2	High	High
3	Medium-High	Medium
4	Medium-High	Low
5	Medium	Low
6	Medium	Low
7	Medium-High	Medium
8	Medium-High	Medium
9	Medium	Low
10	Medium-High	Medium

Fig. 8. Structure-foundation and seismic CoA.

It is possible to notice that all the bridges are characterized by a structure-foundation CoA ranging between Medium and High due to the defectiveness level obtained considering the results of the visual inspections. A more particular aspect is related to the evaluation of the seismic risk CoA, which is high for two bridges, even if Sardinia region is an area with low seismic risk. Also in this case, this result is due to the identified defectiveness level influenced by the state of conservation of the bearings.

4 Conclusions

In this paper, the application of the first three level of the new guidelines on risk classification and management, safety assessment and monitoring of existing Italian bridges is discussed focusing attention on the case of Sardinia. In particular, ten case studies located in north Sardinia have been analyzed in order to evaluate the Class of Attention related to the structure-foundation and the seismic risk.

The influence of the different parameters which regulate the evaluation of the above-mentioned CoAs have been described in detail in order to define the most critical aspects of the IBGs approach.

All the considered case studies are characterized by a structure-foundation risk ranging between medium and high due to the defectiveness level obtained from the visual inspection results.

Also, in the case of seismic risk evaluation some of the bridges fall into a high CoA, even if Sardinia is characterized by a very low seismic risk. This result is influenced by the state of conservation of the bearings that are defined as critical elements in the evaluation of the seismic behaviour of the bridge. For this reason, the IBGs approach developed for the evaluation of the seismic risk could be in some cases overly penalizing. This aspect represents a critical issue for the correct evaluation of the safety level of the existing bridges located in low seismicity zones such as Sardinia. In fact, the seismic risk assessment carried out in this way can lead to an incorrect assessment of the maintenance interventions scheduling process.

Acknowledgments. The studies presented here were carried out as part of the activities envisaged by the Agreement between the High Council of Public Works (CSLLPP) and the ReLUIS Consortium implementing Ministerial Decree 578/2020 and Ministerial Decree 204/2022. The contents of this paper represent the authors' ideas and do not necessarily correspond to the official opinion and policies of CSLLPP.

Disclosure of Interests. The authors have no competing interests to declare that are relevant to the content of this article.

References

1. Palmisano, F., Asso, R., Chiaia, B., Marano, G.C., Pellegrino, C.: Structural assessment of existing R.C. half-joint bridges according to the new Italian guidelines. J. Civil Struct. Health Monit. **13**, 1–25 (2022)

2. Calvi, G.M., Moratti, M., O'Reilly, G., Scattarreggia, N., Monteiro, R., Malomo, D., Calvi, P.M., Pinho, R.: Once upon a time in Italy: the tale of the Morandi bridge. Struct. Eng. Int. **29**, 198–217 (2019)
3. Nuti, C., Briseghella, B., Chen, A., Lavorato, D., Iori, T., Vanzi, I.: Relevant outcomes from the history of Polcevera Viaduct in Genova, from design to nowadays failure. J. Civ. Struct. Heal. Monit. **10**, 87–107 (2020)
4. Thompson, P.D., Small, E.P., Johnson, M., Marshall, A.R.: The Pontis bridge management system. Struct. Eng. Int. **8**, 303–308 (1998)
5. Rossi, P.P., Spinella, N., Recupero, A.: Experimental application of the Italian guidelines for the risk classification and management and for the safety evaluation of existing bridges. Structure. **58**, 105387 (2023)
6. Pregnolato, M.: Bridge safety is not for granted—a novel approach to bridge management. Eng. Struct. **196**, 109193 (2019)
7. Zucca, M., Crespi, P., Stochino, F., Puppio, M.L., Coni, M.: Maintenance interventions period of existing RC motorway viaducts located in moderate/high seismicity zones. Structure. **47**, 976–990 (2023)
8. Costantino, G., Messina, D., Recupero, A., Rossi, P.P., Spinella, N.: A web platform for management and analysis of existing bridges. Procedia Struct. Integr. **44**, 1220–1227 (2023)
9. Italian Ministry of Sustainable Infrastructures and Mobility (MIT): D.M. 17 December 2020. Linee guida per la classificazione e gestione del rischio, la valutazione della sicurezza ed il monitoraggio dei ponti esistenti (2020)
10. Italian Ministry of Public Works: D.M. 17 January 2018. Nuove Norme tecniche per le costruzioni. Gazzetta Ufficiale, vol. 42 (in Italian) (2018)
11. CEN: EC8-Part 1: Eurocode 8. Design provisions for earthquake resistance of structures. In: Part 1–1: General Rules—Seismic Actions and General Requirements for Structures. ENV 1998-1. CEN, Brussels (2005)

Linking Tourism Hotspots and Vulnerability to Climate Change – Case Study Rhodes Island, Greece

Apostolos Lagarias[1]([⊠]) [iD], Akrivi Leka[2] [iD], Dionisia Koutsi[2] [iD],
and Anastasia Stratigea[2] [iD]

[1] Department of Planning and Regional Development, School of Engineering, University of Thessaly, Volos, Greece
lagarias@uth.gr
[2] Department of Geography and Regional Planning, School of Rural, Surveying and Geoinformatics Engineering, National Technical University of Athens, Athens, Greece
{akrleka,stratige}@central.ntua.gr, koutsi.dionisia@gmail.com

Abstract. Tourism in Mediterranean regions is an important developmental lever. Nevertheless, it also constitutes a main source of degradation of the natural/cultural capital, while it exposes tourist destinations to severe pressures (energy/water stress, traffic congestion, urbanization, pollution, etc.) that are mainly due to the prevailing mass tourism model across the Mediterranean coastline. This holds especially true in insular regions, i.e. highly attractive areas due to their natural/cultural wealth and uniqueness, but also extremely vulnerable due to the insularity condition as well as other global-wide challenges, such as Climate Change (CC), coastal urban sprawl, biodiversity degradation, etc. Currently, many islands demonstrate signs of extreme tourism overcrowding, rendering them 'tourism hotspots', a state that threatens sustainability and resilience objectives. Having Rhodes Island, Greece, as a case study – namely a highly reputed tourist destination in the global scenery – this work aims at establishing a methodological framework for 'bridging' tourism hotspot areas with climate change risks. This is accomplished by the use of spatial, quantitative and qualitative, data that forms the ground for: identifying the spatial pattern and dynamics of tourism hotspot areas in Rhodes Island; and linking them with past and potential CC incidents in order for risks to be identified and relevant, more informed policy decisions, serving sustainability and resilience objectives to be articulated. Results designate critical concerns as to the risks inherent in Rhodes tourism hotspots, calling for the deployment of relevant resilience plans, coupled with the discharging of tourism load in relevant areas.

Keywords: Tourism hotspots · Climate change risks · Spatial analysis

1 Introduction

In recent decades, tourist development and its repercussions in spatial, ecological/environmental, economic, social, cultural, psychological, etc. terms have been placed at the heart of the international planning and policy discourse [1–4], in alignment with

O. Gervasi et al. (Eds.): ICCSA 2025 Workshops, LNCS 15897, pp. 197–214, 2026.
https://doi.org/10.1007/978-3-031-97660-5_15

relevant policy directions at the glocal (global-local) level, addressing sustainability, resilience and socio-economic cohesion [5, 6]. At the epicentre of this discussion lay coastal, mostly mass tourism destinations – both in mainland and insular territories –, demonstrating a notably linear form of tourism activity along the coastal part. In fact heavy tourism overload of *coastal space*, especially in Mediterranean coastal and insular regions [7], coupled with the quite dense residential pattern of these regions (more than one third of the population in Mediterranean countries lives in coastal administrative entities) [8], is source of environmental degradation of vulnerable land and marine ecosystems. Further to that, this pattern sets up also the scene for severe sectoral conflicts to emerge in seeking for coastal or marine space from various actors/stakeholders (e.g. residential, fisheries, agriculture, tourism, commercial and passenger port activities). Last, but not least, this overloading of the coastal space results in highly dense built-up patterns, which are definitely heavily exposed to severe Climate Change (CC) incidents [9]. Such incidents are currently a major threat for the Mediterranean region as a CC hotspot [10, 11]; while they constitute a source of multiple socioeconomic stresses [12], burdening the region's stability and prosperity.

As various studies demonstrate [13, 14], *insular regions* in the Mediterranean seem to be more affected by CC repercussions, with islands being perceived as the most susceptible to CC areas of the world. Such regions, being at the heart of this work, are highly endowed and attractive areas, with their charm being associated with their rich maritime heritage and cultural tradition as well as an unrivalled diversity of landscapes and nature-based populations. Based on these remarkable attributes, they act like a magnet to tourism flows, witnessing a continuously escalating volume of visitors. In fact tourism constitutes the 'engine' of islands' economic profile, leading to a Tourism-Led Growth (TLG) model [15], with noticeable contribution to GDP, employment, and foreign exchange earnings. Despite the economic benefits of their popularity, however, such a trend has led to the violation of their carrying capacity constraints, giving prominence to the new threat of overtourism [4], a state that places enormous pressure on local resources while definitely affecting the pursuance of sustainability and resilience objectives.

Within such a context, *tourism planning* nowadays, particularly in fragile insular regions, is grasped as a highly complicated task, taking into consideration vulnerability of the tourism sector in a number of abrupt or long term developments, occurring at the global level. Such developments are the outcome of technological advances and the sharing economy, economic stability, demographic changes and lifestyle/consumers' preferences, migration patterns, health crises, CC and natural disasters, to name but a few. That said, an additional task when tourism planning is conducted involves *vulnerability assessments* of tourism destinations to various threats and their spatial implications in order for more effective policy decisions to be enabled. In fact such assessments can be used from either a proactive tourism planning viewpoint, i.e. plan of tourism products that are properly addressing vulnerabilities of a destination to external and internal driving forces; or a reactive one, i.e. being prepared to effectively cope with adverse incidents of driving forces that can cause severe damages to a destination. In order for this to be attained, more precise estimations of human activity along the coastal strip are needed. However, certain *knowledge gap* is noticed in this respect that hinders effective planning and articulation of developmental strategies for coastal regions [3]. In addition, planning and developmental strategies are rather superficially handling or integrating into the planning practice information on specific risks, e.g. CC, faced by each single region in order for resilience to emerging threats to be incorporated into policy decisions that are coming out from the planning discourse. Thus although the pressures of mass tourism on Mediterranean islands and the increasing frequency of climate-related hazards are well acknowledged, there remains a notable *gap* in the literature regarding spatially integrated approaches that concurrently assess tourism density/intensity and climate vulnerability. Existing studies often examine these dimensions in isolation, lacking a common analytical framework for effectively informing regional spatial planning and resilience strategies. This paper seeks to address this *gap* by proposing a geospatially-informed methodology that overlays tourism hotspot identification with spatial risk assessment of climate-induced hazards—namely floods and wildfires. Applying this approach to the case of Rhodes Island, Greece, the study offers both methodological and empirical contributions to current debates on sustainable tourism development and territorial resilience in coastal and insular contexts.

Having the aforementioned in mind, the *focus* of the present paper is on tracking the human footprint in the coastal part of Rhodes Island, Greece by means of identifying tourism hotspots; and assessing the CC risks related to these hotspots. More specifically, a methodological framework is established aiming at 'bridging' tourism hotspot areas with CC risks, a fact that aims to uncover critical spatial relationships and vulnerability patterns in the study area. Such an experiment results in certain fact-related connotations, namely awareness raising and informing policy reaction for handling CC risks associated with these hotspots; and preparing for the damage such risks can cause to highly populated areas. This effort is accomplished by use of qualitative and quantitative data and GIS tools, properly selected for demonstrating the high exposure of Rhodes' tourism hotspots to combined CC risks.

The structure of the paper has as follows: in Sect. 2 the methodological approach is presented; Sect. 3 elaborates on the tourism supply dynamics of the study region, i.e. Rhodes Island, Greece, aiming at highlighting tourism hotspots; Sect. 4 attempts to gain insights into CC risks inherent in the area of concern from a geospatial perspective and link them to tourism hotspot areas; finally in Sect. 5 discussion of results and certain key conclusions are drawn.

2 The Methodological Framework

The methodological approach of this work consists of the following steps (Fig. 1):

- Step 1 is dedicated to a thorough insight into the study region in order for the social, economic, cultural, environmental, historical etc. *profile* to be grasped.
- Step 2 pays attention to the specifics of the tourism sector per se, exploring its dynamics as well as the tourism density and intensity in the area of concern. In this respect, certain literature-based indicators can be applied, provided that relevant data are available. More specifically, density of tourist accommodation (e.g., hotel and Airbnb beds per km^2), proximity to key attractions, land cover change (e.g., impervious surface expansion), and NDVI loss are frequently used to assess tourism pressure

and environmental stress. Coastal built-up expansion in the study area, as well as the spatial pattern of hotel and Airbnb accommodation, the expansion of large-scale tourism infrastructure through time, etc. are also falling into this step, leading to the identification of *tourism hotspots*.

• Step 3 aims at illuminating *vulnerability concerns* of the study area that are due to CC impacts. Spatial data elaboration is forming the ground for relevant inferences to be drawn with regards to mainly flood and fire risks inherent in the vicinity of tourism hotspots, and the island's soil sealing to the detriment of the agricultural land. In addition, past events (fire, flood) are explored based on information provided by relevant works, elaborating on risk assessment at the case study level.

• Step 4 aims at bridging work carried out in Steps 2 and 3. Out of this step, *vulnerability concerns* of the study area are downscaled to tourism hotspot areas in order for the type and intensity of risk to be roughly sketched.

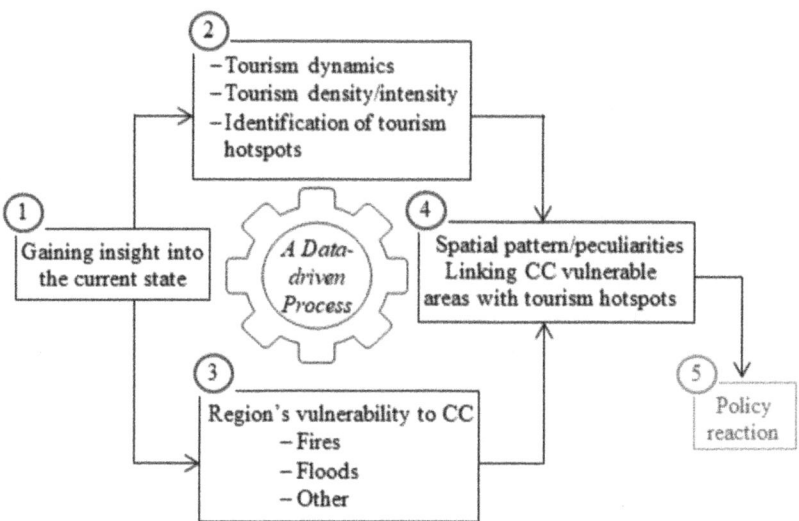

Fig. 1. Steps of the methodological approach.

Results of this process can be utilized for articulating policy reaction at the case study level, i.e. formulating proactive and reactive policy measures for minimizing repercussions of risk incidents and strengthening resilience of tourism hotspot areas.

3   Featuring Tourism Dynamics in the Island of Rhodes

The island of Rhodes is the largest one in the Dodecanese Prefecture, Greece, and is situated in the Southeastern Aegean Archipelagos. Due to its privileged geopolitical location, the island's trajectory through the centuries is marked by a strong maritime presence. In addition, Rhodes has a rich history, ranging from the Hellenistic period to the Byzantine era, the period of the medieval Knights of Rhodes, the Ottoman Empire and the occupation by the Italian conquerors, joining finally the Hellenic Republic in 1948. This history has left remarkable cultural remains on the island's land, which, combined with the rich natural environment, sets up the ground for quite an attractive tourism destination. In addition, in the capital of the island of Rhodes lies the Medieval or Old Town of Rhodes, being the best-preserved medieval town in the world and a UNESCO's World Heritage Site.

The island of Rhodes owns an area of 1401 km^2 and a population of 125,113 inhabitants [16], half of which resides in the island's capital – also capital of the Dodecanese Prefecture – the city of Rhodes. In the time span 2011–2021, the island displayed a population increase of 8.4%, in contrast to the general population of Greece as a whole, which declined by 4.13%.

According to relevant studies [17], the island of Rhodes, together with the one of Kos, falls into the group of Dodecanese islands' complex which demonstrate a high tourism performance. More specifically, Rhodes displays a remarkable tourism and population dynamics, coupled with high rates of built-up expansion. The tourism dynamics is mostly attributed to large scale hotel accommodations, manifesting a high concentration of beds and arrivals and causing a rising seasonal population density as well. In order for this pattern to be grasped, a further insight into the dynamics of the sector is attempted by use of properly selected, literature-driven, absolute indicators demonstrating developments of tourism supply; as well as relative indicators, unveiling tourism density and intensity in the destination [4]. In addition, the spatial distribution of tourism supply is explored in order for *tourism hotspot areas* to be identified.

More specifically, the dynamics of the tourism sector in the island of Rhodes is definitely witnessed by the steadily expanding tourism supply in the island. In fact during the last decade (2014–2023), tourism supply displays an increase of 8.32%, 16% and 20.36% in the number of hotels, rooms and beds respectively (Fig. 2). Worth noticing is the rising of 5* hotels (Rhodes Island rates first in the Dodecanese islands' complex, owing 60% of 5* hotel beds), reaching an increase of 105.9% in this decade; while the increase in 4* hotels amounts to 35.51% (Fig. 2a). A smaller increase of 13.53% is noticed in 3* hotels, while the 1* and 2* hotels display a certain downward trend (−10.41% and −14.03% respectively). A relevant pattern is noticed when considering the number of hotel rooms (Fig. 2b), where 5* hotel rooms display an increase of 113.25%, 4* rooms are rather stabilized (+6.58%) and 3*, 2* and 1* hotel rooms demonstrate a remarkable decrease (−16.79%, −27.73% and −14.89% respectively). A similar to hotel rooms' pattern seems to be followed by the number of hotel beds (Fig. 2c). This tourism supply image demonstrates the pathway of the tourism sector in the island, directed so far towards a mass tourism, high class destination model; while in spatial terms this implies the prevalence of large scale tourism accommodation infrastructure, mainly concentrated in the eastern and north-eastern coastal part.

In addition to the hotel infrastructure, Airbnb accommodation is gradually evolving as an important part of the tourism supply. In 2023, this amounts to 5149 accommodations and 15,447 beds [19]. It should be noted here that Airbnb development in the island of Rhodes, compared to other Greek islands (e.g. Mykonos and Santorini), remains yet relatively low in comparison to the hotel sector. However, alarming is the 19% increase

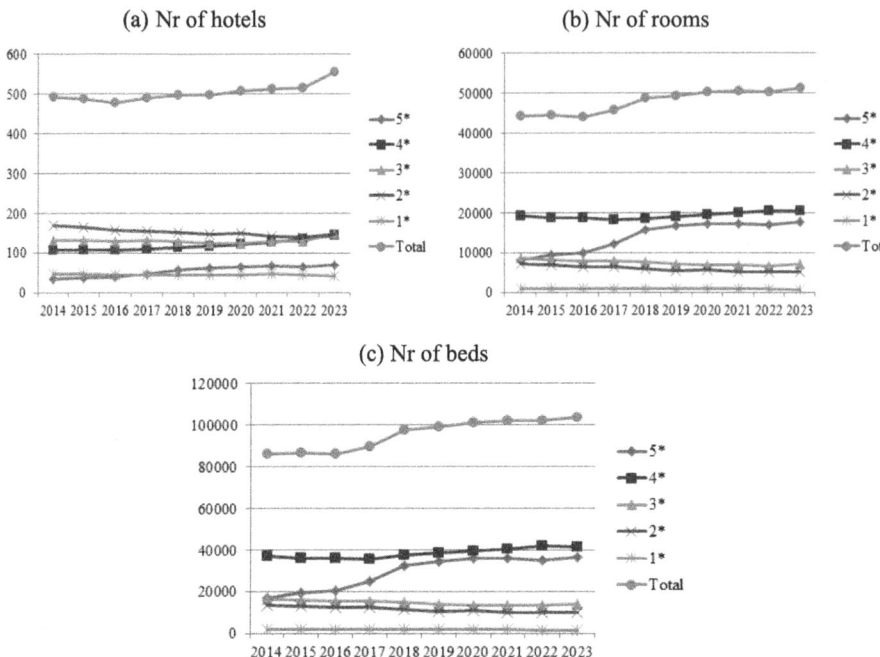

Fig. 2. Tourism accommodation developments in the island of Rhodes in the decade 2014–2023. Source: [18], own elaboration.

of Airbnb accommodation in the time span 2022–2023 [19], displaying the dynamics of Airbnb development.

In order for the tourism pressure in the study region to be identified, the relative indicators depicted in Table 1 are utilized, assessing tourism density and intensity. Performance of the island of Rhodes in these indicators demonstrates the island's position in the Dodecanese complex. More specifically, the island occupies the highest position as to the Tourism Density aspect (indicators TPI3 and TPI4); while with respect to the Tourism Intensity (indicators TPI1 and TPI2) it rates lower that the average value of the Dodecanese islands. Taking into consideration that the Tourism and Airbnb Accommodation Density (TPI3 & TPI4) highlight islands that accommodate mainly mass tourism and are most prominent in terms of land 'consumption', the aforementioned image provided by the values of these indicators reaffirms, in a way, the pressure exerted on the built environment of the island of Rhodes, a fact that is also advocated by the rising of 5* hotel accommodation. This rapidly expanding accommodation type is largely affecting the built space of the island with heavy tourism infrastructure projects, especially in its coastal part (Fig. 3).

The NATURA 2000 regions of the study area and the Human Settlement Layer in 2018 are demonstrated in Fig. 3a, b respectively. In addition, the spatial pattern of the tourism supply, i.e., location of hotel and Airbnb accommodation, is depicted in Fig. 3c, d. Inspection of the human intervention in the island of Rhodes delineates a rather crowded eastern coastal corridor that features specific concentrations – *tourism*

Table 1. Tourism pressure - Position of the island of Rhodes in the Dodecanese Complex.

Tourism Pressure Indicators - TPI	Short Description	Island of Rhodes Value	Dodecanese Island Complex Average Value
TPI1. Tourism accommodation intensity	[Total tourist accommodation (beds) / resident]	1.47	2.3
TPI2. Airbnb accommodation intensity	[Total Airbnb accommodation (beds) / resident]	0.10	0.14
TPI3. Tourism accommodation density	[Total tourist accommodation (beds) / island's surface]	130.96	102.4
TPI4. Airbnb accommodation density	[Total Airbnb accommodation (beds) / island's surface in km^2]	9.39	7.37

hotspots – in the neighbourhood of the Lindos, Afantou, Faliraki and Ialissos settlements as well as in the city of Rhodes (Fig. 3c, d); while part of these concentrations falls into or lays in close contact with NATURA 2000 protected areas (Fig. 3a). Furthermore, both hotel and Airbnb infrastructure deployment displays a similar pattern; while Airbnb accommodation seems to be further expanding to the island's mainland in NATURA 2000 protected areas (Fig. 3d). The same holds for tourism-related entrepreneurship that is in alignment with the Airbnb distribution. This tourism-related infrastructure pattern on coastal land can be also viewed in the Human Settlement Layer performance indicator (Fig. 3b). In fact the degree of urbanization related to any human-made infrastructure represents an average built-up density of 23% that is mostly concentrated along the eastern coastal part of the island of Rhodes.

4   Exploring Areas Exposed to CC Risks in the Island of Rhodes

The island of Rhodes has recently been evidenced to exhibit high vulnerability to climate-induced risks and natural hazards, as a combined result of high systemic socio-ecological exposure and high vulnerability due to the:

- considerable lack of adequate infrastructure that is capable of securing resilience towards the immense tourist flows of the high-season period (May to September),
- inherent vulnerabilities related to geomorphology and climatic parameters with respect to existing land use/land cover patterns.

The exposure to a combination of vulnerability factors is magnified in the middle- to north-eastern coastal rim of the island, currently emerging as a *tourist hotspot corridor*. In this corridor, the most recent waves of development are concentrating, especially since the dawn of the 21st century.

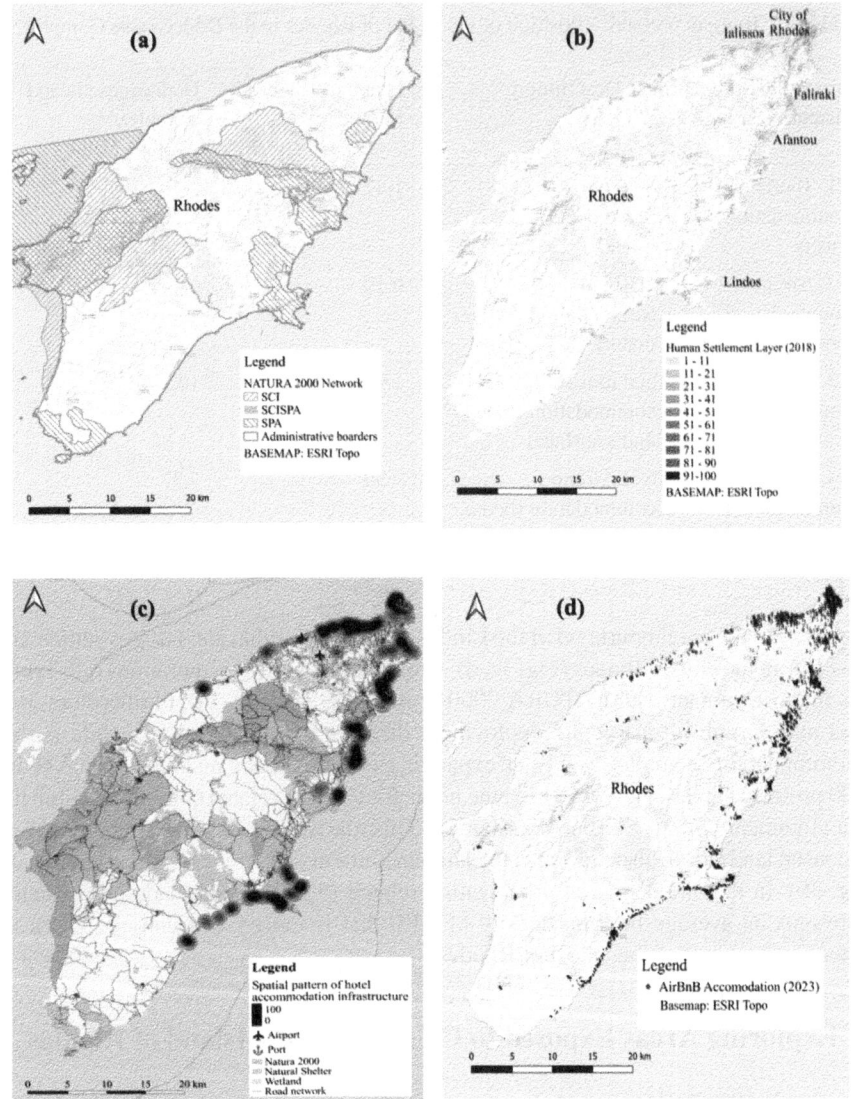

Fig. 3. Island of Rhodes. (a) Natura 2000 regions, (b) Human Settlement Layer (2018), (c) Spatial pattern of hotel infrastructure, (d) Spatial pattern of Airbnb accommodation. Source: Own elaboration based on data from (a) [20], (b) [21], (c) [22] and (d) [19].

The hazardous situation in the island of Rhodes due to CC impacts has been observed and highlighted during the *mega-wildfire* of July 2023 [23]. As witnessed during this wildfire crisis and explicitly stated in the respective report of the Rapid Mapping Service of Copernicus [24], thousands of residents and visitors of inland and coastal villages and large resorts were ordered to evacuate. Fire started on 19/07 in a mountainous inland forest part, reaching after four days the south-eastern coast close to the Glystra

Beach and Genadi Beach in the neighborhood of Lindos peninsula, burning facilities and infrastructure along its way, and ultimately destroying 17,653 ha of forest and transitional scrub land [24]. Evacuation was proven to be a very difficult task for the Civil Protection's agents, as thousands of people were found trapped for several hours between the mountain and the sea [25], with 16,000 people being transported across land and another 3000 by the sea.

However, wildfires are not the only major threat of the urbanized tourist model of the island of Rhodes and the specific coastal corridor. Certain urban constellations of this corridor are also exposed to severe risk of *floods*, particularly affecting specific parts of the coastline zone. Climate change is accentuating both flood and fire risk, while pressure is exerted on coastal wetland ecosystems and woodland areas. In the foreseeable future, estimations at the local level predict considerably lower mean precipitation rates (20–25% reduction) as well as increased drought, accompanied by an increase in Hot Days (i.e. the number of days within a year where Maximum Temperature is greater than 35 °C) [26]. Furthermore, according to Skrimizea & Parra [27], water stress is already high in certain parts of the island. As early as in the 1990s, a study carried out by the United Nations Environment Programme [28], identified signs of saturation in different tourist places around the city of Rhodes, raising concerns regarding the effects of the island's unbalanced socio-economic development on water resources, ascribed to the growth of tourist activities and a concomitant accelerated rate of water use [27].

Within such a context, in this section, the effort is to gain insights and identify such combined risks from a *geospatial perspective*. For a number of well attested reasons, particular focus is placed on the eastern coast/corridor (Fig. 4), due to:

- The higher vulnerability to combined flood and fire risk.
- The less planned character of tourism development and relative urban infrastructure with respect to the northern highly-urbanized part.
- The more intense accentuation of built up activity, as evidenced by new artificial cover during the past decades.
- The higher environmental vulnerability due to the concentration of Natura 2000 and other wildlife sites close to the coast, with important natural areas already impacted by the 2023 fire and previous hazardous events,further affected by large population and tourism constellations falling into these coastal NATURA sites (Fig. 3).

The focus area (eastern coastal corridor - Fig. 4) is actually expanding in a 5-km depth zone along the eastern coastline. This is a large area, of an over 80-min drive (70 km) from the city of Rhodes to the southern end, crossing a relatively rough and heterogeneous landscape. A considerable part of high-valued agricultural land is concentrated in this zone (olives, vineyards, etc.), with the total agricultural land adding up to 26% of the focus area. In addition, significant ecosystems from the mountainous ranges are ending up to the sea; while parts of the coastline are marked by the presence of sandy beaches, thus presenting high vulnerability to soil erosion [29]. Two quite distinct highly-developed coastal tourist areas are situated along this eastern corridor, namely the Lindos peninsula and its surroundings (Fig. 4) and the Faliraki resort.

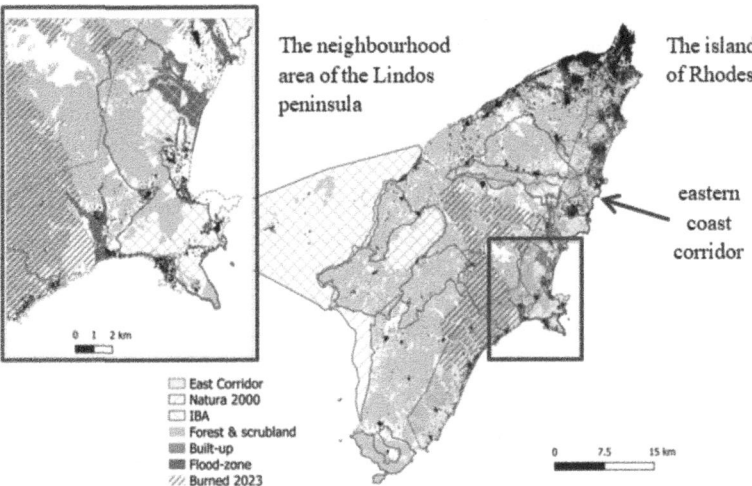

Fig. 4. Combined fire and flood risk in the eastern coastal rim of Rhodes Island in the neighborhood of the Lindos peninsula, Source: Own elaboration.

4.1 Flood-Prone Areas

Flood-prone areas are directly obtained from the official Web-GIS database of the Greek Ministry of Environment and Energy [30]. The Flood Hazard Maps, Flood Risk Maps, and Flood Risk Management Plans are in alignment with the Directive 2007/60/EC [31], setting the general framework for the assessment and management of flood risks; while the geographical unit for implementing the Directive 2007/60/EC as to the flood risks assessment and management is the River Basin District (Water District).

The applied methodology assessed flood risk within the inundation areas, resulting from the hydraulic analysis for the examined return periods, with flood risk depending on [30]:

- The extent and intensity of the flood for the return period within the Flood Risk Management Zone.
- The potential impacts/damages and the significance/value of existing land uses.
- The vulnerability of these land uses to flooding, in terms of their susceptibility based on flood characteristics.

Specifically, for the island of Rhodes almost all flood-prone areas are concentrated on the central eastern part, while the southern one (also considerably less developed and impacted by tourism or urbanization) is less affected. Highly attractive mass tourist areas, like Lindos peninsula (Fig. 4) and Faliraki, situated along the focus corridor in the middle- and north-eastern coast, have been severely flooded during the past decades. These regions constitute *tourism hot spots*, where settlements and tourism infrastructure are raising in adjacent to flood-zones and natural reserves. Severely flooded is also the Ialissos settlement, situated in the north-western coast, close to the city of Rhodes. An estimation of the distribution of flood-prone areas and their relation to built-up areas and tourism facilities (Airbnb) is presented in Tables 2 and 3.

Table 2. Flood-zone statistical data and built-up areas.

	Total Island's Surface		Eastern Island's Zone	
	(ha)	% of total	(ha)	% of zone
Land within flood zone	2396	1.65%	1526	4.38%
Built-up areas within the flood zone	117	4% of total built-up area	52.9	4.8% of zone's built-up area
Tourism facilities within the flood zone	Yes (approx. 150 Airbnb)	2.7% (total 5400)	Yes (approx. 130 Airbnb)	4.7% (total 2728)

Table 3. Built-up area falling into the major flood zones.

Flood_AREA* (ha)	Within the Eastern Focus Corridor (Yes/No)	Built-up area (ha)	% built up area of flood-zone area
219.0	NO	24.0	11.0
195.9	YES	16.8	8.6
418.1	YES	14.6	3.5
123.8	NO	14.1	11.4
171.5	NO	6.6	3.8
132.2	YES	6.2	4.7
168.0	NO	5.9	3.5
145.9	YES	3.5	2.4
7.8	YES	2.7	34.5
17.4	YES	1.8	10.1
116.4	YES	1.2	1.0
19.7	NO	1.1	5.7

* Return Period of 1000 years - T1000 [30] is used due to the fact that Climate Change renders such mega-flood events more probable in the short-term.

By this information, it can be observed that the most extensive flood zones with concentration of built-up areas within them (up to 30% of certain flood zones are covered by structures) are more particularly concentrated in the coastal middle-eastern zone. The same holds for almost all Airbnb accommodations, with 130 out of a total of 150 Airbnb units operating within potential flood zones. Generally, the density of Airbnb per km^2 of land in the studied corridor is around 8 times higher than the overall Airbnb density at the island's level.

4.2   Land Use/Land Cover Analysis

To identify land cover types, the Coastal Zones Land Use/Land cover Database of the European Union's Copernicus Land Monitoring Service [32] is used. The Coastal Zones (CZ) product provides a detailed Land Cover/Land Use (LC/LU) dataset, extracted from high resolution satellite and other available data. Class definitions follow the CORINE Land Cover classification, adapted to the specific characteristics of coastal zones. A Minimum Mapping Unit (MMU) of 0.5 ha and a Minimum Mapping Width (MMW) of 10 m are used. The last available reference year is 2018, including change mapping since 2012.

Specifically, for mapping and analysing the built-up environment several methods and respective datasets have been proposed [33]. To identify recent changes in the island's *soil sealing pattern* through various types of construction, the Imperviousness Classified Change Layer (IMCC database) [34] is used, i.e. a suitable geodatabase for investigating the impact of human activity on the landscape. Imperviousness Classified Change Layer (raster 20 m) covers the period 2006–2018 and provides the degree of imperviousness change in the categories of sealing change (unchanged no sealing, new cover, loss of cover, unchanged sealed, increased sealing, decreased sealing) between each two Imperviousness Density status layers [34]. Rasters of the database were processed according to the methodology described by Lagarias [35].

A comparison of land cover types between the island level as a whole and the focus corridor (Table 4) shows that artificial land along the eastern corridor (6.8%), despite the fact that major urban areas are omitted, is higher than the overall islands' mean percentage (4.0%). Forest land covers this corridor by 10.3%, compared to the 21.5% for the total island; while most of the land cover is classified as semi-natural land, including scrubs and transitional vegetation.

Table 4. Types of land cover in 2018.

	Island of Rhodes in ha & percentage of land	Focus corridor in ha & percentage of land
Forest land (CZ)	30,489 (21.5%)	3571 (10.3%)
Semi-natural land	72,178 (51%)	18,092 (52.1%)
Agricultural land	27,691 (19.6%)	9254 (26.6%)
Artificial land	5666 (4%)	2349 (6.8%)
Other	5458 (3.9%)	1446 (3.9%)
Total area	144,547	34,781

4.3   Identifying the most Recent Built Up Developments

The simple inspection method facilitates a rough evaluation of land-use change area in the most recent period, covering the years beyond 2018, where both CZ and IMCC database ceased to be updated. This process includes the following steps, using a script in the Google Earth Engine platform:

- Creation of a point-based Area of Interest (AOI). An AOI is created with a buffer around it for a larger search area, and the administrative region is selected for clipping.
- Setting the Time Periods & Sentinel-2 Data Filtering. The script defines two periods: summer 2017 and summer 2024 for comparing the *Normalized Difference Vegetation Index* (NDVI). The date ranges are set to focus on the summer months of each year. Sentinel-2 images are filtered based on the AOI and time period, also using Sentinel-2 SCL band to remove clouds and cloud shadows.
- NDVI calculation and comparison. NDVI calculation is processed using the Visible and Near Infrared (B8) and Red (B4) bands. The mean NDVI for both periods is calculated and the difference between them is computed.

Results show that during the period 2017–2024 NDVI loss is observed (Fig. 5) in most of the Rhodes' island territory, a fact that is partly attributed to the drought conditions generally holding in the Southern Aegean Region [4]. Furthermore, in certain parts of the focus corridor of this work, NDVI loss identified is basically attributed to the effect of fires and built up developments, leading to complete loss of existing vegetation coverage. Some plots of agricultural land also exhibit heavy NDVI loss due to ex-cultivation of certain areas, possibly being cleared-off for future development.

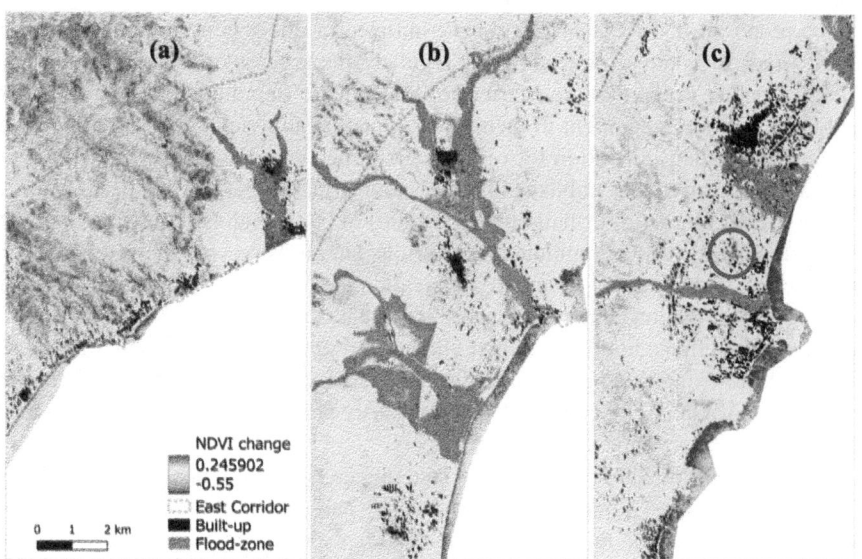

Fig. 5. NDVI change detection map 2017–2024 and flood risk in: (a) the Glystra resort in the southern of Lindos peninsula, (b) Kalathos-Vagies settlement in the northern of Lindos peninsula, (c) Afantou settlement in north-eastern coast and the new tourism development (in red circle). Source: Own elaboration.

That said and despite the dramatic experiences of the 2023 wildfire, but also the documentation and mapping of the flood-risk areas in the middle to north-eastern part of the island of Rhodes and the disastrous flood of 2024, severely affecting, among others, the settlements of Ialissos, Faliraki and Afantou – i.e. tourism hotspots in the study area – it seems that the Tourism-Led-Growth (TLG) model [15] still remains the prevailing direction in the island's economic profile, somehow leaving aside knowledge gained by the already witnessed and actually severe repercussions of Climate Change. This direction is largely supported by both the top-rated position of the island of Rhodes in the global tourism scenery; and the recent policy reforms, being the outcome of a decade of economic austerity Greece has gone through and the effort to 'reboot' the national/regional economy after the recent public debt crisis.

In fact within the focus corridor major new tourism development projects are currently deploying. Among them falls the 'Afantou Project' (Fig. 6a), perceived as one of the greatest projects in the Mediterranean. This is situated in the vicinity of the Afantou settlement, falling into the focus corridor of this work. The Afantou area is adjacent to a Natura 2000 site (GR4210029 - Birds Directive) and an Important Bird and Biodiversity Area (IBA), hosting 66 protected species of the Nature Directives [36], also including two important wetlands (ROD014 and ROD042 of the relevant national database). The site also contains extended archaeological zones and sites (Fig. 6b), as it has been the location of very ancient settlements and fortifications (Hellenistic wall – "Erimokastro, ancient tombs at the "Traounou" site, and ancient walls near the Ladiko Bay - [37]), with Afantou being a major Rhodian town since ancient times.

The proposal of the 'Afantou Project', initiated in 2012, is in alignment with the current Greek legislative framework that regulates the process of urban planning maturation of public properties, transferred to the Hellenic Republic Asset Development Fund [38]; and the assignment to them of an economically viable investment identity, with the aim of their utilization for reasons of significant public interest. The Afantou proposal, as approved and published in the National Gazette 180/AAP/2016 [39] suggests an overall plot ratio (or building coefficient) of 0.09, leading to tens of thousands new square meters; and a combination of various land uses serving the needs of about 5000 tourists, including [40]: tourism – recreation areas; business parks; theme parks; shopping and recreation centers; transport, technical, social, and environmental infrastructure and functions; holiday – tourist village; and public properties with mixed uses (Fig. 6b). A pre-existing old golf course that has been developed by the National Tourism Organization of Greece since the '70 s and is partly abandoned for several decades, is also planned to be revitalized by the developers.

The 'Afantou Project' is mandated to take into consideration possible environmental impacts. However, Climate Change parameters and specific examination of various hazards/risks, impacts on land use transition and new pressure posed on islands' water resources are not adequately addressed. This is totally aligned with other similar new tourism development proposals in Greece, with environmental impacts and hazardous risks being considerably underestimated in order for the license processing and their implementation to be facilitated.

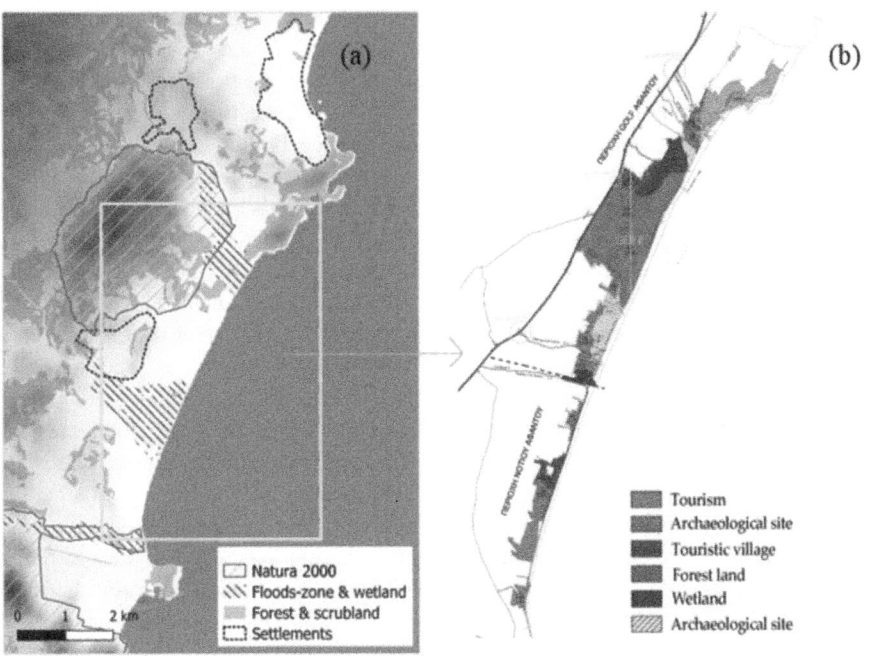

Fig. 6. (a) Location of the Afantou Project (yellow box) in relation to the risk-prone areas (in blue) and natural reserves (in green). (b) The plan of the Afantou Project in the north-eastern part of the island of Rhodes, Source: Own elaboration.

5 Discussion and Conclusions

The tourism supply dynamics of Rhodes Island – i.e., the flagship, together with Kos Island, of the Dodecanese complex, Southern Aegean Region – reflects a traditional mass tourism model, mostly based on large scale, steadily expanding, high class tourism infrastructure investments. This, in turn, implies consumption of valuable land and has adverse impacts on protected areas and other sectoral uses (e.g. agriculture), especially in the eastern coastal rim of the island, where the majority of tourism hotspots are situated. Such a dynamics is the outcome of developments in both the external and the internal decision environment. Speaking of the external environment, as critical issues are considered: the notable position of Rhodes island in the tourism arena, rendering this island a challenging option for tourism investments in the global scene; the role of Information and Communications Technologies (ICTs) as an accelerator of tourism growth, facilitating temporal and geographical concentration of tourist flows in certain well-established tourism destinations as the island of Rhodes; the overdependence on offshore tour operators, rendering local stakeholders less powerful in this bargaining game and rather unable to articulate a diversifying, more sustainable, tourism narrative; and the legislative framework in Greece, especially policies promoted after the 10 years recession period targeting the restart of the Greek economy, which have brought on board new spatial planning instruments for facilitating large-scale investments on both public and privately-own plots. These policy directions surpass regulations of urban and periurban space that emanate by the General Urban Plans carried out at the municipality level; and play a critical role in promoting fast-track processes as enablers for serving global real estate interests and supporting large tourism investments in insular territories in general, including Rhodes. That said, it is noticeable the confined role of local administrations and population as partners in strategic policy decisions at the national and regional level, having thus a say in defining a destination's image that is in alignment with sustainability and resilience objectives at the local level.

In a CC era, Rhodes Island is confronted with the threat of losing off important landscape features and natural resources. More specifically, significant loss of forest land and tree coverage due to wildfires, loss of wetlands and beaches due to the CC impacts in combination with tourism encroachment and coastal erosion problems, and increasing soil sealing in the neighborhood of fire and flood-prone areas are placing resilience to several types of climate-induced crises at stake in the immediate future. In this respect, spatial planning seems to acquire a crucial role in the effort to embed in its processes, in a substantial way, various kinds of CC risks and provide options for ensuring sustainability and resilience objectives in this complex and uncertain environment, undertaking also the role of educating, raising awareness and empowering local communities to realize challenges and react in a risk-minimizing and resilience-maximizing way. Furthermore, future steps of this work could explore the integration, into the proposed framework, of the Urban Heat Islands (UHI) effects, i.e. a particularly relevant topic to such intensively built-up coastal tourist areas and a factor that can potentially exacerbate climate-related vulnerabilities.

References

1. Leka, A., Lagarias, A., Panagiotopoulou, M., Stratigea, A.: Development of a tourism carrying capacity index (TCCI) for sustainable management of coastal areas in Mediterranean Islands – Case study Naxos, Greece. Ocean Coastal Manag. **216**, 105978 (2022). https://doi.org/10.1016/j.ocecoaman.2021.105978
2. Lagarias, A., Stratigea, A., Theodora, Y.: Overtourism as an emerging threat for sustainable Island communities–Exploring indicative examples from the South Aegean Region, Greece. In: Gervasi, O., et al. (eds.) Computational Science and Its Applications – ICCSA 2023 Workshops. ICCSA 2023 Lecture Notes in Computer Science, pp. 404–421. Springer, Cham (2023). https://doi.org/10.1007/978-3-031-37123-3_29
3. Mokhtari, Z., Bergantino, A.S., Intini, M., Elia, M., Buongiorno, A., Giannico, V., Sanesi, G., Lafortezza, R.: Nighttime light extent and intensity explain the dynamics of human activity in coastal zones. Sci. Rep. **15**(1), 1663 (2025). https://doi.org/10.1038/s41598-025-85917-z
4. Leka, A., Lagarias, A., Stratigea, A., Prekas, P.: A methodological framework for assessing overtourism in insular territories—Case study of Santorini Island, Greece. Int. J. Geo-Inform. **14**, 106 (2025). https://doi.org/10.3390/ijgi14030106
5. UNWTO: Tourism and the sustainable development goals–Journey to 2030. (2018). https://www.undp.org/sites/g/files/zskgke326/files/publications/UNWTO_UNDP_Tourism%20and%20the%20SDGs.pdf, last accessed 16 Feb 2025
6. COM(2019) 640 final: The European Green Deal. Communication from the Commission to the European Parliament, the European Council, the Council, the European Economic and Social Committee and the Committee of the Regions, European Commission, Brussels (2019)

7. Lagarias, A., Stratigea, A.: Coastalization patterns in the Mediterranean: a spatiotemporal analysis of coastal urban sprawl in tourism destination areas. GeoJournal. **88**, 2529–2552 (2022). https://doi.org/10.1007/s10708-022-10756-8

8. GRID Arendal: https://www.grida.no/resources/5900, last accessed 11 Feb 2025

9. Theodora, Y., Stratigea, A.: Climate change and strategic adaptation planning in Mediterranean insular territories: gathering methodological insights from Greek experiences. In: Gervasi, O., et al. (eds.) Computational Science and Its Applications – ICCSA 2021 Workshops. ICCSA 2021 Lecture Notes in Computer Science, vol. 12958, pp. 100–115. Springer, Cham (2021). https://doi.org/10.1007/978-3-030-87016-4_8

10. Stratigea, A., Leka, A., Nicolaides, C.: Small and medium-sized cities and insular communities in the Mediterranean: coping with sustainability challenges in the smart city context. In: Stratigea, A., Kyriakides, E., Nicolaides, C. (eds.) Smart Cities in the Mediterranean–Coping with Sustainability Objectives in Small and Medium-sized Cities and Island Communities, pp. 3–29. Springer (2017). https://doi.org/10.1007/978-3-319-54558-5

11. Nastos, P., Saaroni, H.: Living in Mediterranean cities in the context of climate change: a review. Int. J. Climatol. **44**, 3169–3190 (2024). https://doi.org/10.1002/joc.8546

12. Lionello, P., Platon, S., Rodo, X.: Preface – Trends and climate change in the Mediterranean region. Glob. Planet. Chang. **63**(2–3), 87–89 (2008). https://doi.org/10.1016/j.glopla cha.2008.06.004

13. Vogiatzakis, I.N., Mannion, A.M., Sarris, D.: Mediterranean Island biodiversity and climate change: the last 10,000 years and the future. Biodivers. Conserv. **25**, 2597–2627 (2016). https://doi.org/10.1007/s10531-016-1204-9

14. Lazoglou, G., Papadopoulos-Zachos, A., Georgiades, P., Zittis, G., Velikou, K., Manios, E.M., Anagnostopoulou, C.: Identification of climate change hotspots in the Mediterranean. Sci. Rep. **14**, 29817 (2024). https://doi.org/10.1038/s41598-024-80139-1

15. Balaguer, J., Cantavella-Jorda, M.: Tourism as a long-run economic growth factor: the Spanish case. Appl. Econ. **34**, 877–884 (2002). https://doi.org/10.1080/00036840110058923

16. ELSTAT – Population Census 2021. https://www.statistics.gr/documents/20181/17286366/ APOF_APOT_MON_DHM_KOIN.pdf/41ae8e6c-5860-b58e-84f7-b64f9bc53ec4,   last accessed 12 Feb 2025

17. Koutsi, D., Lagarias, A., Stratigea, A.: Assessing the tourism footprint in Dodecanese complex, Greece – An islands' typology approach. In: Gervasi, O., et al. (eds.) Computational Science and Its Applications – ICCSA 2024 Workshops. ICCSA 2024 Lecture Notes in Computer Science, vol. 14822, pp. 388–406. Springer, Cham (2024). https://doi.org/10.1007/978-3-031-65318-6_26

18. Hellenic Chamber of Hotels: https://www.grhotels.gr/category/epicheirimatiki-enimerosi/sta tistika/, last accessed 18 Feb 2025

19. Inside Airbnb Platform: https://insideairbnb.com/, last accessed 18 March 2025

20. European Environment Agency (EEA): Natura 2000 Viewer. https://natura2000.eea.eur opa.eu, last accessed 12 Jan 2025

21. Global Human Settlement Layer: https://ghsl.jrc.ec.europa.eu/, last accessed 25 Feb 2025

22. OSM – OpenStreetMap Data / Geofabric Downloads: https://download.geofabrik.de/europe/ greece.html, last accessed 20 Feb 2025

23. Makineci, H.B.: Investigation of burned areas with multiplatform remote sensing data on the Rhodes 2023 forest fires. Ain Shams Eng. J. **15**(10), 102949 (2024)

24. MSR675: Wildfire on Rhodes Island, Greece. (2023). https://rapidmapping.emergency.cop ernicus.eu/EMSR675/download, last accessed 16 Feb 2025

25. BBC: https://www.bbc.com/news/world-europe-66295972, last accessed 18 Feb 2025

26. Georgoulias, A.K., Akritidis, D., Kalisoras, A., Kapsomenakis, J., Melas, D., Zerefos, C.S., Zanis, P.: Climate change projections for Greece in the 21st century from high-resolution

EURO-CORDEX RCM simulations. Atmos. Res. **271**, 106049 (2022). https://doi.org/10.
1016/j.atmosres.2022.106049

27. Skrimizea, E., Parra, C.: Social-ecological dynamics and water stress in tourist islands: the case of Rhodes, Greece. J. Sustain. Tour. **27**(9), 1438–1456 (2019)

28. United Nations Environmental Programme - UNEP: Guidelines for integrated management of coastal and marine areas - with special reference to the Mediterranean Basin. In: UNEP Regional Seas Reports and Studies No. 161. Split, Croatia, PAP/RAC (MAP-UNEP) (1995) ISBN 92-807-1487-2

29. Zaimes, G.N., Gounaridis, D., Iakovoglou, V., Emmanouloudis, D.: Assessing soil erosion risk for Rhodes Island, Greece with a GIS-based multi-criteria decision analysis. In: Proceedings of the IASTED International Conference on Water Resource Management, Gaborone, Volume: Africa Water Resource Management (AfricaWRM 2012), Botswana (2012). https://doi.org/10.2316/P.2012.762-008

30. Greek Ministry of Environment and Energy: https://gis.floods.ypeka.gr/, last accessed 18 Feb 2025

31. Directive 2007/60/EC. On the assessment and management of flood risks. Off. J. Eur. Union L 288/27, 6.11.2007, 27–34 (2007)

32. Coastal Zones Land Use / Land cover Database of the European Union's Copernicus Land Monitoring Service: https://land.copernicus.eu/en/products/coastal-zones, last accessed 6 Feb 2025

33. Lagarias, A., Stathakis, D.: Towards a more realistic estimation of urban land take by combining cadastral parcels and building footprints. Environ. Plann. B Urban Analyt. City Sci. **52**(5). 1091–1109 (2024). https://doi.org/10.1177/23998083241282092

34. European Environment Agency (EEA) - Copernicus Land Monitoring Service: High Resolution Layer Imperviousness (2018). https://land.copernicus.eu/en/products/high-resolution-layer-imperviousness, last accessed 6 Jan 2025

35. Lagarias, A.: Impervious land expansion as a control parameter for climate-resilient planning on the Mediterranean coast: evidence from Greece. Land. **12**(10), 1844 (2023). https://doi.org/10.3390/land12101844

36. European Environment Agency (EEA): https://eunis.eea.europa.eu/sites/GR4210029, last accessed 28 Jan 2025

37. Archaeological Cadastre: https://www.arxaiologikoktimatologio.gov.gr/, last accessed 13 Jan 2025

38. Hellenic Republic Asset Development Fund: https://hradf.com/, last accessed 5Feb 2025

39. National Gazette 180/AAP/2016: Afantou Project. https://www.technologismiki.com/nomos/pd_9_8_16.php?toc=0&printWindow&, last accessed 2 March 2025

40. Geoplan: Strategic Environmental Impact Study - Afantou Rhodes. (2012) (in Greek). https://docplayer.gr/2595479-Stratigiki-meleti-perivallontikon-epiptoseon-s-m-p-e-afantoy-rodoy.html, last accessed 22 Jan 2025

Developing a Methodological Framework to Assess Social Equity in Regional Spaces Through the Lens of Space Syntax

Chiara Garau[1](✉) (iD), Mana Dastoum[1,2](✉) (iD), and Gianfranco Fancello[1]

[1] Department of Civil and Environmental Engineering and Architecture (DICAAR), University of Cagliari, Via Marengo 2, 09123 Cagliari, Italy
cgarau@unica.it
[2] Department of Construction and Architectural Technology, School of Architecture (ETSAM), Universidad Politécnica de Madrid (UPM), Madrid, Spain

Abstract. Social equity is a fundamental principle of sustainable urban development, emphasising the fair distribution of resources, services, and opportunities to all individuals, regardless of socioeconomic or demographic characteristics. Although many studies utilising social science methods have investigated different aspects of equity in society, the use of Space Syntax analytical method in urban planning has not been well covered in current literature. Space Syntax is a well-established method for analysing spatial configurations and provides particular consistencies to the main indicators of social equity, such as accessibility, connectivity, inclusivity, security, and the equitable distribution of public and green spaces. This study seeks to provide an original methodology linking Space Syntax analysis with the socio-spatial dimensions of social equity in regional contexts. To achieve this, relevant indicators of social equity from a socio-spatial perspective are identified and analysed. The research's originality is combining spatial analysis with the multidimensional concept of social equity. These results show that the socio-spatial equity indicators and Space Syntax used together provide a useful diagnostic tool for identifying spatial inequality and guiding a fair urban development.

Keywords: Social Equity · Social Justice · Space Syntax · Urban Accessibility · Public Space · Sustainable Urban Development

1 Introduction

Social equity is a multidimensional concept within urban and regional planning, reflecting a commitment to justice by recognising the ways in which resources, services, and opportunities are allocated among different people [1–4]. This encompasses multiple

---

This paper is the result of the joint work of the authors. 'Abstract' and 'Finding and Results' (with its subparagraphs) were written jointly by the authors. CG wrote 'Discussion' (with its subparagraphs) and 'Conclusions'. MD wrote 'Material and Methods' (with its subparagraphs), GF wrote 'Introduction'. CG and GF supervised the paper.

attributes like accessibility to basic services [5, 6], connectivity within and between communities [7, 8], inclusion of different social groups [9], personal and security for every individual [10], and the equitable allocation of public amenities or utilities [11] and green spaces [12]. These interact to affect the socio-spatial structure of urban environments and, for that reason, influencing the quality of life as well as more broadly the dynamics of social cohesion and economic opportunity. Conversely, Space Syntax offers quantitative insights of how urban layouts influence accessibility, connectivity, and inclusivity, due to its ability to model and quantify spatial relationships [13–15]. Accessibility, which is a central component of social equity, can be analysed through Space Syntax metrics [16], because they show how the spatial configuration of the built environment (or urban morphologies) enables and constrains movement [17]. Connectivity, a key indicator, can be explored using network centrality measures to understand how well different areas are interconnected [18, 19], shedding light on spatial disparities that may contribute to social exclusion [20]. Moreover, visibility graph analysis (VGA) allows one to assess the inclusiveness and equitable distribution of public and green spaces, consequently emphasising areas where spatial design could either promote or hinder social contact and involvement [21, 22].

Despite the evident alignment between the indicators of social equity and the analytical tools provided by Space Syntax, the integration of these two domains remains largely unexplored in urban research and practice. While Space Syntax has been extensively applied to study spatial accessibility [23–25], connectivity [26, 27], and the inclusivity of urban spaces [28–30] its potential to address the broader and multidimensional concept of social equity has yet to be fully realised. Existing studies often focus on specific spatial metrics without adequately linking these findings to the socio-economic and demographic inequalities that shape access to urban opportunities [17]. This disparity underlines the need of a theoretical framework connecting Space Syntax analysis to the different aspects of social equality. Consequently, the objective of this research is to establish a methodological framework that combines the two (a Space Syntax and socio-spatial approaches to social equity), in an attempt to fill this gap. It is crucial to take such measures because they play a key role in detecting and examining spatial patterns that affect equitable access, connectivity, and inclusivity, particularly at the regional level.

Based on these assumptions, the following research questions are proposed to seek suitable solutions: From a socio-spatial viewpoint, what are the key indicators of social equity and how can they be operationalised within the context of Space Syntax analysis? In what ways it affects fairness in access, connectivity, and inclusivity? How may the combination of Space Syntax metrics with social equity factors reveal new insights into spatial patterns? What methodological framework may be developed to methodically connect Space Syntax analysis with the different aspects of social equity?

This research has a significant insight from both the theoretical and practical point of view. It contributes theoretically by linking space syntax with social equity studies, advancing knowledge on how spatial analysis techniques (Space Syntax analysis) is related to social equity. This paper derives a new theoretical framework for researchers to systematically analyse the relationship between space organisation and the extent to which spaces serve different groups equitably. It extends beyond the typical access metrics to cover a broader range of social accessibility parameters. In practice, this study gives useful insights for urban planners and policymakers. The findings might inform the design of fairer cities, ensuring that all people have equitable access to basic services, green spaces, and public services. The proposed framework can serve as a tool to assess current urban challenges, identify aspects that require improvement, and rank interventions that can help in addressing spatial inequalities. Through mitigating spatial segregation and fostering inclusion, this research is linked to the fulfillment of three Sustainable Development Goals (SDGs): Goal 5: Gender Equality, Goal 10: Reduced Inequalities, and Goal 11: Sustainable Cities and Communities.

The structure of this document is organised in 5 sections. After this introductive section, the section of materials and methods describes the conceptual and analytical approach used by reviewing the most relevant academic literature, consequently specifying the process of defining social equity indicators and relating them to Space Syntax metrics. The Sect. 3 shows the results, namely the methodological framework, by combining Space Syntax analysis with socio-spatial equity indicators. The Sect. 4 critically evaluates the discussion, by considering under the existing urban planning research and practice field, the strengths, limitations, and broader implications of the framework. Finally, Sect. 5 summarises the key findings, highlights the contributions of this research to the field of urban planning, and identifies potential directions for future research.

2 Material and Methods

The research methodology in this study is a qualitative approach that outlines the conceptual and analytical framework adopted to integrate Space Syntax analysis with the socio-spatial dimensions of social equity. The methodology involves four key phases that can be summarised as follow: (1) Overview of the Relevant Literature, (2) Identifying relevant indicators of social equity in regional spaces, (3) Reviewing the space syntax metrics, (4) Linking social equity indicators to Space Syntax metrics, and (5) Constructing and validating the proposed methodological framework through a review of academic literature. Figure 1 presents a brief overview of the research methodology.

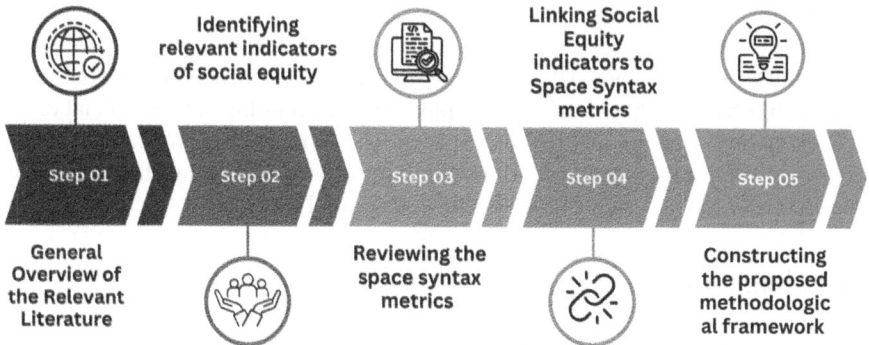

Fig. 1. Visual representation of the research methodology applied in this study.

First, it is essential to develop a clear understanding of social equity. Therefore, the initial stage involves defining social equity and its closely related concepts. Following this, the literature review examines existing research on social equity in urban and regional contexts, identifying gaps and establishing a foundation for integrating these concepts. To build a comprehensive methodological framework, relevant indicators that capture the socio-spatial dimensions of social equity must be identified. Drawing from existing literature, key measures and indicators of social equity are selected, forming the basis for operationalising social equity within the context of Space Syntax analysis. Namely, Space Syntax allows not only to assess quantitatively spatial configurations but also to evaluate their impact on human movement, interaction, and accessibility. In this phase, syntactic measures of Space Syntax are reviewed and analysed to establish a framework that links these measures with social equity indicators. The next phase systematically associates social equity indicators with quantifiable Space Syntax measures to create a robust analytical framework. Finally, based on the findings from the first four phases, a methodological framework is developed to integrate Space Syntax analysis with social equity indicators systematically.

2.1 Search Strategy

Important studies on social equity in urban and regional contexts are analysed using a keyword search strategy in the Scopus database. A carefully chosen set of keywords—including Social Equity, Accessibility, Urban and Regional Spaces, and Space Syntax—was employed for this objective. The initial search yielded only four articles, three of which were not fully relevant to the subject and were excluded. A second search was then conducted, this time removing Space Syntax from the keywords. This process initially identified 448 articles, underscoring the limited exploration of space syntax analysis in relation to social equity. Following the application of selection criteria, including language, subject area, and document type 78 articles were excluded.

The remaining 370 records were extracted and organised in an MS Excel spreadsheet, including their titles, abstracts, keywords, authors' names, affiliations, journal names, and publication years. Duplicate and irrelevant articles were removed, after which the authors manually screened the remaining studies by reviewing their titles, keywords, and abstracts. A total of 56 papers then underwent a detailed eligibility assessment through full-text examination. Ultimately, 19 studies were deemed highly relevant to the research objectives, as they specifically explored the relationship between social equity and accessibility in urban and regional spaces. The process of identification relevant articles, screening and excluding records, eligibility criteria and final inclusion has been depicted briefly in the systematic review flow diagram (Fig. 2).

3 Finding and Results

3.1 General Overview of the Relevant Literature

In recent decades, the concept of social equity has become a central concern in urban planning [31, 32], reflecting the growing need to create more inclusive and just cities [33]. Rapid urbanisation, socio-economic disparities, and uneven access to essential services

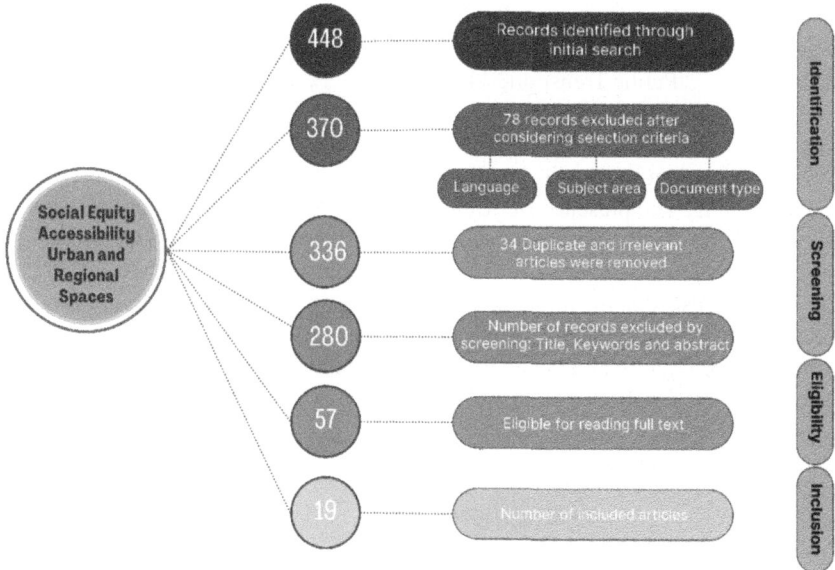

Fig. 2. Systematic review flow diagram

have intensified the urgency to design urban environments that promote fairness and equal opportunities for all [34]. Other closely related concepts to social equity include spatial justice, inclusivity, equitable access, and social fairness, which have been defined in Table 1.

Table 1 . Other closely related concepts to social equity and their definitions

Terms	Definition
Social equity	Fair distribution of resources and opportunities, ensuring all individuals can participate in society regardless of background [35].
Spatial justice	Equitable allocation of spatial resources and infrastructure to provide fair access to services and public space [6].
Inclusivity	Designing environments and policies that accommodate diverse populations, ensuring participation for all [36].
Equitable access	Fair opportunities for all individuals to reach and use public services, removing barriers for disadvantaged groups [37].
Social fairness	Equal treatment and opportunities for all, addressing systemic inequalities in society [38].

The word cloud visualisation (Fig. 1) represents a rapid qualitative overview of the prominent themes emerging from the literature. Word size within the cloud corresponds to the frequency of each term. Prominent terms such as "Social Equity," "Spatial Justice,"

"Equitable Access," and "Accessibility" highlight the fundamental concerns of ensuring fairness in spatial distribution and urban design. Other significant terms, including "Transportation," "Public Transport," "Healthcare," "Educational Services," and "Green Space Equity," emphasise the urban areas which social equity has been investigated predominantly. Additionally, concepts such as "Segregation," "Disparity," "Vulnerability," and "Inequity" reflect the socio-spatial challenges that hinder inclusivity in urban and regional planning. The presence of "Connectivity," "Spatial Pattern," and "Sustainable Development" further underscores the role of spatial analysis in assessing accessibility and mobility dynamics. However, the notable absence of the term "Space Syntax" in this word cloud suggests that the integration of social equity assessment with the space syntax techniques has not been adequately investigated in the existing literature. This gap reinforces the originality and necessity of this research in developing a novel methodological framework that bridges spatial analytics with the multidimensional concept of social equity (Fig. 3).

Fig. 3. Word cloud visualisation of the frequently occurring keywords

3.2   Previous Studies in the Field

This paper explores the relationship between equity, accessibility, and cohesion in urban public spaces, and the possibility of measuring social equity by using space syntax analysis. The connection between equity and transportation, urban green spaces and parks, has been extensively studied by scholars. There are also several studies about social equity of public infrastructures, healthcare and educational services. Since the focus of this study is to develop a new methodological framework only the employed research methods of the existing literature have been represented in this section.

The study of spatial and social equity in urban environments has been extensively explored across various domains, including transportation accessibility, public services distribution, and the built environment. A key theme in this body of literature is the intersection between accessibility measures and equity assessments, highlighting disparities in urban resource allocation. This review synthesises various perspectives, drawing connections among methodologies, findings, and implications, while identifying existing research gaps.

Cavallaro et al. [39] examined the spatial and social equity impacts of High-Speed Railways in north-western Italy, employing Spatial and Social Equity Railway Indexes to assess variations in travel times, connections, and socioeconomic impacts. Similarly, Sharma and Patil [40] investigated spatial and social inequities in access to educational services in Greater Mumbai, using the Lorenz curve and Gini index for spatial equity and a public-private transport accessibility ratio for social equity. Their research underscores how different transport modes contribute to inequities, echoing concerns raised by Wilberg et al. [41] regarding variations in walking accessibility across different population groups in Helsinki, particularly older adults. They integrated seasonal walking speed data with service accessibility, revealing temporal inequities, a dimension that is often overlooked in traditional accessibility studies.

A related concern is how transport infrastructure influences social equity. Cuthill et al. [42] combined quantitative and qualitative approaches using geographically weighted regression to assess local variations in accessibility, reinforcing the notion that equity concerns require localised, context-specific evaluations. This aligns with Sharma and Patil's [43] broader framework analysing accessibility equity in Greater Mumbai, encompassing multiple urban services such as jobs, education, healthcare, and parks. Their spatial autocorrelation analysis further confirms inequities observed in earlier studies, bridging gaps between micro-scale and macro-scale assessments.

Beyond transport, urban infrastructure plays a critical role in spatial equity. Zhao et al. [44] utilised a quantitative approach to examine cycling infrastructure distribution in Canada, correlating infrastructure levels with sociodemographic characteristics using Pearson correlation and multilevel regression. This approach parallels Chang et al. [45], who analysed spatial and social justice dimensions of public service facilities through service area analysis and the Gaussian two-step floating catchment area (G2SFCA) method. These methodologies demonstrate how multi-dimensional accessibility frameworks may be applied to different urban environments, such as in the case of Cai et al. 's [46] study on public charging stations in Shanghai with the use of both a supply-demand gap analysis with equity metrics.

Another important aspect of social equity is healthcare accessibility. Chen et al. [47] assessed accessibility to tertiary hospital services for older adults using a simple gravity model, revealing substantial regional variation. In a similar way, Iraegui et al. [48], who evaluated urban green space (UGS) accessibility in Barcelona, using spatial clustering methods. Such methodological parallels imply that differences in accessibility are neither confined to transport mode choices nor are limited to the distribution of essential services and thus demand more cohesive and holistic policy approaches.

Gu et al. [49] further investigated healthcare accessibility in Kunshan, China with the Balanced Floating Catchment Area (BFCA) method, identifying inequities among hospital types and travel modes. Wang et al. [50] explored similar themes in relation to open spaces, ascertaining how the accessibility of those places affects older adults' visitation in high-density urban settings. This use of GIS and Space Syntax Theory exemplifies the spatial nature at the heart of urban equity.

Using public space accessibility research as an example, Xu and Wang [51] studied public space accessibility in Nanjing Old City beyond the traditional ones, which included socially vulnerable groups. On the other hand, the gravity potential addresses accessibility variability differences, as also highlighted by Rashid [52], based on Space Syntax research that analyses social equity through street networks and urban compactness in 25 cities in England. Unlike Zhao and Gong [53], who used optimisation models to examine urban park accessibility inequalities in Nanchang. This approach shows different methods used in equity studies while demostrating their adaptability.

Recent advancements in accessibility evaluation are evident in Sun et al. [54], who introduced an enhanced three-step floating catchment area (3SFCA) method, integrating Space Syntax metrics with multi-modal transportation analysis. This refinement, in fact, provides better estimation of demand across populations, a problem also noted and addressed by He et al. [55], that applied machine learning along with geostatistical analysis to evaluate accessibility to urban parks in Taiyuan, China. These studies illustrate the ongoing shift in the accessibility assessment paradigm towards the use of cutting-edge computational methods to achieve more accurate measurements.

Beyond spatial metrics, policy frameworks play a significant role in shaping urban equity. Meerow et al. [56] analysed social equity in urban resilience planning, using a qualitative content analysis of resilience plans from North American cities. Their consideration of procedural equity fits with Wan and Titheridge [57], who proposed in a conceptual framework for transport equity in China the need for tripartite equity. They note that equity assessments need to recognise the socio-political context reminding the importance of policy-sensitive analysis, as their findings suggest.

Together, these studies demonstrate how diverse urban equity research can be. While methodologies range from GIS-based accessibility models to regression analyses and machine learning approaches, a common theme emerges: spatial inequities persist across different urban services and infrastructures. Despite significant advancements, gaps remain in integrating multi-dimensional equity assessments that account for temporal variations, socio-political contexts, and evolving urban structures. Future research should prioritise interdisciplinary frameworks that combine spatial, social, and policy-driven analyses to address these persistent inequities comprehensively.

Figure 4 illustrates the frequency of methodological approaches employed in the reviewed studies, using a heatmap with a colour gradient ranging from dark blue (indicating lower frequency) to bright green (indicating higher frequency). The most frequently applied method is GIS-based spatial analysis, followed by equity measurement techniques, such as the Gini index, Lorenz curve, and Moran's I. The floating catchment area methods (e.g., 2SFCA, 3SFCA, G2SFCA) and multi-modal transport and travel time analysis also appear prominently. Regression models and network-based accessibility assessments are moderately frequent, reflecting their role in capturing spatial and socio-economic dynamics. Gravity-based accessibility models and social equity frameworks, such as qualitative content analysis, are applied less frequently. Space syntax analysis, though valuable in urban studies, is among the least used methodologies in the selected literature. The visualisation effectively highlights methodological trends, revealing a preference for quantitative spatial techniques in accessibility and equity research.

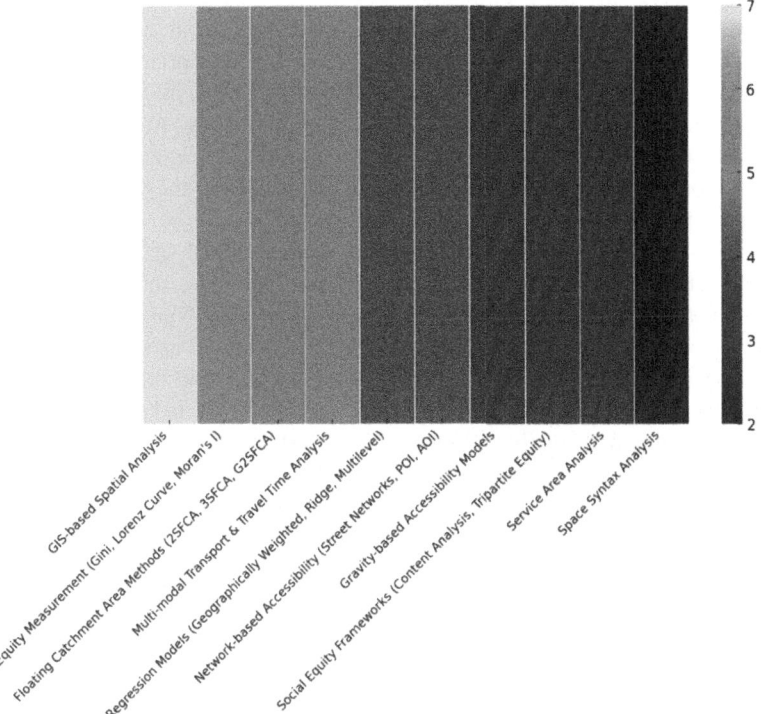

Fig. 4. Frequency of applied methods in previous studies

3.3 Measures and Components of Social Equity

Social equity in urban planning is a multidimensional concept that seeks to reduce disparities and improve the quality of life for marginalised or vulnerable populations [58]. It encompasses various measures that ensure fair access to urban resources, social services, and opportunities for all individuals, regardless of socio-economic status, age, gender, or physical ability. A socio-spatial perspective on social equity considers how urban spaces and infrastructure contribute to or mitigate inequalities, focusing on key dimensions such as accessibility, inclusivity, fair distribution of amenities, and security.

Accessibility is one of the most fundamental indicators of social equity, as it determines the extent to which individuals can reach essential services, work-places, educational institutions, and recreational spaces. Equitable urban accessibility requires a well-connected and affordable public transport system that accommodates diverse demographic groups, including individuals with disabilities, elderly citizens, and lower-income populations who may lack private transport options [11]. Furthermore, pedestrian-friendly environments, cycling infrastructure, and barrier-free urban design enhance mobility and independence, fostering greater participation in social and economic activities.

Inclusivity in urban spaces refers to the design and governance of public areas that welcome and serve diverse communities. Parks, plazas, and streets should be planned with a variety of users in mind, incorporating amenities that support different cultural, recreational, and social needs [59]. Universal design principles play a crucial role in ensuring that individuals with disabilities, parents with young children, and elderly residents can fully engage with urban environments. Additionally, inclusive governance structures that involve local communities in decision-making processes contribute to more socially just urban development by reflecting the voices of historically underrepresented groups [60].

Fair distribution of amenities is another critical aspect of socio-spatial equity, ensuring that essential services such as healthcare facilities, schools, supermarkets, and green spaces are equitably dispersed across urban areas. The most vulnerable and socio-economically disadvantaged communities have limited access to a high-quality public service [61]. Urban policies, such as mixed-income housing and equitable zoning, emphasised investment in disadvantaged neighbourhoods and can help bridge these gaps, by promoting and creating a more equitable urban fabric.

Security is a critical axis of social equity, as this dictates how freely people use and access public spaces. Safety perception, and actual safety, directly influences outdoor participation, especially for women, children and older generations. Crime prevention through environmental design (CPTED) strategies such as better street lighting, active surveillance, and well-maintained public spaces can improve urban security and promote feelings of belonging and trust within communities [62]. Moreover, equitable law enforcement practices and halting discriminatory policing are essential for socially just and safe cities [63].

3.4 Space Syntax Metrics

In the 1980s, Bill Hiller and his collaborators at University College London developed space syntax theory and analytical methods and discovered that space has its own social logic that influence the behaviour of humans, including pedestrian mobility [64]. This theory claims that the configuration of the urban grid itself is the primary generator of movement and social encounters [65]. The Space Syntax approach employs an axial map, which is used to quantify the spatial networks of this map, using the longest and minimally set of straight lines that can pass through all the undivided spaces in the built environment (in this case for the agglomeration of urban areas). These axial lines provide a basis for analysing the configurations of spacetime and function as lines of sight in the space [66]. In contrast, segment-based analysis relies on a segment map, which is derived from the axial map by dividing axial lines into smaller segments at their intersections [67].

Space syntax offers a set of theories, methods, techniques and metrics for analysing urban environments that identify the underlying spatial structures that determine perception, use and experience [68]. It offers a lens through which to understand how different spatial configurations affect human social behaviour and movement [69]. The term "spatial configuration" is used in space syntax when referring to the relationships between individual spatial units and the overall structure of a spatial system [27]. In urban studies, these units typically include axial lines (uninterrupted lines of movement, visibility) and segments (portions of axial lines divided at intersections with other lines). Space syntax has its own rigorous methods for modelling street networks in the form of configurations, via the use of axial lines creating an axial map and via segments producing a segment map [70]. Furthermore, it provides analytical tools to examine the intersection patterns of these lines or segments through various topological and topo-metric measures. Additionally, space syntax enables users to visualise data by applying colour gradients to the map based on the values of specific measures for individual units [71].

Several Space Syntax measures have been applied in previous studies, demonstrating varying degrees of correlation with movement patterns. These include integration, connectivity, choice, control, intelligibility, angular step depth, intensity, and synergy. However, an initial review indicates that four classic Space Syntax metrics integration, connectivity, choice, and control are the most commonly utilised for examining social behaviours [72]. A concise explanation of these key measures is presented below.

Integration is one of the fundamental measures in Space Syntax used to analyse pedestrian and vehicular movement patterns [73] It evaluates to what extent the spatial configuration possesses the capability to absorb human mobility patterns. From a topological perspective, integration calculates distance based on the number of turns and directional shifts required to navigate through the system. A network with fewer axial lines and directional changes tends to be more integrated [13]. Angular integration measures the closeness of each segment to all others by summing angular changes, whereas metric integration considers the straight-line distance between the midpoints of two adjacent segments [74].

Choice refers to the extent to which a particular street is part of the shortest path between any two other streets in a network [75]. Areas with high choice values are positioned along the shortest paths between multiple origins and destinations, making this measure particularly effective in predicting pedestrian and vehicular movement patterns [76]. This metric enables researcher to identify the trajectories which are most likely to be used by citizens who are aware of shortcuts within the spatial network of cities. Connectivity, another key measure, captures the number of direct connections a street or space has with its immediate surroundings [77]. Since this measure evaluates spatial relationships based only on immediate neighbouring areas without considering the broader network, it is classified as a local measure [78]. Thus, it could be considered a critical metric for the measurement of urban accessibility on a local scale.

Lastly, control quantifies how much influence a space has over access to its immediate neighbours, factoring in the number of alternative connections available to each of them [79]. It measures to what degree a space restricts access to neighbouring spaces, considering what alternative links are available for each neighbour space [80]. Higher control values mean significant opportunities for appropriate surveillance of urban areas. Collectively, these measures create a powerful framework for linking spatial configurations to social behaviour.

Other measures include intelligibility, which evaluates the correlation between integration and connectivity of spaces [81]; Angular step depth assesses movement efficiency calculating the distance travelled on a network, and intensity defines the relationship between the rate of entropy change and the total depth [82]. Likewise, the factor of synergy, which captures the relationship between local and global integration, has been addressed to a lesser extent [83].

4   Discussion

4.1   Linking Social Equity Indicators to Space Syntax Metrics

The methodological framework used to evaluate social equity through Space Syntax analysis is analysed in this section. The framework is organised by considering four main indicators: accessibility, inclusivity, equitable distribution of public facilities, and security. All of them are mapped to specific Space Syntax metrics. This approach helps to find spatial patterns in urban environments that either promote or reduce social inequalities.

Based on the literature on both variables, this research identifies customised Space Syntax metrics for each social equity indicator. By considering accessibility, the appropriate metric depends on the scale of analysis. On local or neighbourhood scales studies, the connectivity measure is particularly useful in assessing the accessibility of urban spaces. At a regional or city-wide scale, global integration is a more coherent indicator for understanding the overall accessibility of spaces across a spatial context.

Within the main context of social equity, the inclusivity indicator should be examined via a mix of syntactical criteria (such as integration, connectivity, and choice) and empirical observations. This guarantees a broader understanding of inclusiveness across all demographic groups, including for instance gender and age. Furthermore, universal design principles should be integrated into this assessment to facilitate adaptive solutions that enhance accessibility for individuals with disabilities [84, 85].

For the equitable distribution of public amenities (green spaces, public squares and so on), Space Syntax analysis should be combined with GIS-based land-use distribution evaluations. In this way, it is possible evaluate spatial disparities in service supply.

Finally, security can be assessed through various syntactical measures, by considering its theoretical foundations. Gehl [86] claims that crime rates usually drop in cities with considerable pedestrian movement and social interaction. In the same way, urban contexts with increased visibility and clear sightlines benefit from improved natural surveillance, hence promoting safer environments. In this sense, apart from integration and connectivity, Space Syntax metrics such as choice and control are useful for assessing security. At a local or neighbourhood scale, visibility graph analysis can further contribute to the design of secure built environments. Moreover, to address the subjective dimension of security, a combined methodological approach incorporating CPTED surveys can offer deeper insights into perceived safety levels, thereby strengthening the overall social equity framework. In summary, the methodological approach outlined above allows for a multi-dimensional assessment of social equity through Space Syntax analysis. Depending on the research focus and scale, these methodological strategies can be adapted to ensure a functional and comprehensive evaluation of urban spatial equity.

Figure 5 visualises the framework for linking social equity indicators to space syntax metrics and its methodological procedures.

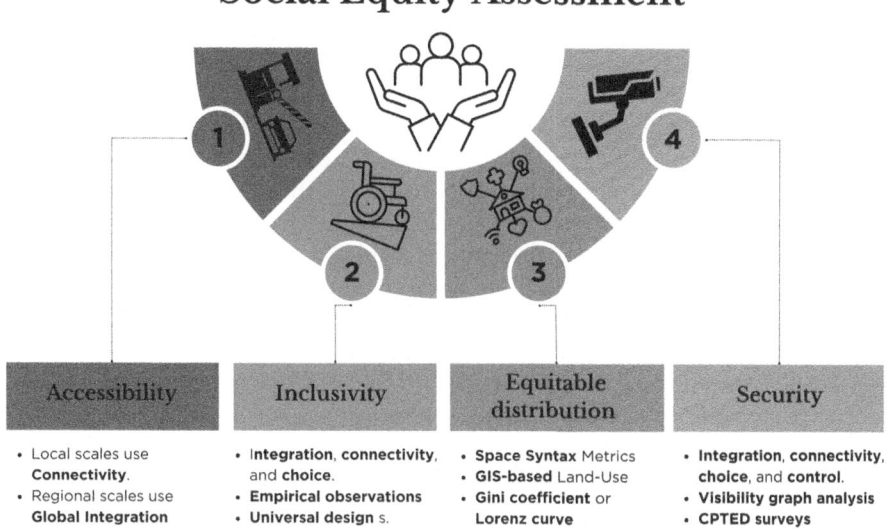

Social Equity Assessment

Accessibility	Inclusivity	Equitable distribution	Security
• Local scales use **Connectivity**. • Regional scales use **Global Integration**	• **Integration, connectivity, and choice**. • **Empirical observations** • **Universal design** s.	• **Space Syntax** Metrics • **GIS-based** Land-Use • **Gini coefficient** or **Lorenz curve**	• **Integration, connectivity, choice, and control**. • **Visibility graph analysis** • **CPTED surveys**

Fig. 5. Framework for linking social equity indicators to space syntax metrics

4.2 Implications, Limitations, and Future Research Directions

One of the main strengths of this research is its interdisciplinary approach, integrating spatial analytics with socio-spatial equity concepts. The framework provides a replicable methodology that urban planners and policymakers can employ to assess and address spatial inequalities. However, certain limitations must be acknowledged. First, Space Syntax analysis primarily focuses on spatial configurations and does not inherently account for socio-economic variables such as income levels, cultural dynamics, or governance structures. To overcome this limitation, the integration of socio-economic data with Space Syntax metrics is recommended for a more comprehensive equity assessment. Additionally, while this research establishes a foundational framework, further empirical validation through multiple case studies is necessary to refine and generalise its applicability.

5 Conclusions

This study responded to a notable research gap in the fields of urban studies by developing a methodological framework that integrates Space Syntax cost-benefit analysis to bear on the socio-spatial aspects of social equity.

In response to the first research question (from a socio-spatial viewpoint, what are the key indicators of social equity and how can they be operationalised within the context of Space Syntax analysis?), accordingly four key indicators of social equity were identified: accessibility, inclusivity, equitable distribution of public facilities, and security.

In that manner, these indicators were operationalised within Space Syntax analysis through specific metrics: accessibility was measured using connectivity and global integration, depending on the scale of analysis; inclusivity was assessed by combining integration, connectivity, and choice values with empirical observations and universal design principles; equitable distribution of public facilities was examined using GIS-based land use distribution coupled with Space Syntax analysis; and security was analysed through visibility graph analysis, choice, and control metrics, with additional insights from CPTED surveys (this sentence replied the second research question: in what ways it affects fairness in access, connectivity, and inclusivity?). By focusing on the third research question (how may the combination of Space Syntax metrics with social equity factors reveal new insights into spatial patterns?), this paper demonstrated that integrating Space Syntax metrics with social equity indicators could uncover spatial disparities that impact urban fairness. Finally, in response to the fourth question (What methodological framework may be developed to methodically connect Space Syntax analysis with the different aspects of social equity?), a structured methodological framework was developed, demonstrating how quantitative spatial analysis can be combined with qualitative empirical observations and socio-economic measures to comprehensively assess urban equity. These findings imply that Space Syntax may have the potential to be an effective diagnostic tool for finding areas of spatial injustice and guiding equitable urban solutions when used with socio-spatial equity indicators.

The originality of this research lies in the convergence of Space Syntax analysis with the various forms of social equity discussed in this study, which goes beyond the traditional accessibility studies to include broader socio-spatial issues.

This research clearly links spatial analysis to social justice, while informing not only the critical debate on the equitable development of cities but also guiding meaningful progress in key Sustainable Development Goals (SDGs).

Future work may strengthen this framework through real-world case studies and more broadly test for applicability across different urban contexts to refine its adoption and replication in policy and practice.

Acknowledgments. This study was partially supported by the MUR through the project SMART3R-FLITS: SMART Transport for Travelers and Freight Logistics Integration Towards Sustainability" (Project protocol: 2022J38SR9; CUP Code: F53D23005630006), financed by the PRIN 2022 (Research Projects of National Relevance) program. This study was also partially supported by the Ecosystem of Innovation for Next Generation Sardinia (e.INS) and received funding from the European Union Next-GenerationEU (PIANO NAZIONALE DI RIPRESA E RESILIENZA (PNRR)—MISSIONE 4 COMPONENTE 2, INVESTIMENTO 1.5—ECS00000038). In particular, the "Finding and Results" was funded by eINS. This study reflects only the authors' views and opinions, and neither the European Union nor the European Commission nor MUR can be considered responsible for them.

References

1. McDermott, M., Mahanty, S., Schreckenberg, K.: Examining equity: a multidimensional framework for assessing equity in payments for ecosystem services. Environ. Sci. Policy. **33**, 416–427 (2013). https://doi.org/10.1016/j.envsci.2012.10.006
2. Stokan, E., Hatch, M.E., Overton, M.: Fifty years as the fourth pillar of public administration: a polycentric extension of the social equity framework. Public Adm. **101**(4), 1427–1442 (2023). https://doi.org/10.1111/padm.12888
3. Garau, C., Annunziata, A., Desogus, G., Rossetti, S.: Spatial smartness and (In) justice in urban contexts? The case studies of Cagliari and Parma, Italy. In: International Conference on Innovation in Urban and Regional Planning, pp. 484–495. Cham, Springer Nature Switzerland (2023)
4. Pinna, F., Garau, C., Annunziata, A.: A literature review on urban usability and accessibility to investigate the related criteria for equality in the city. In: International Conference on Computational Science and Its Applications, pp. 525–541. Springer International Publishing, Cham (2021)
5. Grengs, J.: Nonwork accessibility as a social equity indicator. Int. J. Sustain. Transp. **9**(1), 1–14 (2015). https://doi.org/10.1080/15568318.2012.719582
6. Jian, I.Y., Luo, J., Chan, E.H.: Spatial justice in public open space planning: accessibility and inclusivity. Habitat Int. **97**, 102122 (2020). https://doi.org/10.1016/j.habitatint.2020.102122
7. Kaplan, S., Popoks, D., Prato, C.G., Ceder, A.A.: Using connectivity for measuring equity in transit provision. J. Transp. Geogr. **37**, 82–92 (2014). https://doi.org/10.1016/j.jtrangeo.2014.04.016
8. Eizenberg, E., Jabareen, Y.: Social sustainability: a new conceptual framework. Sustainability. **9**(1), 68 (2017). https://doi.org/10.3390/su9010068
9. Harris, E., Franz, A., O'Hara, S.: Promoting social equity and building resilience through value-inclusive design. Buildings. **13**(8), 2081 (2023). https://doi.org/10.3390/buildings13082081
10. Abed, A., Al-Jokhadar, A.: Common space as a tool for social sustainability. J. Hous. Built. Environ. **37**(1), 399–421 (2022). https://doi.org/10.1007/s10901-021-09843-y
11. Manaugh, K., Badami, M.G., El-Geneidy, A.M.: Integrating social equity into urban transportation planning: a critical evaluation of equity objectives and measures in transportation plans in North America. Transp. Policy. **37**, 167–176 (2015). https://doi.org/10.1016/j.tranpol.2014.09.013
12. Kimpton, A.: A spatial analytic approach for classifying greenspace and comparing greenspace social equity. Appl. Geogr. **82**, 129–142 (2017). https://doi.org/10.1016/j.cities.2022.103839
13. Sharmin, S., Kamruzzaman, M.: Meta-analysis of the relationships between space syntax measures and pedestrian movement. Transplant. Rev. **38**(4), 524–550 (2018). https://doi.org/10.1080/01441647.2017.1365101
14. Huang, B.X., Chiou, S.C., Li, W.Y.: Accessibility and street network characteristics of urban public facility spaces: equity research on parks in Fuzhou city based on GIS and space syntax model. Sustainability. **12**(9), 3618 (2020). https://doi.org/10.3390/su12093618

15. Askarizad, R., Lamíquiz Daudén, P.J., Garau, C.: The application of space syntax to enhance sociability in public urban spaces: a systematic review. ISPRS Int. J. Geo Inf. **13**(7), 227 (2024). https://doi.org/10.3390/ijgi13070227
16. Garau, C., Annunziata, A., Yamu, C.: A walkability assessment tool coupling multi-criteria analysis and space syntax: the case study of Iglesias, Italy. Eur. Plan. Stud. **32**(2), 211–233 (2020). https://doi.org/10.1080/09654313.2020.1761947
17. Karimi, K.: The configurational structures of social spaces: space syntax and urban morphology in the context of analytical. Evid. Based Des. Land. **12**(11), 2084 (2023). https://doi.org/10.3390/land12112084
18. Askarizad, R., Lamíquiz Daudén, P.J., Garau, C.: Exploring the role of configurational accessibility of alleyways on facilitating wayfinding transportation within the organic street network systems. Transp Policy. **157**, 179–194 (2024). https://doi.org/10.1016/j.tranpol.2024.09.001
19. Karimi, K.: Space syntax: consolidation and transformation of an urban research field. J. Urban Des. **23**(1), 1–4 (2017). https://doi.org/10.1080/13574809.2018.1403177
20. Lucas, K.: Transport and social exclusion: where are we now? Transp. Policy. **20**, 105–113 (2012). https://doi.org/10.1016/j.tranpol.2012.01.013
21. Turner, A., Doxa, M., O'Sullivan, D., Penn, A.: From isovists to visibility graphs: a methodology for the analysis of architectural space. Environ. Plan. B Plan. Des. **28**(1), 103–121 (2001). https://doi.org/10.1068/b2684
22. Askarizad, R., He, J.: The role of urban furniture in promoting gender equality and static social activities in public spaces. Ain Shams Eng. J. **16**(2), 103250 (2025). https://doi.org/10.1016/j.asej.2024.103250
23. Jiang, B., Claramunt, C., Batty, M.: Geometric accessibility and geographic information: extending desktop GIS to space syntax. Comput. Environ. Urban. Syst. **23**(2), 127–146 (1999). https://doi.org/10.1016/S0198-9715(99)00017-4
24. Penn, A.: Space syntax and spatial cognition: or why the axial line? Environ. Behav. **35**(1), 30–65 (2003). https://doi.org/10.1177/0013916502238864
25. Morales, J., Flacke, J., Morales, J., Zevenbergen, J.: Mapping urban accessibility in data scarce contexts using space syntax and location-based methods. Appl. Spat. Anal. Policy. **12**, 205–228 (2019). https://doi.org/10.1007/s12061-017-9239-1
26. Yang, T., Jing, D., Wang, S.: Applying and exploring a new modeling approach of functional connectivity regarding ecological network: a case study on the dynamic lines of space syntax. Ecol. Model. **318**, 126–137 (2015). https://doi.org/10.1016/j.ecolmodel.2014.11.015
27. Can, I., Heath, T.: In-between spaces and social interaction: a morphological analysis of Izmir using space syntax. J. Hous. Built. Environ. **31**, 31–49 (2016). https://doi.org/10.1007/s10901-015-9442-9
28. Vaughan, L.: The spatial syntax of urban segregation. Prog. Plan. **67**(3), 199–294 (2007). https://doi.org/10.1016/j.progress.2007.03.001
29. Önder, D.E., Gigi, Y.: Reading urban spaces by the space-syntax method: a proposal for the South Haliç Region. Cities. **27**(4), 260–271 (2010). https://doi.org/10.1016/j.cities.2009.12.006
30. Netto, V.M.: What is space syntax not? Reflections on space syntax as socio-spatial theory. Urban Des. Int. **21**, 25–40 (2016). https://doi.org/10.1057/udi.2015.21
31. Reece, J.W.: In pursuit of a twenty-first century just city: the evolution of equity planning theory and practice. J. Plann. Literat. **33**(3), 299–309 (2018). https://doi.org/10.1177/0885412218754519
32. Mercier, J.: Equity, social justice, and sustainable urban transportation in the twenty-first century. Adm. Theory Praxis. **31**(2), 145–163 (2009). https://doi.org/10.2753/ATP1084-1806310201
33. Lee, N.: Inclusive growth in cities: a sympathetic critique. Reg Stud. **53**(3), 424–434 (2019). https://doi.org/10.1080/00343404.2018.1476753

34. Goel, R.K., Vishnoi, S.: Urbanization and sustainable development for inclusiveness using ICTs. Telecommun. Policy. **46**(6), 102311 (2022). https://doi.org/10.1016/j.telpol.2022.102311
35. Salmi, J., Bassett, R.M.: The equity imperative in tertiary education: promoting fairness and efficiency. Int. Rev. Educ. **60**(3), 361–377 (2014). https://doi.org/10.1007/s11159-013-9391-z
36. Lanteigne, V., Rider, T.R., Stratton, P.A.: Inclusive building performance: a new design paradigm. In: World Congress of Architects, vol. 97, pp. 783–791. Springer International Publishing, Cham (2023, July). https://doi.org/10.1016/j.habitatint.2020.102122
37. Haque, M.N., Sharifi, A.: Barriers and solutions for just and equitable access to urban ecosystem services: a critical analysis. Int J Sustain Dev World Ecol, 1–17 (2025). https://doi.org/10.1080/13504509.2025.2456862
38. O'brien, F.J.: Biomaterials & scaffolds for tissue engineering. Mater. Today. **14**(3), 88–95 (2011). https://doi.org/10.1016/S1369-7021(11)70058-X
39. Cavallaro, F., Sommacal, G., Božičnik, S., Klemenčič, M.: Combined transport in the Alps: reasons behind a difficult acceptance and possible solutions. Res. Transp. Bus. Manag. **35**, 100461 (2020). https://doi.org/10.1016/j.rtbm.2020.100461
40. Sharma, G., Patil, G.R.: Spatial and social inequities for educational services accessibility-A case study for schools in Greater Mumbai. Cities. **122**, 103543 (2022). https://doi.org/10.1016/j.cities.2021.103543
41. Willberg, E., Fink, C., Toivonen, T.: The 15-minute city for all?–Measuring individual and temporal variations in walking accessibility. J. Transp. Geogr. **106**, 103521 (2023). https://doi.org/10.1016/j.jtrangeo.2022.103521
42. Cuthill, N., Cao, M., Liu, Y., Gao, X., Zhang, Y.: The association between urban public transport infrastructure and social equity and spatial accessibility within the urban environment: an investigation of Tramlink in London. Sustainability. **11**(5), 1229 (2019). https://doi.org/10.3390/su11051229
43. Sharma, G., Patil, G.R.: Urban spatial structure and equity for urban services through the lens of accessibility. Transp. Policy. **146**, 72–90 (2024). https://doi.org/10.1016/j.tranpol.2023.10.017
44. Zhao, Q., Winters, M., Nelson, T., Laberee, K., Ferster, C., Manaugh, K.: Who has access to cycling infrastructure in Canada? A social equity analysis. Comput. Environ. Urban Syst. **110**, 102109 (2024). https://doi.org/10.1016/j.compenvurbsys.2024.102109
45. Chang, M., Huang, L., Zhai, T., Zhu, J., Ma, Y., Li, L., Zhao, C.: A challenge of sustainable urbanization: mapping the equity of urban public facilities in multiple dimensions in Zhengzhou, China. Land. **12**(8), 1545 (2023). https://doi.org/10.3390/land12081545
46. Cai, Y., Zhang, J., Gu, Q., Wang, C.: An analytical framework for assessing equity of access to public electric vehicle charging stations: the case of Shanghai. Sustainability. **16**(14), 6196 (2024). https://doi.org/10.3390/su16146196
47. Chen, Y., Ding, Q., Shen, Y.: Assessing accessibility and social equity of Tertiary hospitals for older adults: a city-wide study of Tianjin, China. Buildings. **12**(12) (2022). https://doi.org/10.3390/buildings12122107
48. Iraegui, E., Augusto, G., Cabral, P.: Assessing equity in the accessibility to urban green spaces according to different functional levels. ISPRS Int. J. Geo Inf. **9**(5), 308 (2020). https://doi.org/10.3390/ijgi9050308
49. Gu, Z., Luo, X., Tang, M., Liu, X.: Does the edge effect impact the healthcare equity? An examination of the equity in hospitals accessibility in the edge city in multi-scale. J. Transp. Geogr. **106**, 103513 (2023). https://doi.org/10.3390/ijgi9050308
50. Wang, S., Yung, E.H.K., Sun, Y.: Effects of open space accessibility and quality on older adults' visit: planning towards equal right to the city. Cities. **125**, 103611 (2022). https://doi.org/10.1016/j.cities.2022.103611

51. Xu, N., Wang, P.: Evolutionary characteristics of urban public space accessibility for vulnerable groups from a perspective of temporal–spatial change: evidence from Nanjing Old City, China. Land. **13**(7), 998 (2024). https://doi.org/10.3390/land13070998

52. Rashid, M.: On spatial mechanisms of social equity: exploring the associations between street networks, urban compactness, and social equity. Urban Sci. **6**(3), 52 (2022). https://doi.org/10.3390/urbansci6030052

53. Zhao, Y., Gong, P.: Optimal site selection strategies for urban parks green spaces under the joint perspective of spatial equity and social equity. Front. Public Health. **12**, 1310340 (2024). https://doi.org/10.3389/fpubh.2024.1310340

54. Sun, Y., Li, H., Guo, X., Gao, C.: Bridging the green space divide: a big data-driven analysis of park accessibility inequities in Chinese megacities using enhanced 3SFCA modeling. Sustainability. **17**(5), 2059 (2025). https://doi.org/10.3390/su17052059

55. He, J., Ren, F., Dong, J., Zhang, H., Yan, W., Liu, J.: Social inequity of park accessibility in Taiyuan: highlighting the unfair layout of parks in second-tier cities of China and the relative role of contributors. Geo-spat. Inform. Sci. **27**(4), 1118–1140 (2024). https://doi.org/10.1080/10095020.2022.2125835

56. Meerow, S., Pajouhesh, P., Miller, T.R.: Social equity in urban resilience planning. Local Environ. **24**(9), 793–808 (2019). https://doi.org/10.1080/13549839.2019.1645103

57. Wan, Z., Titheridge, H.: Socially sustainable transport in the context of different-sized cities in China: conceptualisation and operationalisation of equity. J. Transp. Geogr. **115**, 103816 (2024). https://doi.org/10.1016/j.jtrangeo.2024.103816

58. Reckien, D., Creutzig, F., Fernandez, B., Lwasa, S., Tovar-Restrepo, M., Mcevoy, D., Satterthwaite, D.: Climate change, equity and the sustainable development goals: an urban perspective. Environ. Urban. **29**(1), 159–182 (2017). https://doi.org/10.1177/0956247816677778

59. Chang, H.S., Liao, C.H.: Exploring an integrated method for measuring the relative spatial equity in public facilities in the context of urban parks. Cities. **28**(5), 361–371 (2011). https://doi.org/10.1016/j.cities.2011.04.002

60. Askarizad, R., Dastoum, M., Garau, C.: Street puppet theatre shows on the façades of commercial buildings as a novel stimulator for social gatherings in smart cities. Buildings. **14**(9), 1–20 (2024). https://doi.org/10.3390/buildings14092950

61. Cepiku, D., Mastrodascio, M.: Equity in public services: a systematic literature review. Public Adm. Rev. **81**(6), 1019–1032 (2021). https://doi.org/10.1111/puar.13402

62. Lee, J.S., Park, S., Jung, S.: Effect of crime prevention through environmental design (CPTED) measures on active living and fear of crime. Sustainability. **8**(9), 872 (2016). https://doi.org/10.3390/su8090872

63. Askarizad, R., He, J., Dastoum, M.: Gender disparity in public spaces of Iran: design for more inclusive cities. Cities. **158**, 105651 (2025). https://doi.org/10.1016/j.cities.2024.105651

64. Hillier, B., Hanson, J.: The Social Logic of Space. Cambridge University Press (1989)

65. Hillier, B.: Cities as movement economies. Urban Des. Int. **1**(1), 41–60 (1996)

66. Wineman, J.D., Kabo, F.W., Davis, G.F.: Spatial and social networks in organizational innovation. Environ. Behav. **41**(3), 427–442 (2009). https://doi.org/10.1177/0013916508314854

67. Hillier, B., Iida, S.: Network and psychological effects in urban movement. In: International Conference on Spatial Information Theory, pp. 475–490. Springer Berlin Heidelberg, Berlin, Heidelberg (2005, September). https://doi.org/10.1007/11556114_30

68. Karimi, K.: A configurational approach to analytical urban design: 'space syntax'methodology. Urban Des. Int. **17**(4), 297–318 (2012). https://doi.org/10.1057/udi.2012.19

69. Muhuri, S., Basu, S.: Interactional spaces of a high-rise group housing complex and social cohesion of its residents: case study from Kolkata, India. J. Hous. Built Environ. **36**(2), 781–820 (2021). https://doi.org/10.1007/s10901-021-09830-3

70. Jiang, B., Claramunt, C.: Integration of space syntax into GIS: new perspectives for urban morphology. Trans. GIS. **6**(3), 295–309 (2002). https://doi.org/10.1111/1467-9671.00112

71. Tomé, A., Kuipers, M., Pinheiro, T., Nunes, M., Heitor, T.: Space–use analysis through computer vision. Automat. Construct. **57**, 80–97 (2015). https://doi.org/10.1016/j.autcon.2015.04.013

72. Mehrinejad Khotbehsara, E., Yu, R., Somasundaraswaran, K., Askarizad, R., Kolbe-Alexander, T.: The walkable environment: a systematic review through the lens of space syntax as an integrated approach. Smart Sustain. Built Environ. (2025). https://doi.org/10.1108/SASBE-02-2024-0049

73. Koohsari, M.J., Sugiyama, T., Mavoa, S., Villanueva, K., Badland, H., Giles-Corti, B., Owen, N.: Street network measures and adults' walking for transport: application of space syntax. Health Place. **38**, 89–95 (2016). https://doi.org/10.1016/j.healthplace.2015.12.009

74. Hillier, B.: Spatial sustainability in cities: organic patterns and sustainable forms. In: 7th International Space Syntax Symposium, vol. K01, pp. 01–20

75. Hillier, B., Burdett, R., Peponis, J., Penn, A.: Creating life: or, does architecture determine anything? Archit. Comport. Archit. Behav. **3**(3), 233–250 (1987)

76. Al-Sayed, K., Turner, A., Hillier, B., Iida, S., Penn, A.: Space Syntax Method ology, Bartlett School of Architecture, 4th edn. UCL, London (2014)

77. Hillier, B., & Hanson, J.: The social logic of space. Cambridge: Press Syndicate of the University of Cambridge. 2005. Network and Psychological Effects in Urban Movement. International Conference on Spatial Information Theory 475–490 (1984).

78. Yang, C., Qian, Z.: Street network or functional attractors? Capturing pedestrian movement patterns and urban form with the integration of space syntax and MCDA. Urban Des. Int. **28**(1), 3–18 (2023). https://doi.org/10.1057/s41289-022-00178-w

79. Blanchard, P.: Mathematical analysis of urban spatial networks. (2009). https://doi.org/10.1007/978-3-540-87829-2

80. Baran, P.K., Rodríguez, D.A., Khattak, A.J.: Space syntax and walking in a new urbanist and suburban neighbourhoods. J. Urban Des. **13**(1), 5–28 (2008). https://doi.org/10.1080/13574800701803498

81. Jiang, B., Claramunt, C., Klarqvist, B.: Integration of space syntax into GIS for modelling urban spaces. Int. J. Appl. Earth Observ. Geoinform. **2**(3-4), 161–171 (2000). https://doi.org/10.1016/S0303-2434(00)85010-2

82. Hillier, B.: The hidden geometry of deformed grids: or, why space syntax works, when it looks as though it shouldn't. Environ. Plann. B. Plann. Des. **26**(2), 169–191 (1999). https://doi.org/10.1068/b4125

83. Xing, Z., Guo, W.: A new urban space analysis method based on space syntax and geographic information system using multisource data. ISPRS Int J Geo-Inform. **11**(5), 297 (2022). https://doi.org/10.3390/ijgi11050297

84. Pinna, F., Garau, C., Maltinti, F., Coni, M.: Beyond architectural barriers: building a bridge between disability and universal design. In: International Conference on Computational Science and Its Applications, pp. 706–721. Springer International Publishing, Cham (2020)

85. Barbagallo, A., et al.: Evaluation of urban spaces through the integration of universal design and microsimulation: the case study of the marina district in Cagliari (Italy). In: International Conference on Computational Science and Its Applications, pp. 351–370. Cham, Springer Nature Switzerland (2023)

86. Gehl, J.: Life Between Buildings: Using Public Space. Island Press, Washington, DC (2011)

87. Hillier, B.: A note on the intuiting of form: three issues in the theory of design. Environ. Plann. B Plann. Des. Anniv. Issue. **25**, 37–40 (1998)

BIM and Building Heritage Management: Interoperability Issues in Structural Design

Giovanna Concu$^{(\boxtimes)}$ [iD], Federico Lecca, Costantino Carlo Mastino[iD], and Daniel Meloni[iD]

University of Cagliari, 09123 Cagliari, Italy
gconcu@unica.it

Abstract. The construction sector is one of the most polluting in the world. The increase in sustainability of the sector passes through the management of the existing real estate in terms of renovation and efficiency. The problem is particularly evident in Sardinia Island, owner of a largely obsolete and inefficient real estate stock. In this context, BIM (Building Information Modeling) represents the tool to improve the efficiency and quality of the processes of design, construction and management of public works. However, to date, interoperability between software related to the various process elements - architectural, structural, plant engineering, etc. - does not seem adequate. This paper analyzes the level of interoperability between three software for the creation of the BIM model and a structural modeling and calculation software with reference to a reinforced concrete building representative of the Sardinian real estate stock. The results highlight the critical issues still present in the process of exporting and importing models between the various software, which prevent the full effectiveness of the BIM approach. The implications of these aspects on the construction sector in Sardinia are illustrated and discussed.

Keywords: BIM · structural design · existing buildings · buildings sustainability

1 Introduction

Italy is the first country in Europe for the number of homes per capita. According to national institute of statistics (ISTAT) housing stock data, in Italy there are 599 homes per thousand inhabitants against a European average of 506, and including unused buildings, the total number of buildings or building complexes amounts to 14,515,795 [1, 2]. This primacy highlights the centrality of housing policies in Italy, especially considering the gradual loss of value of the building stock, above all in peripheral areas, since over 70% of buildings are over 40 years old. Much of this heritage shows problems of obsolescence that require structural, functional, typological and technological interventions.

In Sardinia Island, more than 60% of residential properties date back to over 44 years ago, and over 30% of properties for civil use are uninhabited [1]. These properties are often in small towns subject to depopulation or are intended for holiday homes. The interventions on the house for the implementation of the so-called Green Buildings

© The Author(s), under exclusive license to Springer Nature Switzerland AG 2026
O. Gervasi et al. (Eds.): ICCSA 2025 Workshops, LNCS 15897, pp. 234–247, 2026.
https://doi.org/10.1007/978-3-031-97660-5_17

Directive [3], which foresees a gradual reduction in energy consumption of residential buildings, will concern two thirds of the houses occupied and built by 1980 on the Island. In view of this, the renovation market currently absorbs approximately 80% of the value of construction production, and represents 64% of the value of regional production, consolidating its relevance in the global insular market and in the regional economy [4].

The old real estate heritage, often in precarious conditions, represents a brake on the transition towards sustainable construction. The renovation and management of this building heritage is one of the great challenges that the construction sector will have to face in the coming years, a complex path that will require innovative solutions and tools, concreteness and feasibility, knowledge and expertise. Buildings cost more than they should to design, build, and maintain, so there needs to be more and better collaboration between the various stakeholders involved in the construction process. In a recent NIST (National Institute of Standards and Technology for the United States) study, lack of interoperability was identified as costing $15.8 billion annually [5]. This aspect can be significantly improved with better information management and a restructuring of management processes to create standard information exchanges between stakeholders.

A tool that can offer a control opportunity for buildings sustainable renovation is Building Information Modeling (BIM), a method for generating and managing information about buildings throughout their life cycle. Based on parametric building modeling technology, BIM uses a relational database combined with a behavioral model to process and represent information about the building in a dynamic way.

When considering structural design, which is a fundamental aspect in the sustainable renovation of existing buildings, it can be noted that this area is lugging in applying the BIM digitalization process due to several factors, including the difficulty of automating processes in which the intervention of the structural engineer is strictly necessary, the schematization of calculation models, the passage of information between architectural, structural, and systems models.

This paper analyzes the problem of BIM interoperability in structural design of existing buildings through the implementation of representative tests and their critical analysis, focusing on the exchange of data between BIM software and structural modeling software. To this end, a sample building, simulating existing reinforced concrete buildings in the Sardinian context, was generated using three different commercial BIM modeling software, then exported and loaded onto a commercial structural modeling software, and the critical issues that emerged in the transition between the two modeling environments were detected and analyzed.

The results obtained allow us to shed light on the state of the art regarding interoperability between architectural and structural models, and to focus on the future steps needed to facilitate the use of BIM in the structural renovation of existing buildings, essential in contexts such as the Sardinian one in which the proper management of the building heritage represents a primary objective towards sustainability.

2 Building Information Modeling (BIM)

The National Building Information Model Standard Project Committee defines BIM as follows: *Building Information Modeling (BIM) is a digital representation of physical and functional characteristics of a facility. A BIM is a shared knowledge resource for information about a facility forming a reliable basis for decisions during its life cycle; defined as existing from earliest conception to demolition [5].*

Declaring the definition in the construction field, Building Information Modeling (BIM) is a process based on intelligent 3D models that provides stakeholders in the sector (architects, engineers, professionals, etc.) with in-depth information and tools to plan, design, construct and manage buildings and infrastructure more efficiently and reduce their overall costs. "Building" refers to the entire life cycle of the structure, including conception, design, construction, functional life, maintenance, renovation and adaptive uses, recycling/disposal, as well as related factors such as investments, risk management, environmental impacts and others. Currently, 10 dimensions of BIM are used (Fig. 1). "Information" refers to the acquisition, use, exchange and creation of information in the form of data, which is the key to the functioning of the system. Relatively recent developments in standardized database schemas have begun to standardize the packaging of information, but further standardized definitions are needed across the various fields related to the construction model for the various functional aspects and participants in the process to work together efficiently. "Modeling" refers to the digital representation of the construction and the management process that revolves around it, meaning that computers can be used to virtually "build" the construction project, visualize and test it, modify it if necessary, and then produce various reports and views for all the phases involved in the process.

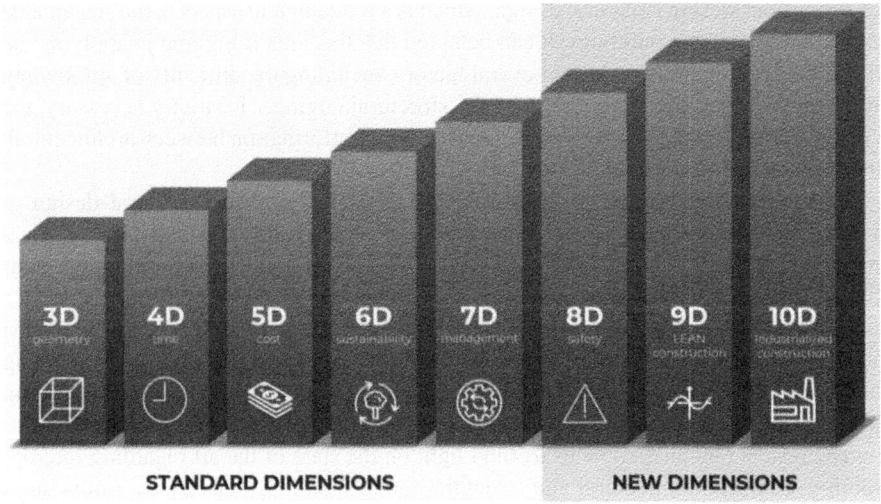

Fig. 1. The 10 dimensions of BIM

BIM therefore offers the possibility of having a virtual dual of the building, allowing the world of construction to be approached from a methodological point of view with all other production sectors and promoting its industrial characterization. The BIM building model, created using entities representing the different building components, can make them relate to each other and integrate them with multiple pieces of information, to allow stakeholders immediate and shared verification of all the choices made. The basis of the effectiveness of the BIM approach is the concept of interoperability, understood as the possibility of exchanging the data contained in the model between the various software work environments related to the different process elements, allowing all stakeholders involved in the design, construction and management process of a building to collaborate efficiently and without loss of information. BIM interoperability is therefore a fundamental requirement to facilitate and guarantee the exchange of information between the different software platforms used in the life cycle of a building project. Therefore, it is necessary that the flow of information capable of fully describing the production and management process of the structure is defined in a universal "language", i.e. understandable by the various software platforms involved. This can be done by encoding information in standardized formats such as IFC (Industry Foundation Classes) [6], a common exchange format defined at international level and continuously evolving. The IFC data model is intended to describe data from the building and construction industry. The main and most important feature of this format is that it is a neutral and open file type, i.e. not under the control of a group or a single supplier but available to everyone. The IFC model is developed by BuildingSMART [7] (International Alliance for Interoperability, IAI) with the aim of facilitating interoperability between the various disciplines that interact during the design, construction and life of a building (engineering, architecture, construction industry, environmental matters, systems and safety, etc.) by defining a system that can be used and understood by all so as to be able to exchange a single file containing all aspects of the building that can be modified and read with maximum ease, based on the BIM methodology. The IFC data model specification is open and available and has been recognized and registered in the international standard ISO 16739:2013 [8] and subsequent amendments and additions.

2.1 Interoperability in the Field of Structural Design

Interoperability is therefore the passage of information from the central BIM model software to the specific software of a given field, in this case the structural field, and vice versa.

To date, the diffusion of BIM in Italy is mainly concentrated in the architectural design sector, where the solutions are increasingly advanced and sufficiently mature for highly professional use. Only in more recent times have proposals for BIM solutions linked to structural and plant engineering aspects seen the light. The use of BIM in the structural field, and in particular the interoperability between the architectural BIM model and the structural calculation model, is a topic still being explored, which certainly needs to be developed further. The central theme is the different vision of modeling between the architectural field and the structural field: while architectural modeling aims to obtain a model as realistic as possible, structural modeling aims to schematize the structure in simple or simplified elements, such as rods and nodes, for the subsequent structural analysis. At present, a way must be found to contemplate both needs, to improve and make the BIM model of the building increasingly efficient. Further complexities arise when it comes to modeling an existing building, for which a survey phase in the broad sense is necessary to identify the actual state of the construction with the greatest possible precision and reliability, so that the structural model can correctly represent the building to be analyzed and predict realistic collapse mechanisms. Although there are some specific studies on the subject in the literature [9–14], the issue of interoperability between the BIM model and the structural model is still an open problem that requires considerable in-depth study, especially when modeling concerns existing buildings.

In this context, the present work aims to analyze the interoperability, relating to the structural aspects of an existing building, between the architectural model created in a BIM software environment and the structural model created using software for structural analysis. To this end, the model of a reinforced concrete (RC) building was generated, representative of the large building stock present in Sardinia, using three commercial BIM modeling software. The BIM model was then exported and loaded onto a commercial structural modeling software, and the critical issues that emerged in the transition between the two modeling environments were then detected and analyzed.

In this research, the software chosen for the creation of the BIM model are Autodesk Revit [15], ALLPLAN [16] and ARCHLine [17], while for the structural modelling and analysis the software chosen is Sismicad [18]. The choice fell on these software by reason of their diffusion among workers in the sector.

3   The Building

The reinforced concrete building structure is a two-level frame 2.95 m apart with a foundation level positioned at −1.50 m from the design level (Fig. 2).

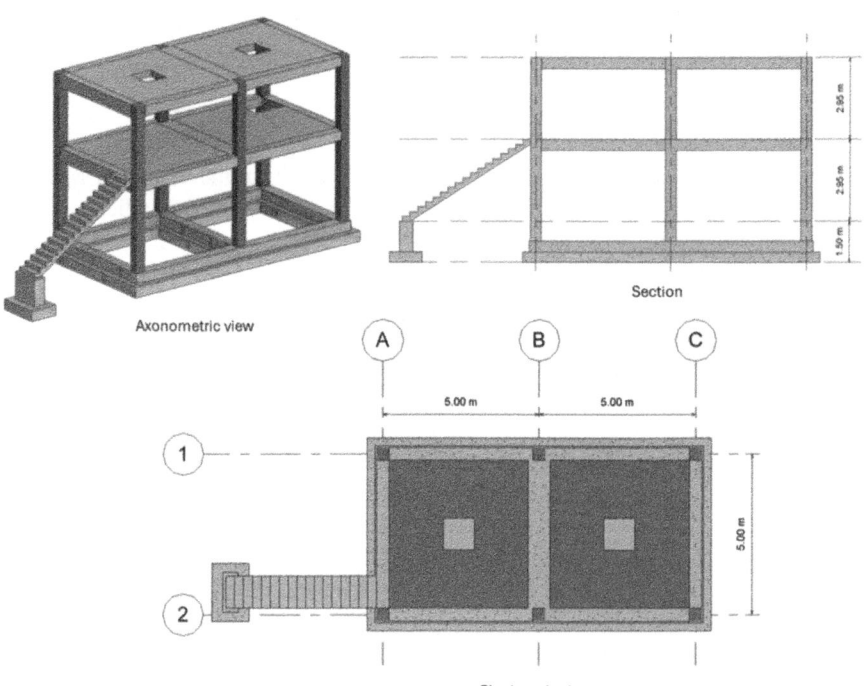

Fig. 2. The reinforced concrete building. Axonometric and planimetric views and section

Each floor frame is made up of six pillars, spaced 5.00 m apart, with a section of 0.40×0.40 m, reinforced with 4 longitudinal bars φ16 mm, stirrups φ8mm every 0.25 mm and a 250 mm concrete cover (Fig. 3a). The longitudinal bars of the pillars extend below the design level to connect with the foundations. There are three types of beams: type 1 beams connecting the pillars along the long sides of the building, type 2 beams connecting the pillars along the external short sides, and type 3 beams connecting the central pillars along the short side. The type 1 beam has dimensions 0.40×0.40 m with 3 φ16mm reinforcing bars in the upper part and 3 in the lower part, the stirrups are φ8mm with variable pitch 0.20 m in the middle and 0.10 m up to 1.5 m from the ends. The type 2 beam has dimensions 0.40×0.50 m and the same reinforcement as beam 1 (Fig. 3b).

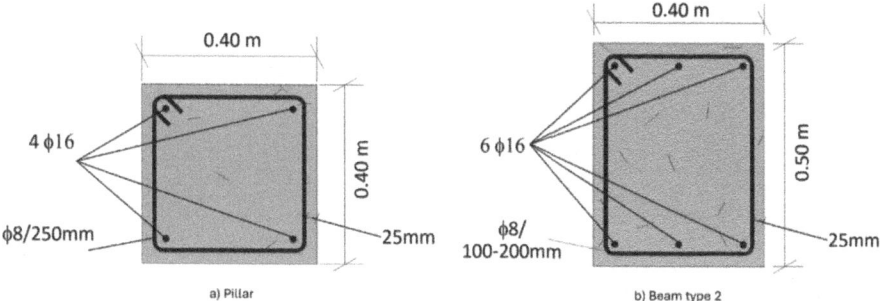

Fig. 3. Pillar (a). Beam of type 2 (b)

The type 3 beam has dimensions 0.70×0.25 m, longitudinal reinforcement made up of 7 φ16mm bars in the upper part and 7 in the lower part, φ8mm stirrups with four arms with pitch 150 mm. The foundation structure is composed of reversed T-beams with a section of 1.00×0.80 m reinforced with 14 longitudinal bars φ16mm divided into two rows of 7 positioned parallel to the design plane, plus 8 bars distributed in the vertical part of the inverted beam, φ8 stirrups with a pitch of 150 mm (Fig. 4).

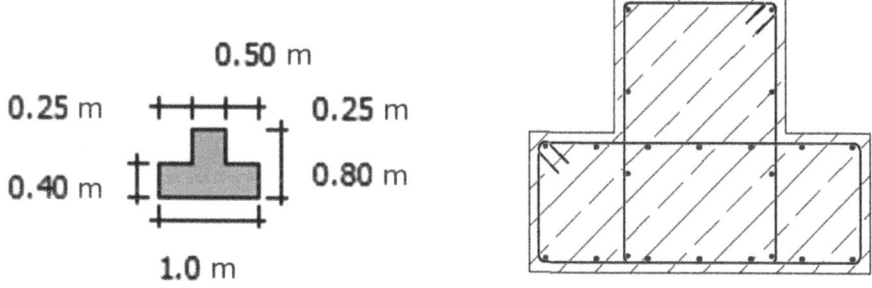

Fig. 4. Foundation beam

The floors of the ground floor are mixed in reinforced concrete with 200 mm hollow cores and 50 mm screed with a total thickness of 250 mm; one of the floors has a hole measuring 1.40×1.40 m. The floors of the upper floor are reinforced concrete slabs with a hole measuring 1.00×1.00 m in the center. The building is equipped with external stairs, 1.00 m wide and with a difference in height of 2.95 m. The stairs consist of a 150 mm thick climbing slab with 17 reinforced concrete steps with a riser of 173.5 mm and a tread of 280 mm. The stairs reinforcement consists of two rows of 10 longitudinal bars φ14mm, adapted to the shape of the ramp and ending in the foundation of the stairs, and a cage of transverse bars φ10mm that continue along the entire slab, while the foundation of the stairs is reinforced with φ8mm stirrups and φ16mm bars (Fig. 5).

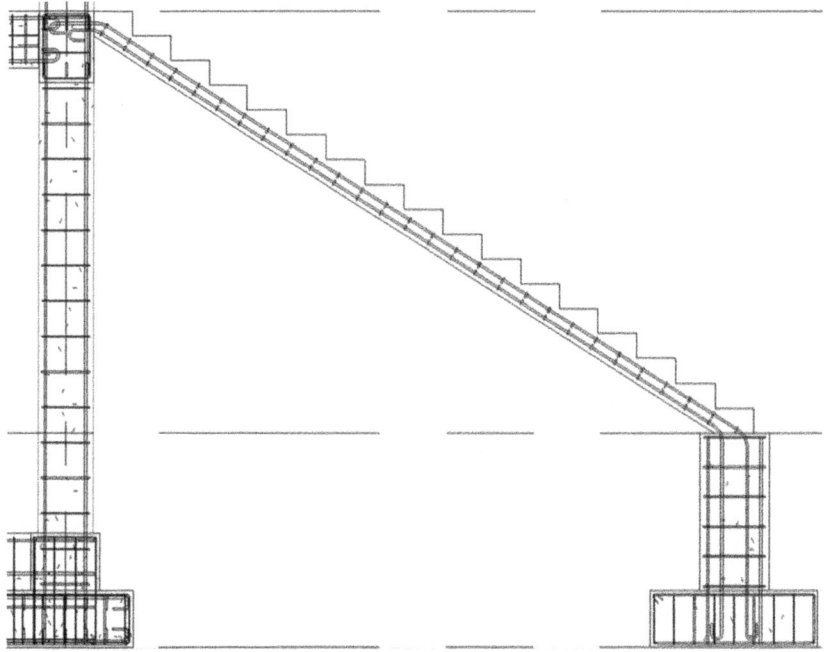

Fig. 5. The stairs reinforcement

4   Methodology

The working methodology is divided into four steps:

- Step 1: creation of the model of the sample building in each of the three BIM software and export of the model in the IFC4 and IFC2x3 formats. The IFC4 format is the most recent, but is not yet supported by several platforms, including Sismicad; the IFC2x3 format is more consolidated, although it has a smaller library than IFC4.

- Step 2: visualization of the exported model using the KITModelViewer software [19], a tool used to visualize semantic data models from the fields of BIM. In addition to the graphical representation, the tool can display properties and relationships between objects and allows various analyses of the data. This visualization tool is very useful in the transition from BIM software to other environment software, such as structural software, to analyze the information contained in the standardized and open data files, evaluate the correctness of the exported model and intervene on the information.
- Step 3: import of the IFC2x3 file into the structural analysis software.
- Step 4: analysis of critical issues related to data export and import.

Figure 6 summarizes the methodological flow.

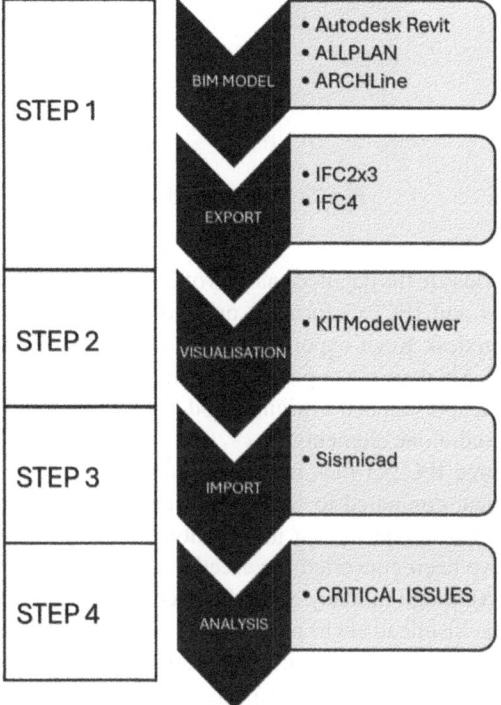

Fig. 6. Methodological flow

5 Results

The results and critical issues encountered in the modeling and data transfer process are reported below.

Figure 7 shows the 3D model created with the three BIM software as exported in the IFC4 format and displayed by KITModelViewer.

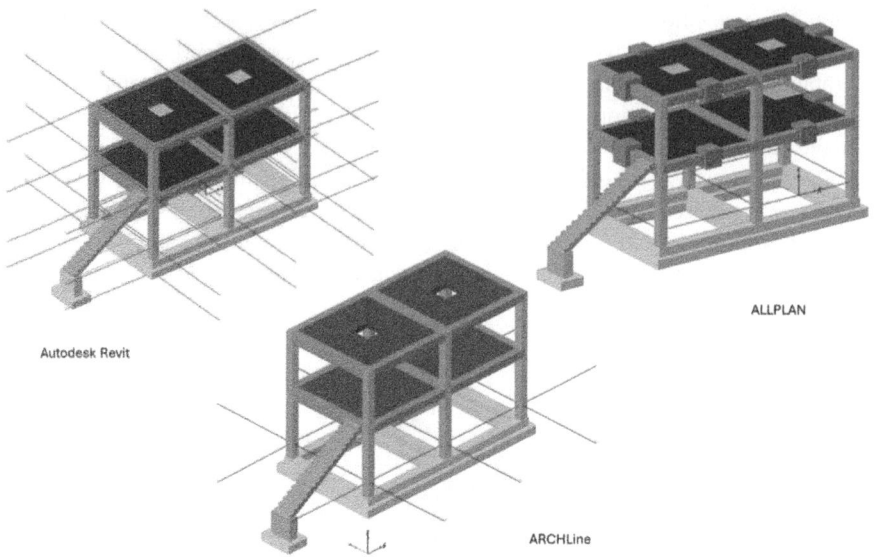

Autodesk Revit

ALLPLAN

ARCHLine

Fig. 7. 3D BIM models

In general, thanks also to the detailed analysis of the various properties of the elements exported in the IFC4 and IFC2x3 formats, omitted for the sake of simplicity, it can be observed that Autodesk Revit exports a greater number of elements than the other two software, ALLPLAN does not export the assignment of objects to work planes and introduces elements not present in the original model, while ARCHLine does not support reinforcements as stand-alone elements.

Analyzing the three IFC2x3 files imported into the structural software Sismicad, it can be observed that, compared to what was detected in the passage through KIT-ModelViewer, there is a further loss of information, as many elements have not been converted, others have been converted incorrectly, and others are not readable by the structural software. Although in many cases the operator can intervene by making corrections directly in the Sismicad environment, this solution represents an additional step that highlights the limits of interoperability between BIM software and structural software, especially considering the simplicity of the modeled building. Figure 8 shows the building models exported from the three BIM software via IFC files and imported into the structural software, while Fig. 9 shows some details of the visualization and layers produced by converting the entities into the structural software.

Therefore, the analysis relating to steps 1 and 2 has allowed us to understand the limits and differences of the BIM formats and software in relation to the IFC file. The analysis relating to steps 2 and 3, on the other hand, is based on importing the IFC2x3 files into the structural software, and has allowed us to observe which elements are recognized and which are not and the degree of adherence of the model imported into Sismicad compared to the models in IFC format, thus understanding the level and limits of interoperability between the various software used.

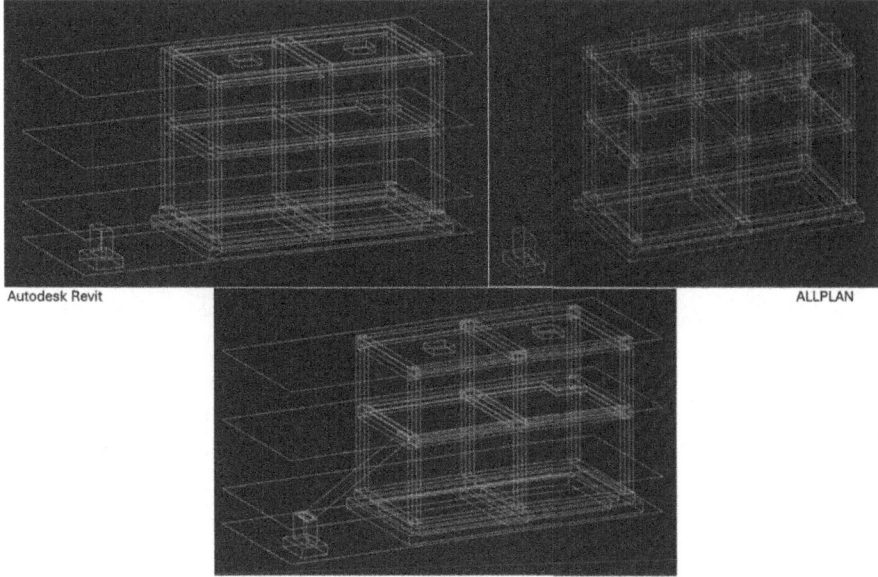

Fig. 8. IFC models imported into Sismicad

Figure 10 summarizes the quality of the model transfer from BIM software to the structural software Sismicad, highlighting the problems encountered element by element.

6 Discussion

From the results previously presented, the following considerations can be drawn.

- The most recent IFC format (IFC4) is not supported by all the software considered in this study, therefore a less recent format (IFC2x3) was chosen, but still suitable for simulation.
- The use of the various software considered was approached from the point of view of a user without specific experience in BIM modeling, so the modeling, export and import options were often kept in the default mode.
- The building chosen as a case study is significant and representative of the real estate heritage of Sardinia but is still a relatively simple building.
- In the export and import phases of the IFC model, some entities are not read, others are not recognized or are recognized only partially, others are inserted even though they are not present in the starting model.
- The major problems are associated with the management of the bars of the reinforced concrete elements.
- The BIM modeling software used in this study manages some types of data differently, therefore the export of such information into the structural software using the IFC file does not occur in a univocal manner.

244   G. Concu et al.

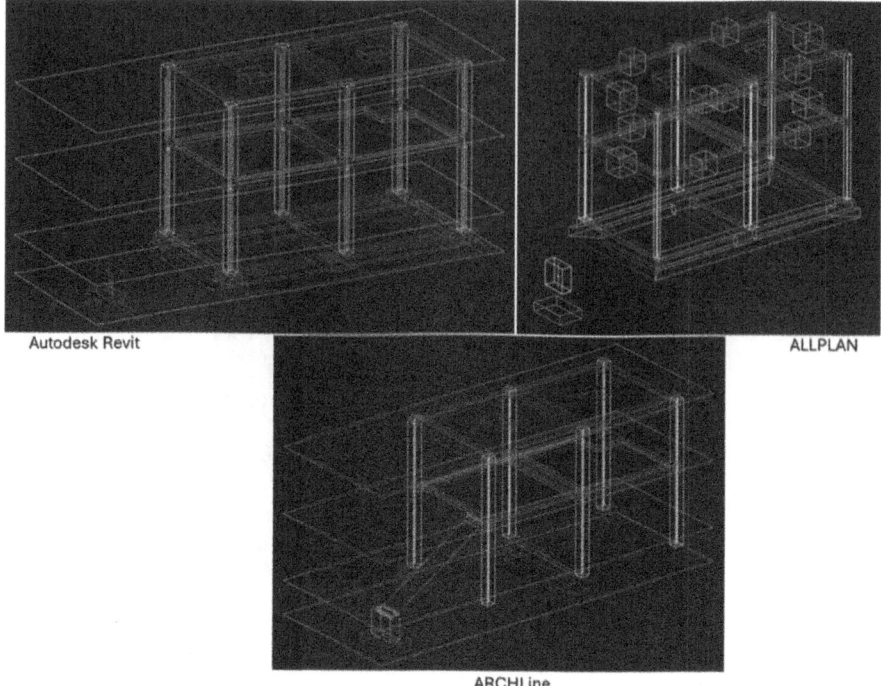

Fig. 9. Details of the imported models

	Autodesk Revit	ALLPLAN	ARCHLine
BEAMS	✓	✓	✓
PILLARS	✓	⚠	O
REINFORCEMENTS	X	X	X
STAIRS	X	X	X
R.C. SLABS	✓	✓	✓
MIXED FLOORS	O	O	O
REVERSED T-BEAMS	O	X	X
FLOOR HOLES	✓	✓	✓

Legend: ERRORS / PROBLEMS ⚠ WARNING / OK

Fig. 10. Quality of the model transfer

In light of these considerations, it can be stated that, in the context of this study, the IFC2x3 format is efficient and allows the transfer from the BIM modeling environment to the structural software of a building model that is consistent with what has been set, unless there are a series of critical issues that can be partially resolved through additional corrective intervention by the user in the structural software. Therefore, the IFC2x3 format can be useful in the construction phase of the structural model of the building as it reduces the operations compared to the implementation of the model from scratch. However, from the point of view of interoperability, understood as the possibility of building a single file containing all the information of the building in a detailed and unambiguous way and manageable by the different software relating to the various areas of analysis while keeping all the types of data unchanged, the road is still long. The achievement of real interoperability will be linked to the possibility and ability to standardize the coding and interpretation of information in the various areas of design.

While the purpose of this study is to evaluate the level of interoperability in the application of BIM to structural engineering, without going into the merits of the capabilities of the individual software used, it can be asserted that, net of some strengths and weaknesses that each software has, the interoperability problems that emerged are common to the software considered, so that, currently, the choice of the BIM software to be used for a given project will generally depend on various factors, such as the specific needs of the project, the level of complexity, the budget, the expectations, the skills of the user.

6.1 Relevance for the Construction Sector in Sardinia

Interoperability in the structural field, still in its early stages, is just one of the key aspects for the introduction and diffusion of BIM in the design, construction and management of buildings and related services throughout Italy and in Sardinia, which has a real estate portfolio often inefficient and obsolete. It should be emphasized that in Italy, starting from 1 January 2025, contracting authorities and granting bodies must adopt digital construction information management methods and tools for the design and construction of new buildings and for interventions on existing buildings with an estimated cost of more than 2 million euros. Therefore, BIM has become mandatory in public procurement of a certain size, but the transition is hindered by digital gaps and regulatory doubts, highlighting the difficulties in implementing the digital challenge by many contracting authorities, which could fuel speculation to the advantage of a few and generate unnecessary rush to superficial training or merely formal certifications. The ANCI (National Association of Italian Municipalities) has even proposed raising the threshold of mandatory BIM to 4 million euros.

This problem is particularly strong in Sardinia, where contracting authorities are mostly small and could find themselves facing a blockage of procedures due to technical and personnel shortages. The OICE BIM 2023 report [20] highlights how in Italy the geographical distribution by macro-regions adopted for the purposes of analyzing the BIM tenders detected in 2023 sees the Central regions in first place, with 30.5% of the total BIM tenders, the South in second place with 27.9%, the North-East in third place with 18.2%, the North-West in fourth place with 13.0%, while at the lowest level are, as in 2022, the Islands of Sardinia and Sicily with only 10.4% of all BIM tenders. Despite this deficit, it is important to underline that Sardinia is moving to promote the introduction and diffusion of BIM and digitalization in the construction sector. For example, within Iscol@, a program of the Sardinia Regional Authority for the Sardinian school, Axis II "Safety interventions and scheduled maintenance of school buildings" is included, aimed at making schools more comfortable and safe places by carrying out safety interventions, maintenance and renewal of furnishings and equipment on school buildings. In the Iscol@ tenders, the Sardinia Regional Authority has foreseen the possibility of introducing BIM as a reward element as early as 2017, and has drawn up specific guidelines [21], for use by Local Authorities, to create BIM models of school projects both for the graphic part and for the information part and the database setup. This best practice should be encouraged and transferred to as many project areas as possible, together with the promotion of interoperability in the structural and other technical fields.

7 Conclusions

This paper analyzes the level of interoperability between the software Autodesk Revit, ALLPLAN, ARCHLine, used for the implementation of the BIM model of a building, and the software for structural modeling and calculation Sismicad. The models are visualized with the software KITModel Viewer.

The building considered is a reinforced concrete construction representative of the existing real estate stock of Sardinia.

The applied methodology consists in the implementation of the BIM model in the three dedicated software, in the export of the model using the IFC4 and IFC2x3 formats and in its import into the structural software.

The results highlight the critical issues related to the process of transferring the model from one design environment to another. In particular, it emerges that in the export and import phases of the IFC model some entities are not read, others are not recognized or are recognized only partially, others are inserted even though they are not present in the starting modeling environment. The major problems are associated with the management of the bars of the reinforced concrete elements. Furthermore, it is clear that BIM modeling software manages some types of data differently, therefore the export of such information to the structural software via the IFC file does not occur univocally.

While the purpose of this study is to evaluate the level of interoperability in the application of BIM to structural engineering, without going into the merits of the capabilities of the individual software used, it can be stated that, net of some strengths and weaknesses that each software has, the interoperability issues that emerged are currently common to the software considered. The choice of BIM software to use for a given project will generally depend on various factors, such as the specific needs of the project, the level of complexity, the budget, the expectations, the skills of the user.

These interoperability gaps between BIM software and structural software are representative of the problems that currently prevent the full effectiveness of the BIM approach in the management of the design, construction and management processes of public works. This also has a significant impact in the case of Sardinia, which holds a real estate portfolio that is often inefficient and obsolete and is characterized by generally small contracting authorities that often have to deal with technical deficiencies and inadequate resources.

Acknowledgments. The authors thank Concrete srl for providing Sismicad Full Pro Pack free of charge.

Disclosure of Interests. The authors have no competing interests to declare that are relevant to the content of this article.

References

1. Caffari, F., Calabrese, N., Murano, G., & Signoretti, P.: La consistenza del parco immobiliare nazionale. ENEA - Dipartimento Unità Efficienza Energetica, Laboratorio Efficienza Energetica negli Edifici e Sviluppo Urbano. ISBN Edizione digitale: 978-88-8286-482-8 ISBN. Edizione cartacea: 978-88-8286-483-5
2. CRESME-Fondazione Symbola: Il valore dell'abitare - La sfida della riqualificazione energetica del patrimonio edilizio italiano (2024). ISBN 9788899265946
3. Directive (EU) 2024/1275 of the European Parliament and of the Council of 24 April 2024 on the energy performance of buildings (recast)
4. CNA Sarda: IL MERCATO DELLE COSTRUZIONI IN SARDEGNA. RAPPORTO ANNUALE 2022 E STIME PREVISIONALI 2023. Cagliari, Giugno (2023)
5. National BIM Standard: https://www.nibs.org/nbims, last accessed 18 March 2025
6. Industry Foundation Classes (IFC): https://technical.buildingsmart.org/standards/ifc/, last accessed 18 Mar 2025
7. buildingSMART International: https://www.buildingsmart.org/, last accessed 18 Mar 2025
8. ISO 16739:2013 Industry Foundation Classes (IFC) for data sharing in the construction and facility management industries
9. Gomes, A.M., Azevedo, G., Sampaio, A.Z., Lite, A.S.: BIM in structural project: interoperability analyses and data management. Appl. Sci. **12**, 8814 (2022). https://doi.org/10.3390/app12178814
10. Sampaio, A.Z., Sequeira, P., Gomes, A.M., Sanchez-Lite, A.: BIM methodology in structural design: a practical case of collaboration, coordination, and integration. Buildings. **13**, 31 (2023). https://doi.org/10.3390/buildings13010031
11. Sampaio, A.Z., Gomes, A.M.: BIM interoperability analyses in structure design. CivilEng. **2**, 174–192 (2021). https://doi.org/10.3390/civileng2010010
12. Wang, D., Lu, H.: Development of a BIM platform for the design of single-story steel structure factories. Buildings. **14**, 747 (2024). https://doi.org/10.3390/buildings14030747
13. Jia, J., Gao, J., Wang, W., Ma, L., Li, J., Zhang, Z.: An automatic generation method of finite element model based on BIM and ontology. Buildings. **2022**, 12 (1949). https://doi.org/10.3390/buildings12111949
14. Ciccone, A., Ciotta, V., Asprone, D.: Integration of structural information within a BIM-based environment for seismic structural e-permits. J. Civ. Eng. Manag. **29**(2), 171–193 (2023). https://doi.org/10.3846/jcem.2023.18460
15. Autodesk Revit: https://www.autodesk.com/eu/products/revit/overview, last accessed 18 Mar 2025
16. ALLPLAN: https://www.allplan.com/products/allplan-2025/, last accessed 18 Mar 2025
17. ARCHLine: https://www.archlinexp.com/, last accessed 18 Mar 2025
18. Sismicad: https://www.concrete.it/prodotti/sismicad/, last accessed 18 Mar 2025
19. KITModelViewer: https://www.iai.kit.edu/english/4561.php, last accessed 18 Mar 2025
20. 7° Report OICE sulla digitalizzazione e sulle gare BIM 2023: https://www.oice.it/849794/2024-oice-7-rapporto-sulla-digitalizzazione-e-gare-bim, last accessed 18 Mar 2025
21. Linee Guida BIM Iscol@: https://www.regione.sardegna.it/sardegna-istruzione/iscol-edilizia-scolastica/bim-building-information-modeling, last accessed 18 Mar 2025

From Street Experiments to Planned Solutions (STEPS 2025)

Planning Guidelines for Parklets Installation: A Possibile Integration into Urban Planning Strategies

Gloria Pellicelli$^{(\boxtimes)}$ ⓘ, Silvia Rossetti ⓘ, and Michele Zazzi ⓘ

Department of Civil Engineering and Architecture, University of Parma, Parco Area delle Scienze, 181/A, 43124 Parma, Italy
gloria.pellicelli@unipr.it

Abstract. In the context of street experiments (SE)—urban interventions that have gained prominence in the new millennium, particularly in the last decade, aiming to create more livable cities by prioritizing vulnerable road users such as pedestrians and cyclists, this study focuses specifically on parklets. Parklets are included within the SE category of "re-purposing parking spaces" and are designed to enhance social interaction, walkability, and the overall quality of life, as widely documented in the literature. This research aims to develop planning guidelines for parklet implementation based on a physical analysis that considers key location criteria derived from existing literature and best practices worldwide. Additionally, the study integrates insights from semi-structured interviews conducted in Parma, Italy, with stakeholders involved in recent parklet initiatives. The purpose of these guidelines is to provide public administrations a comprehensive framework for facilitating the approval process of such interventions, ultimately supporting the integration of tactical urbanism into long-term urban planning strategies. While public authorities currently play a crucial role in approving parklet projects, the approval process remains complex. Although these guidelines are initially designed for medium-sized cities, their neighborhood-based approach allows for potential adaptation to larger urban contexts in the future.

Keywords: Street experiments · Parklets · Sustainable mobility · Planning strategies · Public space

1 Introduction

Recently, the focus on transforming urban mobility has grown exponentially, aiming to reduce the dominance of cars and promote safer and more liveable public spaces. The traditional paradigm, which prioritizes parking near facilities and access to cities, even near historic centres, is being challenged by global initiatives (see, among others, [1]) that emphasize social interaction, the environment, road safety, and the demand for public spaces.

Within this evolving context, Tactical Urbanism (TU) has emerged as a strategic approach to reimagining urban environments. As highlighted in the literature [2–5], one

© The Author(s), under exclusive license to Springer Nature Switzerland AG 2026
O. Gervasi et al. (Eds.): ICCSA 2025 Workshops, LNCS 15897, pp. 251–268, 2026.
https://doi.org/10.1007/978-3-031-97660-5_18

of the most prominent expressions of TU is the concept of street experiments: temporary, low-cost interventions aimed at testing new configurations of public space. Among these, parklets have gained particular attention. They can be described as a type of intervention that falls within the category of street experiments, whose primary purpose is to transform streets, which mainly serve vehicular traffic, into spaces that prioritize active movement and social interaction [6–9]. Parklets convert parking spaces into public areas dedicated to social interaction and active mobility. The concept originated in 2005 in San Francisco during the "Park(ing) Day" event, which temporarily converted a parking space into a public area for two hours. Since then, the idea has spread rapidly, especially from 2020 to present time, in response to the Covid-19 pandemic, which highlighted the need for outdoor spaces for safe social gatherings.

Street experiments, including parklets, offer the possibility to test creative in-field solutions, involving citizens in assessing the effectiveness of such interventions. Regarding mobility, this approach opens a window of opportunity to reduce the number of cars through urban policy changes and the creation of safe and attractive spaces to promote active mobility [10].

This shift has been accelerated by three key global challenges: climate change, rapid population growth, and the Covid-19 pandemic. Mobility infrastructures, such as roads and sidewalks, have undergone a crisis. This context of instability represents an opportunity for cities to rethink their infrastructure systems and urban spaces through a sustainability lens, avoiding further impermeabilization.

However, to transform these temporary interventions into permanent solutions, it is essential to integrate them within the urban mobility plans.

This research focuses on parklets and aims to answer the following research question: how can parklets become a systemic and permanent tool for sustainable urban transformation?

This paper is based on the study presented in the paper by Pellicelli et al. [11], which defined a cognitive framework to specify criteria for identifying priority intervention areas through a protocol applied to the Oltretorrente neighborhood in Parma (Italy). The current research revisits the case study of the same neighborhood and aims to define planning guidelines for installing parklets within neighborhoods. This approach will make it easier for associations, citizens, and potentially the administration to choose the location of the intervention.

Furthermore, the methodology incorporate a qualitative approach, specifically semi-structured interviews conducted with key stakeholders involved in two significant interventions carried out in the neighborhood.

The paper is structured as follows: Sect. 2 identifies, through an initial literature review, the main drivers and barriers influencing the implementation of these interventions. Section 3 outlines the methodology of this study. Section 4 describes planning guidelines for parklets. These guidelines serve as a tool to facilitate collaboration between public authorities and stakeholders, providing the relevant actors with useful resources for the effective location and management of interventions. Section 5 presents the application of the previously discussed findings to a specific neighborhood in the city of Parma. Finally, Sect. 6 summarizes key conclusions and opens up new research questions for future investigations.

2 Drivers and Barriers in Literature

Numerous authors have addressed the drivers and barriers related to parklets. What facilitates the installation of these interventions, and what limits their implementation? An additional question concerns social interaction, specifically the positive and negative perceptions generated by certain interventions.

In their research Steven & Dovey [9], identify five key values: resilience (in terms of space adaptation, such as creating green spaces, bike-friendly, pedestrian-friendly, and safe environments, as well as sustainability), support for local businesses, innovation (the flexibility of parklets to attract new activities), community engagement (the participation of stakeholders), and place identity, strengthened by an attractive intervention that fits within the context. The authors emphasize how these characteristics align with the framework identified by Lynch in 1981 [12].

VanHoose [13] highlights internal enablers within the experiments themselves, such as the involvement of stakeholders in the design and implementation process, which can help reduce resistance from opponents. Additionally, promoting the experiment tends to reduce resistance and prevent conflicts [13, 14].

Finally, embedding experiments in long-term policies is an enabler for street experiments, along with institutional support. Indeed, in the cases analyzed by Glaser and Krizek [15], the cities that aligned street experiments with existing policy goals were able to increase their feasibility. In the case of the Living Streets of Ghent, where the municipality was the initiator and implementer of the experiment, the financial, material and human resources that accompanied their top-down role were crucial to legitimize the experiment [16].

Malamut [17] focuses primarily on streateries and their distinction from outdoor dining, emphasizing the importance of open spaces and their expansion. The primary barrier to outdoor dining arises from the privatization of sidewalk or street spaces, which are public and designated for public use. This barrier, along with gentrification, is also highlighted in other academic analyses [18–21].

VanHoose [13], through a literature review, identifies four barriers that are internal to the experiments themselves: a lack of required resources (the most cited) [14, 15, 23–27], unsuitable design [28–30], a lack of a clear vision [13, 25, 26, 31], and low frequency, because one-time events fail to generate transformative processes that influence other contexts and practices [32].

As a barrier, Van Hoose [13] identifies opposition from stakeholders (related to a preference for private mobility from car owners). Additionally, business owners are often afraid of losing business if car traffic is removed from their street.

Institutional regulations and processes are also seen as barriers. This issue reflects the incompatibility between 'innovative, human-centered approaches' and existing road regulations, because internal municipal procedures obstruct implementation even when the municipality acts as a project partner.

A separate discussion concerns the positive and negative perceptions from the community and users of these interventions. Negative aspects of parklets are often attributed to their physical properties and use. The most frequently cited negative impact is the presence of "antisocial behavior." Business owners report that parklets are used as toilets and sleeping areas, are subject to graffiti, and become unusable in winter, thus representing an inefficient use of street space [33].

Among the risks highlighted by Davidson [34] are that projects reflect one social group's idea rather than being built by the whole community, that "testing first and asking questions later" is harmful, and that there is a deviant quality to these activities.

To explore this, a SWOT analysis has been developed based on existing literature and divided by authors. It is summarized below (Table 1).

Strengths include internal initiatives through which the installation could be a success (e.g., inclusion of stakeholders). Weaknesses, on the other hand, include internal elements that hinder the success of the intervention (e.g., institutional regulations and processes). Opportunities consist of the external elements that contribute to the installation of the intervention (e.g. to discourage crime and undesiderable behaviors). Threats refer to areas that could potentially create problems and are external agents (e.g., antisocial behaviours).

Table 1. SWOT analysis regarding drivers and barriers of parklet realisation process according to the literature.

Analysis	Elements	References
S	They are functional	[17]
	They are crucial sites of democratic assembly	[17]
	They include stakeholders in the decision-making process	From [13]: [14, 25, 29, 35]
	They promote and advertise the experiment	From [13]: [14, 23, 25, 36]
	Calls attention a critical need in the city	[34]
	Highlights problems and test solutions to gain the attention of city and civic leadership	[34]
	Low-cost intervention	
	Temporariness	
	Opportunity to test pilot project	[34]
	Innovative	[34]
W	Privatization of sidewalk space (streateries) and streets	[17]; From [33]: [18–21]
	Business conditions	[37]
	Lack of required resources	From [13]: [14, 15, 22–27]
	Unsuitable design	From [13]: [28–30]
	Lack of clear vision	From [13]: [25, 26, 31]
	Institutional regulations and processes times of approval	From [13]: [14, 16, 22, 24]
	Deviant quality	[34]
	Dangerous in testing first and asking questions later	[34]
O	They allow socialization and facilitate contact with diverse people	[17, 30]
	Reduction of parking	[30]

(continued)

Table 1. (*continued*)

Analysis	Elements	References
	Resilience of street space • green spaces • Safety • physical activity • support for commercial activities etc • innovation • knowing people and creating community • strengthen place identity	[33]
	Disincentive crime and undesirable behaviours	[30]
T	Opposition from stakeholders	From [13]: [14, 16, 22, 24, 25]
	Innovative (The idea is not common to all citizens)	[34]
	Unequal voice in public policy	[34]
	Antisocial behaviour (e.g., used as a dormitory)	[33]
	Unuse during the winter months	[33]
	Low frequency	From [13]: [22]
	Opposition from business owners as they are often afraid of losing business if car traffic is removed from their street	From [13]: [14, 16, 22, 24, 25]

3 Methodology

The methodology adopted for this study consists of three main points, which concur to determine planning guidelines for the installation of parklets in an urban neighbourhood context.

The flow is composed as follows:

- Identification of the planning guidelines, to be applied to a case study to verify their effectiveness and their easiness of replicability. Their structure reflects the selected case study, the *Oltretorrente* district in the city of Parma, Italy.
- Interviews with stakeholders who have actually carried out some interventions. The people to be interviewed have made interventions in the same city as the case study, to uniform the whole methodology.

The definition of the planning guidelines has been developed according to six sub-categories. Each answers a specific question, and together they form a practical tool for the implementation of parklets in urban neighbourhoods. Specifically:

- What: What is the object of the research?
- Who: Who are the commissioners and what needs do they have?
- When: When is the installation of a parklet appropriate?
- Where: Where is it most suitable location?
- Why: Why is it necessary? What needs can it meet?
- How: What is the approval process?

Starting with the guidelines, the methodology also includes a qualitative component based on semi-structured interviews. After an initial quantitative analysis, in which the characteristics of the streets in a neighborhood were categorized to assess the suitability of certain areas for hosting interventions [11], the research also includes a qualitative evaluation through dialogue with stakeholders.

The semi-structured interviews proved to be a valuable tool for gathering information about the interventions by speaking with the creators of the parklets. This type of interview allowed for asking specific questions while giving the interviewee the freedom to answer openly.

This phase, directly related to the case study, aimed to verify and evaluate the implementation of parklets completed in 2024. The questions aimed to understand how the interventions were implemented, what constraints and difficulties were encountered, and how the neighborhood residents experienced the project.

Specifically, the questions addressed:

- how the process of creating the parklets took place, including fundraising, design, and location selection;
- the role of various stakeholders, including the position of the administration;
- what obstacles and drivers were encountered;
- what compensations were adopted to address traffic modification or what could be adopted;
- what feedback was received;
- what alternative processes or improvements could be made in the future.

4   Parklets Planning Guidelines

4.1   What

Parklets are defined as temporary interventions that consist of replacing car parking spaces in public spaces.

They are part of the group of street experiments called "repurposing parking space," along with pop-up plazas and pop-up parks.

They consist of a platform, usually made of wood, that hosts benches or tables. Their purpose is to generate public space for sociality and reduce space for vehicular mobility.

Parklets can be also divided into public and private, depending on location. Public ones include bicycle parklets, social parklets, and pocket parks. Private (or semi-private) are the streateries (Table 2).

Table 2. Identified typologies of parklets.

Location	Typologies
Public	Bicycle parklets Social parklets Pocket parks
Private or semi-private	Streateries

4.2 Who

Interventions such as parklets can help improve sociality. But how to meet everyone's needs?

The question "who?" is answered on the one hand by those who start these initiatives, i.e., the promoters, and on the other hand by those who experience and use public spaces.

Among the commissioners can be identify numerous promoters. Being bottom-up interventions, can be identify merchants, local associations, educational institutions, or the administration. They may have different needs that lead them to request the creation of parklets in the neighbourhood.

Users include students, citizens, pedestrians, cyclists etc.

In Table 3 a division of possible promoters and their needs can be seen.

Table 3. List of possible promoters and their needs.

Promoters	Needs
Commercial traders	-Attracting people to enter the store -Promote consumer comfort (such as nearby parking)
Associations	-Promote students' safety when arriving and leaving school -Promote sociability -Increase school spaces as a place for meeting and outdoor activities
Educational institutions	-Improve the quality of life for one or more categories of people in the neighborhood -Finding community spaces
Administration	-Sharing the visions of various stakeholders -Integrating citizens' requests with existing urban plans

4.3 Where

The urban-scale location protocol has been refined by adding potentially interesting elements involving pedestrian routes and surrounding activities.

The neighborhood-scale protocol can be summarised as follows in Fig. 1. For further explanations concerning the localization protocol, see [11].

4.4 When

The intervention of a parklet is appropriate when certain urban needs emerge, for which the reappropriation of the street by the community is seen as a way to succeed in reviving the city.

Three characterizing aspects are highlighted that consider the context from the urban scale to the local scale, and reflect the location protocol.

- Qualitative aspect: it concerns road characteristics, in particular factors such as the absence of seating, poor road safety, high accident rate and traffic congestion.

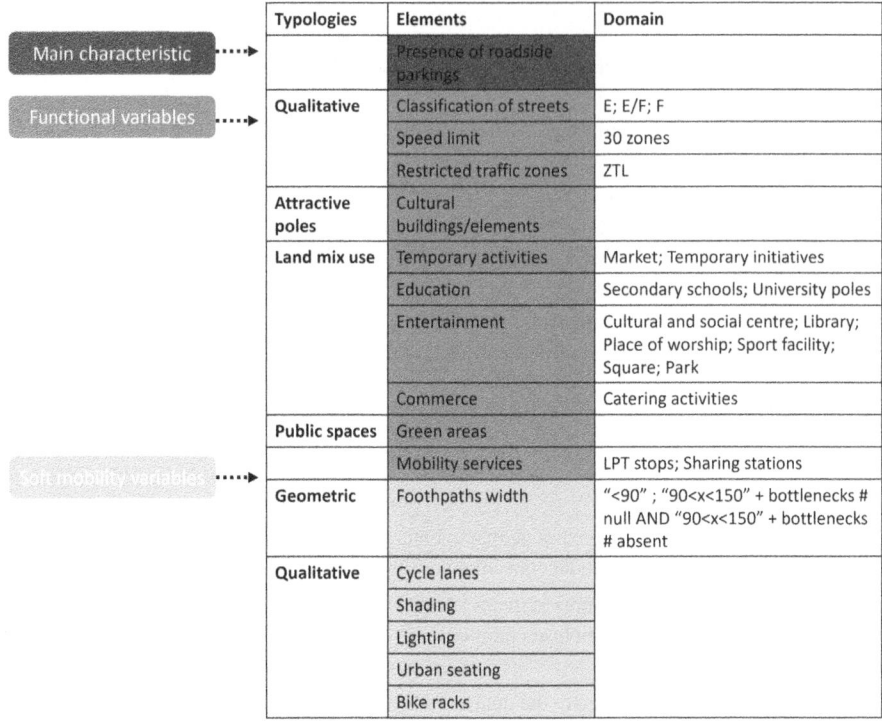

Typologies	Elements	Domain
	Presence of roadside parkings	
Qualitative	Classification of streets	E; E/F; F
	Speed limit	30 zones
	Restricted traffic zones	ZTL
Attractive poles	Cultural buildings/elements	
Land mix use	Temporary activities	Market; Temporary initiatives
	Education	Secondary schools; University poles
	Entertainment	Cultural and social centre; Library; Place of worship; Sport facility; Square; Park
	Commerce	Catering activities
Public spaces	Green areas	
	Mobility services	LPT stops; Sharing stations
Geometric	Foothpaths width	"<90" ; "90<x<150" + bottlenecks # null AND "90<x<150" + bottlenecks # absent
Qualitative	Cycle lanes	
	Shading	
	Lighting	
	Urban seating	
	Bike racks	

Main characteristic ┈┈▶
Functional variables ┈┈▶
Soft mobility variables ┈┈▶

Fig. 1. Synthesis of the localization protocol at the neighborhood scale.

- Urban aspect: concerns urban features such as the presence of schools, catering activities and commerce facilities.
- Local aspect: it's about the context management, meaning what occurs around the street for the project to work. This is the most difficult as it refers to balancing actions to prevent all the traffic and negative externalities from spilling into adjacent streets.

4.5 Why

Why is it worthwhile to implement parklets within our cities? To meet certain urban needs. Urban needs, as defined by Gehl [38], are to create vibrant, safe, sustainable and healthy cities.

Specifically:

- Vibrant cities: Spaces for people, Short distances, Attractive facilities
- Safe cities: Road safety for pedestrians and cyclists, Increased slow mobility, More space for pedestrians, Road safety for vulnerable users
- Sustainable cities: Less emissions, More greenery
- Healthy cities: Improvement and expansion of pedestrian pathways, Less traffic

Figure 2 presents the diagram showing which types of parklets can meet one or more urban needs, through a Sankey diagram.

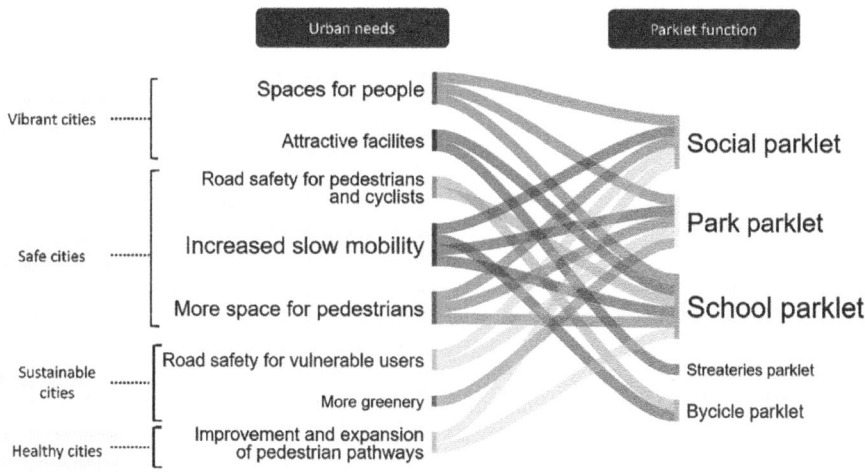

Fig. 2. Urban needs that parklet can address, divided into categories.

4.6 How

The 'How' question aims at identifying the existing approval process for the implementation of parklets.

This paragraph is closely related to the chosen case study, as it was possible to identify the process through interviews with stakeholders.

Thus, eight steps could be identified (Table 4):

1. The idea, which comes from local groups;
2. The request to the administration, which is the turning point, without which the project cannot be allowed to continue;
3-4. If the administration's decision is positive, the design, often commissioned to a professional, begins. In the meantime;
5. Stakeholder recruitment undertakes, along with promoting the project for sources of funds;
6. Often, in fact, funds come not only from stakeholders who are interested but must be sought externally as well;
7. Finally, the actual construction takes place;
8. The project is temporary in nature. However stakeholders and the citizens can apply to the administration to extend the period granted or make the project permanent.

5 Results

In this section, the methodology previously described has been applied to the case study in the city of Parma (Italy). The results achieved regarding the application of the guidelines and the interviews with the promoters of the interventions are reported below. This makes it possible to have an overall picture of the situation regarding parklets that will allow these interventions to be implemented and improved in the future with a perspective of integration with urban plans.

Table 4. Approval process for the installation of a parklet.

Steps	Authors	Description
Initiative	Developer	The initiative comes from the community (associations, citizens, school groups)
Request to the administration	Developer	The administration is approached for permission to carry out the intervention. In particular: mobility/environment, public works, urban green councillorships, and urban police
Approval	Administration	The administration sets the time for occupation of the area. Being included as a partner, the citizens' association does not have to pay for the occupation of public area
Design	Professional	An appointed professional designs the perakelt form an architectural point of view
Stakelholder recuitment	Developer	Awareness-raising campaign on the topic is carried out to find potential partners
Funding search	Developer + stakeholder	Some of the material is given by associations, and the funds to buy the other are raised through donations. One technique used is the online crowdfuning
Building	Community	Once all the material has been collected, the construction and occupation of the site is carried out privately
Durability extension	Developer	The developer group collects petition signatures to ask the administration to turn the intervention permanent

5.1 Case Study in Parma

The case study considered, and on which the analyses described earlier are carried out, is the *Oltretorrente* neighbourhood in Parma (Fig. 3). The neighbourhood delineates the western part of the city's historic centre and is considered as the object of analysis due to its history of street experiments, especially those related to the school environment. Furthermore, in 2023, the neighbourhood has been chosen for the installation of a parklet along Viale Maria Luigia, the street which accommodates most of the area's high schools. The parklet initiative is temporary and stems from a bottom-up approach started by a group of teachers and students from one of the schools situated along the street. Thus, given the complexity and diversity of the neighbourhood, it is interesting to study which types of parklets could be located there and where.

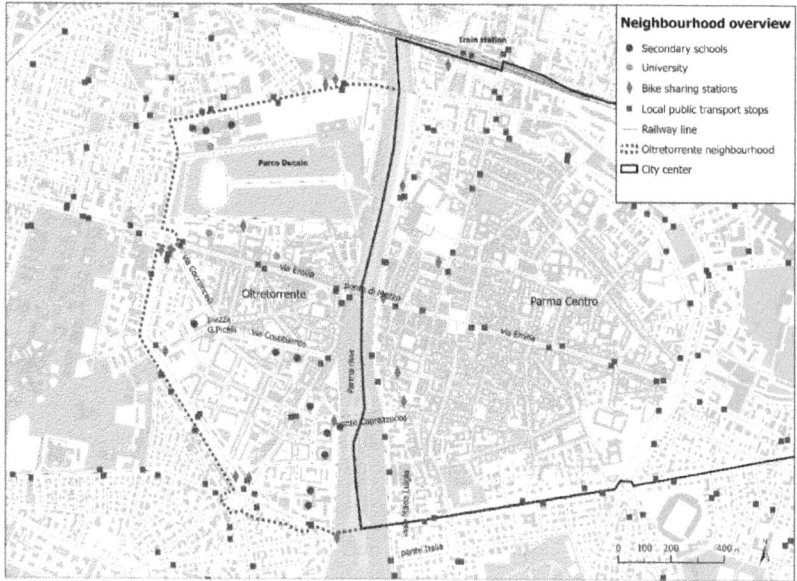

Fig. 3. Overview of Oltretorrente neighbourhood with the main mobility services. Source: authors' elaboration.

Following the adjustment of the localization protocol, the possible localization related to social parklets, the most general category, is shown below in Fig. 4.

The suitability of streets in which it is more or less appropriate to install social parklets (in the figure, from green to red) has been given by the combination of a series of factors such as the presence of pavements, the presence of valuable buildings, urban greenery etc. For all specifications, please refer to [11].

5.2 Interviews Results

This sub-section presents the findings from the semi-structured interviews conducted in January 2025. As interviewees, people who directly contributed to the building of the parklets within the neighbourhood has been chosen, in order to get a precise overview of the process. They are the professor of the high school group who planned the project, and the professional collaborator (Table 5).

The implementation process was particularly long, but the most difficult aspect was the fundraising. In fact, the project was advertised only when the administration's final approval arrived, and raising the funds and materials was particularly challenging. In addition, the private contribution that the creators put in, both in terms of materials and funds, was crucial.

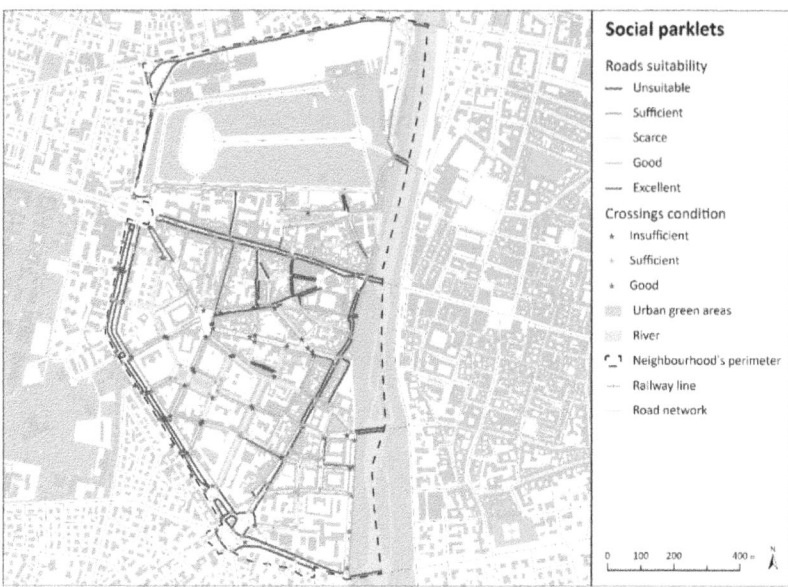

Fig. 4. Level of suitability of roads for the installation of social parklets. Source: readaptation from [11].

Table 5. People interviewed.

Interviewee	Occupation
Eng. Francesco Fulvi, PhD	Freelance professional *Manifattura Urbana* association member
Prof. Niccolò Vernazza	Professor at G. Ulivi scientific high school

1. Parklets experience and process steps:

    The parklets experience in Viale Maria Luigia began in 2022, thanks to the collaboration between Professor Vernazza of the *Change group* of the Ulivi High School (an extracurricular group dealing with topics such as the environment and sustainable mobility) and the students of the Romagnosi High School in Parma. The goal was to create temporary public spaces to reduce the presence of cars and change the mentality of citizens.

    The process saw several steps.

    Concept and authorization: The Change group proposed the idea, and approached the municipality, facing the opinion of several offices (urban regeneration department, mobility department, environment department and the technical department), finally getting the approval for a three-month project. The municipality acting as a partner granted two parking spaces, without the need to pay for the occupation of public land. The project originated as a two-month temporary intervention. After a petition, the municipality agreed to make it permanent.

Social involvement and funds: stakeholders were approached by the professor of the high school group, with a request for their support. Some companies in Parma provided some materials (the rest was raised privately by the developers), but not financial support. The necessary money was raised through a fundraiser on Change.org, which started the promotion of the project on a larger scale.

The project from the architectural point of view was assigned to the professional, supported by students from another high school in the city.

The second parklet built, for which funds won by the proposing high school were available instead, involved the collaboration of more schools, and a more complex and studied architectural configuration. The biggest obstacle was having to apply to the administration for permission by going through the departments of mobility and environment, public works and green analysis. Parking lots have been granted but the parklet is still temporary.

Management and Maintenance: remains a major challenge since vandalism occurred in the first parklet, and in the second, graffiti appeared all along the side of the parklet. Maintenance and cleaning are completely under the responsibility of the proponent. The main barrier to implementation is the municipal authorization, which remains the first obstacle to overcome.

2. Objectives:

Improving air quality: greener areas, and dedicated to active mobility, would benefit air health, as demonstrated recently in Paris.

Social integration: Involvement of students from different schools.

3. Possible compensations:

In the case of Parma, no alternative measures have been considered to reduce the traffic that is inevitably created in the surrounding area. Among the measures proposed by the parties involved is to improve the public transportation system, and to encourage people to leave their cars outside the ring road boundary. This solution turns out to be particularly difficult as it requires considerable effort and funds.

4. Feedback:

No monitoring of use or satisfaction questionnaires have been conducted, but it is noted that people use it, not only students but also citizens.

Therefore, interviewees would like to see such interventions spread to other parts of the city as well, both because they are a virtuous example of participation and because they increase public space. Furthermore, public investment would be very limited for this type of intervention.

They stress the importance of adapting the parklet to the context in which it operates, from a functional, aesthetic and material point of view.

5. Future perspectives:

Permanent School Street: Create a "children's street" with green spaces and benches along the entire length.

Interventions: continue with temporary structures with the prospect of municipal interventions for permanent upgrades.

Ultimately, the parklet project represents an innovative model for transforming urban spaces and promoting sustainable mobility through active participation. The main focus is on persuasive strategies for their dissemination. How to convince people and the administration? For example, by appealing to the healthiness of the air and the related health problems it affects. Finally, interventions must be thought of as a system that shifts public mindset regarding mobility and school travel, otherwise they alone fail to be sufficient to address the problems.

6 Discussion and Conclusions

In order to achieve the goal of improving urban public space, a systemic change in mobility is needed. In this sense, street experiments can be an enabler. Their goal is to give the street back to citizens by promoting active mobility.

Davidson [34] highlights in his research the rewards of tactical urbanism as a tool for change:

- Highlights problems and test solutions to gain the attention of city and civic leadership.
- Opportunity to test pilot project
- As a source of innovation
- Calls attention to a critical need in the city

The present research enriches the source work of Pellicelli [11], attempting to answer the questions left behind.

Firstly, the protocol is enriched through interviews with authors and stakeholders, by including the need to engage the local population in constructive dialogue, and considers punctual elements in the district.

Secondly, the protocol does not take into account only cultural buildings, but also other public buildings that could serve as significant focal points for promoting sociability, such as schools or neighbourhood primary services, which contributes to the protocol's refinement.

Thirdly, some of the data reported in the literature, including the identification of the neighborhood's most frequently visited areas and the monitoring of traffic flows, useful for conducting pre and post-installation analyses of the parklet to assess its impact, have been addressed, only in the area of Viale Maria Luigia, through cycle-pedestrian and vehicular traffic surveys.

Furthermore, the calculation of the parking spaces lost due to the installation of parklets has been carried out. This would be necessary at the time of implementation to determine how many spaces need to be replaced and where. Considering social parklets (the broader category) and the areas where they are classified as 'good' and 'excellent,' the total number of parking spaces in those streets is more than 300. Relocating them is unrealistic—but is it necessary if the ultimate goal is to promote slow mobility instead of vehicular traffic?

The real solution lies in enhancing and expanding the city's infrastructure and public transport connections (such as sharing services, buses, etc.), ensuring that cars are left outside the ring roads. This aligns with the efforts made by local administrations in recent years through initiatives like "ecological days".

One of the main limitations of the current methodology is that, while it identifies suitable areas for intervention, it does not account for specific constraints that may affect certain streets. A clear example is Via Kennedy, south of Parco Ducale, which is deemed suitable for social parklets. However, both sidewalks are enclosed by fences (one belonging to the park and the other to the university) limiting accessibility despite the presence of relevant buildings and services. A study focused on isochrones and spatial permeability could address this issue, revealing how barriers impact accessibility.

Additionally, many key features require on-site data collection, as they are not available through institutional portals or public geodatabases. Continuous data gathering and updating are crucial to maintaining the validity and reliability of this methodology, an essential practice for all research involving on-site analysis.

Regarding future developments, it would have been highly valuable to include citizens in the interviews to understand street experiments from their perspective. A possible recommendation in the guidelines could be to introduce a future survey for users and neighborhood residents, fostering interaction between the administration and stakeholders/citizens.

Future developments will also focus on simplifying the approval process, addressing the commonly cited issue of administrative delays. This aspect, particularly the request for permanence, should ideally be easy in the future through a potential modification of the process, combined with the localization protocol, to support administrations in managing these interventions more efficiently.

Ultimately, the research should aim to answer the following questions:

- How to integrate these guidelines within existing urban plans, to turn these interventions into planned and permanent practices in our cities?
- Can these interventions contribute to climate change adaptation, such as through de-sealing operations?

Acknowledgements. The authors jointly designed and contributed to the paper. Conceptualization: S.R., G.P; M.Z.; Data curation, G.P.; Investigation, G.P.; Validation: S.R.; Methodology, G.P., S.R., and M.Z; Supervision: S.R., M.Z.; Writing—original draft, G.P.; Writing—review and editing, S.R. All authors have read and agreed to the published version of the manuscript.

The authors wish to thank Francesco Fulvi and Niccolò Vernazza for valuable contribution during the interviews, which provided important insights for the case study development.

Attribution. Research funded under the National Recovery and Resilience Plan (NRRP), Mission 4 Component 2 Investment 1.5 – Call for tender No. 3277 of 30/12/2021 of Italian Ministry of University and Research funded by the European Union – NextGenerationEU. Award Number: Project code ECS00000033, Concession Decree No. 1052 of 23/06/2022 adopted by the Italian

Ministry of, CUP D93C22000460001, "Ecosystem for Sustainable Transition in Emilia-Romagna" (ECOSISTER).

Disclosure of Interests. The authors have no competing interests to declare that are relevant to the content of this article.

References

1. United Nations: The 2030 Agenda for Sustainable Development, New York (2015)
2. Furchtlehner, J., Liˇcka, L.: Back on the street: Vienna, Copenhagen, Munich, and Rotterdam in focus. J. Landsc. Archit. **14**(1), 72–83 (2019)
3. Iborra Pallarés, V., Flor García, M., Aragonés Pomares, L., Ortuño Padilla, A.: The healthy city: how sustainable mobility policies gave a resilient response to the COVID-19 crisis through tactical urbanism. In: Cheshmehzangi, A., Sedrez, M., Zhao, H., Li, T., Heath, T., Dawodu, A. (eds.) Resilience vs Pandemics. Urban Sustainability. Springer, Singapore (2023)
4. Silva, P.: Tactical urbanism: towards an evolutionary cities' approach? Environ. Plann. B. Plann. Des. **43**(6), 1040–1051 (2016)
5. Bertolini, L.: From "streets for traffic" to "streets for people": can street experiments transform urban mobility? Transp. Rev. **40**(6), 734–753 (2020)
6. Campisi, T., Caselli, B., Rossetti, S., Torrisi, V.: The evolution of sustainable mobility and urban space planning: exploring the factors contributing to the regeneration of car parking in living spaces. Transp. Res. Procedia **60**, 76–83 (2022)
7. Littke, H.: Revisiting the San Francisco parklets problematizing publicness, parks, and transferability. Urban For. Urban Green. **15**, 165–173 (2016)
8. Peterson, E.F.: Using pilot projects to reclaim public space for pedestrians: lessons from New York City and San Francisco. Thesis, University of British Columbia (2012)
9. Stevens, Q., Dovey, K.: Pop-ups and public interests: Agile public space in the neoliberal city. In: Arefi, M., Kickert, C. (eds.) The Palgrave Handbook of Bottom-Up Urbanism, pp. 323–337. Palgrave Macmillan (2019)
10. Jeruseviciute, G.: An exploratory research on urban street experiments and transitions in urban mobility. Master Thesis in Environmental & Infrastructure Planning. Univeristy of Groningen (2022)
11. Pellicelli, G., Marinelli, L.J., Zazzi, M., Rossetti, S.: From spontaneous to strategic: integrating street experiments into urban planning practices. In: Gervasi, O., Murgante, B., Garau, C., Taniar, D., C. Rocha, A.M.A., Faginas Lago, M.N. (eds.) Computational Science and Its Applications – ICCSA 2024 Workshops. ICCSA 2024. Lecture Notes in Computer Science, vol. 14823. Springer, Cham (2024)
12. Lynch, K.: Good City Form. MIT Press (1981)
13. VanHoose, K.: City street experiments and system change: identifying barriers and enablers to the transformative process. Transp. Res. Interdisc. Perspect. **22**, 100982 (2023)
14. Eyler, A.A., Hipp, J.A., Lokuta, J.: Moving the barricades to physical activity: a qualitative analysis of open streets initiatives across the United States. Am. J. Health Promot.: AJHP **30**(1), e50–e58 (2015)
15. Glaser, M., Krizek, K.J.: Can street-focused emergency response measures trigger a transition to new transport systems? Exploring evidence and lessons from 55 US cities. Transp. Policy **103**, 146–155 (2021)

16. VanHoose, K., Bertolini, L.: The role of municipalities and their impact on the transitional capacity of city street experiments: lessons from Ghent. Cities **140**, 104402 (2023)

17. Malamut, L.Z.: Public space or private profit? 'Streateries' and the need to reclaim the public realm in the post-pandemic city. 41 YALE J. oN REG. 780, pp. 780–832 (2024)

18. Douglas, G.: The Help-Yourself City: Legitimacy and Inequality in DIY Urbanism. Oxford University Press (2018)

19. Mandhan, S., Gregg, K.: Managing the curb – Public space and use of curbside cafes during the coronavirus pandemic. Cities **132**(104070), 104070 (2023)

20. Morhayim, L.: Fixing the city in the context of neoliberalism: institutionalized DIY. In: Zavestoski, S., Agyeman, J. (eds.) Incomplete Streets: Processes, Practices, and Possibilities, pp. 225–244. Routledge (2015)

21. Thorpe, A.: Owning the Street: The Everyday Life of Property. MIT Press (2020)

22. Hipp, J.A., Bird, A., van Bakergem, M., Yarnall, E.: Moving targets: Promoting physical activity in public spaces via open streets in the US. Prev. Med. **103**, S15–S20 (2017)

23. Sarmiento, O.L., Díaz Del Castillo, A., Triana, C.A., Acevedo, M.J., Gonzalez, S.A., Pratt, M.: Reclaiming the streets for people: insights from Ciclovías recreativas in Latin America. Prev. Med. **103**, S34–S40 (2017)

24. Stevens, Q., Leorke, D., Thai, H.M.H., Innocent, T., Tolentino, C.: Playful, portable, pliable interventions into street spaces: deploying a 'playful parklet' across Melbourne's suburbs. J. Urban Des. 1–21 (2023)

25. VanHoose, K., De Gante, A.R., Bertolini, L., Kinigadner, J., Büttner, B.: From temporary arrangements to permanent change: assessing the transitional capacity of city street experiments. J. Urban Mob. **2**, 100015 (2022)

26. Vitale Brovarone, E., Staricco, L., Verlinghieri, E.: Whose is this street? Actors and conflicts in the governance of pedestrianisation processes. J. Transp. Geogr. **107**, 103528 (2023)

27. Zieff, S.G., Hipp, A., Eyler, A.A., Kim, M.S.: Ciclovia initiatives: engaging communities, partners and policymakers along the route to success. J. Public Health Manag. Pract. **19**(3 0 1), S74–S82 (2013)

28. Marcheschi, E., Vogel, N., Larsson, A., Perander, S., Koglin, T.: Residents' acceptance towards car-free street experiments: focus on perceived quality of life and neighborhood attachment. Transp. Res. Interdiscipl. Perspect. **14**, 100585 (2022)

29. Scudellari, J., Staricco, L., Vitale Brovarone, E.: Implementing the Supermanzana approach in Barcelona. Critical issues at local and urban level. J. Urban Des. **25**(6), 675–696 (2020)

30. Smeds, E., Papa, E.: The value of street experiments for mobility and public life: citizens' perspectives from three European cities. J. Urban Mob. **4**, 100055 (2023)

31. Verlinghieri, E., Vitale Brovarone, E., Staricco, L.: The conflictual governance of street experiments, between austerity and post-politics. Urban Stud. (2023)

32. Savini, F., Bertolini, L.: Urban experimentation as a politics of niches. Environ. Plann. A: Econ. Space **51**(4), 831–848 (2019)

33. Stevens, Q., Morley, M.: The contested value of parklets. J. Urban Affairs 1–19 (2024)

34. Davidson, M.M.: Tactical urbanism, public policy reform, and 'innovation spotting' by government: from park(ing) day to San Francisco's parklet program.Thesis (M.C.P.)–Massachusetts Institute of Technology, Department of Urban Studies and Planning (2013)

35. Oliver, A., Pearl, D.S.: Rethinking sustainability frameworks in neighbourhood projects: a process-based approach. Build. Res. Inf. **46**(5), 513–527 (2018)

36. Montero, S.: Worlding Bogota's Ciclovía: from urban experiment to international "best practice." Lat. Am. Perspect. **44**(2), 111–131 (2017)

37. Foneseca, A.: Parking to place: barriers and opportunities for adaptability in new parking structure construction in Los Angeles (2019)
38. Gehl, J.: Città per le persone. Maggioli Editore, Rimini (2017)

A New Definition of a Smart and Healthy City Through a Literature Review on Accessible Urban Green Space

Chiara Garau⬤, Andrea Manca$^{(\boxtimes)}$ ⬤, Maria Serena Pirisino$^{(\boxtimes)}$ ⬤,
and Francesco Pinna

Department of Civil and Environmental Engineering and Architecture (DICAAR), University of
Cagliari, via Marengo 2, 09123 Cagliari, Italy
amanca@unica.it, mariaserenapirisino@gmail.com

Abstract. Urban green spaces (UGS) are part of green infrastructure, public open spaces, and city amenities that may promote health for all urban residents, according to the World Health Organisation (WHO). Therefore, creating urban green areas that are accessible, inclusive, and fairly distributed across the city is vital to designing and building smarter and healthier urban environments. Numerous scientific studies have reinforced the growing awareness of their benefits to residents and their well-being in recent decades. Research has defined green spaces (from urban forests to inner-city green spaces) and highlighted social aspects, including environmental justice and accessibility, by analysing different methodologies and techniques. However, cutting-edge framework for the accessibility and inclusivity of the urban green spaces has not been developed. This work contributes to ongoing research and critically reviewing the literature to solve this gap. Specifically, this research examines the potential of urban green spaces and their accessibility, proposing operative process that establish a scientific definition and facilitate critical reflection on the planned and design solutions needed to transform and enhance urban landscapes in smarter, healthier and more inclusive cities.

Keywords: Accessibility · Inclusivity · Literature Review · Smart and Healthy City · Urban green space (UGS)

1 Introduction

The World Health Organisation defines the *Urban Green Space* (UGS) as «all urban land covered by vegetation of any kind. This covers vegetation on private and public grounds, irrespective of size and function, and can also include small water bodies such as ponds, lakes or streams», and, in addition, it is «a component of green infrastructure, an important part of public open spaces and common services provided by a city and can serve as a health-promoting setting for all members of the urban community» ([1], p. 2). Indeed, its many benefits in the urban environments and its beneficial impacts on behalf of citizens and their well-being have been object in several research, conducted over the last three decades, as analysed and reported by Farkas et al. [2].

O. Gervasi et al. (Eds.): ICCSA 2025 Workshops, LNCS 15897, pp. 269–285, 2026.
https://doi.org/10.1007/978-3-031-97660-5_19

The aforementioned study indicates that several studies have concentrated on defining and analysing green spaces, ranging from urban forests to inner-city green areas, using different methodologies and techniques. Other studies highlight the benefits, positive impacts, and challenges regarding the urban setting, such as health conditions, and the psycho-sociological well-being of the urban resident. Others indicate that the removal of existing urban green spaces, as negative effects, caused by the over-urbanisation, as well as consequent problems such as the inequalities, limited access to public amenities, environmental aspects which destabilise cities' liveability.

Consequently, these studies post the belief that urban green spaces should be equitably distributed, accessible, and inclusive for all residents, and that urban planning should prioritise this goal.

The Covid-19 pandemic has emphasised the importance of creating quality and easily accessible urban green spaces, as evidenced by the many street experiments conducted in many worldwide cities during this period. This reflects a response to the need of change the public spaces, rethinking the urban green spaces as sensitive places for physical and mental recreation [3, 4].

Thus, an increasing number of cities are implementing measures to enhance the quantity, quality, and accessibility of green areas. However, these considerations automatically lead to the following unresolved issues: (1) How can an accessible urban green space be defined? Which parameters and characteristics come into play, such as, in the urban scale, their diffusion and distribution within the cities; in the architectural scale, instead, compliance with the requirements of Universal Design principles; or even, from the environmental justice and the social equity point of view, what aspects need to be analysed? (2) What are the most successful methodologies and technologies used in the investigation and evaluation of urban green spaces? (3) What is the perception of green public areas among residents and general users? Can their involvement in the planning and administration procedures of these places improve the quality and efficacy of the project? (4) With which aspects and elements of our daily lifestyle the urban green spaces are closely connected? How can they contribute to a different perception of the city? Can the presence of accessible urban green spaces in vulnerable contexts, such as historic cities or degraded surroundings, facilitate their transformation into smarter, healthier, and more inclusive landscapes?

Starting from these questions, this paper aims to provide an advanced framework for the accessibility and inclusiveness of urban green spaces via a systematic and critical literature assessment, beginning with these concerns. Specifically, the study investigates the potential of urban green spaces, their accessibility, focusing to establish an operative framework that defines scientific parameters and offers critical insights into planned and design solutions for evaluating the urban environments in smarter, healthier and inclusive cities.

This paper analyses around 125 works in English, categorised as articles, book chapters, and conference papers, as recorded in the Scopus Database, to address the aforementioned research issues. To accomplish this objective, the structure of the paper is delineated as follows: following this *Introduction* (Sect. 1), the *methodology* to process the data is delineated (Sect. 2), subsequently providing an in-depth analysis of *the state of art on accessible urban green spaces* (Sect. 3). Sect. 4, titled *"Conclusion"* discusses the outcomes derived from the literature review, highlights the principal findings of the study, and outlines the research plan.

2 Methodology

This study proposes an analysis of the current literature on accessible urban green spaces, aiming to provide an original framework via a systematic and evaluative literature review that addresses the aforementioned challenges. Figure 1 shows the five stages (1. problem formulation, 2. data collection, 3. data evaluation, 4. analysis and interpretation, and 5. public presentation) into which the literature review is organised in line with the main approaches and methodologies ([5], pp. 4–11).

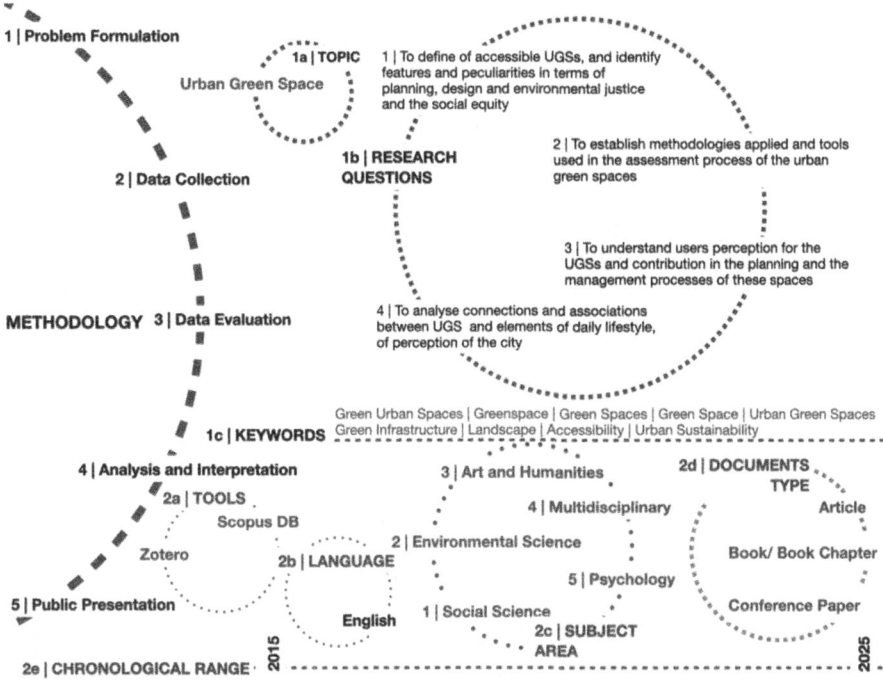

Fig. 1. Methodology's Scheme (MSP).

The first phase, *Problem formulation*, is to define and articulate the research questions that will move the literature review, followed by establishing the criteria for inclusion and exclusion. The primary goals of the literature review are varied. Firstly, the literature review seeks to clarify the definition of accessible urban green spaces by examining their key characteristics and distinct features, particularly in relation to urban planning, landscape design, and broader issues of environmental justice and social equity. Secondly, the review aims to explore the methodologies and analytical tools employed in evaluating urban green spaces. Thirdly, the review considers the role of user perception, investigating how individuals and communities experience green urban environments. Finally, the review investigates the interrelations between urban green spaces and various dimensions of everyday urban life. This includes their influence on public health and safety, their contribution to the perceived quality of the urban environment, and their role within sensitive or complex settings such as historic city centers or socially and environmentally degraded areas. Through this multifaceted analysis, the literature review seeks to shed light on the significance of green infrastructure in shaping resilient, equitable, and liveable urban landscapes.

To achieve these objectives, the literature review first delineates the appropriate topics to refine the study scope, followed by the selection of keywords to further simplify the search results. The first category comprises green urban places; the second includes greenspaces, green spaces, green space, urban green space, green infrastructure, urban green spaces, landscape, accessibility, urban sustainability.

The second phase, *Data collection*, begin with the choice of Scopus as a search database among the many currently available [6]. The searches used for the investigation of pertinent literature on accessible urban green spaces within the Scopus Database are: Green [and] urban [and] spaces.

A significant quantity of results, around 1200, has been gathered in the first search. Consequently, filters have been included to refine the search. The study period spans from 2015 to the first quarter of 2025. The year 2015 was selected as the starting year of the study due to the observation that prior to this date, contributions about the accessibility and the inclusivity of urban green spaces are rather sporadic and not continuous. The topic areas considered include Social Science, Environmental Science, Arts and Humanities, Multidisciplinary Studies, and Psychology. The recommended document types are Article, Book Chapter, Book, and Conference Paper, all in English and from open sources. To further narrow the scope of study topics, the chosen keywords have been examined in the title, abstract, and among the authors' keywords. The final selection comprises around 120 submissions. The diverse and extensive data on various contributions was compiled in an Excel spreadsheet. Furthermore, all contributions were documented in a separate Zotero library [7].

The following part of the study was *Data evaluation*, which was conducted by reviewing the abstracts to assess the utility of the identified sources. Upon identifying a significant publication, the cited sources were scrutinised to include further references into the bibliography. Subsequently, the examination of sources is undertaken to identify those most relevant for inclusion. Finally, the analysis and interpretation of the data were undertaken using a thematic method. Recognising patterns in literature, including repeating themes, persistent arguments, and research deficiencies, has shown to be particularly significant.

3 State of Art on Accessible Urban Green Spaces

3.1 Quantitative Synthesis

This proposed research analyses the existing literature on accessible urban green spaces with the aim of creating a distinctive scheme. A systematic evaluation of the literature from the Scopus Database has identified approximately 125 contributions, in English, categorised as Articles, Book Chapters, Books, Conference Papers, and Reviews. The chronological period from 2015 to the first trimester of 2024 has been examined.

Figure 2a illustrates a notable temporal growth in publications concerning these topics, rising from 1% between 2015 to 26% in 2022, with a high of 32% predicted in 2024. The literature review has been based to identify and define previously the research questions. This phase, characterised by a thematic approach, allowed to identify recurring themes, ongoing debates, and research gaps. The contributions reveal four overarching themes, which are further elaborated upon and summarised here: 1. Spatial Equity, Environmental Justice and Social Equity; 2. Analysis and assessment process; 3. Urban Green Spaces planning and management; 4. Connections, associations and relationships.

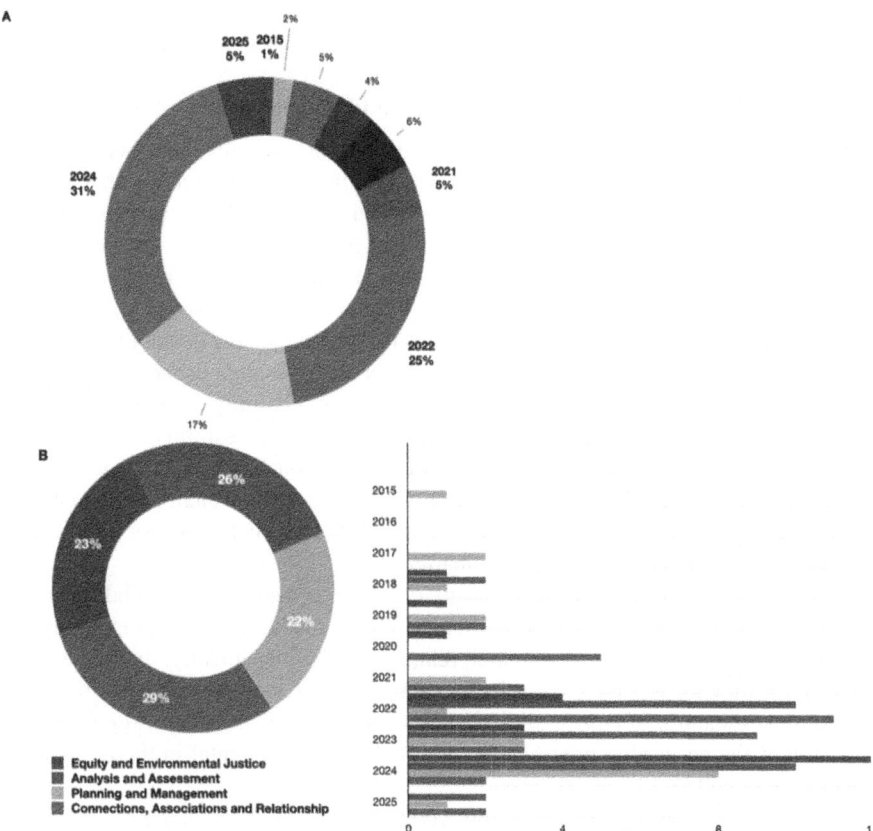

Fig. 2. Graph representations of the study findings. Distribution of the relevant literature selection from: A. Chronological Distribution; B. Topic - Chronological distribution (MSP).

Moreover, as shown in Fig. 2b, among the four topics, following the research issues, exposed above, the contributions are balanced on the different themes. From a chronological point of view, only the thematic in reference to *Planning and management* has a more homogeneous distribution in the decade under consideration. While, for other issue, there has been for all a consistent a significant increase in 2022.

It is interesting to observe that in 2022 the major contributions are divided into *Analysis and assessment* and *Connections, associations and relationship* themes. It should be noted that many of the contributions to this last thematic deal with the topic of Pandemic Covid19 and health.

In 2024, however, most of the contributions, besides addressing the theme of *Analysis and assessment*, are directed towards *Equity and Environmental* justice issues.

The geographical contexts under examination are distinct. Europe and Asia are the principal regions of study, with further examination of other locations including Canada, the United States of America, Latin America, and Australia.

3.2   Towards a Thematic Framework

3.2.1   Spatial Equity, Environmental Justice and Social Equity

The accessibility concept has evolved throughout the years. Initially described by Hansen [8] in 1959 as the potential of opportunities, accessibility was subsequently characterised by Alam et at (2010) as "the convenience of accessing spatially distributed opportunities with a choice of travel. Paez *et al.* (2012) defined the accessibility as the potential for reaching spatially distributed opportunities such as employment and recreation" ([9], p. 2).

Urban green spaces represent opportunities for the sustainable development of local communities, and for their well-being. How can be an accessible urban green space be defined? The literature research indicates that the term accessibility of UGSs is associated with concepts of equality and environmental justice. The accessibility of urban green spaces is closely linked to the varying scales of intervention. The research conducted by Xu S. et al., focussing on the Weidu District of Xuchang City, Henan Province, China. The disparities in accessibility have been studied and evaluated across three scales: subdistrict, community, and residential quarter.

The results indicate that the accessibility of park green space at the subdistrict level differs from that at the community and residential quarter levels regarding geographical distribution features and quantitative relationships. Consequently, their research is crucial for achieving dependable results for subsequent urban green space planning [10].

The dual meaning of *equity*, *spatial equity* and *social equity*, has a key role in the definition of the accessible urban green, and both are fundamental in the urban green spaces planning [11].

Colbert J. *et al* shown in their study conducted in the Auckland Region of New Zealand that inadequate spatial accessibility to urban green spaces adversely impacts disadvantaged groups, who are more susceptible to health inequalities associated with socioeconomic factors. The findings put in evidence that more deprived neighbourhoods were revealed to have lower accessibility to urban green spaces, highlighting the urgency to address the emerging divisions in accessibility and opportunities for these neighbourhoods [12].

Simultaneously, the problem raised by Lu Y. et al., pertains to two study gaps within the green justice field. The first pertains to the spatial equality levels of various forms of urban green spaces, together with their distinctions and geographical distribution features. The second aspect pertains to the disparities in spatial equality levels of urban green spaces between cities at different socioeconomic stages. Their study, contextualised within China, examines three categories of urban green spaces: community green spaces, street greenery, and public parks, investigating the influence of socioeconomic factors on the spatial equity of these areas across various cities. The results indicate that the population growth rate enhances the spatial equity of community green areas and street greenery. Conversely, economic development and increased in-migration can worsen the equity level of public green space accessibility [13].

Several research reported a widespread attention to the social equity and environmental justice in the accessibility of urban green space. Strategies for the planning and design of accessible green space based on Environmental Justice should be include five essential points: 1. community-led, green space development and management; 2. fair and equitable distribution of green spaces; 3. improvement of accessibility; 4. connecting green spaces to benefits of health; 5. and mandatory linkage of built infrastructure with the provision of green spaces [14–18].

However, the literature review has shown that there is a lack of research focused on the accessibility of the urban green spaces in the architectural scale, and on the Universal Design principles.

3.2.2   Analysis and Assessment Process

The definition of accessibility, usually and with reference to green spaces, is quite extensive. This concerns both physical and dimensional aspects, and the environmental justice and social equity issues. Thus, the analysis and assessment processes on accessible urban green spaces are numerous and diversified depending on the aspect of accessibility that is to be investigated.

Specifically, Geographic information system (GIS) data-based approach is widely used [19–21], both as a unique method, and in combination with other methods of analysis such as spatial syntax [22–24], remote sensing, and statistical techniques [25]. Several research have been demonstrated that this kind of analysis is a valuable tool for planning and decision-making at both municipal and regional levels.

A significant example is represented by the Barcelona green axes initiative. This project sought to convert one-third of the streets inside its nineteenth-century expansion grid into green spaces, so enhancing safety and comfort for pedestrians, cyclists, and other social activities in healthier environments. The GIS-based analysis gives a comprehensive framework of the transformations, of the way to connected green infrastructure system, and significantly increase accessibility to green areas [26].

An important example of integrated methodology is the comprehensive analysis of the central urban area of Yuxi City, China, for the evaluation of the establishment of a new green space. This research demonstrates a high association between service level, kind of green space, service pressure, and demand for green space with geographical location, using open data sources such as POI, OSM, and ASTER GDEM, with GIS analysis and Global Mapper. This facilitates the assessment of future planning by integrating population density and land development intensity, thereby enabling the strategic arrangement and planning of park green spaces through the reduction of low-demand areas, expansion of green spaces in high-demand areas, enhancement of public transportation, and improvement of accessibility [27].

Another integrated method used is represented by The Gaussian Two-Step Floating Catchment Area (G2SFCA) method, along with the Lorenz curve and Gini coefficient. Theses methodologies are employed, for example, to measure and evaluate the accessibility and equity, considering both average walking speed and variations in walking speed across different age groups [28, 29].

In addition, many study are based on the application of an improved two-step floating catchment area (2SFCA) method, for estimating the accessibility in the urban green spaces [30, 31].

Other analysis and evaluation methods mentioned by the research considered are such as space syntax approach [32], perception-based survey, aimed to improve access to nature in cities [33], the use of geolocated social media as a rapid indicator of park visitation and equitable park access [34], accessibility of urban green spaces evaluation based on urban morphology [35] or spatial heterogeneity analysis [36], questionnaire method using a social preference approach (SPA) [37], nationwide analysis based on remote sensing, open street map and census data [38].

Finally, it is interesting to mention the research conducted by Mitropoulos L.et al., a district in central Athens, Greece. They deem the incorporation of accessibility in planning and the creation of tools essential for evaluating and measuring accessibility in green spaces. Consequently, their study aims to construct two accessibility indices: the infrastructure accessibility index and the opportunity accessibility index, which use an infrastructure-based approach and a distance-based approach, respectively. These accessibility indices are used for four categories of users and their requirements: pedestrians, People with Disabilities (PWD), cyclists and public transport users. The Infrastructure Accessibility Index (IAI) measures accessibility for sidewalks, crosswalks, bikeways and public transport stops. While the Opportunity Accessibility Index (OAI) quantifies the proportion of various user categories that get diversified opportunities during a certain timeframe. The permissible time restriction for user types is determined based on survey responses for seven distinct categories: green spaces, recreational spaces, education buildings, health buildings, public service building, commercial uses and public transport stops. The findings allow to provide recommendations to improve accessibility levels at local level [39].

3.2.3 Urban Green Spaces Planning and Management

Establishing accessible and inclusive urban green areas has emerged as a primary goal of urban development. In urban green space planning and design, many relevance features and aspect are considered, including the *green*, *connectivity*, *multi*-functionality and *accessibility*.

The complexity of these processes should lead to the definition of an independent operational approach, a sort of *Green Infrastructure* planning. Every local governance should have tools and methodology to implement appropriate UGS planning and operative measures able to design and networking of green spaces, and providing leisure opportunities and other functions, as well as accessibility to all community. This essential aspect can be crucial in metropolitan areas, such as delineated by Papageorgiou M. et al., on Athens and Thessaloniki [40].

Availability, accessibility and quality are among the most important features in the development of UGSs. Some studies propose innovative methods and approaches for increasing data and information useful to support local UGS planning and management. The case discussed by Kajosaari A. et al., on Finland, is a relevant study based on uses data from a large-scale public participation GIS (PPGIS) survey, aimed to understand the mechanisms leading to UGS visitation and the health and well-being benefits gained from UGS use and exposure [41].

Another interesting example on innovative methodology, is the application of the ESTIMAP-recreation model to the city of Trento (Italy), discussed by Cortinovis C. et al. [42]. Their results allow to show significant differences in terms of priority of intervention across the city, with implications on planning decisions.

The accessibility of urban green spaces, as mentioned above, refers to both physical and social and cultural dimensions. Therefore, the common goal is to address urban planning practices and community preferences with an operational approach, based on the engagement methods that prioritizes inclusivity, equity, and community, towards a more cohesive and effective society.

Regard this aspect, there is a wide range of research that highlights the importance of this approach in the urban green space planning process. The engagement methods allow to understand the perceptions and attitudes of the communities towards UGS.

These are often investigated through a comprehensive questionnaire survey, focusing on several and diversified aspects and features, such as socio-demographic factors [43–48], social interaction and engagement phenomena [49]; as well as the level of satisfaction in terms of visual perception (based on landscape quality criteria) [50], location and extension [51], distance and time spent for and in green spaces [52].

While the case of the multicultural landscape of Aotearoa in New Zealand, reported by the authors Cui Y. et al., is significant example of inclusive participatory planning processes, utilising both on-site and online meetings. [53].

Participatory methods are crucial for both users and potential users, such as marginalized groups, in the planning and development of public urban green spaces, as well as their management. This is demonstrated in a research Sweden, where, as several contexts, lack resources and appropriate methods to manage these areas. A process model for user participation in the management of urban green spaces has been developed, with the engagement of not only users, but also marginalised groups and non-users. This process model has become an optimal solution and practically feasible within the daily activity of a municipal organisation. This tested process could serve as a model for local management of urban green spaces, using limited resources [54].

The importance of citizen participation in the management of these spaces at the local level has been emerged in Greek context, such as that Thessaloniki where, through a questionnaire distributed online, it put in evidence as the citizens face the problems in using green space, and they consider the maintaining green spaces in cities is a critical intervention for improving living conditions [55].

And in reference to the Urban Green Space management, some studies have been addressed to establish and to develop evidence-based approach to effectively balance social, environmental, and economic objectives. These aim to support the city administrators, by providing them objective solutions for managing city-scale green spaces, each with its distinct characteristics. Berlin and Melbourne are exemplified by their cases [56].

3.2.4 Connections, Associations and Relationships

The research analysed and the results reported so far show that green urban spaces are closely connected to our lifestyle aspects, such as social interaction, health and safety, and to our perception of cities. And, in this perspective the accessibility of these spaces becomes essential.

Specifically, the urban green spaces are vital places for social interaction, social cohesion, public spirit cultivation, and community formation [57]. For this reason, many researchers argue that three are the significative characteristics of the UGSs: 1. accessibility of elements, 2. functional selectivity, and 3. structural connectivity and shareability. In this regard, it's very interesting the study on Changsha, carried out to Zhang C. et al., focused on the evaluation and the evolution of its urban green spaces publicness pattern in about a decade, in relationship with Changsha's urban development history, environmental, policy, economic, and social factors supported, led, promoted, and guided the formation and evolution of the urban green spaces publicness pattern. This has been provided ideas and methods for the UGS publicness evaluation on the urban scale and becoming a reference for the construction of liveable and sustainable cities [58].

Despite the many benefits of using green urban spaces, some research shows that in some contexts a part of the community, such as ethnic minority groups, as low-income, multi-ethnic populations [59–61], or more vulnerable groups, as older people [62, 63], can have difficulty in accessing these spaces. This is due to different reasons such as fear of crime; antisocial behaviour and accidents; difficulty in social interaction; problems related to unsuitable or unsafe playgrounds; no gardens or safe areas for children's play; poor accessibility; and lack of toilets; difficulties of transporting and caring for young children and poor weather.

There is a significative relationship between the accessibility of urban green spaces and health, and psychological and behavioural well-being benefits of the city dwellers, and many authors highlight the need for improving the existence of high-quality green spaces in urban areas [64–69]. Significant are the results of research in Japan which highlights the association between green space and suicide mortality. The findings, from spatial analyses of municipality-level panel data for the 1975–2014 period, suggest that accessible urban green space has a protective effect against self-harming behaviour [70].

In the last four years, moreover, many studies have been directed to understand the COVID-19 pandemic impact on our lifestyle habits and, therefore, in the way we interact with the urban landscape, particularly with the urban green spaces [71, 72].

These studies highlight the importance to continue to realise, maintain, and monitor UGSs, not only urban ecosystems and biodiversity, but also for the health of all urban residents [73].

The pandemic has significantly changed public priorities, improving the value of accessible, and safe of the urban green spaces, reconciling different aspects.

As the authors Wang et al. claim in their findings, the main objective is now to create multifunctional UGSs that satisfy to diversified interests, connecting heterogeneous features such as child-friendly and leisure facilities for families, and designing vibrant spaces for socialising, air-purifying plants, and scenic pathways, all sustained by enhanced safety and accessibility [74]. At the same time, as emerged from the research of Geneletti D. et al., applied to the city of Trento (Italy), another aim is to suggest standard measures, policy interventions and regulations that should be applied by urban planning to ensure that green space continues to benefit citizens also during emergency conditions [75].

Always in terms of emergency conditions, it is very interesting the study carried out by Cao Y. et al., on the refuge green spaces (RGS), a part of urban green space, located in China, used as refuge. These contribute significantly to the resilience of cities during the natural disasters. The research aim is to assess the equity of these places in relation to their planning layout, and to propose corresponding optimization measures in conjunction with future green space planning, analysing the evacuation capacity [76].

In addition, there is close link between accessible urban green space and crime mitigation: in fact, different study support that the creation of accessible urban green spaces represents a successful strategy towards achieving happier and sustainable cities [77].

However, how does an accessible urban green space affect the perception of the urban landscapes or another context?

Only a few studies have focused on these issues, but their analysis has provided very interesting information that highlights the importance of planning, designing and creating accessible and quality green spaces.

The presence of accessible urban green spaces can improve the perception of some context such as fragile settings [78], historic cities [79], or degraded environments [80], transforming and enhancing them in smarter, healthier and inclusive landscapes.

In these contexts, however, planning and designing accessible green spaces is often a challenge. An example is the one represented by the study of Gargiulo C. et al., applied to Pizzofalcone, a significant area of the city of Naples. This area, despite its centrality and its historical and architectural value, is not integrated with the rest of the historical city. So, the study is focused on identify and classify in a matrix active mobility measure, such as realisation of accessible green spaces, resulting from the study and comparison of the latest strategies and best practices, related to physical, economic, social and functional features of historic districts [81].

4   Conclusions

The Urban Green Space (UGS) is an essential part of the public open spaces. From more than three decades, several research that highlight its benefits, positive impacts, and challenges regarding the urban setting or on behalf of citizens such as health conditions, and the psycho-sociological well-being, are carried out.

So, planning, design and managing urban green spaces, equitably distributed across the city, accessible, and inclusive, has become a priority objective of urban planning.

But, as is well known, defining the accessibility of urban green space is not easy, due to the complexity of the aspects and elements involved such as physical and dimensional aspects, and the environmental justice, social and spatial equity issues.

This paper, part of an ongoing research, aims to examine the potential of urban green spaces, its accessibility with the aim to establish operative process able to define scientific definition and to propose a critical reflection about the planned and design solutions to transform and enhance the urban landscape in smarter, healthier and inclusive cities.

Thus, the first research step is focused on develop a cutting-edge framework for the accessibility and inclusivity of the urban green spaces through a systematic and critical literature review and try to define accessible urban green spaces.

Based on the findings of the analysed research, urban green spaces represent opportunities for the sustainable development of local communities, and for their well-being. Their accessibility is closely connected notions of equity (spatial and social) and environmental justice. In the evaluate process of the accessibility, it is essential considering the different scale of intervention, adequately assessing the elements and issues at each level. At the same time, the spatial equity is to be observed on different types of UGS, and their differences as well as spatial distribution characteristics and socioeconomic stages.

However, a significant feature, not extensively investigated, is the part of the accessibility of the urban green spaces in the architectural scale, and on the Universal Design principles.

These elements should be considered in the accessibility analysis and assessment processes, fundamental step to improve the quality and the accessibility of the UGSs, or to enhance the future operative proposal in the planning and management processes.

With reference to the urban green space planning process and management, it should be noted the importance, for every local governance, of appropriate methodology and tools to implement UGS planning and operative measures able to design and networking of green spaces, and providing leisure opportunities and other functions, as well as accessibility to all community. Participatory methods are crucial for both users and potential users, such as marginalized groups, in the planning and development of public urban green spaces, as well as their management.

In addition, green urban spaces are closely connected to our lifestyle aspects, such as social interaction, health and safety, and to our perception of cities. And, in this viewpoint the accessibility of these spaces becomes essential. So, the UGSs become multifunctional space that satisfy to diversified interests, connecting heterogeneous features such as child-friendly and leisure facilities for families, and designing vibrant spaces for socialising, air-purifying plants, and scenic pathways, all sustained by enhanced safety and accessibility, and ensure that green space continues to benefit citizens also during emergency conditions,

In conclusion, the research agenda aims propose a critical reflection about the planned and design solutions, to analyse the best practices and to suggest strategies able to transform and enhance the urban landscape in smarter, healthier and inclusive cities.

Acknowledgements. This study has been supported by the MUR through 2 projects: SMART3R-FLITS: SMART Transport for Travellers and Freight Logistics Integration Towards Sustainability" (Project protocol: 2022J38SR9; CUP Code: F53D23005630006) and 2) MOVING StEPS: MOVING from Street Experiments to adaptive Planned Solutions (Project protocol: 2022BLK9TS; CUP Code: F53D23005550006), both financed with the PRIN 2022 (Research Projects of National Relevance) program. This research was granted by PNRR-M4C2- I1.1 – MUR Call for proposals n.104 of 02-02-2022 - PRIN 2022 – ERC sector SH7- - Funded by the European Union – Next GenerationEU. This manuscript reflects only the authors' views and opinions, neither the European Union nor the European Commission can be considered responsible for them.

Authors' Contributions This paper is the result of the joint work of the authors. 'Abstract', '1. Introduction', '2. Methodology', '3.1 Quantitative synthesis', '3.2 Towards a thematic framework', and 4. Conclusion were written jointly by the authors. CG wrote '3.2.3 Urban Green Spaces planning and management', AM wrote '3.2.1 Spatial Equity, Environmental Justice and Social Equity', MSP wrote '3.2.4 Connections, associations and relationships, FP wrote '3.2.2 Analysis and assessment process'. CG and FP and coordinated and supervised the paper.

References

1. World Health Organization. Regional Office for Europe: Urban Green Spaces: A Brief for Action. World Health Organization. Regional Office for Europe (2017) https://iris.who.int/handle/10665/344116

2. Farkas, J.Z., Hoyk, E., de Morais, M.B., Csomós, G.: A systematic review of urban green space research over the last 30 years: A bibliometric analysis. Heliyon. **9**, e13406 (2023)

3. Mehta, V.: Unparalled prospect: COVID-19 and the expansion of public space. J. Urban. (2022)

4. Verhulst, L., Casier, C., Witlox, F.: Street experiments and COVID-19: challenges, responses and systemic change. Tijdschrift voor Economische en Sociale Geografie. **114**(1), 43–57

5. Randolph, J.J.: A Guide to writing the dissertation literature review. Pract. Assess. Res. Eval. **14**(13), 1–13 (2009)

6. https://www.elsevier.com/products/scopus

7. https://www.zotero.org/

8. Hansen, W.G.: How accessibility shapes land use. J. Am. Inst. Plann. **25**, 73–76 (1959)

9. Liu, D., Kwan, M.P., Kan, Z.: Analysis of urban green space accessibility and distribution inequity in the City of Chicago. Urban For. Urban Green. **59**, 127029 (2021)

10. Xu, S., Wang, Y.: Influence of spatial scale on the study of access fairness of urban park green space. Front. Environ. Sci. **10**, 1030796 (2023)

11. Patel, S., et al.: The impact of urban design on mental well-being by integrating green spaces in Doha City, Qatar. J. Infrastruct. Policy Dev. **8**, 3147 (2024)

12. Colbert, J., Chuang, I.-T., Sila-Nowicka, K.: Measuring spatial inequality of urban park accessibility and utilisation: A case study of public housing developments in Auckland, New Zealand. Landsc. Urban Plan. **247**, 105070 (2024)

13. Lu, Y., et al.: Inclusive green environment for all? An investigation of spatial access equity of urban green space and associated socioeconomic drivers in China. Landscape and Urban Planning. **241**, 104926 (2024)

14. Bressane, A., Loureiro, A.I.S., Negri, R.G.: Environmental racism in the accessibility of urban green space: a case study of a metropolitan area in an emerging economy. Urban Sci. **8**, 224 (2024)

15. Tang, M., Li, X.: The disparity of greenness accessibility across major metropolitan areas in the United States from 2013 to 2022. Land. **13**(2024), 1182

16. Chen, S., Knöll, M.: Environmental Justice in the Context of Access to Urban Green Spaces for Refugee Children. Land. **13**, 716 (2024)

17. Silva, C.S., et al.: Environmental justice in accessibility to green infrastructure in two European Cities. Land. **7**, 134 (2018)

18. Das, D.K.: Factors and strategies for environmental justice in organized urban green space development. Urban Plan. **7**, 160–173 (2022)

19. Kurniawan, H.B., Roychansyah, M.S.: The social equity of public green open space accessibility: the case of South Tangerang, Indonesia. Geograp. Environ. Sustain. **16**, 45–54 (2023)

20. Pallathadka, A., et al.: Using GIS-based spatial analysis to determine urban greenspace accessibility for different racial groups in the backdrop of COVID-19: a case study of four US cities. GeoJournal. **87**, 4879–4899 (2022)

21. Weber, R., Haase, A., Albert, C.: Access to urban green spaces in Hannover: an exploration considering age groups, recreational nature qualities and potential demand. Ambio. **52**, 631–646 (2023)

22. Huang, B., et al.: Space accessibility and equity of urban green space. Land. **12**, 766 (2023)

23. Askarizad, R., Lamíquiz Daudén, P.J., Garau, C.: The application of space syntax to enhance sociability in public urban spaces: a systematic review. ISPRS International Journal of Geo-Information. **13**(7), 227 (2024)

24. Marinelli, L.J., Annunziata, A., Caselli, B., Desogus, G., Torrisi, V., Garau, C.: Accessibility and polarities of pedestrian network in university campuses. A space syntax application. In: International Conference on Computational Science and Its Applications, pp. 383–400. Springer Nature Switzerland, Cham (2023)

25. Derdouri, A., et al.: Urban green space in transition: a cross-continental perspective from eight Global North and South cities. Landsc. Urban Plan. **253**, 105220 (2025)

26. Magrinyà, F., Mercadé-Aloy, J., Ruiz-Apilánez, B.: Merging green and active transportation infrastructure towards an equitable accessibility to green areas: Barcelona green axes. Land. **12**, 919 (2023)

27. Zhou, J., et al.: Evaluation on the urban green space layout in the central city of Yuxi based on big data. Front. Environ. Sci. **10**, 1068205 (2022)

28. Luo, W., et al.: Accessibility and equity of park green spaces: considering differences in walking speeds across age groups. Land. **13**, 2040 (2024)

29. Cao, Y., Guo, Y., Zhang, M.: Research on the equity of urban green park space layout based on Ga2SFCA optimization method—taking the core area of Beijing as an example. Land. **11**, 1323 (2022)

30. Liao, Y., Furuya, K.: A case study on children's accessibility in urban parks in Changsha City, China: developing an improved 2SFCA method. Land. **13**, 1522 (2024)

31. Yang, Y., et al.: Equity study on urban park accessibility based on improved 2SFCA method in Zhengzhou, China. Land. **11**, 2045 (2022)

32. Long, Y., et al.: Analysis of urban park accessibility based on space syntax: Take the Urban Area of Changsha City as an example. Land. **12**, 1061 (2023)

33. Quezada, C.R., Guajardo, F.J., Steiniger, S.: Walking access to urban wetlands: an opportunity for recreation and wellbeing. Urbano. **25**, 56–67 (2022)

34. Hamstead, Z.A., et al.: Geolocated social media as a rapid indicator of park visitation and equitable park access, computers. Environ. Urban Syst., 38–50 (2018)

35. Łaszkiewicz, E., et al.: Greenery in urban morphology: a comparative analysis of differences in urban green space accessibility for various urban structures across European cities. Ecol. Soc. **27**, 22 (2022)

36. Zhao, W., et al.: Spatial heterogeneity analysis of the multidimensional characteristics of urban green spaces in China—a study based on 285 prefecture-level cities. Land. **13**, 1050 (2024)

37. Addas, A.: Exploring the pattern of use and accessibility of urban green spaces: evidence from a coastal desert megacity in Saudi Arabia. Environ. Sci. Pollut. Res., 55757–55774 (2022)

38. Weigand, M., et al.: Are public green spaces distributed fairly? A nationwide analysis based on remote sensing, OpenStreetMap and census data. Geocarto Int. **38**, 2286305 (2023)

39. Mitropoulos, L., et al.: A composite index for assessing accessibility in urban areas: A case study in Central Athens, Greece. J. Transp. Geograph. **108**, 103566 (2023)

40. Papageorgiou, M., Gemenetzi, G.: Setting the grounds for the green infrastructure in the metropolitan areas of Athens and Thessaloniki: The role of green space. Eur. J. Environ. Sci., 83–92 (2018)

41. Kajosaari, A., et al.: Predicting context-sensitive urban green space quality to support urban green infrastructure planning. Landsc. Urban Plan. **242**, 104952 (2024)

42. Cortinovis, C., Zulian, G., Geneletti, D.: Assessing nature-based recreation to support urban green infrastructure planning in Trento (Italy). Land. **7**, 112 (2018)

43. Xu, Z., et al.: The perceptions and attitudes of residents towards urban green spaces in Emilia-Romagna (Italy)—a case study. Land. **14**, 13 (2025)

44. Uchiyama, Y., et al.: Local environment perceived in daily life and urban green and blue space visits: Uncovering key factors for different age groups to access ecosystem services. J. Environm. Manag. **370**, 122676 (2024)

45. Puplampu, D.A., Boafo, Y.A.: Exploring the impacts of urban expansion on green spaces availability and delivery of ecosystem services in the Accra metropolis. Environ. Challen. **5**, 100283 (2021)

46. Dos Santos, T.B., Do Nascimento, A.P.B., De Mora Regis, M.: Green areas and quality of life: Use and environment perception of an urban park in São Paulo city, Brazil. Revista de Gestao Ambiental e Sustentabilidade. **8**, 132–139 (2019)

47. Wan, C., Shen, G.Q.: Salient attributes of urban green spaces in high density cities: The case of Hong Kong. Habitat Int. **49**, 92–99 (2015)

48. McCarthy, L.J., Russo, A.: Exploring the role of nature-based typologies and stewardship schemes in enhancing urban green spaces: Citizen perceptions of landscape design scenarios and ecosystem services. J. Environ. Manag. **346**, 118944 (2023)

49. Lahoti, S.A., Dhyani, S., Saito, O.: Exploring the factors shaping urban greenspace interactions: a case study of Nagpur, India. Land. **13**, 1576 (2024)

50. Guneroglu, N., Bekar, M.: Visual perception of urban greening in public parks: evidence from Trabzon City, Turkey. J. Environ. Eng. Landsc. Manag. **30**, 124–134 (2022)

51. Žlender, V., Ward, T.C.: Accessibility and use of peri-urban green space for inner-city dwellers: a comparative study. Landsc. Urban Plan. **165**, 193–205 (2017)

52. Cernicova-Buca, M., Gherheş, V., Obrad, C.: Residents' satisfaction with green spaces and daily life in small urban settings: Romanian perspectives. Land. **12**, 689 (2023)

53. Cui, Y., Gjerde, M., Marques, B.: Mapping and assessing effective participatory planning processes for urban green spaces in Aotearoa New Zealand's diverse communities. Land. **13**, 1412 (2024)

54. Randrup, T.B., et al.: ParkLIV–engaging non-users in green space management. Local Environ. **29**, 1008–1025 (2024)

55. Baxevani, M., et al.: Peri-urban and urban green space management and planning: the case of Thessaloniki, Greece. Land. **13**, 1235 (2024)

56. Rambhia, M., et al.: Prioritizing urban green spaces in resource constrained scenarios, resources. Environ. Sustain. **16**, 100150 (2024)

57. Mouratidis, K., Poortinga, W.: Built environment, urban vitality and social cohesion: Do vibrant neighborhoods foster strong communities? Landsc. Urban Plan. **204**, 103951 (2020)

58. Zhang, C., et al.: The evolution and driving mechanisms of the blue-green space publicness pattern in Changsha, China. Land. **13**, 403 (2024)

59. Koprowska, K., et al.: Condemned to green? Accessibility and attractiveness of urban green spaces to people experiencing homelessness. Geoforum. **113**, 1–13 (2020)

60. Cronin-de-Chavez, A., et al.: Not a level playing field: A qualitative study exploring structural, community and individual determinants of greenspace use amongst low-income multi-ethnic families. Heal. Place. **56**, 118–126 (2019)

61. Kim, K., Lee, C.K., Kim, H.W.: Understanding the accessibility of urban parks and connectivity of green spaces in single-person household distribution: case study of Incheon, South Korea. Land. **11**, 1441 (2022)

62. Gao, S., Bosman, C., Dupre, K.: Understanding the well-being of older Chinese immigrants in relation to green spaces: a gold coast study (Australia). Front. Psychol. **11**, 551213 (2020)

63. Zhao, H., et al.: Analyzing urban parks for older adults' accessibility in summer using gradient boosting decision trees: a case study from Tianjin, China. Land. **253**, 105220 (2025)

64. Knight, S.J., et al.: The importance of ecological quality of public green and blue spaces for subjective well-being. Landsc. Urban Plan. **226**, 104510 (2022)

65. Ribeiro, A.I., et al.: Association between neighbourhood green space and biological markers in school-aged children. Findings from the Generation XXI birth cohort. Environ. Int. **132**, 105070 (2019)

66. Acosta, F., Haroon, S.: Memorial parking trees: Resilient modular design with nature-based solutions in vulnerable urban areas. Land. **10**, 298 (2021)

67. Jarvis, I., et al.: Greenspace access does not correspond to nature exposure: measures of urban natural space with implications for health research. Landsc. Urban Plan. **194**, 103686 (2020)

68. Nawrath, M., Elsey, H., Dallimer, M.: Why cultural ecosystem services matter most: exploring the pathways linking greenspaces and mental health in a low-income country. Sci. Total Environ. **806**, 150551 (2022)

69. Kang, M., Kim, S., Lee, J.: Pilot study on the physio-psychological effects of botanical gardens on the prefrontal cortex activity in an adult male group. J. People Plants Environ. **25**, 413–423 (2022)

70. Jiang, W., Stickley, A., Ueda, M.: Green space and suicide mortality in Japan: An ecological study. Soc. Sci. Med. **282**, 114137

71. Zhang, W., et al.: Travel changes and equitable access to urban parks in the post COVID-19 pandemic period: Evidence from Wuhan, China. J. Environ. Manag. **304**, 114217 (2022)

72. Dushkova, D., et al.: Human-nature interactions during and after the COVID-19 pandemic in Moscow, Russia: exploring the role of contact with nature and main lessons from the city responses. Land. **11**, 822 (2022)

73. Talal, M.L., Gruntman, M.: What influences shifts in urban nature site visitation during COVID-19? a case study in Tel Aviv-Yafo, Israel. Front. Environ. Sci. **10**, 874707 (2022)

74. Wang, Y., et al.: Urban green–blue space utilization and public perceptions amid the COVID-19 pandemic: insights from Northwest China. Land. **13**, 540 (2024)

75. Geneletti, D., Cortinovis, C., Zardo, L.: Simulating crowding of urban green areas to manage access during lockdowns. Landsc. Urban Plan. **219**, 104319 (2022)

76. Cao, Y., et al.: Refuge green space equity: a case study of third ring road on Chengdu. Land. **12**, 1460 (2023)

77. Venter, Z.S.: Is green space associated with reduced crime? A national-scale study from the Global South. Sci. Total Environ. **825**, 154005 (2022)

78. Andersson, E., et al.: Neighbourhood character affects the spatial extent and magnitude of the functional footprint of urban green infrastructure. Landsc. Ecol. **35**, 1605–1618 (2020)
79. Zhang, Z., et al.: Cultural heritages lead to less dense and greener cities—evidence from 371 Chinese cities. Land. **14**, 177 (2025)
80. Mohamed Anuar, M.I.N.B., Abdullah, S.A.: The benefits of green infrastructure planning in addressing lost spaces underneath elevated urban highways. Play. Malaysia. **20**, 255–270 (2022)
81. Gargiulo, C., Sgambati, S.: Active mobility in historical centres: towards an accessible and competitive city. Transp. Res. Proc. **60**, 552–559 (2022)

How to Ensure Safety and Promote the Permanence of School Streets?

Melba Cedro[1]([✉]) [iD], Gloria Pellicelli[1] [iD], Silvia Rossetti[1] [iD], and Vincenza Torrisi[2] [iD]

[1] Department of Civil Engineering and Architecture Parco Area delle Scienze, University of Parma, Parco Area delle Scienze, 181/A, 43124 Parma, Italy
melba.cedro@unipr.it
[2] Department of Electric, Electronic and Computer Engineering, University of Catania, Via S. Sofia 64, 95125 Catania, Italy

Abstract. In recent years, research has focused on innovative solutions to ensure the safety of road users, with a particular emphasis on vehicular traffic, pedestrian mobility and the habits of vulnerable users. Among these, school streets represent a highly relevant topic, especially for their ability to combine safety, social interaction and play in proximity to schools.

This study analyses potential scenarios for the permanent implementation of school streets in the Italian context, evaluating their positive and negative externalities, particularly in terms of traffic management, safety and urban livability. The adopted methodology includes a preliminary literature review aimed at identifying international experiences and classifying key variables that influence the development of progressive solutions for managing vehicular and pedestrian flows. A case study is then presented, focusing on a school street located in the *Oltretorrente* neighborhood of Parma (Italy). Analysis through GIS (Geographic Information System) tools and multimodal transport simulation models using the software VISSIM have been developed to analyze the morphological, social and functional characteristics of the area, in order to assess its suitability for experimental interventions. The results of the study provide a basic framework of the essential characteristics for the success of future traffic management scenarios aimed at the permanent adoption of school streets. It emerges that the integration of social and modal analyses can promote more conscious actions that effectively balance the needs of safety, accessibility and urban sustainability.

Keywords: School streets · Street experiments · Traffic simulation · Scenario analysis · Sustainable mobility

1 Introduction

The concept of School Streets as it is understood today, dates back to the 1990s and was already mentioned in Italy with the first interventions in Bolzano and Milan. They are currently referred to as 'school zones'. According to the New Italian Road Code (from Italian "Nuovo Codice della Strada"), a school zone is defined as an "urban area in the proximity of buildings used for educational purposes, in which a special protection of pedestrians and the environment is guaranteed, delimited along the access paths by appropriate start and end signs" [1]. In this context, an integrated urban and transport planning plays a key role in bringing together all the socio-spatial variables that influence strategies related to urban mobility infrastructure and services [2–4]. Promoting walkability, safer environments, and social interaction within the sustainable mobility framework can lead to the creation of new, more efficient solutions for school spaces [5–7]. One of the most well-known negative externalities is traffic congestion, which is a common problem in school environments and typically results from the heavy reliance on the private cars by parents accompanying their children to school [8]. Among the factors leading to these issues, fragmented urban sprawl has certainly had an impact, generating difficulties with longer distances and leading users to feel safer when using a private car. The fragmentation of urban areas has also led to the emergence of monofunctional areas of the city that discourage walking and do not promote adequate accessibility. Promoting active mobility for children would solve many of the problems associated with delayed learning and perception of urban space [9, 10]. For this reason, academics and administrators now point to the need to invest their resources in road safety, an enabling environment and accessibility [11–14]. Among the strategies to promote walkability and accessibility in the surroundings of schools, School Streets have emerged as a valuable measure. These interventions temporarily restrict motorised traffic near school entrances during pick-up and drop-off; times, aiming to create safer, healthier, and more child-friendly environments. As highlighted in the literature [15, 16]. these schemes are typically implemented as pilot projects, and and the transition from temporary to permanent street reallocation is frequently complicated and slowed down by various institutional, social, and technical barriers [17]. Within this context, the present study investigates the processes of permanence of School Street through online and in-field investigations and then performing quantitative and qualitative analysis of the street space through the implementation of a microsimulation model. While school street programs are not new in themselves, what makes this study stand out is its emphasis on the conditions for permanence, rather than just the implementation or short-term outcomes of such interventions. The paper is structured as follows (Fig. 2): Sect. 1 briefly illustrates a collection of the main guidelines adopted at the international level, also applied at the neighbourhood level, concerning the management and localization of School Streets. Section 2 presents the methodology and tools used to analyze the case study. Section 3 identifies the tools and analyses necessary to complete an initial classification of factors supporting possible traffic management scenarios. It also presents the study of the area through the definition of thematic maps of physical elements and study of vehicular and pedestrian flows through field surveys. Section 4 concludes with a discussion of the results obtained and the critical points identified.

2 Methodological Approach

The methodology adopted in this study is articulated in multiple phases and combines both theoretical and empirical components (see Fig. 1). It is designed to investigate the conditions that influence the permanence of School Street interventions through a structured sequence of analyses. The first phase consists of a literature review, aimed at identifying international experiences and classifying the key variables that influence the development of progressive solutions for managing vehicular and pedestrian flows (as further detailed in Sect. 3). This step enables the identification of the main characteristics that may favour or hinder the transition from temporary to permanent interventions.

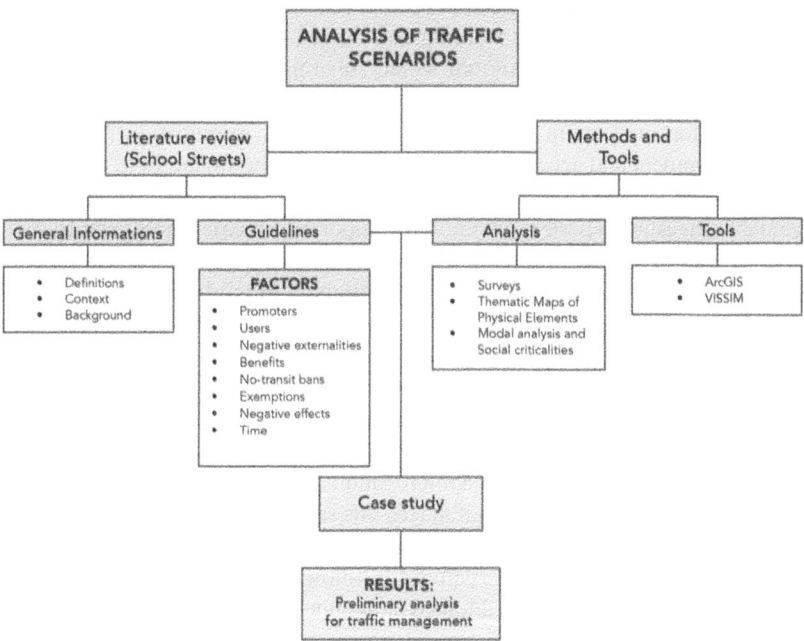

Fig. 1. Workflow and methodological steps. Source: authors elaboration.

Building on this foundation, the methodology included:

• The identification of the tools and analyses needed to make an initial classification of the factors supporting possible traffic management scenarios, as discussed in Sect. 4;
• The analysis of the study of the area through the definition of thematic maps of physical elements and a study of vehicular and pedestrian flows through on-site surveys, as detailed in Sect. 5.

3   School Street Applications and Guidelines at International Level

The main characteristics of the location of School Streets are different and all closely related to sociability and road safety. As already mentioned in the previous paragraphs, this global phenomenon spread rapidly after the COVID-19 pandemic [18–20], with a general increase between 2020 and 2024. Each country has contributed significantly, albeit in different ways, to the management of road space for the protection of vulnerable users. Some of them with measures such as Open Streets, which promote multifunctional spaces to improve the quality of life. Others, instead, have invested more in School Streets, focusing their interventions on the relationship between local authorities and educational institutions. For this reason, a comparative analysis has been carried out between the best practices analysed in literature and the guidelines developed by administrations in mostly local areas [22 – 33]. Among those analysed, a subdivision has been then made according to: (i) the scope of the study, (ii) the type of intervention (e.g. Open Streets or more specific interventions such as Play Streets or School Streets) and (iii) the level of action (global or neighborhood). This activity served to identify potential common factors that could later provide a preliminary framework for studying modal analysis and the degree of success of these interventions for their permanence and sustainability. The study highlighted that most of the guidelines for the establishment and management of School Streets have been defined in the years during and after the pandemic [33]. This aspect is particularly important because, although school zones have been present in the urban landscape for several years, administrations are now more involved through the development of efficient tools for territory management.

In addition, the involvement of school communities and local authorities is interesting, as some guidelines emphasize the process and timelines, and allow for citizens' approval and legitimization of school interventions within the strategic actions of the regional area. One of the most successful cities is certainly London.

As a result of the study, the following key variables have been identified as determinants for the implementation of School Streets:

- **Promoters** - Those who are actively investing in the promotion of school streets or wider urban space redesign processes, often through guidelines or strategic actions. These include local transport authorities, school communities, local government and EU initiatives.
- **Users** - People who regularly use the school environment and are therefore the most exposed to potential hazards. This includes children, parents, and school staff.
- **Negative externalities** - The main negative impacts on school areas, such as traffic congestion, air pollution, road accidents, and low levels of physical activity.
- **Benefits** - All the positive outcomes that result from the implementation of School Streets. These include creating safe and attractive places for vulnerable users, improving social interaction and inclusion, providing training for cyclists and pedestrians, reducing the use of private cars and decreasing air pollution.
- **No-transit bans** - Refers to those who are prohibited from driving during school street closures, i.e. parents/guardians dropping off or picking up students, school staff or other unauthorized drivers.

- **Exceptions** - Categories of vehicles that are allowed to travel during the road closure despite the ban. These include residents, commercial vehicles, emergency and assistance services, bicycles, scooters, refuse collection vehicles and school buses.
- **Negative effects** - Challenges and criticality caused by the road closure, such as traffic congestion in surrounding roads.
- **Time** - The duration of the road closure. This includes whether the closure is total (24 hours) or temporary (e.g., 15–30 min before and after school). In most cases, the time period selected will target congestion around school start and finish times.

Based on the analysis, the international School Street implementation process includes the following key steps (Fig. 2):

1. **Location and use**: the first step is to analyze the factors that influence the location of School Streets. These include the street typology, the level of traffic, the level of air pollution, the local mobility habits of citizens and the most common transport modes in the area. Another necessary action is to identify the traffic devices and road layouts that provide a framework for road safety. The other aspect to be considered in this first step is use, defined as the determination of the predominant type of use of a given area. In this case, it is necessary to interact with the school community, as these are sensitive areas used by vulnerable users such as children. This step is very important as it guarantees an intervention in line with extra-curricular activities that could also be increased or included in educational programs (e.g. outdoor learning, after-school programs etc.).

2. **Identify the stakeholders involved**: closely linked to the users, this step concerns the identification of stakeholders involved in the promotion of School Streets. These include, of course, the local transport authorities, who could guarantee greater protection and legitimacy for the intervention, as well as, in the same way, the school communities. Indeed, gaining local support could guarantee the permanence of the measures adopted. Furthermore, at this stage, it is also necessary to define the methods of communication with the various stakeholders to ensure greater efficiency and promotion of these interventions.

3. **Installation and management**: traffic signage, whether horizontal and/or vertical, is an essential tool for establishing road closures. For example, many guidelines refer to the time needed to prepare for the closure by means of appropriate signage such as barriers and school signals. In addition, during the closure it is necessary to have people who are responsible for traffic management in other areas, or simply to ensure that the orders issued are complied with (e.g. local police, etc.).

Fig. 2. Scheme of the Schools Streets permanence process. Source: authors elaboration.

4. **Monitoring School Street**: this is a fundamental step in determining the permanence of School Streets, as it includes a maintenance plan for interventions and the collection of feedback from users. Il also guarantees the possibility of establishing a degree of efficiency of the intervention, considering its replicability or improvement within the territory.

5. **Guidelines and best practices**: the last step of the permanence process concerns the use of an appropriate toolkit to educate citizens and encourage greater participation by local communities. The aim should be to ensure clear documentation that allows the promotion of practices for the redesign of public space and to provide evidence of other successful projects in the territory.

4   Traffic Survey: Preliminary Analysis

The section presents the activities carried out to collect data and analysis on the above case. Specifically, vehicular and bicycle/pedestrian flows in a neighbourhood were analysed to determine the impact of closing a street (to become a school street) has on surrounding streets. This scheme was followed for both the vehicular and bicycle-pedestrian traffic surveys. The scheme used for the survey is shown below (Tables 1 and 2) and included a division into categories of vehicles and, of course, their direction. The survey was carried out from optical cones corresponding to the focal points of the case study, as will be explained in the following section.

Table 1. Survey Scheme of Vehicular Flow.

	Survey objects	Description
Location	Optical cone	Represent the reference points
	Manoeuvres	Represent the directions
Typologies	Cars	
	Motorcycles	
	Bicycle	
	Bus	
	Trucks	
	Others	Special vehicles like firefighters trucks, ambulances, police etc.

Table 2. Survey Scheme of Pedestrian Flow.

	Survey objects	Description
Location	Optical cone	Represent the reference points
	Manoeuvres	Represent the directions
Typologies	Crossings	
	Pedestrian	
	Bicycle	
	Scooter	
	Others	Other transport means associated to soft mobility

5   Geometric-Functional Factors Analysis with GIS Software

From the field surveys, the geometric-functional characteristics of the study area were divided into road space and pedestrian space (Tables 3, 4 and 5). The latter are:

Table 3. Geometric-functional characteristics of cycle-pedestrian path

Cycle-pedestrian path
Width of cycle path Width of pedestrian path
Parklets

Table 4. Geometric-functional characteristics of pedestrian path.

Pedestrian Path	
Width	Presence of on-street parkings
Accesses	Traffic calming devices
Bike racks	Vertical signage
Speed Limit	Scooter parkings
Carriageways	Parklet
Crossings	
Presence of on-street parkings for vulnerable users	

Table 5. Geometric-functional characteristics of the road space.

Street	
Carriageways	On-street parkings
Crossings	Traffic calming devices
Speed Limit	Vertical signage
Width of the road space	Motorbikes/Scooter parkings
Parkings for vulnerable users	

6 Implementation to the Case Study of Parma

The proposed methodological approach has been implemented on a real-case study, focusing on the Oltretorrente neighbourhood in the city of Parma (Italy), and this section describes in details the study area and presents the results of applying of the methodology. Within the selected neighbourhood, some interventions have been carried out in recent years, but they are still temporary. The aim, as mentioned above, is to test the methodology to make these interventions permanent, and to be able to integrate them into planning strategies.

6.1 Case Study Overview

The chosen case study is the Oltretorrente district of Parma, an area located to the west of the Parma River and part of the city centre. It covers an area of about 1.1 square kilometres and has a population of about 8,496. The district is bordered by urban boulevards to the north, west, and south, while the Parma River forms its eastern boundary. It is divided into two main areas along an east-west axis by Via Emilia. The northern area contains mainly services and public facilities, including the Parco Ducale, while the southern area is predominantly residential.

Oltretorrente is a lively district with a high concentration of activities, particularly along its two main streets, Strada d'Azeglio (Via Emilia) and Via Bixio. Notably, it hosts a significant number of secondary schools located along the eastern edge of the district, near the Parma River. In addition, some poles of the University of Parma are located in the area, especially near the Parco Ducale.

In terms of transport accessibility, the district is largely accessible by car, except for Via Emilia and the area around Ponte di Mezzo, which fall within the Limited Traffic Zone (LTZ). Due to the characteristic narrow streets of the district, the infrastructure for active mobility is limited. However, pedestrian routes are widespread. The public transport system is well developed, ensuring easy access along the main roads, and several bike-sharing stations are also available.

Figure 3 shows some of the key elements within the neighbourhood, while Fig. 4 shows all the pedestrian paths and pedestrian crossings existing in the neighbourhood.

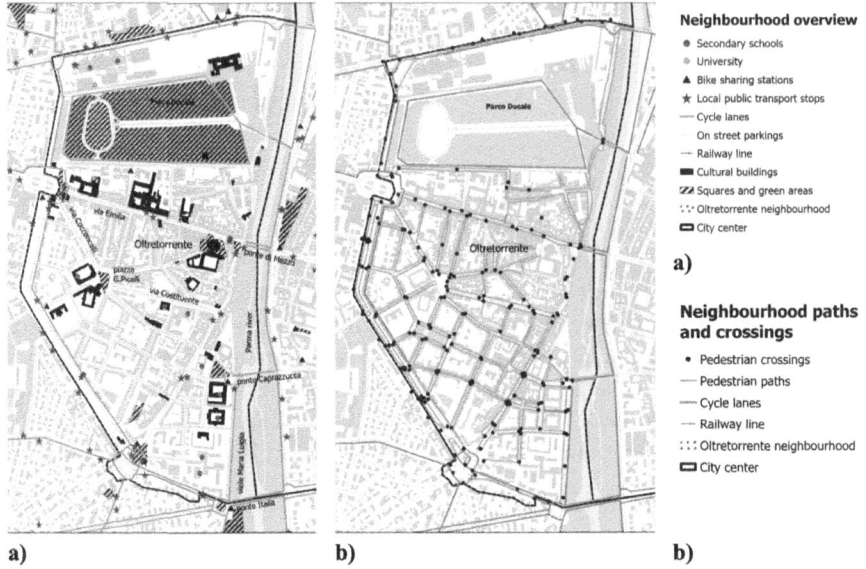

Fig. 3. Neighbourhood overview: a) identification of some important poles that characterized the area and b) pedestrian paths and crossings. Source: authors elaboration.

Fig. 4. a) First parklet (Liceo Scientifico Ulivi) and b) Second parklet (Liceo Classico e Linguistico Romagnosi. Photographs taken by the authors.

School Street: Viale Maria Luigia

To deepen the analysis, let's consider Viale Maria Luigia, the road that is already the subject of a 30-minute school street during school entrance hours. The road is bordered on the one hand, by a large traffic roundabout at Ponte Italia and, on the other hand, it extends to Piazzale Rondani near Ponte Caprazucca. The area is characterised by the presence of several educational institutions, including the Liceo Scientifico Statale

Giacomo Ulivi, the Liceo Classico e Linguistico Romagnosi, the Istituto Tecnico Economico ITA Melloni and the Istituto Tecnico Tecnologico C. Rondani. For this reason, following a municipal ordinance, it has become a School Streets, although this is not yet permanent. The ordinance in question was issued by the Mayor (No. 47) on 04/24/2015 and still in force, despite its initial temporary nature. In detail, the measure provides for a ban on motorised vehicles on school days, from 7:40 a.m. to 8:10 a.m., with the exception of authorised (e.g., emergency vehicles, residents or vehicles assisting users with disabilities). Over the years, schools in the area have promoted initiatives to improve the school street such as the installation of parklets, which help to promote greater sociality and sustainable mobility. The latter are located at two of the schools in the area (Fig. 4 a-b).

6.2 Preliminary Analysis of Vehicular and Pedestrian Traffic Flows

The following research provides the main factors that determine the possible impact of school streets in terms of negative and/or positive externalities through the study of vehicular and pedestrian flows (see Fig. 6 a-b).

Specifically, in-field surveys were conducted during the hour when the road section of Viale Maria Luigia is closed. Specifically, from 7:40 to 8:10 a.m. (when the road is closed to traffic) and from 8:10 to 8:40 a.m. (when the road is open to traffic).

The survey focused on the three main traffic junctions in the southern part of the district (Fig. 5) and on the whole Viale Maria Luigia. They are: Via della Salute, the first access point to the neighbourhood from the beltway to the south and west; the next intersection, and the traffic of the roundabout between the neighbourhood and Ponte Italia, to the south, an important access point to schools and services to the south.

Fig. 5. Location of survey important nodes. Source: authors re-elaboration from Google Earth view.

Numerical results of these traffic surveys will constitute the base for the implementation of a microsimulation model, in order to perform scenario analysis according to the evidences emerged from the following Geometric-functional analysis.

The detected maneuvers and related optical cones are shown in Fig. 6 a-b.

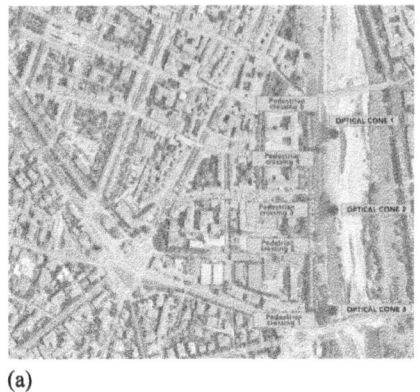 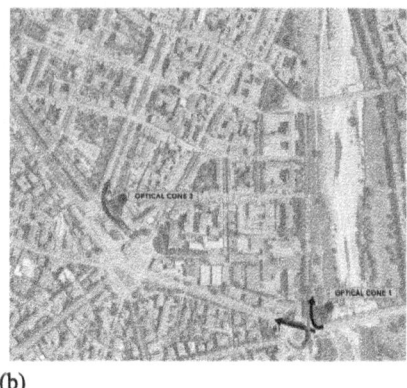

(a)   (b)

Fig. 6. (a – b). Detected vehicles and cyclist/pedestrian detected maneuvers and related optical cones. Source: authors re-elaboration from Google Earth view.

6.3   Results from Geometric-Functional Analysis and Discussions

This section presents the results of the geometric analysis of Viale Maria Luigia. This is useful to identify already positive features and critical elements that can be further improved. Table 6 deals with the Cycle-Pedestrian Path on Parma river side (East side).

Table 6.   Important features of the street with photographic survey. Acquisition date: 29/11/2024. Tools: Laser distance meter.

Geometric-functional elements	Description	Photo
Width of cycle path	2.50 meters	
Width of pedestrian path	2.68 meters The pedestrian space is extremely compromised by obstacles which do not guarantee spatial continuity and accessibility	
Parklet	• Parklet (Liceo Scientifico Ulivi) • Parklet (Liceo Classico and Linguistico Romagnosi) Occupied space = 2 parking spaces per parklet	

Table 7 is about the pedestrian path on the west side of the school (West side).

Table 7. Important features of the street with photographic survey. Acquisition date: 29/11/2024. Tools: Laser distance meter

Geometric-functional elements	Description	Photo
Width	4.78 meters (3.08 meters of pedestrian accessible section + 1.70 metres of space occupied by flowerbeds and/or obstacles)	
Accesses	In correspondence with the accesses of all schools or residential buildings. They are subdivided as follows: <ul><li>Two residential carriageway accesses</li><li>Two residential pedestrian</li><li>Four school carriageway accesses</li><li>Five school pedestrian accesses</li></ul>	
Bike racks	They are placed at school entrances.	

Table 8 is about both sides of street (whole street).

Table 8. Important features of the street with photographic survey. Acquisition date: 29/11/2024. Tools: Laser distance meter

Geometric-functional elements	Description	Photo
Carriageways	1 carriageway (Traffic direction: From Ponte Italia towards Piazzale Rondani)	
Crossings	5 Crossings No obstacles identified that restrict accessibility to the crossing	
Speed Limit	30 km/h (30 Zone)	
Width of road space	7 meters (considering parkings)	
Parkings for vulnerable users	4 On-street parkings: • 2 - ITE Melloni - Istituto Tecnico Economico • 1 - Liceo Scientifico Ulivi • 1- Liceo Classico e Linguistico Romagnosi	

(*continued*)

Table 8. (*continued*)

On-street parkings	Difficult to identify the exact number since they are not individually identified. All car parks are parking fees except those for vulnerable users	
Traffic calming Devices	Two traffic calming devices: • Roundabout (Ponte Italia) • Road hump (Crossing)	
Vertical signage	• Pick-up point • Bicycle crossing • Closure to vehicle traffic from 7:40 am to 8:10 am except for authorised vehicles • Pedestrian crossings • 30 Zones • No-parking zone • Road hump • Transit prohibited for vehicles with a laden mass exceeding a specific weight except authorised • Parking fees (times: 9 a.m.-12.30 p.m./14.30 p.m.-7 p.m. and fees: € 1.20)	
Motorbikes/Scooters parkings	• At the school entrance	

7 Discussion

Among the dangerous elements identified, the traffic roundabout represents an inconvenience that increases traffic congestion and affects with the pedestrian road safety. In addition, it would be useful to measure the number of vehicles parked in the area, which are usually parents pick-up and drop-off their children off at school.

Also, near the roundabout, it is difficult to detect the pedestrian crossing, as it is obstructed by the different traffic flows, which do not provide safety and visibility for the pedestrian and significantly increase the travel time to cross from one side of the roundabout to the other. In general, a high number of vehicles was observed between the 7:40 a.m. and 8:10 a.m., while in the second time slot the number of vehicles decreased by more than 50%.

Among the most common problems are parents' cars struggling to get into the school zone to drop off their children. In fact, there are no parking spaces to facilitate the flow of traffic.

In addition, a large number of bicycles use the road space for transit because of the obstruction of the cycle and pedestrian paths are blocked by students before entering the schools. Given the closure of the road section, this should not pose a danger to cyclists but given the reopening of the school road at different times (8:00/8:05/8:07), it is difficult to predict the transit risk.

During the opening of the road (8:10–8:40 am), almost all the bicycles observed used the cycle-pedestrian path, in contrast to pedestrians, who often cross diagonally despite the presence of 5 pedestrian crossings along Viale Maria Luigia.

Finally, the parklets are not always used at times when the school street is closed, in contrast to other times when the frequency of use is much higher.

Furthermore, direct observations showed that, many vehicles belonging to parents accompanying their children to school, or those needing to reach services further into the neighbourhood, are often not stopped by the traffic officers (who are monitoring the road closure all the time). This is dangerous because it is no longer possible to determine which and how many vehicles actually have permission to enter, and when instead the transit restriction is simply not respected.

8 Conclusions

It can be highlighted how the presence of a school street aims to improve the internal situation of the road, in this case by providing greater safety and allowing social interaction and freer mobility for students. However, it still lacks compensatory measures, and its impact on adjacent streets remains significant and negative.

This research analyses and validates possible solutions for the feasibility analysis study of the intervention, and to hinder the emergence of possible negative externalities from users.

The proposed methodology is considered to be particularly effective in an urban context at a neighbourhood scale, since the size of the neighbourhood itself is appropriate for a specialised analysis, which therefore implies particularly precise analyses and observations. Nevertheless, it is easily replicable in all medium-sized cities, such as Parma. In metropolitan cities, which are much more complex and articulated in terms of school location, it will be necessary to delimit a neighbourhood, or part of it, to performed effective analysis.

Future developments of this research will focus on the development of a micro-simulation model including both current movements of pedestrians and vehicles and perform scenario analysis to qualitative and quantitative assess the impact of interventions such as streets experiments ensuring their permanence. In addition, the analyses of ex-ante and ex-post configurations will consider the analysis of pedestrians behaviours in response to these interventions.

Acknowledgments. This research was granted by PNRR-M4C2- I1.1 – MUR Call for proposals n.104 of 02-02-2022 - PRIN 2022 – ERC sector SH7- Project title: MOVING StEPS - MOVING from Street Experiments to adaptive Planned Solutions - Project Code 2022BLK9TS - CUP Code D53D23011060006 - Funded by the European Union – NextGenerationEU.

This manuscript reflects only the authors' views and opinions, neither the European Union nor the European Commission can be considered responsible for them. Participation of G. Pellicelli was also supported by the project ECOSISTER (ECS00000033). The work of V. Torrisi is funded by the European Union (Next-Generation EU), through the MUR-PNRR project SAMOTHRACE (ECS00000022).

Disclosure of Interests. The authors have no competing interests to declare that are relevant to the content of this article.

References

1. Italian Road Code, L.D. n. 285 of April 30, 1992
2. Smeds, E., Papa, E.: The value of street experiments for mobility and public life: citizens' perspectives from three European cities. J. Urban Mobil. **4**, 100055 (2023). https://doi.org/10.1016/j.urbmob.2023.100055
3. Blečić, I., Congiu, T., Fancello, G., Trunfio, G.A.: Planning and design support tools for walkability: a guide for urban analysts. Sustainability. **12**(11), Article 11 (2020). https://doi.org/10.3390/su12114405
4. Rossetti, S.: How do SUMPs consider factors influencing walkability and cyclability? A review of literature and planning tools. Eur. Transp./Trasporti Europei. **97**, 1–11 (2024). https://doi.org/10.48295/ET.2024.97.9
5. Ceccarelli, G., Messa, F., Gorrini, A., Presicce, D., Choubassi, R.: Deep learning video analytics for the assessment of street experiments: the case of Bologna. J. Urban Mobil. **4**, 100067 (2023). https://doi.org/10.1016/j.urbmob.2023.100067
6. Von Schönfeld, K.C.: On the 'impertinence of impermanence' and three other critiques: reflections on the relationship between experimentation and lasting – or significant? – change. J. Urban Mobil. **5**, 100070 (2024). https://doi.org/10.1016/j.urbmob.2023.100070
7. Schwebel, D.C., Wu, Y., Swanson, M., Cheng, P., Ning, P., Cheng, X., Gao, Y., Hu, G.: Child pedestrian street-crossing behaviors outside a primary school: developing observational methodologies and data from a case study in Changsha, China. J. Transp. Health. **8**, 283–288 (2018). https://doi.org/10.1016/j.jth.2018.01.005
8. Hiep, D.V., Huy, V.V., Kato, T., Kojima, A., Kubota, H.: The effects of picking up primary school pupils on surrounding street's traffic: a case study in Hanoi. Open Transp. J. **14**, 237–250 (2020). https://doi.org/10.2174/1874447802014010237

9. Rossetti, S., Caselli, B., Torrisi, V.: Towards more walkable streets. An assessment method applied to school areas in Parma. TeMA – J. Land Use Mobil. Environ., 149–158 (2024). https://doi.org/10.6093/1970-9870/10911

10. Varma, R.: Reimagining safer school streets with children using the crosswalk program. IATSS Res. **45**(1), 39–48 (2021). https://doi.org/10.1016/j.iatssr.2021.03.003

11. VanHoose, K., Bertolini, L., Straatemeier, T.: Learning through experiments: the case of low-traffic neighborhoods in London. J. Urban Mobil. **7**, 100107 (2025). https://doi.org/10.1016/j.urbmob.2025.100107

12. Zhang, K., Tamakloe, R., Cao, M., Kim, I.: Exploring fatal/severe pedestrian injury crash frequency at school zone crash hotspots: using interpretable machine learning to assess the micro-level street environment. J. Transp. Geogr. **121**, 104034 (2024). https://doi.org/10.1016/j.jtrangeo.2024.104034

13. Collins, P.A., Thompson, C., Humes, M., Frohlich, K.L.: Contrasting stakeholders' perspectives on the first full-year school street initiatives in Ontario, Canada. J. Urban Mobil. **6**, 100094 (2024). https://doi.org/10.1016/j.urbmob.2024.100094

14. Dempsey, N.: Quality of the built environment in urban neighbourhoods. Plan. Pract. Res. **23**(2), 249–264 (2008). https://doi.org/10.1080/02697450802327198

15. Kingham, S., Curl, A., Banwell, K.: Streets for transport and health: the opportunity of a temporary road closure for neighbourhood connection, activity and wellbeing. J. Transp. Health. **18**, 100872 (2020)

16. Thomas, A. (2022a). Making School Streets Healthier: Learning from Temporary and Emergency Closures

17. Staricco, L., Verlinghieri, E., Brovarone, E.V.: Permanently temporary. Street experiments in the Torino Mobility Lab project. TeMA J. Land Use Mobil. Environ. **3**, 159–167 (2024)

18. Combs, T.S., Pardo, C.F.: Shifting streets COVID-19 mobility data: findings from a global dataset and a research agenda for transport planning and policy. Transp. Res. Interdiscip. Persp. **9**, 100322 (2021). https://doi.org/10.1016/j.trip.2021.100322

19. Mehta, V.: Unparalleled prospect: COVID-19 and the expansion of public space. J. Urban. Int. Res. Placemak. Urban Sustain. **1–4**, 153–156 (2022). https://doi.org/10.1080/17549175.2022.2146156

20. Verhulst, L., Casier, C., Witlox, F.: Street experiments and COVID-19: challenges, responses and systemic change. Tijdschr. Econ. Soc. Geogr. **114**, 43–57 (2022). https://doi.org/10.1111/tesg.12542

21. Camden - Healthy School Streets, last accessed 10 Mar 2025

22. Hackney - School Streets, https://hackney.gov.uk/school-streets, last accessed 27 Feb 2025

23. Living Streets Toolkit, https://www.livingstreets.org.uk/media/oryjkyte/school_streets_toolkit.pdf, last accessed: 20 Feb 2025

24. NACTO – Designing Street for Kids, https://globaldesigningcities.org/publication/designing-streets-for-kids/, last accessed 10 Mar 2025

25. NACTO - School Streets, https://nacto.org/wp-content/uploads/200708_School-Streets.pdf, last accessed 10 Mar 2025

26. Reading School Streets Programme, https://www.reading.gov.uk/vehicles-roads-and-transport/travel-to-school/school-streets/, last accessed 10 Mar 2025

27. School Streets for Safe and Sustainable School Trips, https://urban-mobility-observatory.transport.ec.europa.eu/resources/case-studies/school-streets-safe-and-sustainable-school-trips_en, last accessed 1 Mar 2025

28. School Streets: how to set up and manage a scheme, https://www.gov.uk/government/publications/school-streets-how-to-set-up-and-manage-a-scheme/school-streets-how-to-set-up-and-manage-a-scheme, last accessed 23 Feb 2025

29. School Streets Initiative, https://schoolstreets.org.uk/, last accessed 23 Feb 2025

30. School Streets Toolkit, https://www.openplans.org/school-streets-toolkit, last accessed last accessed 10 Mar 2025
31. Slough Borough Council – School Streets https://www.slough.gov.uk/downloads/file/2941/school-street-manual, last accessed 01 Mar 2025
32. Walk'n'Roll Cities Guidebook (2022) – https://urbact.eu/sites/default/files/2023-01/walknroll.pdf, last accessed 27 Feb 2025
33. Thomas, A., Furlong, J., Aldred, R.: Equity in temporary street closures: the case of London's Covid-19 'School Streets' schemes. Transp. Res. Part D: Transp. Environ. **110**, 103402 (2022b). https://doi.org/10.1016/j.trd.2022.103402

CPSO for Innovative Transport Planning and Designing

Tiziana Campisi$^{(\boxtimes)}$ (ID), Giovanni Giuseppe Iacuzzo, Angela Ricciardello$^{(\boxtimes)}$ (ID), and Marianna Ruggieri (ID)

Department of Engineering and Architecture, University of Enna Kore, Cittadella Universitaria, 94100 Enna, EN, Italy
{tiziana.campisi,angela.ricciardello}@unikore.it

Abstract. Mobility and transport systems are becoming increasingly complex. In order to make them more efficient and sustainable, it is necessary to promote studies and research that can improve not only the aspects related to data acquisition but also to data processing and simulation. Several studies in the literature focus on the evolution of mathematical models and traffic simulation tools. This allows planners to use available budgets and resources as efficiently as possible when expanding or rebuilding transport systems. Simulation models help to understand the effects that different measures have on traffic volume and flow under different circumstances. Therefore, traffic simulation creates a sound basis for sound and economic decisions, making traffic and mobility safe, sustainable, equitable and resilient. Starting from the acquisition of traffic data on a case study located at the Municipality of Enna in Sicily, this study focused on the use of the aforementioned dataset for the implementation of a Continuous Particle Swam Optimization algorithm to define a Neural Network model and predict the short-term traffic flow of a smart traffic control region. This approach emphasises that the prediction aspect compared to other methods is more accurate, and the prediction results provide a basis for improved vehicle flow management and intelligent regional traffic control.

Keywords: Particle Swarm Optimization · Neural Network · Traffic Flow Prediction · Sustainable Road Network

1 Introduction

Sustainability is a key factor in modern transport planning. Most regulatory instruments such as Sustainable Urban Mobility Plans (SUMPs) focus on the creation of environmentally friendly, socially inclusive and economically viable transport systems. These plans favor public transport, cycling and walking over car-centred models, with the aim of reducing carbon emissions and improving urban liveability. Implementation of SUMPs involves extensive stakeholder involvement to ensure a balance between community needs and environmental objectives, [1, 2].

O. Gervasi et al. (Eds.): ICCSA 2025 Workshops, LNCS 15897, pp. 304–318, 2026.
https://doi.org/10.1007/978-3-031-97660-5_21

These documents often require preliminary baseline studies that can analyse how some solutions reduce vehicular flows (especially private traffic) by favouring collective and public transport such as bus [3] or demand responsive transport [4] or shared mobility [5].

Various technologies and methodologies have been implemented over the years for the evaluation of vehicle flows, starting with the theory of car following models [6] or even traffic simulation models configured as a management system of graphs and matrix assignments, which makes it possible to carry out simulations of transport networks and thus of the road network, by searching for minimum paths and assigning traffic flows to them on the basis of one or more O/D matrices, which makes it possible, on the basis of these minimum paths, to calculate time, cost and distance matrices [7].

Models for simulating traffic flows are generally tools for analysing and predicting traffic effects. They can be used to plan interventions on transport networks, such as the construction of new roads or the renovation of existing ones.

The increasing volume of urban traffic poses significant challenges in terms of road congestion and environmental impact [8]. The ability to accurately predict vehicle flow is essential for implementing effective management strategies and improving mobility quality. With other words, an accurate prediction of urban traffic is essential for optimizing mobility and reducing pollutant emissions.

In recent years, recurrent neural networks (RNNs), particularly Long Short-Term Memory (LSTM) networks, have demonstrated excellent performance in modeling complex time series, making them ideal tools for traffic forecasting [9].

However, the effectiveness of LSTM networks heavily depends on parameter selection, such as the number of neurons in hidden layers and the learning rate, which affect predictive performance and training time [9,10]. To address this issue, in this study, we propose an optimization approach based on Continuous Particle Swarm Optimization (CPSO) [16,17], a technique inspired by the collective behavior of swarms, to determine the optimal network parameters.

In this paper an original approach based on Deep Neural Networks (DNNs) for modeling vehicle traffic is proposed. In details, for the analysis, a LSTM network optimized through Continuous Particle Swarm Optimization (CPSO) has been implemented in order to select the number of neurons in hidden layers and the learning rate. The efficiency of this approach in traffic analysis and its ability to predict traffic flow have been investigated and applied to a real test-case. It has been shown that the optimization improves the algorithm's performance due to cut of the number of parameters and decreasing the computational cost. It means that the computational efficiency enhance thanks to the lower number of neurons, without compromising predictive performance. In particular, the results reveal a significant reduction in loss and Root Mean Squared Error (RMSE), highlighting the potential of the proposed approach for innovative prediction applications in urban traffic.

2 State of the Art

2.1 Traffic Models

The requirement of making cities more sustainable for the lives of citizens is a major issue in our time, as well as the need of reducing the pollution or minimizing the time wasted in traffic jams. Thus, in accordance with 2030 agenda [29], the research in the filed of sustainable local mobility models held a great appeal and many scientists proposed original ideas in order to support the integration of sustainable mobility into future global policy.

In this context, mathematical models play a key role due to their intrinsic ability in describing the phenomenon under study in a realistic, suitable but also rigorous way. With other words, they have a predictive feature that can be applied, for example, in order to analyze the effect of possible urban planning interventions. Moreover, such mathematical models can be adjusted for the purpose of fitting real data collected from street experiment, that is defining the dynamics of the involved variables (i.e. vehicles and/or pedestrian) and their interactions. It also means that they can simulate realistic scenarios, assess benefit and risk of any kind of approach.

Literature is reach in mathematical models for description of traffic flow, usually classified in microscopic, macroscopic, and kinetic models (see [30]).

The macroscopic mathematical models arise form the fluid dynamics equations or rather are systems of partial differential equations. The microscopic mathematical models are the agent based models, that include for example the cellular automata model and the force based models. They respectively simulate the behavior of vehicles or pedestrians and the timing evolution of the traffic in a road or the crowd in a room. The last ones are the mesoscopic models which are mainly based on the equations of the kinetic theory for gas dynamics.

In this paper an original approach based on DNN is proposed for modeling vehicle traffic. Namely, a LSTM network has been optimized by means of CPSO with the aim of select the minimum number of neurons in hidden layers and the learning rate.

2.2 Deep Learning Approaches for Traffic Flow Prediction

DNNs are a class of artificial neural networks distinguished by the presence of multiple hidden layers between input and output. This architectural depth enables them to model highly complex and non-linear relationships, making them particularly effective in domains such as image recognition and natural language processing. A key strength of DNNs lies in their ability to perform hierarchical feature extraction: lower layers capture basic patterns, while deeper layers progressively learn more abstract representations.

In the context of traffic dynamics modelling, this capacity translates into the ability to detect intricate temporal and spatial dependencies in traffic patterns— relationships that traditional models or shallow networks may fail to capture. Among DNN architectures, RNNs, and specifically LSTM networks, have shown strong performance in time series prediction tasks such as traffic flow forecasting, thanks to their ability to retain long-term dependencies in sequential data.

However, the effectiveness of these models heavily relies on the careful tuning of hyperparameters, including the number of neurons, learning rate, and network depth. Given the high dimensionality of the parameter space, manual optimization is often impractical, leading to the adoption of heuristic and nature-inspired optimization techniques.

In this regard, several studies have explored the integration of algorithms such as Particle Swarm Optimization (PSO) to automatically search for optimal network configurations. For instance, a PSO-Bi-LSTM model has been proposed for short-term traffic flow prediction, achieving improved accuracy and stability compared to conventional approaches [18]. Similarly, PSO-based optimization of LSTM architectures has been shown to enhance forecasting performance and generalization capability [19].

These contributions form the theoretical foundation for the approach proposed in this work, which employs a continuous variant of PSO (CPSO) to optimize both the architecture and hyperparameters of an LSTM network, with the objective of developing an efficient and reliable predictive model suitable for simulating real-world urban traffic scenarios.

2.3   The Evolution of Traffic Data Acquisition

Recent decades have witnessed a profound structural change in transport demand patterns, both for the movement of people and for goods [32]. These phenomena, undoubtedly linked to economic development and the ever-increasing number of vehicles in transit, have led to a gradual increase in vehicle congestion. This has also led to an increasing increase in journey times, road accidents and environmental problems related to pollution, especially around large cities where urban traffic often combines with goods transport and long-distance journeys [33].

In recent decades, various mathematical models have been developed that can support engineers in the delicate task of carrying out accurate analyses on the evolution of traffic flows [34]. These models, the development of which is also attributable to the sudden and unstoppable technological development of sensors and software that make it possible to perform both simulative and predictive analyses.

The first type, the simulative one, analyses how the model behaves when it is stressed by particular external conditions, without these necessarily having to occur in reality. This aspect is of particular interest to a road section manager who needs to know what would happen if, for any reason beyond the everyday, the section in question were temporarily subjected to conditions quite different from the steady state. The second, i.e. the forecasting type, can be achieved by monitoring traffic conditions and, therefore, through it is also possible to make predictions about the occurrence of critical phenomena such as traffic jams or slowdowns, and possibly prevent them, or, if it is not possible to remain in an acceptable flow condition, equip oneself to deal with the criticality in the best possible way.

In this context, traffic models play an active role in the identification of traffic states and critical situations in the system, make it possible to determine which particular measures to take in order to take due account of exceptional situations (an accident or the temporary closure of a lane) and finally to assess the effects of the countermeasures that can be adopted [35,36]. Traffic simulation models can generally be subdivided into

- microscopic models, which describe traffic behaviour at a high level of detail and consider individual vehicles by describing their movements as the result of individual choices and interactions with other vehicles and the road environment [37];
- macroscopic models, which use ensemble relationships and identify global properties and state variables in which traffic is generally described as a flow defined by behavioral rules that are based primarily on the interaction of vehicles with each other and with the infrastructure [41];
- mesoscopic models, which are at an intermediate level of detail between the previous ones, examine the behaviour of groups of vehicles, thus allowing a simplification of the study compared to the micro but a greater level of detail compared to the macro-simulation [38].

Among the models in the literature that are capable of individually representing the movement of each vehicle on the basis of driver behaviour are, for example, those based on the:

- pursuer theory – Car Following,
- lane change theory – Lane Change,
- minimum access interval theory – Gap Acceptance.

Any road traffic flow estimation model requires a road flow survey phase to determine the actual traffic conditions of the network. The collection of traffic data is therefore of fundamental importance for all activities that may affect the complex mobility system in a more or less direct way, both in small areas, such as a single intersection, and in large areas, such as long-distance roads. In particular, the surveys of certain quantities, both quantitative and qualitative, characterising the vehicular flows passing over a road section contribute to the definition of the analytical framework of mobility and, thanks to their continuous and constant updating, may constitute an element of fundamental importance for the development of the territory [39]. Over the years we have witnessed the evolution of survey methods from manual ones to those with advanced sensors or the use of Big Data [40].

Manual traffic data collection methods are based on the use of one or more operators who record certain traffic data such as the number and type of vehicles passing through a given time interval. The recording of traffic data can be carried out using paper forms or using hit counters. There is no doubt that the use of observers has natural limitations that may not guarantee the correctness and accuracy of the information recorded [42].

The need to continuously and accurately collect traffic data has led technological research in the sector to produce increasingly refined instruments and detection systems. Over the years, data acquisition techniques with various technologies and sensors such as inductive loop, pneumatic tubes, triboelectric cables, piezoelectric sensors and others have become widespread.

While traditional automatic vehicle traffic detection technologies offer the undoubted advantage of allowing measurements to be taken over a long period of time and with a good level of reliability, they have the disadvantages of being suited to the measurement of only a few specific flow parameters (mostly flow rate and speed) and of having a rather limited spatial domain of analysis (represented only by the road sections where the detection sensors are positioned).

Since the Second World War, the use of technology in the management and processing of information has become increasingly strategic for organisations and citizens. Since the 1990 s, in conjunction with the internet boom, the term Information and Communication Technology (ICT) has entered common parlance to refer to that complex of sciences, methodologies, criteria, techniques and tools, capable of collecting, processing and transmitting information of various kinds. These types of applications are also used in the transport sector, both with regard to the transport of goods and the movement of passengers [43].

Aerial photography can be considered a particular technique for observing and analysing the traffic flows of a territorial portion, even a very large one, through which it is possible to trace the main parameters of the vehicular flow of each section of the study area.

Traffic monitoring through the use of video cameras is a non-intrusive procedure that, since its first applications in the 1970 s, has made it possible to more accurately analyse the dynamics and evolution of traffic flows over time. A further new traffic monitoring technique developed consists in the use of probe vehicles, i.e. vehicles equipped with GPS (Global Position System) devices capable of detecting the satellite positioning of the vehicle. This detection technique, also known this detection technique, also known by the acronym FCD (Floating Car Data), presents itself as a 'mobile sensor' in the vehicle flow as it does not require any type of installation along the roadway, is cheaper than other monitoring techniques and requires less maintenance [44]. Moreover, it provides the advantage of being able to cover the entire road network, provides more reliable information on journeys in terms of route lengths and travel times, allows the evaluation of origin-destination flows and, finally, gives the possibility of automatically detecting abnormal traffic delays, such as those caused by accidents. In contrast, there are limitations associated with the instruments used in this monitoring technique, i.e. the accuracy of position determination can also be very poor, as in the case of urban canyons or in tunnels where GPS reception is interrupted [45].

In recent years, in conjunction with the sudden spread of web use, both through the use of PCs and mobile devices (smartphones, tablets, etc.), a series of applications have been developed that, although providing in most aggregate or often qualitative data, can be useful for finding information, such as in the case of traffic congestion levels (e.g. google maps and/or waze), [46].

3   Methodology

3.1   Optimization Algorithms

Optimization is a fundamental concept in computer engineering and plays a crucial role in solving a wide range of complex problems. Among the various approaches to address these challenges, heuristic optimization methods inspired by natural processes or social phenomena, proved to be particularly effective in determining optimal solutions in complex research spaces. Heuristic methods are based on general algorithms, i.e. problem-independent, in which the components and their interactions achieve an optimal solution on the strength of practical experience and knowledge. Among others, we can mention for example Tabu Search [20–22], Genetic Algorithm [25,28], Ant Colony Optimization [23,24] and Particle Swarm Optimization (PSO) [26,27].

A stochastic optimization technique inspired by swarm movement was first proposed in 1995 by Eberhart and Kennedy [12]. The latter belongs to the family of evolutionary algorithms and finds application in different areas varying from training of neural networks, from clustering methods for the analysis of large volumes of data to intrusion detection systems.

The PSO simulates the social behavior of a flock of birds flying synchronously in searching for food. The algorithm therefore proposes a cooperative dynamics in which each particle (bird of the flock) moves influenced not only by its own experience (learning of itself) but also by the other members experience. Since 1995, numerous variants of the original method have been introduced to improve quality and efficiency, such as [13–15].

Among these variants, Continuous searching for Particle Swarm Optimization (CPSO) stands out [16,17]. Designed to accelerate the convergence of the swarm towards the optimal solution, that is the search for the maximum or minimum of an assigned function, called objective function, the CPSO uses continuous functions to update the position and speed of the particles. The formulation is derived from the integration of a Cauchy problem associated with a second order differential equation that describes the motion of a damped harmonic oscillator known the angular frequency and damping coefficient. In details, let us denote with $\mathbf{p}(t) = [x_1(t), x_2(t), \ldots, x_n(t)]$ the vectorial function representing the position of each particle of the swarm in a *n-dimensional* space and, analogously, $\dot{\mathbf{p}}(t)$ its velocity and $\ddot{\mathbf{p}}(t)$ its acceleration, then, they are updated in CPSO by the integration of the following Cauchy problem

$$\begin{cases} \ddot{p}(t) + 2\zeta(t)\omega(t)\dot{p}(t) + \omega^2(t)p(t) = f(t) \\ p(0) = p_0 \\ \dot{p}(0) = \dot{p}_0 \end{cases} \tag{1}$$

with $t \in [0, T]$.

The previous problem describes the dynamics of a damped harmonic oscillator with ω the undamped angular frequency of the oscillator and ζ the damping ratio.

If $\zeta(t) = \overline{\zeta}$, $\omega(t) = \overline{\omega}$ and $f(t) = \overline{f}$, $\forall t \in [a, b] \subset [0, T]$, then,

$$p(t) = c_1 e^{\lambda_1 t} + c_2 e^{\lambda_2 t} + \frac{\overline{f}}{\overline{\omega}}, \ \forall t \in [a, b] \tag{2}$$

where, λ_1 e λ_2 denote the solutions of the characteristic equation associated to the homogeneous form of 1 in the case of underdamped or overdamped system (i.e. $\lambda_1 \neq \lambda_2$).

Otherwise, if the system is critically damped, i.e. $\lambda_1 = \lambda_2 = \overline{\lambda}$, then

$$p(t) = (c_1 + c_2 t) \, e^{\lambda_2 t} + \frac{\overline{f}}{\overline{\omega}}, \ \forall t \in [a, b] \tag{3}$$

The values of constants c_1 and c_2, as well as the form for λ_1 and λ_2 are detailed in [16] and [17].

3.2   LSTM Network

For traffic analysis and forecasting, we employed a DNN, leveraging the LSTM's ability to model complex time series. The goal is to provide reliable traffic estimates to prevent congestion and reduce pollutant emissions.

Numerical optimization plays a fundamental role in selecting the network parameters. An incorrect configuration could compromise network performance and significantly increase training time. In this work, we designed a LSTM network to forecast traffic flow based on historical data, with the objective of enabling congestion mitigation and emission reduction strategies. The novelty of the proposed approach lies in the application of the Continuous Particle Swarm Optimization (CPSO) algorithm for hyperparameter tuningan optimization technique that, to the best of our knowledge, has not been previously applied to neural network optimization.

Unlike traditional PSO, the CPSO operates in a continuous domain with a well-defined analytic formulation, allowing for smoother convergence and finer control in the search space. We leveraged CPSO to optimize two crucial aspects of the LSTM architecture:

- The number of neurons in each of the hidden LSTM layers.
- The initialization value of the learning rate.

These parameters play a critical role in determining the network's ability to generalize from data and converge efficiently during training. Poorly chosen values can result in underfitting, overfitting, or excessive training time. CPSO was employed to explore these parameter spaces in a fully automated fashion, minimizing the mean square deviation between predicted and observed values.

The resulting LSTM model consists of three LSTM layers followed by two fully connected layers. Each LSTM layer uses the hyperbolic tangent (tanh) activation function, and the final output layer is linear to support continuous value prediction.

This contribution introduces CPSO as a novel and effective optimization method for neural architectures. The integration of CPSO with LSTM enables a more adaptive and performant prediction model, with potential applications beyond traffic forecasting.

4 The Case Study Analysis

With the aim of validate the proposed procedure, the method has been applied for the traffic prediction in a real case study; namely, the data used to train the neural network were collected on Via Boris Giuliano in Enna, an area characterized by various traffic attraction poles.

The data collection period ran from 3 to 9 February 2025, with acquisitions made from 6:00 am to 12:00 pm. Each hour was divided into 15–min slots to obtain a detailed time series of vehicle flow. In detail, the traffic data was acquired by means of a camera–supported manual count, which was carried out during the aforementioned period from which the peak week emerged.

Through the detection it was possible to validate the hourly peak flows corresponding in the real case to the greatest vehicular flows during the hours of start and end of work and school activities.

The investigated area included two survey stations positioned at the beginning and end of the road arch.

The definition of the O/D matrices was also validated using floating car data (FCD) available on a platform related to the use of Big Data. In particular, the research interrogated a specific 'self-service' web portal with an O/D approach, defining some customized queries, namely:

- the selection of the study area
- the definition of the analysis section
- the survey period (two weeks)
- Times (from which to deduce the peak hours)

The comparison of the acquired data and the interrogation of the portal confirms the choice of the analyzed time period, the object of this study.

5   Simulation and Results

In this section, the presented procedure has been adopted with the aim of traffic prediction in the aforementioned real case study. Namely, the CPSO has been implemented over the time interval $[0, T] = [0, 10]$.

The integration parameters has been chosen as follows:

- Number of particles: 10;
- Sub-interval of integration: 100;
- Integration step: $dt = 0.1$;
- Maximum number of stalls: 5.

As an objective function for optimization, we used the neural network training process, focusing on minimizing the Mean Squared Error (MSE):

$$MSE = \frac{1}{n} \sum_{i=1}^{n} (y_i - \hat{y}_i)^2 \qquad (4)$$

Once the optimal parameters were determined, the network was re-executed with the optimized configurations provided by CPSO.

The following figures, Fig. 1 and Fig. 2, show the trend of loss and RMSE error without applying the optimization process.

The optimization led to a significant reduction in the number of neurons in the hidden layers compared to the initial configuration (from 200, 100, and 50 down to 125, 63, and 35). Moreover, the optimized learning rate was initialized at 0.0537.

This configuration improved computational efficiency while maintaining nearly unchanged predictive performance, enhancing the convergence of the neural network.

In Fig. 1 and Fig. 2 a comparison in terms of performance of the neural network is presented with the aim of underline the improvement gained by introducing the optimization process. Such performance is measured by means of Loss error and RMSE error.

In details, the Fig. 1 illustrates the standard LSTM network training process over 200 epochs.

The Fig. 2 shows the LSTM network training process over 300 epochs when the CPSO is introduced.

A reduction in loss below 0.2 can be appreciated, while the RMSE error, initially above 1, decreases below 0.4.

Finally, Fig. 3 shows the neural network's prediction compared to real data. A good correspondence between estimated and observed values is noted, confirming the model's ability to effectively learn traffic dynamics.

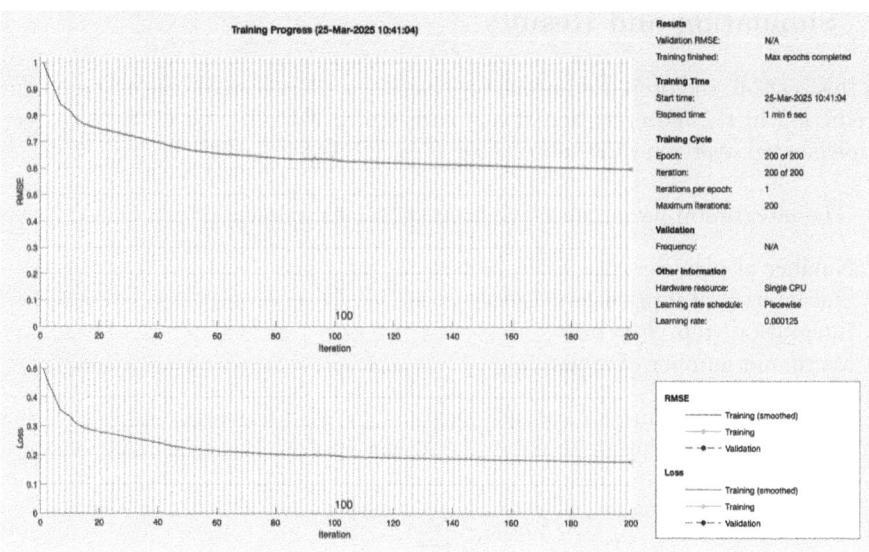

Fig. 1. Loss error and RMSE error trend without optimization process.

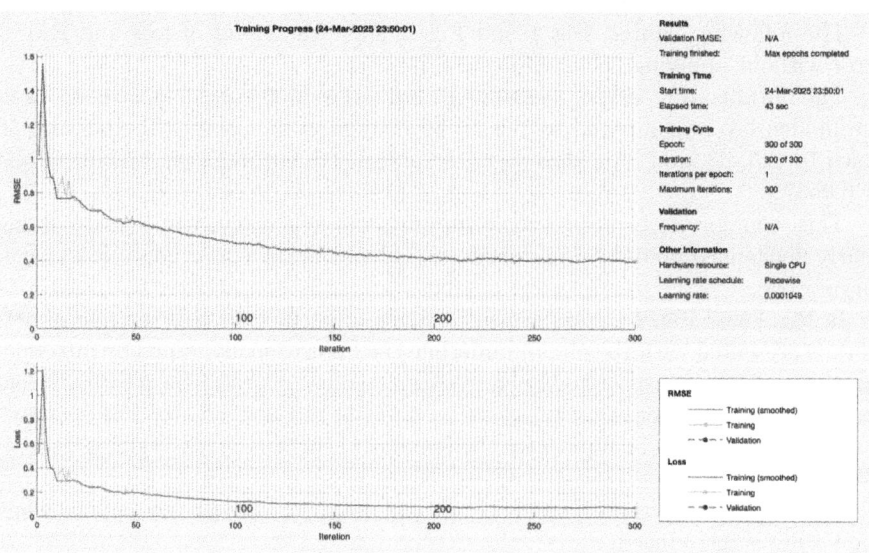

Fig. 2. Loss error and RMSE trend during LSTM network training after CPSO optimization.

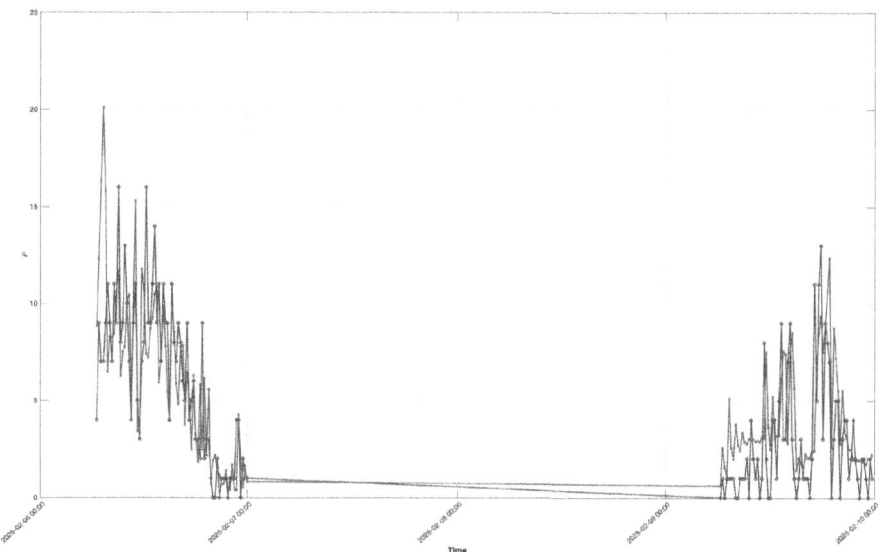

Fig. 3. Neural network prediction compared to real data.

6   Conclusion

The accurate prediction of urban traffic is essential for optimizing mobility and reducing pollutant emissions. In this study, an approach based on DNNs for modeling vehicle traffic on Via Boris Giuliano in Enna has been presented. Data were collected between February 3 and February 9, 2025, with a temporal resolution of 15 min. For the analysis, an LSTM network optimized through CPSO to select the number of neurons in hidden layers and the learning rate has been adopted.

It has been shown that the optimization improves computational efficiency by reducing the number of neurons without compromising predictive performance. The results detail a significant reduction in loss and RMSE error, highlighting the potential of the proposed approach for traffic prediction applications.

The obtained results confirm the effectiveness of CPSO optimization in configuring the LSTM network for urban traffic forecasting. The optimization allowed for a reduction in the number of neurons in hidden layers, improving computational efficiency without compromising prediction quality. The RMSE error, which initially exceeded 1, was reduced to less than 0.4, while the loss dropped below 0.2, demonstrating good model learning capability.

The prediction analysis highlighted a strong correlation between estimated values and real data, confirming the network's ability to model traffic dynamics.

Future developments could include the integration of additional contextual variables, such as weather conditions and special events, to further improve the accuracy of the predictive model.

Acknowledgement. This research was granted by PNRR-M4C2- I1.1 – MUR Call for proposals n.104 of 02-02-2022 - PRIN 2022 – ERC sector SH7- Project title: MOVING StEPS - MOVING from Street Experiments to adaptive Planned Solutions - Project Code 2022BLK9TS - CUP Code J53D23009280008 - Funded by the European Union – NextGenerationEU. The authors A. R., M. R acknowledge the support by G.N.F.M. of I.N.d.A.M.

References

1. Mozos-Blanco, M.Á., Pozo-Menéndez, E., Arce-Ruiz, R., Baucells-Aletá, N.: The way to sustainable mobility. a comparative analysis of sustainable mobility plans in Spain. Transp. Policy **72**, 45–54 (2018)
2. Charradi, I., Campisi, T., Tesoriere, G., Abdallah, K.B.: A holistic approach to SUMP strategies and actions in the post-pandemic and energy crisis era. In: International Conference on Computational Science and Its Applications, pp. 345–359 (2022)
3. Mirza, A.M., Jain, R.K.: Review of public transportation integration and modeling strategies: toward seamless urban mobility. Multi. Rev. **8**(1), 2025018 (2025)
4. Campisi, T., De Cet, G., Vianello, C., Garau, C.: Exploring economic and ethical challenges of implementing demand-responsive transport systems (DRT) in Italy. Eur. Transp./Trasporti Europei **98** (2024)
5. Canitez, F.: Sustainable urban mobility plan for Istanbul: a critical review. J. Intell. Decis. Making Inf. Sci. **2**, 233–249 (2025)
6. Zhang, T.T., Jin, P.J., McQuade, S.T., Bayen, A., Piccoli, B.: Car-following models: a multidisciplinary review. IEEE Trans. Intell. Veh. (2024)
7. Tascione, A.M., Di Costanzo, L., Forcina, D., Pariota, L., Capezza, C., Simonelli, F.:Correlation of OD matrix and traffic volume with functional data analysis: a simulation-based case study in the city of Portici. In: 2024 IEEE International Conference on Environment and Electrical Engineering and 2024 IEEE Industrial and Commercial Power Systems Europe (EEEIC/I&CPS Europe), pp. 1–5 (2024)
8. Anupriya, B.P., Graham, D.: Traffic congestion: how cities can overcome this growing issue. Transp. Res. Part A: Policy Pract. **174** (2023)
9. Dalal, S., Jaglan, V., Agrawal, A., Kumar, A., Joshi, S.J., Dahiya, M.: Navigating urban congestion: optimizing LSTM with RNN in traffic prediction. In: AIP Conference Proceedings, vol. 3217, p. 030005 (2024)
10. Mahajan, D., Pottigar, V.V., Suresh, C., Fahad, A.: Implementing real-time traffic flow prediction using LSTM (2024)
11. Campisi, T., Ricciardello, A., Ruggieri, M., Vitanza, G.A.: Preliminary analysis on parklets: can they contribute to the realisation of a walking friendly city in Italy? In: Lecture Notes in Computer Science, vol. 14823, pp. 168–183 (2024)
12. Eberhart, R., Kennedy, J.: A new optimizer using particle swarm theory. In: MHS 1995. Proceedings of the Sixth International Symposium on Micro Machine and Human Science, pp. 39–43 (1995)
13. Shi, Y., Eberhart, R.: A modified particle swarm optimizer. In: 1998 IEEE International Conference on Evolutionary Computation Proceedings. IEEE World Congress on Computational Intelligence (Cat. No. 98TH8360), pp. 69–73 (1998)
14. Tanweer, M.R., Suresh, S., Sundararajan, N.: Self regulating particle swarm optimization algorithm. Inform. Sci. **294**, 182–202 (2015)

15. Orlando, C., Alaimo, A.: A robust active control system for shimmy damping in the presence of free play and uncertainties. Mech. Syst. Signal Process. **84**, 551–569 (2017)

16. Orlando, C., Ricciardello, A.: Analytic solution of the continuous particle swarm optimization problem. Optim. Lett. **15**(6), 2005–2015 (2021)

17. Orlando, C., Ricciardello, A.: Continuous particle swarm optimization. In: AIP Conference Proceedings, vol. 2293, p. 200009 (2020)

18. Zhao, J., Jiang, X., Wang, W.: Traffic flow prediction based on improved PSO-BiLSTM model. Phys. A: Stat. Mech. Appl. **624**, 129734 (2023)

19. Zhou, F., Chen, Z.: Research on traffic flow prediction method based on LSTM model and PSO-LSTM model. arXiv preprint arXiv:2403.05611 (2024)

20. Glover, F.: Future paths for integer programming and links to artificial intelligence. Comput. Oper. Res. **13**(5), 533–549 (1986)

21. Glover, F.: Tabu search – part 1. ORSA J. Comput. **1**(2), 190–206 (1989)

22. Glover, F.: Tabu search – part 2. ORSA J. Comput. **2**(1), 4–32 (1990)

23. Birattari, M., Pellegrini, P., Dorigo, M.: On the invariance of ant colony optimization. IEEE Trans. Evol. Comput. **11**(6), 732–742 (2007)

24. Dorigo, M., Gambardella, L.M.: Ant colony system: a cooperative learning approach to the traveling salesman problem. IEEE Trans. Evol. Comput. **1**(1), 53–66 (1997)

25. Whitley, D.: A genetic algorithm tutorial. Stat. Comput. **4**(2), 65–85 (1994)

26. Artale, V., Milazzo, C.L.R., Orlando, C., Ricciardello, A.: Comparison of GA and PSO approaches for the direct and LQR tuning of a multirotor PD controller. J. Industr. Manage. Optim. **13** (2017)

27. Artale, V.. Milazzo, C.L.R.. Orlando, C.. Ricciardello, A.: A PSO-PID quaternion model based trajectory control of a hexarotor UAV. In: AIP Conference Proceedings, vol. 1702 (2015)

28. Artale, V., Milazzo, C.L.R., Orlando, C., Ricciardello, A.: Genetic algorithm applied to the stabilization control of a hexarotor. In: AIP Conference Proceedings, vol. 1648 (2014)

29. Sathiyan, S.P., et al.: Comprehensive assessment of electric vehicle development, deployment, and policy initiatives to reduce GHG emissions: opportunities and challenges. IEEE Access (2022)

30. Piccoli, B. et al.: Vehicular traffic: a review of continuum mathematical models. Encycl. Of Complexity Syst. Sci. (2009)

31. Liu, H.Y.: Utilize improved particle swarm to predict traffic flow. Adv. Mater. Res. **756–759**, 3744–3748 (2013)

32. Xie, F., Levinson, D.: Evolving Transportation Networks. Springer, Cham (2011)

33. Xu, S., Sun, C., Liu, N.: Road congestion and air pollution-analysis of spatial and temporal congestion effects. Sci. Total Environ. **945**, 173896 (2024)

34. Yue, W., Li, C., Mao, G., Cheng, N., Zhou, D.: Evolution of road traffic congestion control: a survey from perspective of sensing, communication, and computation. China Commun. **18**(12), 151–177 (2021)

35. Dorokhin, S., Artemov, A., Likhachev, D., Novikov, A., Starkov, E.: Traffic simulation: an analytical review. In: IOP Conference Series: Materials Science and Engineering, vol. 918, no. 1, p. 012058 (2020)

36. Algherbal, E.A., Ratrout, N.T.: A comparative analysis of currently used microscopic, macroscopic, and mesoscopic traffic simulation software. Transp. Res. Procedia **84**, 495–503 (2025)

37. Hasan, U., AlJassmi, H., Hasan, A.: Microsimulation modelling and scenario analysis of a congested Abu Dhabi highway. Engineering **4**(3), 2003–2014 (2023)

38. Varga, B., Tettamanti, T.: Jam propagation analysis with mesoscopic traffic simulation. IEEE Trans. Intell. Transp. Syst. **24**(12), 14162–14173 (2023)
39. Chand, A., Jayesh, S., Bhasi, A.B.: Road traffic accidents: an overview of data sources, analysis techniques and contributing factors. Mater. Today Proc. **47**, 5135–5141 (2021)
40. Bachechi, C., Po, L., Rollo, F.: Big data analytics and visualization in traffic monitoring. Big Data Res. **27**, 100292 (2022)
41. Zhao, C., Liao, F., Li, X., Du, Y.: Macroscopic modeling and dynamic control of on street cruising for parking of autonomous vehicles in a multi-region urban road network. Transp. Res. Part C: Emerg. Technol. **128**, 103176 (2021)
42. Leduc, G.: Road traffic data: collection methods and applications. Working Pap. Energy Transp. Clim. Change **1**(55), 1–55 (2008)
43. Sood, K.: ICT-driven data mining analysis in civil engineering: a scientometric review. Wiley Interdiscip. Rev. Data Min. Knowl. Disc. **15**(1), (2025)
44. Hazenberg, L.W.: The potential of floating car data for calibrating origin-destination matrices. Master's thesis, University of Twente (2025)
45. Yang, H., Zhang, X., Li, Z., Cui, J.: Region-level traffic prediction based on temporal multi-spatial dependence graph convolutional network from GPS data. Remote Sens. **14**(2), 303 (2022)
46. Liu, Y., Hoseinzadeh, N., Gu, Y., Han, L.D., Brakewood, C., Zhang, Z.: Evaluating the coverage and spatiotemporal accuracy of crowdsourced reports over time: a case study of Waze event reports in Tennessee. Transp. Res. Rec. **2678**(4), 468–481 (2024)

Temporary Real Estate Management: Approaches and Methods for Time-integrated Impact Assessments and Evaluations (TREAT 2025)

PS-U-GO's Urban Living Lab: An Educational Space for Urban Commons in Naples (Italy)

Stefano Cuntò[1], Lorenzo Lodato[2], Federica Morra[3], Stefania Ragozino[3], and Maria Cerreta[1(✉)]

[1] Department of Architecture, University of Naples Federico II, Naples, Italy
{stefano.cunto,maria.cerreta}@unina.it
[2] Lido Pola Urban Commons, Naples, Italy
[3] National Research Council, Naples, Italy
stefania.ragozino@cnr.it

Abstract. The contribution is elaborated within the framework of Urban Living Lab (ULL), concerned with the right to the city, co-production processes and collective management models for public resources in complex decision contexts. We present the adopted value-focused thinking methodology and the results regarding the first implemented phase of the PS-U-GO Urban Living Lab Naples "Towards a free and accessible sea". It is one of the four ULLs implemented within the Erasmus+ project "PS-U-GO - Education in Living Labs: Participatory Skills for Sustainable Urban Governance", and it aims at contributing to the process of re-appropriation, democratisation and return of the sea to the city. This experimentation takes place in continuity with the action-research process developed by CNR IRISS in collaboration with Lido Pola - Urban Commons to monitor and implement urban regeneration processes in the Bagnoli neighborhood in Naples, Italy. It is an ongoing experience that involves actors of the quintuple helix: researchers, scholars and students; civic committees, urban commons and associations; public administrations and private; and last but not least, the sea.

Keywords: Commons · Urban regeneration · Collaborative decision-making process

1 Introduction

In recent years, the growing attention towards urban commons has led to a profound redefinition of the relationship between citizenship, urban space, and practices of shared use. The interaction of these three elements, in both their material and immaterial dimensions, often gives rise to project communities [1], capable of producing collective urban resistance and promoting collective practices of care, both understood as forms of affective labour and social reproduction [2, 3]. These practices are expressions of broader movements of resistance within the neoliberal city, capable, in some cases, of safeguarding urban spaces from the risks of gentrification and touristification, as well as from processes of neglect and urban decay [4]. Katsikana defines these concepts as forms of *social reproduction of resistance within the city*: often marginalised activities, yet essential for building common, horizontal, and non-hierarchical spaces that foster mutual learning and shared awareness.

In this perspective, urban commons are not merely material or environmental resources collectively managed; they are also social, political, and spatial devices, what Velicu terms *relational politics* [5], emerging from the continuous interaction between subjects, collective needs, and territories. From this standpoint, the city itself is conceptualised as a commons, no longer merely an object of consumption or appropriation, but a site of shared practices, active participation, and social experimentation [6]. According to Stavrides, common space is generated through the process of communing, that is, collective and horizontal actions producing porous, inclusive, and transformative urban thresholds. These threshold spaces represent moments where social distinctions dissolve, enabling citizens to act as active communitas, challenging and subverting the normalisation of space imposed by exclusionary urban forms [6]. Thus, the city becomes a network of places to be collectively inhabited, freeing it from proprietary logics and reconceptualising it as a living, accessible environment that fosters social bonds and participatory democracy.

Within the theoretical framework outlined by Elinor Ostrom [7], the community management of common resources proves effective when based on shared rules, cooperation, and collective responsibility. However, in the urban context, the relational dimension of urban commons is more complex: the value of space derives from its shared use by citizens, not from its exclusion or appropriation. According to Borch and Kornberger (2015), the urban commons paradigm differs from the classical natural resource model, as it places proximity, social interaction, and co-production of use-value at its core [8].

In Naples, a metropolitan city in southern Italy, this reflection finds fertile ground in the experiences around urban commons fostered by informal communities and the promotion of civic and collective use practices supported by the municipal administration [9–12]. This context has facilitated the emergence of project communities striving to reclaim denied spaces, activating urban regeneration processes starting from existing and collective needs and resources. In a broader scenario in which many Mediterranean coastal cities face persistent challenges such as lack of public services, denied opportunities for ecosystemic regeneration, and the pressures of overtourism, the issue of access to the sea and the management of its usable spaces becomes particularly relevant. The idea that beaches represent one of the most beloved – and contested – forms of public space is widely recognised in the literature, with numerous examples globally [13]. Indeed, worldwide, there is a worrying trend of restricting access to public beach areas to ensure private enjoyment of seafront properties or for commercial development purposes. The coastline of Naples exemplifies this, where the demand for sea access strongly emerges in the claims of social movements. The liminal areas between city and sea, such as beaches, docks, rocks, and tuff cliffs, while legally part of the maritime public domain and therefore recognised as public collective goods, are often subject to concessions that compromise accessibility, with significant impacts on spatial and environmental justice. As highlighted by Pica [14], the Comitato Mare Libero, Pulito e Gratuito Napoli (Committee Free, Clean and For-Free Sea Naples) has activated a network of civic mobilisations which, through mapping practices, legal actions, and collective activism, has reclaimed the right to the sea as a fundamental right, advocating for the inclusion of the coastline within the emerging legal category of commons [14]. In this perspective, treating the coast as a commons represents a cultural and political challenge aimed at reactivating the relationship between spaces, rights, and citizenship. As Lucarelli [15] argues, recognising the social function of the maritime public domain could restore the sea to a public and participatory dimension, freeing it from the market logics that have fragmented access. The experience of the Comitato Mare Libero Napoli shows how collective care, understood as a transformative action and a process of building ties, can redefine the deep meaning of coastal space, turning it into a social infrastructure capable of generating shared value [16]. However, this implies the need to experiment with new forms of collaborative governance. In recent years, Living Labs (LLs) have emerged as experimental spaces capable of enabling urban innovation processes through collaborative approaches, becoming key tools to foster social and environmental transitions, often positioning themselves as operational alternatives to traditional urban governance models, activating reflective and transformative practices [17, 18]. LLs, in this context, emerge as protected environments for experimentation, sociotechnical niches where alternative solutions can be tested, co-created, and potentially transferred into mainstream governance, through a process analogous to the Multi-Level Perspective on socio-technical transitions [19, 20]. Originally developed within the field of computer science [21], the concept of Living Lab has rapidly expanded into social and urban domains. From platforms for technological testing, LLs have evolved into territorial co-creation contexts, where inhabitants are no longer mere users but become actively engaged actors in transformation processes [22, 23]. This evolution reflects a shift from a technology-centred innovation approach towards a social and territorial approach, recognising everyday life, cultural significance of places, and actor plurality as key resources for urban innovation [24, 25]. Urban Living Labs (ULLs) therefore operate as collective learning spaces in urban contexts, where practices of co-design, incremental experimentation, and the production of new urban narratives coexist [26–28].

This contribution presents the methodological approach and the results of the first phase of work dedicated to defining the thematic and operational choices of the PS-U-GO Urban Living Lab Naples – Towards a free and accessible sea (PS-U-GO ULL Naples), conducted from February to October 2025 as part of the Erasmus+ project PS-U-GO – Education in Living Labs: Participatory Skills for Sustainable Urban GovernanceOF.[1] The PS-U-GO project, spanning three years (January 2024 – December 2026), aims to implement four Urban Living Labs as experimental educational spaces, where actors from the quadruple helix – businesses, research, public institutions, and civil society – are involved in processes of self-definition, co-design, and testing of ideas and solutions to address the most pressing urban challenges. The four ULLs are being developed in the European cities of Cottbus (Germany), Naples, Palermo (Italy), and Nicosia (Cyprus) (Fig. 1). The objective of the PS-U-GO project, in its international dimension, is twofold:

---

[1] Information on the project can be found at the following link: https://www.psugo.eu/, The project partnership is composed of academic partners (University of Cyprus, University of Cottbus BTU), research organisations (CNR), Third Sector organisations (SFIUS, Urban Foxes, PUSH) and AESOP; the Neapolitan unit is coordinated by Stefania Ragozino (CNR-IRISS).

on the one hand, to promote the active participation of local communities towards a sustainable and innovative urban governance; on the other, to provide students and other actors involved with advanced tools and skills in the field of civic participation, through innovative educational models based on non-formal learning, tested in real and complex contexts.

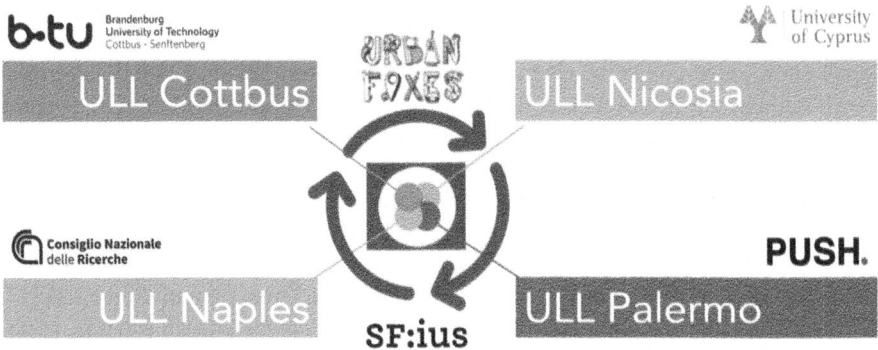

Fig. 1. The four ULL system of the PS-U-GO project

In the specific case of Naples, the ULL1F^2 is conceived as an instrument of social innovation aimed at the re-appropriation, democratisation, and restitution of the sea to the city, through the experimentation of a collective management model of urban commons applied to the liminal areas of access to the sea and through a collaborative pathway fostering knowledge co-construction, civic participation, and collective action. This learning module, inspired by the *learning with political movements* approach [29], is part of a broader system of collaborations and international projects that bring together the world of research and activism in the city of Naples, moving forward towards horizons of mutual learning.

The paper presents the case study of sea accessibility in the city of Naples, positioning the Comitato Mare Libero Napoli within the broader Italian and Neapolitan context. It then details the research methodology underpinning the project and guiding the first phase of the PS-U-GO ULL Naples, the "Theme Choice" phase. The paper concludes with the presentation and discussion of the results.

---

^{2} The ULL builds on the ongoing action-research process promoted by CNR IRISS in collaboration with Lido Pola – Bene Comune (2021 – ongoing), aimed at activating urban regeneration processes in the Bagnoli district, as well as on the activities of the Comitato Mare Libero, Pulito e Gratuito di Napoli, and the AESOP International Conference "Urban Conflicts and Peace: Everyday Politics of Commons", co-organised by CNR IRISS and hosted by DiARC and Lido Pola – Bene Comune in 2023. The ULL is supported, in its educational dimension, by the Evaluab - Evaluation Laboratory of the DiARC, University Federico II of Naples.

2   The Case Study of the Neapolitan Coast

"Il mare non bagna Napoli"2F,[3] the title of the renowned 1953 book by Anna Maria Ortese [30], today stands as an illuminated installation atop the MADRE museum, created by artists Bianco-Valente, and continues to resonate as a powerful monito regarding the city's urban condition. This paradox aptly describes the progressive physical and symbolic separation between Naples and its sea. The city's morphology, shaped by unplanned urban growth and a longstanding orientation towards industrial and port development, has contributed to reinforcing this fracture. The historic centre, which for centuries had developed in close relationship with the waterfront, has been progressively saturated by port infrastructures, shipyards, commercial docks, and logistical areas, transforming the coastline into a technical and functional space, removed from public use.

The same process affected both the eastern and western peripheries: from San Giovanni a Teduccio to Bagnoli, areas once characterised by a direct and daily relationship with the sea have been reconfigured as industrial or residual spaces, now in states of degradation and marked by denied and fragmented access. In parallel, the most scenic coastal stretches, such as those of Posillipo, have been progressively privatised through the development of exclusive residential parks, private beaches, and concessions for hospitality and tourism purposes. This process has turned cliffs, coves, and historical access points into closed, filtered spaces, very often inaccessible to the general public, drastically reducing the availability of free public beaches [14].

The combination of uncontrolled urban growth, coastal industrialisation, and widespread privatisation has resulted in a severe restriction of accessibility and usability of the liminal areas between the city and the sea. The collective right to the landscape, bathing, and relationship with the sea has been reduced to a privilege, denying much of the population the natural proximity that for centuries had defined both the material and immaterial identity of Naples. These dynamics are deeply intertwined with issues of socio-economic status, racial segregation, and climate justice, and reveal how, through illegal actions and exclusionary regulations, the coastline can be transformed from "a strip of nature" into a palimpsest of greed, racism, ecological neglect, and socio-economic discrimination [13].

In 2011–2012, the civic campaign "Una Spiaggia per Tutti" (A Beach for All) promoted a proposal for a popular consultative referendum to establish the "Great Public Beach of Naples in Bagnoli". The proposal was signed by 15,000 citizens and subsequently approved, but then forgotten by the Municipality of Naples. Since 2020, mobilisations for a free, clean, and accessible sea have spontaneously resumed from east to west of the city, in response to the closure of four public beaches by municipal ordinances, starting with the Gaiola Marine Protected Area (AMP Gaiola). The movement "Mare Libero, Pulito e Gratuito Napoli" emerged spontaneously, from the convergence of small, fragmented struggles and the legacy of the historic committee "Una Spiaggia per Tutti". From 2020 onwards, in the context of the Covid-19 pandemic and the resulting emergency management policies, public administrations and private organisations implemented measures to restrict access to both private and public spaces. While such measures were necessary to contain the spread of infections, they were maintained even

---

[3] The Sea Does Not Bathe Naples.

after the end of the pandemic, effectively resulting in privatisation or quasi-private management of public and inalienable spaces that were meant for free public use. Restrictions on access to the sea, beaches, parks, and public gardens generated widespread discontent and frustration among the population, who experienced the erosion of fundamental rights linked to individual and collective psycho-physical well-being. The reservation and access-limitation model for beaches was first adopted by the C.S.I. Gaiola Onlus Association, which manages the Gaiola Marine Protected Area (Natura 2000 Network). This model was then adopted by the Municipality of Naples for the two main public beaches in the city centre: Baia Donn'Anna and Spiaggia delle Monache. From 2021 to 2025, the "Mare Libero, Pulito e Gratuito Napoli" Committee organised dozens of protests to denounce the inadequacy and discriminatory principles of the reservation system. Under this system, the municipality delegated management to private beach concession holders, who developed a digital app allowing only two booking slots: one from 10:00 to 13:00, and another from 14:00 to 17:00. By design, the system excluded both minors and elderly people, due to the technological barrier imposed by digital booking. Over the years, with the support of Co.Na.Ma.L. (National Free Sea Committee), the Neapolitan group filed five legal appeals to the Seventh Section of the Campania Regional Administrative Court; three were won, while two remain pending. It is crucial to note that the Neapolitan committee could pursue these legal actions solely thanks to contributions from thousands of Neapolitan citizens: all court costs were covered through crowdfunding, raising around €30,000 over three years, with each appeal costing over €5,000. Despite the rulings in favour of citizens, the Municipality of Naples and the Port Authority have continued to ignore court injunctions, persisting with reservation systems and access restrictions on the aforementioned public beaches. To date, the committee's achievements include over 50 public mobilisations; 5 legal appeals filed, of which 3 were won; €30,000 raised in donations to cover legal expenses; 4 documentaries broadcast on European public television.

The PS-U-GO ULL Naples community aligns with and integrates into this stream of civic mobilisation and advocacy, forming a close relationship between three main groups of actors, operationally involved across the various methodological phases (Fig. 2): the technical-organisational committee, composed of researchers from CNR IRISS, the Evaluab team at DiARC, and activists from Lido Pola – Bene Comune; the Labor-actors with 15 participants selected via an open call, including university students, recent graduates, post-doc researchers, and professionals from various disciplines (urban planning, architecture, sociology, law, journalism, and psychology); the activist community of the "Mare Libero Napoli" Committee, involved in reclaiming sea access as a commons.

Fig. 2. The core working team of the PS-U-GO ULL Naples.

3 Methodology

The methodology common to the four ULLs of the PS-U-GO project is presented below, followed by the methodological approach developed for the PS-U-GO ULL Naples.

3.1 The PS-U-GO Methodology

The methodology developed for the four Urban Living Labs (ULLs) in Nicosia, Palermo, Naples, and Cottbus is the result of a careful process of analysing existing practices, systematising past experiences, and adapting them to the specific educational and participatory aims of the PS-U-GO project3F.[4] The methodology is founded on four key principles that define the identity of the project's ULLs:

1. *Real-world context*: each ULL is rooted in a specific and real urban context, addressing actual territorial challenges.
2. *Inclusive participation and co-creation*: active involvement of all stakeholders following the quadruple helix model (public, private, research, civic).
3. *Experimentation and evolution*: adoption of an iterative approach, based on cycles of experimentation, evaluation, and continuous learning.
4. *Sustainability and impact*: orientation towards producing concrete and lasting change, both in urban practices and in participants' capacities.

This methodology integrates the learn-make-show approach proposed by project partner Urban Foxes, and was designed to be flexible and adaptable to different local contexts while maintaining a common reference framework. The process is structured into three main steps, developed through a cyclical and iterative approach.

Design and Initiation. In this initial step, preceding the activation of the ULLs, the project team defined the mission, objectives, and expected impacts for each ULL to be developed. In this perspective, an initial "blueprint" was created — flexible and adaptable

---

[4] The partnership produced the deliverable 'Urban Living Labs Methodologies' available at the following link: https://www.psugo.eu/portfolio-item/urban-living-labs-methodologies-del iverable-5/

— intended to guide the activities. A mapping of local needs, with particular attention to young people as the primary target group, enabled the launch of stakeholder engagement strategies within each territory.

Operation. This step pertains to the implementation of a shared yet flexible methodology across the four ULLs. This structure allowed the development of comparable processes, despite significant differences in local-scale specific objectives and expected impacts. The methodology comprises four operational steps (Fig. 3):

– Theme Choice: participatory identification of work themes, giving priority to listening to the emerging priorities from the territory.
– Exploration: urban laboratories, masterclasses, on-site explorations, and co-analysis sessions with external experts to deepen the chosen theme.
– Experimentation and Co-Creation: co-design, prototyping, and testing innovative solutions and practices through collaborative activities with the community and other stakeholders.
– Urban Showcase: public presentation of the processes and outcomes through open events, exhibitions, or other creative and accessible formats.

Fig. 3. The methodology of PS-U-GO ULLs.

Evaluation and Feedback. Within the international project team, a systematic method was defined for collecting both qualitative and quantitative feedback from participants and stakeholders. This step is to be considered transversal to the Operational phase, enabling critical analyses of processes and outcomes from a comparative perspective, thus contributing to the consolidation of learning for continuous improvement, scalability, and transferability of the practices.

3.2 The PS-U-GO ULL Naples Approach

Within the context of the city of Naples, the PS-U-GO ULL Naples has been conceived as an essential device to enable local capabilities [31, 32], by valuing often invisible resources and fostering spaces of trust between citizens, institutions, and the research community [33]. The methodology adopted by the PS-U-GO ULL Naples reflects a vision whereby the territory is not merely the location of intervention, but the very engine of transformation, activated through inclusive participatory pathways sensitive to social, cultural, and economic diversity. Particular emphasis is placed on engagement methods and tools to support collaborative decision-making processes. In this perspective, the Action Research approach [34, 35] is employed to structure continuous cycles of exploration, intervention, and critical reflection, supporting dynamic, adaptive, and mutual learning. In line with these premises, the ULL of Naples promotes several core principles tailored to its specific context:

- Right to research: within reflections on globalisation, this principle refers to guaranteeing, as a fundamental human right, the opportunity for each individual to systematically enhance their knowledge and, more broadly, to actively participate in shaping the future [36].
- Right to the city: this concept goes beyond the mere demand for fundamental needs; it represents a specific quality of urban life, encompassing access to urban resources and the possibility of experiencing a form of urban living alternative to the logics of capitalism and industrialization [37].
- Everyday life: recognising and critically examining the routines and institutions of daily life that have a real impact on urban regeneration practices and urban resistance movements [38, 39].
- Frugality: in the context of co-production, this implies developing effective solutions by valuing local resources and community knowledge, rather than relying on large-scale, long-term solutions often tied to major investments and characterised by limited participation [40].
- Culturality: acknowledging local narratives and place identities as cultural resources and components of a dynamic process involving both individuals and the wider community. This is fundamental for identifying community values and promoting cultural transformation through the formalisation of new shared norms [41].
- Plurality: adopting differentiated approaches in line with the concept of socionatures, to capture the social, cultural, and natural complexity of territories [42].
- Mutual and informal learning: fostering co-creation processes based on continuous, horizontal sharing of experiences and knowledge.
- Transformative social innovation: experimenting with models of participatory and inclusive governance, as well as technological solutions, by promoting deep change processes emerging from the co-evolutionary interaction of factors and narratives towards systemic innovations [43].

The PS-U-GO ULL Naples is therefore based on the idea that stakeholder engagement and the construction of shared visions are indispensable components for activating transformative social innovation processes. To this end, during the Theme Choice phase—the focus of this document—the laboratory adopted a combination of operational tools designed both to facilitate the active engagement of communities and stakeholders and to support the co-creation of future scenarios.

The activities were developed through a progressive cycle of participatory meetings, involving different groups of actors alongside numerous stakeholders and external experts connected to the issue of sea accessibility. Every week, the working group convened for laboratory workshops, seminars, masterclasses, and public assemblies. Each meeting focused on the analysis of specific themes and employed collaborative engagement tools aimed at building a shared knowledge base and initiating the definition of the manifesto's key elements. Specifically, four main stages were structured, during which the Labor-actors and the various actors engaged in dialogue on four key issues deemed fundamental for drafting the manifesto: Shared Values, Preliminary Objectives, Common Problems, and Stakeholder Mapping.

The participatory process was supported by a variety of tools inspired by the principles of "gamestorming" [44], which foster collective creativity, visual communication, and spontaneous interaction among participants. The use of visual artefacts (post-its, canvases, conceptual maps), collaborative workspaces (MIRO, physical workspaces), and the adoption of a simplified visual language facilitated the emergence of ideas, their collaborative reorganisation, and their subsequent translation into operational strategies.

The methodological process adopted for the PS-U-GO ULL Naples is grounded in the adaptation of Value-Focused Thinking (VFT), traditionally developed for systemic decision support [45, 46], to the dynamic complexity of participatory urban governance. Following the latest insights on the operational integration of value-based decision processes, the PS-U-GO ULL Naples interpreted VFT not merely as a decision support tool but as the overarching architecture of the collaborative process. In particular, the VFT methodology [47] was reinterpreted and articulated according to the PS-U-GO methodological structure. The following section describes the four phases of the ULL, with a specific focus on the Theme Choice phase, which concluded in April 2025 (Fig. 4).

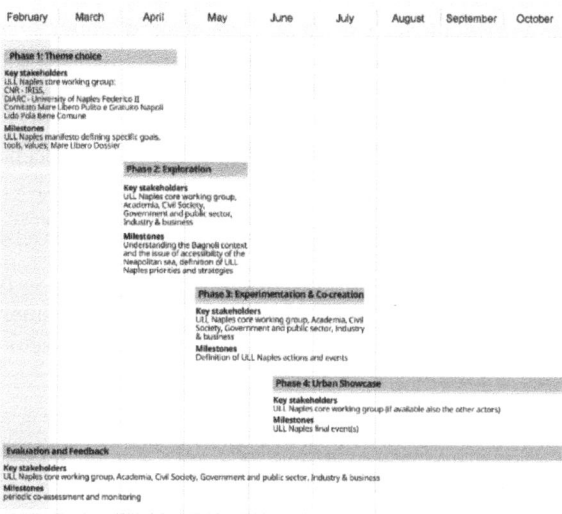

Fig. 4. The PS-U-GO ULL Naples roadmap

Theme Choice – Shared Construction of Objectives. In this initial phase, VFT was used to launch the process, corresponding to the Front-End, which focuses on clarifying the problem situation and establishing the value base of the process, thereby fostering the emergence of shared values. Specifically, the Theme Choice phase was structured around four main activities, which, through a recursive process, led to the drafting of the ULL's Manifesto: (1) building a set of Shared Values; (2) defining Preliminary Objectives aligned with the group's capacities and ambitions; (3) identifying Common Problems relevant to urban commons governance in Naples; and (4) mapping the Quadruple Helix Stakeholders to be engaged according to objectives and issues.

Shared Values. This activity was developed through a participatory approach, based on administering a questionnaire to all members of the Technical-Organisational Committee, the Laborattori, and the activist community of Mare Libero Napoli, during the ULL's first meeting. The activity was structured as follows:

– Initial value set: the questionnaire presented a list of 38 value concepts, derived from a qualitative analysis of the motivation letters submitted by Laborattori during the application phase.
– Individual selection: each participant was asked to select five values that best represented their motivation and personal vision.
– Narrative space: after completing the questionnaire, an open assembly session was held, during which each participant could briefly explain the meaning they attributed to the chosen values, fostering an autobiographical narrative dimension.

Preliminary Objectives. The methodology adopted to define the Preliminary Objectives involved the creation of three working tables, each composed of members of the Technical-Organisational Committee (acting as facilitators), the Laborattori, and the Mare Libero Napoli activists (Fig. 5). Each table followed a facilitated process structured in five main steps:

– Selection of guiding values. In an initial session, groups were asked to identify the main values to use as a reference when formulating objectives. Structured brainstorming. Participants freely expressed ideas and aspirations regarding what the laboratory should achieve, using the selected values as a compass.
– Clustering and synthesis. The ideas were collected, grouped by thematic similarity, and systematised into priority intervention areas.
– Formulation of General and Specific Objectives. For each thematic area, the following were defined: A General Objective that translates the shared value into a broad goal; Several Specific Objectives, more operational in nature, representing intermediate steps necessary to achieve the general objective.
– Validation and prioritisation. The objectives were discussed and validated in plenary through debate, with initial prioritisation based on relevance and feasibility, in relation to available resources, competences, and the temporal horizon of the ULL.

Common Problems. The methodology adopted to identify Common Problems relating to the governance of urban commons followed a sequence inspired by collaborative

Fig. 5. Working tables for the definition of Preliminary Objectives

problem structuring and causal analysis tools. The activity was carried out through three working tables and structured in four main phases:

- Problem brainstorming. During facilitated sessions, the Laborattori, Technical-Organisational Committee, Mare Libero activists, and other relevant actors (including researchers and activists from the Naples Commons Network) were invited to identify perceived problems in urban commons governance and record them using visual supports (post-its, MIRO boards).
- Discussion and comparison of emerging problems. Problems were presented and discussed by participants at each table to clarify meanings, highlight differing perspectives, identify redundancies or overlaps, and map interrelations between issues.
- Selection and prioritisation of Fundamental Problems. Through a structured discussion, the identified problems were ranked by systemic impact, urgency, and relevance, and then grouped into Fundamental Problems, i.e., structural issues synthesising the most critical concerns (e.g. "Disparities in roles for commons management", "Lack of shared governance tools", "Privatisation of coastal access").
- Cause analysis and construction of the Fishbone Diagram. Using the Fishbone Diagram method, the group explored the root causes generating or reinforcing the fundamental problems, grouping them into categories (managerial, regulatory, economic, political, cultural). This provided a visual mapping of the links between systemic issues and underlying causes, creating a collective tool to guide the design of future actions.

Stakeholder Mapping. The stakeholder mapping process for ULL Naples followed an iterative and participatory approach, aimed at identifying, analysing, and positioning key actors according to their interest and influence, to guide engagement and collaboration strategies for the subsequent phases of the ULL:

- Framing the reference structure. The Laborattori, the Technical-Organisational Committee, and DIARC researchers defined the four sectors of the quadruple helix:

Research and innovation: universities, research centres, study groups; Public institutions: local authorities, public agencies, maritime authorities; Private sector: economic actors, maritime concessionaires, entrepreneurs; Civil society: associations, citizen committees, informal groups.

– Identification of priority stakeholders. Through a series of facilitated thematic tables, each group worked on one of the four sectors, identifying: Existing, already active stakeholders relevant to the issue of sea access; Potential stakeholders to be involved or engaged.

– Relevance and influence analysis. Stakeholders were placed on Cartesian grids using two main criteria: Their capacity to influence the achievement of ULL objectives; Their interest in themes related to the access, management, and enhancement of the sea as a common good.

– Development of descriptive profiles. For each priority actor, a descriptive profile was produced, summarising: Their institutional or organisational role; Their current and potential relevance to the ULL objectives; Their preferred engagement modalities (e.g., workshops, interviews, operational collaborations, advocacy).

Exploration – Investigation and Scenario Building. During the Exploration phase, the VFT approach will be enhanced through a combination of collaborative mapping methods, stakeholder engagement on spatial issues, and situated field reflections (urban walkshops, masterclasses). This phase aims to deepen the understanding of the territories and relevant actors to the identified objectives, translating the value framework into initial hypotheses for action and potential transformation scenarios. The construction of causal networks linking problems and objectives, typical of the VFT approach (means-ends networks), is here reinterpreted as a tool for shared exploration of urban complexity.

Experimentation and Co-Creation – Testing Shared Solutions. In the Experimentation phase, the VFT model evolves further by integrating co-design and co-creation moments for activities and operational tools. Building upon the objectives and criticalities explored, participants will be called upon to co-design solutions that, through incremental and iterative processes of feedback and adaptation, aim to develop practices of re-appropriation and civic use of the sea resource. In this phase, as indicated by Keeney [45, 46], the Back-End component of the VFT—dedicated to evaluating alternatives and action strategies—is reinterpreted in a collective and participatory manner.

A distinctive element of the methodology applied is the continuous integration of evaluation and feedback cycles, designed to foster reflective learning and ensure the adaptability and scalability of the practices developed. The iterative VFT-ULL approach thus enables not only the structuring of a collaborative decision-making process but also the consolidation of local capacities and the promotion of transformative social innovation.

4 Preliminary Results

The Theme Choice phase of the Naples Urban Living Lab (ULL) was dedicated to the shared definition of the PS-U-GO ULL Naples Manifesto, a foundational document aimed at clarifying the role, objectives, and modes of action of this temporary community.

The construction of a shared value set represented one of the first and most significant outputs of the PS-U-GO ULL Naples methodological process. This activity aimed to create a common base of ideal and cultural references capable of guiding the entire laboratory process, reinforcing the participants' sense of belonging to the temporary community and making explicit the guiding principles of collective action.

This activity pursued three main objectives: to foster mutual understanding among participants through the language of values; to elicit and systematise the values considered a priority by each actor involved; to build a shared framework to serve as a reference for defining the objectives and operational strategies of PS-U-GO ULL Naples. In this sense, the collective restitution and processing of the questionnaire results followed two main directions: through the sharing of values, participants articulated the personal meanings they attributed to the selected concepts, which were essential for enabling moments of exchange and discussion during the laboratory sessions; through a frequency analysis, the most recurring values within the group were identified, allowing convergences and affinities to emerge. Through this process, a shared value set was constructed, reflecting: attention to the collective dimension and the value of care (care for the territory, relationships, resources); recognition of active participation as a founding principle of citizenship; the importance of social and environmental justice; the promotion of solidarity, collective responsibility, and the autonomy of local communities. The shared value set, in addition to representing a common symbolic and operational asset capable of linking participants from diverse backgrounds, competences, and visions, played a fundamental role in guiding the construction of the preliminary objectives of the laboratory during the Theme Choice phase, as well as in shaping the methodological and operational decisions to be implemented in the Exploration and Co-Design phases. Moreover, the process of eliciting values consolidated the community dimension of the ULL, strengthening the sense of co-responsibility towards future objectives and facilitating a more fluid and conscious collective work in the subsequent phases. The definition of the Preliminary Objectives represented a pivotal stage in the process of drafting the ULL Naples Manifesto, setting the direction for the subsequent development of exploration and co-creation activities. The main aim of this phase was to translate the shared value set that emerged in the first meeting into preliminary objectives that could transcend and connect the laboratory's dual souls: the academic side (research and experimentation) and the operational side (activism and civic action). Furthermore, this action served as an initial framework for defining the ULL's priorities for action.

The process led to the definition of a structured set of Preliminary Objectives and Sub-Objectives for the ULL, which clearly synthesised the pact between the academic community and civic activism. This initial operational framework proved fundamental for shaping the narrative structure that underpinned the final drafting of the ULL Naples Manifesto. This approach also strengthened the collaborative and reflective dimension of the laboratory, promoting not only the construction of shared objectives but also the co-production of meaning among the different actors involved.

In the process of drafting the PS-U-GO ULL Naples Manifesto, the phase dedicated to identifying Common Problems played a central role. This activity was necessary to critically analyse the legal, administrative, and operational context related to the management of urban commons. The shared identification of issues allowed different perspectives to emerge, valuing each actor's situated experience, intending to anchor the definition of objectives to a concrete understanding of existing constraints and create a collective knowledge base useful for the subsequent design of strategies and actions for change. The application of this methodology helped produce a shared and layered framework of the main challenges that the management of the sea as a commons might face. Moreover, the process fostered an important collateral outcome: the construction of mutual trust among actors with different backgrounds and experiences, thanks to the open sharing of criticalities and the opportunity to recognise common problems from diverse perspectives.

Within the methodological framework aimed at drafting the ULL Naples Manifesto, stakeholder mapping represented a key step for consolidating the network of actors involved—and to be involved—in defining strategies oriented towards achieving the laboratory's objectives. This activity drew inspiration from the quadruple helix model—research, public institutions, private sector, and civil society. Accordingly, four thematic tables were structured, one for each sector, with each table also reflecting on integrating a fifth dimension linked to the sea as a thematic and natural actor, whose perspectives would later be explored during the Exploration and Co-Design phases.

The main goals of stakeholder mapping are focused on: identifying actors relevant to the ULL's preliminary objectives; analysing the interest and influence power of different actors relative to those objectives; supporting the design of targeted engagement strategies specific to each actor; strengthening the laboratory's capacity to operate from a systemic and inclusive perspective.

This analysis allowed for the classification of actors as: key actors (high influence, high interest); actors to engage (low influence, high interest); actors to monitor (high influence, low interest); secondary actors (low influence, low interest). The mapping produced: a systemic and updated overview of the actor ecosystem operating in or influencing sea access in Naples; the identification of potential strategic alliances and stakeholders to proactively involve in the subsequent Exploration and Co-Creation phases; the creation of an operational database useful for designing future engagement and collaborative governance activities. Additionally, the mapping facilitated a broader reflection on the need to integrate multi-actor and multi-level approaches, acknowledging the complexity of institutional, economic, and social balances characterising the governance of urban coastal resources.

These activities found an initial synthesis in the National CONAMAL Conference (March 2025), held at the Ex Asilo Filangieri common space. On this occasion, the PS-U-GO ULL Naples promoted a collaborative mapping experiment, administering a questionnaire to actors and participants aimed at exploring perceptions and priorities on the issue of sea access. The conference was followed by an international Training Event4F[5] with the PS-U-GO project partners, during which: the subsequent Exploration phase of the ULL Naples was formally launched; the ULL Manifesto was presented, drafted by the Laborattori based on the knowledge and experiences developed throughout the Theme Choice process.

---

[5] The Training Event 2 Naples was co-organised by the PS-U-GO ULL Naples Organizing Committee and the Croatian partner SF:ius and hosted by the Department of Architecture, University Federico II of Naples.

5   The PS-U-GO ULL Naples Manifesto

The Theme Choice phase, characterised by a collaborative and reflective approach, led to the definition of the PS-U-GO ULL Naples Manifesto, a document that establishes the ULL as a temporary community sharing values, objectives, and modes of action. The Manifesto emerged from the need to give voice to the plurality of actors involved—not only to define common objectives but also as a tool to build, through dialogue and co-production, a shared identity. Specifically, it defines the identity, vision, mission, shared values, operational objectives, involved actors, and methodological tools adopted by the laboratory. This moment marks the starting point for organising the next phases of the presented methodology. In response to the question "Who are we?", the Manifesto describes the group as a heterogeneous network composed of researchers from the IRISS Institute of the CNR, lecturers from the DIARC Department of the University of Naples, students from various faculties, alongside activists from the Neapolitan Commons Network and the Mare Libero, Pulito e Gratuito civic movement. The group was established as an experiment in hybridisation between informal groups, associations, research bodies, and educational institutions, to explore and promote practices of regeneration in situ to increase the accessibility and usability of common goods, particularly the sea, the liminal coastal areas, and the urban spaces connected to them. The group's vision centres on a long-term strategic goal: the formal and substantive recognition of Naples' liminal coastal areas as commons. In this perspective, the collective enjoyment of the sea and its urban interfaces is recognised as a right to be claimed and protected. The mission translates into an operational commitment to building an enabling environment for the production of shared knowledge, through a collaborative, experimental process based on mutual learning and action research. The ultimate goal is to produce evidence capable of supporting and legitimising civic claims regarding the collective use of these spaces. The guiding principles underpinning the laboratory's work reflect those of the commons network and the free sea movement: non-discrimination, mutualism, solidarity, care, self-determination, and community protagonism. The organisational and relational model is based on a horizontal and inclusive approach, rejecting hierarchical logics and promoting active participation. The laboratory pursues a set of concrete objectives: to generate shared knowledge that increases the critical awareness of individuals and groups, encouraging actions for civic protection and mobilisation; to promote relationships based on reciprocity and care for natural resources and people; to encourage direct participation in decision-making processes, moving beyond mere consultation to build truly collaborative practices; to defend and expand the accessibility and usability of common goods, conceived as key elements for an ecological reconnection between nature and the city.

The PS-U-GO ULL Naples's work targets a heterogeneous and diverse audience of actors, involved at various levels in the management and use of public and private assets located in the liminal coastal areas. The group aims to engage, in a synergistic, horizontal, and collaborative way, the multiplicity of actors and entities belonging to the quintuple helix (research, civil society, public institutions, business, and natural resources), to promote the protection and extension of access to the sea and common goods. The group also identifies with a shared methodology, based on engagement tools and techniques that facilitate inclusion and collaboration. The initial phase adopted the Value-Focused

Thinking method, alongside structured discussion tools (brainstorming, causal analysis, visual classification, stakeholder mapping). The Naples Urban Living Lab is expanding its repertoire of engagement tools for the next exploration and co-design phases. These aim to activate collaborative methods capable of stimulating shared reflections and generating collective visions. Among these: Participatory mapping, to visualise socio-territorial relationships and criticalities; Co-design workshops, to foster the integration of expert knowledge and local insights; Walkscapes and urban explorations, as immersive practices in the places under study; Visual and interactive tools (posters, canvases, toolkits, maps), supported by digital platforms, to facilitate communication and collective reflection.

Acknowledgments. This study was funded by the Erasmus+ project PS-U-GO - Education in Living Labs: Participatory Skills for sustainable Urban Governance (ID KA220-HED-FB48E1DA). In the unity of the work, SC, SR and MC conceived the work, SC developed the methodology, SC, SR, LL, FM drafted the manuscript, and SR and MC coordinated the activities and revised the final version.

References

1. Manzini, E.: Politiche Del Quotidiano. Progetti Di Vita Che Cambiano Il Mondo. Edizioni di Comunità (2018)
2. Viderman, T., Knierbein, S.: Affective urbanism: towards inclusive design praxis. Urban Des. Int. **25**, 53–62 (2020). https://doi.org/10.1057/s41289-019-00105-6
3. Ragozino, S., De Vita, G.E., Oppido, S.: «Normality was the problem!» Femminismi e Commoning Nella Riproduzione Sociale Della Città. CRIOS. **24**, 74–81 (2024)
4. Katsikana, M.: Gender in resistance. In: A Fem. Urban Theory our Time, pp. 92–114. Wiley (2021). https://doi.org/10.1002/9781119789161.ch4
5. Velicu, I., García-López, G.: Thinking the Commons through Ostrom and Butler: boundedness and vulnerability. Theory Cult. Soc. **35**, 55–73 (2018). https://doi.org/10.1177/0263276418757315
6. Stavrides, S.: Common Space: The City as Commons. Zed Books, London (2016)
7. Ostrom, E.: Governing the Commons. The Evolutions of Institutions for Collective Actions. Cambridge University Press (1990)
8. Borch, C., Kornberger, M.: Urban Commons. Rethinking the City. Routledge, London/New York (2015)
9. Sciarelli, R.: Caring and commoning in political society: insights from the Scugnizzo Liberato of Naples. Urban Stud. **61**, 1738–1755 (2024). https://doi.org/10.1177/00420980231217375
10. Capone, N.: Dispositivi Giuridici per La Città Pubblica e l'uso Comune Dello Spazio Pubblico. L'esperienza Napoletana Dei Beni Comuni. In: Perrone, C., Masiani, B., Tosi, F. (eds.) Una Geografia delle politiche urbane tra possesso e governo. Sfide e opportunità nella transizione. Urban@it - Centro nazionale di studi per le politiche urbane (2021)
11. Micciarelli, G.: Commoning: Beni Comuni Urbani Come Nuove Istituzioni: Materiali per Una Teoria Dell'autorganizzazione. Editoriale scientifica. (2018) ISBN 8893913623
12. Vittoria, M.P., Ragozino, S., Esposito De Vita, G.: Urban commons between Ostrom's and neo-materialist approaches: the case of lido Pola in Naples, Southern Italy. Land. **12** (2023). https://doi.org/10.3390/land12030524
13. Low, S.: Beach Politics: Social, Racial, and Environmental Injustice on the Shoreline. NYU Press (2025) ISBN 1479821969

14. Pica, K.: Opening the gate to bathers' rights. Community-led process for the coast as a commons. Contesti. Città, Territ. Progett., 170–191 (2024). https://doi.org/10.36253/contest-15663
15. Russo, M.: La Bonifica Come Infrastruttura. Progetto Urbanistico e Pratiche Di Risanamento Ambientale: Il Caso Di Bagnoli. In: Lucarelli, M. (ed.) Siti industriali dismessi: il governo delle bonifiche, pp. 94–114. Centro Regionale di Competenza analisi e Monitoraggio del Rischio Ambientale (2006) ISBN 9788889972038
16. Belingardi, C.: Comunanza Urbane. Autogestione e Cura Dei Luoghi. University of Florence (2014)
17. Sabel, C.F., Zeitlin, J.: Experimentalist governance. In: The Oxford Handbook of Governance. Oxford University Press (2012)
18. Torkkeli, K., Karvonen, M., Pritup, D., Enqvist, J.: 'It benefits every moment': understandings of and engagements in science-related practices in everyday life. Public Underst. Sci. (2025). https://doi.org/10.1177/09636625241309055
19. Bourdieu, P.: Il Senso Pratico. Armando Editore, Rome (2021) ISBN 886677328X
20. Savini, F., Bertolini, L.: Urban experimentation as a politics of niches. Environ. Plan. A Econ. Sp. **51**, 831–848 (2019)
21. Markopoulos, P.; Rauterberg, M. Livinglab: A White Paper; 2001;
22. Franz, Y.: Designing social living labs in urban research. Info. **17**, 53–66 (2015). https://doi.org/10.1108/info-01-2015-0008
23. Edwards-Schachter, M.E., Matti, C.E., Alcántara, E.: Fostering quality of life through social innovation: a living lab methodology study case. Rev. Policy Res. **29**, 672–692 (2012). https://doi.org/10.1111/j.1541-1338.2012.00588.x
24. Cognetti, F., Maranghi, E.: Adapting the Living Lab Methodology: The Prefix 'Co' as an Empowerment Tool for Urban Regeneration in Large-Scale Social-Housing Estates Urban Book Series, pp. 69–82. Springer Science and Business Media Deutschland GmbH (2023)
25. Ostanel, E.: Spazi Fuori Dal Comune: Rigenerare, Includere, Innovare. FrancoAngeli, Milano (2018) ISBN 8891765120
26. Cerreta, M., Panaro, S.: Collaborative decision-making processes for local innovation: the CoULL methodology in living labs approach. In: Amenta, L., Russo, M., van Timmeren, A. (eds.) Regenerative Territories. GeoJournal Library, vol. 128. Springer, Cham (2022). https://doi.org/10.1007/978-3-030-78536-9_12
27. Cerreta, M., Elefante, A., La Rocca, L.: A creative living lab for the adaptive reuse of the Morticelli church: the SSMOLL project. Sustain. For. **12**(24), 10561 (2020). https://doi.org/10.3390/su122410561
28. Mazzarella, C., La Rocca, L., Ventre, S., Cerreta, M.: Heritage communities urban living lab (HeCo ULL): a circular methodological approach for co-design through social multi-criteria evaluation. In: Calabrò, F., Madureira, L., Morabito, F.C., Piñeira Mantiñán, M.J. (eds.) Networks, Markets & People. NMP 2024 Lecture Notes in Networks and Systems, vol. 1186. Springer, Cham (2024). https://doi.org/10.1007/978-3-031-74679-6_4
29. Santamarina, A.: Learning with political movements: social reproductive politics as a scholar-activist methodology. Soc. Mov. Stud., 1–17 (2025). https://doi.org/10.1080/14742837.2025.2470248
30. Ortese, A.M., Nozzoli, A.: Il Mare Non Bagna Napoli, vol. 77. Adelphi, Milano (1994) ISBN 8845910547
31. Sen, A.: Commodities and Capabilities. Oxford University Press, Oxford (1985)
32. Nussbaum, M.: Creating Capabilities: The Human Development Approach. Belknap Press: An Imprint of Harvard University (2013) ISBN 8178243296
33. Hinrichs-Krapels, S., Bailey, J., Boulding, H., Duffy, B., Hesketh, R., Kinloch, E., Pollitt, A., Rawlings, S., van Rij, A., Wilkinson, B., et al.: Using policy labs as a process to bring evidence

closer to public policymaking: a guide to one approach. Palgrave Commun. **6** (2020). https://doi.org/10.1057/s41599-020-0453-0

34. Lewin, K.: Action research and minority problems. J. Soc. Issues. **2**, 34–46 (1946). https://doi.org/10.1111/j.1540-4560.1946.tb02295.x

35. Saija, L.: La Ricerca-Azione in Pianificazione Territoriale e Urbanistica. Franco Angeli, Milano (2016) ISBN 9788891710734

36. Appadurai, A.: The future as cultural fact: essays on the global condition. Rass. Ital. Sociol. **14**, 649–650 (2013)

37. Lefebvre, H.: Le Droit à La Ville. L'Homme la société. **6**, 29–35 (1967). https://doi.org/10.3917/pal.110.0039

38. Lefebvre, H.: The Critique of Everyday Life. Verso Books, London/New York (2014) ISBN 1781686505

39. Federici, S.: Reincantare Il Mondo: Femminismo e Politica Dei Commons. Verona, Ombre corte (2021) ISBN 8869481956

40. Concilio, G.: Urban living labs: opportunities in and for planning. In: Human Smart Cities: Rethinking the Interplay between Design and Planning, pp. 21–40. Springer (2016)

41. Magnaghi, A.: Il Progetto Locale. Bollati Boringhieri, Torino (2000)

42. Minervini, D.: Socionature. Percorsi Di Sociologia Dell'ambiente. Morlacchi Editore, Perugia (2024) ISBN 9788893925402

43. Avelino, F., Wittmayer, J.M., Pel, B., Weaver, P., Dumitru, A., Haxeltine, A., Kemp, R., Jørgensen, M.S., Bauler, T., Ruijsink, S., et al.: Transformative social innovation and (dis)empowerment. Technol. Forecast. Soc. Change. **145**, 195–206 (2019). https://doi.org/10.1016/j.techfore.2017.05.002

44. Gray, D., Brown, S., Macanufo, J.: Gamestorming a Playbook for Innovators, Rulebreakers, and Changemakers. Sebastopol, O'REILLY (2010) ISBN 978-0-596-80417-6

45. Keeney, R.L.: Give Yourself a Nudge: Helping Smart People Make Smarter Personal and Business Decisions. Cambridge University Press, Cambridge/London (2020) ISBN 1108715621

46. Keeney, R.L.: Value-Focused Thinking. Harvard University Press, Harvard (2022)

47. Vieira, G.B., de Souza, Y.L., Simões, A., de Almeida, J.A., Belderrain, M.C.N.: Using value-focus thinking in an integrated process to support decisions. Pesqui. Operacional. **44** (2024). https://doi.org/10.1590/0101-7438.2023.043.00276110

A Game-Based Collaborative Decision-Making Approach for Cultural Heritage Reuse

Maria Cerreta[✉], Federica Guglielmi, Ludovica La Rocca, and Sveva Ventre

Department of Architecture (DiARC), Federico II University of Naples, Naples, Italy
{maria.cerreta,ludovica.larocca,sveva.ventre}@unina.it

Abstract. Preserving cultural heritage plays a crucial role in sustaining the identities of communities and individuals while also nurturing belonging, civic participation, and collective memory. This paper explores the application of gamification as a tool for enhancing community engagement in the valorisation of cultural heritage. It addresses the need for innovative strategies to promote active participation and foster a sense of belonging, contributing to sustainable and inclusive development models. The research investigates the potential of gamification to bridge the gap between local communities, cultural heritage sites, and relevant stakeholders on a local level. A methodology for assessing the impact of gamification projects is presented, drawing upon a pilot study focused on the *Colommunity* project in Bacoli, Italy. A *game-based* collaborative decision-making approach has been implemented to encourage the co-exploration and co-management of the Colombario del Fusaro, an ancient Roman funerary site, which is currently completely inaccessible due to the absence of a suitable management plan. The study integrates the gamification approach with the Theory of Change to analyse the relationship between project activities, outputs, outcomes, and resulting social and cultural impacts. The findings highlight the effectiveness of gamification in creating engaging experiences that motivate community involvement in cultural heritage. The research emphasises the importance of co-creation processes that involve local communities, experts, and institutions to ensure the development of valuable and sustainable initiatives. Furthermore, the paper contributes to the ongoing discussion about the long-term impact of gamification in the cultural heritage sector.

Keywords: Archaeology · Faro Convention · Heritage Community · Gamification · Collaborative Decision-making process

1 Introduction

Cultural heritage preservation underpins the recognition of shared values, strengthening ties between people and places and encouraging more inclusive forms of civic engagement. The symbolic and historical value that these cultural resources often manifest represents a heritage of vital importance not only in terms of culture but also in terms of education and strengthening territorial economies, providing a fundamental context for many everyday activities. At the European level, already in 2015, the report *Cultural*

© The Author(s), under exclusive license to Springer Nature Switzerland AG 2026
O. Gervasi et al. (Eds.): ICCSA 2025 Workshops, LNCS 15897, pp. 340–355, 2026.
https://doi.org/10.1007/978-3-031-97660-5_23

Heritage Counts for Europe (CHCfE) [1] recommended in principle 5 of the 5 strategic recommendations to maximise the cross-sectoral impact of cultural heritage by integrating it into all sectoral policies, through participatory governance and by recognising the strategic value of culture for sustainable, inclusive and smart development at the local and regional level.

This approach is also confirmed by the European Agendas for Culture [2], which calls for the identification of guidelines for the management and enhancement of cultural heritage, because it constitutes a shared resource, a common asset and responsibility, and its preservation is a priority for national, regional and local self-governments [3]. Furthermore, the structured involvement of local actors, including civil society, in the management strategies, valorisation and creative and innovative reuse of heritage plays a crucial role in the regeneration processes of urban spaces and socio-cultural processes [3].

The Faro Convention, adopted in 2005 by the Council of Europe, emphasises the importance of cultural heritage as a fundamental resource for the well-being of communities. It introduced a significant change in the way cultural heritage is conceived. The Convention has redefined the role of cultural heritage by emphasising its relational dimension with its community, which means understanding how people interact with and derive meaning from heritage [4]. In this way, culture becomes a strategic investment sector to achieve a sustainable and regenerative heritage development model, to contribute to the building of a peaceful and democratic society. By introducing the concept of the Heritage Community, the Convention brings about a real revolution and redefines the paradigms of heritage conservation. The latter is no longer considered a mere object of contemplation, but an integral part of our collective identity [5], recognising the right of people to enjoy and contribute to its protection.

The continuous threats brought about by the processes of abandonment, deterioration, deconstruction or alteration that attack material cultural heritage, especially when minor and unrecognised, make it a more vulnerable resource due to natural factors as much as human actions [6] among which the lack of appropriate management and valorisation certainly stands out.

These phenomena risk the disappearance of the memory of these sites and the loss of their historical value and cultural identity. As pointed out by Garcia-Fernandez and Medeiros, the fragility of these assets requires new tools for awareness-raising and valorisation, including through innovative languages and technologies. To make this happen, Sacco and Teti [7] stress the importance of investment in Europe as well as in Italy for the promotion of new business models, so that cultural and creative production becomes the dynamic incubator of heritage valorisation [8, 9].

According to the Culture 3.0 framework, integrating emerging sectors like digital media and gaming into cultural production is key to unlocking culture's developmental potential. This also allows the integration of 'new human and artistic skills within the new value creation processes' [7] to overcome a passive protection model and foster a dialogue between past and present.

Artistic and cultural promotion depends first and foremost on the citizenship, which plays a fundamental role as the primary user of cultural resources, thus making it necessary for these resources to become part of citizens' daily lives [10]. Out of a static and detached logic of heritage, innovative approaches such as gamification can be a key tool to make cultural heritage alive and dynamic, stimulating the involvement of local communities and trying to keep up with the socio-cultural changes of the context in which they are inserted, generating new forms of collective value [11]. In this logic, game-based approaches that offer place-based experiments, to attract not only the "educated tourist", but also the non-specialist visitor and primarily residents [10] must be favoured and enabled instead of standardised strategies divorced from contexts.

Several programmes at the European level - such as Horizon 2020 and Creative Europe - have adopted strategies for cultural valorisation through innovation and digitisation. Italy, too, has developed an extended partnership called Cultural Heritage Active Innovation for Sustainable Society (PE5 - CHANGES), which promotes a regenerative approach aimed at responding to contemporary heritage challenges by fostering collaboration between research, enterprises, institutions and citizens.

This contribution is part of one of these research projects, the extended partnership PE5 CHANGES - Cultural Heritage Active Innovation for Sustainable Society - promoted by the PNRR (National Recovery and Resilience Plan), conducted by the Department of Architecture (DiARC) of University of Naples Federico II in the Campi Flegrei area of the Campania region, near Naples.

This region is rich in archaeological, historical, cultural, and natural heritage, attracting significant attention due to frequent archaeological discoveries and ongoing excavations by various international research institutions. The research project focuses on exploring a unique aspect of this "distributed" heritage, emphasising its collective value over individual monuments. This objective moves beyond the traditional concept of "minor heritage"- a term that once referred to less significant or overlooked elements of cultural heritage - by recognising the value of the landscape and its layers of historical sedimentation. It advocates for a broader understanding of heritage that includes not only individual artefacts but also the collective and systemic value of entire territories. This shift challenges the notion of "monuments" as isolated objects of preservation, highlighting instead the importance of the broader cultural and natural context in which they exist [12].

Starting from this context, the research proposes to explore the role of gamification as a tool to stimulate the active involvement of the community in the valorisation of its heritage. Furthermore, the most effective strategies to stimulate a sense of belonging and activate participatory dynamics are investigated to understand how culture and heritage affect collective wellbeing, strengthen social cohesion and promote sustainable and inclusive development models.

The article is structured in different sections exploring the involvement of communities in heritage enhancement through gamification. In Sect. 2, the research methodology will be analysed, focusing on the specific case of a pilot project that the contributors carried out within the PE5 CHANGES project, using gamification as a participation tool; the evaluation approach to measure the project impacts used in the case study will also be analysed. In Sect. 3, the *Colommunity* platform will be analysed in detail, exploring why it came into being, its structure and how it works. The results of the project will be discussed, presenting the design of *Colommunity* and the digital system developed to monitor social impacts, as well as the theoretical framework on the impacts of gamification. Finally, in Sect. 4, the conclusions will discuss the operative implications and future directions for research.

2 Materials and Methods

2.1 Gamification

Since antiquity, games have been regarded as fundamental activities, although traditionally been seen as mere leisure activities. However, the influence of play goes far beyond its specific context, thanks to what sociologist Roger Caillois has described as the "social vocation" of games [13]. By taking on a collective dimension and not just a connotation of personal distraction, games become a moment of sharing, meeting and interaction between people, even outside the dynamics of the game itself. The term "gamification", which was popularised after 2010 within the digital media industry, has increasingly gained attention across various domains, including education, marketing, and cultural heritage [11, 14].

The success of gamification is closely linked to the growing integration between the digital world and everyday life, where the influence of video games on society has helped to profoundly transform both individual habits and modes of communication [15]. On the other hand, games, which are designed for entertainment, manage to create engaging experiences and motivate people to participate in an activity for long periods. Consequently, gameful-design has been widely adopted as an effective strategy to make even non-game products and services more engaging and motivating [16]. As an illustration of this, gamification is an approach already widely used within the education system, helping students to develop their skills and immerse themselves more deeply in their studies, benefiting their cognitive functions considerably and making learning a more engaging activity [17].

The effectiveness of gamification is based on some principles of game psychology, a discipline that studies the motivations and psychological mechanisms that drive people to play and feel involved in the activity. To understand its potential, it is essential to distinguish between the concepts of play and game: the former refers to a free form of activity, the latter to a structured activity with defined rules and objectives [16]. Within these concepts, there are different practices: toys, understood as simple objects to play with, belong to play without imposing a fixed purpose or structure; on the contrary, games involve regulated and purposeful systems, as in serious games, real video games developed for educational, training or social purposes, going beyond the mere function of entertainment [18] and gamification, which consists of game-design techniques - like scoring systems, challenges, and rewards - in non-game settings to increase user engagement and motivation [16].

An interesting theoretical model is the MOAR! - Motivation, Occasion, Action, Response - developed by Viola and Cassone to understand user involvement in training processes and video games (Fig. 1). The MOAR! model is a cycle consisting of four phases, Motivation, Occasion, Action and Response, which, through a constant and calibrated repetition of actions, can transform them into stable and lasting behaviour.

This scheme highlights how involvement is not only linked to the moment of play but arises from a continuous interaction between desires, context, activity performed, and feedback received, thus generating a motivating and potentially transformative experience. It starts with motivation, which may be internal (i.e. dictated by curiosity or passion) or external (understood as the promise of a reward or recognition), followed by the presence of a concrete opportunity to act, i.e. a favourable context suited to the person's capabilities.

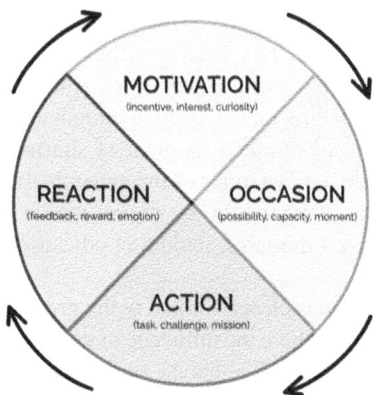

Fig. 1. The MOAR! scheme (source: Viola and Cassone, 2017)

The individual then performs an action, which must be well-structured, rewarding and possibly repeatable, so that it can turn into a habit. Finally, the response (feedback) represents the perceived return of the action: it can be immediate or emotional but must always close the loop by generating new motivation. If the loop is well designed following this model, the scheme fosters sustainable engagement, turning the interaction into an engaging and potentially transformative experience.

This circular process makes actions motivating and attractive, especially when considered boring or unpleasant [15], as a management or learning process might be. The establishment of a physical and emotional bond - engagement - between the object of the game-design process and the individual, making it long-lasting, makes gamification an important tool for engagement and the promotion of virtuous behaviour in different and numerous fields. If we analyse the scientific literature regarding the application of gamification in the field of cultural heritage, some studies [14] have pointed out that this is indicated as an effective means both for the interpretation of cultural heritage in its historical contexts, but also as an understanding device for learning. Applications of this methodology usually occur more within cultural institutions such as museums, which host archives, exhibitions and permanent collections that tend to be more readily available to gamification experts.

Another notable finding to emerge from the analysed literature is the experimentation of this game-based approach within tourism experiences for the enhancement and valorisation of the visit to the heritage site [14].

Drawing on the methodology currently being applied within PE5 CHANGES project – developed by the research group to which the authors belong – the methodology presented in Fig. 2 represents an adaptation of the MOAR! framework (Fig. 1), endowing it with a more dynamic and fluid progression between phases, rather than a strictly cyclical structure.

This revised framework is grounded in the methodology proposed by Mazzarella et al. [9], which aims to foster interaction between Urban Living Labs (ULLs) and cultural landscapes to support the formation of Heritage Communities. It is articulated in three iterative phases and embeds the Social Multicriteria Evaluation within the ULL process to guide activities, strengthen stakeholder collaboration, and enhance sustainability assessment. By doing so, it outlines the principal phases of a collaborative decision-making process oriented towards implementing circular economy principles in the development of Heritage Communities. Following the MOAR framework, the phases are simplified and adapted to support the application of the methodology to the construction and development of the case study, ensuring contextual responsiveness and operational clarity throughout the process.

Fig. 2. Authors' elaboration of the MOAR! scheme, based on the methodological framework of the Phases and Steps of the Heritage Community Urban Living Lab (HeCo-ULL) by Mazzarella et al., 2024.

Despite the already widespread application and growing maturity of gamification in the field of cultural heritage, there is still much to experiment with regarding the use of game-based approaches in this field. In addition to the technological challenges, studies on serious games and gamification of cultural heritage have shown the importance of a collaborative approach, so that content creation is accessible to a wide public without losing historical accuracy and cultural sensitivity [19].

In this perspective, the inclusion of different stakeholders within the creative process is of relevant importance, which makes it clear that a co-creation process allows cultural institutions - promoters of the game-based approach - to generate a relationship between community and technology developers, making the results more effective and enabling the generation of shared values [19].

2.2 Impact Assessment

Impact evaluation is an essential tool for understanding and measuring whether and how interventions and projects generate significant changes in the contexts in which they operate. In particular, social impact evaluation has become increasingly widespread in recent years, not only among scholars but also in response to the demands of the European Commission [20], new funding bodies, and, in Italy, as a result of legislative developments such as Law 106/2016 and the guidelines on the evaluation of social impact (d.lgs. 24 July 2019) [21]. While most definitions describe social impact as a positive social change [22], some authors define it as a reduction in negative effects [23], confirming the variety of perspectives that contribute to the complexity of defining social impact.

Generally, social impact refers to any change that "affects the way people live, work, relate to one another, organise to meet their needs and generally cope as members of society. The term also includes cultural, political, environmental, health, and psychological dimensions" [24]. According to Italian Law No. 106 of 6 June 2016, the evaluation of social impact is understood as the "qualitative and quantitative evaluation, in the short, medium and long term, of the effects of the activities carried out on the reference community with respect to the identified objective".

It is therefore especially important to design projects with impact in mind when engaging in processes of reuse and valorisation of heritage that aim to activate local communities around the recognition of shared values.

In this perspective, the Theory of Change (ToC) [25] is a valuable tool for its ability to stimulate the development of solutions to complex social problems [26], while also helping organizations understand how their work and relationships contribute to complex, long-term social change and how their actions relate to the broader ecosystem of activities [27]. Technically, ToC can be considered both a theory and a practice, a process and a product [28], and it serves both as a tool for planning and framing problems as well as for monitoring and evaluation. A key feature of ToC is its ability to represent the entirety of the process needed to produce the desired change, breaking down complexity into small, manageable steps, while focusing on short-, medium- and long-term changes and linking program activities to results at each stage of the process [29].

Through the impact value chain, the ToC breaks down the process of generating social impact into five main stages, enforcing an approach that begins with a forward-looking vision and then works backwards to construct the steps needed to achieve the expected impact. This includes identifying the long-term changes (impacts) and medium-term outcomes, then constructing and measuring the project's performance through immediate results (outputs), activities and processes capable of triggering change, and the resources needed to implement them.

The construction of the impact value chain thus reflects a paradigm shift in how we approach heritage valorisation, no longer solely through a conservation lens, but through a dynamic process capable of activating social capital, generating participation, and producing tangible benefits for local communities [30, 31].

Among the key impact dimensions relevant to the ongoing research, two are particularly significant for investigating the formation of heritage communities through gamification-based activation processes: the **social** and **cultural** dimensions.

On the social level, particular attention is given to the increase in social cohesion resulting from civic engagement processes, which can lead to greater individual and collective empowerment. Equally relevant is the enhancement of the sense of belonging to the cultural asset residents feel, as this emotional connection strongly influences their attitudes of care and respect for the territory in which they live. Furthermore, the collaboration among residents to overcome individual and collective challenges in pursuit of a common goal can strengthen cooperation networks between citizens and institutions, leading to increased mutual trust.

On the cultural level, the reappropriation of the historical and symbolic meanings of places supports intergenerational transmission and, at the same time, contributes to the growth of competences among individuals within the heritage community [32, 33].

Within this framework, it becomes evident that ex-post impact assessment, and even more importantly, the ex-ante design of an impact-driven process, is fundamental in heritage enhancement pathways, which require new tools to guide political decision-makers and attract funding.

In this regard, the active involvement of citizens in heritage communities plays a central role in improving the quality of life through actions aimed at achieving the shared goal of enhancing their heritage. This research explores technology as a tool for engagement, involvement, and co-evaluation of experiences that are designed and implemented with and by local communities to promote the value of heritage.

3   The Case Study

3.1   A Heritage Community Project for the Valorisation of the Colombario del Fusaro: Colommunity

The work presented was developed within the framework of a master's thesis and curricular internship carried out by Federica Guglielmi at the Faculty of Architecture of the Federico II University of Naples. The thesis project is part of the extended partnership PE5 CHANGES - Cultural Heritage Active Innovation for Sustainable Society - promoted by the PNRR (National Recovery and Resilience Plan), aimed at stimulating the valorisation of cultural heritage, promoting a national network involving universities, research organisations, companies, institutions and citizens, and fostering multidisciplinary synergies and collaborations. The CHANGES project aims to amplify the impact of culture not only in the academic but also in the social context, promoting a dialogue between knowledge, territory and community. Cultural heritage is conceived as a dynamic element that can achieve innovation, inclusion and sustainable development. In particular, Spoke 1, which is where the research fits in, is titled 'Historical landscapes, traditions and cultural identities' and, in line with the principles of the Faro Convention, has among its objectives the development of strategies, methods and tools for the preservation of cultural sites through Heritage Communities, the realisation of historical and archaeological research involving the local population and the development of a digital platform for the management and enhancement of cultural heritage.

An initial mapping of the archaeological heritage of the Campi Flegrei area in Campania, undertaken during an internship, served as the starting point for a more in-depth investigation into a poorly valorised yet historically and culturally significant asset of the territory: the Colombario del Fusaro in Bacoli (Figs. 3 and 4).

Fig. 3. Colombario del Fusaro, Bacoli (Naples, Italy). Photograph by Federica Guglielmi, depicting the archaeological site in its urban context.

This site represents an extraordinary example of Roman funerary architecture and is distinguished by its circular plan, a highly unusual configuration for buildings of this type, which typically exhibited rectangular or quadrangular forms. Notwithstanding its importance, however, it exists in a condition of limited accessibility and restricted collective knowledge. The analysis of this site thus offered an opportunity to reflect upon the necessity for novel valorisation and engagement strategies.

Through a preliminary phase of on-site exploration and analysis, structured through diverse instruments such as site visits, bibliographic research, press mapping, stakeholder mapping, surveys, and structured interviews, it was possible to identify the principal issues contributing to the site's inadequate valorisation.

The integration of hard and soft analysis tools facilitated the collection of pertinent data and enabled an understanding of, simultaneously, the perceptions, expectations, problems, and values that the various stakeholders involved attribute to the Colombario del Fusaro. A key finding that emerged is that the values most attributed to the asset are of a historical and archaeological nature. However, values related to the recreational, emotional, and identity dimensions are significantly less associated, despite being essential for strengthening the bond between the community and the cultural heritage.

Fig. 4. Colombario del Fusaro, Bacoli (Naples, Italy). Photograph by Federica Guglielmi, depicting the underground section of the archaeological site.

The overall evaluation of the data collected led to the identification of two main issues that compromise the relationship between the archaeological asset and the community: the limited knowledge of the site by both residents and visitors, which prevents its recognition from a cultural and identity perspective, and the inaccessibility of the park and archaeological site, which hinders active management by interested third-sector organisations.

Starting from the needs that emerged, a Value Chain was designed (Fig. 5) by listening to the main stakeholders involved in the territorial exploration phase. Among the long-term impact objectives identified is, above all, the increase in the sense of belonging felt by the inhabitants of Bacoli towards the cultural heritage of the Colombario, along with the activation of reuse and management experiments for the site.

A set of criteria and indicators has begun to take shape, to guide impact-oriented design by incorporating integrated qualitative and quantitative data collection mechanisms within the application's digital system, such as short questionnaires or quizzes, to monitor levels of acquired skills, heritage knowledge, and perceived satisfaction and well-being while experiencing the Colombario's spaces.

In the short term, there was a shared recognition of the need to experiment with small-scale actions, both inside and outside the Colombario, intending to engage an initial group of residents in the re-recognition of the abandoned site, starting with the most relevant clusters, such as local associations, committees, and schools.

To engage these stakeholders, the Colommunity platform, based on gamification dynamics, was designed as a digital infrastructure capable of converting users from online to offline participation. It enables groups of citizens to propose initiatives for the enhancement of the site, ranging from storytelling and historical dissemination to collaborative clean-up actions and shared memory mapping, among others.

To achieve this, the main necessary resources were identified, from financial ones for building the digital platform, to human resources, namely professionals and volunteers to be involved in the development of the app and the implementation of activities to be promoted through it.

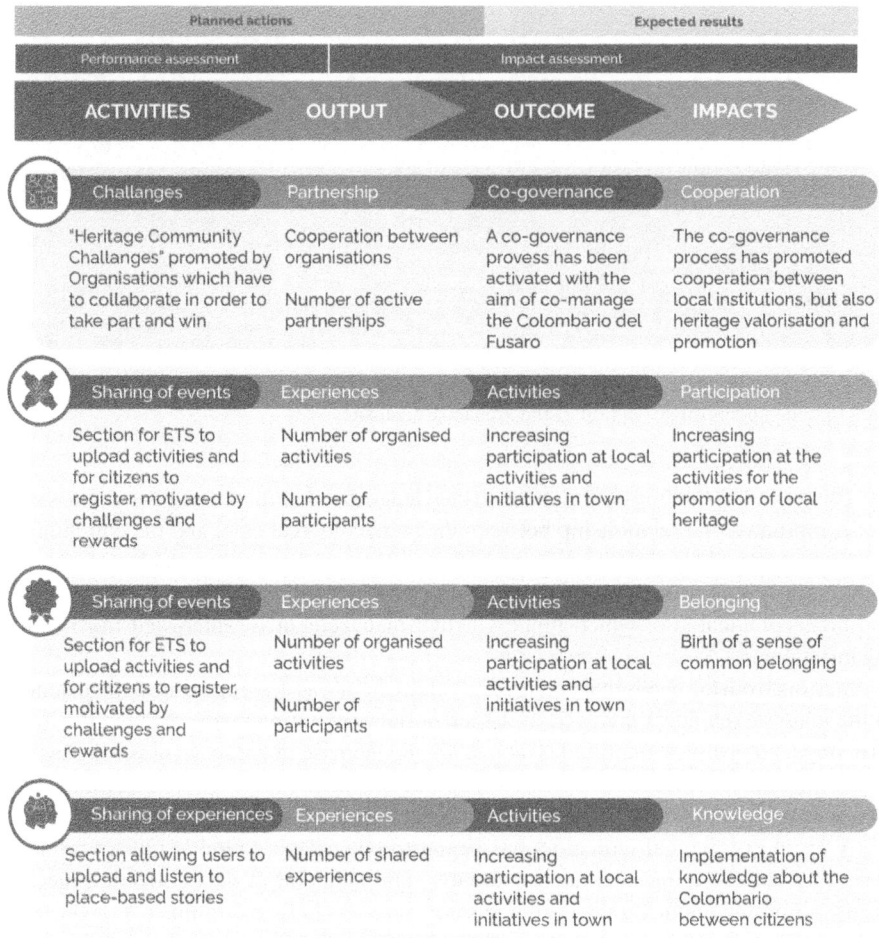

Fig. 5. The Value Chain process

Drawing upon these premises emerges Colommunity (Fig. 6), a mutual-learning interactive platform that hybridises a game-based approach to territorial exploration, akin to geocaching, to actively engage the community of Bacoli in the valorisation of the Colombario del Fusaro. The platform leverages gamification, incorporating scores, leaderboards, and quizzes, to offer cultural experiences that valorise the tangible and intangible heritage of Bacoli.

The principal aim is to establish a nexus between the local community, third sector organisations, and the Colombario del Fusaro, allowing citizens not only to rediscover their history but also to cultivate a genuine sense of belonging to it. In this manner, each individual can actively contribute to the creation of value for the territory and foster the development of a Heritage Community.

Colommunity is designed to instigate tangible actions within the territory through "challenges" conceived for the co-exploration of cultural heritage. These challenges are structured to co-create an itinerary centred on the Colombario del Fusaro and to enhance knowledge of the local area. Furthermore, the platform offers "rewards" intended to augment player agency: complimentary tickets to heritage sites, priority access to local cultural events, and discounts on typical local products. This is made feasible through the realisation of rewards in collaboration with local partners and associations, which not only incentivises active participation but also establishes a virtuous cycle of value, concurrently stimulating a circular economy.

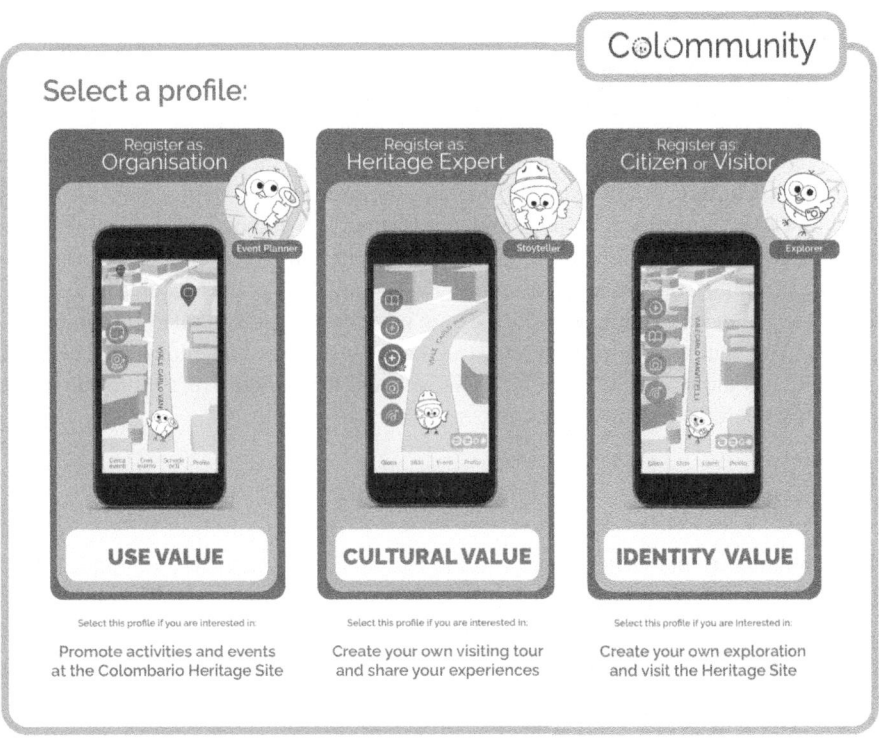

Fig. 6. Colommunity digital platform itinerary

This approach facilitates the construction of a collaborative network amongst local entities, generating novel value for the community and fostering the growth of a sense of belonging and collective identity. In an initial phase, users have the option to register under three distinct profiles (Fig. 6), each conceived to address the diverse needs and contributions that each category of participant can bring to the project.

The first profile is dedicated to the local community, which plays a fundamental role in transmitting the identity-related and affective values associated with their territory. Members of this profile, through the creation of "story experiences", help to bring to life narratives, experiences, and connections that reinforce their sense of belonging.

The second profile is intended for experts in history and archaeology, whose historical and cultural knowledge is fundamental for narrating and interpreting the local heritage. These users can input "story gems" and serve as creators of cultural content (narratives and audio guides) that enrich the player's experience, deepening the understanding of its roots and development through the centuries.

Finally, the third profile is aimed at third sector entities, which have the objective of generating use values for the territory. These players are essential for the creation of initiatives, events, and projects that involve the community, contributing to the promotion of a shared and sustainable management of cultural heritage. Consequently, the platform becomes a point of reference for cooperation between local authorities, citizens, and institutions, generating social and economic value for the territory.

The initial challenge guides the player, through the method of geocaching and the use of GPS, to the primary point of interest: the Colombario del Fusaro. This introduces the player to the historical and cultural significance of the site and promotes a form of experiential learning. Upon reaching the site, the user has the opportunity to deepen their knowledge of the local heritage and, concurrently, to unlock new opportunities for interaction with the platform, accessing new functions and increasing their score.

Players within Colommunity can continuously enrich the pathway, contributing content and experiences. Simultaneously, they are informed about cultural events and activities promoted within their territory, constructing a dynamic and interconnected network that facilitates the realisation of joint initiatives and the building of a more informed, active, and aware community.

4   Conclusions

The Colommunity platform exemplifies the potential of gamification to engage local communities in the preservation and valorisation of cultural heritage. By combining a game-based approach with territorial exploration, the platform successfully encourages active participation in discovering and promoting the rich history of Bacoli, specifically through the Colombario del Fusaro.

By integrating gamified elements such as scores, leaderboards and quizzes, Colommunity not only enhances cultural experience, but also strengthens the connection between local citizens, third sector organisations and the heritage site.

The proposed approach fosters a deeper sense of belonging and empowers individuals to actively contribute to creating value for the community. Ultimately, Colommunity exemplifies a sustainable and inclusive model for developing a heritage community and highlights the transformative potential of interactive, community-driven initiatives in heritage conservation.

The research shows that gamification can serve as a powerful tool to enhance community engagement in the preservation, valorisation and reuse of cultural heritage. By fostering collaboration and encouraging active participation, gamification can bridge the gap between local communities, heritage sites and stakeholders, creating opportunities for sustainable and inclusive development.

Results from the pilot study of the Colommunity project in Bacoli highlight the potential of game-based approaches to engage diverse audiences in the co-exploration and co-management of cultural assets, highlighting the positive social and cultural impacts of such initiatives and reinforcing the importance of co-creation between local communities, experts and institutions.

This research contributes to the wider discourse on the long-term potential of gamification in shaping the future of citizen activation in cultural heritage enhancement, highlighting the need for innovative strategies that align with community-driven approaches to heritage management.

Acknowledgements. The obtained results of this research have been developed in the Project PE 0000020 CHANGES - CUP [E53C22001650006], NRP Mission 4, Component 2 Investment 1.3, Funded by the European Union -NextGenerationEU.

Author Contributions. The authors jointly conceived and developed the approach and decided on the overall objective and structure of the paper: Conceptualization, M.C., F.G., L.L. and S.V.; Methodology, M.C., F.G., L.L. and S.V.; Software, F.G., L.L. and S.V.; Validation, M.C., F.G., L.L. and S.V.; Formal Analysis, F.G., L.L. and S.V.; Investigation, F.G., L.L. and S.V.; Data Curation, M.C., F.G., L.L. and S.V.; Writing-Original Draft Preparation, F.G., L.L. and S.V.; Writing-Review and Editing, M.C., F.G., L.L. and S.V.; Visualization, F.G., L.L. and S.V.; Supervision, M.C. All authors have read and agreed to the published version of the manuscript.

References

1. CHCFE Consortium: Cultural Heritage Counts for Europe: Full Report, Krakow (2015)
2. Council of the European Union: Council Resolution of 16 November 2007 on a European Agenda for Culture (2007)
3. Cerreta, M., Daldanise, G., Giovene di Girasole, E., Torre, C.M.: A cultural heritage low entropy enhancement approach: an ex post evaluation of creative practices. Sustain. For. **13**, 2765 (2021). https://doi.org/10.3390/su13052765
4. Bonacini, E.: Partecipazione e co-creazione di valore culturale. #iziTRAVELSicilia e i principi della Convenzione di Faro / Participation and co-creation of cultural value. #iziTRAVELSicilia and the principles of the Faro Convention. Il Capitale Culturale. **17**, 227–273 (2018)
5. Cerreta, M., Giovene di Girasole, E.: Towards heritage community assessment: indicators proposal for the self-evaluation in Faro convention network process. Sustain. For. **12**, 9862 (2020). https://doi.org/10.3390/su12239862
6. Garcia-Fernandez, J., Medeiros, L.: Cultural heritage and communication through simulation videogames - a validation of Minecraft. Heritage. **2**, 2262–2274 (2019). https://doi.org/10.3390/heritage2030138
7. Sacco, P.L., Teti, E.: Cultura 3.0: un nuovo paradigma di creazione del valore. Econ. Manag. **1**, 79–95 (2017)

8. Ventre, S., Cerreta, M.: Participatory art and co-creation methodology in the "Viale delle Metamorfosi" project. In: Computational Science and Its Applications – ICCSA 2023 Workshops. ICCSA 2023 Lecture Notes in Computer Science, vol. 14108. Springer, Cham (2023). https://doi.org/10.1007/978-3-031-37117-2_20

9. Mazzarella, C., La Rocca, L., Ventre, S., Cerreta, M.: Heritage communities urban living lab (HeCo ULL): a circular methodological approach for co-design through social multi-criteria evaluation. In: Networks, Markets & People. NMP 2024 Lecture Notes in Networks and Systems, vol. 1186. Springer, Cham (2024). https://doi.org/10.1007/978-3-031-74679-6_4

10. Lerario, A., Maiellaro, N.: Mappe interattive per la promozione turistico-culturale. SCIRES-IT Sci. Res. Inform. Technol. **4**, 85–96 (2014)

11. Cerreta, M., Daldanise, G., La Rocca, L., Panaro, S.: Triggering active communities for cultural creative cities: the "Hack the City" play ReCH Mission in the Salerno Historic Centre (Italy). Sustain. For. **13**, 11877 (2021). https://doi.org/10.3390/su132111877

12. Devoti, C., Scientifiche, E.: Dai 'Beni Minori' Al Patrimonio Diffuso: Conoscere e Salvaguardare Il 'Non Monumentale'. In: Patrimonio e Tutela in Italia A Cinquant'Anni Dall'Istituzione Della Commissione Franceschini (1964–2014), pp. 143–154 (2017)

13. Caillois, R.: Man, Play and Games. University of Illinois Press (2001)

14. Marques, C.G., Pedro, J.P., Araújo, I.A.: Systematic literature review of gamification in/for cultural heritage: leveling up, going beyond. Heritage. **6**, 5935–5951 (2023)

15. Viola, F., Cassone, V.I.: L'arte del coinvolgimento, emozioni e stimoli per cambiare il mondo. Ulrico Hoepli Editore S.p.A (2017)

16. Deterding, S., Dixon, D., Khaled, R., Nacke, L.: Gamification: toward a definition. In: CHI 2011 Gamification Workshop Proceedings, pp. 1–12 (2011)

17. Padaya, A., Chbaklo, H.: Innovation & integration of video games in education. In: Innovation & Integration of Video Games in Education, Bournemouth, UK (2022)

18. McGonigal, J.: Reality Is Broken: Why Games Make us Better and How They Can Change the World. Penguin, New York (2011)

19. Kosti, M.V., Diplaris, S., Georgakopoulou, N., Runnel, P., Marini, C., Rovatsos, N., Barakli, A., de Lera, E., Vrochidis, S., Kompatsiaris, I.: i-game: redefining cultural heritage through inclusive game design and advanced technologies. Electronics (Basel). **14**, 1141 (2025). https://doi.org/10.3390/electronics14061141

20. European Commission, G: Approcci proposti per la misurazione dell'impatto sociale, Luxembourg (2015). https://doi.org/10.2767/29077

21. Impronta Etica e SCS Consulting: Le linee guida per la misurazione dell'impatto sociale. In: Una guida pratica per le organizzazioni, Bologna (2016)

22. Santos, F.M.: A positive theory of social entrepreneurship. J. Busi. Ethics. **111**(3), 335–351 (2012). https://doi.org/10.1007/S10551-012-1413-4

23. Bartling, B., Weber, R., Yao, L.: Do markets erode social responsibility? Q. J. Econ. (2015). https://doi.org/10.5167/uzh-85623

24. Vanclay, F.: International principles for social impact assessment: their evolution. Impact Assess. Proj. Apprais. **21**, 3–4 (2003). https://doi.org/10.3152/147154603781766464

25. Reeler, D.: A Three-Fold Theory of Social Change with Implications for Planning, Monitoring and Evaluation. (2007)

26. Anderson, A.A.: The community builder's approach to theory of change. A practical guide to theory development. In: The Aspen Institute Roundtable on Community Change, New York (2006)

27. Keystone: Developing a theory of change. A guide to developing a theory of change as a framework for inclusive dialogue, learning and accountability for social impact. www.KeystoneAccountability.org (2009)

28. Vogel, I.: Review of the use of "theory of change" in international development. Rev. Report. (2012)

29. Weiss, C.H.: Theory-based evaluation: past, present, and future. New Dir Eval., 41–55 (1997)
30. Sacco, P.L., Ferilli, G., Tavano Blessi, G.: Cultural participation, relational goods and individual subjective well-being: some empirical evidence. Rev. Econ. Finan. **4**, 33–46 (2014)
31. Merli, P.: Evaluating the social impact of participation in arts activities. Int. J. Cult. Policy. **8**, 107–118 (2002). https://doi.org/10.1080/10286630290032477
32. Cerreta, M., Panaro, S., Cannatella, D.: Multidimensional spatial decision-making process: Local shared values in action. In: Lecture Notes in Computer Science (including subseries Lecture Notes in Artificial Intelligence and Lecture Notes in Bioinformatics), 7334 LNCS (PART 2), pp. 54–70 (2012). https://doi.org/10.1007/978-3-642-31075-1_5
33. Cerreta, M., Panaro, S., Poli, G.: A spatial decision support system for multifunctional landscape assessment: a transformative resilience perspective for vulnerable inland areas. Sustainability. **13**(5), 1–23. https://doi.org/10.3390/su13052748

Good Practices Inventory and Why It Matters to Urban Health and Inclusivity

Mine Derin Sönmez[✉] [ID], Ayşıl Sara Kerimi, and Pınar Börü [ID]

Izmir Planning Agency, Akdeniz, Cumhuriyet Blv No:120, 35210 Konak, Izmir, Turkey
minederinarch@gmail.com

Abstract. This paper presents a structured methodological approach to constructing thematic good practices inventories for urban transformation, based on two guidebooks developed by the Izmir Planning Agency in coordination with the Turkish Healthy Cities Association and Izmir Metropolitan Municipality. The series operationalizes the Sustainable Development Goals (SDGs), the One Health framework, and the WHO Healthy Cities Phase VII themes (6Ps), addressing contemporary urban challenges through an equity-focused lens.

The first volume, Good Practices for the Healthy Cities of the Future, centers on projects that integrate environmental, human, and animal health, while the second, Good Practices for Disability-Inclusive Cities of the Future, extends the framework to include rights-based urban design and inclusive governance. Across both volumes, a multi-phase evaluation process was applied, incorporating SDG alignment, replicability, digital visibility, and spatial scale.

The findings demonstrate how good practices, when systematically categorized, support comparative learning and local policy adaptation. Key insights highlight the importance of thematic breadth, the underrepresentation of certain dimensions such as animal health, and challenges in scaling successful pilots due to institutional, regulatory, or funding barriers. Future volumes will expand on these lessons, including a forthcoming guide on elderly health.

Izmir Metropolitan Municipality also plans to implement local healthy city solutions based on these good practices, aligning global insights with its urban development strategies. Overall, the Good Practices series contributes to an emerging urban planning culture in which health, inclusivity, and sustainability are jointly pursued as central public priorities.

Keywords: Healthy Cities · One Health · Sustainable Urban Development ·
Good Practice Inventories

1 Introduction

The growing urgency for inclusive and health-oriented urban development has encouraged local governments to seek practical and adaptable models grounded in international collaboration and evidence-based strategies [3, 6]. In response, the Good Practices series was initiated to systematically compile and evaluate global urban projects that demonstrate how cities can respond effectively to challenges such as public health, climate

O. Gervasi et al. (Eds.): ICCSA 2025 Workshops, LNCS 15897, pp. 356–369, 2026.
https://doi.org/10.1007/978-3-031-97660-5_24

change, and social inequality [5, 6]. These guides aim to translate international objectives such as the Sustainable Development Goals (SDGs) and the One Health approach into actionable insights for municipal governance and spatial planning.

The first volume, Good Practices for the Healthy Cities of the Future, examined how urban health can be strengthened through environmental awareness, digital transformation, mental well-being strategies, and community-based resilience efforts. It introduced a classification system organized around health dimensions, spatial impacts, thematic keywords, and measurable alignment with global goals. The approach emphasized the importance of integrated planning, intersectoral cooperation, and localized implementation.

Following this groundwork, the second volume, Good Practices for Disability-Inclusive Cities of the Future, expands the framework by addressing disability as a key factor in equitable urban development. Instead of limiting the scope to physical accessibility alone, it brings forward a rights-based and inclusive design perspective, incorporating a wide range of needs including those of people with invisible disabilities. This volume reinforces the methodological coherence of the series by using the same categorization system and by addressing health, access, and representation together.

Together, the two books present a structured body of knowledge designed to support cities in designing healthier and more inclusive environments. This coherence enables thematic comparability while also allowing each volume to explore distinct policy dimensions, from environmental resilience to social equity. The Good Practices series will continue to grow, addressing additional aspects of urban sustainability through future volumes. Although the selected practices originate from diverse urban contexts, their alignment with the SDG framework and their emphasis on scalable, rights-based, and participatory approaches enhance their potential for replication across different cities facing similar challenges. By focusing on actionable models and cross-contextual applicability, the series serves as a long-term resource for local governments, practitioners, and researchers who aim to create cities that leave no one behind (Figs. 1 and 2).

1.1 Background Motivation

Urban areas play a critical role in addressing contemporary environmental and societal challenges. The Turkish Healthy Cities Association actively works to improve urban health, enhance social well-being, and protect the environment. In an era marked by multiple crises, cities are expected to develop balanced strategies encompassing social justice, environmental sustainability, public health, and economic development. This guide has been inspired by the "One Health" approach, which acknowledges the interconnectedness of human, animal, and environmental health.

Fig. 1. Cover of Good Practices for the Healthy Cities of the Future

Encouraging the collection of exemplary international practices, this guide aims to support cities in achieving the Sustainable Development Goals (SDGs). Selected projects focus on enhancing social resilience and delivering integrated solutions that reflect ecological, social, and economic priorities. These examples serve not only local governments but also academia, civil society, and all relevant stakeholders as a resource for capacity-building and knowledge-sharing.

Urbanization and Public Health. The historical transition to settled life has driven the evolution of urban models shaped by infrastructure systems, technological progress, biological and social needs, planning practices, and urban aesthetics. Public health interventions have long influenced city design, for instance, the development of sewerage systems to prevent mass diseases like plague. As of 2022, approximately 57% of the world population resides in urban areas, with projections indicating an increase to 66% by 2050. Rapid urbanization, especially in developing countries, contributes to the emergence of unsustainable and unhealthy living conditions that affect not only humans but also nature and other species. Since the mid-twentieth century, movements addressing environmental protection, animal rights, and climate change have questioned the human-centered development framework. Planning cities to support all forms of life humans

Fig. 2. Cover of Good Practices for Disability-Inclusive Cities of the Future

and non-humans alike, has become an ethical and practical necessity. David Attenborough, a prominent advocate of biodiversity, has emphasized that protected areas alone are insufficient to halt ecological degradation, urging the use of everyday spaces such as gardens and roadside areas for wildlife conservation. In line with the One Health approach, cities must become part of the solution.

From an ethical standpoint, protecting the rights of non-human beings and creating healthy habitats for all species is paramount. Ecologically, natural systems provide essential resources such as water, food, and air, underlining the urgency of preserving ecosystem functions. The sustainability of cities depends on maintaining these life-supporting systems. Cultural and natural heritage are also interlinked. Studies have observed that individuals residing in areas with preserved ecological and cultural assets tend to experience higher mental well-being and increased cultural productivity. Therefore, the notion of "cultural health" emerges at the intersection of the three axes of the One Health approach.

Contemporary urban development is increasingly influenced by technological advancements, including artificial intelligence, infrastructure systems, and innovations in energy, water, and waste management. Alongside these changes, global trends such as climate change, loss of natural spaces, migration, and rising health demands redefine the parameters of livable urban environments. Within this context, adopting a holistic One Health perspective is no longer optional but essential to shaping sustainable cities and their future ecosystems.

2 Literature

The integration of health, inclusivity, and sustainability into urban governance has prompted a growing emphasis on practice-based frameworks that bridge local action with global development goals. Within this context, structured good practice inventories have emerged as a crucial mechanism for analyzing how urban projects respond to challenges such as climate change, inequality, and access to services [1, 2]. However, while the SDGs provide a normative framework, there remains a lack of systematic tools that translate them into actionable and localized guidance for municipalities.

Good Practices for the Healthy Cities of the Future and Good Practices for Disability-Inclusive Cities of the Future respond directly to this need. Both volumes were developed through a rigorous multi-phase review of over 10,000 international examples drawn from curated databases as seen on Table 1, including WHO Urban Governance Initiatives, UN-Habitat's Urban Agenda Platform, Connective Cities, SmartCitiesWorld, and the International Disability Alliance. Selection criteria were tightly coupled with SDG targets particularly SDG 3 (Health), SDG 10 (Reduced Inequalities), and SDG 11 (Sustainable Cities) along with indicators such as digital visibility, replicability across contexts, and thematic relevance to the One Health framework.

Informed by the WHO's 2016 Global Report on Urban Health and the Phase VII themes of the Healthy Cities Project (People, Planet, Place, Participation, Prosperity, and Peace), the first volume emphasized cross-sectoral health interventions, including urban biodiversity restoration, mental health in public spaces, and integrated food systems [3]. The second volume advanced this structure by focusing on disability-inclusive design, preventive disability services, and universal accessibility, adopting a rights-based perspective consistent with the UN Convention on the Rights of Persons with Disabilities [7].

Recent literature has also pointed to the growing urgency of data-informed policy design in urban health. Urban SDG platforms and regional innovation networks (e.g. BABLE, Metropolis, and UCLG-Agenda 21 for Culture) have contributed significantly to the visibility of localized experiments; however, few have offered a classification model that incorporates thematic keywords, spatial typologies, and multidimensional health impacts as comprehensively as this series.

Both guides propose a scalable and transferable model for documenting good practices, characterized by a matrix of meta-keywords, One Health axes (human, environmental, and animal health), and SDG alignment scores. This model aligns with ongoing research emphasizing the importance of knowledge infrastructures and transdisciplinary learning mechanisms in urban governance.

Table 1. List of Databases

Database of Good Practices for the Healthy Cities of the Future	
World Health Organization & UN-Habitat. (2016).	AbilityNet: A digital world accessible to all
World Health Organization: Case studies	BABLE
WHO initiative on urban governance for health and well-being	Best Buddies
Centre for International Climate Research (CICERO)	C40
Connective Cities	Common Ground
European Commission Intelligent Cities Challenge	Connective Cities
Global Cities Hub	The World Bank
International Observatory on Participatory Democracy Metropolis	European Commission of Mayors for Climate Challenge
Project for Public Spaces (PPS)	Tech4Good Marketplace
SmartCitiesWorld	Global Covenant of Mayors for Climate and Energy Southeast Asia
UCLG - Agenda 21 for Culture	Global Disability Rights Now
UN Department of Economic and Social Affairs (UN DESA)	Humanity & Inclusion

(continued)

2.1 Historical and Conceptual Background

The transformation of cities from early settlements to contemporary urban systems has not only been a story of demographic and technological shifts but increasingly of aligning urban development with planetary sustainability and social justice. At the heart of this shift is the global commitment to the United Nations 2030 Agenda and its 17 Sustainable Development Goals (SDGs), which serve as a framework for integrating ecological, social, and economic priorities into urban governance.

Among these goals, SDG 11 (Sustainable Cities and Communities) specifically addresses urban areas, advocating for inclusive, safe, resilient, and sustainable cities. However, as emphasized in both volumes of Good Practices for the Healthy Cities of the Future and Good Practices for Disability-Inclusive Cities of the Future, meaningful implementation of this goal is deeply entangled with other SDGs, such as SDG 3 (Good Health and Well-being), SDG 10 (Reduced Inequalities), SDG 13 (Climate Action), and SDG 6 (Clean Water and Sanitation). These interconnections demand holistic governance approaches that acknowledge health as a cross-cutting issue and cities as critical actors in global sustainability.

Table 1. (*continued*)

Database of Good Practices for the Healthy Cities of the Future	
UN Framework Convention on Climate Change (UNFCCC)	Inclusive Design Research Centre
UN-Habitat - Urban Agenda Platform	International Disability Alliance
UN-Habitat - Waste Wise Cities	Metropolis
University of Oxford - Nature-based Solutions Initiative	Observation of Public Sector Innovation
Urban SDG Knowledge Platform	SmartCitiesWorld
Whitley Fund for Nature	Special Olympics
NetZero Cities	UN Disability Studies
One Health 4 Cities	UN Department of Economic and Social Affairs (UN DESA)
Oppla	UNICEF
Urban Future - CityChangers.org	

SDGs, while universally adopted, often lack localized frameworks that can translate their ambitious targets into practical urban strategies. This gap becomes especially visible in cities experiencing rapid urbanization, where infrastructural strain, socio-economic inequalities, and environmental degradation compound the complexity of sustainable development. UN-Habitat's 2022 World Cities Report projected that by 2050, over two-thirds of the global population will reside in urban areas, placing unprecedented pressure on city systems. The climate crisis amplifies this pressure, as urban areas currently account for nearly 70% of global carbon emissions, largely from buildings and transportation sectors [5].

In this context, the SDGs are increasingly interpreted not as isolated goals, but as an integrated roadmap requiring transdisciplinary, equity-centered responses. The One Health framework emphasizing the health linkages between people, animals, and ecosystems has emerged as a critical interpretive lens for understanding the urban role in addressing global challenges.

3 Methodology

The good practice guides developed under the Izmir Planning Agency follow a standardized, multi-step methodology designed to maintain consistency, thematic clarity, and applicability across different urban contexts. Each volume is grounded in the One Health framework and contributes to the United Nations Sustainable Development Goals (SDGs), with thematic emphasis adapted to the specific focus of each guide. This approach is used in both volumes of the series: Good Practices for the Healthy Cities of the Future and Good Practices for Disability-Inclusive Cities of the Future.

3.1   Database Identification and Review

The first step involved a systematic review across multiple international databases that catalogue good practice initiatives launched after 2015, ensuring alignment with the institutionalization of the SDGs in global policy discourse. This review covered over 10,000 examples from sources such as WHO Urban Governance Initiatives, UN-Habitat's Urban Agenda Platform, Connective Cities, SmartCitiesWorld, and the International Disability Alliance [1, 2]. The sources were filtered using the following criteria. Sources had to include actionable, implemented practices that contribute to various SDGs, not only conceptual or policy-level frameworks. Databases were required to provide systematically structured listings and demonstrate geographic diversity. Practices that were not yet implemented or were still in observation or data collection phases were excluded. Sources lacking concrete good practice content, such as those containing only academic articles or news items, were eliminated. Duplicative sources based on identical datasets were excluded to preserve originality.

As a result, **5,693** practices were recorded for the *Healthy Cities* guide and **4,703** for the *Disability-Inclusive Cities* guide across verified databases.

Initial Filtering Phase. An initial filtering phase was conducted to ensure thematic alignment.

For the Healthy Cities guide, practices aligned with SDG 3 (Health), SDG 14 (Life Below Water), SDG 15 (Life on Land), and intersected with SDG 13 (Climate Action) were prioritized.

For the Disability-Inclusive Cities guide, practices had to align with SDG 3 and SDG 10 (Reduced Inequalities), especially those targeting disadvantaged populations.

In both guides, examples contributing to SDG 11 (Sustainable Cities and Communities) although not strictly under the One Health framework were retained due to their relevance to urban well-being and intermunicipal learning objectives.

Final Selection Criteria. Shortlisted practices were evaluated using standardized criteria as presented in Table 2 of the guide. These included digital visibility, defined as the project's presence and accessibility on verified platforms, replicability, defined as the adaptability of the initiative across different locations and institutions, geographic balance, ensuring that no single region was overrepresented, and award or recognition, which applied mainly to the Healthy Cities projects and indicated preference for initiatives with international acknowledgment.

Table 2. Evaluation Criteria for Good Practice Selection

Evaluation Criteria	Description
Digital Visibility	Open accessibility and presence on verified platforms
Replicability	Potential for geographic and institutional adaptation
Geographic Balance	Avoidance of regional overrepresentation
Award & Recognition	(For Healthy Cities) Preference for internationally recognized initiatives

This phase finalized 440 practices for Healthy Cities and 400 for Disability-Inclusive Cities.

Categorization and Thematic Structuring. Each selected practice was assessed for its relevance to the **One Health framework** including contributions to human, animal, and environmental health. Their distribution was analyzed to support thematic balance across the guide.

- The *Healthy Cities* guide classified practices under **16 inclusive keywords,** including climate, biodiversity, digitalization, food security, energy, housing, and social participation.
- The *Disability-Inclusive Cities* guide used a **tiered categorization:** 5 **primary keywords** (accessibility, participation, planning, basic needs, environment) and 20 **secondary thematic tags,** including policy, education, mobility, and safety.

Proportional representation based on these classifications guided the final selection of practices included in the printed guides.

One Health Distribution Analysis. Human, Animal, and Environmental Health. To ensure thematic alignment with the One Health paradigm, each shortlisted case was categorized according to its primary health dimension: human health, animal health, and environmental health. The distribution analysis allowed for the identification of gaps, thematic saturation, and potential synergies across practice areas.

In the Healthy Cities guide, the percentage distribution of selected cases across the three One Health dimensions is as follows (Table 3).

Table 3. Health Dimension for Good Practice Selection – Healthy Cities Guide

Health Dimension	Percentage of Cases
Human Health	66%
Environmental Health	21%
Animal Health	13%

In contrast, the Disability-Inclusive Cities guide showed a stronger concentration on human and environmental well-being, reflecting the specific focus of the volume (Table 4).

This distribution analysis not only reinforces the guides' adherence to the One Health framework but also offers municipalities and practitioners a quantifiable overview of where most interventions are currently concentrated. The results help highlight underrepresented dimensions, particularly animal health and provide a basis for rebalancing future programmatic focus areas.

Publication and Knowledge Sharing. To balance analytical depth and reader accessibility:

The *Healthy Cities* guide presented **50 practices**, while The *Disability-Inclusive Cities* guide presented **40 practices** in their respective publications.

Table 4. Health Dimension for Good Practice Selection – Disability-Inclusive Cities Guide

Health Dimension	Percentage of Cases
Human Health	74%
Environmental Health	19%
Animal Health	7%

In both volumes, the **full database** of evaluated practices was made accessible through an **open online platform** to support broader learning, benchmarking, and policy transfer.

4 Discussion and Limitations

The comparative analysis of the two volumes, Good Practices for the Healthy Cities of the Future and Good Practices for Disability-Inclusive Cities of the Future, reveals a shared methodological architecture that enables a layered interpretation of urban health and inclusivity [1, 2]. Both books utilize a matrix-based classification system that incorporates SDG relevance, thematic keywords, spatial scale, and One Health dimensions, allowing each project to be situated within broader urban governance frameworks [3, 4].

A key finding across both volumes is the operationalization of the One Health approach beyond public health discourse. In the first volume, the concept is illustrated through interventions that integrate environmental restoration, active mobility, urban food systems, and mental well-being strategies [1]. Projects such as the Clean Urban Waterways initiative, which harnesses natural water flows and wind currents to capture plastic waste before it reaches the oceans [9], or Mexico City's Green Challenge, which strengthens urban green infrastructure and biodiversity through large-scale revegetation efforts (Green Challenge), are not only environmentally sustainable but also enhance social cohesion and mental resilience. These examples underscore the interdependence of urban ecology and collective health.

In the second volume, the One Health framework is expanded to include rights-based urban design, where physical, sensory, and cognitive accessibility are recognized as health determinants [2]. Projects like the M4Guide mobility assistant app in Berlin (M4Guide) or the Sense Maps initiative in the United Kingdom demonstrate how inclusive infrastructure and social service models contribute to population-level well-being, particularly in contexts where urban services are fragmented or unevenly distributed [2]. The emphasis on invisible disabilities and preventable disability services marks a novel contribution to urban health literature, linking early intervention strategies with long-term sustainability goals [7].

Both volumes highlight the value of transferring international practices to local planning contexts [4]. While the first guide leans toward ecological and systemic transformations such as food sovereignty, heat-resilient design, and green infrastructure [1], the second focuses more on institutional innovation, including inclusive service governance, social care protocols, and rights-based digital accessibility [2]. This difference in orientation illustrates the flexibility of the good practice framework in accommodating both structural and service-level reforms.

Another point of convergence lies in the attention to spatial justice. Projects in both volumes are not merely technical interventions but also responses to social inequities manifested in space, whether through unequal access to green areas, uneven distribution of health services, or the inaccessibility of urban infrastructure for persons with disabilities [4]. The inventory system's inclusion of spatial typologies such as neighborhood, district, and city-wide scales allows for assessing the replicability of interventions across geographies with different levels of institutional capacity [1, 2].

However, when examined in depth, many individual projects reveal context-specific limitations that affect their replicability, scalability, or long-term effectiveness. In the Healthy Cities guide, Mexico City's Green Challenge highlights difficulties in sustaining long-term maintenance due to the need for cross-sector collaboration and consistent community engagement [8]. The Clean Urban Waterways initiative faces challenges in balancing ecological waste interception technologies with local financial constraints and the need for sustained community engagement and education efforts [9]. GreenQuays, Breda's urban river regeneration project, while highly innovative in integrating nature-inclusive quay design, is situated in a European context with strong institutional support, raising questions about its adaptability to municipalities with fewer financial or technical capacities [10].

In the Disability-Inclusive Cities guide, the M4Guide project in Berlin depends heavily on robust municipal data infrastructures and high levels of technical literacy, limiting its applicability in cities with less developed digital ecosystems [11]. The Sense Maps project in the United Kingdom identifies barriers related to retrofitting historic urban areas, where regulatory constraints and physical limitations complicate implementation. Additionally, the Bogotá Urban Governance for Health program, despite its strong emphasis on citizen participation, has reported challenges in institutionalizing participatory mechanisms within formal governance frameworks, especially after external donor support ends.

A further thematic limitation emerges from the underrepresentation of animal health within the One Health framework [6]. While examples such as the Walkin' Pets initiative address mobility aids for disabled animals, they remain isolated cases, and there is little integration of animal health concerns into broader urban sustainability planning.

Overall, the series demonstrates a strong link between data transparency and policy learning [4]. By prioritizing cases with publicly available evaluation tools, participatory elements, and verifiable outcomes, the inventories function not only as repositories of inspiration but also as instruments of accountability and policy transfer [3].

These findings suggest that when good practices are methodically categorized and critically analyzed, they not only highlight what has worked elsewhere but also support the development of context-sensitive planning frameworks [1, 2]. Moving forward, future editions of the Good Practices series could enhance their relevance by systematically including critical lessons from implementation, broadening thematic representation (particularly in underexplored areas like animal health), and capturing more diverse regional perspectives. Such improvements would strengthen the series' contribution to an emerging planning culture in which urban health and inclusion are not siloed concerns but jointly negotiated public values.

5 Conclusion

The Good Practices series offers a concrete contribution to urban policy development by systematizing international examples through a shared, multi-dimensional framework [1, 2]. Rather than presenting isolated case studies, the series introduces a structured method for cataloging, analyzing, and contextualizing projects using thematic focus, spatial impact, and replicability [3, 4]. This approach enables local governments, researchers, and practitioners to address complex planning challenges such as climate adaptation, public health, and social inclusion through real-world applications that align with the Sustainable Development Goals (SDGs) and the One Health framework [3].

From the Healthy Cities volume, Mexico City's Green Challenge demonstrates how large-scale urban revegetation can strengthen climate resilience and biodiversity, although the project also highlights coordination challenges across municipal departments and stakeholder groups [8]. The Clean Urban Waterways project shows how engineered interception systems can prevent plastic waste from entering marine environments while offering environmental benefits and raising community awareness [9]. The GreenQuays Project in Breda illustrates how nature-inclusive urban river regeneration can enhance environmental goals and climate resilience, although its implementation relies on specialized design methods and institutional partnerships, which may limit its immediate transferability to less-resourced cities [10].

In the Disability-Inclusive Cities volume, Berlin's M4Guide project shows how digital mobility tools for visually impaired users can enhance urban accessibility but depend on strong digital infrastructures and cross-sector data cooperation [11]. The AT2030 Inclusive Infrastructure initiative in Ulaanbaatar, Varanasi, and Surakarta demonstrates that inclusive infrastructure can be advanced when paired with policy reforms and community-level participation [12]. The Street Rehab initiative in India presents an innovative example where physical rehabilitation spaces are combined with accessible street design, improving quality of life and raising community awareness [13].

The series applies a consistent multi-phase evaluation process, incorporating SDG alignment, One Health relevance, spatial scale, and intervention type (Akarsu et al.; Abacıgil et al.). This creates a knowledge base that supports comparative insights across geographic and institutional settings [4].

Future volumes could strengthen the contribution of the series by addressing thematic gaps such as the underrepresentation of animal health [3] and by expanding the inclusion of case studies from informal settlements or cities in the Global South [4]. Including more detailed lessons on implementation barriers such as regulatory difficulties, financial limitations, and social resistance would enhance the value of the series as a learning tool for local adaptation and resilience planning [5].

A forthcoming volume focusing on elderly health is planned, which will explore how cities can design inclusive, supportive, and resilient environments for aging populations by addressing issues such as age-friendly infrastructure, social inclusion, preventive health services, and intergenerational solidarity [1]. In addition, Izmir Metropolitan Municipality intends to use the knowledge drawn from these good practice examples to guide the implementation of healthy local city solutions, aligning global insights with the city's ongoing urban transformation efforts [2].

In summary, the Good Practices series helps reframe best practices as context-sensitive and adaptable planning resources [3, 4]. It supports an evolving urban planning approach in which health, inclusivity, and sustainability are understood as shared public priorities. For cities working to translate global goals into local strategies, the series offers a practical and structured reference for designing interventions that are spatially grounded, socially responsive, and environmentally sustainable [1, 2].

Acknowledgments. This guide was prepared by the Izmir Planning Agency (IZPA) on behalf of the Turkish Healthy Cities Association.

Disclosure of Interests. The authors have no competing interests to declare that are relevant to the content of this publication.

References

1. Akarsu, F., Kerimi Bodur, A.S., Sönmez, M.D., Börü, P., Balatacı, T., Uslu, H.Ö.: Geleceğin Sağlıklı Kentlerine Dünyadan İyi Uygulama Örnekleri. Türkiye Sağlıklı Kentler Birliği, Bursa (2024)
2. Abacıgil, F., Akarsu, F., Aktaş, E., Kerimi Bodur, A.S., Börü, P., Emre, A.S., Sönmez, M.D., Tezer, Ç.Ş., Yıldız, F.: Geleceğin Engelli Dostu Kentlerine Dünyadan İyi Uygulama Örnekleri. İzmir Büyükşehir Belediyesi, İzmir (2024)
3. World Health Organization (WHO): Global Report on Urban Health: Equitable, Healthier Cities for Sustainable Development. WHO, Geneva (2016)
4. UN-Habitat: World Cities Report 2022: Envisaging the Future of Cities. UN-Habitat, Nairobi (2022)
5. Intergovernmental Panel on Climate Change (IPCC): Climate Change 2023: Synthesis Report. IPCC, Geneva (2023)
6. WWF: Living Planet Report 2024 – A System in Peril. WWF, Gland (2024)
7. United Nations: Convention on the Rights of Persons with Disabilities (CRPD). UN, New York (2006)
8. Green Challenge, Mexico City – Urban Revegetation and Green Infrastructure Program. USE Metropolis (2021), https://use.metropolis.org/case-studies/green-challenge
9. Clean Urban Waterways Project – Preventing Plastic Waste through Natural Flow and Wind Capture Technologies. Urban Agenda Platform (2021), https://www.urbanagendaplatform.org/best-practice/clean-urban-waterways
10. GreenQuays Project, Breda – Urban River Regeneration through Nature-Inclusive Quays. Urban Agenda Platform (2021), https://www.urbanagendaplatform.org/best-practice/greenquays-urban-river-regeneration-through-nature-inclusive-quays
11. M4Guide – Mobile Multi-Modal Mobility Guide: Case Study on Urban Sustainability Exchange. USE Metropolis (2021), https://use.metropolis.org/case-studies/m4guide-mobile-multi-modal-mobility-guide

12. AT2030 Global Disability Innovation Hub: Inclusive Infrastructure and Accessibility in Ulaanbaatar, Varanasi, and Surakarta. GDI Hub (2022), https://at2030.org/inclusive-infrastructure
13. Street Rehab in India – Global Disability Innovation Hub: Street Rehab Project Overview. Global Disability Innovation Hub (2021), https://www.disabilityinnovation.com/projects/street-rehab-in-india

Transdisciplinary Impact-Oriented Strategies Through a Design-Evaluation Approach: The Case Study of Confiscated Assets from the Mafia in Naples

Piero Zizzania$^{(\boxtimes)}$, Simona Capaldo, Benedetta Grieco, Laura Di Tommaso, Caterina Loffredo, Orfina Fatigato, and Maria Cerreta

Department of Architecture, University of Naples Federico II, Naples, Italy
{piero.zizzania,simona.capaldo,benedetta.grieco,laura.ditommaso, caterina.loffredo,orfinafrancesca.fatigato,cerreta}@unina.it

Abstract. This contribution presents the results of the research group's activities carried out within the PRIN 2022 project "Confiscated Asset in Transition: from the Anti-city to the Third Heritage", as part of a research agreement with the Municipality of Naples and the Agency for Confiscated Assets. The research activity involved students from the Department of Architecture of Naples and several local stakeholders, and it entailed the development of a transdisciplinary and multi-actor decision-making process. This process hybridised different methodologies such as multi-criteria and multi-group evaluations, economic assessments, and urban and architectural design. The methodological approach was implemented starting from the selection of assets confiscated from organised crime within the municipality of Naples. In line with the need to "return these assets to the community", as prescribed by Italian legislation on this topic, the aim was to define time-based strategies for incremental reactivation and adaptive reuse, with particular attention to the direct and indirect benefits generated in the local context. Through the identification of different phases of evaluation and design, several future scenarios were developed to ensure multidimensional impacts, economic, environmental, social, and cultural. The paper explores the potential of a multidisciplinary approach to decision-making in defining scenarios for the regeneration of disused urban assets, highlighting the tools adopted throughout the research and educational process.

Keywords: Social Multi Criteria Evaluation (S-MCE) · Evolutionary Evaluation (EE) · Social Impact Evaluation (SIE) · Time-based strategy · Urban regeneration

1 Introduction

The introduction presents the general theme of impact-oriented strategies within the field of urban studies, design disciplines, and evaluation. It highlights the need for a transdisciplinary approach to the development of integrated urban regeneration processes.

O. Gervasi et al. (Eds.): ICCSA 2025 Workshops, LNCS 15897, pp. 370–388, 2026.
https://doi.org/10.1007/978-3-031-97660-5_25

When the physical transformation goals of urban spaces, the city, and the landscape intertwine with the desire to generate social change, it becomes necessary to adopt an impact-oriented approach [1] for the design and evaluation of interventions. This approach allows for supporting decisions and guiding actions towards greater effectiveness and a stronger ethical responsibility towards the future [2] on the part of the actors and practitioners involved, legitimising public-private partnerships through the definition of common objectives and actions [3].

In evaluative disciplines, territorial studies, and social sciences, the concepts of impact and impact evaluation are central to understanding the causal links between actions undertaken and the effects produced over the long term, whether direct or indirect, positive or negative, intentional or unintentional [4–6]. Vanclay [7] defines social impact as a change capable of influencing lifestyles, culture, communities, political systems, the environment, health, well-being, rights, and individual and collective fears and aspirations. It is, therefore, a perspective centred on the human dimension that permeates all spheres of existence. In this sense, social impact becomes synonymous with positive social change [8], and impact evaluation acts as a guiding tool to promote regeneration processes aimed at social innovation [9], territorial cohesion, spatial justice, institutional learning [10], collective well-being, and the active involvement of citizens [11].

Many authors have emphasised how the city and the spaces we inhabit play a crucial role in ensuring well-being and justice. The complex correlation between urban forms and social, economic, and cultural structures is widely documented [12]. In Reassembling the Social, Latour [13] highlights how social interactions are always mediated by artefacts such as the city, landscape, welfare, and economy. Every time these artefacts are transformed, they reveal their political, ethical, and normative dimensions because, by their nature, they raise questions about the goodness of the project, its consequences, and its impact on communities. From this perspective, Lefebvre [14] asserts the "right to the city" as a collective right to actively participate in the transformations of inhabited spaces, recognising the need for active involvement of territorial actors in a multi-group and multi-level logic. When a territorial transformation aspires to all of this, it becomes essential to equip oneself with transdisciplinary tools and mixed methods [15] capable of supporting the strategic decisions necessary for building a process that not only intervenes on the physical matter and characteristics of the built environment, but also recognises the directly or indirectly involved subjects, anticipates, if possible, the effects, and monitors the triggered socio-economic and political dynamics.

If the goal of regeneration is to generate positive impacts and mitigate negative ones [9], then through impact evaluation tools and methodologies integrated into the process, design choices could be guided towards interventions and strategic actions capable of generating significant and sustainable changes over time. Bazzini and Curti [16] emphasise the fundamental role of evaluation in multi-objective regeneration processes, highlighting how the integrated use of multidimensional indicators - capable of capturing social, economic, and environmental value - can orient transformations towards sustainability, social innovation, and economic compatibility. Urban regeneration processes [9, 17], when supported by evolutionary and transformative evaluative processes [18–20], can transform into opportunities for the grafting of new forms of civil and circular economy, the recovery of abandoned properties and areas, the redistribution of opportunities and well-being, emancipation, empowerment, civic participation, re-appropriation, and care, giving voice to new needs and emerging subjectivities.

However, despite growing sensitivity towards sustainability issues and an increasingly pressing demand for accountability in urban and territorial transformation processes, the limitations of the most widespread impact evaluation methodologies emerge strongly, often stemming precisely from their relationship with complex design processes [21]. On the one hand, there is a structural lack of data, methodological tools, and social infrastructures adequate to ensure awareness, transparency, and traceability of long-term impacts, both in the ideation phase (ex-ante) and in the subsequent implementation and verification phases (in-itinere and ex-post). Furthermore, many impact evaluation methodologies are still rooted in economic-financial theories, based on mechanistic predictive models that shape reality on criteria of stability and linear cause-effect chains, struggling to grasp the dynamic, relational, and systemic nature of the social phenomena triggered by urban transformations [22]. The emotional, perceptual, psychological, and behavioural dimensions that characterise the experience of space and social relationships are difficult to objectify and measure and are often excluded from standardised evaluation systems. Added to this is the radical uncertainty that accompanies both design and evaluation processes: the evolution of contexts, the plurality of actors involved, and the instability of objectives and resources make it necessary to adopt flexible, adaptive evaluation tools capable of changing over time and guiding decisions even during the work [23].

This highlights the need for a design-evaluation approach through adaptive and dynamic methodologies and tools. Therefore, the research aimed to structure an integrated decision-making process to support the design process, broadening strategic horizons towards multidimensional impact scenarios. The adopted methodology allowed for the definition of a set of time-based strategies, capable of combining tangible and intangible actions. The patrimony of confiscated assets represents an opportunity to critically examine design and evaluation tools, attempting to combine them within inclusive transition strategies that consider the multiplicity of actors and stakeholders, are open to temporary and transitory use, and can address uncertainty and generating positive, sustainable, and lasting impacts.

The following contribution presents: Section 2, dedicated to the case studies, which frames the topic of Confiscated Assets concerning the need for an impact-oriented and design-evaluation strategy; Section 3, Materials and Methods, which outlines the general methodology and the workflow of research and design process; Section 4, Results, which describes the initial outcomes of the adopted methodology; Section 5, Conclusion, which discusses the results based on the premises of the contribution.

2   The Case Studies: Confiscated Assets as Research Context

This contribution is part of the PRIN PNRR 2022 research project "Confiscated Assets in Transition: from the Anti-city to the Third Heritage", involving three research units affiliated with the Departments of Architecture at the University of Naples Federico II, the University of Palermo, and the Mediterranean University of Reggio Calabria. The focus is specifically on the progress made by the UniNA research unit and the educational experience developed within the Master's Degree Program in "Architecture for

Communities, Territories, and the Environment" through the design studio Architecture for the Circular and Inclusive City, where architectural and urban design is integrated with impact assessment practices. This contribution interprets the issue of assets confiscated from the mafia - especially in the city of Naples - as a laboratory for experimenting with an impact-oriented and design-evaluation approach.

The growing number of assets confiscated from organised crime represents both a complex challenge and a strategic opportunity. These assets constitute an atypical form of heritage: often critical and problematic, yet rich in symbolic and civic value [24, 25]. Their social reappropriation can activate transformative processes capable of generating positive impacts at both urban and territorial scales. In Italy, the National Strategy for Confiscated Assets, closely linked to public policies for social and urban cohesion, and the Laws 109/1996 and 296/2006, represent the main regulatory pillars. These laws provide for the reuse of confiscated assets for public and social purposes, ensuring their retention as public property while promoting objectives of justice, governance, institutional functions, culture, and social inclusion. Following their transfer to the National Agency for the Administration of Seized and Confiscated Assets, these properties are assigned to local authorities. Some are used for institutional purposes - such as schools, public services, and administrative offices - while others are entrusted to third-sector organisations for socially beneficial projects.

Within this political and regulatory framework, the potential of certain repurposed confiscated assets to serve as urban hubs that promote legality, local development, welfare, culture, and social cohesion is now well-established and widely recognised. However, the broader debate on this issue reveals several critical challenges that highlight the need to innovate existing procedures. From a regulatory standpoint, some mechanisms introduced to ensure transparency and effectiveness in the reassignment process have instead contributed to excessive procedural complexity [26]. This occurs for several reasons, including: the lack of multilevel knowledge and decision-making tools to support integrated regeneration projects; insufficient public funding; the physical and spatial criticalities of the assets, which are often illegally altered, structurally compromised, or unsuitable for collective or public use; and the absence of a long-term strategic vision. Moreover, the time lag between the seizure, confiscation, and eventual reassignment of the assets is frequently uncertain and problematic, often resulting in conditions of neglect and decay that further undermine the liveability of already fragile urban neighbourhoods [26].

Throughout the activities conducted, the set of assets confiscated from criminal organisations in Naples has been increasingly interpreted not merely as a collection of isolated elements, heterogeneous in nature, size, and location, but as a dispersed and diffuse system embedded within the urban fabric. Despite their fragmentation, these assets share a common trajectory: their reassignment to the public domain and their potential to contribute to positive social transformation. From an impact-oriented perspective, this body of confiscated assets can be reinterpreted as a unique civic resource. When embedded within a multiscale strategy for urban regeneration and social innovation, these properties may function as a distributed infrastructure capable of supporting community-driven development.

The central hypothesis for those case studies is that such transformation is possible only through the adoption of an impact-oriented design process, one that meaningfully integrates design and evaluation within an open, multi-stakeholder, dynamic, and iterative decision-making framework.

3   A Hybrid Methodology to Implement an Evolutionary Social Multi-criteria Evaluation

The research work involved the development of a transdisciplinary and multi-stakeholder collaborative decision-making process. In this regard, impact evaluation methodologies based on Multi-Criteria Decision Analysis (MCDA) approaches [27], combined with an Evolutionary Evaluation (EE) approach [28], fostered the development of an evaluative and design research process through the selection of a complex design theme concerning assets confiscated from organized crime in Naples, generating a transdisciplinary design-evaluation approach for defining impact-oriented strategies.

With this approach, the centrality of not only integrating project approaches and tools with those of sustainability evaluation, but also the necessity of designing the evaluative process through an innovative interpretative practice and hybridisation of approaches, methodologies, and tools, aimed at accommodating the operational specificities of intervention contexts, becomes paramount. Thus, impact evaluation goes beyond an *accountability* approach for program verification and becomes a tool for *inquiry* [29], as it supports the understanding of the socio-economic dynamics it triggers, analyses conflict, identifies the strengths and weaknesses of project proposals, and creates opportunities for discussion and reflection on emerging issues, engaging diverse forms of knowledge and expertise.

As highlighted by Patton [30], impact evaluation itself can enable change by facilitating the generation of intentional, conscious, and positive impacts, not only for the direct target, but that are also continuous and incremental over time. In this sense, impact evaluation constitutes a design tool within an impact-oriented perspective. Furthermore, the role of evaluation is central to design education, both for its ability to support and guide the design process and because it becomes a privileged formative tool that accompanies actors throughout the entire formative-design process, fostering the preventive verification of proposed solutions and generating mutual learning [31].

This highlights the need for recursive evaluations aimed at the progressive refinement of design alternatives and the gradual increase in the level of detail of the proposals under assessment, to follow the stochastic and uncertain nature of the project process as it evolves. This approach aligns with a formative evaluation perspective [32], where particular importance is placed on the logic of action. In this way, all actors involved in the design process can progressively become more aware of the values at stake, the impacts generated by each design decision, and the diversity of possible approaches and viewpoints. Within this framework, design alternatives are not seen as fixed or univocal choices, but rather as equally viable scenarios, whose relevance depends on how the design process unfolds over time.

In this sense, MCDA approaches and, more specifically, the Social Multi-Criteria Evaluation approach (SMCE) [23] become the methodological framework within which the evaluative process finds the opportunity to develop. Among the various application methods, a recent evolution of SMCE, known as the *SOcial multi-CRiteria AssessmenT of European policieS* (SOCRATES) [33–35] method, is adopted. SOCRATES allows for the recursive experimentation of multi-criteria evaluations (MCE), multi-group evaluations (MGE), and local and global sensitivity analyses [36]. More specifically, MCEs facilitate the construction of preference rankings based on the setting of a system of evaluation criteria articulated into dimensions, objectives, and criteria. The impact matrix, in this sense, calculates the preferability of alternatives for the adopted system, potentially also considering the relative importance assigned to each criterion, using diversified qualitative-quantitative evaluation scales for each criterion. MGE, in parallel, allows for the calculation of the preferability of different alternatives, based on the scores/judgments assigned by the various groups (or individuals) involved in the decision, which constitute the equity matrix, where values can be assigned through the adoption of diversified qualitative-quantitative evaluation scales. This fosters the integration between "expert" evaluation and "social" evaluation and - therefore - the combination of objective and subjective evaluations, using qualitative-quantitative data.

Alongside SMCE integrated with EE, the evaluation is supported by other evaluation and co-design tools, such as the decision tree or financial analysis, which allows for the optimised visualisation of strategic objectives and actions, and the criterion system used to measure long-term effects (Fig. 1).

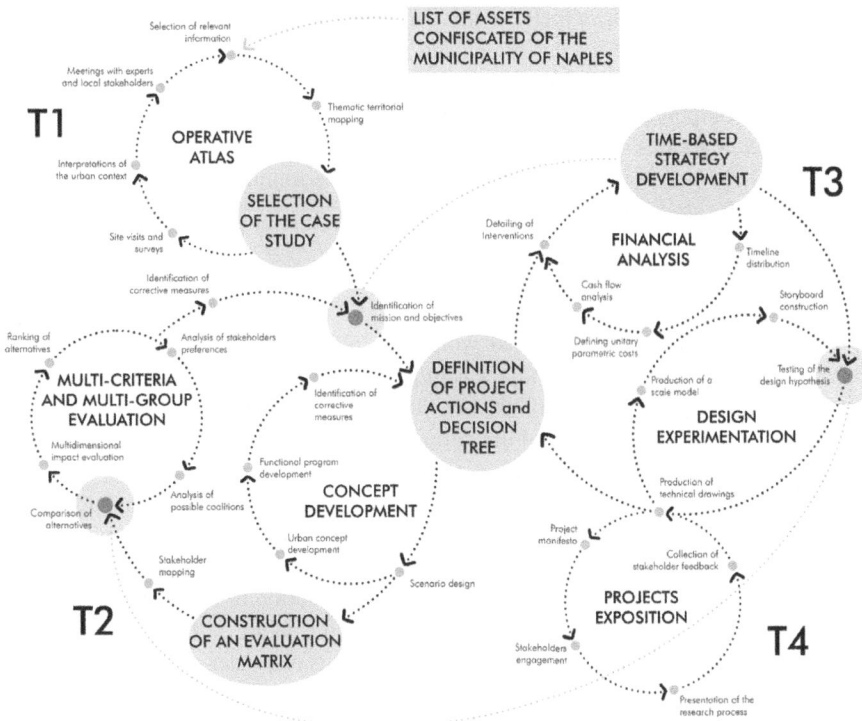

Fig. 1. Workflow diagram of the design-evaluation methodology loops for impact-oriented strategies.

The output consists of a hybrid methodology that integrates diverse approaches, models, methods, and tools, and is structured into four key phases that contribute to generating an evolutionary evaluative loop. This loop fosters the development of a deeper decision-making process, capable of concretely capturing the uncertainty that characterises decision-making processes aimed at urban transformations and public policies. The four phases consist of: Exploration and Immersion (T1); Design and Evaluation (T2); Project Experimentation (T3); Dissemination and Storytelling (T4). The proposed methodological steps and the corresponding results are described in the following section.

4   Results

The results emerging from the research activities were organised into four fundamental operational phases, corresponding to the main points of the methodological workflow developed. This process led to the definition of 14 design strategies, each of which was conceived as a dynamic and evolutionary path over time. The proposals developed scenarios that could synergistically integrate methodological approaches and operational tools of architectural and urban design with those of urban valuation, financial analysis, and impact assessment.

Each phase of the process produced specific results, consistent with the adopted design-evaluation approach, which centres on the progressive construction of design knowledge through iterative cycles of analysis, ideation, evaluation, and reformulation. Below, the key outcomes of each phase are summarised, highlighting the pivotal moments and significant outputs produced in the integrated path between design and evaluation. The evaluation started with the reconstruction of the entire project's process, both in chronological terms and its activities, starting from the municipal call to the analysis carried out by the associations at the end of the event.

4.1   Exploration and Immersion (T1)

The first phase of the methodological workflow, called Exploration and Immersion, involved a dual process: on one hand, the acquisition and deepening of transdisciplinary theoretical knowledge, and on the other, a critical and interpretative reading of the urban context under study. This phase laid the knowledge foundations for the construction of impact-oriented regeneration scenarios.

Starting from the public list of confiscated assets acquired by the Municipality of Naples, an exploratory analysis was conducted, leading to the selection of relevant information and the production of a series of thematic maps within a GIS environment. These maps allowed for the description of the territorial distribution of the assets, their typological composition, the extent of usable surfaces, and the nature of the building or land. The analysis revealed the fragmented and heterogeneous character of the heritage, presenting it as a widespread system, stratified within the complexity of the contemporary city.

To date, 140 assets have been assigned to the Municipality of Naples, allowing for the identification of six types of properties: 85 apartments, 38 ground-floor units, 4 buildings, 7 villas, 2 plots of land, and 4 car boxes. These assets are unevenly distributed across the city's ten districts, with a predominant concentration in District 2 and District 4, corresponding to some of the most densely populated and fragile central areas of the city.

Based on these findings, a representative sample of 13 assets, yet to be assigned, was selected, considering their type, location, and transformation potential. These were organised into five project themes, around which 14 working groups, composed of students from the laboratory, were established. Each group tackled a specific theme, developing an independent design proposal while considering it within an incremental and circular urban strategy, mindful of the systemic potential of the different initiatives (Fig. 2).

       ● Confiscated Assets of the Municipality of Naples
       ● Confiscated Assets of the Municipality of Naples | Case studies

Fig. 2. Cartographic reworking of the data reported in the public lists of confiscated assets acquired by the Municipality of Naples.

The process included site visits, surveys, morphological analyses, socio-demographic readings, and discussions with local stakeholders, integrating an interpretative analysis of the urban context with the identification of key actors and potential beneficiaries. Additionally, moments of exchange were organised with experts and third-sector organisations already involved in managing confiscated assets.

One of the main outputs of this phase is the creation of an Operational Atlas (OA) [37] for the selected case studies, supported by a set of decision-support tools. The OA was conceived as a tool that enables an informed comparison between experts and non-experts in the pre-design phase, when the final purpose of the asset has not yet been defined. The primary goal is to overcome the rigid and sterile normative approach, steering choices from the early stages towards an impact-oriented perspective.

The Atlas offers a multidimensional and multiscale reading of each confiscated asset, integrating both qualitative and quantitative data through analytical charts, evaluation grids, and thematic maps. For each asset, the OA provides a detailed description of its intrinsic and extrinsic characteristics: type, conservation status, accessibility, architectural configuration, and spatial adaptability. This is complemented by an analysis of spatial relationships with the surrounding urban context, through mapping proximity to transport nodes, essential services, social infrastructures, and cultural attraction hubs.

The Atlas also identifies constraints, challenges, and transformative potentials from architectural, urban, and socio-economic perspectives. It serves as a knowledge-sharing tool that enables comparative analysis between the various case studies, facilitating the emergence of priority intervention criteria and the activation of synergies with ongoing or future regeneration projects. In this way, the OA becomes a strategic device for guiding design choices, stakeholder engagement, and the co-construction of alternative scenarios, rooted in the specificities of the places and the needs of the communities (Fig. 3).

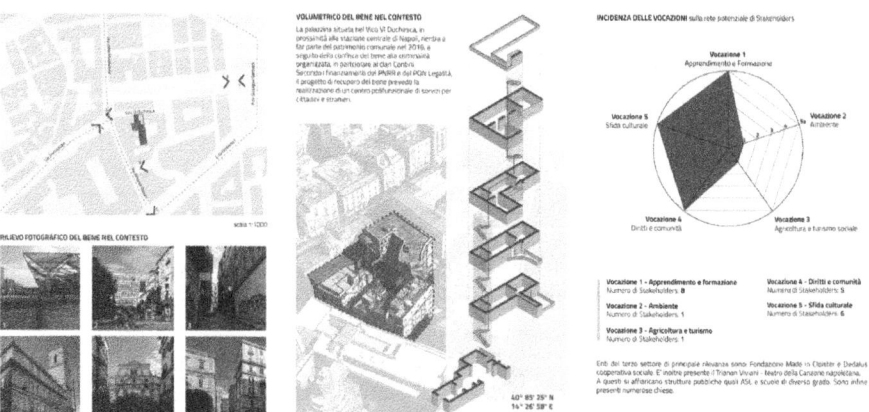

Fig. 3. Example of some deliverables contained within the Operational Atlas. Authors: Y. Danchenko and R. D'Antuono.

4.2   Design and Evaluation (T2)

The second phase of the process, called Design and Evaluation, represented a central moment of the laboratory, where the knowledge acquired during the exploration phase (T1) was reworked with a design-oriented approach. The objective was twofold: on one hand, to activate the creative process of defining strategies through the involvement of different actors, spaces, and visions; on the other, to initiate the concrete experimentation of the evolving evaluation approach, integrating design and evaluation from the early decision-making stages.

A key element was the use of the SOCRATES framework [33], employed not only as a tool for selecting between alternatives but also as a reflective and generative device: it enabled the exploration of the strengths and weaknesses of each proposal, identified common elements among different projects, and suggested targeted adjustments through the analysis of both qualitative and quantitative indicators. In this regard, SOCRATES was used as a dynamic, incremental, and user-centred tool, facilitating the understanding of preferences and synergies between real and potential stakeholders.

In parallel, tools from the social sciences - such as stakeholder mapping - were used to map interests, decision-making power, and potential alliances surrounding each asset being analysed. The groups constructed multidimensional evaluation matrices that allowed for the comparison of design alternatives based on environmental, social, cultural, and economic criteria. The activity was partly conducted through an intensive workshop ("Play SOCRATES"), which helped test the usability of the tool in a collaborative environment, simulating scenarios, preferences, and decision-making implications (Figs. 4 and 5).

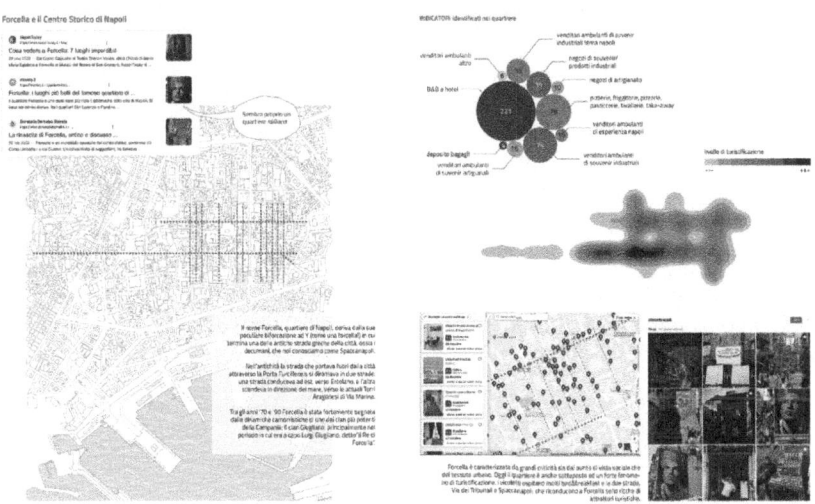

Fig. 4. The "Forcella o'GAS!" group analysed the touristification of Naples' historic centre, identifying a strategic goal to promote sustainable tourism. Authors: C. Maseda Juan, L. Prisco, C. Palmieri.

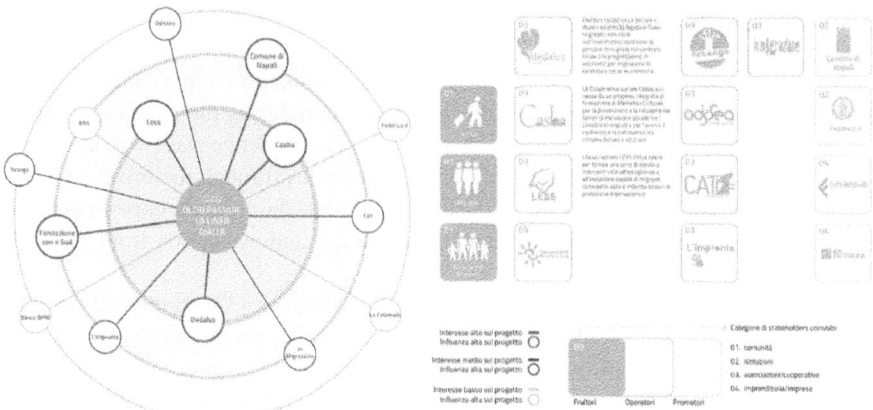

Fig. 5. An example of stakeholder analysis for a project alternative. Authors: Y. Danchenko and R. D'Antuono.

Additionally, a Decision Tree [38] was developed as a design tool to support the process. This tree allowed for the representation of connections between objectives, actions, evaluations, and expected impacts, highlighting how the project evolves over time and is subject to recursive feedback and revisions. This diagram played a fundamental role in supporting the progressive detailing of the project while maintaining a systemic and flexible vision.

In line with the impact-oriented approach, the design strategies were not seen as unique solutions, but as possible alternatives to be activated depending on external conditions (funding, partnerships, active policies). Some alternatives focused on low-budget scenarios with high civic involvement; others, more complex, required institutional synergies or support from foundations. This plurality was seen as a value, useful in building a portfolio of adaptive scenarios consistent with the principles of incremental regeneration and circular sustainability.

Each proposal was repeatedly discussed and collectively verified through graphic outputs, comparisons with the evaluation matrix, and analysis of consistency with the stakeholder and beneficiary system outlined. The interaction between phases T2 and T3 was constant and fluid: the boundary between design and evaluation proved to be porous and recursive, in line with the stochastic and systemic nature of the decision-making and creative process intended to be explored.

4.3 Project Experimentation (T3)

The third phase of the process, called Project Experimentation, focused on the spatial, technical, and economic validation of the strategies developed earlier. Using advanced architectural and urban design tools - including plans, elevations, sections, exploded axonometric views, and 3D representations - the working groups refined their proposals, testing their morphological and compositional consistency, technical feasibility, and long-term sustainability.

This phase saw a strong integration between design languages and evaluation tools, particularly through the introduction of a time-based strategy with multiple operational phases. Sequential axonometric diagrams, stakeholder maps (promoters, operators, users), and storyboards helped to describe the temporal evolution of the project, imagining a gradual transition from light, temporary, low-impact actions (events, installations, ephemeral activities) to more structured, long-lasting interventions that consolidate long-term objectives [39]. This approach captured the incremental and adaptive nature of the project, in line with the principles of circular urban regeneration and impact-oriented design.

Another innovative aspect was the dialogue between traditional design representation tools and financial evaluation tools. The financial sustainability analysis not only tested the intervention's feasibility but also guided the design choices toward management models aligned with the context and capable of fostering new forms of shared, circular economy. In this phase, the information collected and developed allowed for the integration of quantitative indicators into the multicriteria matrix from Phase 2, enriching the evaluation with objective and verifiable elements.

Furthermore, the increased definition of the project enabled a more precise redefinition of stakeholders' roles over time, highlighting strategic alliances, potential synergies, and flexible governance mechanisms. The decisions made in this phase were subjected to a reiterative verification process through the combined use of tools tested in Phase 2, reinforcing the integrated and recursive nature of the methodological workflow (Fig. 6).

4.4 Dissemination and Storytelling (T4)

The Dissemination and Storytelling phase focused on the creation of an articulated system for communicating the main results of the project. It employed graphic, visual, perceptive, and textual content to reach diverse audiences, highlighting the transdisciplinary nature of the work and the contribution of all participants (Fig. 7).

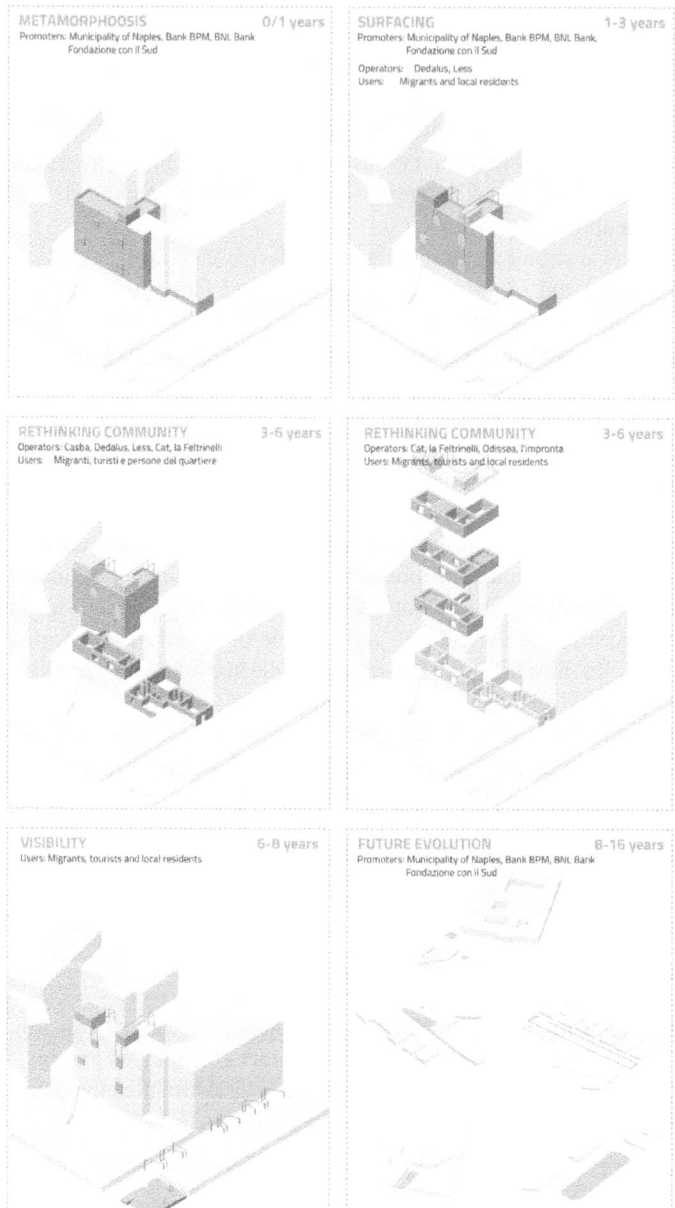

Fig. 6. Examples of final project outputs highlight the temporal evolution of interventions and their associated costs and revenues. Authors: Y. Danchenko and R. D'Antuono.

The core of phase T4 was the final exhibition, a public event that showcased the outcomes of the studio experience and the progress of the research. The exhibition presented both collective and individual outputs - maps, drawings, and scale models -reflecting the

Fig. 7. Some photos from the final exhibition, particularly during the moments of discussion with local stakeholders.

work carried out throughout the process. A key feature of this phase was the engagement of local stakeholders, identified as key interlocutors for the exhibition and a shared brainstorming session. The participation of representatives from the Italian universities involved in the PRIN project, artists, school principals, and members of institutions and associations enriched the debate. The exhibition became an opportunity for knowledge exchange and collective engagement, fostering encounters between otherwise disconnected communities interested in the issue of confiscated assets. This event acted as a moment of collective learning, awareness-raising, and critical reflection, particularly concerning the fight against organised crime and the role of architectural design in the transformation of confiscated property into public heritage.

Among the tools developed, the Manifesto stands out as a key medium to provide a concise overview of the business model underlying each design proposal. It coherently integrates architectural, evaluative, and impact dimensions, including the project abstract, an evocative 3D visualisation of the design idea, and a stakeholder engagement map. Furthermore, the Business Model Canvas [40] illustrates the project's technical and economic feasibility, regarding its temporal evolution, serving as a roadmap for long-term development.

Additionally, the exhibition generated valuable feedback on the process, confirming—through dialogue with local stakeholders—the importance of an impact-oriented approach that integrates diverse knowledge and disciplinary perspectives. It highlighted the effectiveness of the design-evaluation process in developing integrated, time-based strategies. The outcomes of the project's four phases represent an important milestone in the ongoing research on confiscated assets in Naples, providing a solid foundation to retrace the iterative and dynamic process, and to identify further refinements for the proposed strategies (Fig. 8).

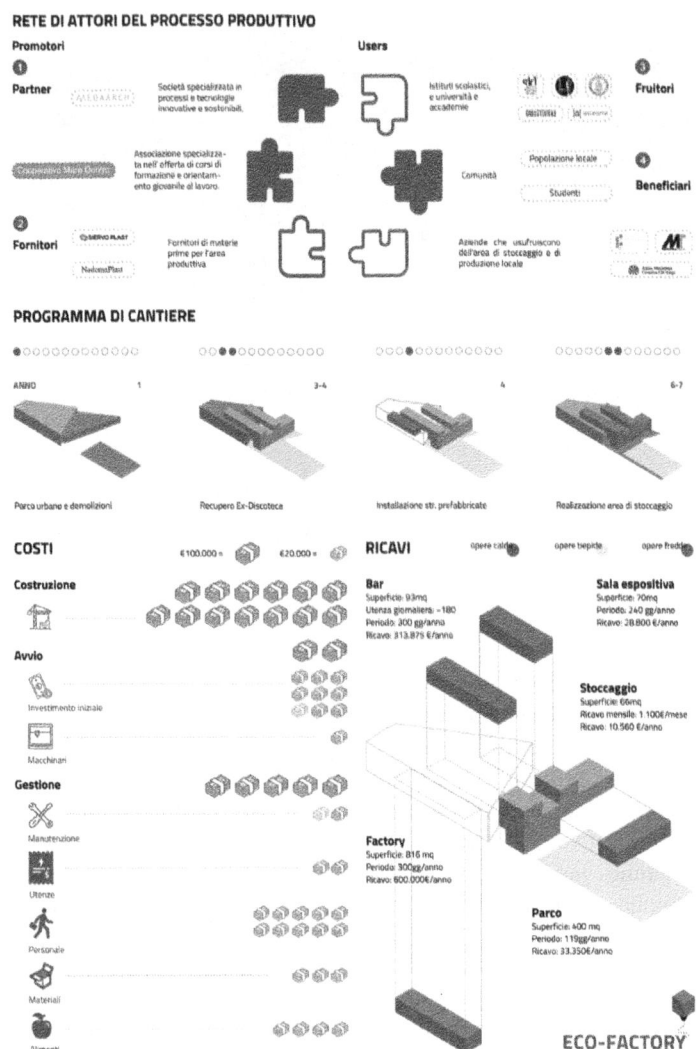

Fig. 8. An example of a project manifesto summarising the design concept, the functional organisation, and the main dimensions of impact generated. Authors: M.C. Piccolo, N. Russo Spena, S. Vecchione.

5 Conclusions

The research and educational activities conducted within the framework of the PRIN PNRR 2022 project underscore the critical role of integrated approaches in addressing the multifaceted challenges of urban regeneration in fragile contexts. Confiscated assets, often situated at the intersection of socio-economic marginalisation and urban decay, represent both a symbolic and practical opportunity to reimagine the relationship between space, community, and governance.

The exploration of these spaces through the laboratory "Architecture for the Circular and Inclusive City" demonstrated the potential of a design-evaluation process to generate innovative strategies that are not only technically and functionally sound but also socially and culturally meaningful. By adopting a transdisciplinary perspective, the research emphasised the importance of engaging with diverse stakeholders as co-creators of knowledge. This participatory framework allowed for the identification of latent values within confiscated properties, facilitating their reactivation as inclusive and circular urban spaces.

From a methodological standpoint, the integration of impact evaluation into the design process proved essential in addressing the complex and layered nature of these contexts. The laboratory's approach, structured around phases of exploration, immersion, and projection, enabled participants to critically assess the existing conditions, uncover hidden dynamics, and envision sustainable and resilient futures. This iterative process bridged qualitative and quantitative dimensions, merging spatial analysis with socio-cultural insights to produce a comprehensive understanding of the challenges and opportunities of regeneration projects.

One of the most significant contributions of the study lies in its ability to frame confiscated assets not merely as physical structures to be rehabilitated but as arenas for the negotiation of new social values. The reactivation of these spaces involves the redefinition of their symbolic and functional roles within the urban fabric, transforming them into drivers for positive social changes.

Moreover, the cross-scalar approach adopted in the study allowed for a nuanced understanding of the interactions between local dynamics and broader socio-political frameworks. This perspective was particularly evident in the analysis of impact dimensions, which extended beyond immediate functional outcomes to include relational, temporal, and symbolic aspects. By situating confiscated assets within larger narratives of urban transformation and social innovation, the research highlighted their potential to act as catalysts for systemic change.

In conclusion, this work affirms the relevance of integrated design-evaluation methodologies in addressing the complexities of urban regeneration, particularly in contexts characterised by socio-spatial vulnerability. It calls for the establishment of hybrid spaces of experimentation, where academic, institutional, and community actors can collaboratively develop and implement transformative strategies. The findings advocate for a paradigm shift in the management and reactivation of confiscated assets, moving towards models that prioritise inclusivity, resilience, and long-term impact.

By framing confiscated assets as resources for circular and inclusive urban futures, the study contributes to a broader discourse on the role of architecture and urbanism in promoting social and spatial justice. It challenges conventional approaches to urban regeneration, proposing instead a holistic framework that values the interconnections between space and community as fundamental to the pursuit of equitable and sustainable urban development.

Acknowledgements and Contributions. This research is part of the PRIN PNRR 2022 project "Confiscated Assets in Transition: from the Anti-city to the Third Heritage", which involves a research group coordinated by Professor Marina Tornatora at the Mediterranean University of Reggio Calabria, the group led by Professor Orfina Fatigato at the Department of Architecture,

University of Naples Federico II, and the team coordinated by Professor Zeila Tesoriere at the University of Palermo. In particular, the contribution presents the ongoing work of the Neapolitan team, carried out as part of the course "Architecture for the Circular and Inclusive City", coordinated by prof. Orfina Fatigato and prof. Maria Cerreta, with PhD candidates: Simona Capaldo, Laura Di Tommaso, Benedetta Grieco, Caterina Loffredo, and Piero Zizzania, within the Master's Degree Program in "Architecture for Communities, Territories, and the Environment".

The activities were conducted with the students: Michele Annunziata, Carmela Avagnano, Mariantonietta Bartolomeo, Raffaele Cimmino, Roberta D'Antuono, Yuliya Danchenko, Alessia Maria Del Peschio, Alessandra Di Costanzo, Chiara Esposito, Gabriella Girardi, Noemi Lubrano, Sara Maiuri, Federica Manenti, Salvatore Marciello, Clara Maseda Juan, Marco Mazzia, Chiara Mirra, Luca Oliva, Maria Ottaiano, Emauele Sirio Palescandolo, Carmen Palmieri, Antonio Pellecchia, Muthuthantrige Sahasri Idan Peris, Valeria Duran Pérez, Maria Chiara Piccolo, Marianna Pignataro, Teresa Portoghese, Ludovica Prisco, Anghjulina Rovere, Camilla Russo, Sabrina Russo, Naomi Russo Spena, Rosanna Santoro, Annachiara Sarnataro, Federica Sarro, Valentina Serafini, Maria Letizia Sibillo, Giuseppina Tedesco, Piergiorgio Tiano, Chiara Tornese, and Sara Vecchione.

The research was jointly framed and developed by the authors: Conceptualization, M.C., O.F., S.C., and P.Z.; Development of case studies, M.C., O.F., S.C., L.D.T., B.G., C.L., and P.Z., with all the students of the course; Methodology, M.C., L.D.T., and P.Z.; Original Draft Preparation, L.D.T., S.C., and P.Z.; Review and Editing, L.D.T., S.C., B.G., P.Z., O.F. and M.C.; Supervision and Final Review, M.C and O.F.. All authors have read and agreed to the published version of the manuscript.

References

1. Coscia, C., Rubino, I.: Fostering new value chains and social impact-oriented strategies in urban regeneration processes: What challenges for the evaluation discipline? Smart Innov. Syst. Technol. **178 SIST**, 983–992 (2021). https://doi.org/10.1007/978-3-030-48279-4_92/FIGURES/2
2. Jonas, H.: Das Prinzip Verantwortung. Versuch einer Ethik für die technologische Zivilisation. Insel, Frankfurt am Main (1979)
3. Iaione, C.: The CO-City: sharing, collaborating, cooperating, and Commoning in the City. Am. J. Econ. Sociol. **75**, 415–455 (2016). https://doi.org/10.1111/ajes.12145
4. Stern, E., Stame, N., Mayne, J., Forss, K., Davies, R., Befani, B.: Broadening the Range of Designs and Methods for Impact Evaluations: Report of a Study Commissioned by the Department for International Development (DFID). Working Paper 38. DFID, London (2012)
5. Glewwe, P., Todd, P.: Impact Evaluation in International Development: Theory, Methods and Practice. World Bank, Washington, DC (2022). https://doi.org/10.1596/978-1-4648-1497-6
6. EEAC: Working Group Governance: Impact Assessment of European Commission Policies: Achievements and Prospects. (2006)
7. Vanclay, F.: International principles for social impact assessment. Impact Assess. Proj. Apprais. **21**, 5–12 (2003). https://doi.org/10.3152/147154603781766491
8. Santos, F.M.: A positive theory of social entrepreneurship. J. Bus. Ethics. **111**, 335–351 (2012). https://doi.org/10.1007/S10551-012-1413-4/TABLES/1
9. Vicari Haddock, S., Moulaert, F. (eds.): Rigenerare la città: pratiche di innovazione sociale nelle città europee. Il Mulino (2009)
10. Ostanel, E.: Spazi fuori dal comune: rigenerare, includere, innovare. F. Angeli (2017)
11. Cerreta, M., La Rocca, L.: Urban regeneration processes and social impact: a literature review to explore the role of evaluation. In: Gervasi, O. (ed.) Computational Science and Its Applications – ICCSA 2021 Lecture Notes in Computer Science, vol. 12955, pp. 167–182. Springer, Cham (2021). https://doi.org/10.1007/978-3-030-86979-3_13

12. Secchi, B.: La città dei ricchi e la città dei poveri. Laterza, Roma - Bari (2013)
13. Latour, B.: Reassembling the Social: An Introduction to Actor-Network-Theory. Oxford University Press, Oxford (2005)
14. Lefebvre, H.: Il diritto alla città. Ombre Corte (2014)
15. McKay, P.A., Schmitt Olabisi, L., Vogt, C.A.: Assessing improvements in socio-ecological system governance using mixed methods and the quality governance framework and its diagnostic capacity tool. Environ. Syst. Decis. **40**, 41–66 (2020). https://doi.org/10.1007/s10669-019-09744-0
16. Bazzini, D., Curti, I.: Misurare l'impatto delle infrastrutture sociali per rigenerare la città, https://www.che-fare.com/articoli/impatto-infrastrutture-sociali-rigenerare-citta, last accessed 10 May 2025
17. Evans, G., Shaw, P.: The Contribution of Culture to Regeneration in the UK: A Review of Evidence: A Report to the Department for Culture Media and Sport, p. 10.13039/501100004623. London Metropolitan University, London (2004)
18. Urban, J.B., Hargraves, M., Trochim, W.M.: Evolutionary evaluation: implications for evaluators, researchers, practitioners, funders and the evidence-based program mandate. Eval. Program Plann. **45**, 127–139 (2014). https://doi.org/10.1016/j.evalprogplan.2014.03.011
19. Mertens, D.M.: Transformative Research and Evaluation. Guilford Press (2008)
20. Venturi, P.: La valutazione d'impatto sociale come pratica "trasformativa". Welfare Oggi. **19** (2019)
21. Zizzania, P., Muccio, E., Sacco, S., Cerreta, M.: Prediction and Uncertainty in Social Impact Evaluation: A Classification Framework Lecture Notes in Networks and Systems. 1186 LNNS, pp. 49–58 (2024). https://doi.org/10.1007/978-3-031-74679-6_5/FIGURES/1
22. Hirschman, A.O.: Development Projects Observed. Brookings Institution Press (1997)
23. Munda, G.: Multi-criteria evaluation as a multidimensional approach to welfare measurement. In: Economy and Ecosystems in Change (2023). https://doi.org/10.4337/9781035303571.00014
24. Tesoriere, Z.: Architettura per i beni confiscati. Figure del progetto nei territori del conflitto fra democrazia e criminalità. IN_BO. Ricerche e progetti per il territorio, la città e l'architettura. **14**, 236–255 (2023). https://doi.org/10.6092/ISSN.2036-1602/14841
25. Tesoriere, Z.: Heritage and the anti-city. Pizzo Sella in Palermo between modern ruins tourism and civic reappropriation. In: Marzo, M., Ferrario, V., Bertini, V. (eds.) Between sense of time and sense of place, pp. 426–433. Lettera 22, Siracusa (2022)
26. Tornatora, M., Amaro, O.: Il progetto dei beni confiscati: per una metamorfosi urbana e architettonica. Culture della Sostenibilità. **30** (2022). https://doi.org/10.7402/CDS.30.008
27. Mecca, B.: Assessing the sustainable development: a review of multi-criteria decision analysis for urban and architectural sustainability. J. Multi-Criteria Decis. Anal. **30**, 203–218 (2023). https://doi.org/10.1002/MCDA.1818;REQUESTEDJOURNAL:JOURNAL:10991360;WGROUP:STRING:PUBLICATION
28. Poli, G., Zizzania, P., Vannelli, G., D'Agostino, A.: Exploring transformative potentials of urban cemeteries through an evolutionary evaluation approach: the case study of "Poggioreale" in Naples (Italy). In: Lecture Notes in Computer Science (including subseries Lecture Notes in Artificial Intelligence and Lecture Notes in Bioinformatics) (2023). https://doi.org/10.1007/978-3-031-37117-2_22
29. Bezzi, C.: Il nuovo disegno della ricerca valutativa. FrancoAngeli (2010)
30. Patton, M.Q.: Utilization-focused evaluation. In: International Handbook of Educational Evaluation, pp. 223–242. Springer Netherlands (2003). https://doi.org/10.1007/978-94-010-0309-4_15
31. Scholz, R.W.: The mutual learning sessions. In: Transdisciplinarity: Joint Problem Solving among Science, Technology, and Society, pp. 117–129 (2001). https://doi.org/10.1007/978-3-0348-8419-8_11

32. Sánchez, L.E., Mitchell, R.: Conceptualizing impact assessment as a learning process. Environ. Impact Assess. Rev. **62**, 195–204 (2017). https://doi.org/10.1016/J.EIAR.2016. 06.001

33. Munda, G., Azzini, I., Cerreta, M., Ostlaender, N.: SOCRATES manual. Publications Office of the European Union (2022). https://doi.org/10.2760/2694059

34. Di Tommaso, L., Daldanise, G., La Rocca, L., Panaro, S., Cerreta, M.: A Co-governance Process for the Adaptive Reuse of Cultural Heritage: The Experience of St. Michael Cloister in Anacapri Lecture Notes in Computer Science (including subseries Lecture Notes in Artificial Intelligence and Lecture Notes in Bioinformatics). 14824 LNCS, pp. 236–252 (2024). https:// doi.org/10.1007/978-3-031-65332-2_16/FIGURES/5

35. Mazzarella, C., La Rocca, L., Ventre, S., Cerreta, M.: Heritage communities urban living lab (HeCo ULL): a circular methodological approach for co-design through social multi-criteria evaluation. In: Lecture Notes in Networks and Systems. 1186 LNNS, pp. 38–48 (2024). https://doi.org/10.1007/978-3-031-74679-6_4/FIGURES/3

36. Azzini, I., Munda, G.: Sensitivity and robustness analyses in social multi-criteria evaluation of public policies. J. Multi-Criteria Decis. Anal. **32**, e70006 (2025). https://doi.org/10.1002/ MCDA.70006;CTYPE:STRING:JOURNAL

37. Kollectiv Orangotango: This Is Not an Atlas: A Global Collection of Counter-Cartographies. Transcript: Independent Academic Publishing (2018). https://doi.org/10.14361/978383944 5198-FM

38. Rokach, L., Maimon, O.: Decision trees. In: Maimon, O., Rokach, L. (eds.) Data Mining and Knowledge Discovery Handbook, pp. 165–192. Springer, Boston, MA (2005). https://doi. org/10.1007/0-387-25465-X_9

39. Besson, R., Bordage, F., Bouchain, P., Clément, G., Gwiazdzinski, L., Lindgaard, J., Nicolas-Le Strat, P., Perez, P., Viveret, P., Zaska, J.: Infinite Places Costructing Buildings or Places? Éditions B42, Paris (2018)

40. Saleh, R., Ost, C.: Innovative business model for adaptive reuse of cultural heritage in a circular economy perspective. Int. J. Entrep. Small Bus. **48**, 39–77 (2023). https://doi.org/10. 1504/IJESB.2023.10053086

Transforming Urban Analytics: The Impact of Crowdsourced Mapping and Advanced AI Techniques on Future Cities (Tr-UrbAna 2025)

Predicting Visitors' Digital Footprints Using Spatial Features and Synthetic Pedestrian Data

Müslüm Hacar$^{(\boxtimes)}$ (iD)

Yildiz Technical University, Esenler, Istanbul 34210, Türkiye
mhacar@yildiz.edu.tr

Abstract. Assessing digital footprints of visitors has often depended on a pedestrian count data representing the human density in urban environment. The data is commonly generated via sensor, cellular phone network, or CCTV technologies, which involves high costs and raises concerns regarding personal data protection. This study presents a novel approach for predicting visitor ratings of eating and drinking out venues in Bakırköy, Istanbul, without relying on a real pedestrian counting system. In our work, a synthetic pedestrian count measure is generated by interpolating the overall review volume data extracted from a complete set of points-of-interest data via Google Maps API. This measure is aggregated to streets, and additional spatial measures are used to further describe the urban environment. Some street geometric features (i.e., sinuosity and street length) that showed limited predictive value in earlier studies were removed from the analysis. A random forest machine learning model was applied to predict visitors' high/low ratings, achieving a 76% F1-score. The results suggest that digital traces left by visitors can be effectively predicted through alternative spatial measures and synthetic data. The proposed approach provides a cost-effective and privacy-respecting method that can support business decision-making in the context of digital consumer behavior.

Keywords: Synthetic Pedestrian Count · Digital Footprint · Urban Analytics · Street Network · Point of Interest

1 Introduction

Digital records left by visitors play a significant role in understanding urban life. In recent years, the analysis of digital footprints, which refers to the records of online behavior that individuals leave behind, including reviews and rating, has become a popular method for evaluating consumer behavior [1–6]. These records offer valuable information about consumer satisfaction and service quality, which can be used by urban planners and business stakeholders [3–6]. In particular, eating and drinking out (EDO) venues generate a considerable amount of digital data that can be used to analyze consumer satisfaction and guide planning decisions. In recent years, studies described below have shown that digital records provide an effective measure for assessing urban dynamics and visitor behavior. This section follows with (1) a literature review part on digital footprint research

© The Author(s), under exclusive license to Springer Nature Switzerland AG 2026
O. Gervasi et al. (Eds.): ICCSA 2025 Workshops, LNCS 15897, pp. 391–402, 2026.
https://doi.org/10.1007/978-3-031-97660-5_26

studies, specifically in urban areas, then (2) describes the gaps in the current analysis, and (3) concludes with the motivations to propose a novel approach to generating synthetic pedestrian data which can be used as a feature for the prediction of visitor ratings.

The use of digital footprints for urban analysis is supported by several studies. Valanarasu [1] examined the potential of the footprint for personality prediction. In his study, he investigated the growing use of social media digital footprints to predict user personality traits by analyzing publicly accessible posts and status updates from multiple platforms, including Facebook, Twitter, and YouTube. His work introduced a novel hybrid machine learning approach that integrates dynamic multi-context information to achieve higher accuracy in personality prediction. Adikari et al. [2] proposed an approach that leverages Natural Language Processing to transform unstructured hotel reviews into a structured representation of emotions and hotel attributes. Their method, validated on 22,450 reviews from 44 hotels, enables segmentation of customer and hotel profiles to support targeted management strategies and informed decision-making. Di Clemente et al. [5] introduced a framework that applies text compression techniques on credit card transaction sequences, capitalizing on Zipf-like distributions to reveal significant purchasing patterns. Their method successfully clusters consumers into groups with similar demographic and behavioral characteristics based on the temporal order of their transactions. Khan and Loan [6] examined how public library users in Delhi utilize Google Maps to share opinions about facilities and services, using content and sentiment analysis to classify the reviews. Their findings indicate that the platform serves as an effective interactive feedback system, with the majority of reviews expressing positive sentiments while highlighting specific areas for improvement. Hacar et al. [7] investigated how urban spatial configurations, including street prominence and place type, influence the digital footprints captured through online reviews and ratings. By applying Space Syntax metrics to Google Maps points of interest (POIs) in Sassi di Matera, Italy, they demonstrated that the relationship between urban form and visitor review behavior varies significantly depending on the type of place. Muhammed et al. [8] developed a conceptual framework through a systematic literature review to identify the key factors that influence customers' willingness to leave digital footprints on social media. Their study finds that intrinsic psychological traits, technological convenience, social influences, and concerns about privacy and security are critical determinants of this behavior. Girardin et al. [9] presented innovative methods for analyzing spatiotemporal data derived from user-generated sources like cell phone networks and georeferenced photos. Their approach effectively reveals tourist presence and movement patterns, providing valuable indicators of urban dynamics. Martí et al. [10] proposed a reference framework that uses volunteered user-generated content from multiple location-based social networks to identify and characterize tourist activity centers in urban settings. Their method enables a fine-grained analysis of tourism dynamics, thereby offering a complementary tool for urban planning decision-making. Jia and Liu [11] investigated the roles of online review valence and usefulness in influencing consumer behavior, suggesting that the positivity of a review offers more diagnostic value than its usefulness rating. Their mixed-method research, which combines large-scale panel data with experimental studies, demonstrates that highly useful reviews increase consumer adoption only when perceived as positive. Li and Hecht [12] investigated discrepancies between restaurant ratings on Google Maps and Yelp, revealing that ratings on Google Maps are on average 0.7 stars higher, particularly for chain restaurants. Their study also shows minimal overlap in top-ranked lists across platforms, questioning the reliability of using a single review source for local searches. Akkaya et al. [13] proposed a machine learning method that uses Google Maps Reviews to extract structured insights on park features and social structures in Istanbul. This approach offers a practical alternative to traditional, labor-intensive public feedback collection methods, supporting urban planning decisions. Owour and Hochmair [14] reviewed 110 social media apps to evaluate their potential for geospatial research, highlighting that only a fraction provided robust APIs and relevant spatial data. Their findings suggest that several lesser-known apps merit further exploration, as they could uncover underexplored aspects of urban dynamics. Tang et al. [15] applied deep learning techniques to segment panoramic urban images and analyzed how built environment attributes affect restaurant popularity. Their results indicate that pedestrian flow is the most critical factor influencing restaurant ratings, while higher densities of traffic signs negatively correlate with review counts. Rajabi et al. [16] assessed healthcare center accessibility in Tehran using Google POI data and clustering algorithms, revealing a significant imbalance in service distribution across the city. Their analysis underscores a misalignment between healthcare resources and population density, emphasizing the need for targeted urban planning. Tse et al. [17] examined Canadian acute care hospitals by correlating Google Reviews with hospital characteristics and patient experience scores, uncovering substantial variability among hospitals. Their study demonstrates that online reviews can serve as a readily accessible, real-time tool for monitoring and improving patient care. Leiras and Eusébio [18] analyzed over a thousand online traveler reviews from Aveiro and A Coruña to assess the perceived image of Accessible Tourism Destinations. Their findings revealed that key accessibility features, such as parking availability and disability adaptations, significantly impact visitor satisfaction, offering a strategic framework for tourism management. Öztürk Hacar et al. [19] analyzed how urban spatial characteristics, such as pedestrian counts, residential density, and street geometry, influence digital consumer behavior at EDO places. Their random forest model applied to Google Maps reviews in Melbourne's city center indicates that pedestrian counts and residential density are strong predictors of review volumes and visitor ratings, while measures of street centrality and geometry exhibit varied effects, suggesting a promising alternative for urban planning and business decision-making.

Many municipalities and private enterprises are interested in using digital footprints for strategic planning and decision-making. Assessing digital footprints of visitors has often depended on pedestrian count data which are commonly generated via sensor, cellular phone network, or CCTV technologies, involving high costs and raising concerns regarding personal data protection. Instead of using a count data, using a predicted pedestrian volume can play a critical role in reducing those disadvantages. Jiang et al. [20] developed a spatiotemporal machine learning model to estimate pedestrian volume in Melbourne. On the other hand, in contexts where historical sensor data are unavailable, digital footprints from location-based platforms can serve as a valuable proxy for modeling pedestrian activity. This paper proposes an approach to generating synthetic pedestrian data derived from Google POI review volumes and supportive spatial features to predict the visitor ratings at EDO places in Bakırköy, Istanbul. By avoiding the use of direct and indirect pedestrian counting technology, the proposed approach addresses key issues related to cost and privacy while offering businesses a practical framework for digital analytics.

2 Materials and Methods

2.1 Study Area and Data Structures

The study is conducted in Bakırköy, a prominent center on Istanbul's European side, particularly renowned for its dense clustering of university preparatory, post-graduate courses, and shopping facilities (see Fig. 1). This concentration of mobility has resulted in a high volume of pedestrian movement, which in turn has spurred the emergence of numerous alternative eating and drinking venues to meet the dynamic needs of the population.

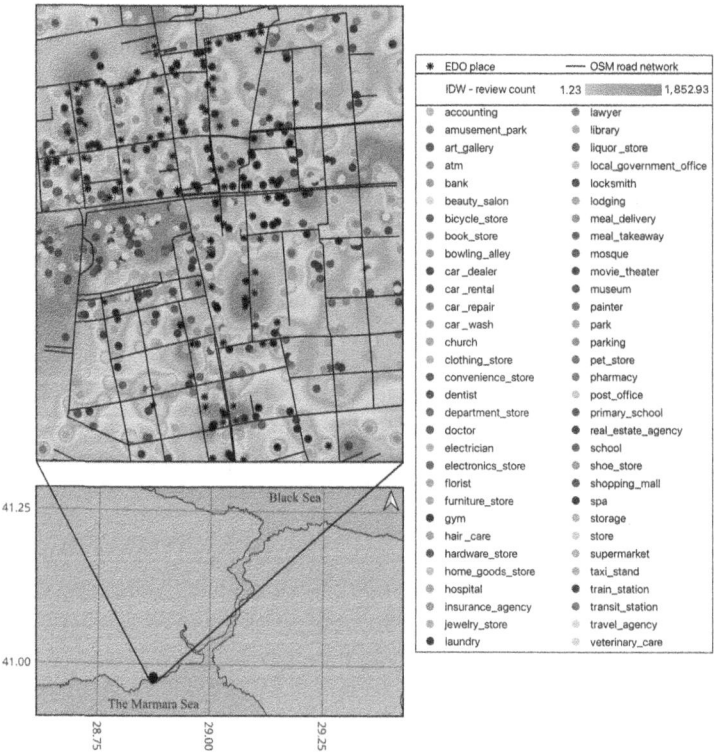

Fig. 1. Study area and the data representations.

Data for this study are primarily sourced from POI points obtained via the Google Maps API [21] and OSM road networks downloaded via OSM Export [22]. The POI records include essential attributes such as review count, rating, and type, which are utilized as the key features in the analysis. In particular, the rating attribute is categorized into two classes: High and Low, using a quantile approach. These categories serve as the dependent variable for predicting visitors' digital footprints. Moreover, OSM road network offers a comprehensive representation of urban transportation. In this study, an arc-node topology of the road network was constructed by first applying a dissolve operation followed by split operations by each junction. All road-based features are derived from the road network topology.

2.2 The Proposed Approach to Feature Generation and Prediction Model

Google POIs data is specifically for EDO establishments, which provides semantic details like place type, review count, and rating [21]. To ensure the reliability of our analysis on visitor behavior, we included only the places that have accumulated at least 10 reviews. This threshold helps us concentrate on consumer-focused locations, facilitating a deeper investigation into the correlation between the spatial distribution of places and consumers' digital footprints.

Instead of employing direct pedestrian count data, typically gathered from sensors, cellular networks, or CCTV, review count data of all types of POIs is used as a surrogate metric to indicate the intensity of consumer presence across the urban landscape. Additionally, to prepare the count data for the following spatial analysis, we applied an Inverse Distance Weighting (IDW) interpolation in a QGIS (version 3.28) environment, which allows to generate continuous surfaces that approximate pedestrian density patterns [23]. Unlike Kriging, IDW does not require complex statistical assumptions or parameters such as spatial autocorrelation or variogram models. IDW assumes that the influence of each data point decreases with distance, which fits well with the idea that areas near popular places with high review counts are likely to have more pedestrian activity. Each grid point's weighted value on the surface is associated to its closest street. Thus, a mean value of several grid points, which is hereafter referred as synthetic-PC, is assigned to each street (see Fig. 2).

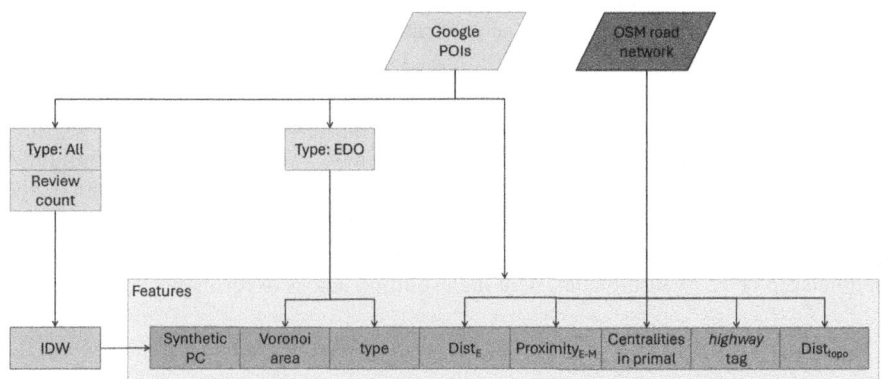

Fig. 2. Workflow of the feature generation.

The review counts at the places within the shopping malls (i.e., Carousel and Capacity shopping malls) are included in the synthetic-PC process to represent the crowd pedestrian population. However, the places are excluded in the target EDO establishment list since they are relatively independent from the neighboring streets but more depended on the indoor locations inside the building of shopping mall.

Voronoi polygons are created to express local proximity as a feature for each place. The area of each polygon is assigned to the regarding central node, POI. Also, the type of EDO POIs (i.e., bakery, bar, café, and restaurant) is used as a feature expressing the diversity of source data and is considered that it may represent the unique properties among others.

OSM road network data includes *highway* tags that classify roads based on their functional type [24]. These types are assumed to have different influences on visitor behavior and accessibility to services. To further quantify the connectivity and importance of individual street segments, centrality measures using a primal graph representation through the Python NetworkX package (version 3.2.1) are computed [25]. Eight metrics to reveal the representation of connectivity within the network are used: betweenness (B), closeness (C), degree (D), eigenvector (E), harmonic (H), Katz centrality (K), load (L), and PageRank (P). These metrics help explain how integrated or isolated each place is within the urban grid [19].

Rest of the features are generated by using both Google POIs and OSM. Firstly, $Dist_E$ is the Euclidean distance between the place and the closest node which has the degree of connectivity as more than two. It is considered to detect the closest potentially densified junctions. Secondly, $Proximity_{E-M}$ is the binary code referring whether the place is close to an end node (E) or middle node (M) of the closest street (see Fig. 3). This measure helps to depict a significant proximity information about an EDO place if it is more like around the junction of a street or not. Thirdly, $Dist_{topo}$ is the topological distance, which gives total number of steps over the street network from an EDO place to the closest pedestrian-friendly roads (i.e., *footway*, *living_street*, and *pedestrian*). The lower $Dist_{topo}$ value means that the place has a high potential to reach higher pedestrian costumers. Finally, since Öztürk Hacar et al. [19] mentioned about lower effect of the direct geometric properties of the closest street, the sinuosity and street length were removed from the prediction model.

Primary goal is to predict visitor scores: rating, which are classified into two categories (i.e., High and Low) using quantile-based segmentation. We employed a random forest classifier, a robust model capable of handling heterogeneous features by using the interrelations among spatial characteristics, network properties, and synthetic-PC. For reproducibility, the random_state parameter is fixed at 42, while the model is configured with 100 trees (n_estimators = 100), the Gini impurity criterion for split evaluation, and the square root of the total number of features considered at each split [26]. Additionally, the dataset is partitioned into training and testing sets using an 80–20% split, with a fixed random seed of 42 to ensure consistent data splitting across experiments.

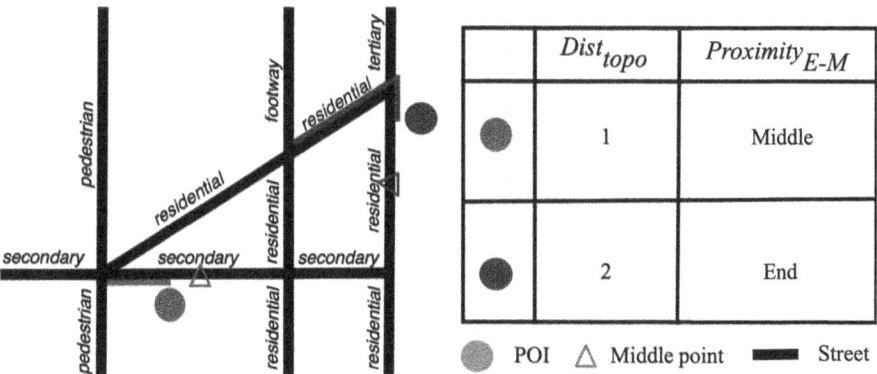

	$Dist_{topo}$	$Proximity_{E\text{-}M}$
●	1	Middle
●	2	End

● POI   △ Middle point   ▬▬ Street

Fig. 3. $Proximity_{E\text{-}M}$ and $Dist_{topo}$ feature descriptions.

3 Experimental Results

Following the methodological framework outlined in Sect. 2, the proposed approach was applied to the Bakirköy study area to evaluate how various spatial features, synthetic-PC, and centrality measures relate to digital consumer behavior at EDO places. The procedures involved extracting and processing POI information from Google Maps, generating an arc-node topology for the OSM road network, and computing both distance-based and network-based features to serve as independent variables for the random forest classification model.

This study employs a selected set of centrality measures, each highlighting a distinct facet of network structure. B emphasizes those segments most frequently used in shortest paths, often corresponding to key thoroughfares. C identifies nodes that are situated relatively near all other nodes, while D highlights the number of direct connections at each node. E reflects a node's importance based on the influence of its neighbors, whereas H modifies the concept of closeness by placing greater emphasis on short distances. K further extends eigenvector centrality by introducing a damping factor that weighs distant connections. L is similar to betweenness but considers distributed flow rather than single shortest paths. Finally, P evaluates node importance by factoring in the significance of inbound connections [27–40]. Figure 4 illustrates the distribution of these eight centrality metrics across the street network. In each subfigure, streets are rendered in red, green, and blue to represent higher or lower centrality values. Taken together, as Öztürk Hacar et al. [19] stated, these distributions reveal how certain streets stand out as major connectors within Bakirköy's urban layout, remarking the network's structural hierarchy and the potential influence of these thoroughfares on consumer movement on the network.

Table 1 summarizes the prediction model's classification performance for the Low and High rating categories. The model is notably effective at identifying venues that fall into the Low rating category. However, the result on the prediction of the High rating category gives a more moderate performance in recognizing the places. Overall, the weighted F1-score of 0.76 demonstrates a balanced level of accuracy across both classes, although there is room for improvement in capturing High-rated venues.

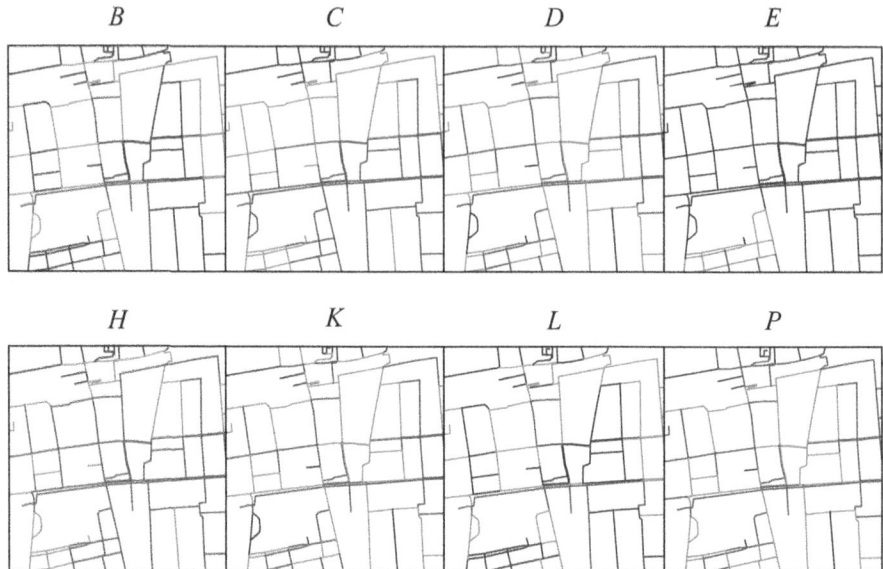

Fig. 4. Distribution of centrality measures across the street network: red as high, green as midrange, and blue as low.

Table 1. Performance metrics of the prediction model

Rating	Precision	Recall	F1-score
Low	0.79	0.86	0.83
High	0.70	0.58	0.64
Weighted	0.76	0.76	0.76

Figure 5 presents the mean decrease in impurity for each feature, revealing how they contribute to distinguishing between High and Low rating classes. $Dist_E$, the distance to a potentially densified junction, emerges as the most influential factor, implying that EDO places located nearer to such junctions are more likely to exhibit distinct rating patterns. Voronoi area and synthetic-PC follow closely, highlighting the relevance of local catchment size and approximate pedestrian activity for rating prediction. The categorical type of an EDO establishment also shows substantial importance, suggesting that different venue types attract varied consumer feedback. Centrality metrics: B, H, E, L, P, K, and C occupy mid-range positions, indicating that network connectivity and integration exert a measurable, though less dominant, effect. Meanwhile, $Proximity_{E-M}$, functional road classification, topological distance to pedestrian-friendly roads ($Dist_{topo}$), and the centrality metric D rank lower, but still contribute to the classification. Notably, the black lines on each bar represent the standard deviation, illustrating the variability of these importance scores across the ensemble. While $Dist_E$ and synthetic-PC exhibit relatively small deviations, indicating more consistent contributions, certain centrality metrics display wider error lines, suggesting that their impact may fluctuate depending on the specific data subsets used in individual decision trees.

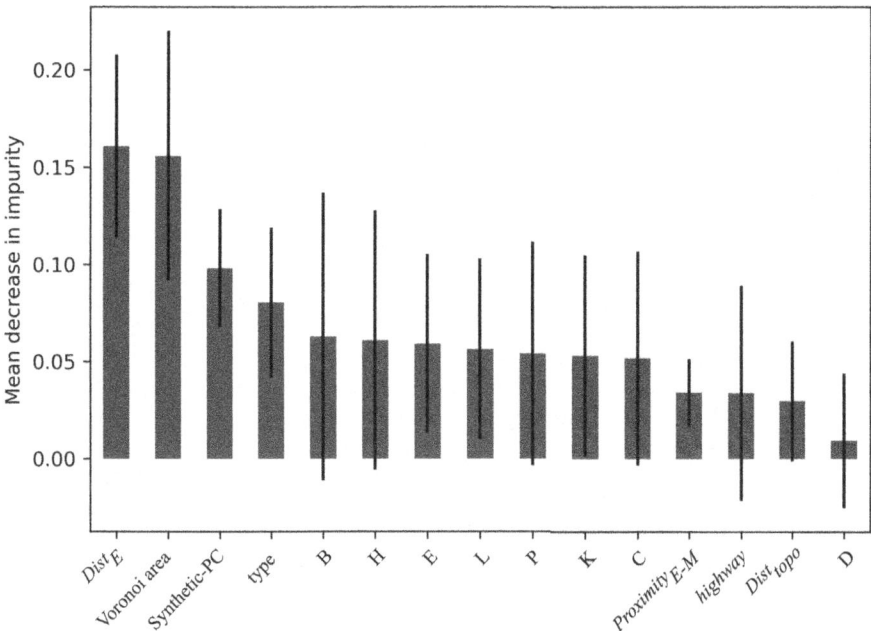

Fig. 5. Sorted feature importances with standard deviation across trees.

4 Conclusion

This study presents a novel approach for predicting visitor ratings at EDO venues by leveraging integrated spatial data derived from Google POIs and an OSM road network, along with a synthetic pedestrian measure. The approach was tested in Bakırköy, Istanbul, a district known for its high pedestrian flows due to the concentrations of educational institutions and shopping facilities. It offers key urban characteristics that influence digital consumer behavior. The analysis demonstrated that factors such as the proximity to densified junctions, local catchment areas, and synthetic pedestrian data play a pivotal role in shaping consumers' digital ratings, with centrality and various spatial metrics further complementing these insights.

The proposed approach can be employed as a decision support tool for entrepreneurs considering the location of new EDO business. By estimating the potential consumer rating at various candidate properties, entrepreneurs can identify the most promising sites based on projected visitor scores. This capability allows for data-driven decisions that align with consumer preferences, ultimately supporting higher success rates for newly established venues.

A key strength of this study is its avoidance of sensor-based, cellular network, or CCTV data collection, thereby reducing financial overheads and privacy concerns. Nonetheless, several limitations warrant attention. The synthetic pedestrian measure may not capture short-term time changes during a day in foot traffic. Future work should consider additional data inputs, such as temporal factors, land use variations, and consumer demographics, to validate and expand upon the present findings. Overall, this research offers a practical, privacy-conscious, and cost-effective strategy for understanding and forecasting digital consumer behavior, supporting the way for more informed urban planning and commercial decision-making.

Disclosure of Interests. The author declares no conflict of interest.

References

1. Valanarasu, M.R.: Comparative analysis for personality prediction by digital footprints in social media. J. Inform. Technol. Digit. World. **3**, 77–91 (2021)
2. Adikari, A., Nguyen, S., Nawaratne, R., De Silva, D., Alahakoon, D.: Transforming customer digital footprints into decision enablers in hospitality. Appl. Sci. **14**(3114) (2024). https://doi.org/10.3390/app14073114
3. Lazer, D., Pentland, A., Adamic, L., Aral, S., Barabási, A.L., Brewer, D., Christakis, N., Contractor, N., Fowler, J., Gutmann, M., Jebara, T., King, G., Macy, M., Roy, D., Van Alstyne, M.: Computational social science. Science. **323**, 721–723 (2009). https://doi.org/10.1126/science.1167742
4. Pentland, A.S.: The data-driven society. Sci. Am. 309, 78–83 (2013). https://www.jstor.org/stable/26018109
5. Di Clemente, R., Luengo-Oroz, M., Travizano, M., Xu, S., Vaitla, B., González, M.C.: Sequences of purchases in credit card data reveal lifestyles in urban populations. Nat. Commun. **9**, 3330 (2018). https://doi.org/10.1038/s41467-018-05690-8
6. Khan, A.M., Loan, F.A.: Exploring the reviews of Google Maps to assess the user opinions about public libraries. Libr. Manag. **43**, 601–615 (2022). https://doi.org/10.1108/LM-05-2022-0053
7. Hacar, M., Öztürk Hacar, Ö., Altafini, D., Pappalardo, L., Gülgen, F., Cutini, V.: From streets to screens: A deep dive into urban configuration and Google reviews. In: Proceedings of the 14th Space Syntax Conference, Nicosia, Cyprus (2024)
8. Muhammad, S.S., Dey, B.L., Weerakkody, V.: Analysis of factors that influence customers' willingness to leave big data digital footprints on social media: a systematic review of literature. Inf. Syst. Front. **20**, 559–576 (2018). https://doi.org/10.1007/s10796-017-9802-y
9. Girardin, F., Calabrese, F., Fiore, F., Ratti, C., Blat, J.: Digital footprinting: uncovering tourists with user-generated content. IEEE Pervasive Comput. **7**, 36–43 (2008). https://doi.org/10.1109/MPRV.2008.71
10. Martí, P., García-Mayor, C., Serrano-Estrada, L.: Taking the urban tourist activity pulse through digital footprints. Curr. Issue Tour. **24**, 157–176 (2021). https://doi.org/10.1080/13683500.2019.1706458
11. Jia, Y., Liu, I.: Do consumers always follow "useful" reviews? The interaction effect of review valence and review usefulness on consumers' purchase decisions. J. Assoc. Inf. Sci. Technol. **69**, 1304–1317 (2018). https://doi.org/10.1002/asi.24050

12. Li, H., Hecht, B.: 3 stars on yelp, 4 stars on Google Maps: a cross-platform examination of restaurant ratings. Proc. ACM Human Comput. Interact. **4**, 254 (2021). https://doi.org/10.1145/3432953

13. Akkaya, M., Özçevik, Ö., Tepe, E.: A machine learning application to Google Maps Reviews as a participatory planning tool. Int. J. Urban Sci. **28**, 379–402 (2024). https://doi.org/10.1080/12265934.2024.2320916

14. Owuor, I., Hochmair, H.H.: An overview of social media apps and their potential role in geospatial research. ISPRS Int. J. Geo Inf. **9**(526) (2020). https://doi.org/10.3390/ijgi9090526

15. Tang, Y., Zhang, J., Liu, R., Li, Y.: Exploring the impact of built environment attributes on social followings using social media data and deep learning. ISPRS Int. J. Geo Inf. **11**(325) (2022). https://doi.org/10.3390/ijgi11060325

16. Rajabi, F., Hosseinali, F., Rabiei-Dastjerdi, H.: An examination and analysis of the clustering of healthcare centers and their spatial accessibility in Tehran Metropolis: Insights from Google POI Data. Sustain. Cities Soc. **117**, 105845 (2024). https://doi.org/10.1016/j.scs.2024.105845

17. Tse, M.P., Dhalla, I., Nayyar, D.: Google star ratings of Canadian hospitals: a nationwide cross-sectional analysis. BMJ Open Qual. **13**, e002713 (2024). https://doi.org/10.1136/bmjoq-2023-002713

18. Leiras, A., Eusébio, C.: Perceived image of accessible tourism destinations: a data mining analysis of Google Maps reviews. Curr. Issue Tour. **27**, 2584–2602 (2024). https://doi.org/10.1080/13683500.2023.2230338

19. Öztürk Hacar, Ö., Hacar, M., Gülgen, F., Pappalardo, L.: Where we rate: the impact of urban characteristics on digital reviews and ratings. Appl. Sci. **15**(2), 931 (2025). https://doi.org/10.3390/app15020931

20. Jiang, F., Ma, J., Li, Z.: Pedestrian volume prediction with high spatiotemporal granularity in urban areas by the enhanced learning model. Sustain. Cities Soc. **79**, 103653 (2022). https://doi.org/10.1016/j.scs.2021.103653

21. Google LLC, Google Maps API, Available online: https://developers.google.com/maps last accessed 15 Mar 2025

22. OpenStreetMap, OSM Export, Available online: https://www.openstreetmap.org/export last accessed 15 Mar 2025

23. QGIS, Firenze Version 3.28 LTR, Available online: http://www.qgis.org/en/site/index.html last accessed 15 Mar 2025

24. OpenStreetMap Wiki, Map Features, Available online: https://wiki.openstreetmap.org/wiki/Map_Features last accessed 15 Mar 2025

25. NetworkX Python Package, Available online: https://networkx.org/ last accessed 15 Mar 2025

26. Pedregosa, F., Varoquaux, G., Gramfort, A., Michel, V., Thirion, B., Grisel, O., Blondel, M., Prettenhofer, P., Weiss, R., Dubourg, V., Vanderplas, J., Passos, A., Cournapeau, D., Brucher, M., Perrot, M., Duchesnay, E.: Scikit-learn: machine learning in Python. J. Mach. Learn. Res. **12**, 2825–2830 (2011)

27. Porta, S., Crucitti, P., Latora, V.: The network analysis of urban streets: a primal approach. Environ. Plan. B Plan. Design. **33**(5), 705–725 (2006). https://doi.org/10.1068/b32045

28. Buhl, J., Gautrais, J., Reeves, N., Solé, R.V., Valverde, S., Kuntz, P., Theraulaz, G.: Topological patterns in street networks of self-organized urban settlements. Eur. Phys. J. B. **49**, 513–522 (2006). https://doi.org/10.1140/epjb/e2006-00085-1

29. Crucitti, P., Latora, V., Porta, S.: Centrality measures in spatial networks of urban streets. Phys. Rev. E. **73**, 036125 (2006). https://doi.org/10.1103/PhysRevE.73.036125

30. Jiang, B.: A topological pattern of urban street networks: universality and peculiarity. Phys. A Statist. Mech. Appl. **384**(2), 647–655 (2007). https://doi.org/10.1016/j.physa.2007.05.064

31. Barthélemy, M., Flammini, A.: Modeling urban street patterns. Phys. Rev. Lett. **100**, 138702 (2008). https://doi.org/10.1103/PhysRevLett.100.138702

32. Masucci, A.P., Smith, D., Crooks, A., Batty, M.: Random planar graphs and the London street network. Eur. Phys. J. B. **71**, 259–271 (2009). https://doi.org/10.1140/epjb/e2009-00290-4

33. Masucci, A.P., Stanilov, K., Batty, M.: Limited urban growth: London's street network dynamics since the 18th century. PLoS One. **8**, e69469 (2010). https://doi.org/10.1371/journal.pone.0069469

34. Strano, E., Nicosia, V., Latora, V., Porta, S., Barthélemy, M.: Elementary processes governing the evolution of road networks. Sci. Rep. **2**(296) (2012). https://doi.org/10.1038/srep00296

35. Corcoran, P., Mooney, P., Bertolotto, M.: Analysing the growth of OpenStreetMap networks Spat. Statist. 3, 21–32 (2013) 10.1016/j.spasta.2013.01.002

36. Zhao, P., Jia, T., Qin, K., Shan, J., Jiao, C.: Statistical analysis on the evolution of OpenStreetMap road networks in Beijing. Physica A. **420**(59–72) (2015). https://doi.org/10.1016/j.physa.2014.10.076

37. Hacar, M., Kılıç, B., Şahbaz, K.: Analyzing OpenStreetMap road data and characterizing the behavior of contributors in Ankara, Turkey. ISPRS Int. J. Geo-Inform. **7**(10), 400 (2018). https://doi.org/10.3390/ijgi7100400

38. Freeman, L.C.: A set of measures of centrality based upon betweenness. Sociometry. **40**, 35–41 (1977)

39. Brandes, U.: On variants of shortest-path betweenness centrality and their generic computation. Soc. Networks. **30**, 136–145 (2008). https://doi.org/10.1016/j.socnet.2007.11.001

40. Hacar, M., Altafini, D., Cutini, V.: Network-based hierarchical feature augmentation for predicting road classes in OpenStreetMap. ISPRS Int. J. Geo Inf. **13**(12), 456 (2024). https://doi.org/10.3390/ijgi13120456

Crowdsourced Data for Urban Planning: A Critical Evaluation of OpenStreetMap Accuracy and Completeness

Federica Deri$^{(\boxtimes)}$ ⓘ, Federico Mara ⓘ, and Chiara Anselmi ⓘ

Department of Energy, Systems, Territory and Construction Engineering, University of Pisa,
Largo Lucio Lazzarino, 56122 Pisa, Italy
`federica.deri@phd.unipi.it`

Abstract. Urban planning relies on accurate and comprehensive spatial data to analyse existing urban configurations, design new development scenarios, and evaluate their feasibility. OpenStreetMap (OSM), the largest freely accessible and editable geographic database, is increasingly used to support such tasks. However, as a crowdsourced platform, OSM presents both strengths and vulnerabilities, particularly regarding the consistency and reliability of its data. This study assesses the accuracy of OSM data in the municipalities of Massa and Viareggio (Tuscany, Italy) – focusing in particular into commercial activities and amenities related to the 15-min city concept – with the objective of identifying and characterizing errors within the dataset. The analysis involved a comparative evaluation between point of interests (POIs) extracted from OSM and a ground-truth dataset obtained through extensive on-site surveys. Rule-based manual matching in a GIS environment was applied to align POIs entries across the two datasets and to quantify discrepancies. For each unmatched OSM entry, the type of error was classified, and results were further disaggregated by functional category. Findings reveal a general underrepresentation of POIs in the OSM dataset, along with frequent positional inaccuracies and outdated information. A limited number of redundant entries were also identified. These results underscore the inherent limitations of Volunteered Geographic Information (VGI), which can be affected by contributor discretion and uneven data coverage. Given that such data increasingly inform spatial analyses and planning decisions, their unreliability poses a critical risk to evidence-based urban design.

Keywords: Crowdsource · Open data · OpenStreetMap · Volunteered Geographic Information · Urban Planning · Evidence-based Urban Design

1 Introduction

Geospatial data are fundamental to urban planning. The greater the accuracy and completeness of available datasets, the more reliable the models become for simulating how urban systems and environments respond to specific planning decisions. Accurately interpreting the current configuration of urban areas provides the necessary foundation for designing new settlement scenarios and assessing their feasibility in terms of infrastructure, mobility, environmental impact, and sustainable development.

© The Author(s), under exclusive license to Springer Nature Switzerland AG 2026
O. Gervasi et al. (Eds.): ICCSA 2025 Workshops, LNCS 15897, pp. 403–420, 2026.
https://doi.org/10.1007/978-3-031-97660-5_27

Recent planning paradigms, such as the "15-min city" model, emphasize the development of pedestrian-oriented urban environments where multifunctional land use and sustainable mobility networks ensure residents have easy access to essential services and amenities. Implementing and testing such models requires up-to-date data on public services, transportation infrastructure, commercial activities, and mobility patterns.

The rise of big data has enabled access to vast and varied sources of spatial information, often more accessible than traditional authoritative datasets. Among these, crowdsourced data have become particularly relevant. Crowdsourcing refers to the practice of collecting information through voluntary user contributions, typically via digital platforms. In the field of geographic information, this practice is known as Volunteered Geographic Information (VGI).

Notable examples of VGI used in urban planning include OpenStreetMap (OSM), Wikimapia, Mapillary, and Geo-Wiki. OpenStreetMap, in particular, is an open-source, collaborative mapping project where anyone can contribute to building a freely available and editable global map. Due to its large volume of data, ease of access, and zero cost, OSM is widely used across a range of sectors, including academic research, environmental disaster response, game development, traffic simulation, navigation, and urban planning [1–4].

Within urban planning, OSM is frequently employed to obtain large volumes of geographic data [5–7]. Numerous studies have used the OSM database to investigate various topics such as urban morphology [6–9], urban amenities [10, 11], street network configurations [12, 13], and mobility and traffic management [14, 15]. Contributions by Hacar et al. [16] have also enriched the methodological tools available for evaluating spatial data in urban contexts.

However, the extensive and diverse use of open data also raises critical concerns about their reliability, which can significantly affect the outcomes of spatial analyses and policy decisions. Validating the accuracy of such data – or, once their limitations are understood, establishing protocols for their improved use – would strengthen the legitimacy of existing findings and encourage a more systematic adoption of these sources in applied research.

This issue has led to a growing body of literature focused on evaluating and improving data quality [17–19]. Researchers have developed metrics to assess dataset characteristics [20–23] as well as methods for data cleaning and enhancement. At the European level, the Open Data Maturity Report provides a benchmark for assessing the maturity of national open data portals, including aspects such as data quality, governance, impact, and technical features [24].

In the specific case of OpenStreetMap, a vast literature has explored data quality by comparing OSM datasets with institutional or commercial mapping sources [5, 25–30]. Key dimensions of evaluation include completeness, consistency, positional accuracy, temporal accuracy, and attribute accuracy, typically in reference to roads, points of interest (POIs), and buildings.

In this vein, the present paper investigates the reliability of OSM data on commercial activities in two Italian municipalities – Massa and Viareggio – by comparing OSM records with ground-truth data – hereafter referred to as 'real data' – obtained through on-field surveys. The paper is structured as follows: Sect. 2 introduces the structure and characteristics of the datasets used; Sect. 3 outlines the methodology, including the selection of case studies and amenities selection (3.1) and the procedural steps for data processing and database construction (3.2); Sect. 4 discusses the results; Sect. 5 summarizes the key findings and suggests directions for future research.

2   Datasets

2.1   OpenStreetMap

OpenStreetMap (OSM) is one of the most significant crowdsourced projects for the collection and dissemination of geographic data, categorized under the broader concept of Volunteered Geographic Information (VGI). The project is based on the principle of creating a free, editable, and constantly updated global map, maintained through the voluntary contributions of users worldwide [2, 31]. As of December 2024, the platform had registered more than ten million users [32].

OSM maps are composed of three fundamental elements – nodes, ways, and relations – each described through user-defined tags, consisting of key–value pairs. Tag creation in OSM follows a folksonomy-based approach, allowing contributors considerable flexibility. Although this openness allows for extensive customization, tools such as Taginfo provide summaries of the most commonly used tags to guide user contributions [2, 33].

Due to this flexibility, each feature in OSM may potentially be described by an unlimited number of attributes. As a result, the OSM database lacks a unified or formally standardized classification. However, the OSM community has defined conventions for frequently used key–value combinations, grouping them into broad functional categories such as amenity, building, emergency, highway, and leisure, among others [34].

Data can be added or edited using a range of software tools. The iD editor, a browser-based application, is OSM's default editing interface and is designed for beginners [2]. In 2024, approximately 204,810 users – accounting for 78% of all mappers – used iD, contributing around 426 million edits (33.1% of total edits) [35]. The editor provides a guided interface for choosing existing tags or creating new ones, enabling contributors to describe geographic features in increasing detail.

Although the iD editor has the highest number of users, the desktop-based Java OpenStreetMap (JOSM) editor – more suitable for advanced users – accounts for the majority of edits, with 761 million edits in 2024 (59.1%) [35].

The open and flexible nature of OSM, which allows anyone to contribute without technical expertise, is both a strength and a limitation [2, 31]. On the one hand, it facilitates continual data updates; on the other, it introduces variability and subjectivity, which can compromise data reliability [27, 36, 37].

Once submitted, OSM data are immediately published in the database without undergoing any formal peer review. Data reliability is instead managed by the OSM community through quality assurance tools, which identify potential errors and inconsistencies that must then be validated and corrected by users [2].

As an open-source platform, OSM offers several methods for free data extraction. The official website allows for manual selection and download of specific areas. PlanetOSM provides a large, continuously updated dump of the full database. Alternatively, services such as GeoFabrik.de and BBBike.org offer regional extracts – GeoFabrik by continent, country, and region; BBBike by custom-defined areas. For tailored data extractions based on specific tags or features, users can employ Overpass Turbo, which queries the OSM database through the Overpass API [2]. A convenient QGIS plugin, QuickOSM, integrates Overpass Turbo into the GIS environment, allowing for easy and customizable data downloads.

For this study, various extraction methods were compared to determine the most suitable for the project. Data downloaded directly from the OSM website, based on predefined geographic bounding boxes, proved to be partial and inconsistent. Although the datasets from GeoFabrik and BBBike were more compact and better organized, they lacked completeness when compared to those obtained through Overpass Turbo. For this reason, the final dataset was downloaded using the QuickOSM plugin in QGIS, with a Quick Query configured to extract nodes, ways, and relations represented as points and multipolygons.

2.2   Real Data

An ideal benchmark for evaluating OSM data reliability would be a national authoritative database. However, in Italy, due to privacy regulations, official datasets of commercial activities – which represents the main category tested in this contribution – are not publicly available in full. The *Camera di Commercio* (Chambers of Commerce) maintain the *Registro delle Imprese* (Business Register), which contains legal and fiscal data on all companies operating in the country. However, this information is accessible to the public only through limited, case-by-case queries or partial datasets made available on specific portals.

In the absence of comprehensive government data, a custom reference dataset was constructed through on-field surveys, designed to directly verify the presence and exact location of POIs in the study areas. This method ensured an accurate and up-to-date snapshot of the local business landscape at the time of the research.

The surveys were conducted during the first two weeks of February 2025, on weekdays and during standard business hours (approximately 9:00–12:00 and 16:00–19:00). The data collection was independently carried out by the three authors on separate dates to reduce errors due to business temporary closures or observer oversight. Each observation recorded the address, business name, and type of POIs based on its category.

After cross-verifying the observations, the three individual datasets were merged to create a definitive, validated ground-truth database. Each activity was then manually geocoded in QGIS, using the recorded address information (street name, number, and any secondary street identifiers). The spatialization was manually performed using the Ortophoto from Geoscopio [38] as a cartographic base for manual geolocation, which was applied consistently throughout the process.

3 Methods

3.1 Case Studies and Amenities Selection

This study focuses on two municipalities in Tuscany, Italy: Massa and Viareggio. Both are located along the coastal strip of the Versilia area, with Massa situated in the northern sector and Viareggio in the southern sector.

The municipality of Massa covers an area of 93.58 km^2 [39] and features a longitudinal spatial development extending from the coast to the mountains. The coastal zone includes the district of Marina di Massa, while the compact historical centre of Massa lies in the foothills. The eastern portion of the municipality includes part of the Apuan Alps mountain range. The suburban agricultural plains are mainly characterized by urban sprawl, whereas the area north of the *Frigido* River has both industrial functions – linked to marble processing – and tourism, with numerous campsites along the coast.

The municipality of Viareggio covers an area of 32.48 km^2 [39] and, in contrast to Massa, follows a coastal-parallel development restricted to the flat alluvial plain. The *Burlamacca* Canal divides the municipal territory in two: the majority of the city lies to the north, where the railway separates the compact historical centre from the suburban zones, which are marked by dispersed settlements and agricultural lands. The southern part of the municipality includes both the port area and the *Migliarino-San Rossore-Massaciuccoli* Natural Park, which borders the coastal area. The surrounding agricultural-productive plain is fragmented by suburban neighbourhoods such as *Versilia*, *Ex Campo d'Aviazione*, and the village of Torre del Lago Puccini.

Both municipalities are integrated within a continuous infrastructural network that connects them to the broader Versilia area and neighbouring provinces. Key infrastructures include the A12 motorway, which links Genoa (Liguria) to Cecina (Tuscany, province of Livorno); the Strada Statale 1 – Via Aurelia, which follows the route of the ancient Roman consular road and connects Rome with France through the entire Tuscan coastline; and the coastal road, which connects the seaside towns of the Versilia conurbation, from Viareggio to Marina di Massa. Additionally, the area is crossed by the Genoa–Pisa railway line and the Lucca–Viareggio line, as Fig. 1 shows [40].

As explained in Sect. 2.2, the present research required the construction of a custom reference dataset that faithfully represented the real-world situation. Due to the complexity and workload involved, the study was limited to the urban centers of Massa and Viareggio, represented in Fig. 2.

The investigation focused on proximity-based services and facilities considered essential for the implementation of the 15-min city model, particularly referring to the 'Commerce' and 'Entertainment' categories defined by Moreno et al. [41]. Given the lack of a unified and widely accepted classification of such functions in the literature – and considering the topic remains actively debated [42] – this study adopted the macro-categories proposed by Papadopoulos et al. [42] as a basis for grouping OpenStreetMap elements by tag values (see Table 1). In both the OSM and real datasets, vacant lots were also mapped and included in the analysis.

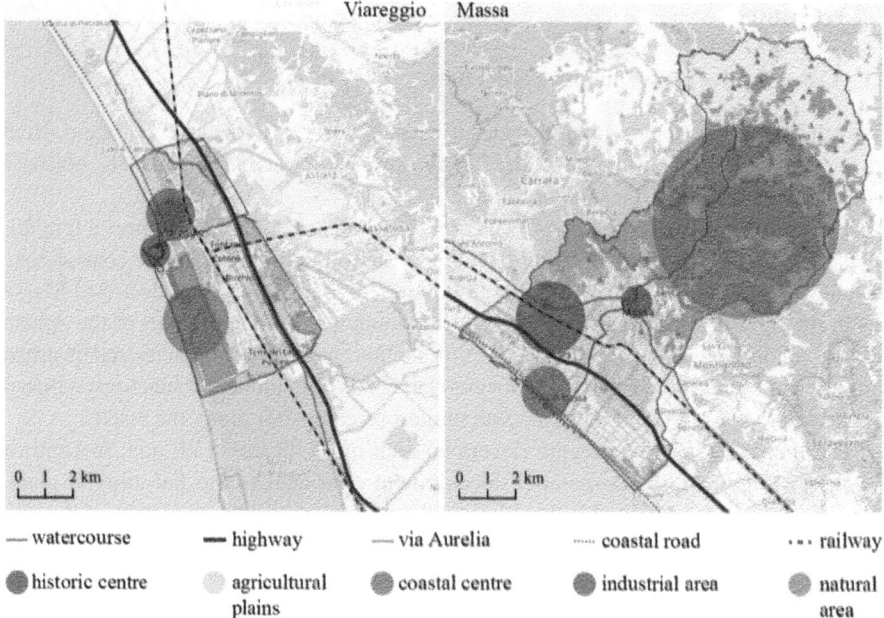

Fig. 1. Territorial framework of Viareggio and Massa municipalities.

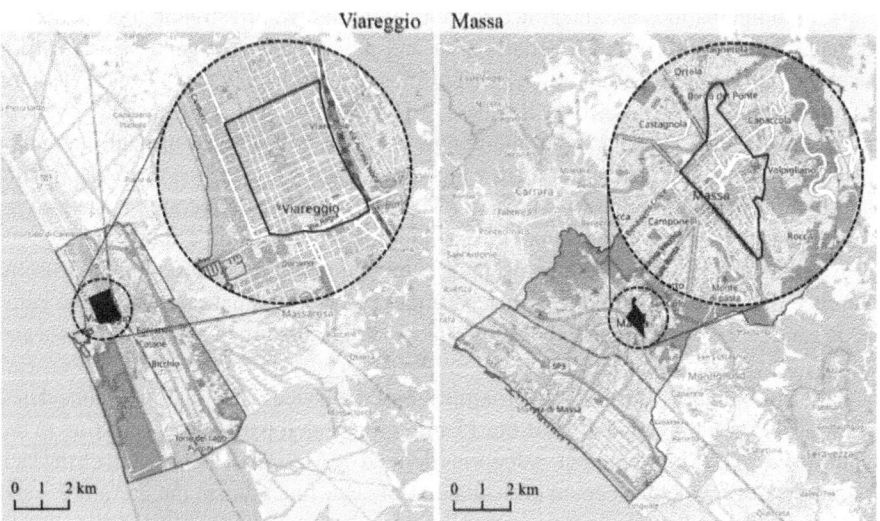

Fig. 2. Study areas within Viareggio and Massa municipalities.

Table 1. Urban amenities examined.

Moreno et al. (2021)	Papadopoulos et al. (2023)
Commerce	food/grocery stores
	retail services/trade
Entertainment	recreational areas
	green spaces
	parks
	sports facilities
	restaurants
	cultural facilities
	entertainment facilities

3.2 Database Processing

As mentioned in Sect. 2.1, the OSM data were extracted using the QuickOSM plugin in QGIS, based on specific values of the keys amenity, craft, leisure, shop, sport, and tourism, which were then assigned to the macro-categories outlined by Papadopoulos et al. [42], as presented in Table 1.

To enable comparison with the real-world data, each surveyed activity was assigned a unique identifier (ID) composed of the municipality acronym (VI for Viareggio, MS for Massa), followed by the letter R (for real data) and a progressive number in the format xxx. Based on spatial proximity and name correspondence between the two datasets, the same ID was manually assigned to matching entries in the OSM dataset. It was not possible to rely on address information for the matching procedure, as OSM entries often lacked address data or included incomplete or incorrect information.

An ID was also assigned to OSM elements that could not be matched with any surveyed activity. In these cases, the ID was composed of the municipality acronym and the prefix UR_ (for "unmatched OSM record"), followed by a progressive number (xxx).

This unique ID system made it possible to identify errors in both datasets related to the presence/absence of individual features and to their incorrect positioning on the map. To further qualify the nature of each discrepancy, an additional field named mismatch was added to the attribute table of the OSM layer.

The following error types were identified:

- "excess": when an OSM feature had no corresponding real-world activity in the vicinity;
- "ceased": when the mapped feature corresponded to a location currently vacant.
- "replaced/inconsistent": when an OSM feature corresponded to a business at the same location but with a different name. This category includes both businesses that have changed over time and those whose name differs from what is recorded on the shop sign.
- "redundant": when two or more OSM entries referred to the same real-world activity;

- "relocated/moved": when an activity's name was found in both datasets but associated with non-adjacent locations, suggesting either a move or an incorrect geolocation;

with the terms "vicinity" or "adjacent" referring to features located on the same side of the street and within a radius of 5 m from the actual activity.

By performing a join operation between the OSM and real-world vector layers using the unique ID as the linking field, a unified table was generated. This table includes all real activities (some of which match with OSM features, while others not), plus all unmatched OSM elements. The analysis results presented in the following section are based on this final integrated dataset.

4   Results and Discussion

The mapping of the real-world dataset yielded 651 entries for Viareggio and 333 for Massa. In Viareggio, these are evenly distributed across the entire study area, with notable concentrations around *Piazza Cavour*, *Corso Giuseppe Garibaldi*, *Via Cesare Battisti*, and *Via Giuseppe Mazzini*. In Massa, four main clusters were identified: *Galleria Leonardo da Vinci*, *Via Dante Alighieri*, *Via Agostino Ghirlanda*, and the intersection of *Viale Europa* and *Largo Giacomo Matteotti* – as depicted in Fig. 3 –, while Table 2 provides the number of mapped entries by functional category.

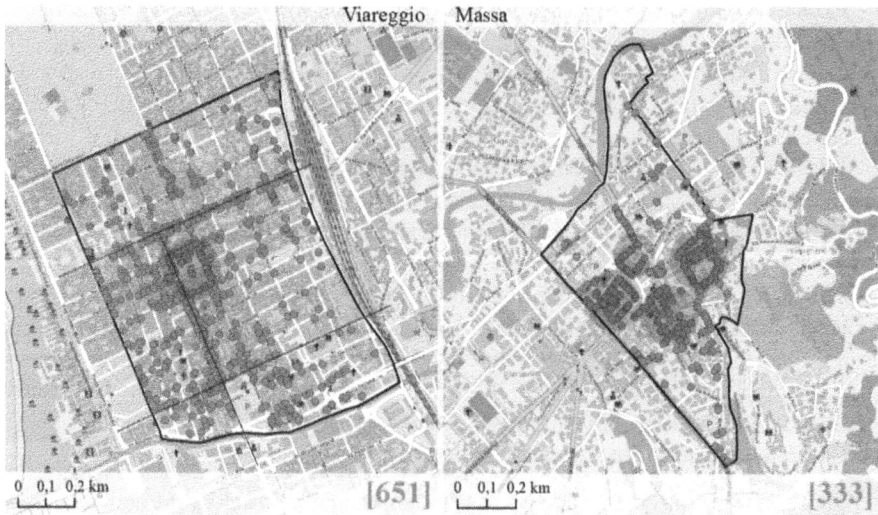

Fig. 3. Real data with an indication of highest density areas.

Table 2. Number of items of the real database based on functional categories.

Papadopoulos et al. (2023)	Number of items	
	Viareggio	Massa
food/grocery stores	50	26
retail services/trade	348	204
recreational areas	1	1
green spaces	0	0
parks	9	0
sports facilities	4	3
restaurants	54	27
cultural facilities	8	12
entertainment facilities	50	49
vacant	129	14

The OSM dataset extraction returned 93 entries for Viareggio and 117 for Massa, as illustrated in Fig. 4. Table 3 shows the number of OSM features per functional category.

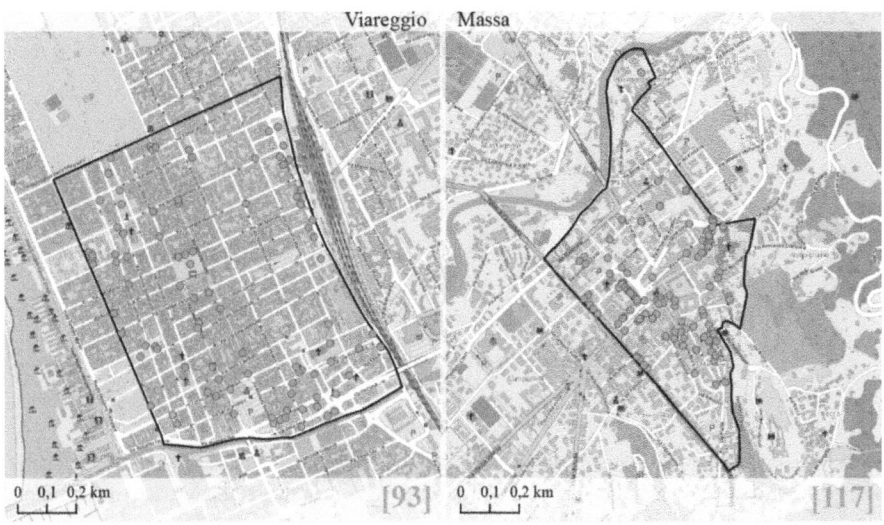

Fig. 4. OpenStreetMap (OSM) data.

While the amount ratio (i.e., the number of extracted OSM entries divided by the number of real entries) was higher in Massa than in Viareggio, the percentages remain quite low: 14.3% for Viareggio and 35.1% for Massa. The figures decrease further when considering the accuracy ratio (i.e., the number of correctly matched OSM features to real-world entries): 9.1% for Viareggio and 17.1% for Massa, as synthetized in the diagrams in Fig. 5.

Table 3. Number of items of the OSM database based on functional categories.

Papadopoulos et al. (2023)	Number of items	
	Viareggio	Massa
food/grocery stores	6	10
retail services/trade	16	46
recreational areas	1	1
green spaces	0	0
parks	14	2
sports facilities	0	1
restaurants	17	29
cultural facilities	14	11
entertainment facilities	20	17
vacant	3	0

Viareggio

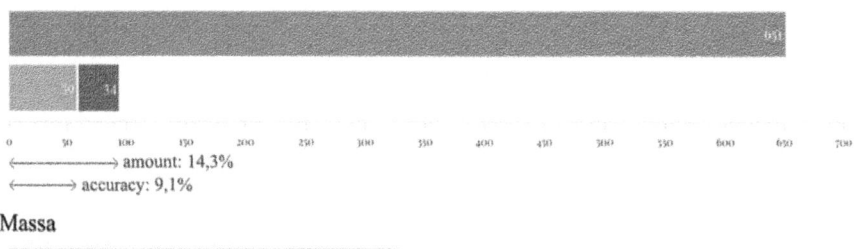

Massa

Real data   matched OSM data   unmatched OSM data

Fig. 5. Real data and OSM data. 'Amount': ratio between total extracted activities and real activities, expressed as a percentage; 'accuracy': ratio between matched extracted activities and real activities, expressed as a percentage.

Following the matching process between the two datasets, which distinguished matched and unmatched OSM entries through the assignment of unique IDs, a more detailed analysis was conducted on the unmatched entries to classify the types of errors present in the crowdsourced dataset.

As shown in Table 4, in both case studies the majority of unmatched OSM features were classified as "excess", meaning they could not be associated with any real-world activity. Compared to Viareggio, Massa showed a higher number of entries classified as "replaced/inconsistent", referring to activities that had either changed over time or were recorded in OSM with a name different from the one observed on the actual shop sign. No "relocated/moved" features were identified in either of the two study areas, i.e., no entries in OSM were found at a significantly different location from their real-world counterparts.

Table 4. Mismatch categories for Viareggio and Massa case studies.

mismatch	Viareggio	Massa
excess	20	39
ceased	8	7
replaced/inconsistent	2	10
redundant real (R)	2	3
redundant unmatched (UR)	0	1
relocated/moved	0	0

These evaluations were extended to the functional categories (see Table 1) in order to identify potential trends. Table 5 reports the values for amount and accuracy—as defined above—for each functional category. While the overall scarcity of OSM data was already observed in the general case study metrics, the category-level analysis reveals interesting patterns.

In Viareggio, for example, the "retail services/trade" category yielded very few results in OSM, with an amount of only 4.6%. The accuracy was even lower, at 2.3%, as not all extracted OSM entries were successfully matched to real-world businesses. However, all matched entries in this category were functionally correct (AC_C = 100.0%).

In contrast, in Massa, the "restaurants" category showed a higher number of OSM entries than those recorded in the field (107.4%), yet only 44.4% of these corresponded to actual existing establishments, and among these, 75.0% were correctly classified in terms of function.

Figure 6 shows the correspondence between real and OSM entries based on functional category, as indicated by the trend of the AC_C parameter defined in Table 5. The image highlights discrepancies in the categorization of urban amenities; in the case of Viareggio, for instance, only 17 out of 20 entertainment facilities listed in the OSM database correspond to those identified through on-site survey. However, not all of these are correctly categorized, as some are actually food/grocery stores and others fall under retail services/trade.

These findings suggest that the incompleteness and inaccuracy of OSM data are not evenly distributed across functional categories, varying significantly in terms of both amount and accuracy.

Table 5. Evaluation of 'amount' (A), 'accuracy' (AC) and the accuracy of the categorization (AC_C) between real and OSM data in relation to functional categories. AC_C: ratio between extracted activities with correct categorisation and matched activities, expressed as a percentage.

	Viareggio			Massa		
	A [%]	AC [%]	AC_C [%]	A [%]	AC [%]	AC_C [%]
food/grocery stores	12,0	12,0	83,3	38,5	19,2	100,0
retail services/trade	4,6	2,3	100,0	22,5	13,2	96,3
recreational areas	100,0	100,0	100,0	100,0	100,0	100,0
green spaces	–	–	–	–	–	–
parks	155,6	88,9	100,0	*	*	*
sports facilities	0,0	0,0	-	33,3	0,0	-
restaurants	31,5	24,1	100,0	107,4	44,4	75,0
cultural facilities	175,0	75,0	83,3	91,7	58,3	71,4
entertainment facilities	40,0	34,0	70,6	34,7	16,3	100,0

* the on-field survey recorded 0 parks, while OSM returned 2 entries; therefore, the percentage cannot be calculated.

Figure 7 illustrates the distribution of mismatch types across functional categories. In Viareggio, different cases must be considered when mismatch values are zero for a specific category. For example:

- in "food/grocery stores" and "recreational areas", all extracted OSM entries were matched with real-world data, resulting in no recorded mismatches;
- for "sports facilities", the mismatch count was zero because OSM did not return any entries for this category;
- in the case of "green spaces", neither the field survey nor the OSM extraction yielded any data.

Similar observations apply to the case of Massa.

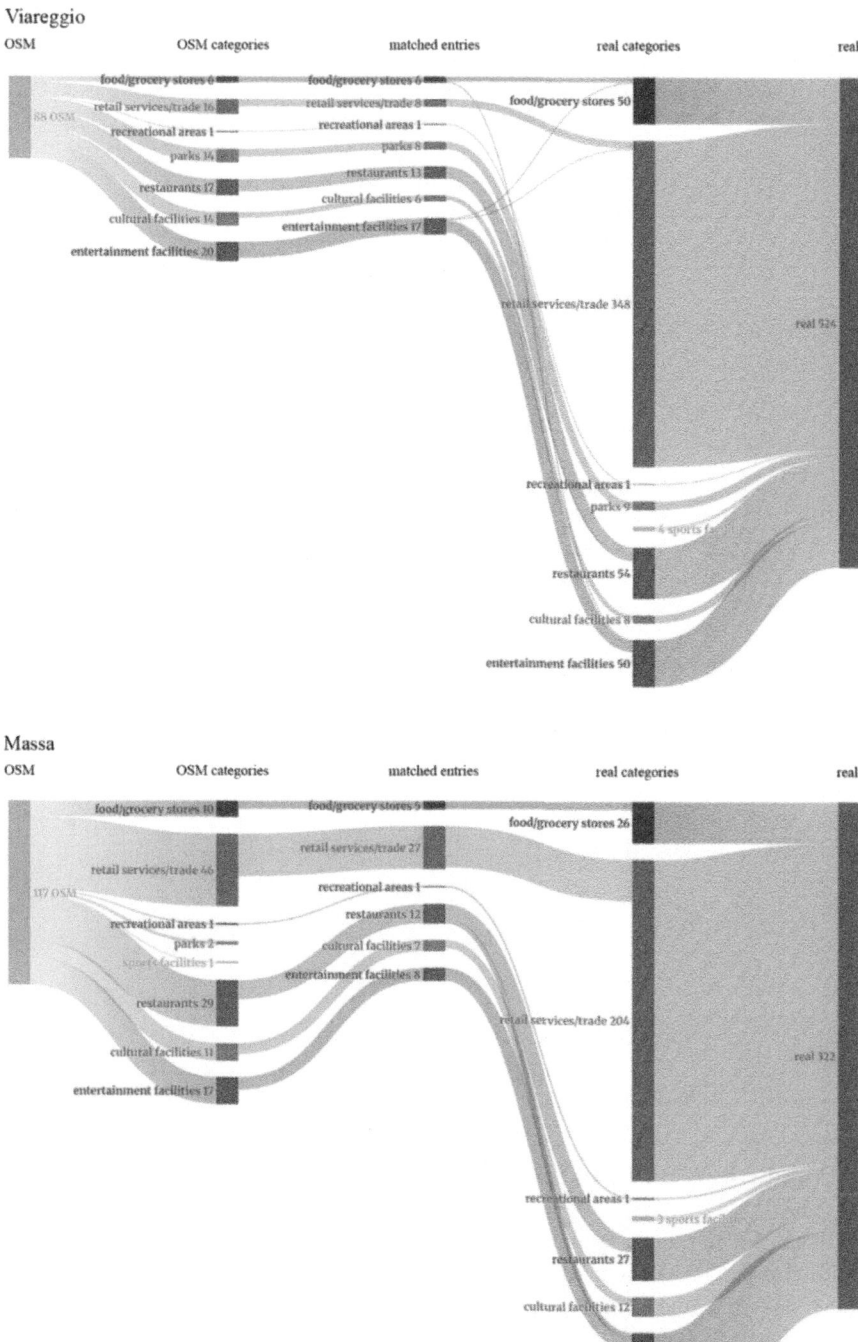

Fig. 6. Correspondence between real and OSM entries based on functional category.

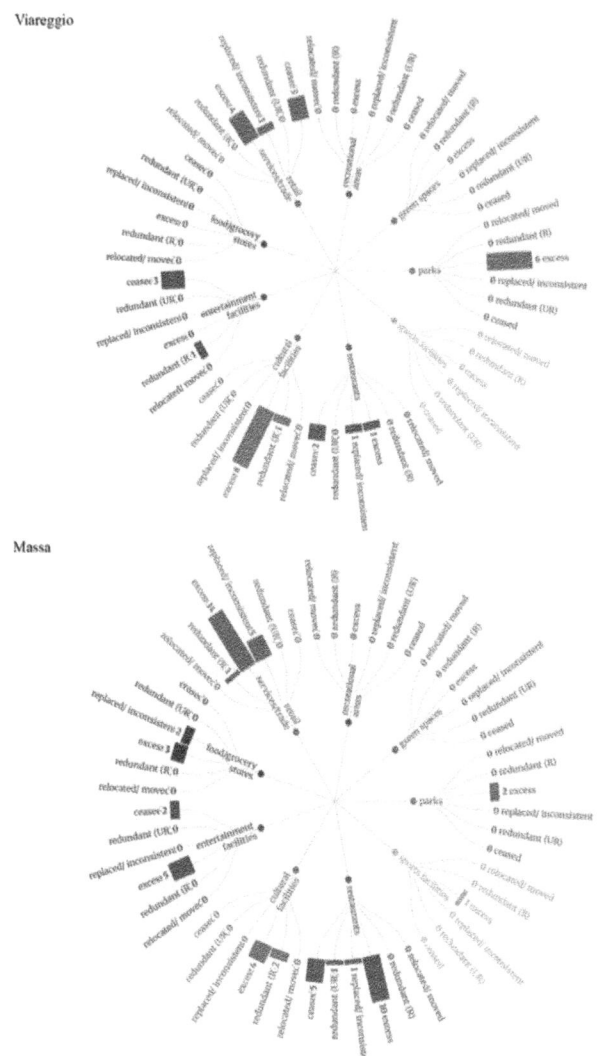

Fig. 7. Mismatch categories based on functional category.

5   Conclusions and Further Developments

The issue of data reliability is a fundamental concern in the design and execution of scientific research. Understanding the quality of available data and recognizing their limitations is essential not only for methodological consistency but also for ensuring the robustness and reproducibility of research outcomes.

This study highlights the importance of conducting detailed evaluations of spatial datasets used in urban planning, with the aim of producing geographically accurate information layers that can effectively support decision-making. In particular, at the urban or micro-urban scale – such as when analysing the proximity of essential services or planning for proximity-based models like the 15-min city – data quality plays a crucial role. The implementation of pedestrian-oriented settlement strategies requires urban planners and decision-makers to rely on accurate, up-to-date representations of distributions and functions of urban amenities. This is essential for identifying which services may be lacking, for assessing neighbourhood suitability, and for comparing the functional structure and organization of different urban areas, needed for promoting evidence-based planning processes.

Focusing on the Italian municipalities of Massa and Viareggio, the study assessed the accuracy and completeness of one of the most widely used open-access databases in spatial analysis: OpenStreetMap (OSM). The evaluation was based on a field-validated comparison between OSM entries and a custom-built reference dataset of real-world urban amenities.

The results clearly indicate that the vast availability of data does not necessarily translate into data quality. Although OSM offers a vast and continuously growing amount of spatial information – exceeding 9.7 billion nodes as of February 2025 [32] – the findings show a general shortage of data and multiple inaccuracies, particularly regarding feature positioning, updates, and redundancy.

The goal of this research was not to identify the underlying causes of these inaccuracies but rather to document the data quality issues within two specific urban contexts, with a close comparison with the real situation. These results are not intended to be generalized, as they respond to a focused research question and reflect localized conditions. In this sense, the adequacy of OSM should be assessed based on the specific analytical or planning objectives, as data reliability can vary significantly depending on the case study context or the types of amenities considered – just to name a few of the parameters that may affect the overall quality of the OSM dataset.

Considering this, future research directions could include the expansion of the amenity types analysed, as well as the application of the same validation procedure to a wider range of case studies – both in terms of geography and urban morphology – to more comprehensively assess the extent and causes of OSM data deficits. Additionally, OSM data comparison with other data sources – including institutional datasets or commercial mapping services – could prove valuable in evaluating whether some sources are systematically more accurate or complete than others. Such comparisons would help assess the context-specific effectiveness of different data types and, ultimately, enhance the reliability of data-driven decision support tools in urban and regional planning.

Although the findings of this study are robust, they should not be generalized, as the present case studies may not fully represent other urban contexts. In different cities or regions, the availability and accuracy of OpenStreetMap (OSM) data may vary significantly depending on factors such as the level of community participation, local territorial characteristics, or socioeconomic conditions. Future research should investigate how these variables affect data completeness and reliability through a broader and more systematic analytical framework. Such work would contribute to a deeper understanding of the strengths and limitations of Volunteered Geographic Information (VGI), helping to define the conditions under which it can be considered usable and trustworthy – depending on the context, the mode of use, and the specific goals for which the data are employed.

Acknowledgments. This work was part of the EMC2 project, funded by ANR (France), FFG (Austria), MUT (Italy), and Vinnova (Sweden) under the Driving Urban Transition Partnership, which has been funded by the European Commission.

Disclosure of Interests. The authors have no competing interests to declare that are relevant to the content of this article.

References

1. Niu, H., Silva, E.A.: Crowdsourced data mining for urban activity: review of data sources, applications, and methods. J. Urban Plan. Dev. **146**(2), 04020007 (2020)
2. Mooney, P., Minghini, M.: A review of OpenStreetMap data. In: Foody, G., See, L., Fritz, S., Mooney, P., Olteanu-Raimond, A.-M., Fonte, C.C., Antoniou, V. (eds.) Mapping and the Citizen Sensor, pp. 37–59. Ubiquity Press, London (2017)
3. Sehra, S.S., Singh, J., Rai, H.S.: Using latent semantic analysis to identify research trends in OpenStreetMap. ISPRS Int. J. Geo-Inform. **6**(7), 195 (2017)
4. Biljecki, F., Chow, S.Y., Lee, K.: Quality of crowdsourced geospatial building information: a global assessment of OpenStreetMap attributes. Build. Environ. **237**, 110295 (2023)
5. Ciepłuch, B., Jacob, R., Mooney, P., Winstanley, A.C.: Comparison of the accuracy of Open-StreetMap for Ireland with Google Maps and Bing Maps. In: 9th International Symposium on Spatial Accuracy Assessment in Natural Resources and Environmental Sciences, p. 337 (2010)
6. Boeing, G.: Spatial information and the legibility of urban form: big data in urban morphology. Int. J. Inform. Manag. **56**, 102013 (2021)
7. Biljecki, F., Chow, Y.S.: Global building morphology indicators. Comput. Environ. Urban Syst. **95**, 101809 (2022)
8. Crooks, A., et al.: Crowdsourcing urban form and function. Int. J. Geograph. Inform. Sci. **29**, 720–741 (2015)
9. Over, M., Schilling, A., Neubauer, S., Zipf, A.: Generating web-based 3D city models from OpenStreetMap: the current situation in Germany. Comput. Environ. Urban Syst. **34**(6), 496–507 (2010)
10. Burke, J., Alomà, R.G., Yu, F., Kruguer, J.: Geospatial analysis framework for evaluating urban design typologies in relation with the 15-minute city standards. J. Busi. Res. **151**, 651–667 (2022)
11. Pezzica, C., Altafini, D., Mara, F., Chioni, C.: Travel-time in a grid: modelling movement dynamics in the "minute city". In: International Conference on Innovation in Urban and Regional Planning, pp. 657–668. Springer Nature Switzerland, Cham (2023)
12. Boeing, G.: A multi-scale analysis of 27,000 urban street networks: Every US city, town, urbanized area, and Zillow neighborhood. Environ. Plan. B Urban Anal. City Sci. **47**(4), 590–608 (2020)
13. Mara, F., Anselmi, C., Deri, F., Cutini, V.: The spatial roots of urban growth: modelling urban dynamics with space syntax. In: International Conference on Computational Science and Its Applications, pp. 61–76. Springer Nature Switzerland, Cham (2024)

14. Carlino, D., Depinet, M., Khandelwal, P., Stone, P.: Approximately orchestrated routing and transportation analyzer: large-scale traffic simulation for autonomous vehicles. In: 15th International IEEE Conference on Intelligent Transportation Systems, pp. 334–339. IEEE (2012)

15. Ferster, C., Fischer, J., Manaugh, K., Nelson, T., Winters, M.: Using OpenStreetMap to inventory bicycle infrastructure: a comparison with open data from cities. Int. J Sustain. Transp. **14**(1), 64–73 (2020)

16. Hacar, M., Mara, F., Altafini, D., Cutini, V.: Preprocessing open data for optimizing estimation times in urban network analysis: Extracting, filtering, geoprocessing, and simplifying the road-center lines. In: International Conference on Innovation in Urban and Regional Planning, pp. 551–562. Springer Nature Switzerland, Cham (2023)

17. Cai, L., Zhu, Y.: The challenges of data quality and data quality assessment in the big data era. Data Sci. J. **14**, 2 (2015)

18. Sadiq, S., Indulska, M.: Open data: quality over quantity. Int. J. Inform. Manag. **37**(3), 150–154 (2017)

19. Quarati, A., De Martino, M., Rosim, S.: Geospatial open data usage and metadata quality. ISPRS Int. J. Geo-Inform. **10**(1), 30 (2021)

20. Senaratne, H., Mobasheri, A., Ali, A.L., Capineri, C., Haklay, M.: A review of volunteered geographic information quality assessment methods. Int. J. Geograph. Inform. Sci. **31**(1), 139–167 (2017)

21. Antoniou, V., Skopeliti, A.: Measures and indicators of VGI quality: an overview. In: ISPRS Annals of the Photogrammetry, Remote Sensing and Spatial Information Sciences, vol. 2, pp. 345–351 (2015)

22. Ostermann, F.O., Granell, C.: Advancing science with VGI: reproducibility and replicability of recent studies using VGI. Trans. GIS. **21**(2), 224–237 (2017)

23. Fonte, C.C., et al.: Assessing VGI data quality. In: Foody, G., et al. (eds.) Mapping and the Citizen Sensor, pp. 137–163. Ubiquity Press, London (2017)

24. European Commission: Open Data Maturity Report 2024. Publications Office of the European Union (2024). https://data.europa.eu/en/publications/open-data-maturity/2024

25. Sehra, S.S., Singh, J., Rai, H.S.: Assessment of OpenStreetMap data-a review. Int. J. Comput. Appl. **76**(16) (2013)

26. Kaur, J., Singh, J., Sehra, S.S., Rai, H.S.: Systematic literature review of data quality within OpenStreetMap. In: International Conference on Next Generation Computing and Information Systems (ICNGCIS), pp. 177–182. IEEE (2017)

27. Haklay, M.: How good is volunteered geographical information? A comparative study of OpenStreetMap and Ordnance Survey datasets. Environ. Plan. B Plan. Design. **37**(4), 682–703 (2010)

28. Brovelli, M.A., Minghini, M., Molinari, M., Mooney, P.: Towards an automated comparison of OpenStreetMap with authoritative road datasets. Trans. GIS. **21**(2), 191–206 (2017)

29. Girres, J.F., Touya, G.: Quality assessment of the French OpenStreetMap dataset. Trans. GIS. **14**(4), 435–459 (2010)

30. Fan, H., Zipf, A., Fu, Q., Neis, P.: Quality assessment for building footprints data on OpenStreetMap. Int. J. Geograph. Inform. Sci. **28**(4), 700–719 (2014)

31. Haklay, M., Weber, P.: Openstreetmap: user-generated street maps. IEEE Pervas. Comput. **7**(4), 12–18 (2008)

32. OpenStreetMap – Stats. https://wiki.openstreetmap.org/wiki/Stats. Accessed March 2025

33. Ballatore, A., Mooney, P.: Conceptualising the geographic world: the dimensions of negotiation in crowdsourced cartography. Int. J. Geograph. Inform. Sci. **29**(12), 2310–2327 (2015)

34. OpenStreetMap - Map features. https://wiki.openstreetmap.org/wiki/Map_features. Accessed March 2025

35. OpenStreetMap - Editor usage stats. https://wiki.openstreetmap.org/wiki/Editor_usage_stats. Accessed March 2025
36. Jacobs, K.T., Mitchell, S.W.: OpenStreetMap quality assessment using unsupervised machine learning methods. Trans. GIS. **24**(5), 1280–1298 (2020)
37. Ballatore, A., Zipf, A.: A conceptual quality framework for volunteered geographic information. In: 12th International Conference, COSIT, pp. 89–107. Springer (2015)
38. Regione Toscana. Direzione Urbanistica e Politiche Abitative - Sistema Informativo Territoriale e Ambientale – SITA.: Ortofoto. https://www502.regione.toscana.it/geoscopio/ortofoto.html. Accessed March 2025
39. Istat,   https://www.istat.it/classificazione/principali-statistiche-geografiche-sui-comuni/. Accessed March 2025
40. Regione Toscana: Piano di Indirizzo Territoriale. Deliberazione Consiglio regionale 27 marzo 2015, no. 37 (2015), https://www.regione.toscana.it/-/piano-di-indirizzo-territoriale-con-valenza-di-piano-paesaggistico. Accessed March 2025
41. Moreno, C., Allam, Z., Chabaud, D., Gall, C., Pratlong, F.: Introducing the "15-Minute City": sustainability, resilience and place identity in future post-pandemic cities. Smart Cities. **4**(1), 93–111 (2021)
42. Papadopoulos, E., Sdoukopoulos, A., Politis, I.: Measuring compliance with the 15-minute city concept: state-of-the-art, major components and further requirements. Sustain. Cities Soc. 104875 (2023)

Urban Digital Twins and Data Spaces: Shaping the Future of Sustainable Cities (TwinAbleCities 2025)

GATE Mobility Toolbox for QGIS: Calculation of Walking Accessibility Using Slope-Adjusted Algorithms

Teodora Koleva, Evgeny Shirinyan[(⊠)], and Dessislava Petrova-Antonova

Sofia University, GATE Institute, 1164 Sofia, Bulgaria
{evgeny.shirinyan,dessislava.petrova}@gate-ai.eu

Abstract. Walking accessibility gains significant attention in recent years in urban planning. Various software tools provide accessibility analysis based on network graphs. However, the slope component is often overlooked. This paper introduces an open-source QGIS plugin which automates calculation of isochrones and an Accessibility Index, inspired by the 15-min city concept. The Accessibility Index evaluates access to various services within predefined distance ranges, weighted by service importance. Four computational methods are available: buffer analysis, network analysis and slope-adjusted network analysis using Tobler's hiking function and the Naismith-Langmuir rule. The QGIS plugin allows straightforward implementation and a high level of reproducibility, resulting in optimized computing time and resources. The tools Average altitude of point features, Slope calculation of network segments, Split network with points, and Accessibility Index can be used together or separately for the assessment of the urban environment. The calculations showed a significant decrease in Accessibility Index in the case of hilly terrain compared to the typical network analysis without considering the slope.

Keywords: Accessibility Index · walkability · Tobler's hiking function · Naismith-Langmuir rule · QGIS · Python

1 Introduction

The concept of walking accessibility has a key role in the scope of urban planning for the sustainable development of cities. Generally, accessibility can be defined as the ability to reach relevant activities, individuals or opportunities, which might require traveling (or walking) to the place where those opportunities are situated [1]. An urban environment can be described using 5Ds: density, diversity of land use, design, destination accessibility, and distance to transit [2]. In residential areas it is important to allocate various amenities within walking distance such as supermarkets, kindergartens, schools, parks, bus stops, restaurants, etc. In addition, walking accessibility can affect property prices [3, 4]. Terrain features such as slope can alter not only the walking speeds, but also the preferences for choosing a certain route [5].

© The Author(s), under exclusive license to Springer Nature Switzerland AG 2026
O. Gervasi et al. (Eds.): ICCSA 2025 Workshops, LNCS 15897, pp. 423–437, 2026.
https://doi.org/10.1007/978-3-031-97660-5_28

This study introduces an open-source QGIS plugin for the calculation of the Accessibility Index (AcsI). It is implemented with the Python API for QGIS (PyQGIS) as a part of the GATE Mobility plugin for QGIS. Pedestrian accessibility is evaluated at the building level using a slope-adjusted network analysis. Among the 5 D's the GATE Mobility plugin implements 3 of them: diversity, destination accessibility and distance to public transport are acknowledged.

The developed index of accessibility aggregates services available around a residential building and the distance calculated to them based on the pedestrian network. In order to distinguish the importance of different services a weighting system of points of interest was established. The plugin allows the use of four methods for the calculation: simple buffer analysis, network analysis, and the slope-adjusted network analysis (based on Tobler's hiking function and the Naismith-Langmuir rule). In addition, the study quantitatively compares these methods using the case of a hilly terrain.

The rest of the paper is organised as follows. Section 2 reviews the related work. Section 3 describes data and the methodology utilised. Section 4 presents the implementation of the plugin in QGIS. Section 5 features the outcome of the implementation, a quantative comparison of all the methods, and visualisation of the outputs. Section 6 provides an overview of the study and potential developments for the future.

2 Related Work

In general, the evaluation of Accessibility index is a calculation related to the concept of walkability. Numerous methods for assessing walkability have been developed with diverse variables considered for the final result [3, 6–8]. Some studies include such factors as pedestrian comfort, condition of the pedestrian network and target groups for index calculations [9, 10]. In terms of the evaluation of accessibility, network analyses, often conducted in GIS, provide a realistic dimension to the assessments. Various methods of network analyses and spatial aggregating functions were implemented as software tools [11–13].

A widely used routing application is represented by Openrouteservice and its QGIS plugin for network analysis ORS Tools. An isochrone can gather population data and avoid features and boundaries. However, it does not consider the slope as a factor for creating itineraries and isochrones [14]. Another network analysis plugin for QGIS, QNEAT3 [15], supports networks, provided by a user, and speed-adjusted analysis. Therefore, slope-adjusted calculations can be performed with some preprocessing steps.

There are other QGIS plugins related to walking accessibility, such as OS-WALK-EU [16]. The software utilises data from OpenStreetMap for services and calculates a walkability index for neighbourhood areas with population represented as a variable. The tool uses a grid of 500 × 500-m cells conforming to the European INSPIRE Grid. To measure residential walkability, OS-WALK-EU incorporates the concept of the 5 D's.

More specialised tools such as PST or Space Syntax explore connectivity and networks rather than calculation of indices. Another toolbox performing diverse spatial analyses developed for Rhino Grasshopper software is the DeCodingSpaces toolbox [17]. 15 min City Score Toolkit, a plugin for calculating urban metrics in QGIS such as pedestrian accessibility and walkability, also leverages the service area of various categories of points of interest (POIs) [18].

A web-based service Aino.World applies the 15-min city concept for any location in the world and enriches the result with recommendations generated by large language models [19]. The calculation of isochrones is conducted using Mapbox services. Several studies consider Sofia, where the terrain is hilly in the southern part of the city, but the slope is not integrated into calculations [20–24].

In general, prior research implies the impact of slope in urban environments and how it affects walking [5, 25]. Şahin Körmeçli [26] integrates Space Syntax metrics with slope values and shows that the longest and main roads with low slope values have higher rates of accessibility. For steep slope regions, a coverage area is lower than for flat regions [27]. In Barcelona, a sidewalk network model realistically captures the pedestrian environment: an undirected graph of the city, whose edges are enriched with sidewalk width, length, slope, a level of accidents, and crosswalk locations [28]. Nevertheless, most of the tools do not consider the characteristics of slope, which is an important component of accessibility, especially in hilly regions.

The Naismith-Langmuir rule and Tobler's hiking function are commonly used approaches for considering the slope in accessibility studies and planning hiking activities. Tobler's hiking function is a more recent development and is often used in various scenarios for walking speed estimation [29, 30]. For instance, in ArcGIS Pro the Tobler's hiking function is implemented [31, 32].

The integration of slope-adjusted network analysis in the calculation of AcsI addresses the limitations of flat-surface assessments. This approach provides more accurate and realistic evaluations of heterogeneous and hilly urban landscapes.

3   Methodology

3.1   Study Area and Data

Sofia is the capital city of Bulgaria, with a population of nearly 1.27 million and 24 districts. Given its heterogeneity in geometry, infrastructure, and environment, the district Lozenets is chosen as a case study. The northern part of the district is occupied by mid-rise residential buildings with dense vegetation. On the south, the district is represented by intensive construction, where accessibility and availability of the road infrastructure, public spaces, and public services are not sufficient. The terrain of the study area varies between 549 m and 668 m above sea level.

The data needed for the calculation comprises the following datasets in the form of ready to use layers in QGIS:

- Residential buildings dataset – prepared by GATE Institute with data from the Bulgarian cadastre;
- POIs dataset (various amenities) – gathered by the researchers in GATE Institute from state and municipal registers.
- Weights of POIs – estimated by experts in GATE Institute.
- Pedestrian network dataset – provided by the municipal enterprise "Sofiaplan".

The count of the residential buildings in the dataset is 5710 features, whereas the count of POIs in the respective dataset is 5203.

POIs are divided into 8 groups and 49 subgroups. Groups are as follows – Green, School, Kids, Health, Mobility – defined as primary groups of importance and consequently with higher weights assigned; the remaining - Sport, Culture and Service are of secondary importance and with lower weights. Within each group another weighting system is used for the subgroups from 0 to 1 with a total sum equal to 1 (Fig. 1).

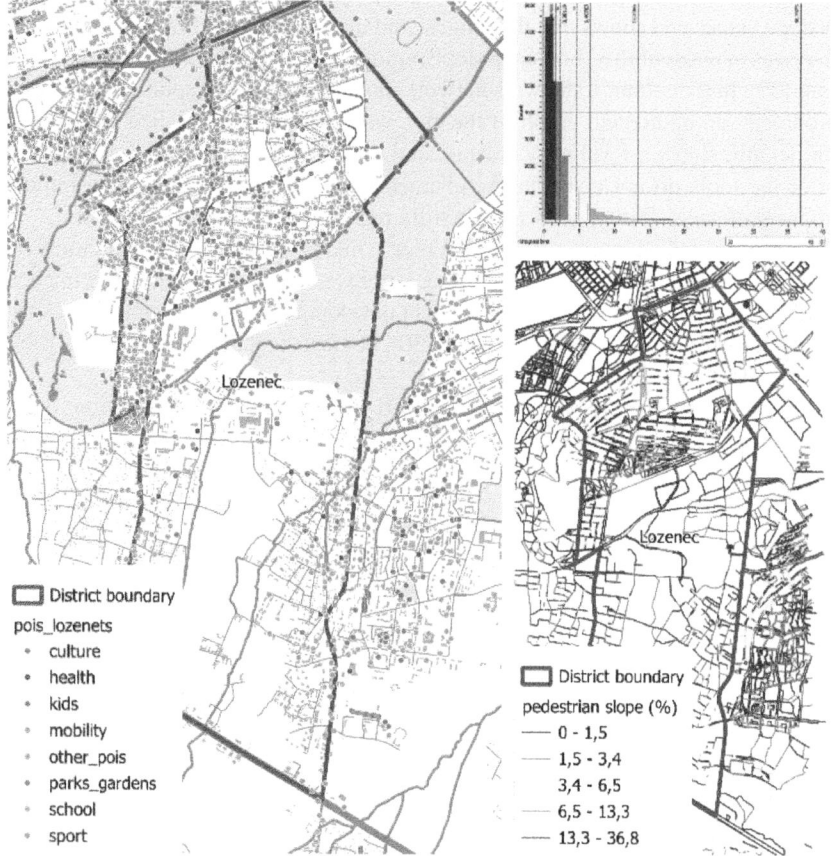

Fig. 1. Study area. Left: points of interest in the district; top right: a histogram of slope values of network segments; bottom right: a slope map of segments

3.2 General Workflow

This section describes the methodology followed for the calculation of AcsI. The main processing steps of the pipeline are shown in Fig. 2.

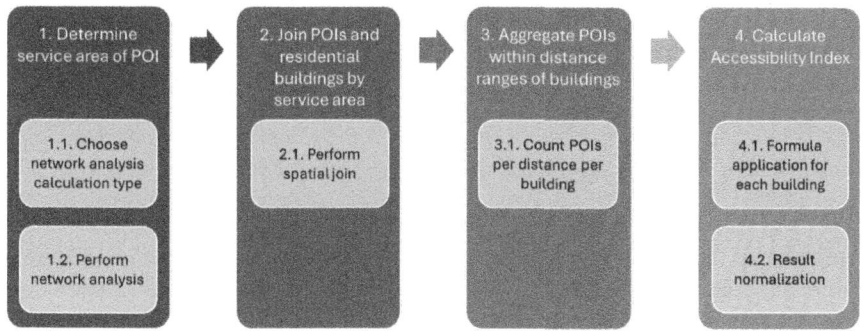

Fig. 2. General workflow

3.3 Determine a Service Area of a POI

The service area itself shows the distance extent within which a residential building would benefit from a certain POI. Four methods for determining a service area are used in the current study: buffer analysis, network analysis, and network analysis with slope in two variants. Service areas of sampled POIs were calculated with three distance steps of 500 m, 1000 m and 1500 m both for all types of analysis.

Buffer analysis is the simplest one as it does not take into consideration the pedestrian network but uses distance by air.

Network analysis uses the pedestrian network for the calculations which results in a more accurate service area. Dijkstra's algorithm calculates a shortest path over a weighted graph. Additionally, distance steps are also used as in buffer analysis with the same values.

The third and fourth methods of network analysis with slope incorporate the slope/inclination of every segment of the pedestrian network and thus impacts the distance. The estimated speed of walking is represented as a function of the slope, with two different calculation approaches applied: Tobler's hiking function and the Naismith-Langmuir rule.

Tobler's hiking function (THF) is formulated in 1993 by Waldo Tobler and has become a popular method to calculate speed in recent research. THF is defined as follows:

$$W = 6^{(-3.5|S+0.05|)} \tag{1}$$

where W is the speed and S is the slope.

According to THF, the maximum speed that can be developed is 6 km/h which is achieved at $-2.86°$ in descent, and the average speed on flat terrain is 5 km/h.

The Naismith-Langmuir rule (NLR) is a combination of the work of two persons – William Naismith and Eric Langmuir. The first input was made by Naismith in 1892 for ascent and states:

"an hour for every 3 miles forward, with an additional hour for every 2,000 feet of ascent".

This means that on flat terrain, the approximate base speed is 5 km/h, with travel time increasing by 0.1 min per 1 m of ascent. In 1984, Langmuir extended the rule with terms for descent that state:

> *"0.03 min should be added per 1 m of descent for slope angle greater than 12°*
> *and 0.03 min should be subtracted per 1 m of descent for slope angles between 5°*
> *and 12°".*

A limitation of the NLR is its prediction of the maximum walking speed of 12 km/h on shallow slope and at the threshold of a 12° slope an abrupt change from 12 km/h down to 3 km/h takes place which seems to be unrealistic.

This third method also uses Dijkstra's algorithm for the network analysis where the edges are weighted with the travel times according to the speeds. Table 1 reveals a sample of the pedestrian network with calculated speeds following THF and the NLR.

Table 1. Street segments with speeds calculated using THF and the NLR

fid	id	type	slope_percent	length	THF	NLR
13677	114806	road	-5.380042414	38.727	5.917	5
13678	114807	road	-2.960065746	19.587	5.594	5
13679	114807	road	0.347647693	0.847	4.983	4.859
13680	114807	road	0.071644611	23.744	5.018	4.97
13681	114807	road	0.409492245	1.974	4.966	4.835
13682	114807	road	3.711535743	0.058	4.422	3.819
13683	114807	road	0.638499088	53.916	4.931	4.747
13684	114808	sidewalk	3.057700387	3.467	4.516	3.985
13685	114808	sidewalk	3.607642024	44.308	4.437	3.844
13686	114808	sidewalk	2.949741138	51.989	4.548	4.013
13687	114813	sidewalk	0.747040771	36.879	4.914	4.707
13688	114813	sidewalk	0.688988874	5.182	4.914	4.729
13689	114813	sidewalk	2.239638063	2.55	4.661	4.214
13690	114813	sidewalk	1.53703794	7.814	4.778	4.432

Figure 3 shows a slope map of the area, service areas calculated as simple buffers, isochrones calculated without slope and isochrones calculated with the slope according to THF and the NLR respectively.

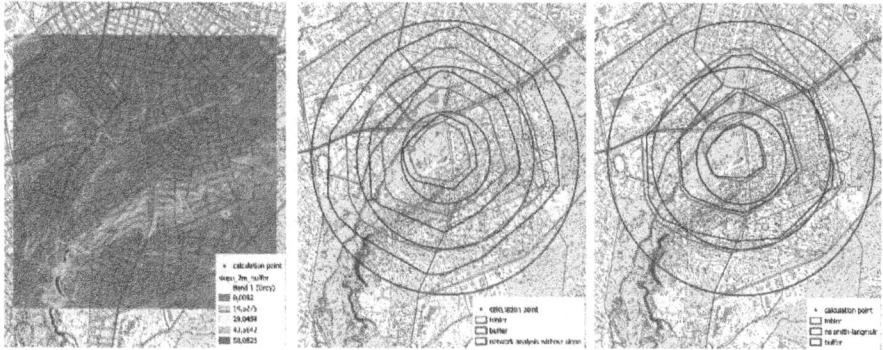

Fig. 3. From left to right: slope map of the area; network analysis compared to THF; the NLR compared to THF

3.4   Join POIs and Residential Buildings by Service Areas

Once the service area has been evaluated for each POI, the residential buildings that fall within every service area should be detected with the corresponding distance range. The spatial join is performed that examines the relations between the geometries of join features (residential buildings) and target features (service areas). It is a one-to-many operation that joins all the features from the join features into the target features by producing several overlapping records. In this case the algorithm seeks for all residential buildings that are within a considered service area. The type of POIs, the distance range, and the count of POIs are also integrated with a building.

3.5   Aggregate POIs within Distance Ranges of Buildings

Having the data from step 3.4 it needs to be summarised so that counts of POIs per building per distance range can be obtained. An aggregate function for counting is utilised. Aggregate functions execute a calculation on a dataset and return a single summary value as a final result. The dataset can be divided into groups on a specific basis and thus the aggregate functions return a single value for each group of the dataset.

Table 2 presents a sample list of buildings (id 278, 387, 2233) with aggregated counts of POIs. For example, a building with id 278 has one pharmacy in 500 m, 1000 m, and 1500 m; 4, 13, and 2 bus stops in 500 m, 1000 m, and 1500 m, respectively.

Table 2. Buildings with POI count

id	phrm_500	phrm_1000	phrm_1500	b_stp_500	b_stp_1000	b_stp_1500
278	1	1	1	4	13	2
387	1	1	1	6	7	4
2233	0	4	1	0	5	2

3.6 Calculate Accessibility Index

AcsI uses the following formula for the calculation:

$$AcsI = \frac{\Sigma(\Sigma(Subgroup\,Weight \times Step\,Weight\,) \times Group\,Weight)}{\Sigma(Subgroup\,Weight) \times Group\,Count} \qquad (2)$$

where *AcsI* is the Accessibility index, Subgroup Weight is the weight assigned to the subgroup, Step Weight is the weight of the distance range, Group Weight is the weight of the group and Group Count is the count of the groups present. For instance, a residential building has access to a playground in 500 m, a health centre in 1000 m and a pharmacy in 1500 m. The playground is a part of the subgroup "playgrounds" with a weight of 0.15 within the group "Kids" with a weight of 15. The distance step weight for 500 m is 1, for 1000 m is 0.75 and for 1500 m is 0.5. The result for this group will be $(0.15 \times 1) \times 15 =$ 2.25. The health centre and the pharmacy are part of group "Health" with a weight of 15 in subgroups "health centres" with a weight of 0.30 and "pharmacies" with a weight of 0.20 respectively. The calculation for the group is $((0.30 \times 0.75) + (0.20 \times 0.50)) \times 15$ $= 4.875$. The final equation will be $(2.25 + 4.875) / ((0.15 + 0.30 + 0.20) \times 2)$ which will result in Accessibility Index of 5.48. The formula does not consider the number of POIs from a specific subgroup type available within a distance range, but whether there is a POI (from a specific subgroup type) available in the certain distance range.

After the calculation of AcsI for all the residential buildings the values are normalised from 0 to 100 through the subsequent equation:

$$Value_{normalised} = \frac{Value}{Value_{max}} \times 100 \qquad (3)$$

where *Value* is the result of the AcsI calculation and *Value_{max}* is the maximum possible value of the index for the current dataset.

4   Implementation

The AcsI calculation is entirely executed in the scope of QGIS using the GATE Mobility plugin, which contains a collection of automated geospatial analyses. Currently, there are four algorithms developed within the plugin that perform diverse spatial tasks: Average altitude of point features, Slope calculation of network segments, Split network with points, Calculation of Accessibility Index.

The calculation of Accessibility Index algorithm is facilitated by the Python libraries *math* and *pandas* together with PyQGIS short for the QGIS Python API (Fig. 4).

According to the methodology, the algorithms applied through QGIS and PyQGIS for the automated calculation of AcsI are described below.

For **determining service area of POIs** with buffer analysis the algorithm "Multi-ring buffer (constant distance)" is implemented from Processing Toolbox.

If network analysis is applied instead of buffer analysis, the Service area (from layer) algorithm is executed. This calculation implements the "shortest path" method. The resulting service area is generated as a Multiline geometry and converted to a polygon

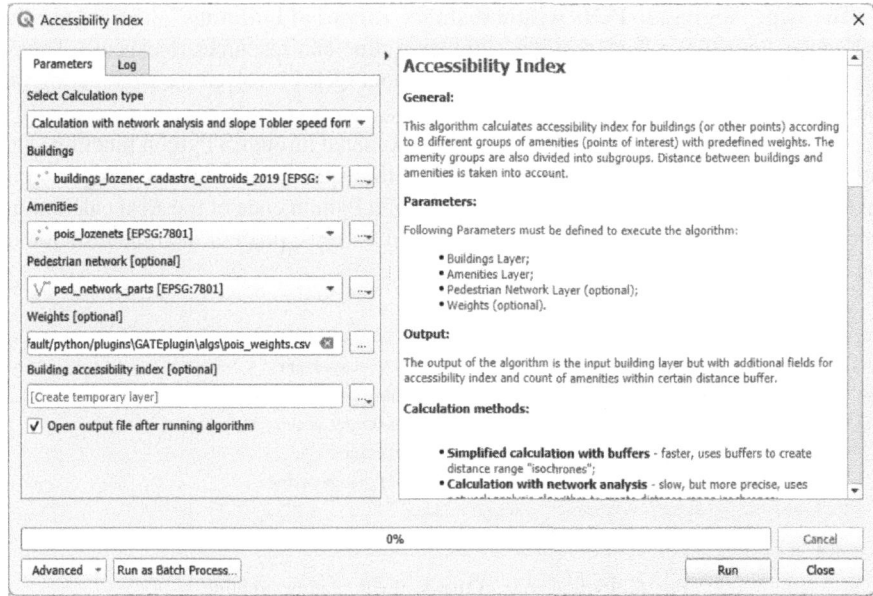

Fig. 4. An interface of the plugin – Accessibility Index

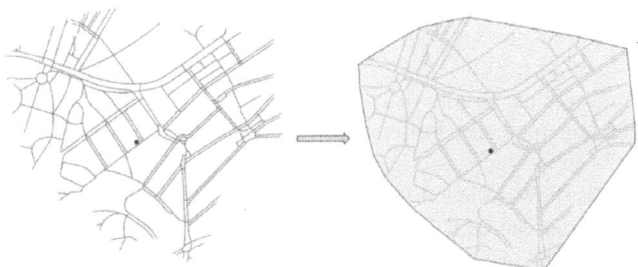

Fig. 5. Lines from Service area and the resulted convex hull polygon

using the Convex Hull algorithm. Figure 5 presents the conversion of the service area from lines to a polygon.

The service area assessment with network analysis and slope calculations also deploys Service area (from layer) algorithm followed by the Convex Hull algorithm. However, it implements the "fastest path" method so that speed and therefore slope can affect the service area. Once the speed is calculated using either THF or the NLR, it is saved as an additional attribute field for each section of the pedestrian network. Slope details are obtained with the Slope calculation algorithm in the GATE Mobility plugin.

For the step "**Join POIs and residential buildings by service area**" the algorithm used is known as "Join attributes by location" from the Processing Toolbox in QGIS.

The step **"Aggregate POIs within distance ranges of buildings"** does not use the Aggregate algorithm, which requires significant time and resources to execute. Therefore, a complete Python solution is adopted without QGIS involved for aggregating the counts of POIs.

The calculation of **Accessibility Index** is automated through a Python function. The weights of the POIs are defined in a .csv file with a specific structure and imported in the function. Figure 6 demonstrates a fragment of a Python code of the AcsI calculating function. In addition, calculations can be executed as "qgis_process" commands without a graphical user interface.

```
1. result_numerator += group_amenity_weights_sum * group_weight
2. result_numerator_max += group_amenity_weights_sum_max * group_weight
3. result_denominator = amenity_weights_sum * len(amenity_groups_to_count)
5. accessibility = result_numerator / result_denominator
6. accessibility_max = result_numerator_max / result_denominator
7. feature["accessibility_index"] = accessibility
8. feature["accessibility_normalized"] = accessibility / accessibility _max * 100
```

Fig. 6. Python code of the AcsI calculating function

5   Results

This section presents the results of calculating of the AcsI for the whole district of Lozenets using four methods: buffer analysis, network analysis, THF, and NRL, as shown on Fig. 7.

Buffer analysis shows a clear differentiation between the northern part and the southern part of the district can be noticed. The northern part is older and closer to the city center, consequently residential buildings situated there have greater access to services which results to higher AcsI scores. On the other hand, the southern part is still developing and is known for its problems with pedestrian network which explains the lower results of AcsI. As for buffer analysis, calculations took approximately 5 min for the whole district of Lozenets.

In the case of the network analysis method, AcsI scores are generally higher in the northern part of Lozenets compared to the southern part. The resulting values vary between 30 and 91.50. The high scores of buildings indicate an access to almost all types of services in every distance range. The calculation of the index for the southern part results in minimum value of 3.1 and a maximum value of 59.6. It can be observed a similar distribution of the values as for the whole district – northern parts with higher scores and southern parts with lower scores. Calculation of the whole district took approximately 30 min.

THF and the NRL demonstrate the same distribution pattern. The calculation time took 40 min to be completed. Overall, calculation with the NLR predicts more residential buildings with AcsI score in the lower ranges compared to THF.

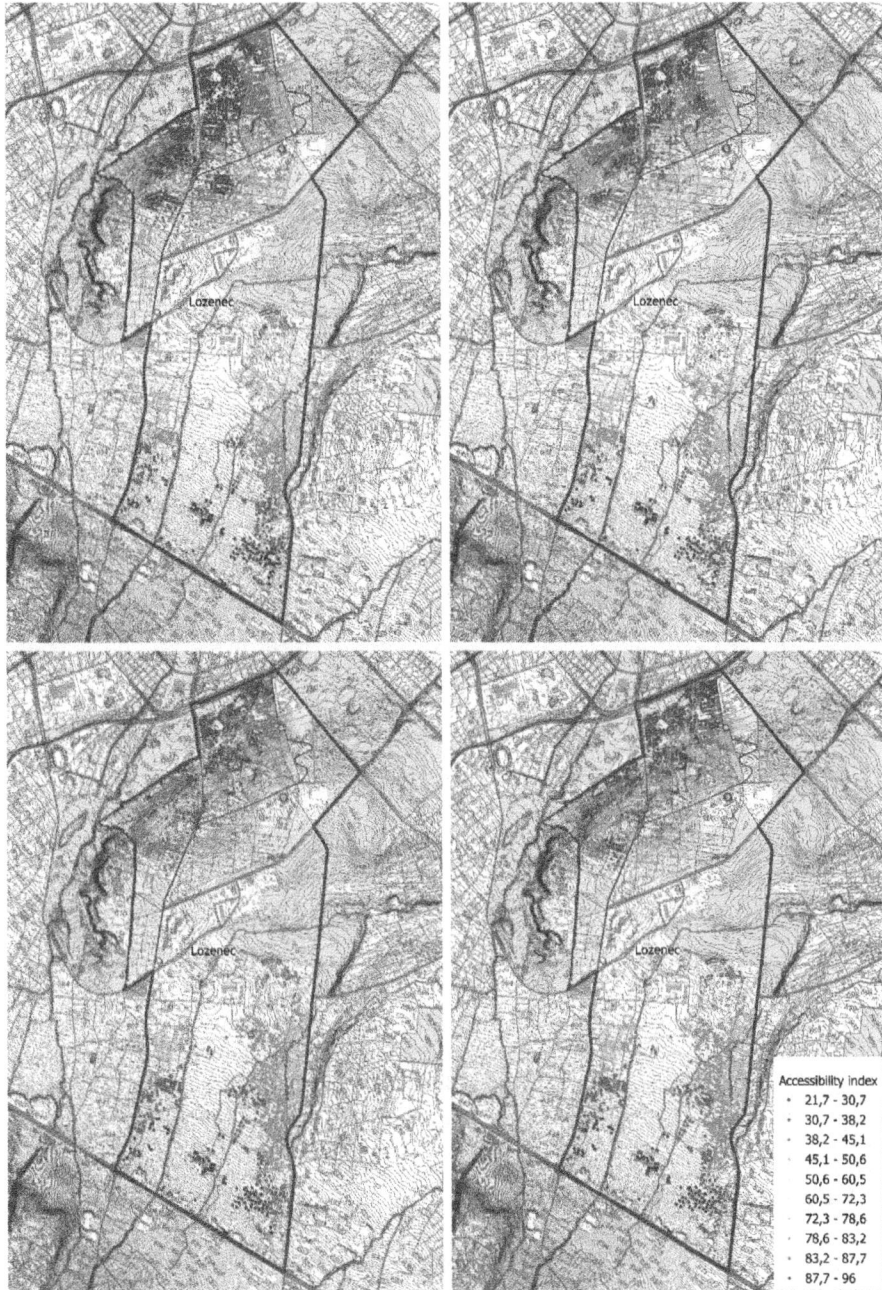

Fig. 7. AcsI scores of the Lozenets district: buffer analysis (top left), network analysis (top right), THF (bottom left), NRL (bottom right)

Figure 8 demonstrates the distribution of scores across all the types of the analysis. Buffer analysis yields too optimistic results, with values reaching up to 96 points, with mean value of 76.3. Similar results can be observed in the network analysis without slope. The lowest maximum belongs to the NLR with 80.4, followed by the THF-based method with 85. The largest group of values in the case of the NLR clusters around 76. Buildings with high AcsI values are distributed in the northern part of the district including sloped areas. In the case of THF the northern flat part with high values is more articulated, which shows higher sensitivity to terrain variations. Finally, the ratio between network analysis and THF shows up to 2.5 times decrease of AcsI in the southern parts of the district.

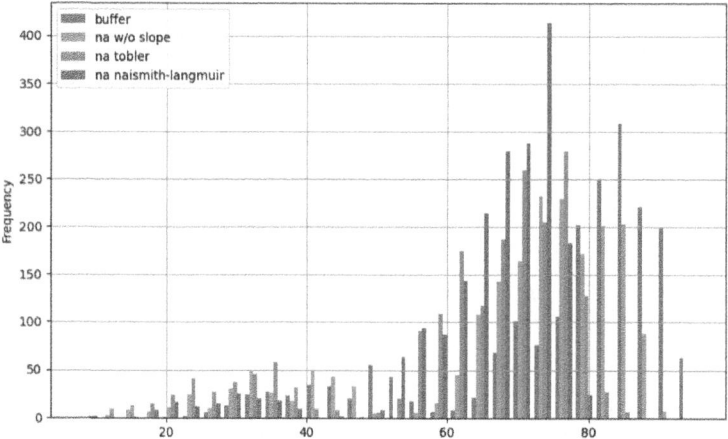

Fig. 8. Ratio of AcsI without slope and with slope considered

5.1 Limitations

The main limitation of the method is the significant computation time at the district scale. Therefore, the possibility of batch processing should be envisioned. In addition, the weights of POI are not present in the user interface, which limits ease of customisation for end-users. Currently, the plugin does not consider steps or elevators.

6 Conclusion and Future Work

This paper introduces a comprehensive approach for calculating AcsI, a key metric for assessing urban environment and development. The methodology is universal and by incorporating multiple calculation methods – buffer analysis, network analysis and network analysis with slope (Tobler's hiking function and the Naismith-Langmuir rule) – it offers a flexible framework that adapts to various urban conditions and datasets. The QGIS built-in network analysis toolbox with implementation of Dijkstra algorithm is preferred combined with several custom changes. The incorporation of the slope into calculations decrease AcsI up to 2.5 times in hilly areas compared to a regular network analysis.

The suggested AcsI focuses on urban morphology and pedestrian networks, providing a universal methodology applicable across various urban scenarios. AcsI evaluates the ease of reaching various points of interest (POIs) within a 15-min walk along pedestrian pathways. The significance of each category of POIs is represented by the weights allocated for the accessibility evaluation.

The plugin is openly available on GitHub where the latest version can be downloaded and utilised in QGIS. Automated algorithms within GATE Mobility plugin are beneficial for both urban and rural use cases.

The case study conducted in Lozenets District proves that the AcsI calculation method is transferable and offers perspectives on conducting calculations not only for the entire city of Sofia, but also for other cities. Consequently, comparisons across distinct cities can be performed. Integration of resulting datasets can be visualised in 3D city models as well. The GATE Mobility plugin operates with user provided data for services, pedestrian network and residential buildings to calculate an index for each building in the dataset. Furthermore, the weighting system for the services can also be modified according to the users' preferences, as well as accounting for staircases or the physical quality of sidewalks.

Future work entails refinements in the calculation process of the index by combining additional factors involved in the 15-min city concept. The GATE Mobility plugin upcoming developments are focused on optimizing the calculation time for certain algorithms including the Accessibility Index calculation and automatisation of further geospatial analyses. Moreover, developments of automated computations for Shannon Diversity Index and Simpson Diversity Index will be explored.

Acknowledgments. This research is part of the GATE project funded by the Horizon 2020 WIDESPREAD-2018-2020 TEAMING Phase 2 programme under grant agreement no. 857155 and the programme "Research, Innovation and Digitalization for Smart Transformation" 2021-2027 (PRIDST) under grant agreement no. BG16RFPR002-1.014-0010-C01.

Disclosure of Interests The authors have no competing interests to declare that are relevant to the content of this article.

References

1. Handy, S.: Planning for Accessibility: In Theory and in Practice. In: Levinson, D.M., Krizek, K.J. (eds.) Access to Destinations, pp. 131–147. Emerald Group Publishing Limited (2005)
2. Ewing, R., Cervero, R.: Travel and the built environment: a meta-analysis. J. Am. Plan. Assoc. **76**, 265–294 (2010). https://doi.org/10.1080/01944361003766766
3. Carr, L.J., Dunsiger, S.I., Marcus, B.H.: Walk score™ as a global estimate of neighborhood walkability. Am. J. Prev. Med. **39**, 460–463 (2010). https://doi.org/10.1016/j.amepre.2010.07.007
4. Gilderbloom, J.I., Riggs, W.W., Meares, W.L.: Does walkability matter? An examination of walkability's impact on housing values, foreclosures and crime. Cities. **42**, 13–24 (2015). https://doi.org/10.1016/j.cities.2014.08.001

5. Meeder, M., Aebi, T., Weidmann, U.: The influence of slope on walking activity and the pedestrian modal share. Transp. Res. Proc. https://doi.org/10.1016/j.trpro.2017.12.095

6. U.S. Environmental Protection Agency National Walkability Index: Methodology and User Guide. https://www.epa.gov/sites/default/files/2021-06/documents/national_wal kability_index_methodology_and_user_guide_june2021.pdf

7. Space Syntax Space Syntax Walkability Index. https://spacesyntax.com/project/walkability-index/

8. Lam, T.M., Wang, Z., Vaartjes, I., Karssenberg, D., Ettema, D., Helbich, M., Timmermans, E.J., Frank, L.D., den Braver, N.R., Wagtendonk, A.J., Beulens, J.W.J., Lakerveld, J.: Development of an objectively measured walkability index for the Netherlands. Int. J. Behav. Nutr. Phys. Act. **19**, 50 (2022). https://doi.org/10.1186/s12966-022-01270-8

9. Alves, F., Cruz, S., Ribeiro, A., Bastos Silva, A., Martins, J., Cunha, I.: Walkability index for elderly health: a proposal. Sustainability. https://doi.org/10.3390/su12187360

10. Kang, C.-D.: The S + 5Ds: spatial access to pedestrian environments and walking in Seoul, Korea. Cities. **77**, 130–141 (2018). https://doi.org/10.1016/j.cities.2018.01.019

11. Urban Network Analysis Toolbox for ArcGIS. In: City Form Lab. http://cityform.mit.edu/pro jects. Accessed 27 Jan 2025

12. PST plugin for QGIS. https://smog.chalmers.se/projects/pst-plugin-for-qgis/. Accessed 15 Nov 2024

13. Space Syntax Toolkit for QGIS. https://plugins.qgis.org/plugins/esstoolkit/

14. Openrouteservice. https://openrouteservice.org/

15. QNEAT3. https://root676.github.io/

16. Fina, S., Gerten, C., Pondi, B., D'Arcy, L., O'Reilly, N., Vale, D.S., Pereira, M., Zilio, S.: OS-WALK-EU: an open-source tool to assess health-promoting residential walkability of European city structures. J. Transp. Health. **27**, 101486 (2022). https://doi.org/10.1016/j.jth. 2022.101486

17. DeCodingSpaces Toolbox. https://toolbox.decodingspaces.net/

18. Albashir, A., Messa, F., Presicce, D., Pedrazzoli, A., Gorrini, A.: 15min City Score Toolkit – Urban Walkability Analytics. Zenodo (2024)

19. Aino. World 15-munite city walkability. https://www.15mincity.ai/

20. Karamitov, K., Petrova-Antonova, D.: PEDESTRIAN ACCESSIBILITY ASSESSMENT USING SPATIAL AND NETWORK ANALYSIS: A CASE OF SOFIA CITY. The International Archives of the Photogrammetry, Remote Sensing and Spatial Information Sciences. **XLVIII-4-W5-2022**, 53–60 (2022). https://doi.org/10.5194/isprs-archives-XLVIII-4-W5-2022-53-2022

21. Boyukliyski, S., Petrova-Antonova, D., Somanath, S.: Evaluation of social facilities coverage: a case study of Sofia city. IFAC-Papers OnLine. **55**, 48–53 (2022). https://doi.org/10.1016/j.ifacol.2022.08.047

22. Karamitov, K., Petrova-Antonova, D., Hristov, E., Borukova, M.: Supply-demand analysis of urban amenities based on walking accessibility. In: 2023 IEEE International Conference on Big Data (BigData), pp. 3973–3979 (2023)

23. Kumalasari, D., Koeva, M.N., Vahdatikhaki, F., Petrova-Antonova, D., Kuffer, M.: GENERATIVE DESIGN FOR WALKABLE CITIES: A CASE STUDY OF SOFIA. The International Archives of the Photogrammetry, Remote Sensing and Spatial Information Sciences. **XLVIII-4-W5-2022**, 75–82 (2022). https://doi.org/10.5194/isprs-archives-XLVIII-4-W5-2022-75-2022

24. Kumalasari, D., Koeva, M., Vahdatikhaki, F., Petrova Antonova, D., Kuffer, M.: Planning walkable cities: generative design approach towards digital twin implementation. Remote Sens. **15**, 1088 (2023). https://doi.org/10.3390/rs15041088

25. Zoppellaro, G.: Lisbon accessibility analisys - an application of the 15-Minute City concept

26. Şahin Körmeçli, P.: Analysis of walkable street networks by using the space syntax and GIS techniques: a case study of Çankırı City. ISPRS Int. J. Geo Inf. **12**, 216 (2023). https://doi.org/10.3390/ijgi12060216

27. Coelho, P.S., Oliveira, L.K., Nobrega, R.A.A.: Influence of slope on pedestrian access to public transportation systems. Latin Am. Transp. Stud. **3**, 100029 (2025). https://doi.org/10.1016/j.latran.2025.100029

28. Rhoads, D., Solé-Ribalta, A., Borge-Holthoefer, J.: The inclusive 15-minute city: walkability analysis with sidewalk networks. Comput. Environ. Urban. Syst. **100**, 101936 (2023). https://doi.org/10.1016/j.compenvurbsys.2022.101936

29. Higgins, C.: Hiking with Tobler: Tracking Movement and Calibrating a Cost Function for Personalized 3D Accessibility. https://doi.org/10.1016/j.landurbplan.2018.12.011

30. Higgins, C.D.: A 4D spatio-temporal approach to modelling land value uplift from rapid transit in high density and topographically-rich cities. Landsc. Urban Plan. **185**, 68–82 (2019). https://doi.org/10.1016/j.landurbplan.2018.12.011

31. VfBidirHikingTime. https://pro.arcgis.com/en/pro-app/latest/arcpy/spatial-analyst/vfbidirhikingtime-class.htm

32. Adjust the encountered distance using a vertical factor. https://pro.arcgis.com/en/pro-app/latest/tool-reference/spatial-analyst/adjust-the-encountered-distance-using-a-vertical-factor.htm

Location-Allocation of Social Amenities Based on Constraint Programming

Dessislava Petrova-Antonova$^{(\boxtimes)}$ ⓘ and Mihail Stamenov ⓘ

GATE Institute, Sofia University "St. Kliment Ohridski", Sofia, Bulgaria
{dessislava.petrova,mihail.stamenov}@gate-ai.eu

Abstract. The social amenities allocation problem is a challenge in urban planning, requiring an optimal distribution of their locations to accommodate demand while ensuring accessibility. This paper presents a novel approach to solving this problem using Constraint Programming (CP). The constraint modeling language MiniZinc is used to formulate the problem, and the Gecode and Chuffed solvers are utilized to identify feasible allocations. To improve computational efficiency, a bounding strategy is applied, determining upper and lower limits on the number of required kindergartens, leveraging a 0/1 knapsack model and combinatorial search techniques. In addition, a clustering-based preprocessing step is introduced that enhances the selection of candidate kindergartens.

The proposed approach is evaluated on real-world data from Sofia, Bulgaria, demonstrating its ability to produce optimal allocations for kindergartens while maintaining computational feasibility. It is implemented within the urban planning use case of the Urban Digital Twin pilot project of the city. The results highlight the advantages of CP for solving complex spatial allocation problems, offering a scalable framework for future applications in urban infrastructure planning.

Keywords: Constraint Programming · Location-Allocation of Social Amenities · Spatial Optimization · Urban Planning

1 Introduction

Urban planning plays a crucial role in shaping the livability and functionality of cities, with social amenities serving as key determinants of residents' well-being. Access to essential services such as schools, healthcare facilities, and recreational spaces influences quality of life, economic opportunities, and social equity. Among these, kindergartens are particularly significant as they provide early childhood education and facilitate the participation of the parents' workforce. However, ensuring equitable access to kindergartens poses a major challenge for urban planners, requiring careful consideration of spatial distribution, demographic trends, and infrastructure constraints. Effective planning of these facilities is essential to foster inclusive and sustainable urban environments.

Optimizing kindergarten allocation is a complex problem that requires advanced computational techniques to balance accessibility, capacity, and efficiency. Traditional approaches often struggle with the combinatorial nature of

O. Gervasi et al. (Eds.): ICCSA 2025 Workshops, LNCS 15897, pp. 438–455, 2026.
https://doi.org/10.1007/978-3-031-97660-5_29

the problem, where multiple factors must be considered simultaneously, such as population density, travel distance, and available infrastructure. Modern urban planning increasingly relies on data-driven methodologies to improve decision-making and resource allocation. In this context, CP provides a powerful framework for solving large-scale spatial optimization problems. Using CP, optimal kindergarten placements can be identified, minimizing inequality in access while ensuring efficient use of resources.

The kindergarten allocation problem is a critical optimization challenge in Sofia, Bulgaria. The objective is to determine the optimal locations to build new kindergartens from a predefined set of possible sites while efficiently distributing children to these kindergartens. The allocation must consider constraints such as capacity limits, proximity, and fairness in distribution. This problem is particularly relevant in densely populated areas where the demand for kindergarten placements exceeds the available slots, requiring an optimal location-allocation strategy.

In this paper, a novel approach is proposed to solve the kindergarten location-allocation problem using CP. The problem is formalized based on MiniZinc, a high-level constraint modelling language, and leverages the power of the Gecode and Chuffed solvers to find optimal solutions. To enhance computational efficiency, Python's multiprocessing module is employed, enabling parallelized execution where each process independently explores solutions for different numbers of required kindergartens. This parallelization significantly accelerates the solution process, making it feasible to handle larger problem instances. The proposed approach provides a scalable and efficient solution to the allocation problem, offering a practical framework that can be adapted to various real-world scenarios. Through experimental evaluation, its effectiveness is evaluated in terms of solution quality and computational performance.

The remainder of the paper is structured as follows. Section 2 introduces the related work. Section 3 is dedicated to the formulation of the problem and the description of the methods used. Section 4 presents the implementation of the proposed approach, while Sect. 5 describes the results obtained. Finally, Sect. 6 concludes the paper.

2   Related Work

This section presents the related work, including the traditional methods like integer programming, deferred- acceptance Algorithms and capacitated P-median models, followed by an alternative to the proposed approach models and finishing with CP applications.

2.1   Traditional Methods

Integer Programming (IP) models have been extensively used for kindergarten allocation, optimizing assignments while considering constraints such as proximity and capacity. For example, [1] applied IP models in Norway to automate the allocation process, demonstrating improved results over manual methods. However, IP models can become computationally expensive when dealing with large-scale problems, necessitating heuristic methods to improve scalability. *Deferred-Acceptance (DA) Algorithms* are commonly used for stable matching problems, where allocation is based on predefined priorities such as sibling attendance and distance. These algorithms have been successfully implemented in Estonian municipalities, as shown by [2], improving fairness and efficiency. However, balancing trade-offs between fairness and overall efficiency remains a challenge, and the effectiveness of the method depends on the priority rules used.

Capacitated P-Median Models focus on minimizing the overall commute distances for children while ensuring that kindergarten capacities are not exceeded. [3] demonstrated the application of such models in school allocation systems in Greece. While effective in optimizing proximity-based allocation, these models require extensive preprocessing of data and are highly sensitive to parameter settings, making implementation complex. *Hybrid Evolutionary Methods*, such as combining genetic algorithms (GA) with traditional optimization techniques, have been explored for capacitated location-allocation problems. [4] proposed a hybrid GA method that improves solution quality while maintaining computational efficiency. However, these methods require careful tuning of parameters and may struggle with convergence, especially for large problem instances.

The *Spatial Decision Support Systems (SDSS)* combine Geographic Information Systems (GIS) with optimization techniques to assist in making location-allocation decisions. [3] demonstrated the integration of SDSS for school placement problems, leveraging spatial data to optimize placements. However, implementing SDSS requires expertise in both spatial analysis and optimization, making it a resource-intensive approach.

2.2 Alternative Methods and Their Limitations

Several other methods have been explored in the literature for solving similar allocation problems.

The *Genetic Algorithms (GA)* are used to encode potential solutions as chromosomes and evolve better allocations over generations [5, 7]. However, GAs require careful parameter tuning and can be computationally expensive, making them less reliable for large-scale problems [6]. Data Envelopment Analysis (DEA) is applied to evaluate the efficiency of kindergarten allocation by analyzing input-output relationships [8]. However, DEA primarily serves as a benchmarking tool rather than a direct solution method. *Particle Swarm Optimization (PSO)* simulates the movement of particles in a search space to optimize allocation decisions [8]. However, PSO struggles with handling discrete constraints like capacity limits and can converge prematurely to suboptimal solutions.

Mixed-integer programming (MIP) has been used for modeling the problem as a set of linear equations, optimizing objectives like travel distance and capacity balancing [1]. Despite its accuracy, MIP becomes computationally infeasible for large-scale problems without heuristic adaptations.

2.3   Constraint Programming

CP is highly effective in solving various types of optimization and decision-making problems. There are several areas, where CP excels.

In the context of *Scheduling Problems*, CP is widely used in scheduling tasks, such as nurse scheduling, operating room scheduling, and production scheduling. It provides flexibility in handling complex constraints and improves efficiency in generating optimal schedules according to [13–15]. For *Resource Allocation*, CP is effective in resource allocation problems, such as tool allocation in manufacturing systems [16] and resource scheduling in high-performance computing [17]. It handles constraints like resource capacities and deadlines efficiently according to [18]

In *Combinatorial Optimization*, CP is powerful for solving combinatorial problems [19], including the traveling salesman problem, knapsack problem, and crew rostering [20]. It ensures optimal solutions through systematic search and constraint propagation [21]. Regarding the *Planning and Decision-Making*, CP is used in planning tasks, such as maintenance scheduling for heritage buildings and traffic incident management, where it optimizes resource use and meets complex constraints [22, 23]. For *Hybrid Approaches* CP is often integrated with other techniques, such as reinforcement learning and integer programming, to enhance its performance in solving large-scale problems [24].

Following the advances of CP, the proposed approach aims to provide a scalable and efficient solution to the kindergarten allocation problem, offering a practical framework that can be adapted to various real-world scenarios.

3   Study Area and Data

3.1   Study Area

The study area is the most populous city in Bulgaria, with a population of more than 1 221 785 in the year 2020, according to [25]. This city is spread over 245.5 km2 [26]. It builds upon previous work, extending the spatial analysis of kindergarten accessibility in Sofia [27,28]. The data consists of three main components: the pedestrian network, residential buildings, and kindergartens.

3.2   Datasets

The *pedestrian network* serves as the foundation for accessibility analysis. It was developed by Sofiaplan for network analysis purposes, ensuring proper connectivity using GIS topology checks. Previous work on network analysis details the preprocessing steps, including calculating travel distances and times while resolving overlapping vertices.

To estimate demand, the number of residents per statistical unit was obtained from the National Statistical Institute. Using cadastral data, the gross floor area (GFA) of *residential buildings* is calculated and distributed demographic data accordingly. The number of children per building was estimated based on age distribution data, resulting in a floating-point approximation of potential kindergarten demand.

On the supply side, due to the lack of precise capacity data, the potential *kindergarten* capacities are estimated based on lot area and legal regulations. This estimation provides insight into the maximum possible capacity expansion without acquiring additional land. The spatial distribution of kindergartens and their potential capacities form the basis for the subsequent allocation analysis.

3.3   Data Preprocessing

To integrate the datasets into a unified framework, residential buildings and kindergartens were mapped onto the pedestrian network as graph vertices. Dijkstra's algorithm was used to compute the shortest walking distances from each building to every kindergarten. Distances exceeding 15 min were set to a high constant value (1,000,000) to effectively represent inaccessibility. The final dataset consists of:

- A distance matrix containing walking distances between buildings and kindergartens.
- An array representing the capacities of potential kindergartens.
- An array indicating the estimated number of children per residential block.

The complete dataset comprises 83,089 buildings and 26,084 potential kindergarten placements. From this dataset, two smaller subsets were extracted: a **neighborhood-level dataset**, consisting of 348 buildings and 59 kindergartens, and a **street-level dataset**, containing 17 buildings and 5 kindergartens. All experiments in this study are conducted exclusively on these smaller datasets.

Figure 1 and Fig. 2 illustrate the spatial distribution of buildings and kindergartens in the neighborhood-level and street-level datasets, respectively.

4   Problem Formulation and Methods

The problem of selecting optimal locations for kindergartens in an urban setting is considered, with the objective of **minimizing the number of kindergartens constructed while simultaneously reducing the total walking distance for children.**

The problem can be formally described as follows:

- Let B denote a set of buildings, each with a given number of children.
- Let K denote a set of potential locations where kindergartens can be located.
- Let d_{ij} denotes the distance from each building i to each potential kindergarten location j.
- Let $\bar{C}_j$ denotes maximum capacity of kindergarten j and the number of children in building i is given by c_i.

Fig. 1. Spatial representation of the neighborhood-level dataset (348 buildings and 59 kindergartens).

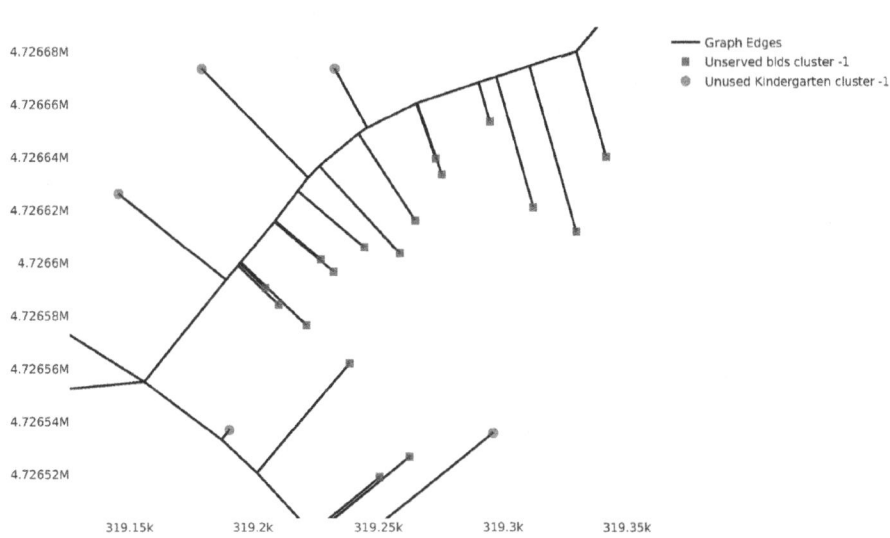

Fig. 2. Spatial representation of the street-level dataset (17 buildings and 5 kindergartens).

The objective is to **select a subset K' of K** and **assign each building to exactly one selected kindergarten** while minimizing the total distance the children have to walk. It can be formalized as two consecutive **p-median problems**. A function-based perspective can also be formulated, where the objective is to identify a function defined as follows:

$$f : B \rightarrow K' \tag{1}$$

where $K' \subseteq K$ is the set of selected kindergartens. This function must respect feasibility constraints while optimizing the objective.

4.1   p-Median Formulation

Since the objective is to minimize both the number of newly established kindergartens and the total walking distance for all children, a two-step optimization approach is necessary. First, the minimum number of required kindergartens is determined. Once this value is obtained, it is incorporated as a constraint in the subsequent optimization step, which focuses on minimizing the total distance between children and their assigned kindergartens. Both steps rely on the same set of decision variables:

-   Let $x_{ij} \in \{0, 1\}$ is 1 if children from building i are assigned to kindergarten j, 0 otherwise.
-   Let $y_j \in \{0, 1\}$ is 1 if kindergarten is built at location j, 0 otherwise.

Minimization of New Kindergartens. The number of new kindergartens is minimized as follows:

$$\min \sum_{j \in K} y_j \tag{2}$$

where y_j is a binary decision variable indicating whether a kindergarten is established at location j ($y_j = 1$) or not ($y_j = 0$). The set K represents the potential locations where kindergartens can be built.

Each building must be assigned to exactly one kindergarten, which is represented by the following constraint:

$$\sum_{j \in K} x_{ij} = 1, \quad \forall i \in B \tag{3}$$

where x_{ij} is a binary decision variable indicating whether building i is assigned to kindergarten j ($x_{ij} = 1$) or not ($x_{ij} = 0$). The set B represents the set of buildings, and K denotes the set of potential kindergarten locations.

The buildings must be assigned only to selected kindergarten plots where kindergartens will be built, ensuring that no assignments are made to unused plots, as defined by the following constraint:

$$x_{ij} \leq y_j, \quad \forall i \in B, \forall j \in K \tag{4}$$

Moreover, the total number of children assigned to a kindergarten j must not exceed its capacity $\bar{C}_j$, and if $y_j = 0$ (the kindergarten is not built), then no children can be assigned to it, which is represented by a third constraint as follows:

$$\sum_{i \in B} d_i x_{ij} \leq \bar{C}_j y_j, \quad \forall j \in K \tag{5}$$

where d_i represents the number of children in building i, and $\bar{C}_j$ denotes the maximum capacity of kindergarten j. The constraint ensures that the total demand for kindergarten seats at a specific location does not exceed its capacity. Additionally, when $y_j = 0$, the right-hand side of the inequality becomes zero, enforcing that no children are assigned to plots where kindergartens are not constructed. This effectively prevents the allocation of buildings to non-selected plots while ensuring that capacity constraints are respected. Although constraint (5) inherently prevents assignments to unbuilt kindergartens by ensuring that the total number of assigned children does not exceed the available capacity, it does not explicitly forbid individual assignments to non-selected plots. The constraint (4) directly enforces that a building cannot be assigned to a kindergarten unless that kindergarten is constructed. Without this constraint, an assignment could still be technically feasible as long as the total assigned children remain within a capacity of zero, but this does not explicitly restrict individual building assignments. Therefore, constraint (4) is necessary to establish a strict logical dependency between x_{ij} and y_j at the assignment level.

Minimization of Distances. After optimizing the first problem, the number of required kindergartens is determined. To incorporate this result into the second optimization step, an additional parameter, p, is introduced, representing the exact number of kindergartens to be built.

The total weighted walking distance is minimized through the following objective function:

$$\min \sum_{i \in B} \sum_{j \in K} c_i d_{ij} x_{ij} \tag{6}$$

where c_i denotes the number of children in building i, d_{ij} represents the walking distance from building i to kindergarten j, and x_{ij} is a binary decision variable indicating whether the children from building i are assigned to kindergarten j ($x_{ij} = 1$) or not ($x_{ij} = 0$).

To enforce that exactly p kindergartens are built, a new constraint is introduced:

$$\sum_{j \in K} y_j = p \tag{7}$$

where y_j is a binary decision variable indicating whether a kindergarten is constructed at location j ($y_j = 1$) or not ($y_j = 0$). By integrating Equation (7) into the optimization model, the solution guarantees that exactly p kindergartens are selected while minimizing the overall walking distance, as defined in o (6).

4.2   Constraint Programming for Feasibility of a Given Kindergarten Count

CP can struggle with scalability when dealing with large or highly complex problems, as the computational effort required for constraint propagation and search can grow exponentially with problem size. For this reason, no direct CP formulation is provided for minimizing the number of kindergartens needed.

Instead, different methods were used to determine bounds for p, the required number of kindergartens. A binary search is performed over p to efficiently find the minimal feasible number of kindergartens. In this formulation, p is treated as a parameter, and the model verifies whether a given number of kindergartens is sufficient to accommodate all children while satisfying the problem constraints.

Decision Variables. The initial approach to formulating the CP model considered an array of size $|B|$, where each element represented the index of the assigned kindergarten. However, this formulation resulted in a search space of $|K|^{|B|}$, leading to significant computational complexity. Furthermore, enforcing a global constraint to limit the number of utilized kindergartens increased propagation overhead, further complicating the model's efficiency.

To mitigate these challenges, a more structured approach was adopted by introducing two separate arrays. The first array tracks the selected kindergartens, while the second assigns buildings to the indices of these selected kindergartens. Given that the number of kindergartens to be used, denoted as p, is predefined, the length of the first array is explicitly set to p, ensuring that exactly p kindergartens are utilized in the final allocation.

Formally, each building $i \in B$ is assigned to one of the p selected kindergartens, represented by the variable:

$$x_i \in \{1, \ldots, p\}, \quad \forall i \in B \tag{8}$$

where x_i denotes the index of the kindergarten assigned to building i. Simultaneously, the indices of the selected kindergartens are stored in an array of length p, where each entry corresponds to a kindergarten from the original set of potential locations:

$$y_j \in K, \quad \forall j \in \{1, \ldots, p\} \tag{9}$$

This formulation significantly reduces the search space while maintaining flexibility in the assignment process, ensuring computational feasibility while adhering to the problem constraints.

Constraints. Two constraints are defined related to the kindergarten capacities and uniqueness of the selected kindergartens. The kindergarten capacity is constrained as follows:

$$\sum_{\{i \in B | x_i = j\}} c_i \leq C_{y_j}, \quad \forall j \in \{1, \ldots, p\} \tag{10}$$

where the total number of children assigned to kindergarten j must not exceed its capacity c_j.

The second constraint ensures that each selected kindergarten is unique (no duplicates), enforcing an ordering among the selected kindergartens:

$$y_j < y_k, \quad \forall j < k, \quad j, k \in \{1, \ldots, p\} \tag{11}$$

where y_j and y_k represent the indices of the selected kindergartens from the set of potential locations. This constraint guarantees that the kindergartens are chosen in a strictly increasing order, preventing the same kindergarten from being selected multiple times.

By enforcing this ordering, the search space is significantly reduced. Without this constraint, the model would differentiate between permutations of the same set of selected kindergartens, treating different orderings of the same selection as distinct solutions. This would result in a search space of:

$$|B|^p \times P(p, |K|) = |B|^p \times \frac{|K|!}{(|K| - p)!} \tag{12}$$

where $|B|^p$ accounts for the possible assignments of buildings to the selected kindergartens, and $P(p, |K|)$ represents the number of ways to arrange p kindergartens from the set K.

By enforcing an increasing order among selected kindergartens, we eliminate duplicate permutations and instead consider only unique combinations, reducing the search space to:

$$|B|^p \times C(p, |K|) = |B|^p \times \frac{|K|!}{p!(|K| - p)!} \tag{13}$$

where $C(p, |K|)$ represents the number of ways to choose p kindergartens from K without considering order. This reduction significantly improves computational efficiency, as the number of valid kindergarten selections decreases from permutations to combinations, leading to a more manageable search space in the constraint programming model.

Satisfaction vs. Objective Function. Unlike the previous formulations, there is no need for an objective function here since the purpose of the model is to satisfy the constraints proving that the given number of kindergartens used is a possible solution.

5 Implementation of Methods

The proposed approach is implemented in Python, utilizing several libraries to handle different aspects of the problem. GeoPandas is used for processing GeoPackage files, while NetworkX facilitates graph-based operations. NumPy supports matrix computations, and clustering is performed using the K-Means algorithm from Scikit-learn. The constraint programming model is formulated in MiniZinc and executed via the corresponding Python library.

5.1   Data Preprocessing

The first step in data processing involves computing the shortest paths between all buildings and kindergartens using Dijkstra's algorithm. Given that the problem is approached through constraint programming, it is crucial to establish meaningful bounds on the number of kindergartens required.

To determine an upper bound, we apply a greedy 0/1 knapsack approach. The kindergartens are sorted by capacity in descending order, and starting from the largest, they are filled sequentially until all children are assigned. In this formulation, kindergarten capacity corresponds to the knapsack size, while the number of children per residential block represents item weights. Since the number of children is stored as a floating-point value, direct application of the knapsack model was not possible. However, analysis of the dataset showed that child counts were precise up to two decimal places, allowing us to scale all values by a factor of 100 to convert them into integers.

The lower bound is derived by systematically generating all possible selections of kindergartens for a given number and evaluating feasibility. The process begins by computing the minimum number of kindergartens required to accommodate all children. This value serves as the initial bound. All possible selections of kindergartens of this size are then generated, and buildings that have access to only one kindergarten are assigned accordingly. A selection is considered valid if this assignment does not violate capacity constraints and all buildings have access to at least one kindergarten. If no feasible combination is found, the process repeats with an incremented number of kindergartens. The complexity of verifying a single combination is linear, while the number of combinations follows the standard binomial coefficient:

$$\binom{|K|}{p} = \frac{|K|!}{p!(|K| - p)!} \tag{14}$$

where $|K|$ is the total number of kindergartens, and p is the selected subset size.

5.2   Kindergarten Selection and Constraint Programming Model

Once the search space is bounded, the final selection of kindergartens is determined using a constraint programming model in MiniZinc. The process iteratively searches for the minimum number of kindergartens required by solving the feasibility problem for a given number. If a solution exists, this number becomes the new upper bound, and the search continues within the updated range.

Two distinct MiniZinc models were developed. The first model performs a pure feasibility check, determining whether a given number of kindergartens can accommodate all children while maintaining accessibility constraints. The second model incorporates a clustering-based approach to improve efficiency. Kindergartens are grouped using a feature space based on their distances to buildings, and the largest kindergarten from each cluster is selected as a representative candidate. Buildings that have access to only one kindergarten are immediately assigned. The remaining buildings are sorted by their proximity to the selected kindergartens, forming preference-based clusters where each building expresses a ranked preference for nearby facilities. If an entire cluster of buildings can be assigned to their top choice without violating capacity constraints, the assignment is finalized. The MiniZinc model then takes the pre-assigned buildings and the selected kindergartens as input to optimize the final allocation.

This structured approach ensures that the search for an optimal solution remains computationally feasible while preserving real-world constraints on accessibility and kindergarten capacity.

6   Experimental Setup and Results

The proposed approach is evaluated on two datasets: the **neighborhood-level dataset**, which consists of 348 buildings and 59 kindergarten plots, and the **street-level dataset**, a smaller toy example containing 17 buildings and 5 kindergarten plots. The experiments compare different preprocessing methods, as well as the performance of two constraint programming models in solving the kindergarten allocation problem.

6.1   Preprocessing Evaluation

To improve computational efficiency and guide the constraint programming solver, a clustering-based preprocessing step was applied using K-Means. Two preprocessing strategies were tested: one where the data was log-transformed and scaled, and another where standard scaling was applied without logarithmic transformation. Additionally, experiments were conducted using both a weighted and an unweighted distance matrix to assess the impact of weighting on clustering quality.

The results indicate that **scaled clustering** of the kindergartens performed slightly better then the **log-transformed clustering** for the neighborhood-level dataset, leading to more balanced groups and improving the efficiency of the subsequent constraint programming models. The usage of weighted matrix is not improving the performance. Figure 3 illustrates the clustering results for **scaled clustering** preprocessing method and Fig. 4 illustrates the clustering results for **log** preprocessing.

Fig. 3. Visualization of kindergarten clustering using scaled data for the neighborhood-level dataset.

6.2 Comparison of Constraint Programming Models

Two CP models were compared. The first model directly attempts to solve the allocation problem by determining the optimal selection of kindergartens and assigning buildings to them. The second model incorporates additional preprocessing steps, including clustering, pre-assignment of buildings that have access to only one kindergarten, and prioritization of larger kindergartens within clusters.

The results show that the first CP model struggles with computational feasibility for the neighborhood-level dataset, failing to compute a solution for scenarios requiring three kindergartens. In contrast, the second CP model, which incorporates clustering and additional heuristics, performs significantly better, producing solutions efficiently for the same dataset. Both models, however, successfully solve the allocation problem for the smaller street-level dataset, indicating that the first model is only viable for small-scale instances.

6.3   Solver Performance

The CP models were executed using two different solvers: **Chuffed** and **Gecode**. Experimental results indicate that Chuffed outperformed Gecode in terms of computational speed, consistently solving the allocation problem slightly faster across different scenarios. However, both solvers produced the same optimal solutions, demonstrating that the choice of solver impacts runtime performance but not solution quality.

Fig. 4. Visualization of kindergarten clustering using log-transformed data for the neighborhood-level dataset.

6.4   Evaluation Metrics

To fairly assess the quality of the obtained solutions, the results were evaluated based on how well the kindergartens were distributed across the city. Instead of relying solely on standard optimization metrics such as total walking distance, the clustering balance of the selected kindergartens was also examined to ensure an equitable spatial distribution. The goal was to allocate kindergartens in a way that minimized local congestion while maintaining accessibility for all buildings.

Figures 5 and 6 illustrate the spatial assignment of buildings to kindergartens after clustering and pre-assignment, demonstrating the final distributions used in the second MiniZinc model.

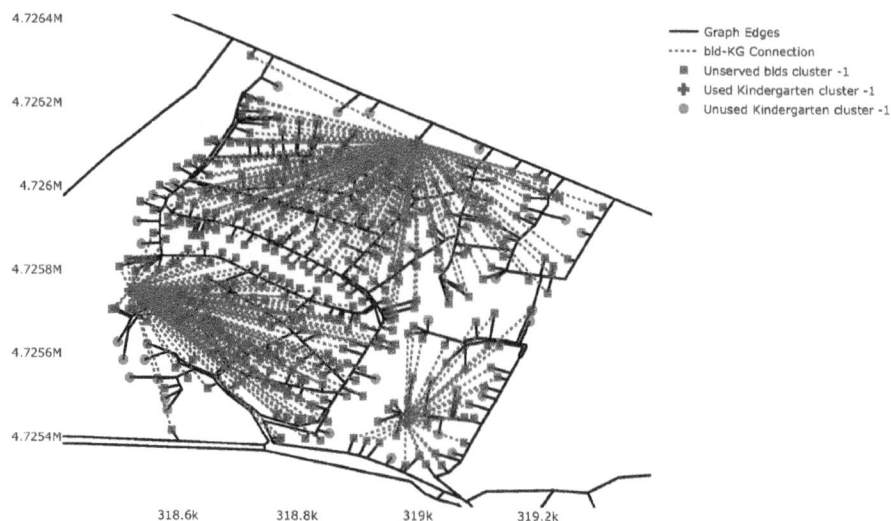

Fig. 5. Final assignment of buildings to kindergartens for the neighborhood-level dataset after clustering and pre-assignment.

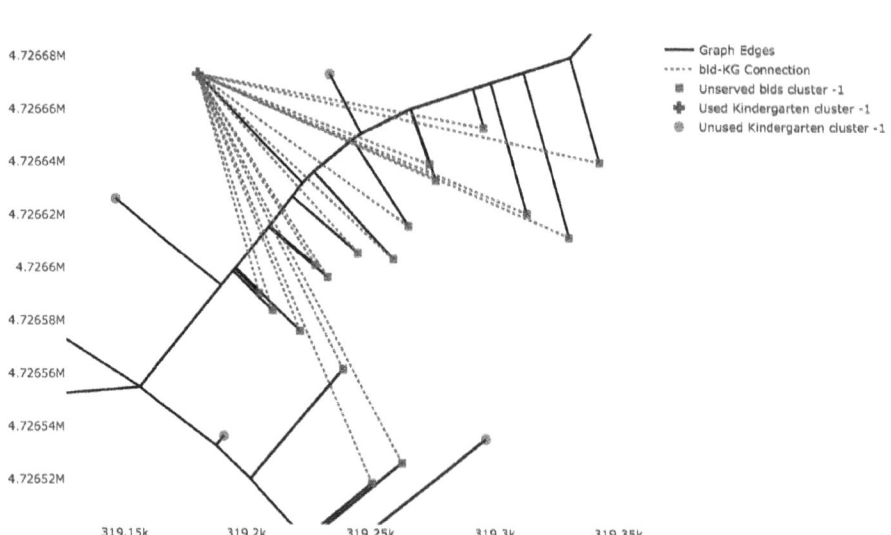

Fig. 6. Final assignment of buildings to kindergartens for the street-level dataset after clustering and pre-assignment.

6.5   Future Considerations

While the clustering-based preprocessing approach significantly improves computational performance, further refinements could be explored. Future work could integrate demand forecasting models to dynamically adjust the number of required kindergartens based on projected population changes. Additionally, alternative clustering techniques, such as hierarchical clustering or density-based methods, could be tested to determine whether they provide more balanced kindergarten distributions.

The experimental results demonstrate that constraint programming is a viable approach for solving the kindergarten allocation problem, particularly when combined with preprocessing techniques that reduce search complexity. The findings suggest that additional heuristics and domain-specific constraints could further enhance solution quality and computational efficiency.

7   Conclusion

This paper presents a CP-based approach to the kindergarten allocation problem, ensuring optimal placement of kindergartens while maintaining accessibility and capacity constraints. By formulating the problem in MiniZinc and leveraging CP solvers, we achieve efficient solutions within a computationally feasible framework.

The proposed method introduces a bounding strategy that effectively narrows the search space by determining realistic upper and lower limits on the number of kindergartens required. Additionally, the integration of a clustering-based preprocessing step improves solution efficiency, reducing computational complexity. The experimental evaluation on real-world data from Sofia confirms the effectiveness of our approach, demonstrating its ability to optimize both the number of kindergartens and the total walking distances for children.

Future work will explore extending the model to incorporate additional constraints, such as land-use regulations and budgetary limitations. Furthermore, adapting the method to dynamic scenarios, where population densities and demand fluctuate over time, could enhance its applicability to long-term urban planning. The combination of CP techniques with machine learning-based predictions for demand forecasting is another promising direction for further research.

Acknowledgments. This research is part of the GATE project funded by the Horizon 2020 WIDESPREAD-2018-2020 TEAMING Phase 2 Programme under grant agreement no. 857155 and the programme "Research, Innovation and Digitalization for Smart Transformation" 2021–2027 (PRIDST) under grant agreement no. BG16RFPR002-1.014-0010-C01, and the CU project, funded by Digital Europe Programme DIGITAL-2023-CLOUD-AI-04 under grant agreement no. 101168005.

References

1. Geitle, A.H., Johnsen, Ø.K., Ruud, H., Fagerholt, K., Julsvoll, C.A.: Kindergarten allocation in Norway: an integer programming approach. J. Oper. Res. Soc. **72**(7), 1664–1673 (2020)
2. Veski, A., Biró, P., Põder, K., Lauri, T.: Efficiency and fair access in Kindergarten allocation policy design. J. Mech. Inst. Design **2**, 57–104 (2017)
3. Batsaris, M., Kavroudakis, D., Hatjiparaskevas, E., Panagiotis, A.: Spatial decision support system for efficient school location-allocation. Eur. J. Geogr. **12**, 31–44 (2021)
4. Gong, D., Gen, M., Yamazaki, G., Xu, W.: Hybrid evolutionary method for capacitated location-allocation problem. Comput. Industr. Eng. **33**(3–4), 577–580 (1997). ISSN 0360-8352
5. Vasanthi, T., Arulmozhi, G.: Optimal allocation problem using genetic algorithm. Int. J. Oper. Res. (IJOR) **5**(2) (2009)
6. Wang, K.-J., Lin, Y.-S.: Resource allocation by genetic algorithm with fuzzy inference. Expert Syst. Appl. **33**(4), 1025–1035 (2007). ISSN 0957-4174
7. Sharma, J., Singhal, R.S.: Genetic algorithm and hybrid genetic algorithm for space allocation problems- a review. Int. J. Comput. Appl. (0975 – 8887) **95**(4) (2014)
8. Wang, L., Liu, T.: Optimization algorithm of preschool education resource allocation based on data envelopment analysis model. Sci. Program. **2022**, 3858664 (2022)
9. Alp, O., Erkut, E., Drezner, Z.: An efficient genetic algorithm for the p-median problem. Ann. Oper. Res. **122**, 21–42 (2003)
10. Avella, P., Sassano, A., Vasil'ev, I.: Computational study of large-scale p-median problems. Math. Program. **109**, 89–114 (2007)
11. Correa, E.S., Steiner, M., Freitas, A.A., et al.: A genetic algorithm for solving a capacitated p-median problem. Numer. Algorithms **35**, 373–388 (2004)
12. Yaghini, M., Karimi, M., Rahbar, M.: A hybrid metaheuristic approach for the capacitated p-median problem. Appl. Soft Comput. **13**(9), 3922–3930 (2013)
13. Weil, G., Heus, K., Francois, P., Poujade, M.: Constraint programming for nurse scheduling. IEEE Eng. Med. Biol. Mag. **14**(4), 417–422 (1995)
14. Hanset, A., Meskens, N., Duvivier, D.: Using constraint programming to schedule an operating theatre. In: 2010 IEEE Workshop on Health Care Management (WHCM), Venice, Italy, pp. 1–6 (2010)
15. Chan, W.T., Hu, H.: Constraint programming approach to precast production scheduling. J. Constr. Eng. Manage. **6**, 513–521 (2002)
16. Quiroga, O., Zeballos, L., Henning, G., A constraint programming approach to tool allocation and resource scheduling in FMS. In: Proceedings of the 2005 IEEE International Conference on Robotics and Automation, Barcelona, Spain, pp. 3715–3720 (2005)
17. Heinz, S., Beck, J.C.: Solving resource allocation/scheduling problems with constraint integer programming (2011)
18. Galleguillos, C., Kiziltan, Z., Soto, R.: A constraint programming-based job dispatcher for modern HPC systems and applications (2020)
19. Cappart, Q., Moisan, T., Rousseau, L.-M., Prémont-Schwarz, I., Cire, A.A.: Combining reinforcement learning and constraint programming for combinatorial optimization. In: Proceedings of the AAAI Conference on Artificial Intelligence, vol. 35, no. 5, pp. 3677–3687 (2021)

20. Caprara, A., et al.: Integrating constraint logic programming and operations research techniques for the crew rostering problem. Softw. Pract. Exp. **28**(1), 49–76 (1998)
21. Michel, L., Hentenryck, P.V. Constraint-based local search. In: Martí, R., Pardalos, P., Resende, M. (eds.) Handbook of Heuristics. Springer, Cham (2018)
22. Ozbay, K., Xiao, W.: Probabilistic programming models for response vehicle dispatching and resource allocation in traffic incident management (2004)
23. Liu, S.-S., Utami, P., Budiwirawan, A., Arifin, M., Perdana, F.S.: Optimization model of maintenance scheduling problem for heritage buildings with constraint programming. Buildings **2023**, 13 (1867)
24. Hooker, J., Ottosson, G., Thorsteinsson, E.S., Kim, H.-J.: On integrating constraint propagation and linear programming for combinatorial optimization. In: AAAI/IAAI (1999)
25. Kalchev, Y.: Cities and their urbanized areas in the Republic of Bulgaria 2010 – 2020, Sofia (2022). https://www.nsi.bg/sites/default/files/files/publications/Urban2010-2020.pdf. Accessed 03 July 2025
26. https://www.sofia.bg/en/web/tourism-in-sofia/more-information-on-sofia. Accessed 03 July 2025
27. Karamitov, K., Petrova-Antonova, D., Hristov, E., Borukova, M.: Supply-demand analysis of urban amenities based on walking accessibility, 3973–3979 (2023)
28. Boyukliyski, S., Petrova-Antonova, D., Somanath, S.: Evaluation of social facilities coverage: a case study of Sofia city. In: IFAC Workshop on Control for Smart Cities CSC 2022. IFAC-PapersOnLine, vol. 55, no. 11, pp. 48–53 (2022)

Urban Digital Twins and Data Spaces: Shaping the Future of Sustainable Cities (TwinAbleCities 2025)

Urban and Valuation Aspects of an Illegal Neighborhood: The Case of Campo Sorbo in Ancient Capua

Claudia de Biase[1]([📧]), Antonetta Napolitano[2], Zomorrouda Redouane[2], and Daniela Menna[2]

[1] Urban Technique and Planning at the Department of Architecture and Industrial Design, University of Campania "Luigi Vanvitelli", Caserta, Italy
claudia.debiase@unicampania.it

[2] Department of Architecture and Industrial Design, University of Campania "Luigi Vanvitelli", Caserta, Italy
antonetta.napolitano@unicampania.it,
zomorrouda.redouane@unicampani.it,
daniela.menna@studenti.unicampania.it

Abstract. Unplanned urbanization and illegal settlements have, for many years, represented one of the most complex challenges for local administrations in Italy, and they are at the center of strong interest from urban planners. Beyond the legal aspects, these phenomena are seen as sources of territorial disorder and urban imbalance (de Biase, Losco, 2023, p.3). The paper describes sustainable solutions for the regeneration of the settlements illegally built and is divided into five sections, beginning with the definition and quantification of illegal settlements worldwide and in Italy. The extent of this type of settlement highlights the centrality of the issue within the broader challenges of urban regeneration across the globe. Particular focus is placed on the Italian context, examining the regulatory and planning framework in place in the country and in the Campania region. With deep roots in the history of our country, building and urban planning violations have affected numerous municipalities, where entire neighborhoods have sprung up spontaneously and often outside the bounds of legality. The South of Italy, in particular, experiences a state of distress that touches on various aspects, and looking to the future in an effort to improve this condition holds significant meaning, especially at the local level. The social and economic factors driving the expansion of illegal settlements are deeply rooted in the dynamics of exclusion and vulnerability that characterize many areas of Italy. These settlements often arise without building permits, in contexts lacking urban planning and control, and develop without access to essential infrastructures, such as connections to the water supply, sewage systems, and energy services. The focus is on a neighborhood that developed illegally within a municipality in the province of Caserta, an area notably affected by this type of phenomenon. The neighborhood, Campo Sorbo, located in the municipality of Santa Maria Capua Vetere, is analyzed both in terms of urban planning tools and the illegal evolution of its settlements. Campo Sorbo's construction began to take shape in the early 1980s and has since evolved into a true urban settlement. However, it lacks the necessary infrastructure and services, creating a context of marginalization and hardship for its residents.

© The Author(s), under exclusive license to Springer Nature Switzerland AG 2026
O. Gervasi et al. (Eds.): ICCSA 2025 Workshops, LNCS 15897, pp. 459–482, 2026.
https://doi.org/10.1007/978-3-031-97660-5_30

The last two sections are aimed at the analysis, classification, and design of both the illegal settlements and the agricultural context in which the neighborhood is located. The analyzed neighborhood, like most illegally established neighborhoods, shows a series of characteristics common to this type of area: there is a lack of efficiency in the urban service network, which requires innovation and improvement; there are issues related to the protection of landscapes, historical heritage, and protected natural areas, which are often poorly managed; there is outdated infrastructure that needs upgrading; and finally, the problem of illegal construction still persists, with unclear procedures for the regularization of unauthorized settlements, even in protected areas. Being aware of these challenges is essential in order to demand and design new solutions. These solutions must be incorporated into municipal urban planning policies to effectively address future challenges and improve the overall situation. (Forte, 2012, p. 17). The project currently being developed as part of the urban planning policies of the municipal administration is set within a broader context of recovery and redevelopment. It includes the implementation of primary urban infrastructure—a fundamental step toward integrating the area into the official urban fabric and improving the living conditions of residents, who have so far been disadvantaged by the absence of essential services such as a water supply system, sewage network, and access to electricity. This study aims to propose comprehensive regeneration strategies by exploring the phenomenon of illegal construction through a detailed analysis of the neighborhood, with particular attention to the urban planning policies adopted by the municipal administration. The goal is to outline a methodological approach that takes into account the ongoing social and urban transformations.

Keywords: Informal settlemets · Illegal settlemets · Multi-criteria evaluation.

1 Illegal Settlments

According to the *World Urbanization Prospects: The 2018 Revision* report published by the United Nations, in 2018, 55% of the world's population lived in urban areas, marking a significant increase from 30% in 1950. Projections indicate that by 2050, this share will reach 68%, highlighting a globally growing trend of urbanization. However, levels of urbanization vary significantly across different regions. The most urbanized areas include North America (82%), Latin America and the Caribbean (81%), Europe (74%), and Oceania (68%). In contrast, Asia and Africa have lower urbanization rates, around 50% and 43% respectively, with Africa remaining the least urbanized region globally (United Nation, 2018). Europe is characterized as a continent in continuous expansion, although there is a prevalence of unplanned urban development, particularly in Eastern and Southern Europe, where informal settlements and illegally constructed buildings—often built without proper permits or in violation of building regulations—are common (Forte, 2015, pp. 153–164).

These critical issues have been widely acknowledged at both international and national levels, leading to the inclusion of urban challenges within sustainable development programs, such as the United Nations' 2030 Agenda and the New Urban Agenda promoted by UN-Habitat. In these contexts, the concept of urban sustainability is interpreted broadly, as outlined by Allen and You (2002), who propose a multidimensional vision based on five interconnected pillars: economic, social, ecological, physical, and political sustainability (Allen, You, 2002). Particularly relevant is the dimension of physical sustainability, or the sustainability of the built environment, which refers to the ability of urban interventions to improve the livability and functionality of buildings and infrastructure for the entire population, while avoiding negative impacts on the surrounding natural environment. This dimension also includes consideration of the efficiency and resilience of the built environment in supporting local economic development. Although informal settlements and illegal housing are part of the built environment, they represent a dysfunctional and often precarious form of it. Their definition varies depending on the legal, regulatory, and cultural contexts of the countries where the phenomenon occurs. According to the definition provided by UN-Habitat, informal settlements are residential areas where a group of housing units has been constructed on land to which the occupants have no legal claim, or which they occupy illegally or without planning, as well as areas where the dwellings do not comply with current urban planning and building regulations (UN-Habitat, 2015, p.3). According to UN-Habitat's latest report, in 2024, 24.8% of the world's population lives in informal settlements. (https://data.unh abitat.org/pages/housing-slums-and-informal-settlements).

The difference between informal settlements and illegal (or unauthorized) settlements lies primarily in the political approach, as both are illegal phenomena but differ significantly in terms of the ownership of the land on which they are built. Some informal settlements, such as slums, are often located on public land (clearings, buffer zones, etc.) or land expropriated from private owners, while illegal settlements are almost always built on privately owned land, either purchased or directly occupied by builders or the inhabitants themselves. This distinction highlights the issue of public land management and the fight against illegality. The problem of informal settlements, together with the dynamics of illegal construction, has a strong territorial impact with significant effects on both individual and collective well-being (urban sustainability, quality of life, safety, etc.).

In Italy, according to the BES – Equitable and Sustainable Well-Being report (ISTAT, 2022), illegal building constitutes a marginal practice in the northern regions, while it assumes significantly greater relevance in the rest of the country, particularly in the South and in the Islands. In fact, in these areas, the incidence of illegal building is particularly high: 42.1 illegal dwellings are recorded for every 100 authorized in the South and 36.3 in the Islands. The analysis highlights a net increase in illegal dwellings equal to 9.1%, a figure not seen since 2004, and this growth could indicate a possible link between the post-pandemic recovery of residential construction and the expansion of illegal building, suggesting a new phase in the spread of this structural issue, caused by the lack of urban plans and/or the absence of building permits. The Campania Region is the one where the greatest spread of this phenomenon has been recorded (after the Basilicata and Calabria Regions). In fact, it is estimated that the share of illegal building is almost equal to half of those legally built. The provinces in Campania most affected by this issue are: Naples and Caserta, with many small and medium-sized municipalities that have lost their administrative boundaries, while peri-urban areas are frequently transformed for urban uses by landowners, without any official building permit or license. In line with what happens in other European countries, also in Italy the current legislation provides a plurality of approaches to tackle the problem of illegal settlements, namely: the repressive one, which involves the demolition of illegally built structures; the mitigative one, that is, the confiscation of illegal buildings and their regeneration through a detailed urban plan; and finally, the comprehensive one, which provides for regularization based on the payment of a monetary penalty to obtain a "retroactive building permit" (Forte, 2014, pp. 600–606). The comprehensive approach should be implemented especially in territories like that of Caserta, where the phenomenon affects entire peri-urban areas beyond municipal boundaries, and where residential settlements are characterized by low construction quality, lack of public services, and absence of minimum urban planning standards (de Biase, Forte, De Paola, 2019, pp. 264–271). Of particular concern are the figures provided by the 3rd Report by Legambiente on illegal building, which states that in the province of Caserta, 887 demolition orders for illegal buildings were issued between 2004 and 2022, but only 116 were actually carried out (Legambiente, 2023).

2   Illegal Settlements in Italy

In Italian language dictionaries, the term *abuso* (abuse) is defined as an "excessive, unlawful, or arbitrary use," meaning the improper use of something, often to the detriment of others. In an urban context, the expression *abusivismo edilizio* (illegal building), in common language, refers to the practice of arbitrarily carrying out an activity that is regulated by legal norms (Devoto, Oli, 1966, p.372); It takes shape in the actions of many citizens who carry out construction works in the absence of, or in violation of, existing regulations. The issue of illegal building is highly relevant today, though it does not have recent origins, and it directly or indirectly concerns the protection of Italy's environmental and cultural heritage, quality of life, and citizen safety. The phenomenon may involve "the treatment of a building structure—the single illegal house, the individual eyesore, which has always been too central to the debate and inevitably destined to trigger paralyzing oppositions—to the territorial project in its many dimensions. A territory that has been affected by illegal construction and, as a result, urbanized in a disorderly way, poorly provided with infrastructure, polluted in soil and water, and depleted of its environmental resources" (Curci, Formato, Zanfi, 2017).

Although it is a term that entered the public imagination following the landslide and building chaos in Agrigento in 1966—when the Girgenti hill collapsed under the weight of speculation—it was actually in Fascist-era Rome that illegal construction began to take shape. In 1931, Rome approved a city plan that envisioned an enormous size of 14,500 hectares, and Article 14 of the technical implementation regulations explicitly stated that subdivisions outside the boundaries of the master plan were prohibited unless authorized by the governing authority. This, combined with the regime's official policy against urban migration, the introduction of laws prohibiting Italian emigration abroad or to other municipalities in the Kingdom, and unclear technical regulations, led to the "natural" emergence of entire residential settlements outside the official urban plan boundaries, creating new footholds for further city expansion. When the new city plan was approved in 1965, urban restructuring zones were established precisely to account for illegal construction. It was found that such violations (44 urban areas) occupied about 3,800 hectares and housed over 200,000 people. But after World War II, with the beginning of the Italian economic boom, the massive migration toward the capital, and the total absence of public policies to regulate it, another 84 illegal boroughs (*borgate*) sprang up. This led to the emergence of the so-called "abuse out of necessity," aimed at solving the housing problems of many workers, who often took part in the construction of illegal housing themselves (Berdini, 2010, pp. 17–29). It was in the wake of the aforementioned collapse—caused by the construction of 8,500 units in violation of planning regulations—that many scholars of the time began to take an interest in the phenomenon, and some political efforts were made to slow its growth and transformation. One of the most determined was the Christian Democrat Fiorentino Sullo, who proposed allowing local authorities to expropriate, in advance, all buildable areas included in urban plans. His reform proposal was the only attempt to counter speculation, but due to the opposition from property owners, Sullo was sidelined within both the government and his own party.

Even though Article 26 of the fundamental law then in force—Law 1150 of 1942—provided for the suspension or demolition of works built without a construction license or in violation of it, these measures were not systematically applied. Therefore, a different solution had to be found, and in March 1985, under Prime Minister Bettino Craxi and Public Works Minister Giovanni Prandini, Law No. 47/85 was passed by Parliament. This marked the first national legislative approach to the issue of illegal building. Before being a law of amnesty and regularization, it represented an attempt at reforming the regulation of urban violations. It made it possible to legalize buildings constructed up until October 1, 1983 (de Biase, Losco, 2023, p.107); more than 4 million applications for regularization were submitted across Italy. The building violations that occurred after the 1985 amnesty then provided ample material for further legalizations, and Laws No. 724/1994 and No. 326/2003 were passed, allowing for the regularization of additional abuses. These laws effectively reversed the goal of combating illegal building (Berdini, 2010, pp. 40–41). From the "natural" illegality of the Fascist era to the "necessity-driven" illegal construction of the economic boom years, up to the outright real estate speculation of today, the phenomenon has taken on increasingly uncontrollable dimensions and influence. It has attracted the interests of criminals, opportunists, and politicians of every party, all at the expense of citizens' well-being and the livability of urban spaces.

Regarding the third building amnesty, provided for by Law No. 326/2003, the Campania Region, then led by President Antonio Bassolino, decided not to implement it. The Regional Council, through a resolution dated September 30, 2003, introduced an absolute ban on the regularization of building violations, establishing that it was not possible to legalize construction works carried out without the necessary permits or in violation of urban planning instruments. However, the Constitutional Court, with ruling No. 199 of 2004, annulled the Region's act, considering it to be in conflict with the constitutional powers of the State. The Campania Region responded with a new Regional Law, No. 10 of 2004, which further restricted the scope of the building amnesty, but this law was also declared unconstitutional by the Constitutional Court in 2006. In the meantime, the deadlines to apply for the amnesty had already expired, and many citizens of Campania were unable to take advantage of the regularization. To this day, the situation of illegal construction in Campania remains high, partly due to these regulatory obstacles. However, Regional Law 16/2004[1], in Article 23, paragraphs 3, 5, and 7, it sets out important provisions concerning illegal settlements, with the aim of regulating and planning the recovery of such areas, in particular:

> *"3. The Urban Municipal Plan (PUC) identifies the boundaries of unauthorized settlements existing as of December 31, 1993, subject to amnesty pursuant to Law No. 47 of February 28, 1985 (chapters IV and V), and Law No. 724 of December 23, 1994 (article 39), with the purpose of:*
>
> *a) Implementing adequate primary and secondary urban infrastructure;*
>
> *b) Respecting historical, artistic, archaeological, landscape-environmental, and hydrogeological interests;*
>
> *c) Achieving rational territorial and urban integration of these settlements.*
>
> *5. The Urban Municipal Plan (PUC) may condition the implementation of urban and building rehabilitation interventions for unauthorized settlements, delineated pursuant to paragraph 3, on the drafting of specific Urban Implementation Plans (PUA), known as Recovery Plans for Unauthorized Settlements, whose preparation procedure follows the provisions outlined by the implementing regulation referred to in article 43-bis.*
>
> *7. The Urban Municipal Plan (PUC) defines the procedures for urban and building rehabilitation of unauthorized settlements, the mandatory redevelopment interventions, and the related implementation procedures, including coercive measures, also through the establishment of building compartments as provided for in Article 33".*

The delimitation of illegal settlements, although not defined by law in terms of specific criteria, aims to plan projects that ensure proper urbanization, while respecting historical, artistic, archaeological, landscape, and hydrogeological aspects. It also seeks to allow for the rational integration of these settlements into the territory and into urban planning. This approach represents a significant cultural shift, as it acknowledges that illegal construction is not solely a matter of building violations, but also involves urban transformations that must be integrated into the general planning of the PUC (Municipal Urban Plan) and the PUA (Implementation Urban Plan). In this way, the category of *urbanistic illegality* is introduced. If illegal construction is limited to a single building violation, it can be dealt with separately; however, when illegality becomes the norm for territorial expansion, the issue must be addressed at the urban planning level. In such cases, the PRIA (Plan for the Redevelopment of Illegal Settlements) is the regional tool

---

[1] *With the recent amendment to Regional Law 16/2004 (Law 5/2024), these actions are confirmed in Article 22, paragraph 2-ter, letters m, n, o, q, as follows:*m) In paragraphs 3, 5, and 7, the word "PUC" is replaced with the word "PSU"; n) In paragraph 3, the phrases "abusivi esistenti al 31 dicembre 1993 e oggetto di sanatoria" and "ai sensi della legge 28 febbraio 1985, n. 47, capi IV e V, e ai sensi della legge 23 dicembre 1994, n. 724, articolo 39" are deleted; *o) In paragraph 5, after the words "recupero urbanistico ed edilizio degli insediamenti," the word "abusivi" is deleted; q) In paragraph 7, the word "abusivi" is replaced with the following: "di cui al comma 3".*

required to redevelop the area and the building stock, and to obtain the necessary titles for amnesty (de Biase, Losco, 2023, p.157).

3   Campo Sorbo in Santa Maria Capua Vetere (CE)

This contribution investigates a case study located in Santa Maria Capua Vetere, an Italian municipality in the province of Caserta, in the Campania region, with a population of 32,113. As part of the development of the PTCP (Provincial Territorial Coordination Plan) of Caserta, approved by Provincial Council Resolution No. 26 on April 26, 2012, the issue of illegal construction was examined in relation to its territorial significance. The spontaneous and uncontrolled growth of these settlements is at the root of the extremely low urban quality in the main urban agglomerations of the province. Moreover, this growth has almost always occurred at the expense of land with strong agricultural and rural value, and in some cases, it has compromised ancient and highly valuable crops, typical of the local agricultural landscape. The investigation into illegal construction was carried out through a cartographic analysis of the urban planning of existing settlements, represented in Table B5.2 *Settled Territory. Settlement Types*, extended to the entire province. This document classifies the existing urban fabrics to date into the following categories: historic urban fabric, non-residential urban fabric, recent urban fabric developed in the presence of a Master Plan (PRG), and recent urban fabric developed in the absence of PRG (PTCP Report, 2012, pp. 233–234) (Fig. 1).

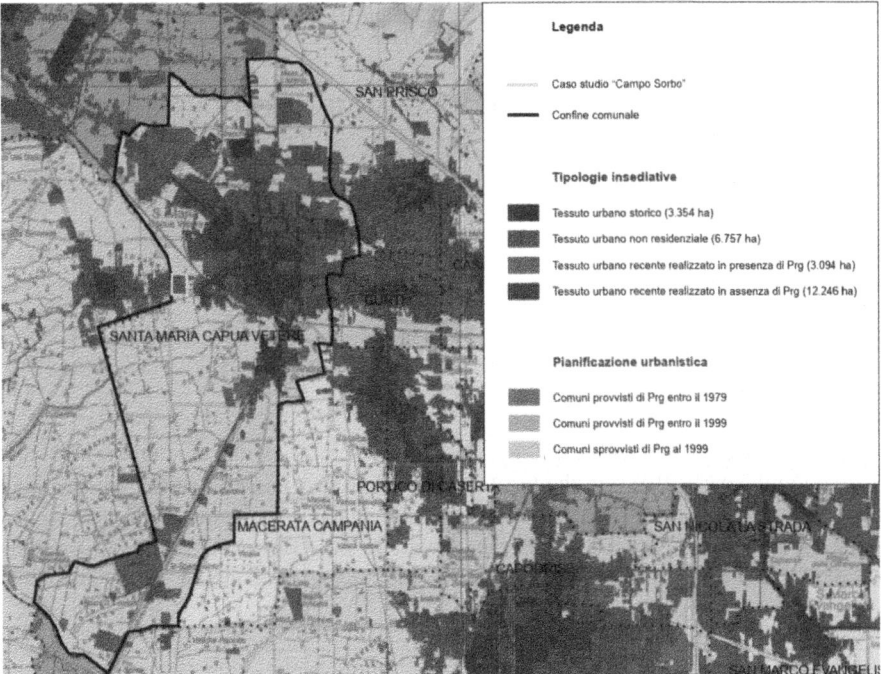

Fig. 1. Zoom on the case study of Table B5.2.2 of the PTCP

The phenomenon of illegal construction in the city of Santa Maria Capua Vetere is characterized by a fragmented distribution across the entire territory. There have been no notable cases of speculative nature; however, many applications for building amnesty were submitted for violations and the construction of small structures, extensions, and changes of use. To gain an indicative understanding of the phenomenon within the municipal area, it is possible to aggregate some recent indicators related to the spontaneous emergence of illegal construction, particularly during the periods of the building amnesty laws (Law 47/85; Law 724/94; Law 326/2003).

Analyzing the applications submitted, we observe that under the first law, Law No. 47/85—which covers a relatively long time span—the number of submitted applications was 1,176, of which 160 were still unresolved as of 2017. For the subsequent amnesties (Law 724/94 and Law 326/03), which cover a nine-year period, the number of applications submitted under Law 724/94 was 420, with 63 still unresolved as of 2017; while for Law 326/03, the number of applications submitted was 132, of which 49 remained unresolved as of 2017. From this analysis, it appears there has been a reduction in the number of applications, and consequently, a considerable decrease in the number of violations committed. In particular, data from the applications show that over 80% refer to violations for residential use, with various types of abuse identified—from very rare cases of new construction to more frequent cases of additions (such as the construction of verandas, upward extensions, enlargements with new rooms), and changes in building use. (Report PUC SMCV, 2023, pp. 115–116).

Table 1. Data on building amnesties Source: Strategic Document Report, Municipal Urban Planning Plan of Santa Maria Capua Vetere, May 2023.

CONDONI EDILIZI – REGULARIZATION OF UNAUTHORIZED CONSTRUCTIONS	
DOMANDE DI CONDONO L. 47/85 (Periodo dal 1942 al 1985)	1176
DOMANDE DI CONDONO L. 47/85 (Periodo dal 1942 al 1985)	420
DOMANDE DI CONDONO L. 47/85 (Periodo dal 1942 al 1985)	132
TOTALE	**1728**

This article aims to analyze the case of "Campo Sorbo," an illegal neighborhood that emerged in the early 1980s in the territory of Santa Maria Capua Vetere. Starting from the current satellite view (Fig. 2), a retrospective analysis was carried out to trace the evolution of the neighborhood, comparing it with the most recent date available from the National Geoportal, which goes back to 1988 (Fig. 3), and we will note that the situation was already present in that year.

Fig. 2. Google Earth View 2025

Fig. 3. National Geoportal 1988

Even in the aerial photogrammetry by the Military Geographic Institute dating back to 1984 (Fig. 4), the situation is clear: a built-up neighborhood already exists.

But the old General Master Plan from 1983 (Fig. 5) classified the area under examination as a "Zone C4," that is, new development expansion areas; according to the Technical Implementation Standards of the Master Plan: *"In these areas, any intervention is conditional upon a prior detailed implementation plan or subdivision plan approved through a regional agreement. The minimum area required for such a plan is 8,000 square meters, or the total area of the entire subzone if it is less than 8,000 square meters. This implementation plan shall identify and specify facilities and urbanization works according to the percentage quotas established in the plan's table, in compliance with applicable standards."*

We find it particularly striking that, at the time of the drafting of the 1983 Master Plan, no official buildings were recorded, this could indicate that, during the period in which the municipality lacked urban planning regulations, there was a widespread phenomenon of settlement construction without proper authorization, a hypothesis that seems even more plausible in light of the high number of amnesty applications submitted in 1985. This

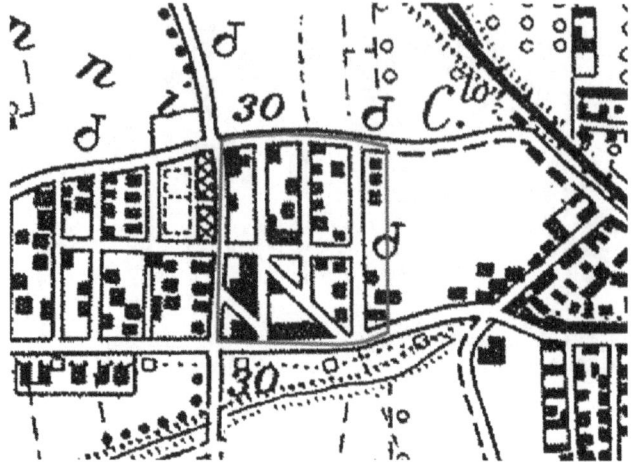

Fig. 4. Programmatic topographic map, IGM 1984

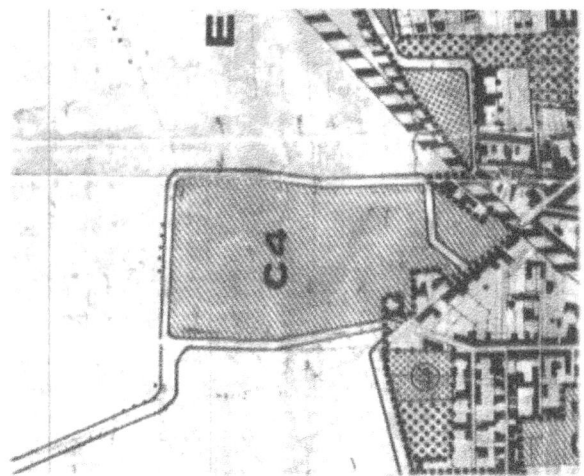

Fig. 5. Zoning map, PRG 1983

prompted us to deepen our analysis by searching for aerial photographs predating 1983. We considered those made available by the National Cartographic Portal which, although not very clear due to a 1:26,000 scale, still allow us to clearly identify the beginning of the neighborhood's development. The 1954 aerial image (Fig. 6) shows no signs of urbanization, while in 1974 (Fig. 7), the road layout begins to emerge, indicating the first signs of unauthorized urban development, accompanied by a few scattered dwellings. It is in the 1981 photo (Fig. 8), however, that the construction of new illegal buildings becomes evident; from this last frame, it is estimated that the built-up land represents about 80% of the currently urbanized area.

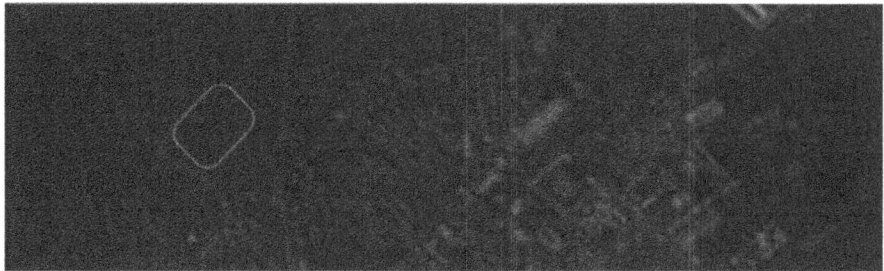

Fig. 6. Aerial view, National Cartographic Geoportal, 1954

Fig. 7. Aerial view, National Cartographic Geoportal, 1974

Fig. 8. Aerial view, National Cartographic Geoportal, 1981

We can therefore create an accurate mapping of the development of the settlements within the neighborhood (Fig. 9), which allows for a more detailed and comprehensive view of the formal and functional evolution of the various spaces, thus offering a clearer understanding of the urban dynamics and ongoing transformations.

The settlement is located in a peripheral area of the municipality of Santa Maria Capua Vetere, to the west of the historic center. It is bordered by the SP20 road, the boundary with the municipality of San Tammaro, and a railway viaduct. As can be seen from the aerial photogrammetry, in relation to the general urban context, the area is situated in a marginal position with respect to the city's development—both in terms of road connections and building density. It covers a surface area of 50,000 square meters, divided into 56 lots inhabited by 57 households (approximately 200 people).

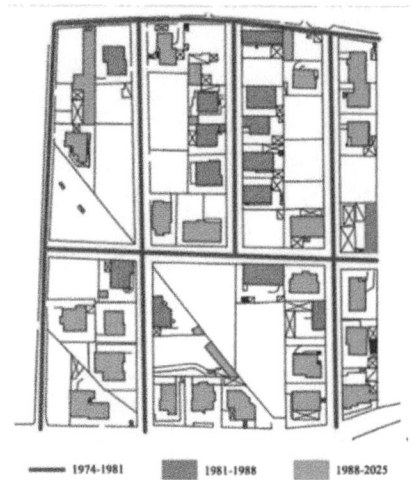

1974-1981   1981-1988   1988-2025

Fig. 9. Development of the settlements

It includes 36 residential structures (13 single-story single-family homes, 6 multi-story single-family homes, 4 single-story two-family homes, 9 multi-story two-family homes, and 4 multi-story multi-family buildings), 17 undeveloped plots of land, 2 structures used as warehouses, and 1 structure used exclusively for commercial purposes. In the analysis of the current state, an assessment was carried out of the primary[2] and secondary[3] urban infrastructure present in the area, which reveals a situation of absolute deficiency. For the primary urban infrastructure, the situation is as follows: the road network consists solely of dirt tracks, often uneven, and in some sections, bituminous material has been laid. However, this intervention, promoted by the residents, is inconsistent and ineffective, as it lacks an organized project. There is a significant safety hazard for internal circulation

---

[2] Primary urbanization works are defined (Art. 4, Law of September 29, 1964, no. 847) as follows: Roads serving settlements, including connections to the main road network of building plots; Spaces necessary for stopping and parking vehicles, in relation to settlement characteristics; Pipelines suitable for the collection and discharge of wastewater (black water) and their connections to the main urban network, including wastewater treatment plants; Water network, consisting of pipelines for the distribution of potable water and related works for abstraction, lifting, and accessories, as well as the necessary connection pipelines to the main urban network; Network for the supply and distribution of electricity for domestic and industrial uses, including secondary substations; Domestic fuel gas network and related connection pipelines; Telephone network, including telephone exchanges serving buildings; Public lighting, including networks and systems for illuminating public areas and streets open to public use; Equipped green spaces, areas serving individual buildings maintained as green spaces with trees and possible facilities.

[3] Secondary urbanization works are defined (Art. 44, Law no. 865/1971 and subsequent amendments) as follows: Nurseries; Kindergartens; Compulsory schools; Neighborhood markets; Municipal buildings; Churches and other religious buildings; Neighborhood sports facilities; Social centers and cultural and health facilities; Neighborhood green areas; for which Ministerial Decree 1444/1968 specifies the minimum standards to be respected to ensure the entire population a minimum endowment of urban standards.

within the area and for the safety of residents. Access to the external road network is not regulated by appropriate signage, nor are pedestrian pathways defined, while both horizontal and vertical signage is completely absent. There are no designated parking or stopping areas, and vehicles are left in various places, along the roadside and in front of gates and pedestrian entrances. The public sewer system is non-existent, and each housing unit is equipped with an Imhoff tank for wastewater disposal. There are no drainage works along the road to manage rainwater, which stagnates along the roadway, making it impassable for many months of the year. There are no connections to the main urban network nor to any water treatment facilities.

The potable water supply network is absent, and each housing unit has a well for water procurement. As for the electricity network, it has been granted by the national electricity provider, but along the formerly unauthorized subdivision, there are long, thick cables running on old wooden poles. There is no public lighting network, and street lighting relies on a few scattered spotlights installed by the residents, which do not provide regular or sufficient lighting for the entire area. Furthermore, there is no equipped green space; the road network is also used as a play area for children, a walking path for the elderly, and a refuge for domestic and stray dogs. Moreover, no secondary urban infrastructure has ever been built: for nurseries, kindergartens, and compulsory schools, residents must travel to the historic center of Santa Maria Capua Vetere (1.5–2 km away). For neighborhood markets, they must go either to the market area of the municipality of Santa Maria Capua Vetere (3 km) or to the market area of the municipality of San Tammaro (2 km). The municipal offices of Santa Maria Capua Vetere are located in the "Tribunal area" (1.5 km away). Churches, as well as sports facilities and cultural centers, are mostly located toward the center of Santa Maria Capua Vetere or, alternatively, in the direction of San Tammaro. In the area under consideration, there are no commercial activities, not even for the sale of essential daily goods. There is only a bakery-pizzeria and a car wash. Currently, the area is in a state of degradation due to the lack of essential urban infrastructure, and these deficiencies negatively affect the quality of life in the neighborhood. They contribute to situations of housing and social hardship and limit the functionality of public spaces, making the area deficient in its ability to serve as a place for community gathering and socialization. This also has direct consequences on the surrounding landscape, both in terms of environmental quality and usability of open spaces. Not surprisingly, given the current state of affairs, the municipal administration has included this area within the "Urban Redevelopment Zones" in the Municipal Urban Plan, approved by Municipal Council Resolution No. 126 of December 30, 2023 (Fig. 10), for which Article 63 of the Technical Implementation Standards (NTA) of the current PUC explicitly states:

1. The homogeneous zone identified as "Urban Redevelopment Areas," except as provided by the following article, defines two parts of the city, "Campo Sorbo" and "Cappuccini," characterized by urbanization phenomena requiring detailed implementation planning.

2. In this homogeneous zone, the Urban Municipal Plan (PUC) pursues the following objectives:

- Improving comfort, safety, and quality of the existing urban fabric;

- Enhancing accessibility and internal connections;

- Strengthening the tree-planting system to improve the environmental and landscape quality of the area and, where appropriate, to mitigate the impact of built-up areas.

3. The implementation of interventions in this homogeneous zone is contingent upon the execution of a Recovery Plan, which must first verify the urban legitimacy of existing buildings, and subsequently carry out urban redevelopment that integrates standard areas, suitable road systems, etc., all in compliance with current national and regional legislation. Properties that cannot be regularized according to Article 23, paragraph 6 of Regional Law 16/04 are excluded from the boundaries of the Recovery Plans.

4. The Recovery Plan aims to:

- Integrate and upgrade primary and secondary urbanization works;

- Define the permissible uses and categories of intervention for each existing building;

- Respect historical, artistic, archaeological, landscape, environmental, and hydrographic interests;

- Achieve rational territorial and urban integration of settlements.

5. The Recovery Plan involves identifying standard areas within the perimeter of the plan, designated for equipped green spaces, parking areas, and facilities of common interest.

6. The objective of the Recovery Plan is to outline actions and interventions aimed at the conservation, rehabilitation, and urban reorganization of the settlement, in order to enhance the livability of the area.

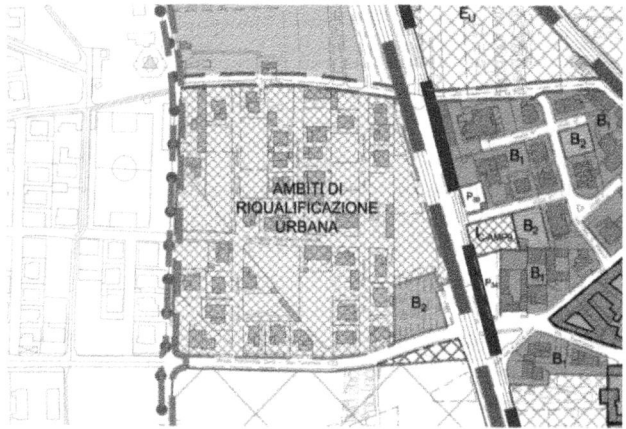

Fig. 10. Stralcio della Zonizzazione del PUC, 2023

7. Regarding the "Cappuccini" Recovery Plan, provisions will be made, in agreement with the Superintendence, for the protection, conservation, and enhancement of archaeological findings identified in the archaeological report.

8. On existing buildings within the areas described in this article, pending approval of the Urban Implementation Plans (PUA), ordinary and extraordinary maintenance interventions are permitted, as well as changes in intended use, exclusively within those allowed in the ATO D2 zone, subject to verification of compliance with urban standards pursuant to Article 5 of Ministerial Decree 1444/68.

4 Land-Use Classification for Urban Agriculture

The neighborhood is still located today in a peri-urban area, surrounded by a vast portion of agricultural land that represents a fundamental resource for the sustainability and development of the area. For this reason, it is extremely important to conduct in-depth studies on the surrounding agricultural territory, in order to promote its improvement and enhancement. Such interventions have also been included in the guidelines of the Provincial Territorial Coordination Plan (PTCP), which promote urban agriculture and the protection of agricultural spaces in the peri-urban fringe, emphasizing the importance of a rational use of these resources and their integration with urban development (PTCP, 2012, p. 125).

To systematically assess the agricultural land within the study area, a land-use-based classification was developed to categorize different land typologies based on their current function and potential for urban agriculture. This classification framework was designed to address the specific challenges of informal urban expansion into agricultural zones while maintaining a focus on the feasibility of reintegrating agricultural activities into the urban fabric. The classification consists of four primary categories: Active Agricultural Land, Abandoned/Degraded Agricultural Land, Mixed-Use Land (Urban-Agricultural Interface), and Built-Up Areas (Encroached Land). These categories were established based on a synthesis of existing urban agriculture and land-use planning literature (FAO, 2007; Simon et al., 2006; Zasada, 2011) and were adapted to suit the localized conditions of a neighbourhood-scale study, where land-use transitions are highly dynamic. The rationale for this classification is twofold. First, it enables a detailed assessment of the study area's agricultural potential by distinguishing between actively cultivated land, deteriorated but recoverable land, and areas where urban expansion has significantly altered the landscape. Second, it serves as a decision-making framework for identifying appropriate urban agriculture interventions, ensuring that recommendations align with each land category's physical and environmental characteristics (see Table 1). Active Agricultural Land consists of plots currently under cultivation, offering the highest potential for agricultural reinforcement or community-led farming initiatives. Abandoned or Degraded Agricultural Land includes areas where farming has ceased, requiring rehabilitation efforts such as soil restoration or improved irrigation. Mixed-Use Land refers to transitional spaces where informal construction coexists with pockets of agricultural activity, presenting opportunities for integrating small-scale urban agriculture through community gardens or agroforestry. Built-Up Areas encompass land fully converted into informal housing, where agricultural interventions would require alternative approaches like rooftop gardening or vertical farming (Zasada, 2011) (Table 3).

Table 2. Classification of the lands with characteristics Source:Author (2025)

Category	Description	Key Characteristics
Active Agricultural Land	Land currently used for farming or food production	Cultivated plots, presence of crops, orchards, or small farms
Abandoned/Degraded Agricultural Land	Previously used for agriculture but now underutilized or degraded	Unmaintained soil, signs of erosion, lack of recent cultivation
Mixed-Use Land (Urban-Agricultural Interface)	Areas where informal settlements and agriculture coexist	Scattered farming within built-up areas, fragmented land use
Built-Up Areas (Encroached Land)	Former agricultural land that is now occupied by illegal/informal buildings	Dense informal housing, little or no open green space

Table 3. Land Suitability classification Source:Author (2025)

UAPI Range	Potential Level	Criteria Considered	Recommended Applications
0.0–0.4	Low Potential	Land availability < 10%, population density < 2,000 people/km^2, road density < 1 km/km^2	Container gardening, vertical farming, microgreens, educational programs, indoor farming
0.4–0.7	Moderate Potential	Land availability 10–30%, population density 2,000 - 5,000 people/km^2, road density 1–3 km/km^2	Community gardens, rooftop farming, small-scale aquaponics, urban orchards, edible landscaping
0.7–1.0	High Potential	Land availability > 30%, population density > 5,000 people/km^2, road density > 3 km/km^2	Large-scale urban farms, agroparks, greenhouses, farm-to-table programs, urban agroforestry

The map (Fig. 11) illustrates the land-use-based classification of the study area. As shown, the Built-Up Areas (Encroached Land) are concentrated in the center of an agricultural zone, leading to further fragmentation of agricultural land. This encroachment reduces the availability of cultivable land, directly threatening local and regional food production (Seto et al., 2011). The expansion of built-up areas into agricultural zones also alters the ecological balance of landscapes, particularly by replacing active agricultural lands (Foley et al., 2005). The transformation of these areas into unplanned urban settlements contributes to soil degradation, habitat fragmentation, and the loss of essential ecosystem services, such as water regulation and soil fertility (Lambin & Meyfroidt, 2011). These impacts are also evident in the category of Abandoned/Degraded

Agricultural Land, where former agricultural plots have deteriorated due to urban pressure and environmental degradation. In the pattern of the built-up area, we observe the presence of unused agricultural interfaces, which are classified as Mixed-Use Land. These areas can be designated for small-scale urban agriculture to benefit the community, thereby integrating built-up spaces with agricultural functions such as agrihoods that integrate agriculture into residential neighborhoods, facilitating food production and preserving green spaces, thereby maintaining the agricultural identity within urban developments(Sangroniz, A. P.,2024).This approach preserves the original use of these areas while maintaining continuity with the agricultural identity of Active Agricultural Land.

Fig. 11. The map of the land use based classification Source:Author (2025)

4.1 Determining Land Suitability Through the Multi-criteria Evaluation (MCE)

This study applies a multi-criteria evaluation (MCE) approach to assess land suitability for urban agriculture, following established frameworks in spatial decision-making (Carver, 1991; Malczewski, 1999; FAO, 2007). The criteria considered include land availability, population density, and road density, which are commonly used indicators in land suitability studies (Chen et al., 2010; Pramanik, 2016). Suitability is classified based on a normalized score ranging from 0.0 to 1.0, with three levels of potential: Low (0.0–0.4), Moderate (0.4–0.7), and High (0.7–1.0) see (Table 2).

The classification thresholds were determined by adapting criteria ranges from urban agriculture and land-use planning studies (FAO, 2007; Pramanik, 2016). Land availability is categorized as low if vacant land is less than 10%, moderate between 10–30%, and high above 30% (Pramanik, 2016). Population density is considered low below 2,000 people/km^2, moderate between 2,000–5,000 people/km^2, and high above 5,000 people/km^2, following urban land-use classifications by the FAO (2007) and United Nations-Habitat (2013). Road density, a key factor for agricultural accessibility, is classified as low below 1 km/km^2, moderate between 1–3 km/km^2, and high above 3 km/km^2, based on urban transport planning studies (Chen et al., 2010; Geurs & van Wee, 2004).

Based on this classification, different urban agriculture strategies are recommended. Low-potential areas (0.0–0.4), characterized by low land availability, sparse population, and weak road networks, are suited for vertical farming, indoor agriculture, and educational programs. Moderate-potential areas (0.4–0.7), where land availability and accessibility are relatively balanced, are ideal for community gardens, rooftop farming, and small-scale aquaponics. High-potential areas (0.7–1.0), which feature abundant land, high population density, and strong road networks, are optimal for large-scale urban farms, agro-parks, greenhouses, and farm-to-table initiatives. This classification aligns with existing urban agriculture studies, ensuring a practical and context-sensitive approach to land reuse (Pramanik, 2016; FAO, 2007).

5   Neighborhood Redevelopment Proposals

"With Determination No. 413 of 10/08/2022 – General Registry No. 1131 of 10/08/2022, the Municipal Administration intends to carry out a market survey for the awarding of a contract concerning THE SOCIAL AND CULTURAL REDEVELOPMENT PLAN FOR DEGRADED URBAN AREAS REFERRED TO IN ART. 1, PARAGRAPHS 431 AND FOLLOWING, OF LAW NO. 190 OF DECEMBER 23, 2014 – REDEVELOPMENT AND RECOVERY PROJECT: 'CAMPO SORBO', with the aim of identifying, in compliance with the principles of non-discrimination, equal treatment, proportionality, transparency, and rotation, the economic operators to be invited to a subsequent negotiated procedure pursuant to Art. 63 of Legislative Decree 50/2016, without prior publication of a call for tenders, in accordance with Art. 1, paragraph 2, letter B) of Decree Law 76/2020, converted into Law No. 120/2020 and subsequently amended by Art. 51 of Decree Law 77/2021, converted into Law No. 108/2021." (https://comune. santa-maria-capua-vetere.ce.it/it/news/1380096) The main objective is to redevelop this area and integrate it into the existing residential context by adding infrastructure and services that can benefit the entire community. The idea is to promote a use of the land that is both sustainable and respectful, aiming to reduce phenomena of social and cultural marginalization, and to prevent the deterioration of buildings, which should be considered not only as part of the landscape but also as safe and healthy places to live.

The goal is for this area to be not only functional for its residents but also to become an integral and shared part of the entire municipal territory. In this regard, the Administration has already initiated works to implement the necessary primary urban infrastructure, and to continue in this direction, this contribution aims to provide guidance developed by the authors, together with students and graduates from the Department of Architecture and Industrial Design, located in Aversa (CE), at the University of Campania "Luigi Vanvitelli," which are part of the ARPAE[4] project funded by the Campania Region in 2023.

First Design Proposal

As part of a recovery strategy, having assessed the needs and expectations of users, the potential of the area, and the resilience capacity of a context lacking organized urban space, design proposals were developed to support the interventions already planned by the administration.

The first project was developed with the aim of reversing the relationship between pedestrian space and vehicular space by reorganizing the hierarchy of traffic flows through a functionally efficient and flexible distribution of the road section. The transformation process of the internal road network within the area envisions a shared public space, equally accessible to a wide range of users (pedestrians, people with disabilities, children, the elderly, residents and non-residents).

A one-way traffic loop was proposed, characterized by neighborhood streets designed to connect different parts of the settlement. This category specifically includes roads intended to serve, through appropriate complementary road elements, the main urban neighborhood settlements (services, facilities, etc.). All types of traffic are allowed, including the parking of private vehicles, provided it is organized within designated areas, evenly distributed, and equipped with dedicated maneuvering lanes. For direct service to residential settlements, two local roads were designed. These are reserved exclusively for the use of residents of the respective streets: one is two-way, ending in a roundabout to facilitate turning, while the other is one-way.

Several existing vehicular roads have been removed and replaced with pedestrian paths, which are part of a green and eco-sustainable design plan (Figs. 12 and 13).

Indeed, in an era where the environmental emergency has reached such a critical level, it is appropriate to envision a strong alternative strategy, represented by the extensive use of green areas capable of providing real healing for environmental degradation. This kind of remedy, combined with the introduction of urban agriculture, the recovery of rainwater, the use of renewable energy sources, and energy savings, could truly bring about the creation of a new urban ecosystem and represent a real opportunity for the sustainable development of the city. An "urban reforestation," therefore, becomes the guiding design concept. In line with this logic, a "green lung" has been designed at the center of the settlement, within which different areas have been envisioned based on the functionality they are intended to serve. In a composition alternating between shades of greenery, bodies of water, and paved zones, the residential buildings are meant to blend with facilities for sports, social interaction (for both youth and adults), and cultural and educational activities. These structures, in the authors' vision, are to be designed as symbols of the neighborhood's rebirth. For this reason, they will feature an architecture that breaks from the existing built environment, characterized by curved and sinuous

---

[4] The project "Public Residential Architecture between Naples and Caserta" (ARPAE), funded by the Campania Region in 2023, is coordinated by the Department of Architecture and Industrial Design of the University of Campania "Luigi Vanvitelli." The project aims to study and map public urban areas that have significantly influenced territorial transformation and the history of contemporary architecture, with the goal of promoting their enhancement and regeneration.

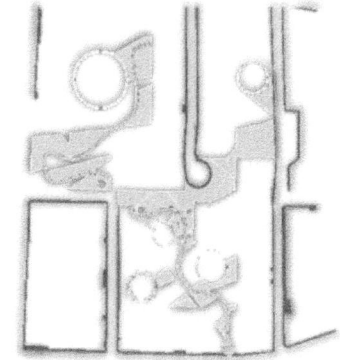

Fig. 12. Hypothesis of vehicular mobility and parking

Fig. 13. Hypothesis of pedestrian mobility

lines in contrast with the linearity of the current buildings. This plan involves not only the design and reclamation of existing green areas but also the use of greenery as a true architectural element, both horizontally and vertically. It is a vision that merges new architectural construction with green spaces into a single concept of an urban eco-park. The starting point is the idea of covering and reconnecting the housing units, which are defined by spontaneous, unregulated architecture due to their illegal origins. As a unifying element among the heterogeneous components, a wall structure has been envisioned, taking on various functions and forms depending on its location. It becomes a bench in pedestrian areas, a storage space in residential zones, and a space for technological networks; stylistically, it takes on different colors—some sections tiled, others green, and others left plain white (Figs. 14 and 15).

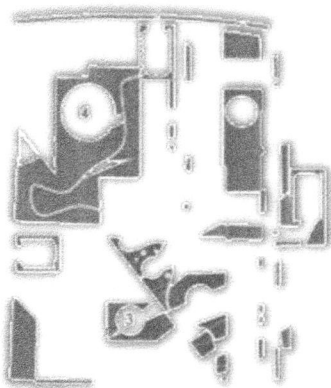

Fig. 14. Hypothesis of equipped public green spaces for sports

Fig. 15. Hypothesis of common interest facilities

An additional element of sustainable development is the idea of innovative zero-kilometer agriculture, made possible through the introduction of urban gardens, distributed in specially reclaimed areas or even on rooftop gardens of the new architectural structures. The availability of the water needed for both greenery and agriculture can be ensured by the creation of distributed water basins of various sizes, capable of hosting a wide range of biodiversity. Given these design elements, a drastic reduction in the "urban heat island" phenomenon is expected—a condition that creates a microclimate several degrees warmer within urban areas compared to surrounding peripheral zones. Grass surfaces and plants, in fact, provide protection not only from solar radiation but also from extreme temperature fluctuations, helping to ensure an ideal microclimate and resulting in energy savings. The principle of environmental sustainability involves exploring alternatives to traditional construction technologies, envisioning new structures made of load-bearing glulam (glued laminated timber), now a viable option even for multi-story buildings, and the widespread use of green roofs, offering enormous environmental benefits, improved living comfort, and a strong visual impact on the urban landscape. The public lighting system will also be designed with cost and pollution reduction in mind, relying on modern technology powered by a photovoltaic panel system capable of meeting the entire area's public energy needs (Fig. 16).

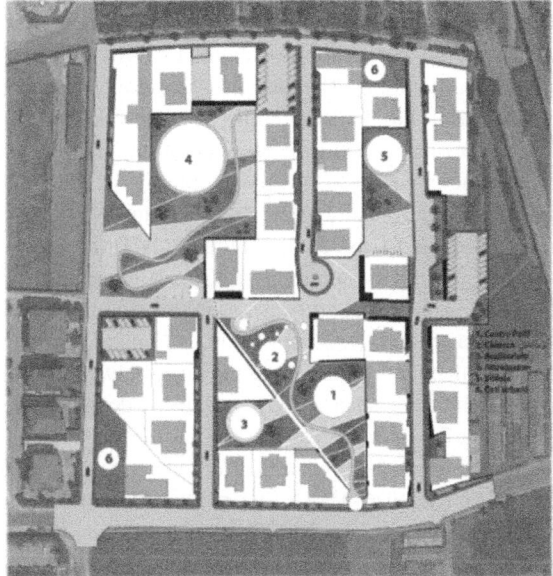

Fig. 16. Masterplan first design proposal Produced by the graduate student: Michele Iannotta

The current state, therefore, presents a condition of total neglect and degradation, failing to meet the minimum requirements for livability. From this need for transformation, the thesis topic focuses on the proposal of a recovery plan based on ecological sustainability, aiming to provide the area with at least the minimum urban planning standards. The proposed recovery plan aims to achieve these standards by equipping the area with a 450 m² compulsory school, 600 m² of facilities for common use, 1,800 m² of equipped green spaces, and 1,900 m² of public parking areas. Subsequently, from the estimated cost analysis, it is determined that the implementation of the urban redevelopment interventions in the area will require an approximate expenditure of €2,800,000.00.

Second Design Proposal

The second proposal concerns the urban regeneration project of abandoned and degraded green areas near Campo Sorbo, with the aim of revitalizing these spaces, responding to the needs of the community, and promoting connection between the two neighboring municipalities. The planned actions focus on the integration of new public spaces, the adoption of eco-sustainable solutions, and the creation of new services, in order to reduce degradation and improve the quality of life for residents. The site includes several abandoned areas, including the one beneath the railway, which represents one of the key critical points to be redeveloped. The choice to intervene specifically in this area stems from the need to enhance a marginal yet strategic space with the potential to become a gathering point. The project aims to address the site's critical issues through a series of targeted interventions, with the goal of restoring vitality and functionality to the entire area. The introduction of new plants and trees will help improve environmental quality, increase biodiversity, and create a favorable microclimate. To ensure sustainable and efficient lighting, solutions using renewable energy sources—such as solar panels to power public lighting—are planned. New playgrounds, areas for sports equipment, and spaces for social events will be created to meet community needs. New urban furniture, such as benches, waste bins, and decorative elements, will be installed to make the area more welcoming and functional. The currently abandoned area will be cleaned and transformed into a space useful to the community, with the addition of playgrounds and sports facilities. To support this transformation, eco-sustainable parking lots will also be built, featuring permeable surfaces and green solutions. A new sports complex will be built, including two padel courts, a basketball court, and two tennis courts, adjacent to the area that already hosts an 11-a-side football field. Additionally, new locker rooms and bleachers will be constructed to encourage public participation. The new urban parks will be designed to ensure soil permeability, avoiding overloading the sewer system and improving rainwater management. New pedestrian and bicycle paths will be created to promote sustainable mobility and improve connections between the different areas of the project. To further enhance connectivity between the designed areas, new rows of trees will be planted along the main access roads (Fig. 17).

Produced by the students in the course of Methods and Tools of Urban Planning, academic year 2023/24: Crescenzo Maisto, Francesco Mancino, Francesco Giovanni Pezone, Carmine Sgariglia, Zeynep SarikanMasterplan seconda ipotesi progettuale.

In general terms, the project has the potential to serve as a link between the municipalities of Santa Maria Capua Vetere and San Tammaro, promoting integration and connection between these two areas. The sustainable approach and the enhancement of the surrounding environment will contribute to making the area a point of reference for the entire community. It therefore represents a key opportunity to restore vitality and usability to a peripheral area that has long suffered from the lack of adequate services and infrastructure. Through targeted interventions focused on redevelopment and

Fig. 17. Masterplan second design proposal

sustainability, the area will be transformed into a hub for social, cultural, and sports activities, capable of strengthening the ties between the two communities and promoting a greener, more inclusive model of urban development.

Brief Concluding Reflections
Through the integration of these projects, it would be possible to address the various challenges of the neighborhood in a coordinated and synergistic way, such as the recovery of public spaces, building redevelopment, environmental sustainability, and the creation of new opportunities for the community. Moreover, a comprehensive regeneration program would allow for the maximization of available resources and ensure a long-term positive impact, transforming the neighborhood into a model of innovation, inclusiveness, and sustainability.

Attributions
Introduction C.DB.; Paragraph 1 D.M.; Paragraph 2 A.N.; Paragraph 3 C.DB.; Paragraph 4 Z.R.; Paragraph 5 A.N.,; Brief Concluding Reflections C.DB., A.N., Z.R., D.M.

Disclosure of Interests.   The authors declare no conflict of interest.

References

1. Allen, A., You, N.: Sustainable Urbanisation: Bridging the Green and Brown Agendas. UCL Development Planning Unit in collaboration with DFID and UN-Habitat, London (2002)
2. Devoto, G., Oli, G.C.: Il dizionario della lingua italiana, Le Monnier, Firenze (1966)
3. Foley, J.A., DeFries, R., Asner, G.P., et al.: Global consequences of land use. Science, **309**(5734), 570–574 (2005)

4. Simon, D., McGregor, D., Thompson, D.: The Peri-Urban Interface: Approaches to Sustainable Natural and Human Resource Use. Earthscan (2006)
5. Food and Agriculture Organization (FAO). Urban and Peri-Urban Agriculture: A Briefing Guide. FAO (2007)
6. Un-Habitat, Global Report on Human Settlements 2009. Planning Sustainable Cities, Earthscann UK-USA (2009)
7. Berdini P., Breve storia dell'abuso edilizio. Dal ventennio fascista al prossimo futuro, Donzelli editore, Roma (2010)
8. Seto, K.C., Güneralp, B., Hutyra, L.R.: Global forecasts of urban expansion to 2030 and direct impacts on biodiversity and carbon pools. Proc. Natl. Acad. Sci. **109**(40), 16083–16088 (2011)
9. Lambin, E.F., Meyfroidt, P.: Global land-use change, economic globalization, and the looming land scarcity. Proc. Natl. Acad. Sci. **108**(9), 3465–3472 (2011)
10. Zasada, I.: Multifunctional peri-urban agriculture—a review of societal demands and the provision of goods and services by farming. Land Use Policy **28**(4), 639–648 (2011)
11. Forte, F., Vetere, S.M.C.: Studi per la formazione del piano urbanistico generale comunale, gennaio (2012)
12. Forte, F.: Illegal buildings and local finance in new metropolitan perspectives. In: Bevilacqua, C., Calabrò F., Della Spina, L. (eds.) New Metropolitan Perspectives. Advanced Engineering Forum, vol. 11 (2014)
13. UN-Habitat, Habitat III Issue Paper 22: Informal Settlements (2015)
14. Forte F.: The management of informal settlements for urban sustainability: experiences from the Campania Region (Italy), The Sustainable City X (2015)
15. Curci, F., Formato, E., Zanfi, F., (a cura di).: Territori dell'abusivismo. Un progetto per uscire dall'Italia dei condoni, Donzelli Editore, Roma (2017)
16. de Biase, C., Losco, S.: Abusivismo urbanistico e pianificazione comunale. Verso la Rigenerazione, Edizioni Le Penseur, Brienza (2023)
17. United Nation, World Urbanization Prospect, The 2018 , United Nations (2018)
18. de Biase, C., Forte, F., De Paola, P.: Informal Settlements: The Potential of Regularization for Sustainable Planning. The Case of Giugliano, in the Metropolitan City of Naples, Springer (2019)
19. ISTAT: Il benessere equo e sostenibile in Italia. ISTAT (2022)
20. Legambiente, III Report "Abbatti l'Abuso" (2023)
21. Relazione Documento Strategico, Piano Urbanistico Comunale di Santa Maria Capua Vetere, pp. 115–116, maggio (2023)
22. Sangroniz, A.P., Ebel, R., Stein, M.: Barriers and opportunities to agrihood development in growing cities of the rocky mountain region: a comparative case study. J. Agric. Food Syst. Community Dev. **13**(3), 271–288 (2024). https://doi.org/10.5304/jafscd.2024.133.03

Author Index

O. Gervasi et al. (Eds.): ICCSA 2025 Workshops, LNCS 15897, pp. 483–484, 2026.
https://doi.org/10.1007/978-3-031-97660-5

The manufacturer's authorised representative in the EU is Springer
Nature Customer Service Centre GmbH, Europaplatz 3, 69115 Heidelberg,
Germany. If you have any concerns regarding our products, please
contact ProductSafety@springernature.com

Printed and bound by CPI Group (UK) Ltd, Croydon, CR0 4YY
24/04/2026
02096374-0002